EUROPE by EURAIL
How to Tour Europe by Train

Twenty-Fourth Edition

written by
LaVerne Ferguson-Kosinski

edited by
Stephanie Bell

rail schedules by
Matthew C. Palma
and
H. Milton Peek

The Globe Pequot Press

Guilford, Connecticut

DEDICATION

This book is dedicated to the memory of my former husband, George Wright Ferguson. In the travel industry he was known as "Mr. Eurail."

Until 1993, George was coauthor of *Europe by Eurail* and *Britain by BritRail*. He was instrumental in educating the public about how to maximize the economy, convenience, and pure enjoyment of rail travel in Continental Europe and Britain.

The staff of RailPass Express, Inc., and I pledge to continue George's legacy and passion for train travel into and beyond the millennium by providing the most current rail information combined with the best customer service.

Rail nomad and adventurer, great educator and friend,
we all miss you!

The author and the publisher gratefully acknowledge the kind permission of the *Great Britain Passenger Railway Timetable,* of Eurostar Passenger Service and its Web site, and of the *Deutsche Bahn Kursbuch* to use their resources in the compilation of the timetables in this text. Station maps courtesy Deutsche Bahn.

Cover photographs: Photonica © C. Rosenstein
Cover design: Laura Augustine

ISSN: 1081–1125
ISBN: 0-7627-0501-9

Manufactured in the United States of America
Twenty-Fourth Edition/First Printing

Contents

About the Author

Author LaVerne Ferguson-Kosinski and her former husband, Lt. Col. George Ferguson, first co-authored this unique and comprehensive guide to touring Europe by train in 1976. Sadly, after battling a long illness, George, who was globally and affectionately known as "Mr. Eurail," passed away in 1997. He was buried with full military honors at Arlington National Cemetery near Washington, D.C.

LaVerne wanted to ensure accurate British and European rail travel information would continue to be available. She has diligently continued this legacy along with her international research team by providing the best products and guidebooks for the independent rail traveler or armchair dreamer. Her technical writing and editorial background, academic education in English, world history, and communications, plus her experience in research and development for an international research institute have added considerable substance to her twenty-four years of traveling the rails in Britain and Europe.

LaVerne first had visions of exploring the world in third-grade geography class. She pursued that goal by first collecting travel brochures, then through higher education at The Ohio State University followed by traveling throughout Europe. She currently resides in Fort Myers living *Brady Bunch*–style with her husband, Joe "Cool" Kosinski, a structural engineer, and two of their six children. Even though she now calls sunny Florida home, Europe will always be her "backyard."

LaVerne enjoys hearing from her readers. Please send your comments and suggestions directly to:

LaVerne Ferguson-Kosinski
RailPass Express, Inc.
2737 Sawbury Blvd., Columbus, OH 43235-4583, USA
or via e-mail at laverne@railpass.com

About the RailPass Express Team

LaVerne Ferguson-Kosinski is President and Chief Executive Officer of RailPass Express, Inc., in Columbus, Ohio. An extraordinary small-business success story, RailPass Express was created in 1980 from a humble beginning in the basement of the Ferguson home with a couple of desks, a toll-free telephone number, and a singular idea to provide the best customer service for their readers and travelers. Incorporated in 1986 by the Fergusons, RailPass Express has blossomed into one of the largest independent, consumer-focused European railpass sales outlets in the world.

LaVerne's dedication to staying on track with the latest rail information by continuing to update her successful guidebooks—*Europe by Eurail* (now in its twenty-fourth edition) and *Britain by BritRail* (in its twentieth edition)—has provided the driving "engine" for the RailPass Express success story. As proven by both books' continuing best-selling status, LaVerne's popular Base City–Day Excursion™ concept really works.

The expertly trained (pun intended) and well-traveled staff at RailPass Express provides the informational resources and rail travel products necessary to pursue the concepts and itineraries as outlined in her guidebooks. LaVerne's team of international researchers and employees share her enthusiasm for the exciting world of British and European train travel. *Europe by Eurail's* team is devoted to producing a comprehensive, practical, yet friendly guidebook to touring Europe by train:

Stephanie Bell, Promotional Editor, employs her editorial and research skills on the guidebooks and maintains an extensive European and British database and research library. A multifaceted graduate of fine arts with an extensive publicity and creative background, Stephanie also contributes her valuable abilities in the marketing of RailPass Express, Inc.

A special note of thanks goes to our colleague **Matthew Palma.** Off on a journey to further his education, Matt verified the timetables of both guidebooks.

Researchers for *Europe by Eurail* also included **Major Robert Bean** and **H. Milton Peek,** true train enthusiasts who have played ongoing, much-appreciated roles with both guidebooks. Their love for British and European rail travel is contagious and we value their input. The additions of **Morton Brown** were included in this edition as well. We say *gracias* to **Jeff Lehman** for his editorial assistance with the tourist boards. Jeff has since resumed his English teaching career in central Mexico.

Mary Kish, General Manager, has applied her managerial excellence and ingenious business acumen for years to RailPass Express, Inc. We commend her for streamlining our operations and give her a standing ovation for keeping the company moving at such high speed. She has helped keep us right on track while making our blue-ribbon customer service standards even better. Amazing!

With all of our recent expansion and growth, we cheerfully welcomed **Lesley Tate.** Lesley is now offsetting some of the administrative functions as Financial Assistant, while integrating new operational systems and procedures.

Kevin Siegmann designs and maintains our award-winning Web site: www.railpass.com. The site contains *Europe by Eurail* and *Britain by Britrail* information for visitors, an extensive rail-related database, plus a *secure* online ordering system for rail travel products. Kevin's dual role as Graphics/Systems Designer enables him to play an integral part in the marketing arena, as well as in the development and implementation of innovative operational upgrades.

Sheila Clowes is the mysterious "Lady of the Lines" on the RailPass Express voice mail system. Originally from London, she is our "resident expert" on all things British. Her official title is Training Supervisor, and we credit her with maintaining the highest customer service standards in our representatives.

Assisting **Ellie Byrnes** in the Point-to-Point and Reservations Office of RailPass Express are **Mary Ellen Baker** and **Susan Beougher.** Our rail information experts personally and meticulously decipher complicated timetables for the best and most convenient trains, schedules and itineraries. They love to share travel and globetrotting stories while assisting travelers. Call (614) 793–7650 for an enjoyable and easy way to make your seat and sleeper reservations.

Other rail customer service specialists at RailPass Express include **Colleen Beader, Laura Biemel, Heidi Anne Bookwalter, Donna Heap, Rich Jacko, Heidi McDannald, Michael Modula, Linda Rence, Sonal Shah** (a genuine thank you for your research and editing assistance), **William**

Stafford, Rohini Vagarali and **Debbie Wanstrath-Norwich.** Call (800) 722–7151 with questions or to order rail passes.

Our most recent exciting and expanding area is European Vacation Tours & Groups, where **Mary DiThomas** and **Karen Cherdron** grace us with their enthusiasm and comprehensive knowledge of the travel industry. Both are well traveled and happy to assist groups or individuals in arranging the best itineraries and accommodations for trips abroad. Euro-pean Vacation offers a wealth of tours throughout Britain and Europe. Visit www.europeanvacation.com on the Internet or call (888) TOUR–404 toll-free for more details.

In North America, we wish to extend thanks to **Heinz Wisner, Barbara Schmidt, Mary Stiller, Cathy Featherstone,** and the entire staff of DER Travel Services. One more gracious thank you to our many friends in the tourist offices and to the travel partner professionals throughout Europe and Britain.

Introduction

"To travel by train is to see nature and human beings, towns and churches and rivers, in fact to see life." —Agatha Christie

Europe by Eurail reflects the "new" Europe and the energy and exuberance of its rail system. It's dynamic, it's futuristic, and it's on the move—accelerating into the millennium with the high-tech boldness and immense speed of the world's finest transportation system.

Train travel is an enigma for most non-Europeans who either have forgotten or have never had an opportunity to learn what travel by train is like. *Europe by Eurail* takes the puzzlement out of European rail travel—like having a friend along who takes you by the hand and shows you how to use the world's finest transportation network to see and learn about European life and culture. Toward that end, it provides specific, pragmatic information with step-by-step directions.

Europe by Eurail is a train traveler's how-to guidebook. It is not a hotel/restaurant guide, but rather tells you *how* to locate them. Certain hotels and restaurants do occasionally gain mention, however, especially if they add to the graciousness and enjoyment of a train trip or a stay in a city. *Europe by Eurail* deals primarily with the necessities of train travel in Europe and offers guidance for appreciating the educational and cultural sites and events that abound along the right-of-way of the Continent's magnificent rail system.

"See Europe by Train" has been a favorite slogan of Europe's railways for decades, but never has it been as full of meaning as it is today. You will never be bored traveling on a high-speed train, because rail travel is still leisurely enough to fully enjoy the constantly changing scenes of hills and hamlets, farms and forests, and cities and countrysides that make the European landscape fascinating. Each country has its own special attractions to offer rail travelers as they speed through, ensconced in comfort and free from worry. Added to the passing scenes is the opportunity for leisurely dining and drinking while chatting with fellow passengers, most of whom are the Europeans you hoped to meet.

Travel by train in Europe is a unique and pleasurable experience. All aboard—and take your imagination with you.

WHY EURAIL?

Many visitors to Europe fail to realize that the European rail network (which we refer to simply as "Eurail"), can take you to practically every nook and cranny on the Continent, so they insist on renting a car. At first glance, those European fly-drive packages might appear enticing, but the more you investigate them, the less appealing they become. The more you open your eyes to rail travel, we think, you'll find there is no better way to go.

Consider that the number of European road traffic fatalities is more than four times that in North America, and that watching the road ahead is not really what most folks go to Europe to do nor is deciphering the signs an easy feat. Most European automobiles are small, compact vehicles. That four-passenger economy car you're thinking of renting could never carry four passengers *and* their luggage—so, bring on the Mercedes at three times the price and double the gas. Prepare yourself for another shock—the price of gasoline in Europe is about three times that in the United States, and gasoline stations are not nearly as numerous as they are stateside.

Another very important facet of a fly-drive package is the VAT (value added tax), which ranges from 6 to 33 percent in European countries. In some countries, foreign tourists are eligible for refunds on certain purchases, but there are no VAT refunds on car rentals. Reference to the VAT may be tactfully avoided in car-rental information or perhaps hidden in the fine print of the terms. Whether or not it's hidden, after determining the low, low cost of a rental car with unlimited mileage privileges (which also includes the privilege of buying unlimited gasoline), don't forget to multiply the bottom line by the VAT of the country and add that figure into the equation.

Another item frequently overlooked is insurance. To assure yourself of the minimum personal protection, plan to add several dollars a day for that coverage. By now, you will realize why Europeans park their own cars and ride the trains.

One key reason for going to Europe is to mingle with Europeans. Traveling day after day in a motor coach filled with other American tourists or riding for hours in a small rental car with your spouse helping you navigate and the kids crammed in with the suitcases is not, in our opinion, the best way to mingle. Europeans use their trains. They will be sitting next to you or across from you in the diner. You will be sharing the same experiences, so conversation will come easily. It's a great way to make new friends.

Those traveling with children across the continent will find the trains to be a blessing as well as fun and intriguing. The kids can eat, get a drink, take a nap or go to the bathroom just as often as their little hearts desire while you enjoy the scenery en route.

Trains have always held an aura of romance and charm about them that cannot be experienced in any other mode of transportation. The mere mention of *The Orient Express,* for example, sparks visions of glamour, intrigue, mystery—and sumptuous dining. Although many of the original famous trains have been replaced by high-speed, high-tech international express trains, that special thrill of rail travel is still there.

The Europeans know how to run a railroad. The Eurail network connects more than 30,000 cities, villages, and hamlets with well over 90,000 daily train departures on more than 160,000 miles of track. That's awesome—and the system is getting faster, more efficient, and more elegant. Unlike the airlines' sardinelike accommodations, European trains are comfortable, stylish, and loaded with amenities to please the tourist and business traveler alike.

Originally, the idea of purchasing a pass for unlimited travel by train within a specified time period, for example, 1 month, on the Eurail system was a simplistic one. One type of railpass, called a **"Eurailpass,"** was offered to non-European residents as a way to encourage independent travelers to use Europe's rail network.

Although today's European railpasses encompass a wide variety of options, time periods, and countries, using a pass is still the most economical, convenient, and flexible way to get the most out of the European rail network. A point-to-point ticket enables you to travel from one point to another but does not provide the flexibility to change your plans.

Railpasses, on the other hand, provide unlimited rail travel each day within a specified time frame. They eliminate the hassle of standing in long lines to purchase tickets, and they can save you a bundle of money if you make long or frequent journeys.

For details on the various kinds of European railpasses available to non-European residents, please consult the European RailPasses section later in this introduction, or contact RailPass Express, Inc., (800) 722–7151, (614) 889–9100; *Internet:* **www.railpass.com.**

Remember . . . Purchase your railpasses before leaving for Europe!

Speeding into the next century, the Base City–Day Excursion Concept™ combined with the appropriate railpass provides greater flexibility to see more of Europe at its best—by train. Many of our cost-conscious readers modify the concept by using the less expensive suburban area of a major city or one of our day-excursion points as their "base." With any one of the various types of railpasses available today, it's easy to modify our comfortable rail travel concept to suit your budget and itinerary. Armed with a railpass and a current copy of *Europe by Eurail,* you become your own tour guide, packing and moving on only when you want to. For the experienced traveler and the novice, it's the only way to go.

HOW TO USE *EUROPE BY EURAIL*

Base City–Day Excursion Concept™

In 1976 *Europe by Eurail* first launched a new concept for easy, comfortable, hassle-free train travel by combining the economy of a Eurailpass with the Fergusons' Base City–Day Excursion™ method of touring Europe. Now in its twenty-fourth edition, *Europe by Eurail* has proven to be a most useful tool for travelers using any type of railpass that allows access to any or all of the 17-country Eurail system.

We identify base cities throughout Europe in which you can stay in comfort and from which you can make numerous day excursions to interesting places, returning each night to the same hotel room. This concept eliminates the hassles of daily packing and unpacking and luggage lugging. This more relaxed approach to rail travel is not only an enjoyable way to visit Europe but also affords the time to see and do a delightful variety of things outside of the major cities.

You do not have to be a geographer to use *Europe by Eurail*. It is conveniently arranged alphabetically—first by country, then by Base City. Rail system maps accompany each country chapter.

Europe by Eurail picks up the traveler disembarking from the train on arrival from another base city (or at the airport if it is the traveler's entry point to Europe) and leads him or her *step-by-step* through the essentials of European rail travel.

We take a pragmatic approach to European rail travel by providing explicit walking directions and explanations based from rail stations. For example, a bewildered tourist standing on a train platform in one of Brussels' *three* train stations needs practical, no-nonsense information—in a hurry:

> *The Grand' Place? How do I get there?*
>
> *Where's the tourist information office?*

Europe by Eurail leads you with specific directions: "To reach the Grand'Place from Gare Centrale (Central Station), walk downhill in the direction of the Town Hall's spire until you reach the square. The tourist office is to the right of the spire when you are facing the Town Hall."

Country sections explain what types of tourist railpasses are accepted, specify what kinds of bonuses are available, and provide specific information about rail travel within that country. These sections also list each country's tourist information office locations in North America, their telephone/fax numbers, and, where applicable, internet site addresses.

Some base cities have a single train station; others have multiple stations. Under **train station descriptions** are the subsections concerning

- Exchanging money and using ATMs
- Locating tourist information

- Luggage facilities
- Securing hotel accommodations
- Train information and reservations
- Railpass validation

Base city **tourist information offices** and **hotel reservation information** are listed with addresses, telephone and fax numbers, Internet and e-mail addresses (if available), hours of operation, and, of utmost importance, how to reach those offices from the rail station.

Connections from each base city to others are listed at the end of each base city section. Not all base cities can be reached from another in the same day, although most can.

A **sightseeing, attractions,** and **special tour** information section for each base city provides a general introduction to what to see and do and how to do it.

Day excursions begin with the distance and average train time and include train schedules to/from the base city. Trains departing a base city are usually in the morning, and trains returning from the day excursions are usually in the late afternoon or early evening.

A brief history and highlights of each day excursion enable you to decide which ones are of the most interest. Then, *Europe by Eurail* again provides *step-by-step* directions on how to get from the rail station to the tourist information offices and to the day excursion sights and attractions.

Special Features

Special features in the Appendix of this edition of *Europe by Eurail* include
- **Sample 15-Day Itineraries**
- **International Calling & Dialing Codes**
- **Glossary of Rail Terminology**—In four languages.
- **Point-to-Point Fares**—Cost of a single train trip between base cities to aid in determining if a railpass is more economical than purchasing separate tickets. Nine times out of ten, a railpass will come out dollars ahead.
- **European Tourist Offices in North America**—Where to get advance destination information.
- **U.S. Passport Offices**
- **Airline** and **Hotel Information**
- **Reader Card**—We want to know more about our readers' travel needs, and we appreciate any comments and/or suggestions. We'll send you additional information about any special promotions and discounted rail travel in Europe—FREE! Please answer the questions on the card and mail it to **RailPass Express, Inc.,** 2737 Sawbury Boulevard, Columbus, OH 43235. Or, if you have Internet access, e-mail us at **laverne@ railpass.com.**

PLANNING A EURAIL TRIP

Planning Pays Off

Depending on who you are, your concept of a "plan" can vary. We have observed two general types of rail travelers—one conservative, the other adventurous. One traveler may require a detailed, hour-by-hour schedule for a day's activities; another may merely get up in the morning and see what happens that day.

One of the first questions to answer when planning a trip is, "When can I go and how much time can I spend there?" April through October are the most popular months for touring in Europe and for many events. When planning your trip, take bank holidays into consideration, since banks, postal services, most shops, and many attractions are closed, and some transportation services are reduced.

Whether or not you admit it, everyone has a problem budgeting vacation time. It's human nature to try to see as much as possible in as little time as possible. This "sightseer's syndrome" could be dangerous to your vacation. Avoid it by planning an itinerary that allows ample "free time." Also, vary the day excursions by going on a short one following a particularly long outing away from the base city. Press too hard by trying to see and do too much on your vacation and you will return home looking as if you desperately need another one.

How long should your Eurail tour be? There are many factors bearing on such a determination, the most important being the individual. How much annual vacation time do you have? How do you use it—all at one time or in two or more segments? Railpasses can accommodate just about anyone's personal needs, with Eurailpasses ranging from 15 consecutive days to 3 months of travel and flexible Europasses with options of 5, 6, 8, 10 or 15 days of travel in 2 months. When you add the wide variety of regional and individual country railpasses available, it may, at first, seem confusing. But *Europe by Eurail* and the experts at **RailPass Express, Inc.** can help you.

Even if you don't have 2 weeks or more for that grand tour of Europe, travel magazines and the travel sections of the Sunday newspapers plus the Internet are usually loaded with 1-week bargain fares to almost anywhere, mainland Europe included. By coupling our Base City–Day Excursion™ mode with a railpass, you can maximize the time that you do have to spend in Europe.

After determining the length of time you will have for your European rail trip, the next step is to develop a clear idea of **where you want to go,** what you want to see, and what you want to do. Develop your objectives well before your departure date. We disagree with those who believe that anticipation of travel is more rewarding than its realization. But we do agree that the planning phase can also be a fun part of your trip. Properly done, this "homework" will pay substantial dividends when travel actually begins.

To get things started, write to, telephone, or visit the Web sites of the **tourist offices** of each country you plan to visit (addresses in North America are listed in the Appendix). Be specific. In your request, indicate **when** you will be going, **where** you wish to go, and **what** in particular you would like to see. If you have any special handicaps or interests and hobbies, be sure to mention them. By spelling out your information needs, you will obtain better responses.

Don't overlook the **Internet** and your local library as valuable information sources. Travelers who have computers and access to the Internet can do an incredible amount of research and planning in the comfort of their own homes or offices. The great "information highway" is at your disposal.

You may want to start with some basic Web sites about each country in general and then do city-specific searches. For example, to obtain general information on Germany, start with the German National Tourist Office Web site: **www.germany-tourism.de.** Other sources of information can be found in each country chapter of this edition.

If you want to know more about European rail travel and railpasses, call **(800) 722–7151;** write to **RailPass Express, Inc.,** 2737 Sawbury Boulevard, Columbus, OH 43235; or check out the Web site at **www. railpass.com.**

Seek out friends and neighbors who have been to Europe. No doubt you'll find their experiences flavored with their own likes and dislikes. A great way to enhance this guidebook and your railpass is to get an inside look at European rail travel with the video *Europe by Train.* This video demonstrates tips and practical information on the services offered, and includes footage of the premier, scenic and Eurostar trains. To order, call (800) 722–7151 or visit www.railpass.com.

You are now ready for the decisive phase of your trip planning—**constructing an itinerary.** For Internet users, we have found that downloading the personal travel planner **EuroData** is extremely easy, understandable, and beneficial. Go to www.railpass.com, then scroll down to "Planning Your Trip" and click on EuroData. The Windows-based software program is simple to download. Changes are quickly and easily updated as you finalize travel plans with the help of icons for air, rail, and lodging, plus maps. Print when finished (the program even includes any notes you may have entered) and voilà— instant travel itinerary! Your limitations during this portion of the planning phase are only the lack of more than 24 hours in a day and the fact that the week contains only 7 days.

No computer handy? Then, **draw a blank-calendar–style form** covering a period from at least 1 week prior to your departure to a few days following your return. Make extra copies of the form—you'll need them.

Changes are common in this project!) Now begin to block your itinerary into the calendar form, being mindful that the itinerary can be changed but the number of days in a week remains fixed. Possibly by the third time through the exercise, you'll begin to see the "light at the end of the tunnel." It's only human to try to cram too many activities into a day, but it's better to discover your planning errors *before* starting your trip rather than in the middle of it.

With your itinerary in a calendar format, you can now determine your housing requirements, seat and sleeper reservations, and other facets of your forthcoming trip. The days blocked out in advance of your departure can show your "countdown" items—stopping the newspaper, having mail held at the post office, and so on. Make several copies of your completed itinerary and leave some behind for the folks with whom you want to stay in touch. Above all, take copies of your itinerary with you—you'll be surprised how beneficial they are and you will refer to them frequently.

One item that you can't leave home without is a **passport.** If you do not have one or if yours has expired, write immediately to one of the U.S. passport offices listed in the Appendix. Allow a minimum of 1 month to obtain your passport. There are ways to expedite the process, but be safe by planning ahead and making this the first order of business when you've decided to make your trip abroad. U.S. citizens are admitted to European countries with only a passport; a visa is not required.

Great resources for passport and visa first-timers are available for 50 cents each from the Consumer Information Center, Pueblo, Colorado 81009. Just ask for the pamphlets *Passports: Applying for them the Easy Way* and *Foreign Entry Requirements* for the scoop on how, when, and where to apply for these travel documents.

"Know before you go"—the slogan of the U.S. Customs Service pertaining to what you can return with—also applies to the financial aspects of vacation planning. The fluctuation of the dollar's purchasing power in Europe over the past few years has left a lot of us wondering whether or not we could afford a vacation on the other side of the Atlantic. It is sometimes difficult to determine what effect Europe's inflation will have on your dollars once you're there. Planning in advance and purchasing most of your vacation needs in advance (particularly transportation) in American dollars are probably the most effective ways to combat inflation and price fluctuations. Buy as many of your vacation needs as you can before you go and plan to limit your out-of-pocket costs paid in foreign currency to a minimum. This way, you are protected against fluctuating currency values.

The idea of putting $50 worth of gas in a Ford Escort reinforces the notion that train travel in Europe can be the best means of effectively stabilizing your travel dollars. Prepayment plans, such as the railpasses, are ideal. Not only do you purchase the pass with American dollars *prior to* departure, but a railpass also provides the most inexpensive and the quickest way to travel in Europe.

Many travel agents still want to sell a *fly-drive* program to clients who want to vacation in Europe. In general, car rentals have one basic fault—the price you are quoted may not be the price you pay; it usually is higher. As a rule of thumb, add to the quoted price another 20 percent for personal accident insurance, collision insurance, and taxes. After that consider that fuel costs about three times what you'd pay in the United States. And don't forget about the VAT (value added tax). Now order an economical railpass by calling the European rail experts at RailPass Express, Inc. (800) 722–7151 (Internet secured online ordering address: **www.railpass.com**)!

Accommodations usually account for the greatest share of a traveler's budget. Low-cost airfare and transportation bargains like railpasses can get the traveler to and around Europe, but the real bite out of the buck comes when the visitor opens his or her wallet to pay for a night's lodging. Attractively priced accommodations packages are being offered by some tour operators; but too few suit the needs of independent travelers, as is the case for travelers on a rail vacation. With advance planning and advance payment, however, you can realize significant savings if you are willing to put forth the extra time and effort to do your "homework."

Well ahead of your intended departure date—preferably 2 months in advance, but no less than 6 weeks—write to the tourist offices listed in the Appendix and request information regarding lodging in the areas you intend to stay during your rail journey. Or you may call **(888) TOUR–404** to make hotel bookings or arrange accommodations by mail or fax with central booking offices. The best assurance that you will have a room waiting upon arrival is to make an advance deposit directly to the hotel, then take care of the balance with the hotel's cashier when checking out. And always ask the hotel to confirm the room rate when you check in; doing so will avoid delays and possible financial embarrassment when leaving.

One final bit of advice on reducing the cost of accommodations in Europe: **Use your railpass.** A railpass can provide exceptional savings in housing costs by permitting you to stay *outside* the base city's center, where hotel rooms, pensions, bed-and-breakfast housing, and the like are far less expensive than their downtown counterparts. Lodgings in the suburbs, a la RailPass, can be more economical and just as convenient as those in the base cities.

Keep in mind that tourist information offices maintain extensive current lists of all types of accommodations, from hostels, bed-and-breakfast establishments or pensions, to 5-star luxury hotels.

When inquiring as to availability, you will be asked the inevitable question, "Where do you want to be near to?" Naturally, when you're traveling by rail, your response will be, "Near the rail station." You are in for a surprise—most major cities have multiple primary rail stations. A better site-selection statement might be to ask for a hotel near one of the major lines of the metro, or subway.

The budget-minded traveler may write to the European tourist offices in North America listed in the Appendix and ask for information about budget accommodations in the countries to be visited while in Europe. The plenitude of modestly priced lodgings and inexpensive restaurants, even in Europe's most expensive cities, will amaze you.

Those interested in international hostels must join Hostelling International. Adult (age 18-54), $25; senior citizen (age 54 and over) $15. You may purchase the above memberships from RailPass Express, Inc., at (800) 722–7151 or get junior (age 17 and under) memberships for $10 and family memberships for $35 from HI-AYH at (202) 783–6161 or visit ww.iyh.org.

We recommend having a confirmed accommodations reservation in your European arrival city for wherever you will be spending the first night.

How to Get There

Transatlantic air traffic is so frequent and varied today that no description of it—short of an entire book—could do it justice. Excursion fares are available in a multitudinous variety. Charter flights are available, too, and they are still mostly money savers. But some excursion rates are less expensive than charters. It is not uncommon on a regularly scheduled airliner winging its way to Europe to find that every passenger in your row of seats paid a different fare for the same flight on the same schedule with the same service!

If you've dealt with a reputable travel agency over the years, contact them for air-excursion-fare options. Or, at your leisure, you can call the various airlines' toll-free "800" telephone numbers and ask them for suggestions and fare information. We have listed the 800 numbers of a few airlines in the Appendix. Don't be disturbed if you receive a variety of responses. Internet users can search the net for those bargain fares. Many airlines have their own sites.

Regarding charter flights, inquire about them but investigate thoroughly before making any final decisions. Here again, get your travel agent involved, even if it's only to obtain the tickets. Even some of the most reputable air-charter carriers still operate on a "Go–No Go" basis. This means that if enough passengers sign up for the flight, it will go as scheduled; if not enough passengers are booked, the flight will be scrubbed.

EUROPEAN RAILPASSES

A railpass provides flexibility and economy if you are making several trips, especially any over long distances. A point-to-point ticket is, of course, good for travel from one point to another. You can, though, consult the fares between major cities listed in the Appendix of this edition or visit our more extensive point-to-point fares database at **www.railpass.com**. Add up the cost of your journey and then compare it to the cost of a railpass to see what works best for your trip.

Today's rail traveler has a wide choice of railpasses available, from the 17-country Eurailpass to regional passes encompassing groups of countries and individual, or national, country passes.

A comprehensive list of prices and types of railpasses is listed in the Appendix of this edition and on the above-listed web site.

How Long Is a Railpass Day?

There are many different types and price ranges of railpasses available that provide *unlimited* rail transportation for a specified number of days. A "railpass day" runs from midnight to midnight, during which time it is possible to make unlimited on-and-off-the-train journeys. Those with flexible railpasses can extend the use of their pass by taking advantage of the overnight bonus. This rule allows passengers boarding overnight trains departing after 1900 to count the trip toward the next day of train travel. This is a great way to get the most out of your pass on long treks, plus be rested for a full day of sight-seeing. Flexible passes are described later in this section.

Railpass Validation

You have 6 months from the issue date of the railpass (the date of purchase stamped on your pass) in which to begin using it. Prior to boarding your first train in Europe, present your pass for validation at the rail station. Allow for a little extra time for the validation process, but once your pass is validated, that ends standing in line to buy another ticket—a real convenience.

- Do not make any entries (such as filling in your passport number) prior to validation.
- Although it is not a part of the validation process, write the starting and ending dates of your pass validation period on a piece of paper and hand it to the clerk along with your pass and passport. (Remember Europeans write the day before the month; thus, 10/07/00 would mean July 10, 2000.)
- Be certain the clerk agrees to the dates before he or she enters the validity period on your pass.
- Double-check the validation dates before accepting the pass. If an error is made in either the dates or your passport number, have it corrected immediately.
- The clerk then enters your passport number and stamps the pass.
- Sign the pass only after the rail official has asked you to do so.

Once validated, your pass is neither refundable nor replaceable.

Pass Protection Program

Guard your railpass with the same attention you give to your cash, traveler's checks, and passport. Lost or stolen passes are not refundable; RailPass Express, however, offers a pass protection program that reimburses its clients in full for the unused portion of the railpass in case of loss or theft, and the cost is only an additional $12 per pass.

Eurail Passes

There are two basic types of Eurailpasses—consecutive-day and flexible passes. **Consecutive-day passes** are valid for an unlimited number of rail journeys during the number of rail pass days you purchased, which constitutes the pass's "validity" period. For example, if you purchased a 15-day Eurailpass and took your first train trip on January 1, your pass would be valid for use as many times as you want in any of the 17 countries listed below until midnight on January 15. We call it the "tick-tock" pass. All of the Flexipasses preceded by the word *Eurail* cover any or all of the 17 European countries. Rates for children ages 4–11 are 50 percent off the adult fares of both passes.

Consecutive-Day Eurail Passes

Austria	Hungary	Spain
Belgium	Ireland (Rep. of)	Sweden
Denmark	Italy	Switzerland
Finland	Luxembourg	
France	The Netherlands	
Germany	Norway	
Greece	Portugal	

Unlimited **first-class** rail travel (some trains may require a special supplement) throughout any or all of **17 countries**:

Choose from these validity periods: **15 days, 21 days, 1 month, 2 months**, or **3 months**. Eurailpass also provides access to many steamers, ferries, and buses, either entirely free or at reduced rates. (Eurailpass bonuses are detailed in each country introduction in this edition.) Go as you please; stop where and when you want. This pass is an excellent value for anyone visiting several countries.

Eurail Saverpass

Unlimited **first-class** rail travel for 2, 3, 4, or 5 people traveling together at all times in any or all of the previously listed 17 European countries, with the same privileges and choice of validity periods as the Eurailpass.

Eurail Youth Pass

For those who are still **under age 26** on their first day of train travel, this pass provides unlimited **second-class** rail travel in any or all of the above-listed 17 countries. It entitles you to the same privileges and choice of validity periods as the first-class Eurailpass, except it is valid for second-class travel only.

Flexible Eurail Passes

Flexible-type Eurail passes provide exactly what the "Flexipass" name implies—flexibility. The Flexipasses work especially well if you plan to stay in one place and not travel for a few days. You choose the number of travel days that can be used at any time either 10 or 15 days within a 2-month validity period. Thus, while you're not traveling, your railpass is not "ticking" away. For example, if you purchase a 10-day Eurail Flexipass, you will have 10 boxes on your pass in which you write the dates of the days you use the train. We recommend that you write in the date *on* the date that you travel, rather than in advance, just in case you want to change your travel plans at the last minute.

Eurail Flexipass

Unlimited **first-class** rail travel in any or all of the aforementioned 17 countries. Buy either 10 or 15 travel days and use them within 2 months.

Eurail Saver Flexipass

Unlimited **first-class** rail travel for 2, 3, 4, or 5 people traveling together at all times in any or all of the aforementioned 17 countries. Purchase either 10 or 15 travel days to be used within 2 months.

Eurail Youth Flexipass

Unlimited **second-class** rail travel for passengers under age 26 on their first date of travel. Purchase either 10 or 15 days of travel to be used within 2 months.

Eurail/Drive Pass

Designed for those who use the rail network for most of their travels but who occasionally want an automobile to explore the local countryside. Includes 4 days of unlimited first-class rail travel throughout the 17 Eurail countries and 2 days of car rental vouchers that can be used at any time, and not necessarily consecutively, within a 2-month period. You can purchase up to 5 additional rail days and an unlimited number of more car days.

Europass

If your rail travel will be limited to **Germany, France, Italy, Spain, and/or Switzerland**, consider this "design-your-own" flexible multicountry pass for unlimited **first-class** rail travel. Choose 5, 6, 8, 10 or 15 days of rail travel to be used within 2 months. As with the other Flexipasses, the travel days need not be consecutive.

You can really get creative by now adding up to 2 of the geographical "zones" listed below to your pass for an additional fee (see the list in the Appendix for all prices):

Benelux Zone (includes Belgium, the Netherlands, and Luxembourg)
Danube Zone (Austria and Hungary)
Greece Plus (Greece and includes ferry crossing from Italy to Greece)
Portugal

Youth Europasses for unlimited second-class rail travel are available to those under age 26 as above.

Europass Saverpass

Unlimited first-class rail travel for two to five persons traveling together at all times to the five countries covered by the Europass plus up to two additional zones listed above are available as well. Choose 5, 6, 8, 10, or 15 days of unlimited first-class rail travel within a 2-month period.

Europass Rail/Drive

Similar in concept to the Eurail/Drive Pass but valid only in the same countries as the regular Europass. It includes 3 days unlimited first-class rail travel and 2 days of car rental vouchers. Unlimited additional car rental days may be purchased, up to 7 additional rail days. Zones are not available.

EUROPE'S PASSENGER TRAINS

Many European trains run at speeds in excess of 100 mph, and the high-speed French **TGV** (*train a grande vitesse*, or train of great speed) *Atlantique*, which normally cruises along at 186 mph, holds the world's speed record at 320 mph with the Thalys, Eurostar, and the Cisalpino following close behind. The basis for high-speed rail traffic is a flawless rail bed, and Europe's tracks sing as trains move smoothly enough to permit dining without fear that the next curve might slosh your coffee. Most rail lines throughout Western Europe today are equipped with endless, welded track. The old "clickety-clack" of the track, regardless of its nostalgic value, is gone forever.

Europe's passenger trains range from the sleek, high-speed, high-tech **AVEs, Eurostar, Thalys TGVs,** and international express trains, running on the main lines, to the perky little omnibus rail cars that ply the suburban lines. In between are national **InterCity** and regional trains that provide express services within a country's borders. The newer trains include a whole stable full of various passenger car (carriage) types, including plush compartment interiors, comfortable seats, and businesslike amenities. Each of the new double-deck TGVs, for example, can carry 545 passengers and feature telephones, a children's play area, and computer hook-ups.

Germany's **InterCity Express (ICE)** service provides cars with increased leg room, headphones, and even some video systems built into the seat backs. Italy has not only a "tilting tower" (the Leaning Tower of Pisa) but also a "tilting" train, termed *Pendolino*. You can sit back and relax with complimentary snacks and an espresso while this comfortable train whisks you to your destination at an operating speed of 155 mph. And the powerful dual-voltage **Cisalpino** trains, the world's first international tilting trains, easily climb the mountain routes between Italy and Switzerland.

The British-Belgian-French–modified TGVs, known as "Eurostar" trains, connect Britain with Continental Europe. Connecting through London and the English Channel tunnel (Chunnel) to Paris, Brussels, Amsterdam, and Cologne (Köln), the Eurostar trains make the British connection between London's Waterloo International station in the city's center and Paris' Gare du Nord station in under 3 hours. Even the airlines can't get you there any faster if you consider the amount of time it takes from city center to the airport, going through security and customs, and then transportation from the arrival airport to city center.

Seat Reservations

Most international and long distance trains *require* seat reservations, including TGVs, Eurostars, InterCity and AVEs EuroCity trains, Cisalpino and Pendolino trains, some ICEs and specialty sightseeing trains such as those in Switzerland (*Glacier Express, Bernina Express, Crystal Panoramic,* and *The William Tell Express*).

A computerized reservation system linking the European rail routes is available in every major rail terminal in Europe. Check the train departure board—if there is an **"R"** next to that train, then seat reservations are mandatory, and you should not board without one. Seat reservations for TGVs and many other types of trains can be made at automatic reservation-ticket dispensers in the rail stations.

Seat reservations in Europe cost about $5.00 each, and this cost is *not* included in a railpass. Advance seat reservations may be made from North America, but they are more expensive and nonrefundable. If, however, you choose to make seat reservations from North America, you may make them through the same place you purchase your railpass. The Point-to-Point and Reservations Department of RailPass Express can help with itinerary planning and seat reservations. Tel: 614–793–7650 from 0900 to 1600 EST Monday through Friday.

The farther south you travel in Europe, the more important it becomes to have seat reservations even if they are not required. *Always* have seat reservations when traveling in Italy and Greece. Seat reservations are not, however, accepted for most local trains, nor for trains traveling *within* the borders of Belgium, the Netherlands, Luxembourg, or Switzerland, with the exception of specialty trains.

To ensure that you receive the proper reservation,

- **Determine the day and date of your travel.** Remember, Europeans reverse the order of the month and day when writing dates. Day, month and then year is the standard reading. For example, June 15, 2000, appears as 15/06/00 and *not* as 06/15/00.
- **Check the train schedules** posted in the rail stations for the train number, its departure time, and arrival time at your destination.
- **Print this information** on a piece of paper, starting with the date, the train number, and the departure time. Draw a short arrow, and then add the arrival time of the train and the name of your destination.
- **Indicate the number of seat reservations required.** Your seat reservation will identify the class of travel (first or second), smoking or non-smoking, car number, and, in most cases, the seat number(s).

Plan to be on the train platform several minutes prior to scheduled departure. European trains stop only for a short time at intermediate stations to let passengers on and off, and stops of only 1 or 2 minutes are usual. To save a lot of scurrying around when the train arrives, **check the illustrated train composition diagrams** displayed on the platforms to determine the approximate positioning of your train's first- and second-class coaches.

Then, as your train approaches, look for *either* a large number **"1"** on or near the doors *or* a yellow stripe above the train windows to indicate first class cars if you have a first class railpass and/or a first class seat reservation. Second class cars are indicated with a large **"2"** on or near the doors.

Train Schedules

Every European rail station has train arrival and departure times prominently posted, usually by huge digital display boards. The printed ones posted are easily recognized by their background color—**departure times are printed on yellow; arrival times on white**. Intermediate stops, train platform, and track numbers are posted as well. In case of discrepancy, the digital display boards take precedence. Although the time schedules may change, the track numbers seldom change.

Schedules are listed chronologically in **24-hour time** from 0001 (1 minute after midnight) to 1200 (noon) and to 2400 (midnight)—for instance, a departure time of 1843 would be equal to 6:43 P.M.

Train information and reservation offices in the stations also provide printed mini–schedules listing rail services between two specific points. They're free. These offices have national and international schedules as well.

Train schedules presented in this edition of *Europe by Eurail* are updated to press time. They are, however, for planning purposes only. When purchasing a railpass, you are entitled to receive a **free pocket timetable and map** of the major rail connections.

Train Splitting

When international trains in Europe have multiple destinations, sometimes passenger coaches are "split" en route, with cars going to different cities. To make certain you end up where you want to be:

- **Check the train sideboards** displaying the departure point, stops en route, and the final destination.
- **Announce your destination** to the conductor as he or she checks your railpass.
- **Stay in your seat** when the train halts at a terminal for "splitting" the coaches. Since the splitting process occurs quickly, if you are in another part of the train you could easily end up at the wrong destination—sans suitcase and your fellow travelers.

There may also be times when two trains are scheduled to depart on the same track—one in each direction, of course. Check for your train's departure position; otherwise you might be standing at the wrong end of the track as your train departs.

Europe's Night Trains/Hotel Trains

Although we usually advocate going to Europe to see it, not sleep through it, today's European overnight trains provide a most comfortable and convenient means of transport over long distances. And there's an aura of romance on Europe's luxurious hotel trains.

There is a great variety of accommodations on night trains, ranging from **sleeperettes** (comfortable reclining seats) to the luxury-hotel–style trains complete with a hotel lobby area and concierge. Traditional nighttime trains usually do not have full restaurant service, but the steward can provide drinks and snacks. They are normally comprised of standard sleeping cars, **couchette cars** (with four berths per compartment in first class and six berths in second class), and regular seats. The couchette cars usually offer washrooms and toilets at the ends of the cars. You get a place to lie down, a blanket, and a pillow.

EuroNight (EN) trains are usually air conditioned and provide additional comfort and services with the same basic facilities as the traditional sleeping car trains. EN trains complement EuroCity daytime trains and offer a wash basin with soap, towels, and a power plug; a real bed with sheets, pillows, and blankets; complimentary mineral water, snacks and a continental breakfast served in the cabin.

For luxury, comfort, and privacy, Europe's high-tech, high-comfort hotel trains are top of the line—InterCity Night (German Rail), CityNightLine (based in Switzerland), and Trens Hotel (Spanish Rail). An InterCity Night cabin contains its own private shower, toilet, and wash basin, and beds are aligned in the direction of travel. Popular routes include Berlin–Munich and between Berlin–Dortmund, Essen, Dusseldorf, Cologne (Köln), or Bonn. Railpass holders receive about a 50 percent discount on cabin rates.

CityNightLine trains feature high-quality, double-decked, hotel-style sleeping accommodations and single-level sleeperette cars. Luxury Category A provides spacious compartments on the upper deck with one or two wide beds, shower, toilet, and panoramic windows. Railpass holders receive about 30 percent discount. For budget travelers, Category C has large reclining seats with a canopy, containing a reading lamp to enhance a feeling of privacy. Railpass holders pay only about $20. CityNightLine routes include Berlin–Zürich, Zürich–Vienna or Hamburg, and Vienna–Cologne/Dortmund.

The tilting Spanish **Trens Hotel** trains operate within Spain and internationally into Portugal, France, Italy, and Switzerland. The Gran Clase sleeping cars include private toilet and shower facilities; Turista Class offers four-berth compartments; or, for economy, choose the sleeperette seats. Trains carrying the Gran Clase cars include the famous *Pablo Casals* (Barcelona–Geneva, Bern, and Zürich), the *Antonio Machado* (Barcelona–Seville/Malaga), and the *Lusitania Express* (Madrid–Lisbon).

Generally speaking, the least expensive trains with sleeping accommodations are in Southern and Eastern Europe; Northern and Central Europe are the most expensive. The sleeperette, or reclining seat, is the least expensive type of accommodations, and Luxury Class on hotel trains is the most expensive.

Remember: *Railpasses do not cover the costs of sleeping accommodations*; in most cases, however, they do provide a discount.

The "Chunnel" and Eurostar Services (Internet: www.eurostar.com)

In 1888, Louis Figuier proclaimed that "linking France and England will meet one of the present day needs of civilization." On May 6, 1994, England's Queen Elizabeth II and France's President François Mitterand brought Figuier's words to life and inaugurated a new era in European train travel—the linking of England and France via a tunnel that runs underground and beneath the English Channel. More than 17 million tons of earth were moved to build the two rail tunnels (one for northbound and one for southbound traffic) and one service tunnel. The Chunnel has proven to be one of the world's largest undertakings. The project cost more than $13 billion and took 7 years to complete.

Napoleon's engineer, Albert Mathieu, planned the first tunnel in 1802, incorporating an underground passage with ventilation chimneys above the waves.

For obvious reasons the British were nervous. Later, in 1880, the first real attempt at a tunnel was undertaken by Colonel Beaumont, who bored 2,000 meters into the earth before abandoning the project. When work on another tunnel began in 1974, the Beaumont tunnel was found to be in good condition. Construction of the current tunnels began in 1987; they are 38 kilometers in length undersea and have an average depth of 40 meters under the seabed.

Operated by a British railway operating company and by the French (SNCF) and Belgian (SNCB) railways, the Eurotunnel provides three different types of service between England and the Continent. Eurostar provides passenger service, and Le Shuttle provides automobile, coach, and lorry service between Folkstone and Calais. International rail freight rounds out the list.

Travel times from London to Paris are reduced from more than 9½ hours to 3 hours; Brussels is only 2 hours and 45 minutes away, thus making a European Capitals tour nothing more than a day excursion. *Eurailpass* holders receive a discount on Eurostar tickets. Eurostar also serves Lille and Calais in Northern France and Ashford, Kent, in England. To order tickets contact RailPass Express at (800) 722–7151 or visit www.railpass.com; for Eurostar day and overnight tours call (888) TOUR–404 (see Special Itineraries/Tours chapter).

The Eurostar Trains

The sleek Eurostar trains *(Trans Mache Super Trains)* each carry 766 passengers (24 in premium first class, 182 in first class and 560 in second class) and reach speeds of nearly 200 mph in France and 100 mph through the Chunnel and into England. The train is based primarily on the TGV but was redesigned to accommodate the three different voltage types encountered en route. The trains are accessible to handicapped passengers and those requiring special needs. Arrangements may be made up to 48 hours prior to departure by calling Eurostar Complimentary Assistance Service in the U.K. at 44 (1233) 617575. Sufficient storage for luggage is provided.

Families traveling with children may opt for coaches 1 through 18 where facilities are offered for baby changing and flip-up seats allow more room for kids. Ask the train manager for a children's pack of things to do while traveling.

You are required to check in at the Eurostar terminal at least twenty minutes prior to departure. After check-in and passing through the security and passport control, you will find a boarding area lounge, cafeteria, bar, and shops.

Those taking advantage of a trip from Paris or Brussels to London on a Eurostar train are in for a treat. The trains offer the comfort and amenities comparable to few other trains in the world. From departure you're in store for a smooth, quiet ride, and even when you enter the tunnel, the only noticeable change is the sudden darkness outside the windows. Those concerned with changes in air pressure needn't worry. Air flow through the tunnel is regulated to minimize changes in pressure, and few passengers, if any, notice discomfort.

Eurostar staff are multilingual and are available to provide assistance from the minute you enter the terminal to the minute you exit the platform. You'll notice them right away, dressed in navy blue uniforms with accented yellow scarves or ties. If you have any questions, don't be shy—they're there to serve you, and serve you they do.

Passengers traveling first class are treated to an onboard meal ranging from breakfast to dinner, depending upon the time of day. Second-class passengers won't starve either, as a buffet car and roving refreshment cart services are available at reasonable costs.

Given the frequency of rail service and the speed of travel, it's easy to see how a "quick trip" to Paris, Brussels, or any continental destination can be accomplished. Following is the schedule for Eurostar trains running between London and Brussels; then between London and Paris. To purchase one-way or round-trip Eurostar tickets or for scheduling information on trains to other cities, *Tel:* (800) 722-7151, *Fax:* (614) 764-0711, or visit www.railpass. com/eurostar.

Note: Be certain to check in at your departure station at least 20 minutes prior to departure.

LONDON WATERLOO STATION—BRUSSELS MIDI/ZUID

Depart London	Eurostar Train No.	Arrive Brussels	Notes
0614	9108	1002	Mon–Sat
0653	9110	1037	Mon–Sat
0827	9116	1210	
1027	9124	1405	
1227	9132	1610	
1423	9140	1802	
1627	9148	2010	
1719	9152	2106	Departs at 1723 Sat, 1727 Sun
1827	9156	2210	Except Sat
1927	9160	2310	

TRIP TIPS

Before You Go

If there have been any break-ins in your neighborhood, you should take steps to ensure that a break-in doesn't happen to you while you are gone. Alert the neighbors to keep a watchful eye for suspicious people and their activities. Many professional thieves have been known to park in a driveway in broad daylight with a moving van. The police should be advised regarding your absence. Also, check with the insurance agency that writes your home-

BRUSSELS MIDI/ZUID—LONDON WATERLOO

Depart	Eurostar Train No.	Arrive	Notes
0702	9109	0850	Mon–Sat, arrives 0843 Sat
0803	9113	0939	Mon–Sat
0857	9117	1039	
1102	9125	1243	
1302	9133	1443	
1456	9141	1639	
1702	9149	1843	
1756	9153	1939	Except Sat
1856	9157	2039	
2102	9165	2243	Arrives 2239 Fri & Sun

PARIS NORD—LONDON WATERLOO

Depart	Eurostar Train No.	Arrive	Notes
0637	9005	0846	Mon–Sat
0716	9007	0909	Mon–Sat
0813	9011	1013	1
0910	9015	1113	
0943	9017	1143	Mon, Fri, Sat, Sun
1019	9019	1213	
1143	9025	1343	
1219	9027	1413	
1304	9031	1509	
1416	9035	1609	Fri, Sun
1443	9037	1643	
1519	9039	1713	
1543	9041	1743	Fri
1607	9043	1813	
1710	9047	1913	
1743	9049	1943	Sun
1819	9051	2013	
1843	9053	2043	Except Sat
1919	9055	2113	
2007	9059	2213	
2043	9061	2243	Fri, Sun
2113	9063	2316	

1. Departs 0807 on Sunday

LONDON WATERLOO—PARIS NORD

Depart	Eurostar Train No:	Arrive	Notes
0515	9078	0823	Mon–Sat
0619	9002	1023	Mon–Sat
0723	9006	1123	
0753	9008	1147	Mon–Sat
0823	9010	1223	
0853	9012	1253	
0923	9014	1323	Mon, Fri, Sat
0953	9016	1353	
1023	9018	1417	
1053	9020	1453	Fri–Sat
1157	9024	1556	
1253	9028	1653	
1327	9030	1720	Fri, Sun
1357	9032	1756	
1523	9038	1923	
1553	9040	1947	Fri–Sun
1623	9042	2023	
1715	9046	2117	Mon–Fri, 1
1748	9048	2153	2
1823	9050	2223	Sun
1853	9052	2253	
1923	9054	2323	Fri, Sun
1953	9056	2347	

Departures are daily unless otherwise noted. The times shown above are local times. France is 1 hour ahead of Great Britain.

1. Departs 1723 Sundays
2. Departs 1753 Fridays and Saturdays

owner's policy. Ask the same question they ask in those television commercials: "Am I covered?" You may need additional coverage during your absence. One final caution: Don't announce your forthcoming vacation plans in the newspapers. Thieves can read, too. Save the social column for your return.

What to Take?

Half the clothes and twice the money! Obviously, the practical answer to this question is, "As little as possible." We usually tend to pack everything we might conceivably use during a vacation, lug it everywhere, use it very little,

Eurostar Fares

Eurostar fares are provided in U.S. dollars one-way, in either direction. For schedules or tickets, contact RailPass Express, Inc. at (800) 722-7151 or www.railpass.com. Call (614) 793-7650 for Eutostar fares to other cities services, including Ashford, Lille, Calais-Frethun, and Marne-la-Vallee.

LONDON TO PARIS OR TO BRUSSELS

Fare	First Class	Second Class	Notes
Adult	$219	$149	
Senior	$159	$120	1
Youth	—	$79	2
Child	$105	$65	3
Adult Passholder	$155	$95	4

1. Senior: Age 60 and over.
2. Youth: Age 12–25; ticket discount not available for youth.
3. Child: Age 4–11; ticket discount not available for children.
4. Discounted ticket available with the purchase of a Eurailpass, Europass, or BritRail Pass.

- Seat reservations are mandatory on all Eurostar trains.
- Tickets issued include reservation on the same voucher (inclusive price).
- Youthpass holders can utilize second class only.
- First class includes a gourmet meal.

and return home with longer arms. In these days of wash-and-wear fabrics (and deodorants), such an approach is not necessary. A good rule of thumb is to take **one medium-size suitcase with wheels** and a shoulder bag. Hold to this rule and you will have a more comfortable trip. Regardless of how comfortably warm you expect the weather to be at your destination, pack a **sweater.** Brief cold spells in Europe are not uncommon. Stow a small pocket **flashlight** in your shoulder bag together with a collapsible **umbrella** or rain hat in the "unlikely event" that you may need them.

Bring a **washcloth** if you normally use one, since they generally are not found in European hotels. Take an **electrical converter** and **adapter plugs** for your **electrical appliances,** such as electrical razors and hair dryers. Travel-size, dual-voltage hair dryers are convenient—you only need to switch the voltage to the European 220 and add the appropriate adapter plug.

If you must take expensive jewelry with you, take a copy of its **insurance appraisal** as proof of purchase to customs officials upon your return. The same for watches produced by foreign manufacturers. You may have bought that solid-gold Rolex in a St. Louis pawnshop for a song, but the customs inspector could have you singing a different tune if you can't come up with the paperwork! Also bring **proof of purchase** on any expensive items you are traveling with, such as your laptop computer or video cameras.

If you wear prescription eye glasses or contact lenses, **take a copy of the eyeglass or contact lenses prescription** with you. The same applies for **prescription medications.** Even if you use only over-the-counter drug products, we suggest taking an adequate supply of the item in its original container. Many such products are not available in Europe or are sold under a different label or packaging.

For rail travelers, we heartily recommend luggage with wheels. Samsonite, the luggage manufacturer, has published an interesting booklet on the subject of suitcases and travel. With the catchy title, *Lightening the Travel Load—Travel Tips and Tricks,* it is crammed with helpful tips, everything from analyzing your packing and luggage needs to safeguarding your possessions on a trip. Helpful hints on carry-on luggage, how to tip, how to clear customs, and how to stay healthy are also included. For a free copy, write to Samsonite Traveler Advisory Service, P.O. Box 39603, Denver, CO 80239. Include a self-addressed business envelope with postage affixed to cover up to 2 ounces first-class.

Cash, Cards, and Credentials

Right now both the Euro and individual country currencies exist in Europe. The Euro will become legal tender for 11 European countries (over 280 million people) in the next two years. Currently, the Euro is used on major electronic transactions at an exchange rate of $1 USD = 0.98 EUR. Until the Euro becomes the unified currency for Europe, (supposedly by 2002) consult the "Cheat Sheet for Travelers," online at **www. oanda.com/cgi-bin/travel**, for **foreign exchange rates.** You can print out the conversion rates in a wallet-size format for each country you intend to visit. Then just cut them out and place them in your wallet for a convenient reference guide. Another great conversion site is www.xe.net.

Don't carry more cash than you can afford to lose; use **ATMs** (automated teller machines) or carry traveler's checks. You will, of course, need some cash on your flight to pay for tips, snacks, refreshments, and taxi fares at your arrival city. U.S. currency will usually do, but don't carry it all in one big roll—distribute it around in pockets, briefcase, money clip, and/or money belt. A money belt is an ideal way to carry larger notes. Getting some smaller denominations of the local currency is always a great idea for tipping, plus those coins and bills will make great souvenirs once the Euro is in place!

ATMs offer the best exchange rate on foreign currencies, but if you plan to use them, do your homework first. Ask your bank for a list of ATM locations in the countries where you plan to travel and whether or not your magnetic imprint needs to be modified to work in foreign ATMs. Be certain to know your PIN number, and inquire if the bank will charge you per overseas cash withdrawal. Also, remember that ATM PIN numbers in Europe are four digits; six digits will not work. The two largest international ATM networks are Visa/Plus and MasterCard/Cirrus. To find out which network your bank uses, you can look on the back of your card for the network logo. To find the ATM locations abroad for Visa/Plus, write to Visa International, 900 Metro Center Boulevard, M1-9C, Foster City, CA 94404, or access the Web site at www.visa/com/cgi-bin/vee/vw/products/atm/wrld.html?2+0; for Master Card/Cirrus, call (800) 4–CIRRUS, or access its Web site at www.master card.com/info/atm-form.htm.

Although U.S. banks levy surcharges for the luxury of using their machines, these charges do not extend to U.S.-issued cards at machines overseas. Remember, though, that a cash withdrawal on a credit card is like a "temporary mini-loan," and there is an interest charge.

You can avoid interest charges by using a **debit card** (whereby cash withdrawals and purchases are deducted from your checking account). You probably will still pay a fee of around $2.00 per withdrawal with a debit card. If you do carry traveler's checks, cash them at the branch-bank facilities located in or near railway stations and airports. Banks and official currency-exchange services are government supervised and are required to pay the official exchange rates. Hotels and stores seldom give you the full exchange value and often add substantial service fees. Credit cards are handy for paying the larger expenses, such as hotels and restaurants. The charge is converted into dollars at the applicable exchange rate on the date the charge is posted.

Make a list of credit card, traveler's check, airline ticket, and railpass numbers that you plan to take. When purchasing your railpass inquire about Pass Protection, a type of travel insurance covering any unused portion of the pass in case of loss or theft while abroad. Leave a copy of your list at home and pack one in your suitcase or carry-on bag. Make **two copies of your passport.** Leave one copy at home and take the other one with you. Carry a certified copy of your birth certificate and a few extra passport photos. Taking the time to do this will save you days of delay on your trip if your passport is lost or stolen. If your passport *is* lost or stolen, report it to the local police and contact the nearest U.S. Embassy or Consulate.

Cameras, Film

If you plan to take an expensive foreign-made camera that you purchased in the United States, bring the sales slip. Otherwise, go to a U.S. Customs

Office before leaving the country and have your equipment registered. Carry a copy of the sales slip or the registration form with your passport and keep a spare copy tucked away in the camera case or your shoulder bag.

Despite what airport officials tell you, their electronic luggage-checking devices could fog your film. The best way to avoid that is to not have film in your camera when you go through airport security, and place unboxed film in clear plastic bags. Ask that your cameras and film be inspected by hand. Above all, do not pack film in your check-through luggage. Although special lead-lined bags are available at most camera stores, luggage is subjected to a high level of radiation, and the film can still be damaged.

Color film in Europe includes processing and is usually more expensive than you can buy at home. The solution? Prepare and take all the film you'll need with you. The same principle applies for those videotaping their adventures. We found it to be a stress reliever to have extra film and extra batteries on hand. Just recharge every evening and you won't miss a shot.

We have had fun with the new digital cameras. Just carry a box of computer disks, which takes up as little room as 4 rolls of film, and have a go at it. Review pictures as soon as you take them and delete any that are not up to par. Plus, you can label the disk immediately with the city and site names for reference. When home, enjoy viewing them on your PC, use as screensavers, or take to a local photo lab and have actual prints made from the images on your disk files.

En Route Tips

With all the luxuries of flight that aircraft offer, something about flying makes it more demanding on your system than a similar amount of time spent at home or in the office. A transatlantic trip with a minimum of inconveniences is what we're after. Here are some suggestions that we've found helpful on our flights.

In-Flight Comfort. If you plan to catch some shut-eye en route, ask for a seat alongside a bulkhead. Bulkheads don't mind being leaned on, but passengers do. If you need more legroom, sit in an emergency exit row, but only if you are physically capable of standing and opening the exit hatch if necessary. Also, be sure your seat reclines. On some planes the seats in front of the emergency exits do not recline. Opt for seats in the forward section of the airplane; passengers in the forward section generally experience less vibration and engine noise.

Wear loose clothing. Unfasten your shoes, but don't take them off. Your feet will swell following several hours of immobility at airplane altitudes. The best remedy is to walk the length of the aisle in the airplane every hour or so. Try deep knee bends. To reduce swelling, consider wearing elastic stockings.

Flying dehydrates your body. Drink lots of water and watch what you mix with it—alcohol dehydrates, too. Special meals for special diets are no problem with the airlines, but requests should be made at the same time as reservations.

Tax-Free Purchases. Tax-free shopping in Europe was abolished in July 1999 between European Union (EU) countries. This change should have little if any effect on U.S. and other non-EU travelers as long as travel is to or from a non-EU destination. The EU consists of Austria, Begium, Denmark, Finland, France, Germany, Great Britain, Greece, Holland, Ireland, Italy, Luxembourg, Portugal, Spain, and Sweden. Every international airport, as well as many ferry ports and train stations, currently has a "tax-free" shopping service. The routine is generally the same: You select your purchase, pay for it and add it to your carry-on luggage, find safe storage for it during the flight, and then haul it off the airplane. There are variations.

For example, at JFK in New York you select the items from a sample or catalog. The items are then delivered "for your convenience" to your departure gate for pickup. The hazards of this system are many. If the delivery person gets things mixed up and fails to make the right gate at the right time, you'll be off into the wild blue yonder sans purchases. Or if you are late passing the pickup point, sometimes an unknown "benefactor" will try to help by taking your purchases onboard the plane ahead of you—then finding this so-called benefactor can prove to be difficult.

Solution? Buy your "booty" aboard the airplane while en route. Most international airlines carry aboard a good stock of "tax-free" items, that you can purchase from the cabin crew. It's always best to check at the airline counter, however, to be certain that this in-flight service will be available on your particular flight. *Tax-free,* by the way, is a misused term. Most items, with the exception of alcohol and tobacco, normally may be purchased cheaper in the arrival city. Many airports are planning to create specialty shopping outlets to compensate for revenue losses. If taking any Eurostar or Channel crossing trips while abroad, the taxes in Belgium and France are lower than in Britain.

Keep in mind everything you purchase, "tax-free" or otherwise, is subject to customs duty when returning home. Items shipped are processed separately. Consequently, know your quotas and attempt to stay within them to avoid paying duty and experiencing the ensuing delays involved. Good luck with customs. And remember, honesty is always the best policy!

Prior to Landing. Fill out all the customs and immigration forms your flight attendant may give you and keep them with your passport and airline ticket. Keep this packet handy but secure, until your credentials are required by the customs or immigrations officials at the arriving airport.

Jet Lag—What to Do About It

For North Americans it takes an entire day to reach Europe by air and an entire day to return. Although the flying time aboard most commercial jet airliners ranges from 7 to 8 hours, airport to airport, it will be Day 2 before you arrive in Europe. (There are a few daytime eastbound transatlantic flights, but most depart at night during Day 1 and arrive the following morning, that is, Day 2.) During the flight you will be exposed to a cocktail hour, a dinner hour, and a break for an after-dinner drink, followed by a full-length feature movie. In the morning, as the sun rises in the East over Europe, you'll be awakened an hour or so before landing for breakfast.

Add up the time consumed by all the scheduled events while en route and you'll quickly conclude that your night spent in the sky over the Atlantic Ocean consisted of many things—except sleep. Even if you did manage to sleep during the entire trip instead of eating, drinking, and watching movies, your body and all its functions will be arriving in Europe a few hours after midnight by North American time. You will crave adjustment to the phenomenon known as jet lag, which will be trying its best to interrupt your plans for a carefree vacation.

The following explanation of what jet lag is and some means to combat it should prove helpful to any traveler undergoing 4 or more hours of time change.

The human body has numerous rhythms; sleep is one of them. Even without sunlight, as in a cave, the body will still maintain a 24-hour awake/asleep cycle. The heart rate falls to a very low ebb in the early hours of the morning, when you are usually asleep. Body temperature, which affects the mental processes, also drops during this time. Consequently, if an air traveler is transported rapidly to a time zone 5 or 6 hours ahead of that of the departure point, even though it may be 8:00 or 9:00 A.M. at the arrival point in local time, the traveler's body functions are at a low ebb. As a result, the traveler feels subpar, and this feeling can persist for as long as 2 or 3 days unless something is done to correct it.

To cope effectively with jet lag, start varying your normal sleep-eat-work pattern a week or so before your departure. If you are normally up by 7:00 A.M. and in bed around 11:00 P.M. or so, get up earlier and go to bed later for a few days. Then reverse the procedure by sleeping in a bit in the morning and going to bed ahead of your normal time. Vary your mealtimes, possibly putting off breakfast until lunchtime. This will condition your body to begin accepting changes in routines. In turn, when the big transatlantic change comes, it won't be as much of a shock on your system.

To lessen the effects of jet lag en route, avoid excessive drinking and eating. Set your watch to local time at your destination as you descend on your flight. By doing this, you subconsciously accelerate your adjustment to the new time zone. For example, how many times have you looked at your watch and *then* realized you were hungry? After your arrival, exercise the first day by taking a vigorous walk, followed by a long nap. Then take it easy for the rest of your arrival day. From now on begin doing everything you normally do back home according to the new local time.

Some seasoned transatlantic travelers take even stronger precautions to avoid jet lag. They follow the rule of "no coffee, tea, food, wine, beer, or liquor" on the day of the flight to Europe. They do, however, advocate lots of fruit juices, vegetable juices, and water (no carbonated drinks). This method follows the theory that your body clock will then go on hold, waiting for you to restart it with breakfast the day you arrive in Europe.

Resist the temptations of the airlines up to the point of breakfast and try to get some sleep. Some current studies have shown the hormone melatonin to be useful in combatting jet lag, but as with any other over-the-counter drug, you should first consult your physician. And then there's the "light theory"—that using a blue light source behind your elevated kneecaps will eliminate jet lag. Regardless of which remedies you choose, respect jet lag by taking some precautions and you'll enjoy your vacation.

Train Travel Tips

"What affects men sharply about a foreign nation," wrote G. K. Chesterton, "is not so much finding or not finding familiar things, it is rather not finding them in the familiar place."

Going to Europe for the first time can mean a confusion of terminology that causes us to learn too late that what we sought was actually available throughout our visit. Our problem can be merely not knowing where to look and what to ask for. The following tips should help you enjoy your rail adventures:

Handicapped Travel. Rail travel is becoming more and more a chosen method of transportation and recreation for disabled persons. Many aids for the handicapped have been incorporated into rail station design. Trains are being designed with wider doors for wheelchair access; some even have a removable seat to make room for a wheelchair. Ramp access to toilets, buffets, and other facilities is being provided. Folding wheelchairs are also available at main stations so that occupants can be transferred to a regular seat once aboard the train.

The European railways are eager to provide as comfortable a journey as possible for the disabled passenger. To do this, advise authorities of your intended travel plans before departure.

In the United States contact Mobility International USA, P.O. Box 10767, Eugene, OR 97440 (tel. 503–343–1284) for information about services and referrals to international affiliates. They also produce a book, *A World of Options for the 90s: A Guide to International Educational Exchange, Community Service, and Travel for Persons with Disabilities.*

If you plan to travel in Europe with a handicapped person, as soon as you establish your itinerary, contact one of the tourist offices listed in the Appendix and begin making arrangements. The same applies to the airline you'll be using for your transatlantic flight. Give details of your itinerary, the nature of the disability, and any other information that will help them to help you, such as whether a wheelchair is needed at departures and arrivals. Specifically, provide information regarding special diets, medications, and toilet and medical-attention requirements. With these details attended to, you can look forward to a pleasant journey.

Baggage Carts. Many otherwise able train visitors to Europe impose a severe disadvantage upon themselves by arriving with more luggage than anyone could possibly carry. Train porters are nearly an extinct species, and their demise was expedited by the luggage trolley—Europe's version of our baggage cart—an elusive device that, whatever your position on the train platform, haunts the extreme opposite end and requires insertion of coins to use. Our number-one trip tip to all train travelers is to "go lightly." We repeat: At most, take **one medium-sized suitcase with wheels,** augmented by a modest shoulder bag. There will still be times when you wish you could discard your suitcase. Pack lightly and leave room for souvenirs or you'll just need to purchase another piece of luggage.

If you have purchased a model with built-in wheels, however, it usually will follow at your heels like a well-trained dog as you apply minimum pulling power. Unlike a dog, the wheeled suitcase cannot climb stairs by itself, so be prepared to lift it on and off the train and in some stations without elevators.

Consider investing in your own baggage cart to take with you if you wish to use the luggage you have. There are many types available. You will see more and more train travelers proceeding through rail stations in Europe with wheeled equipment.

When loading your luggage onto a baggage cart or station trolley, keep the load as narrow as possible. The trolleys provided by the station should not be taken aboard the train, although we've seen it tried. Again, if you are taking your own cart with you, fold it before boarding. If you don't, you may spend an embarrassing 10 minutes or so on the station platform extracting a hapless fellow traveler from it as your train eases out of the station without you.

Porter Services. Porter service is on the wane but still available in some train stations, particularly the larger ones. The best way to locate a porter is to inquire at the "Left Luggage" (baggage storage) area. Most stations also offer luggage lockers (some stations have stopped this service and, for security reasons, have even removed trash containers). If your luggage has been checked in at the station, there will be a handling charge, but the tip remains a personal transaction between you and the porter.

Most porters will take your bags to the train and place them aboard in the luggage racks over your seat. Porters are rather scarce on arrival platforms. If you must have assistance, approach the stationmaster's office or the train conductor prior to departure, with the request that a porter be asked to meet your train upon arrival at your destination.

If you are transferring between base cities or changing hotels from one city to another, you can request the hall porter at the hotel you are leaving to arrange for the arriving hotel's hall porter to meet your train upon arrival. A small tip should arrange everything.

A Few More Train Travel Tips. A few more train travel tips to make your trip more enjoyable:

• Show your pass or rail ticket, upon request, and in the case of the pass, have your passport handy should the conductor want to see it.

• Don't place your feet on the seats of the train unless you have removed your shoes or have provided a protective covering for the seat.

• Place your luggage in the overhead racks (or the luggage vestibules) provided for that purpose—not on the seats so that other passengers won't be able to crowd you.

• Observe the smoking/nonsmoking areas and rules. There are rather stiff fines that can be imposed for smokers who violate the nonsmoking regulations.

• Observe seat reservations. Seating that has been reserved is marked, usually by a ticket inserted at the top of the seat. Even though it is apparent that a seat is unoccupied, if there are other passengers seated opposite, ask whether the seat is open—doing so will avoid embarrassment later if the person holding the reservation happens to return.

• Regarding dining-car reservations, on long-distance trains it is best to arrange for them soon after boarding. Ask the conductor. If he or she cannot make the reservations for you, a member of the dining-car crew will do so. Generally, these crew members pass through the train prior to the first serving for that purpose. Usually there are two servings, so be prepared to select the one to your liking. You can also ask about the menu at the same time. The second serving is scheduled so that the dining-car crew has time to tidy up before the train reaches its destination. Therefore, the first serving is preferred by many because it does not seem to be as rushed.

• If you plan an overnight journey on a sleeper, ask the attendant to explain how the equipment in your compartment operates. For example, newer sleeping cars have electric shades. A push of the button and they open; another push of the same button and they close. If you did not know the button's function, you just might try pushing the button while the train was standing in a station and you were not dressed for the occasion! Tip the attendant for his or her services; the appropriate time to do so is when breakfast is served.

Not by Bread Alone

Oddly enough, the reader who exists on hamburgers and milk shakes back home will find such a diet expensive to maintain in Europe. Europe abounds in good, wholesome food. Practically every major railway station has a cafeteria where the food is displayed along with the prices. "Order the spaghetti Bolognese," was the advice of one tourist official in Switzerland. "You can't go wrong," he declared, and he was right.

Many of the railway stations have dining-room facilities, and some even have gourmet restaurants. Most European restaurants offer a tourist menu at a fixed cost. Look for the MENU sign, posted outside, showing the prices and food selections.

If you are puzzled by foreign menus, take heart. Many European restaurants have menus that have been translated into your language. Although the translated versions may take some of the "adventure" out of eating in a foreign country, they may save an embarrassing moment—such as ordering the poulet, which you recognize as chicken, and ending up with a whole roasted chicken!

To help hold the food price line, determine if your hotel includes breakfast with the accommodations and if so, what kind of breakfast and how much the room is without it.

On day excursions, pack a picnic-style lunch. Bread, cheese, pastry, cold cuts, fruits, soft drinks, and beer or wine—all are available from local shops. If you give advance notice, perhaps the hotel will prepare a basket lunch for you.

For the most part, meals served aboard the trains are, naturally, on the expensive side. In many cases, though, the food is excellent and well worth the premium you pay for enjoying it as you speed along with the scenic countryside. Many trains provide buffet and cafeteria services, and you can usually count on a food trolley being aboard for drinks and sandwiches. On some trains, such as the TGV Thalys, gourmet meals are served at your seat—airline style. One fact remains: The least expensive food aboard a train is that which you brought. Again, plan ahead and save.

Dos & Don'ts Safety Tips

• Picking pockets is an art that is seemingly practiced throughout the world and most commonly occurs in crowded public places. Be leery of being bumped or of someone causing a distracting incident. Don't carry anything more valuable than a handkerchief in hip pockets. Money belts, holster wallets, or pouches that can be hidden are the safest way to carry cash and other valuables.

• If you do not have a concealable money belt, holster wallet, or pouch, women should place the straps of their purses across their chests and carry the purses in front—not on the side with the straps only on the shoulder. Motorcycle thieves can grab the purse from your shoulder very easily. Men should modify the inside pocket of a coat or jacket with a zipper or Velcro. Or sew a medium-size button both above and below the pocket opening. Loop a piece of shoestring or other strong string around the buttons when carrying valuables. Don't let the thought of someone picking your pocket alarm you. Just be aware of it and take the proper precautions.

• Don't leave cash, cameras, and other valuables in the hotel room or locked up in a suitcase. Take them with you or leave them in the hotel safe. We advocate leaving expensive jewelry at home, but if you must take it with you, leave it in the hotel safe when you're not wearing it.

• Don't dangle your camera from around your neck or wrist; keep it in an inexpensive-looking camera bag.

• Don't designate one individual to carry everyone's passport or other valuables, and don't carry all of your own valuables in one place. Split up documents and money in various safe holding locations.

Stay alert.

For further peace of mind we suggest reviewing the Web site http://travel. state.gov/asafetripabroad.html for insightful tips and suggestions for "A Safe Trip Abroad." It contains ideas on what to bring and leave behind, what to learn and arrange before you go, as well as helpful tips for public transport safety.

Remember, visitors are always subject to the law of the land, so pay attention to media reports and research some of the local laws and customs prior to departure. Also consider visiting the U.S. State Department's internet site, www.state.gov, which contains up-to-date information on foreign affairs. You may also contact the U.S. Department of State Consular's Office for information on travel warnings and public announcements by calling (202) 647–5225; *fax* (202) 647–3000; or visit www.travel.state.gov.

Several pamphlets are available as well from the Superintendent of Documents, US Government Printing Office, Washington, DC 20420, tel: (202) 512–1800. At about $1.00 each, they include, *Your Safe Trip Abroad, A Safe Trip Abroad, Tips for Americans Residing Abroad,* and *Travel Tips for Older Americans.*

Austria

Austria's central location in Europe and its six international airports of the Imperial Cities—Vienna (Wien), Graz, Innsbruck, Klagenfurt, Linz, and Salzburg—make it a convenient gateway country for European travelers. Although German is the native language of Austria, most tourism officials also speak English. With a smile on your face, try the informal German greeting "Grus Gott," and ask slowly and distinctly, "Do you speak English?" A smile almost always elicits a cooperative attitude.

Austria is more than museums and antiques; it is also music, gorgeous scenery, and gourmet foods. Austria is a country where one can easily overindulge in temptingly tasty pastries and piles of *schlagrahm* (whipped cream)—and what a way to go. We discovered why the *schlagrahm* is so delicately delicious—it's the *real* thing.

As the Austrian National Tourist Board succinctly states: "Austria is more than 1,000 years old. So far, so good." For more information and pretrip planning tips, be sure to visit Austria's Web site: **www.anto.com** or contact the Austrian Tourist Offices in North America:

New York: New York, NY 10110. *Tel:* (212) 944–6880; *Fax*(212) 730–4568; *E-mail:* antonyc@ibm.net

Montreal: Office National Autrichien du Tourisme, 1010 Ouest Rue Sherbrooke, Suite 1410, Montreal, Quebec H3A 2R7, Canada. *Tel:* (514) 846–3709; *Fax:* (514) 849-9577

Toronto: 2 Bloor Street East, Suite 3330, Toronto, Ontario M4W 1A8, Canada. *Tel:* (416) 967–3381; *Fax:* (416) 967–4101

Vancouver: 200 Granville Street, Suite 1380, Granville Square, Vancouver, BC V6C 1S4, Canada. *Tel:* (604) 683–5808; *Fax:* (604) 662–8528

Banking

- **Currency:** Austrian schilling (ATS)
- **Exchange rate at press time:** 12.82ATS = $1.00 U.S.
- **Hours:** 0800–1230 and 1330–1500 Monday–Friday; closing at 1730 on Thursday; closed Saturdays and Sundays. Banks in most airport and rail terminals are open 7 days a week, 0800–2000; until 2200 in Vienna.

Communications

- **Country Code:** 43
  For telephone calls within Austria, dial a zero (0) preceding area code.
- **Direct dial:** AT&T Direct: 022 90 30 11; Canada Direct: 022 90 30 13; MCI WorldPhone: 022 90 30 12; SprintExpress: 022 90 30 14

  What's the best way to phone home? Telephone calls to the United States made from a private or a public phone at the post office cost ATS 18 (about $1.50) per minute (rates for Alaska and Hawaii are higher). It may be worth your while to buy a green Telephone–Wertkarte for ATS 50 (approx. $3.75) or the gold one for ATS 100 (approx. $7.50) at a post office and make your calls from a card-operated pay phone. Collect and credit card calls are possible from Austria; special overseas operators can be reached by dialing 09 nationwide.

  Avoid placing lengthy long-distance phone calls from your hotel, since hotel surcharges can be astronomical.

Rail Travel in Austria

The Austrian Federal Railways, or Österreichische Bundesbahnen (ÖBB) operates the 5,800 kilometer rail system and accepts the **Austrian Railpass,** the **European East Pass,** the variety of **Eurailpasses,** and **Europasses** with purchase of the **Danube zone.** (See Appendix for list of railpass types and prices or consult the RailPass Express Web site at www.railpass.com). Remember to purchase your railpasses prior to your departure for Europe. For ÖBB information on the Internet: www.oebb.at.

The basic **Austrian Railpass** is valid for 3 days of rail travel within a 15-day period. First Class, $154; Second Class, $104. Additional rail days available for $22, First Class; $16, Second Class. Child rates are half of the adult fare for ages 4–12; under age 4 travel free.

A **Eurailpass** includes the following discounts within Austria:
- Boats between Melk, Krems, and Vienna (Wien), operated by DDSG Blue Danube Schiffart (First Danube Steamship Company)—15 percent discount
- Wurm and Köck steamers on the Danube River from Linz to Passau (Germany)—50 percent discount
- Rack railroads Puchberg am Schneeberg–Hoschneeberg—10 percent discount; and St. Wolfgang-Schafbergspitze—15 percent discount
- Rent-A-Bike (130 stations)—40 percent discount
- Steamers on Lake Wolfgang (Wolfgang See)—20 percent discount
- Steamers on Lake Constance (Bodensee)—50 percent discount

Purchase of the **Europass** or **Europass Saverpass** with the Danube zone added also includes the above discounts.

Rail seat reservations cost approximately ATS 30; both national and international reservations may be made at any rail station. Eurail Aid offices are located in Innsbruck Hauptbahnhkof, Salzburg Hauptbahnhkof, and Wien Westbahnhof (Vienna West Station).

Base City . . .

Vienna (Wien)

City Dialing Code: 1
www.info.wien.at

Arriving by Air

Schwechat Airport, *Tel:* 7007–2231 or 7007–2232 (24 hours)

Located 19 kilometers from the city center, Schwechat Airport is the home base for Austrian Airlines, which offers nonstop flights between the United States (New York) and Vienna and serves more than 30 other international airlines.

Airport–City Links: Trains run every 30 minutes from the airport into Wien Mitte and Wien Nord stations. The price to Mitte is approximately $3 U.S. During heavy morning and evening traffic, the train is the best way to go. At other times, we recommend the airport bus service, which connects with the Westbahnhof (West Station) and Südbahnhof (South Station), as well as with the city air terminal (Hilton Hotel). The fare is ATS 70; time en route, 20 minutes. The bus-departure point is immediately outside and to the left of the arriving-passenger exit. Purchase tickets on the bus.

If you purchase a Vienna Card in the baggage claim area of the airport ("Tourist Corner") you'll pay only ATS 60 on the Vienna Airport Lines bus. See "Getting Around in Vienna" for details about the Vienna Card.

Arriving by Train

The Westbahnhof (West Station) and Südbahnhof (South Station) are Vienna's major railway terminals. Westbahnhof is the gateway to Germany, Switzerland, and the rest of northern and central Europe; Südbahnhof is the gateway to southern and eastern Europe. Wien Mitte and Wien Nord are commuter-type stations. For **train information** by telephone, dial 1717 (24 hours).

Westbahnhof has two levels. Arriving by train, you will be on top of the elevated level. The taxi stand is on the left as you leave the train platform. The main station concourse is at street level.

- **Baggage storage** located on main station concourse level. After descending on the escalator from track level, turn right and go to the far end of the concourse just before the station restaurant. The facility will be to your immediate right.
- **Money exchange** (*Exchange-Wechselstube*) located to the right of the escalators on the top level. Daily hours: 0700–2200.
- **Train information, reservations, and railpass validation** may be made at *Reisebüro am Bahnhof,* located in the glass kiosk.
- **Südbahnhof** is a three-level terminal with the train platforms located on the middle and top levels.
- **Money exchange** located in lower level immediately to the right of the main staircase. Daily hours: 0630–2200.

Tourist Information/Hotel Reservations

- Schwechat Airport, opposite the baggage carousels in the arrivals hall. Daily hours: 0830–2100. Hotel reservations.
- Verkehrsbüro Travel agency in the Westbahnhof (West Station). Daily hours: 0700–2200. Hotel reservations. Located in the entrance hall on the ground floor.
- City center main tourist office: Kärntner Strasse 38, Vienna 1 (behind the Vienna State Opera House). Daily hours: 0900–1900. *Tel:* 51 38 892. To get there by public transport, take the U-bahn (underground) Line U3 to Volkstheater and on the Ringstrasse you can take tram 2, D or J for the two stops to the Opera House. From Südbahnhof (South Station), only tram D will take you to the Opera House.
- Tourist information by telephone: 211 140 (Monday–Friday 0800–1600).

Getting Around in Vienna

The most economical and convenient way to discover Vienna is to purchase the **Vienna Card.** At a cost of only ATS 210, you'll have access to Vienna's entire public transportation network for 72 hours, plus discounts at many museums, sights and attractions, concerts, shops, theaters, restaurants, cafes, and *Heurigen* (wine taverns). All the benefits are more fully described in the 64-page Vienna Card coupon book.

Purchase the Vienna Card at tourist information offices, your Vienna hotel, or **Vienna Transport** *(Wiener Linien)* information offices, located in many underground stations, such as Stephansplatz, Karlsplatz, the Westbahnhof rail station, and the Landstrasse/Wien Mitte station. These offices are open

Monday–Friday 0630–1830 and Saturday–Sunday 0830–1600. Or order the Vienna Card with your credit card by telephoning 43 (Austria country code) (179) 844–0028. For Vienna Transport information, dial 7909–105.

Vienna's efficient city transportation network includes the U-Bahn underground, trams, S-Bahn (rapid-transit intracity trains), and bus service. The best bargain is the Vienna Card that covers more than just the transportation network. But there are other choices for transportation only: A single ticket is ATS 17, a 24-hour network pass is ATS 50, a 72-hour network pass is ATS 130, and an 8-day strip ticket is ATS 265. Children under 6 travel free.

These transportation tickets can be purchased from tobacconists, at vending machines in the underground stations, or even from reception desks in many Viennese hotels. Single-trip tickets from the ticket vending machines in trams and buses cost ATS 20. A punched single ticket is valid for one trip, including changing lines. Purchase a public transportation map for ATS 15.

Sights/Attractions/Tours

The Vienna Tourist Guides are highly qualified professionals who can help you find a variety of ways to see Vienna, and one of the best ways to really get to know the city is on foot. Ask for the brochure *Walks in Vienna* and choose from sixty walking tours; each has a different theme spanning the spectrum from "Pure Hapsburg, The Hofburg and its Emperors" to "Chow-houses, Boozers, Brothels, and Other Houses of Ill Repute." Reservations are not required; just show up at the point mentioned in the brochure for the particular tour you choose. Cost: ATS 130 per person; under age 18, ATS 70; with a Vienna Card, ATS 115. Duration of the walking tours is 1½–2 hours. Private guided tours may also be arranged. For a real moving experience, tour Vienna by bicycle. Call Vienna-Bike at 319 12 58 to book your bike.

For a leisurely view of Vienna, take a cruise aboard the ship MS *Vienna* from the Little Danube onto the Big Danube. The ship departs from Schwedenplatz for a cruise to Reichsbrucke. You can return to the city via the underground or the MS *Vienna*. Departures are at 1000 and 1400. One way ATS 120; round trip ATS 170 (10 percent discount with Vienna Card; reduced rates for children). Ask the tourist office for the DDSG Blue Danube Ships' brochure detailing their cruise programs or call 588 80 222.

Vista of Vienna

The pace is slower in Vienna; Vienna developed the waltz and the city's tempo has moved in leisurely three-quarter time ever since.

Vienna's coffeehouses are oases of good living at a leisurely pace. Visiting them during your stay is a must. Our favorite coffeehouse happens to be the original one in Vienna, the **Sacher Café,** a part of Hotel Sacher immediately behind the Opera House. It has a semiformal but friendly atmosphere. By all means try the sugar tarts and don't miss the *Apfelstrudel* (apple cake). Expensive? Well, yes, but it's worth it.

The Viennese "invented" coffee. According to legend, in 1683 the Turks were defeated and abandoned their three-centuries quest to conquer the heart of Europe at the gates of Vienna. In their hasty departure, they left some bags of coffee beans behind. The local folks swarmed out of the city and carried the bags back behind its protective walls and began experimenting. A gentleman by the name of Kolschitzky evolved a clear brew—unlike the Turks who, to this day, serve it with the grounds—and the people of Vienna were so elated that they erected a bronze statue to his memory.

The Viennese like to eat well, and they take great pride and pleasure in giving their visitors every opportunity to do likewise. Choose from a dazzling array of eateries from stand-up snack bars and simple little pubs, known as *Beisel,* to ethnic specialties and gourmet restaurants. Since good food deserves good libation, try the tasty and strong Austrian beer or some of Austria's great vintages. These are bottled and aged; but young, fresh wine is rushed to the taverns, where locals and visitors alike consume it as though it might lose its freshness between sips.

Vienna is many things, but primarily it is music. Visit the **State Opera**, a preeminent point of European music, or visit the **Strauss home** where the *Blue Danube Waltz* was written. Thrill to the harmonious voices of the **Vienna Boys' Choir,** or marvel at the white **Lipizzan stallions** as they dance to music in the **Spanish Riding School**. Vienna is a memory that will waltz through your dreams forever.

Since Hungary accepts Eurailpass and Europass (if the Austria/Hungary associate zone option has been purchased), many Eurail travelers transit Vienna on through trains such as the *Wiener Walzer* without stopping. Take advantage of the frequent rail service and stop for a few hours in Vienna en route to Budapest. Baggage can be stored in the *Gepackaufbewahrung* (temporary baggage storage facility) in the Westbahnhof main concourse level.

Day Excursions from Vienna

Because of its location on the Danube River and the eastern reaches of the Alps, Vienna can offer some unusual day-excursion opportunities. Among them are cruises on the Danube to **Melk** or tours through the Vienna Woods and the **Austrian Alps** by train.

Local trains can take you to **Baden,** one of the most famous sulfur-bath spas in Austria or to the Tyrolean center of **Innsbruck**. Express trains can whisk you from Vienna to Salzburg in time for lunch—followed by dinner—and still return you in time to slumber in your base city Vienna.

Train Connections to Other Base Cities from Vienna (Wein)

Depart from Vienna West station (Wien Westbahnhof), unless otherwise noted

DEPART	TRAIN NUMBER	ARRIVE	NOTES
Amsterdam Centraal			
1920	EN 224	0940+1	R, Sleeper
Berlin Zoobahnhof			
1110★	EC 172	2125	
2125	EN 228	0906+1	R, Sleeper
Bern (Berne)			
0720	EC 160	1746	1
0920	EC 162	1946	2
Brussels (Bruxelles) Midi/Zuid			
1920	EN 224	0935+1	R, Sleeper
Budapest Keleti			
0815	EC 229	1113	
0907	D 263	1203	
1007	D 345	1303	
1435	EC 63	1720	
1607	EC 25	1852	
1800	D 343	2138	
2007	D 347	2303	
Hamburg			
1020	ICE 90	1952	
1950	EN 490	0746+1	R, Sleeper
Munich (München) Hauptbahnhof			
0550	EC 16	1036	
0850	EC 64	1336	
1550	EC 62	2036	
2028	D 262	0120+1	
2330	D 248/D 268	0630+1	
Paris Gare de l'Est			
0850	EC 64	2222	
2028	D 262	1023+1	
Rome (Roma) Termini			
0730★	EC 31	2115	
1930★	EN 235	0933+1	

DEPART	TRAIN NUMBER	ARRIVE	NOTES
Zürich Hauptbahnhof			
0720	EC 160	1625	
0920	EC 162	1826	
2120	EN 466	0625+1	

Daily, including holidays, unless otherwise noted
R Reservations required
★ Departs from Vienna South station (Südbahnhof)
1. Arrive in Zurich at 1625. Change to IC 732 departing at 1634.
2. Arrive in Zurich at 1826. Change to IC 736 departing at 1834.

Day Excursion to

Austrian Alps Tour   VIA VILLACH AND SALZBURG

Depart from Vienna South Station (Südbahnhof)

Distance by train: 541 miles (871 km)
Average train time: 14 hours, 40 minutes

The Austrian Alps probably provide more beauty than all of the fine art masterpieces in the world laid end to end. The fact that you can watch the splendor of their Alpine panorama unfold from the comfort of a train compartment makes this a most unusual and thrilling day excursion.

Take an adequate, large-scale map of Austria along, and try to select a day when good visibility is forecast. For the latter, your hotel should be able to provide a weather forecast, and an ideal map is the one published by Kummerly and Frey. You'll find it in newspaper kiosks or station newsstands.

This day excursion requires changing trains in Salzburg with the option of changing trains en route to Salzburg at Villach. The time between trains in Villach and Salzburg varies according to the schedule you select. Consider having lunch in Villach followed by dinner in Salzburg. Dining aboard is also possible, since all of the trains listed on the schedule haul dining cars.

The Alps in Austria are divided from north to south into three chains: the **northern limestone Alps, the central high Alps**, and **the limestone Alps of the south**. These chains are separated from each other by the great furrows that form the river valleys of the Inn, the Salzach, and the Enns in the north and the Drava and Mur in the south. The route we have selected for this day excursion takes you through all three alpine chains.

Even if the weather is good when you leave Vienna, the climate of the Alps varies considerably with differences in altitude. Expect some changes in the tem-

Vienna (Wien)—Austrian Alps Tour

DEPART VIENNA SÜDBAHNHOF	TRAIN NUMBER	ARRIVE VILLACH
0658	IC 531	1148
0858	IC 597	1348
1058	IC 599	1548

DEPART VILLACH	TRAIN NUMBER	ARRIVE SALZBURG
1200	EC 10	1446
1400	IC 597	1646
1600	IC 599	1846

DEPART SALZBURG	TRAIN NUMBER	ARRRIVE VIENNA WESTBAHNHOF
1532	EC 163	1845
1610	IC 941	1935
1710	IC 547	2035
1732	EC 569	2045
1805	EC 65	2118
1932	EC 161	2245
2005	EC 17	2315
2025	IC 945	2400

Daily, including holidays
Distance: 541 miles (871 km)

---

perature and visibility while en route. It is not unusual to enter a tunnel with the landscape bathed in sunlight only to emerge at the other end into a storm.

Vienna is 580 feet above sea level. Leaving the city, the train moves along the edge of the Vienna woods. Before arriving in Bruck, you will get an occasional glimpse of the **Raxalpe Peak** (6,630 feet). This steep-sided limestone massif, due to its proximity to Vienna, has become very popular with city-based mountain climbers. Here, the train follows the first mountain railway (**Semmeringbahn**) built in Europe (1848–54), which runs between Gloggnitz and Murzzuschlag.

From Murzzuschlag to Bruck, the train parallels the Murz River through the last really mountainous pass leading out of the Alps and on to the broad plains fed by the Danube. Bruck lies at the confluence of the Mur and the Murz rivers in the pleasant setting of the **Styrian Alps**. After passing

Unzmarkt, the peaks of the Zinken (7,255 feet) and the Greimberg (8,115 feet) Alps are visible. You then arrive in **Klagenfurt**, 1,472 feet above sea level. Summers here are extremely hot, for the town lies in a basin shielding it from the moderating effects of the Mediterranean.

Between Klagenfurt and Velden, the train passes along **Lake Woerth** before arriving in Villach. Leaving Villach and approaching the Tauern Tunnel (5 miles long), you will be able to view Mount Hochalm (11,020 feet). As you exit the tunnel, Edelweiss-Spitz (8,453 feet) stands guard on the left while Mount Gamskarspitze (9,296 feet) looms on the right.

After pausing briefly at **Badgastein**—the highest en route station, at 2,838 feet above sea level—the train gradually descends into Schwarzach and parallels the Salzach River, which flows past Bischofshofen and the city of Salzburg. Your return train to Vienna arrives at Westbahnhof (West Station).

Day Excursion to

Baden
BATHS, CURES, AND CASINO

Depart from Vienna South Station (Südbahnhof)

Distance by Train: 17 miles (27 km)
Average Train Time: 20 minutes
City Dialing Code: 2252 or 2258
Tourist Information Office: Brusattiplatz 3, Leopoldsbad, A-2500 Baden bei Wien
Tel: 44531 57 or 44531 59; *Fax:* 80733 or 44531 49
Internet: www.tiscover.com/baden-bei-wien
E-mail: touristinfo.baden@netway.at
Hours: May 1–October 31, 0900–1800 Monday–Saturday; 0900–1200 Sunday;
   November 1–April 30, 0900–1700 Monday–Friday; closed Saturday & Sunday.

Proceed to level 3 for trains departing on tracks 11 and 19 for Baden in direction of Graz. To get to the tourist information office from the rail station, use the station underpass to the town side of the tracks. Walk directly through the park in front of the station and bear right onto Bahnstrasse (Station Street) at the end of the park. Two blocks farther along, you will see a Fussgängerzone (pedestrian area). Turn right and walk to the town square. Pass the Rathaus (city hall) on its left side and proceed toward the end of the pedestrian area through Grüner Markt (the marketplace). The tourist office is just behind Gruner Markt.

Baden is situated on the eastern edge of the Vienna woods and surrounded by extensive vineyards and woodlands. Because it also lies on the edge of Europe's great eastern Pannonian plain, it enjoys a moderate climate, much sunshine, and favorable temperatures. In fact, Baden is in the warmest part of Austria and it is well known as a health resort.

Baden sits on 15 ancient **thermal water springs**—with a regular temper-

Vienna (Wien)—Baden

DEPART VIENNA SÜDBAHNHOF	TRAIN NUMBER	ARRIVE BADEN
0740	E2951	0804
0840	E2953	0904
0940	E2955	1004
1040	E2957	1104
1240	E2961	1304

Trains depart daily every 40 minutes past the hour. Plus commuter trains departing at 0810, 0815, 0910, 0915, 1010, 1015 and other services at the same frequency until late afternoon. Check schedules for track Nos. 11 and 19 on top (third) level of the Südbahnhof (South Station). Most trains departing for Graz stop at Baden.

DEPART BADEN	TRAIN NUMBER	ARRIVE VIENNA SÜDBAHNHOF
1455	E2962	1520
1655	E2966	1720
1755	E2968	1820
1855	E2970	1920
2055	E2974	2120

Trains depart daily every 55 minutes past the hour. Plus commuter trains departing at 1512, 1525, 1533, 1555, 1612, 1625, 1633, and continuing until late evening. Check schedules in Baden railway station.

Distance: 17 miles (27 km)

---

ature of 36 degrees Celsius (97 degrees Fahrenheit). These sulfurous thermal springs form the basis for treatments and cures; some 4 million liters of it are used daily. The early Romans were always keen on baths and they spent legions of hours soaking in the medicinal, hot sulfur springs of the area they called "Aquae" and its thermal springs. In the nineteenth century, Baden became the center of social life for Vienna's growing sphere of influence. Today, it is a world-renowned spa and vacation spot, full of charm, flowers, and more swimming pools than one can possibly enter in a single day excursion.

Swimming is a year-round pastime, either outdoors in the thermal and mineral pools or indoors at **Römertherme**. The thermal public swimming pool (Thermalstrandbad), with its Art Deco–style, 5,000-square-meter pool area and extensive sandy beach, is an adventure-bath for the whole family. In 1930 a section of the park lands of Castle Weilburg was added, making it one of the largest open-air baths in Austria.

Baden offers other forms of relaxation, ranging from quiet paths leading in and around the eastern edges of the Vienna woods to a lively game of Black Jack in the **Casino Baden** opposite Kurpark. The casino opens daily at 1500, and for ATS 260 you can buy welcome chips worth ATS 300. Baden is also ideal for shopping—its entire center is a pedestrian zone filled with small specialty shops. When you tire of bargain hunting, retreat to the city rose garden in **Doblhoff Park** to watch chess played on a larger-than-life chess board.

Another interesting pastime is visiting the informal **wine taverns** scattered throughout the town. Since the Middle Ages, every citizen of Baden has had the right to sell self-produced wine, as well as meat and sausage specialties. These "taverns" are identified by a pole decorated with fir twigs, or you can seek them out by following the tavern signs displayed throughout the town. With even more wine taverns in Baden than swimming pools, visitors engaged in "researching" taverns might do well to come to Baden as early as possible and leave only when they have discovered the best vintage—or spend the night in Baden, depending upon how much research they conducted.

Day Excursion to

Innsbruck   JEWEL OF THE ALPS

Depart from Munich, Germany   From Vienna Westbahnhof

Distance by Train: 107 miles (172 km)   *Distance by Train:* 319 miles (513 km)
Average Train Time: 1 hour, 53 minutes   *Average Train Time:* 5 hours
City Dialing Code: 512
Tourist Information Office: Burggraben 3, A–6021
Tel: (0512) 59850; *Fax:* (0512) 598507
Internet: www.tiscover.com/innsbruck
E-mail: info@innsbruck.tvb.co.at
Hotel Information: Innsbruck Hauptbahnhof
Tel: (0512) 583766; *Fax:* (0512) 583767
Hours: Monday–Friday 0800–1600

A tourist office is located in the train station on the east side. One is also on the outside of the station. To get to the other offices, leave the main station hall by the exit on the left-hand side and proceed past the "Checked Baggage" area. To get to the office in town, follow Salurner Strasse to the Triumphal Arch; make a right and follow Theresien Strasse directly to the tourist office at the Burggraben crossroad.

Located less than 2 hours away by train, Innsbruck is a convenient excursion to make from Munich (München), Germany. Translated, *Innsbruck* means "bridge over the Inn River." Situated at the junction of the Inn Valley and the Sill Gap, on the road and railroad route running into Italy through the Brenner Pass, the city is the cultural and tourist capital of the Austrian Tyrol.

Innsbruck is surrounded theatrically by its mountains. There is a mountain view from nearly every street, corner and every window in town. Looking northward from its main street, **Maria–Theresien Strasse**, you will confront the towering Alps, which seem to encroach upon the city. The scene is breath-taking.

This day excursion offers an opportunity to explore the **Tyrolean Alps** in a cable car—plus a visit to one of the most picturesque "old towns" in Austria. To top it off, a circuitous return on the **Mittenwald railroad** is possible; it takes you on a fantastically scenic rail route straight through the heart of the Austrian and Bavarian Alps en route back to Munich via Garmisch-Partenkirchen.

You are in for an eye-filling day. Even the regular rail line running out of Munich is loaded with Alpine scenery. Take a seat on the right side of your coach outbound from Munich for the best views. Keep your eyes on the edges of the pine forest for families of deer. The fawns venture farther into the clearing but scamper back faster into the woods as the train passes.

Most of the shops and restaurants in Innsbruck accept German currency. If you want to change money into Austrian schillings, however, the exchange office is located at your far left just as you exit from the trains. Hours are 0730–2000 daily. The Hotel-Information office located in the station is an official exchange, too.

The **Innsbruck Card** includes admission fees for many sights, museums, and other attractions (even a free welcome drink at the casino) and unlimited use of the public transportation network within the city. The card is valid for periods of 24, 48, or 72 hours at 230, 300, and 370 schillings, respectively.

Also purchase the large guide map if you plan a walking tour of the city, then head west for a few blocks to Innsbruck's **Arc de Triumph**. From this point, turn north and wend your way slowly through the Altstadt (Old Town), which lines both sides of the street all the way to the **Goldenes Dachl** (Golden Roof) at the end of Herzog-Friedrich Strasse. It may come as a disappointment, but the so-called Golden Roof is made of heavy, gilded copper.

Bus tours of the city are available throughout the year. Biking tours are a great way to see Innsbruck, too. For an excursion that takes you back in time, telephone (0512) 530–7134 to make reservations for the Nostalgic Tram.

We suggest you eat lunch in the **Goldener Adler** (Golden Eagle), the oldest inn in the city, founded in 1390! It is around the corner on the left and can best be described as a delicious experience. If you go there for dinner, enjoy Tyrolean music in the cellar restaurant. It will complete a perfect evening.

In the winter Innsbruck is an Alpine sports paradise, with 7 skiing regions, including the magnificent Stubai Glacier, 62 lifts, 55 marked ski runs, 130 kilometers of well-maintained ski trails, and 9.5 kilometers of high-altitude cross-country trails. Telephone, fax or e-mail the Innsbruck Tourist Office or visit **www.europeanvacation.com** for holiday and ski package information.

Vienna (Wien)—Innsbruck

DEPART VIENNA WESTBAHNHOF	TRAIN NUMBER	ARRIVE INNSBRUCK	NOTES
0510	EC 562	1030	1
0650	EC 662	1151	
0720	EC 160	1230	
0920	EC 162	1430	
1120	EC 564	1630	

DEPART INNSBRUCK	TRAIN NUMBER	ARRIVE VIENNA WESTBAHNHOF
1530	EC 569	2045
1706	EC 663	2220
1730	EC 161	2245
1930	EC 661	0050+1

Daily, unless otherwise noted
1. Monday–Saturday only
Distance: 319 miles (513 km)

Munich (München), Germany—Innsbruck

DEPART MUNICH HAUPTBAHNHOF	TRAIN NUMBER	ARRIVE INNSBRUCK
0729	EC 81	0922
0929	EC 85	1122
0944	EC 483	1138
1129	EC 87	1322

DEPART INNSBRUCK	TRAIN NUMBER	ARRIVE MUNICH HAUPTBAHNOF
1437	EC 12	1630
1637	EC 84	1830
1837	EC 86	2030
2037	EC 80	2230

Daily, including holidays
Distance: 107 miles (172 km)

Day Excursion to

Melk

ALTERNATIVE CRUISE UP THE DANUBE

Depart from Vienna West Station (Westbahnhof)

Distance by Train and Boat: 102 miles (192 km)
Total Time: 7 hours, 40 minutes
City Dialing Code: 27
Tourist Information Office: Rathaus (town hall)
Tel: 525–2307
Internet: www.tiscover.com/melk
Hours: Daily 0900–1200 and 1500–1800
DDSG ship line: Tel: (4315) 8880; *Fax:* (4315) 888–0440;
E-mail: ddsg.blue.danube@telecom.at

As you emerge from the bahnhof (rail station), walk toward the abbey, which dominates the foreground. The town hall sits at the base of the abbey, three blocks from the station.

The Danube is Europe's grand river, second in length only to the Volga and stretching almost 1,800 miles across eight countries. As plains, hills, and mountains succeed one another along its course, the Danube can be sluggish, swift, or even wild. The Danube rises in Germany's Black Forest—the length of a football field away from the watershed of the Rhine. By the time its waters reach the German city of Ulm, the Danube becomes navigable by river craft. Between Ulm and Vienna, the Danube takes on an Alpine character. The Danube is unusual among the rivers of the world in that it flows from west to east. At its delta, it empties into the Black Sea.

"The Blue Danube Waltz" is a musical expression of the attractiveness and charm of Austria along the banks of the Danube. The vast countryside—fringed by the Austrian Alps on the south—offers a vista of natural beauty. Although the waters of the river, especially in times of flood, do not always display the color of which the song sings, the beauty of the countryside through which the Danube flows makes it easy to forget that the waters are actually milky white throughout most of the spring and summer.

We recommend taking the 0827 train to Melk, the point from which the cruise down the Danube begins. It will bring you to Melk in time for unhurried connections with the ship, but Melk itself is steeped in history and warrants your visit. The earlier train will permit you to wander about Melk's ancient streets, still guarded by the watch towers of its town wall, and to visit Melk's **Benedictine Abbey**, the epitome of Baroque architecture in Austria.

Melk marks the beginning of the **Wachau region** of the Danube Valley, where ancient castles watch over the steep vineyards and orchards that stretch down to the banks of the river. It is the most picturesque section of the Danube.

Vienna (Wien)—Melk—Up the Danube (Donau)

There is no longer a regular Danube (Donau) steamer service between Wien and Melk. However, on Sundays from May through Sept, there may be a sailing if sufficient passengers request reservations. Should such sailings occur, the timetable would be:

Depart Vienna Reichsbrücke dock at 0830, arrive Krems an der Donau at 1340. A regularly scheduled service sails from Krems an der Donau from May through Oct; depart Krems an der Donau at 1550 and arrive at Melk Altarm dock at 1840. Take a taxi or bus from Melk Altarm dock to the Melk Bahnhof (station) for return to Vienna by train.

Return train schedules from Melk Bahnhof to Vienna (Wien) Westbahnhof are:

DEPART MELK	TRAIN NUMBER	ARRIVE VIENNA WESTBAHNHOF	NOTES
1911	2033/IC547	2035	1, Mon–Fri
1910	E1709	2022	1, Mon–Fri
2007	E1627/EC65	2116	1
2102	2047/IC647	2235	1
2207	E1629/EC17	2315	1
2259	IC945	2400	1

Daily, unless otherwise noted
1. Change trains at St. Polten
Distance: 53 miles/85 km

Have lunch and sample the fine regional wines in one of Melk's charming *"Heurigen"* taverns before you walk or taxi to the DDSG pier, known locally as "Schiff Station." Check with the information desk on the pier for boarding instructions.

European Cruise Ships of the DDSG Blue Danube Schiffart (see phone, fax, and e-mail information at the beginning of this section) ply regularly between Melk and Vienna from mid-May through the end of September. The Eurailpass is accepted under certain conditions and becomes your boarding ticket. The trip from Melk to Vienna is downstream in the Danube's swift current. It takes 5½ hours to complete the cruise portion; the train time to Melk from Vienna is about 1 hour.

Carry a map of the Danube and refer to it often, for it's one fine scene after another. The market town of **Spitz**, on the Danube's left bank, is readily recognizable because it nestles at the base of the Tausendeimer mountain. The name of the mountain (a thousand vessels) doesn't refer to the river traffic—it refers to the fact that the vineyards on its sides, in a good year, can produce a thousand vessels of wine.

When the ship calls at **Durnstein**, with its red roofs, you should recall that it was here that King Richard I, the Lionhearted of England, was captured and held prisoner when he returned from the Third Crusade. The next port of call will be **Krems**, which marks the eastern area of the Wachau. Since olden times, Krems has been the hub of the Wachau wine trade. Here, the Danube becomes dotted with islands as the ship draws nearer to Vienna.

Day Excursion to

Salzburg

FORTRESS CITY

Depart from Vienna Westbahnhof

Distance by Train: 196 miles (315 km)
Average Train Time: 3 hours, 23 minutes
City Dialing Code: 662
Train Information: Hauptbahnhof, Südtiroler Platz 1
Tel: 662–1717; *Fax:* 662 88 87 31 69
Tourist Information Offices:
Hauptbahnhof (Central Station) Tourist Office, Platform 2a; *Tel:* 88987–340
Mozartplatz Information Office, Mozartplatz 5; *Tel:* 88987–330
Salzburg-Mitte Information Office, Münchner Bundesstrasse 1; *Tel:* 88987–350
Salzburg-Süd Information Office, Park & Ride Terminal, Alpensiedlung-Süd, Alpenstrasse; *Tel:* 88987–360
Internet: www.salzburginfo.at
E-mail: tourist@salzburginfo.at
Hours: Daily 0845–1945 or 2100 (depending on time of the year)

If Vienna gives you the impression that it is musically inclined, wait until you see and hear Salzburg. It has been described as a music festival that never seems to end. No wonder—Salzburg is the birthplace of Mozart. His home is now a museum, and his music has become the very soul of Salzburg.

Music isn't the only thing that makes Salzburg an interesting city. It has the largest completely preserved fortress in Central Europe—the **Hohensalzburg Fortress** (circa 1077). You can reach the fortress by taking the cable car from Festungsgasse 4 (*tel:* 84 26 82), located right behind the **Neptune Fountain.** Directly behind the Neptune Fountain, you will find the cable-car station. These conveyances can whisk you to the top of Salzburg and the Hohensalzburg Fortress in a minute. There is a foot path leading to the top, but it takes a lot of huffing and puffing. Conducted tours include the **State rooms, Fortress Museum,** and **Rainer Museum.** The tour with an audio guide takes about 40 minutes. Opening hours: June 15–September 14, 0900–1800;

September 15–March 14, 0930–1700; March 15–June 14, 0930–1730. Tour costs: adults, ATS 40; children 6–15, ATS 25; Family Pass (2 adults and up to 5 children), ATS 100. In summer there is a terrace restaurant on the fortress's south side where you may view the mountains as you dine.

The trip to Salzburg aboard the *Mozart* is an event in itself. Between Vienna and Linz the train skirts the fertile Danube Valley. When the train leaves the river at Linz, you are treated to a rolling tableau of farmland followed by a magnificent view of the Alps as you skirt their northern escarpment.

The Salzburg Card, available at the tourist information offices, provides admission to all of the attractions in Salzburg, as well as free access to public transportation and many discounts. Choose a 24, 48, or 72-hour card for ATS 200, 290, or 380, respectively. If you're using Salzburg as a base city, inquire about the all-inclusive Salzburg Plus Card to include accommodations, all meals, attractions, and one concert. Prices start at ATS 1,560.

To conduct your own tour, begin in the old section of the city. Board bus No. 1, 5, 6, or 51 at the bus stop in front of the railway station and ride to the Staatsbrucke, the fifth stop. This places you on the perimeter of the Old Town, where most of the sightseeing is located. Orient yourself with the **Kapitelplatz** (Capital Place), and you are right in the center of everything.

The music-festival season starts in January and ends in December. In other words, it never ends. Afternoons in Salzburg may be spent in one of its comfortable coffeehouses watching theatergoers and opera buffs flocking to a performance—everyone in formal attire. In Salzburg, elegance is the way of life.

Salzburg has a charming narrow street, **Getreidegasse,** which is lined with gilt and wrought-iron trade signs, pictorial devices dating back to the time when few people could read. This is one of the best areas in town to find authentic Austrian souvenirs.

Mozart's birthplace, Mozarts Geburtshaus, is located at No. 9 Getreidegasse (*tel:* 84 43 13) and is probably one of the most visited houses in the city. Open daily 0900–1800 (until 1900 in July and August). Birthplace of Wolfgang Amadeus Mozart in 1756, it is now a museum. The Mozart family lived in the third-floor apartment from 1747 to 1773. Here you will see paintings and original instruments belonging to Mozart, including his childhood violin.

Only about five minutes from Mozart's Birthplace, Amadeus movie fans won't want to miss The Mozart Residence, or Mozart-Wohnhaus (*tel:* 87 42 27 40). It's across the Salzach River at No. 8 Markartplatz. Special audio and visual exhibits document the life of the Mozart family. It was here that Mozart lived and composed until 1780. His famous piano-forte, Mozart family portrait, and instruments from that era are on exhibit in the Dancing Master's Hall.

Mozart died a pauper in Vienna at age thirty-five and his body was dumped into an unmarked grave. His life story supports the expression applicable to too many of the world's great artists: "To be appreciated, one must die first."

Vienna (Wien)—Salzburg

DEPART VIENNA WESTBAHNHOF	TRAIN NUMBER	ARRIVE SALZBURG	NOTES
0510	EC 562	0828	1, 2
0550	EC 16	0855	2, 3
0628	IC 842	0950	4
0720	EC 160	1028	2
0728	IC 640	1050	2
0828	IC 844	1150	4
0850	EC 64	1155	2, 4
0920	EC 162	1228	2
0928	IC 540	1250	2

Salzburg—Vienna (Wien)

DEPART SALZBURG	TRAIN NUMBER	ARRIVE VIENNA WESTBAHNHOF	NOTES
1510	IC 645	1834	4
1532	EC 163	1845	2
1610	IC 941	1935	2
1710	IC 547	2035	4
1732	EC 569	2045	2
1805	EC 65	2118	2,4
1810	IC 649	2135	
1910	IC 647	2235	4
1932	EC 161	2245	2
2005	EC 17	2315	2, 3
2025	IC 945	2400	4
2132	EC 661	0050+1	1, 2

1. Train runs Mon–Sat only.
2. Restaurant car in this train.
3. Snacks and drinks available on this train.
4. EC 64 and EC 65 are named the *Mozart,* a popular train; seat reservations are suggested.

Belgium

Belgium may be small in size—about the size of the State of Maryland in the United States—but it is large in its significance to the European Community. Belgium played an important role in creating the European Union, which now comprises fifteen members. The Treaty on the European Union was signed in Maastricht in 1992 in an effort to safeguard peace in Europe and to move toward economic and monetary union with intergovernmental cooperation. Belgium's capital city, Brussels, is the seat of the European Union, NATO, and many other world trade and finance companies.

In 1830, Belgium gained its independence. No longer a part of the Netherlands, Belgium became a federal state of communities and regions. The three communities are based on the Dutch, French, and Germanic languages and culture—the Flemish Community, the French Community, and the German-speaking Community. The three regions (Flemish, Brussels Capital, and Walloon) were based on economical concerns.

Belgium has a hereditary constitutional monarchy, but the king does not "govern"; he serves as protector of the country's unity and independence. King Albert II became Belgium's sixth king in 1993.

Perhaps not as well known is Belgium's significant gastronomic role in Western Europe. After all, it was the Flemish Benedictine monks who invented beer, and the beers considered to be "the best" are the ones still brewed traditionally in Belgian monasteries. Restaurants of the Ardennes are well known for their wild game and the coastal restaurants serve some of the finest North Sea fish and shellfish dishes. A not so well known culinary fact about Belgium: The ratio of restaurants to population is equal to that of France.

For more information about Belgium use the Internet address **www.visitbelgium.com** or contact the Belgian Tourist Offices in North America:

New York: 780 Third Avenue, Suite 1501, New York, NY 10017. *Tel:* (212) 758–8130; *Fax:* (212) 355–7675; *E-mail:* info@visitbelgium.com

Banking

- **Currency:** Belgian Franc (BEF)
- **Exchange rate at press time:** 37.58 BEF = $1.00 U.S.
  Hours 0900–1530 or 1600 Monday–Friday; closed Saturday, Sunday, and holidays.

Communications

- **Country Code:** 32
  For telephone calls within Belgium, dial a zero (0) preceding area code.
- **Direct dial:** AT&T Direct: 0-800-100-10; MCI: 0-800-100-12; Sprint: 0-800-100-14

Rail Travel in Belgium

The Belgian railways were the first to be constructed on the continent of Europe, and Belgian National Railways (SNCB) is said to operate one of the densest rail networks in the world (3,396 kilometers). Brussels serves as an international crossroads. InterCity (IC) trains connect the main towns and regions of Belgium; the Inter-Regional (IR) trains include stops at local stations. Rail service is frequent—usually every hour between most major cities and towns, and with SNCB's integrated schedules, you need not wait long for train connections.

TGV Thalys trains link Brussels to Paris in 1 hour and 25 minutes and to Amsterdam in the Netherlands in only 2 hours and 40 minutes; the high-speed Eurostar trains can whisk you from Brussels to London in only 3 hours.

The Belgian National Railways accepts **Eurailpass, Europass** (with the purchase of the Benelux [Belgium/Netherlands/Luxembourg] Associate Zone), and the regional **Benelux Tourrail Pass,** which provides unlimited rail travel for any 5 days within a 1-month period in Belgium, the Netherlands, and Luxembourg. If you are two adults traveling together, purchase the special "Tourrail for Two" pass and save a total of $109 first class or $78 for second class passes.

Benelux Tourrail Pass

5 days in 1 month	1st Class	2nd Class
Adult	$217	$155
Youth (age 4–25)	—	104

Benelux Tourrail for Two Pass

5 days in 1 month	1st Class	2nd Class
2 people traveling together	$326	$233

Base City . . .

Brussels (Bruxelles)
City Dialing Code: 2
Internet: www.tib.be

Brussels has stood for more than 1,000 years as a signpost of ideals and ideas, a crossroad of people and events. Less than 150 miles from Amsterdam and 200 miles from Paris, Brussels is a bonanza for travelers desiring to see Europe by train. Few people realize how short distances actually are in Belgium, of which Brussels is the capital. Its most opposite points are only 195 miles apart.

Latin and Nordic cultures meet in Brussels, making it a city of contrasts. French is spoken by the Walloon people of French origin, and Flemish is the tongue of the nation's Germanic inhabitants. French, German, and Flemish are official languages in Belgium. Consequently, all signs are bilingual in Brussels. English is spoken in all of the train stations, hotels, and (the majority of) public places.

Brussels is old; it celebrated its millennium in 1979. Brussels is new; it's the headquarters of the European Common Market and the North Atlantic Treaty Organization (NATO). It is amazing that the people of Brussels have been able to preserve the city's quaint atmosphere while immersed into all this international activity. Having played vital cultural and commercial roles in Europe for more than 1,000 years, it is appropriate that Brussels was selected as a European City of Culture in 2000.

Arriving by Air

Brussels National Airport, B-1930, Zaventem, *Tel:* (322) 753–3913 (0700–2200), **www.brusselsairport.be**. Located 14 kilometers from city center.

Airport–City Links: Airport City Express trains depart from the airport every 20 minutes for Brussels Gare du Midi (South Station), Gare du Nord (North Station), and Gare Centrale (Central Station). Journey time—about 20 minutes. Fare one-way BEF 140 1st class; BEF 90 second class. (Eurailpass/Europass not accepted).

Bus station located on ground floor, beneath Arrivals Hall. Take escalators/elevators through the Diamond Area of the terminal.

Taxis about 1,100 BEF, tip included. Available outside Arrivals Hall. Look for yellow and blue logo on taxi. Save 20–50 percent by phoning for a Brussels taxi instead of using the vehicles waiting at the airport. *Tel:* (322) 721–4190. Avoid using unmetered taxis!

Money Exchange: "GWT" located in Arrivals Hall

Arriving by Train

Brussels has three train stations along its main line: one in the north (Gare du Nord), one in the south (Gare du Midi), and a midcity underground station (Gare Centrale). EuroCity trains and the major express trains do not stop in the central station. Change at either the north or south station and then transfer to a local train if Gare Centrale is your destination. Those arriving in Brussels on the Eurostar train from London will arrive at Brussels Midi.

North Station (Nord Bruxelles or Gare du Nord), Rue du Progrès, 85
Gateway to Holland, Germany, Switzerland, Italy, and eastern France.
- **Money exchange:** in a corridor to the left when exiting from the trains into the main station area. Hours: daily, including Sunday, 0800–2000.
- **Hotel reservations:** at the information booth in the departure hall. Hours: 0900–1700 Monday–Friday.
- **Train information:** in the corridor off the left-hand side of the main station area as you exit from the trains. Hours: 0700–2100 daily, except Sunday.
- **Train reservations:** ticket window No. 3 or No. 4 in the main station area.
- **Railpass validation** is at window No. 3 or No. 4.

A railway museum is located on the mezzanine of the North Station. Turn right when entering the main station from the train area and walk up the stairs at the end of the concourse. The museum holds an interesting collection of rail-transportation vehicles, ranging from the first Belgian steam locomotive to some of the present-day diesel and electric traction units. The museum is well worth the time of your visit. Admission is free.

Central Station (Gare Centrale), Carrefour de l'Europe 2. Links both North and South Stations via underground trackage. Many of the express trains do not stop here. You may, however, board any of the local trains as a shuttle to either of the main stations and vice versa. Therefore, it is possible to establish yourself in one of the downtown hotels or pensions quite near Central Station yet be able to make any train connection with a minimum of inconvenience.
- **Money-exchange:** Center hall of the station. As you stand looking at the train information board above the ticket windows, the office is on your right. Hours: daily, 0800–2000.
- **Hotel reservations** can be made at the Reservations booth in the center hall of the station. Hotel accommodations can also be obtained by visiting the tourist information center in the town hall facing the Grand'Place. (Refer to the section "Tourist Information/Hotel Reservations.") Open daily 0900–2100.
- **Train information** is displayed in the main station area immediately above the ticket windows. This is hourly information. Regular printed schedules are also displayed.

- **Train reservations:** Available only at North and South (Midi) Stations.
- **Railpass validation** must be completed at either North or Midi Station.

South Station (Gare du Midi), Rue de France 2. Gateway to Great Britain (via Eurostar trains through the Channel tunnel), France, and Spain. On the main floor you will find all the necessary train and tourist services. The tracks are located on the floor above and each track has its own escalator leading to it. The underground metro station is underneath the rail station.

- **Money–exchange:** Left side of the main hall as you enter from the street. Daily hours: 0700–2300.
- **Hotel reservations:** "Information" booth in the center of the main hall. Hours: 0900–1700 Monday-Friday. If this booth is closed, use the Brussels Tourist Information Office (T.I.B.) in the Grand'Place.
- **Train reservations and railpass validation:** local trains, at the ticket counters in the main hall. Reservations for international trains including the Eurostar must be made in the Relations Internationales Office on the far right-hand side of the main hall. Take a number from the ticket machine to wait for your turn. Railpasses may be validated at this office; Eurostar has its own terminal where its tickets are validated.
- **Eurostar Terminal:** Right side of the main hall as you enter from the street. Automatic ticket check-in (a simple insertion of your ticket into a machine) begins one hour prior to departure. Then enter the main terminal, which consists of a large waiting room, cafes, and duty-free stores. Keep in mind that you will carry your luggage onto the train as there is no baggage check-in. If you did not purchase your Eurostar tickets before departing for Europe, they may be purchased at the Relations Internationales Office.

Tourist Information/Hotel Reservations

Tourist and Information Office of Brussels (T.I.B.): Town Hall, Grand'Place, 1000 Brussels
Tel: 32 2 513 89 40; *Fax:* 32 2 514 45 38; *Internet:* www.tib.be
Hours: 0900–1800 Monday–Saturday; Sundays 0900–1800 April 1–September 30 and 1000–1400 October 1–November 30; hotel reservations available.

To reach the Grand'Place from Gare Centrale (Central Station), walk downhill in the direction of the Town Hall's spire until you reach the square. The tourist office is to the right of the spire when you are facing the Town Hall.

The T.I.B. has everything you will need to make your visit to Brussels enjoyable. In addition to tourism information and hotel reservations for Brussels, this office can also provide guides to restaurants, museums, and monuments; tickets to shows; city tours; public transport information; and books and maps.

Belgian Tourist Office: Rue du Marché-aux-Herbes, 63, B-1000 Brussels. Information/hotel reservations for all of Belgium.
Tel: 504 03 90; *Fax:* 504 02 70.
Internet: www.opt.be
Hours: June 1–September 30, daily 0900–1900; November 1–March 30, Monday–Saturday 0900–1800; Sunday 1300–1700; April–May and October, daily 0900–1800.
Located one block north of the Grand'Place.

Getting Around in Brussels

Brussels boasts a highly efficient public transport system encompassing metro, tram, and bus (STIB, Societé des Transports Intercommunaux Bruxellois). **Transport information:** *Tel:* (322) 515–2000. A free map is available from the tourist office. The signs for the metro are blue with a white letter "M"; tram and bus stop signs are red and white. Many of the metro lines also have above-ground bus and tram connections. Note that the trams and buses stop "on request." This means you should raise your hand to signal the driver to stop.

Purchase transport tickets at metro stations, STIB offices, or newsstands: one single ticket, BEF 50; card for five journeys, BEF 240; card for ten journeys, BEF 330; one-day card for use on all STIB transport whenever you wish during the same day, BEF 130. The one-day pass is also available at tourist information offices.

Sights/Attractions/Tours

The city abounds in things to see and do, ranging from its elegant **Grand'Place** to historic **Waterloo**. If you visit Brussels during the summer, sign up at the tourist office for what we believe is the best way to browse Brussels—"Summer Routes"—attractive, unique theme packages and tours incorporating trams, coaches, boats, or bikes, as well as feet. These are not the usual whistle-stop tours; you get off the beaten track and you can choose the theme tour that appeals to you. The T.I.B. also conducts other city tours—in 14 languages!

If you want to conduct your own tour, arm yourself with maps and information from the T.I.B. Then head for the Grand'Place. You can reach it from the Central Station (Gare du Centrale) by walking downhill toward the spire of the Town Hall. When you reach the square, take a minute to drink in the splendor of the ornate medieval guild houses facing the square. You will realize immediately why it is called the most beautiful square in all of Europe. If you are looking for a souvenir or a gift for someone, we can suggest pralines (hand-dipped chocolates), speculoos (brown sugar biscuits), or some fine Brussels lace. All three of these Belgian specialties are available from shops in and around the Grand'Place.

Following your map, proceed down C. Bulstraat (just to the left of the Town Hall as you face it). The name changes to Stoofstraat. At the corner of Eikstraat and Stoofstraat, you can view one of Brussels' most beloved, albeit somewhat irreverent, symbols—**Manneken Pis**. It's a fountain statue—sometimes costumed—doing just what its name implies.

Want to see Brussels and the rest of the European Community in one day? You can. Ask the tourist information office for details about **Mini-Europe** (*Tel:* 478 05 50) in Bruparck (metro stop: Heysel). You'll see Europe in miniature—more than 300 models of famous buildings and monuments of the European members constructed on a scale of 1:25, complete with animation and sound effects. Watch a TGV glide by, an Airbus take off, or Mt. Vesuvius erupt simply by pushing a button. Open April–December; admission 395 BEF (children under 12, 295 BEF). *Internet:* **www.minieurope.com.**

Bits and Bites of Brussels

Having played vital cultural and commercial roles in Europe for more than 1,000 years, it is appropriate that Brussels was selected as a European City of Culture in 2000. Brussels' cosmopolitan population knows how to enjoy itself. Eating and drinking well in Brussels is not a problem. Succumbing too easily to gastronomic temptation is the real difficulty. Bruxellois, it is said, is like French cuisine served in German portions—although some lighter touches of the nouvelle cuisine have inched their way into Brussels' menus. For the finest gourmet dining, experience the city's most famous culinary establishment, **Comme Chez Soi** at 23 Place Rouppe. For reservations, call 512 29 21 (closed Sunday and Monday). It's only a 15-minute walk from the Grand'Place, at the end of rue du Midi.

In Belgium, beer is not just beer; it's an art form, and the local cafes and bistros are as much an attraction as are the brews they dispense. In Brussels, some offer more than one hundred different labels of Belgian beer alone. Curious? Order a "gueuze," "lambic," or a "krik" (cherry beer?).

For bistro-type dining with a modest price tag, we suggest that you head for the pedestrian-only **Rue des Bouchers** (Street of the Butchers), a stone's throw from the Grand'Place. For lobster with morels or shrimp served in an art-deco atmosphere, try **Aux Armes de Bruxelles** at No. 13 (*Tel:* 511 55 98). Or, if you prefer quaint, rustic decor, try **Le Marmiton** (*Tel:* 511 79 10) at No. 43. Don't miss having mussels in Brussels—**Chez Leon** on Rue des Bouchers serves mussels a myriad of ways, and we love them all. Along with the gastronomy, in the evening the area presents numerous sidewalk displays by local artisans.

If you've never eaten a **Brussels waffle**, you haven't lived a full and rewarding life. We are not referring to the "Belgian waffle" that you'll find at concession stands in every state fair, nor do we refer to the highly touted desserts served by fancy restaurants using a waffle as a base piled high with candied

Train Connections to Other Base Cities from Brussels

Depart from Brussels (Bruxelles) Midi/Zuid South Station unless otherwise noted

DEPART	TRAIN NUMBER	ARRIVE	NOTES
Amsterdam Centraal			
0640	606	0940	1
and then hourly at 40 min after the hour until 2140			
0828	Thalys 9309★	1108	R
1228	Thalys 9325★	1508	R
1728	Thalys 9345★	2008	R
1828	Thalys 9349★	2108	R
2028	Thalys 9357★	2308	R
Barcelona Sants			
1740	Thalys 9348★	0900+1	R, 2
Berlin Zoobahnhof			
0825	Thalys 9409★	1650	R, 3
1025	Thalys 9417★	1850	R, 3
1225	Thalys 9425★	2050	R, 3
1425	Thalys 9433★	2250	R, 3
2254	521/243	0916+1	R, 4
Bern (Berne)			
0715	EC 91	1512	
1216	97	1825	5
2223	499	0709+1	Sleeper
Budapest Keleti			
0654	411	2303	3
1911	EN225	1303	Sleeper
Hamburg Hauptbahnhof			
0825	Thalys 9409★	1507	R, 3
1025	Thalys 9417★	1707	R, 3
1225	Thalys 9425★	1907	R, 3
1425	Thalys 9433★	2107	R, 3
1625	Thalys 9441★	2307	R, 3
Luxembourg			
0636	2106	0933	
and hourly at 36 min. past the hour until 2036			
other trains:			
0715	EC 91	0952	
1215	97	1452	
1915	299	2152	
Lyon Part-Dieu			
0744	TGV 9526	1213	R
0925	TGV 9532	1333	R
1513	TGV 9542	1910	R

Milan (Milano) Centrale
| 0715 | EC 91 | 1925 | |
| 1915 | 299 | 0710+1 | Sleeper |

Munich (München) Hauptbahnhof
1025	Thalys 9417★	1911	R, 3
1225	Thalys 9425★	2111	R, 3
1911	EN 225	0624+1	Sleeper

Nice Ville
| 0925 | TGV 9532 | 1848 | R |

Paris Gare du Nord
0711	Thalys 9306★	0835	R, 6
0740	Thalys 9308★	0905	R
0840	Thalys 9312★	1005	R
0911	Thalys 9414★	1205	R

and hourly at 40 min. past the hour until 2040; also

| 1811 | Thalys 9350★ | 1935 | R |

Vienna (Wien) Westbahnhof
0654	411 EC 29	0946	3
0825	Thalys 9409★	2145	3
1654	431	0845+1	7
1911	EN 225	0945+1	Sleeper

Zürich Hauptbahnhof
0715	EC 91	1500	8
1215	97	2000	
1610	295	0006+1	
2230	499/469	0643+1	Sleeper

Daily, unless otherwise noted

R   Reservations mandatory

★   Thalys high-speed train, supplement required

+1 Next day

1. Daily, except Sunday.
2. Change to sleeper train 477 in Paris Austerlitz station, departing 2047.
3. Change trains in Cologne (Köln).
4. No change of trains required; sleeper cars of train 521 merge with train 243 at Liège.
5. Change trains in Basel, Switzerland.
6. Monday–Friday only.
7. Change to sleeper train CNL 213 in Cologne (Köln) departing 2023.
8. Change to EC 103 in Basel, Switzerland.

fruits and buried in whipped cream. These confections are good, mind you, but nothing in the world can surpass the kind of waffle that Brussels offers. There's nothing fancy about a Brussels waffle. The vendor will hand it to you wrapped in a small napkin.

Brussels waffles are a part of the environment—you can buy them from several small waffle shops located in the area around the city's opera house, and you should only buy them from a shop that actually makes the waffles right on the premises. Look for the sign GAUFRES in French or WAFELS in Flemish.

Day Excursions

It is difficult to choose from the numerous day excursions Brussels has to offer. With its central location and plentiful trains available, a day excursion to Paris, Amsterdam, Luxembourg, or Köln (Cologne) is quite feasible. Via the Channel Tunnel and its Eurostar trains, even London becomes a day excursion. We, however, present four day excursions going to various points within Belgium itself. We offer **Antwerp**, city of diamonds and Rubens; **Bruges** and its famous Markt; **Ghent** with its Flower Show; and **Namur**, gateway to the beautiful Ardennes.

Day Excursion to

Antwerp (Antwerpen) THE DIAMOND CITY

Depart from Brussels Midi/Zuid Station

Distance by Train: 35 miles (57 km)
Average Train Time: 40 minutes
City Dialing Code: 3
Tourist Information Office: Grote Markt 15, B–2000 Antwerp
Tel: 232 01 03; *Fax:* 231 19 37
E-mail: toerisme@antwerpen.be
Internet: www.dma.be/english
Hours: Monday–Saturday 0900–1800; Sunday 0900–1700

To get there on foot, the walk takes about 15 minutes. Antwerp's metro system can also get you there, but first stop at the metro office in the railway station for fare and routing information. In a hurry? Follow the pictograms to the taxi queue.

Train-departure information for your return trip to Brussels can be found on the many train bulletin boards located throughout the station. A train information office is on the street side of the station, between the two main exits. The train information office does not dispense tourist information, but they can assist you in finding the tourist office.

Brussels (Bruxelles)—Antwerp (Antwerpen)

DEPART BRUSSELS MIDI/ZUID	TRAIN NUMBER	ARRIVE ANTWERP CENTRAL	NOTES
0740	607	0820	
0752	2007	0844	Mon–Fri
0813	2007	0856	Sat–Sun
0840	608	0920	
0852	2008	0944	Mon–Fri
0913	2008	0956	Sat–Sun

and the pattern continues hourly until 2340.

DEPART ANTWERP CENTRAL	TRAIN NUMBER	ARRIVE BRUSSELS MIDI/ZUID	NOTES
1440	635	1520	
1504	2036	1547	Sat–Sun
1516	2036	1608	Mon–Fri
1540	636	1620	
1604	2037	1647	Sat–Sun
1616	2037	1708	Mon–Fri

and the pattern continues hourly until 2316.

Daily, unless otherwise noted.
All departing trains en route to Antwerp also stop at Brussels Central Station and then at Brussels Nord Station; trains returning to Brussels from Antwerp stop first at Nord, then at Central, and then at Midi/Zuid Station.
Distance: 35 miles (57 km)

If you are convinced that diamonds are a girl's best friend or the kids are hankering to see one of Europe's finest zoos—go to Antwerp. Be certain the train you take from Brussels is marked "Antwerp Central." EuroCity and other through trains continuing to Amsterdam stop only at stations on the edge of Antwerp. The central station is right in the city center. If you do end up in one of Antwerp's suburban stations, board an inbound local train.

The city's name is spelled three ways: "Antwerp" is the English version; in French it is "Anvers"; and its Flemish title is "Antwerpen." Call it what you will, this fine city with nearly half a million people is a marvelous place to visit. Its contrasts will amaze you. Antwerp is Belgium's second city, the third largest port in the world, reputed to be the world's diamond center, and a Renaissance treasure house.

Because Antwerp is one of the world's major seaports, it offers an unusual harbor tour that the entire family can enjoy. During the summer, motor launches depart from the Steenplein on the river. With more than 3,000 acres of docks, seventeen dry docks, and six locks (including the largest in the world), the harbor is a spectacle you should not miss. There are a variety of waterborne tours to select from and a short trip on the river Scheldt takes fifty minutes. The port sightseeing tour that we recommend takes two and a half hours. A combination zoo-harbor ticket is available, too. This will take care of the kids, but we doubt that anyone will forget the diamonds.

Antwerp boasts twenty museums, among them the **Plantin-Moretus,** featuring a sixteenth-century printing press. Most of Antwerp's museums are closed on Mondays, but the zoo, which is just to the right as you exit from the railway station, is open daily until sunset. If you are interested in the **Zoo-Harbor Tour** combo ticket, check with the city tourist information office and pick a time to participate.

Most seasoned travelers put **Rubens's House** (open Tuesday–Sunday, 1000–1645) at the top of their list of sightseeing "musts." Rubens bought a beautiful patrician dwelling where he lived with his family from 1615 until his death in 1640. Works of the great Flemish master also are kept in many of the museums and churches in Antwerp. Rubens is buried in **St. James Church,** where you may view the painting *Madonna with Child and Saints,* which shortly before his death, he directed be placed on the altar. Rubens and Antwerp remain inextricably linked.

Other sightseeing musts are the **Cathedral of Our Lady** (largest Gothic church in Belgium), containing four Rubens masterpieces; the **Grote Markt** (marketplace); and the **Open Market** (known locally as the Birds Market). The **Birds Market** is open on Sunday mornings, when miscellaneous wares are sold. All these city highlights will be on the map you receive at the city tourist office, and all are within reasonable walking distance.

The Flemish term, *De Rubenswandeling,* means **The Rubens Walk.** It's all laid out for you in a colorful brochure, its map detailing eleven points of interest associated with Rubens. For a bit of variety, there is a *Stadswandeling/Rondwandeling*—city round-trip walking tour—prepared in a similar format. Both are available at the tourist office.

According to legend, the site of Antwerp was once inhabited by a giant who extracted tribute from all who navigated the river and cut off a hand of those who refused to pay. He was slain by a Roman soldier, who cut off the giant's hand and threw it into the river. Thus, the city's name: *Ant* (hand) and *werpen* from the verb "to throw." In support of the legend, the city fathers erected a statue of the Roman soldier, **Silvius Brabo,** in front of the city hall. Those not subscribing to the legend say the name was derived from *Aenwerpen* (higher land). There's always someone who doesn't believe in the tooth fairy.

Day Excursion to

Bruges (Brugge)   OLD LACE AND CHURCH SPIRES

Depart from Brussels Nord Station

Distance by Train: 65 miles (105 km)
Average Train Time: 1 hour, 7 minutes
City Dialing Code: 50
Tourist Information Office: Burg 11, B–8000 Brugge
Tel: 44 86 86; *Fax:* 44 86 00
E-mail: toerisme@brugge.be
Internet: www.brugge.be
Hours: April 1–September 30: 0930–1830 Monday–Friday; 1000–1200 and
    1400–1830 Saturday–Sunday; October 1–March 31: 0930–1700 Monday–Friday;
    0930–1300 and 1400–1730 Saturday–Sunday

Arriving in Bruges, check schedules posted in the station for your return train to Brussels. Train information office inside the station on the left side as you exit from the train platform (Tel. 50 38 23 82). Tourist information is available outside the station near the Video Palace, or go to the central tourist office in Burg Square.

To get to the tourist office in Burg Square, board any bus stopping in front of the railway station that is marked CENTRUM at the entrance side of the bus. The bus will take you to the Markt. It stops in the center of the square in front of the Provincial Palace. To return to the station, board the bus marked O STATION at the library on the square close to the Markt, which can be reached by walking through Kuiperstraat off the Markt.

Bruges has magnetic attractions—many of which date from the Middle Ages and the Renaissance—as well as picturesque canals, art treasures, and antiques shops. Probably the most interesting sight is the **Burg**, where history has been in the making since the ninth century. Surrounding the Burg are museums of all descriptions, spectacular church spires, peaceful canals, and fascinating alleyways. Next to the Burg is the **Markt** (Marketplace), where you will find the **Town Hall** and the **Belfry,** a remarkable building that dominates the Markt with its famous 280-foot-high octagonal tower. If you are up to it, climb up the Belfry for a panoramic view.

During the thirteenth and fourteenth centuries, Bruges stood at the crossroads of traffic between the Mediterranean and the Baltic. Rich cargoes piled high on its docks and in its warehouses held treasures of spices, cloth, and other luxuries. Bruges was bursting at the seams during this period. Hundreds of ships dropped anchor in its harbor. In its medieval magnificence, Bruges boasted a population double that of London. There was no equal to the grandeur of its court—and no one seemed alarmed that the estuary linking Bruges with the North Sea was growing narrower and shallower as the silt from the River Zwyn slowly oozed seaward.

Inexorably, the waterway began to close. Deep-draft ships could no longer navigate the estuary. The docks were abandoned and Bruges became a victim of its own progress, a landlocked city. Today, Bruges is a museum of the Middle Ages, with gabled roof lines casting shadows on its cobblestone streets. Despite the loss of its commerce with the sea, Bruges has managed to maintain its former opulence.

Remnants of grand days past, the canals of Bruges weave in and around the city graced by a bevy of swans. Oddly enough, the birds' presence is attributable to a murder. In 1488, the good people of Bruges beheaded a tyrant named Langhals ("Long Neck"). Miffed by this deed, the counts of Flanders decreed that the "long necks," the symbolic swans, would be kept at public expense forever—and they are.

Although walking is the best way to see Bruges, there are other interesting ways of getting around the city, one being by canal boat—board behind the Belfry. The trip lasts thirty-five minutes. Or, if pedal power appeals to you, rent a bicycle at the station. Yet another, and no less pleasant, way of seeing the city is by horse-drawn cab. The cabs wait on the Burg (city square) in front of the tearoom directly in front of the Belfry.

In addition to all the sights of historic significance in Bruges, there are many stores selling exquisite, handmade Flemish lace, excellent reproductions of Flemish paintings, and colorful ceramics. In general, prices are slightly lower than in Brussels, and the quality is as high.

Brussels—Bruges (Brugge)

Two or more trains per hour from Brussels Midi/Zuid to Bruges; at 8 and 36 min after the hour; journey time 55-60 min. The same trains depart first from Nord station, then Central, and finally Midi/Zuid.

Returning trains (2 or more each hour) depart Brugge at 34 and 59 min after the hour; journey time 50 to 55 min. Trains arrive first at Midi/Zuid, then Central, and then Nord.

Note: The rail route from Brussels to Bruges is the main line to the port of Oostende. Consequently, most of the trains going in that direction stop at all three of the main Brussels stations. Check departure information in the station you plan to depart from in Brussels.

Distance: 65 miles (105 km)

Day Excursion to

Ghent (Gent)

HISTORIC BEAUTY

Depart from Brussels Nord Station

Most trains from Brussels to Ghent stop in all three of Brussels' metropolitan train stations. Check departure information in your station.

Distance by Train: 40 miles (64 km)
Average Train Time: 45 minutes
City Dialing Code: 9
Tourist Information Office: Botermarkt 17A, B–9000 Ghent
    Inquiry desk in the Crypt of the Belfry
Tel: 266–52 32
E-mail: toerisme@gent.be
Internet: www.gent.be
Hours: November 8–March 31, 0930–1630 daily; April 1–November 5, 0930–1830 daily
    To reach the tourist office, take tram No. 10, 11, 12, or 13 to the town center at Korenmarkt.

Ghent is one of the true Flemish water towns. Three rivers—the Schelde, the Lys, the Lieve—plus a canal flow through it. This accounts for its more than one hundred bridges and its Celtic name, "Ganda," meaning a place of confluence. In the fourteenth century, Ghent was the second largest city, after Paris, north of the Alps. In 1827, the cutting of the Terneuzen canal made Ghent the second largest seaport in Belgium. In more modern times, Ghent has become world-famous for its flower show and the International Ghent Fair. Both are held in the Flanders Expo, a trade fair complex a few kilometers from the center of Ghent.

Ask for a free brochure "All Information for Tourists" at the tourist office. The brochure includes a map with different walking tours. Each is color-coded, and places of interest are indicated. During the season, guided walking tours for individuals start at the tourist office every day. Or what about enjoying a carriage trip, a boat excursion, or a tour by taxi bike? If you are visiting in the spring be sure to visit the 32nd international horticultural exhibition, "The Ghent Floralies" at the Flanders Expo fron April 22–May 1.

Saint Michael's Bridge, in the heart of the city, is a good place to begin your walking tour. The view from here is impressive, with church towers and guild houses rimming the skyline. In the distance you can see the **Castle of the Counts,** one of the most imposing feudal fortresses in Europe today. It played a prominent role in Ghent's history during feudal times. The tradespeople had united in a number of strong guilds and could offer armed resistance against their feudal lords, the counts, when said gentry came to collect the rent. The town hall and the Belfry, symbols of civic freedom, were also erected during that period. The Castle of the Counts was completely restored in 1887 and is well worth your inspection.

The **Kouter** is a favorite place for the citizens of Ghent to start their Sunday walks. Every morning there is a flower market here, which on a Sunday takes over the whole area. In the summer, bands from Ghent and the province play in the wrought-iron bandstand in the middle of the square. The vegetable and fruit markets are open Monday through Saturday at the **Groentenmarkt.** As the commercial activity diminishes, the social activities gain tempo.

In early times Ghent, like many other Flemish towns, was involved in warding off the Norse invaders coming off the beaches of the North Sea to loot and plunder. Later, Ghent was able to turn to more peaceful activities. Growing in opulence, Ghent fostered the emerging artists of Flanders and today is considered the cradle of Flemish art.

Along with many other events, the Millennium includes the 500th birthday celebration of "Charles V Year." Following are just a few of the highlights to take place in Ghent (please contact the tourist office for details):

December 12, 1999–March 19 "Charles V and the Imagination of the 19th Century," Museum of Fine Arts, Citadelpark.

March 31–June 30 "Popular Figures in Folklore," Museum of Folklore, Kraanlei 65.

April 1–June 3 "Over the Edge," current art displayed on street corners organized by SMAK Museum.

April 21–June 25 "The Gardens of Eden from Charles V up to the Present," Museum for Industrial Archaeology and Textile, Minnemeers 9.

May 28–June 7 "Wine and Gastronomy in the Empire of Charles V" in the city center.

June 7–11 Millennium Town Criers Championship in the city center.

June 24–25 Final weekend of "Charles V Year 1500–2000."

Brussels—Ghent (Gent)

At least three trains per hour depart Midi/Zuid at 8, 18, and 36 min after the hour; journey time approximately 30 min. Trains depart first from Nord, then Central, and then Midi/Zuid.

Returning trains (at least three each hour) depart Ghent at 9, 24, and 57 min after the hour; journey time approximately 30 min. Trains arrive first at Midi/Zuid, then Central, and then Nord.

Distance: 40 miles (64 km)

Each September and October, Ghent plays host to the **Flanders Festival of Music.** Some of the world's greatest musicians and the most celebrated Belgian orchestras and choirs perform. Many other annual events take place. International regattas are held every May at the **Georges Nachez Aquatic Stadium.** From April 1–October 31 daily and during the winter season on Fridays and Saturdays many of the city's historic places, such as the Castle of the Counts, are illuminated at night. The **Ghent Festivities** are staged each year from the third Saturday to the fourth Monday in July. The town is alive with music, all sorts of entertainment, and cultural happenings at every street corner. It's a great time to visit Ghent.

Hungry? With more than 350 restaurants to choose from, something will suit your tastebuds—Italian, Greek, French, Chinese, vegetarian—you name it, you can find it. Opposite the town hall, try the **Hotel Cour St. Georges.** Although Ghent lies inland from the North Sea, it is, in fact, a seaport and offers some exceptional seafood. If you enjoy shellfish, order the Belgian specialty, *moules mariniers* (steamed mussels).

Day Excursion to

Namur

GATEWAY TO THE ARDENNES

Depart from Brussels Midi Station

Distance by Train: 43 miles (69 km)
Average Train Time: 50 minutes
City Dialing Code: 81
Tourist Information Office: Square de l'Europe Unie B–5000
Tel: 22 28 59 or 24 64 49; *Fax:* 24 65 54
Hours: 0930–1800 daily
Internet: www.ftpn.be

In the Namur station, leave the train-platform area via an underground ramp. Once on the ramp, walk past sortie 1 to sortie 2 and take the escalator to the street level. Bear right around the "C & A" store and proceed to the park, where the tourist office will be in plain view.

If you would like to revisit the eighteenth century, go to Namur. It is one of the most attractive towns in Belgium. The tourist office offers several excellent walking tours and theme tours. It can also provide personalized tours upon request. The year 2000 presents Namur as Tourist Year of Parks and Gardens. Brochures and event schedules are available from the tourist office. For the footsore and those wanting to range farther afield, book an **"All-in-One"** ticket that includes boat tours, cable-car ascensions, and a traction-train ride around and through the Citadel of Namur, complete with underground explorations.

On Saturday mornings, don't miss the colorful flower market at the **Place du Palais de Justice** and the **Leopold Square** shopping center. Probably you will not find such a concentration of museums and monuments anywhere else in Europe.

The dominating landmark of Namur—**the Citadel**—looms on its skyline. It is in the center of the **Parc du Champeau**. The walk there can be delightful, particularly if you ascend via the cable car that departs from the Place Pied-du-Chateau. The tourist bureau will provide full details. You can also reach the Citadel by bus. Board bus No. 3 in the town square, adjacent to the railway station. A tour of the Citadel is included in the "All-In-One" ticket, too.

The Citadel of Namur sits at the confluence of the Meuse and the Sambre. Two thousand years of history are contained within its walls. Originally a Celtic stronghold with primitive fortifications, it was altered into a strongly defensive castle. Underground fortifications were added in the fifteenth century and again expanded century after century until modern weaponry brought a cessation of such defenses in the eighteenth century. Throughout its history, however, the Citadel, as one of the most important strongholds of Europe, faced twenty sieges!

Namur's tourist office has a wide selection of excursions for you to select from. Here are but a few: **The Gardens of Annevoie,** famous for their eighteenth-century style of flowers and fountains, are open 0900–1900; a visit can be made in minutes. A restaurant and tavern are on the grounds. **Cruises on the River Meuse** are available in a variety of schedules, including a picnic onboard or ashore.

Continuing with Namur's excursion offerings, the city is justly proud of its space-telecommunications ground station and offers a tour of the facility that includes guide service plus a documentary film. The visit requires one and a half hours; food and beverage self-service is available.

For aquatic buffs, a kayak or boat trip down the river Lesse is available, with departures daily throughout the season at 1000 and 1400. Looking for some-

---

Brussels—Namur

At least two trains hourly depart Midi/Zuid at 6 and 36 min after the hour; journey time 1 hr. Trains depart first from Midi/Zuid, then from Central, and then from Nord.

Returning trains depart Namur at 25 and 55 min after the hour; journey time 1 hr. Trains arrive first at Nord, then Central, and then Midi/Zuid.

Distance: 43 miles (69 km)

thing a bit less strenuous? Perhaps a water tour of the **Caves of Neptune** would fill the bill. It's a 45-minute tour and includes a 20-minute boat ride plus a sight and sound show.

Namur is the gateway to the Ardennes, the forests and mountains of Belgium, with all the amenities of a holiday resort. Should you find yourself with time to spare (a very unlikely thing), take a stroll on the **Boulevard de la Sambre,** an attractive, tree-lined avenue. If, on the other hand, you are looking for exquisite gifts, the **Rue de l'Ange** has excellent shops. Or enjoy Brasseries (Breweries) du Bocg and des Fagnes.

We highly suggest visiting Namur during the season of festivals. This is the best way to experience the local folklore of the Stiltwalkers of Namur; or the looming giants, the Royal Society of Moncrabeau, the bright-yellow uniformed Canaris regiment, or the choreographed lunacy of the dancing Chinels.

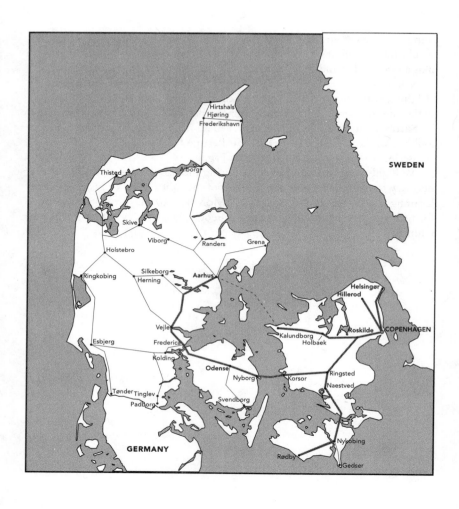

Denmark

Danes are a fun-loving people, and their sparkling humor is unsurpassed. For example, Victor Borge, one of Denmark's leading exponents of such jocularity, explains that his ultra-expensive, concert grand piano is "every bit as good as a Rolls-Royce, except," quips Victor, "it has smaller wheels." This is typical Danish humor, and this fairy-tale land of Denmark abounds in it. No doubt you will find the Danes to be the most happy and humorous of all Europeans. Why are they that way? One of our Danish friends explains it in this manner: "For centuries, we Danes were the most feared of the Vikings, destroying and plundering at will. Now, we've got that all out of our system and have nothing left to do except to be happy!" This happy attitude seems to exist throughout the country.

Legend has it that the ancient Vikings, fierce as they were, never missed the chance to throw a party, and apparently their descendants are just as enthusiastic when it comes to having a good time. In summer, there are festivals throughout Denmark where eating, drinking, singing, and dancing are the orders of the day. In winter, the Danes go inside for their celebrations, where eating, drinking, singing, and dancing are the orders of the day. Oddly enough, this never seems to be monotonous to the Danes—or their visitors. With the completion of the Oresund Fixed Link—the bridge linking Copenhagen, Denmark, with Malmo, Sweden, in 2000, it will be even more convenient to visit both countries.

For more information about Denmark, contact the newly merged Danish and Swedish Tourist Board in North America:

New York: P.O. Box 4649, Grand Central Station, New York, NY 10163–4649. *Tel:* (212) 885–9700; *Fax:* (212) 885–9710; *E-mail:* info@goscandinavia. com; *Internet:* **www.goscandinavia.com** or **www.dt.dk**

Banking
- **Currency:** Danish Kroner (DKK)
- **Exchange rate at time of press:** 6.92 DKK = $1.00
- **Hours:** 0930–1600 Monday–Friday; Thursday until 1800

Communications
- **Country Code:** 45

- **No city codes** required for calls within Denmark. Danish phone numbers are usually 8 digits. Direct dial: AT&T Direct: 8001–0010

Shopping

- **Hours**: Monday–Thursday, 0900/1000–1730/1800; Friday, 0900/1000–1900/2000; Saturday, 0900/1000–1200/1300/1400 (until 1700 for most shops in Copenhagen)

Denmark has a hefty 25 percent VAT (value added tax). It may be avoided in two different ways. Have your purchases sent home. This way, you pay only the purchase price of the item plus shipping and insurance. Second plan, take the goods home yourself by paying the VAT; save your purchase slips and get the VAT refunded at the Copenhagen Kastrup Airport tax-free shop. In that case, plan to arrive at the airport an hour ahead of your original reporting time.

Rail Travel in Denmark

The dynamic Danish State Railways (DSB) is on the move. In June 1997, the newly opened tunnel and bridge made crossing the Great Belt by train more than an hour faster than going by ferry. The "Lyntog" (high-speed diesel) trains cruise from Copenhagen to Aarhus in only 2½ hours instead of 4. On July 1, 2000, the 16-kilometer rail and motorway tunnel/bridge complex connecting northeast Denmark and southern Sweden will be completed. The Øresund Bridge will merge Copenhagen and Malmö creating the largest domestic market in northern Europe (equalling Berlin, Hamburg, and Amsterdam).

Denmark's InterCity and Lyntog trains feature seats with headphones for listening to music, 220-volt outlets for computers, and play areas for children. In first class, passengers can help themselves to tea, soft drinks, and newspapers. The DSB wants to make your trip fast but comfortable. It is advisable to have seat reservations on all IC and Lyntog trains.

The following bonuses apply if you have a **Eurailpass:**
- **Stena Line** ships, Frederikshavn–Göteburg (Sweden); Frederikshavn–Oslo (Norway)—50 percent discount
- **Scanlines** ships, free ferry transport: Aarhus–Kalundborg; Helsingør– Helsingborg (Sweden); Rodby Faerge–Puttgarden (Germany)
- **Color Line** ships, 30 percent discounts on: Frederikshavn/Skagen–Larvik (Norway); Hirtshals–Kristiansand (Norway); Hirtshals/Frederikshavn–Moss (Norway) day sailings only
- **Hjorring Privatbanen** railways, Hjorring–Hirtshals v.v.—50 percent discount

- **Flyvebådene** (catamarans), Knudshoved–Halskov v.v.—Free;
  Kobenhavn (Copenhagen)–Malmö (Sweden)—25 percent discount
- **DFDS Scandinavian Seaways** ships, København (Copenhagen)–
  Oslo (Norway) and Esbjerg–Harwich (Great Britain)—50 percent
  discount on lowest available cabin category or couchette

If your European travels are all within Scandinavia, consider the **ScanRail Pass** that you can purchase in North America. It provides unlimited rail travel in Denmark, Finland, Norway, and Sweden, plus discounts on certain ferry crossings and private railways. Although you can purchase a Scanrail Pass at train stations in Scandinavia, it is considerably more expensive than if you purchase it in North America. Call toll-free 800–722–7151 or contact RailPass Express, Inc. online at www.railpass.com to order.

ScanRail Pass

	Adult	Child	Senior	Youth
5 days within 2 months				
1st Class	$270	$135	$241	$203
2nd Class	200	100	178	150
10 days within 2 months				
1st Class	$420	$210	$374	$315
2nd Class	310	155	276	233
21 days consecutive				
1st Class	$486	$243	$432	$365
2nd Class	360	180	321	270

ScanRail 'n Drive Pass

(Purchase only in North America; car rental not available in Finland.) Prices are per person. Valid for 5 days of unlimited rail travel and 3 days of car rental to be used within a 15-day period. Able to add unlimited number of car days.

	1st Class		2nd Class		Additional
	2 Adults	1 Adult	2 Adults	1 Adult	Car Day
Economy	$304	$354	$242	$297	$60
Compact	324	399	262	337	78
Intermediate	344	419	272	357	88

Base City . . .

Copenhagen (København)

Internet: www.copenhagencity.dk

Arriving by Air

Kastrup Airport. *Tel:* 3231–3231; *Fax:* 3231–3132; *Internet:* www. cph.dk

Located 12 kilometers southeast of city center. Most international flights to and from Denmark use Kastrup (Copenhagen) Airport. About 60 airlines have regular services to Copenhagen and there are several daily connections to/from all other major European airports.

Airport–City Links: The airport rail terminal links the airport to the Copenhagen main railway station (Københaven H.) by train; departures every 20 minutes. Frequent airport-coach, public-bus, and taxi service is available also. A shuttle bus operates between Kastrup Airport and City Central Railway Station 0630–2310 (weekends/holidays 0545–1110). Journey time: 20–30 minutes. Intervals: 10–15 minutes. From Central Railway Station to Kastrup Airport 0542–2145 daily. The ride to the downtown SAS terminal (located at the main railway station) costs 40 kroner (DKK). For only 15 DKK, public bus No. 250S will take you from the airport to the Town Hall Square, near Tivoli Gardens, and to the railway station, where your ticket still entitles you to transfer to any other bus within one hour from the time of purchase. Taxi service has a minimum charge of 7.15 DKK per kilometer plus a 20-DKK "start" charge.

The airport has money-exchange facilities, and you may obtain hotel reservations at the service department in the airport's arrival hall. The airport operates a tax-free shop, but only departing or in-transit passengers are permitted to use it. The shopping area is one of the largest and most attractive in Europe, perhaps because the experts from Tivoli influenced its design.

Arriving by Train

There are direct train connections from Copenhagen to major cities in Europe, including Stockholm, Oslo, Hamburg, and Basel.

Copenhagen has four major railway stations, but, unlike the situation in Paris, primarily the central station, **København Hovedbanegaard**, is of concern to railpass travelers. Signs in and approaching the station are marked KØBENHAVN H. The abbreviation of Hovedbanegaard (Central Station), an "H," reflects the efficiency of this huge train complex right in the heart of the city. The tracks run below street level, and the architecture of the station blends well with the locale. København H. is suggestive of a great Viking hall with two great wooden archways that span its enclosed area.

The station is served by twelve tracks joined by six exits as you ascend from train level to the station's arrival area. *For your orientation, upon arrival you may exit in a northerly or an easterly direction.* Tivoli Gardens flank the station's east side, and a huge square fronts the station to the north. The arrival hall serves mainly for baggage handling. The lost-and-found office and the *politi* (police station) are alongside tracks 11 and 12.

Most services are located in the north departure area. Here you will find the SAS coach terminal, a cafeteria, and an excellent restaurant in the northwest corner. Taxi service is available at both the north and the east exits. City bus lines also serve the station, but inquire at the train information office before using one. Train arrival-and-departure information is displayed in bulletin form at both the arrival exits and the east and west entrances. Modern, airport-style digital displays give train-departure information automatically at each departure gate and on the train platforms. Elevator service, as well as stairways, is available between the station and the train platforms. If you are using a baggage cart, be certain to use the elevators to move your baggage.

- **Baggage Storage.** Lockers are available in two sizes—the small one, 20 DKK; the large one is 30 DKK for 24 hours.
- **Money Exchange.** Den Danske Bank is located along the north side across from McDonald's. It also has an ATM. The hours of operation are 0700–2100 daily. A similar banking facility may be found in the row of shops on the ground level. Hours are 0900–2200. There is a 40 DKK charge for cashing traveler's checks, so you may want to utilize the ATM.
- **Train Information.** *Tel:* 3314–1701. Between the entrances to tracks 3/4 and 5/6 on the departure (north) side of the station. One or more of the windows is open daily 0700–2100. Train information departures (yellow) and arrivals (white) bulletins are displayed. During the times that international trains are arriving or departing, the Danish State Railways personnel wearing "Information" hats will be seen in the station. They speak English and are eager to assist you.
- **Train Reservations.** RejseCenter on the north side of the station, just opposite the departure gates for tracks 1/2 and 3/4. Inside the office, take a number for domestic or international assistance. Hours: 0800–1900 daily. International Reservations: *Tel.* 3314–3088; Domestic Reservations: *Tel:* 3314–8800.
- **Railpass validation** is in the same office where international tickets are purchased, 0630–2400 daily.
- **Inter-Rail Center,** in the middle section of the south side of the station between tracks 2 and 4. Enter by showing your railpass. You can pick up information on what's going on in the *Copenhagen This Week* pamphlet, and

the center personnel can help with reservations for youth hostels. For a few kroner, you can even take a shower.

Through-passengers to the Swedish ferry port of Helsingborg (via Helsingør north of Copenhagen) need only ensure that they are in a coach properly marked for the crossing. Frequently (such as is the case at Helsingør), seven or eight coaches arrive at the ferry dock, but only three or four are loaded for the trip. Check before boarding the train and also advise the conductor of your destination. If you do miss the connection, the ferry service is very frequent.

For hydrofoil service between Copenhagen and Malmö, check with the train information office. Connections may be made either by public bus from the central station to the hydrofoil pier or by taxi directly from your hotel. If you are burdened with luggage, the taxi would be the service to use.

For rail service between Oslo or Stockholm and Copenhagen, it's a toss-up between using the hydrofoil or taking the ferry crossing between Helsingborg (Sweden) to Helsingør (Denmark). The hydrofoil route is about one hour faster—aside from the time spent getting from the station to the pier. We still prefer the ferry. You don't have to change conveyances, railpasses are accepted, and tax-free shopping is onboard.

Tourist Information/Hotel Reservations

København Turistinformation: Bernstorffsgade 1, DK–1577 København V, Denmark. *Tel:* 3311–1325; *Fax:* 3393–4969; *Internet:* www.copenhagencity.dk. Hours: May 1–September 15, 0900–2100 daily; September 16–April 30, 0900–1700 Monday–Friday, Saturdays 0900–1400, closed on Sunday.

To reach the tourist office on foot, exit the central station and walk toward the corner on the right side, toward the front of the Tivoli Gardens. Turn right at this point. The office will be on your right and readily identifiable by the familiar **i** sign.

Hotel reservations (*Tel:* 3312–2880; *Fax:* 3312–9723) can be made at the tourist office. The personnel are authorized to accept advance payments on behalf of the hotels to ensure reservations.

For convenience and comfort, we can recommend the four-star hotel Plaza at Bernstorffsgade 4, DK–1577 (*Tel:* 3314–9262; *Fax:* 3393–9362). Room rates range from 1550 DKK and up for a single; doubles begin at 1750 DKK and go up to 2000 DKK for a deluxe room.

Getting Around in Copenhagen

In Copenhagen an electrified metropolitan S-train railway network connects the city center with the suburban areas at frequent intervals and when the Metro is completed in 2000, City Line will run every 1.5 minutes during rush hour.

A great convenience is the **Copenhagen Card,** which entitles you to unlimited travel by buses and trains in the entire metropolitan area as well as the whole of North Zealand, Roskilde, and Køge, plus free entrances to more than 60 museums, attractions, and sights, including Tivoli and Tivoli Museum, Believe It or Not!, Danish Toy Museum, Frederiksborg Castle, and many more. A four-color, 88-page guide booklet accompanies the card and includes a map of the city. And that's not all—you also receive a 25–50 percent discount on four ferry crossings to Sweden and a 20 percent discount on canal tours and the city tour. What a bargain! Cards are issued for 24 hours (140 DKK), 48 hours (255 DKK), or 72 hours (320 DKK). Children age 5–11 pay 70, 125, or 160 DKK.

Copenhagen has invested heavily in providing bicycle paths alongside many of its main streets and the city provides more than 2,000 free bicycles for visitors to use while sightseeing. Look for one of the 110 Citybike parking areas located throughout the city center, deposit a 20-DKK coin, and start pedaling. When you return the bike, you get your money back. Check with the tourist office for more details.

Sights/Attractions/Tours

Tivoli Gardens (*Tel:* 3315–1001; *Fax:* 3393–1881) is open from May through mid-September. It's not the world's largest amusement park, but it is unique. It has been in business since 1843. Each year, people come from all over the world to enjoy its very special blend of attractions old and new. Tree-lined walks, resplendent with flowers and sparkling illuminations, form the backdrop to its theaters and open-air amusement areas. There are more than twenty restaurants to choose from. Four evenings each week, the park closes with a giant display of fireworks.

During its day of entertainment for young and old alike, international artists appear at the Tivoli Concert Hall, Gilbert & Sullivan scenarios are acted out at the Pantomime Theater, and the Tivoli Boys Guard parades frequently to the delight of all. There's also an impressive assembly of quality rides to thrill you, games to play, and seven great restaurants to select from when you get hunger pangs. Tivoli cannot be described adequately in words; it must be experienced.

Amalienborg Palace is a beautiful example of Rococo architecture and has served as the permanent residence of the Danish royal family since 1794. See the changing of the Royal Guard at 1200 every day in the palace square.

Those with more prurient interests may want to visit the **Museum Erotica** at Købmagergade 24, 1150 København K, *Tel:* 3312–0311, to experience the "Love Life of Homo Sapiens." Hours: 1000–2300.

Tour the colorful **Nyhavn canal** area with its quaint restaurants or take the city harbor tour—a comfortable way to see beautiful Copenhagen.

Want more? Tour the city's world-famous breweries, Carlsberg and Tuborg. Get details from the tourist office. Yes, they provide samples of their products.

Contact Carlsberg in advance by calling 3327–1314.

Year-round, visit *Den Lille Havfrue* (**"The Little Mermaid"**), symbol of today's Copenhagen. It is an enchanting, soul-touching statue, and next to Queen Margrethe it is probably Denmark's most famous female.

Copenhagen Condensed

Shopping? Copenhagen can accommodate you. You'll learn quickly about **Stroget** (pronounced "stroy-it"). It's not one but actually five different shopping areas, each designated pedestrian-only and lined with shops that might make you want to hide your credit cards. All the well-known Danish specialties are in profusion here. Just north of the Stroget in the Latin Quarter there are some good cafes and restaurants, so you can get anything from a hot dog to a five-course banquet. Try the world-famous Danish delicacy "smorrebrod," which usually consists of rye bread topped with marinated herring or liver pâté and onion rings.

For the best salmon specialties, we enjoyed the **Queen's Restaurant & Pub** at Vester Voldgade 25. For reservations, telephone 3312–5902. For an extraordinary evening, **St. Gertruds Kloster** at 32 Hauser Plads can provide you with an unforgettable dinner in a fourteenth century atmosphere—in medieval monastery vaults—accompanied by the romantic light of 1,500 candles. For reservations, call 3314–6630 or *Fax:* 3393–9365.

If you have a sweet tooth, please, don't go home before you have tried the Danish waffle–ice cream combination.

Day Excursions

Five delightful day excursions await whenever you can break away from the charm that is distinctly Copenhagen's. Admittedly, this is a difficult thing to do because the Danish capital has so much to offer, what with its Tivoli Gardens, and pedestrian-only shopping streets; but leave it you must. The entire country is a fairyland. Go out and enjoy it.

Jutland is the Danish mainland, the tip of the European continent that reaches northward toward the Scandinavian peninsula. **Aarhus** is Jutland's cultural center and Denmark's second largest city. Fans of William Shakespeare will, no doubt, make **Helsingør** (Elsinore) their prime day-excursion choice. Castle buffs will head for **Hillerød** and its gracious Frederiksborg Castle. **Odense,** birthplace of Hans Christian Andersen, will delight day excursioners of all ages. **Roskilde** is loaded with Danish folklore and history, including a Viking-ship museum, Museum Island, and Denmark's most important medieval building—the Roskilde Cathedral—for centuries the final resting place of Denmark's royalty.

Train Connections to Other Base Cities from Copenhagen
(København)

DEPART	TRAIN NUMBER	ARRIVE	NOTES
Amsterdam Centraal			
0755	EC 38	1849	R, 1
1055	EC 36	2249	R, 1
2013	EN 232	0957+1	R, Sleeper, 2, 3
Berlin Zoobahnhof			
0755	EC 38	1528	R, 3, 4
1055	EC 36	1528	R, 3, 4
1355	EC 34	2128	R, 3, 4
Brussels (Bruxelles) Midi/Zuid			
2013	EN 483	1035+1	R, Sleeper, 5
Hamburg Hauptbahnhof			
0755	EC 38	1215	R, 3
1055	EC 36	1524	R, 3
1355	EC 34	1815	R, 3
1755	EC 30	2215	R, 3
1848	EN 483	0041+1	
2200	EN 232	0914+1	
Munich (München) Hauptbahnhof			
0755	EC 38	1843	R, 3, 4
1055	EC 36	2206	R, 3, 4
1848	EN 483	0920+1	Sleeper
Oslo Sentral			
2205	392	0707+1	R, Sleeper
Paris Gare du Nord			
1755	EC 30	0908+1	R, 6
2018	EN 232	1205+1	R, Sleeper, 5
Stockholm Central			
1021	286	1841	R
2205	284	0741+1	R, Sleeper
Vienna (Wien) Westbahnhof			
1555	EC 32	0850+1	R, 6
Zürich Hauptbahnhof			
0755	EC 38	2003	R, 4

Daily, unless otherwise noted.
R Reservations required.
Thalys high-speed trains require supplement.
1. Change trains in Hamburg and Osnabruck.
2. Change in Duisburg to EC 140 departing 0751
3. Snacks and drinks available on this train.
4. Change trains in Hamburg.
5. Change trains in Cologne (Köln) to Thalys 9420★ departing 0802.
6. Change to sleeper train in Hamburg.

Day Excursion to

Aarhus (Århus)   WORLD'S SMALLEST BIG CITY

Depart from Copenhagen H. Station

Distance by Train: 139 miles (223 km)
Average Travel Time: 2 hours, 30 minutes
No city code required
Tourist Information Office: Town Hall, DK–8000 Aarhus
Tel: 8940–6700; *Fax:* 8612–9590
Internet: www.aarhus-tourist.dk; *E-mail:* tourist-aarhus@aar-turist.dk
Hours: June 19–September 10, 0930–1800 Monday–Friday, 0930–1700 Saturday, and
    0930–1300 Sunday; September 11–April 30, 0930–1630 Monday–Friday,
    1000–1300 Saturday; May 1–June 19, 0930–1700 Monday–Friday, 1000–1300
    Saturday.

To reach the tourist office, exit the station and cross the street. Turn left, proceed
to the first traffic light, and cross the street to the SAS building. From this point, you
will see the town hall close by on the left. Entrance is at the tower. Money-exchange
service is available in the tourist office when banks are closed.

The Great Belt Tunnel decreased the travel time between Copenhagen and
Aarhus from 4 hours to 2½ hours. And travel aboard the Danish Railways
(DSB) InterCity trains is comfortable and a pleasant way to see the Danish
countryside. When you arrive in Aarhus, disembark and follow the signs to the
main rail station, where you mount stairs leading to the station's main concourse. Lift (elevator) service and escalators are available. After turning left,
walk to the end of the corridor. The train-information office is to the left at
the end of the corridor (open daily 0800–1900).

Aarhus has many other worthwhile attractions. It's Denmark's second largest
city and Jutland's uncontested cultural center.

People have lived in Aarhus ever since the Vikings settled at the mouth of
the river, where it meets the bay. There the Norsemen constructed a harbor,
built houses, and erected a church. During the 1960s, contractors excavating
under a bank in Aarhus came upon the remains of a semicircular rampart that
the Vikings of a thousand years ago used to protect their small community.

Today the site is a museum where you can see the reconstructed ramparts
with a typical house of that time, together with tools and other belongings
used by the first inhabitants of Aarhus. In addition to this museum, there is a
collection of seventy-five historic buildings that have been transferred there
from every region of the country to re-create an entire seventeenth-century
Danish market town, complete with narrow cobbled streets, shops, public
squares—even a millrace. Known as **The Old Town,** it is the largest museum in Jutland. Here you can wander through Danish history from the Vikings
to Hans Christian Andersen.

Copenhagen (København)—Aarhus (Århus)

DEPART COPENHAGEN H	TRAIN NUMBER	ARRIVE AARHUS STATION	NOTES
0700	IC 121	1008	
0751	Lyn 23	1033	Mon–Fri
0800	IC 125	1108	
0851	Lyn 27	1132	Mon–Fri
0900	IC 129	1208	
0948	IR 1333	1404	Sat–Sun
1000	IC 133	1308	
1100	IC 137	1408	

DEPART AARHUS	TRAIN NUMBER	ARRIVE COPENHAGEN H	NOTES
1402	IC 140	1718	
1440	Lyn 42	1727	Mon–Fri
1502	IC 144	1818	
1540	Lyn 46	1827	Mon–Fri
1602	IC 148	1922	
1644	Lyn 50	1918	Mon–Fri
1702	IC 152	2018	
1740	Lyn 54	2027	Mon–Fri
1802	IC 156	2118	
1902	IC 160	2218	
2002	IC 164	2318	

Daily, unless otherwise noted
Note: Reservations are recommended for travel on all IC and Lyntog trains in Denmark. Passengers may board the train without a reservation but are not guaranteed a seat.
Distance: 139 miles (223 km)

To reach The Old Town, follow the city map for a 10-minute walk, or take bus No. 3. In June–August it is open 0900–1800 daily; May and September, 0900–1700; April, October, and December, 1000–1600; January–March and November, 1100–1500. Admission: 55 DKK adults; 15 DKK children.

Admission to the **Viking Museum** is free and it's only three blocks from the tourist office at Clemens Torv in the basement under Unibank.

You may want to visit other attractions by taking the bus. You can purchase a **Tourist Ticket** (45 DKK), which is valid for an unlimited number of bus rides in the Borough of Aarhus for 24 hours. It includes a two-and-one-half-hour guided city-bus tour, which departs daily from Park Allé, the tourist office, at 1000 from June 23 to August 31. Buy it at most newsstands or at the tourist office. Remember to make a reservation in advance either by telephone or in person at the tourist office. If you plan to stay longer or make Aarhus your base city, you can buy the **Aarhus Passport** for one day (adults, 88 DKK; children under age 16, 44 DKK), two days (adults, 110 DKK; children, 55 DKK), or for one week (adults 155 DKK; children, 75 DKK), which gives you unlimited access to public transport as well as free entrance to many of the town's attractions.

South of Aarhus you'll find the **Prehistoric Museum** at Moesgård, one of Denmark's top attractions. (Hours: daily 1000-1700 in summer; closed Mondays during winter.) The museum contains collections from the Stone Age, the Bronze Age, the Iron Age, and the Viking period. To get there, take bus No. 6 from the railway station.

Between Kalundborg and Aarhus, there is a hydrofoil ferry service that takes only 90 minutes. You can return to Copenhagen via this same route, but we recommend the "great circle" tour, which includes stops at the cities of **Fredericia** and **Odense.**

Day Excursion to
Helsingør
HAMLET'S HIDEAWAY

Depart from Copenhagen H. Station

Distance by Train: 26 miles (44 km)
Average Train Time: 45 minutes
Helsingør Turistbureau: Havnepladsen 3, DK–3000 Helsingør
Tel: 49 21 13 33; *Fax:* 49 21 15 77
Internet: www.helsingorkommune.com or www.helsingoerhavn.dk
Hours: June–August, 0900–1800 Monday–Friday; 0900–1500 Saturday.
September–May, 0900–1600 Monday–Friday and 0900–1300 on Saturday.
Located just across the street on the left side of the station. Look for the TURIST AGENCY sign at the end of tracks 1 and 2 for more explicit directions. Words of caution—obey the traffic signals when crossing to the tourist office, and use the designated walkway. A local, private railroad uses the street as a siding, and it could be hazardous to your health.

Helsingør is one of Denmark's oldest populated places. Documents dating back to 1231 record its development. In the vaults under **Kronborg Castle,** there is a statue of Holger Danske, a Viking chieftain who voyaged to the Holy Land as a crusader about A.D. 800, and there are many buildings of ancient vintage. For example, nearby No. 27 Strandgade is the oldest half-timbered house in town. It was built in 1577. Other structures date back to the fifteenth century.

It's the lure of Shakespeare's Hamlet that usually brings visitors to Helsingør (Elsinore). The town has many other attractions, however, not the least of which is the world's biggest and best ice cream cone. Read on, Macbeth!

Local train service between Copenhagen and the town of Helsingør (sometimes referred to by its older name, "Elsingore" or "Elsinore") runs every 20 minutes throughout the day and is interspersed with frequent express train service.

The Helsingør railway station is the terminus for the train ferries that ply between Denmark and the town of Helsingborg in Sweden. The distance across the sound between the two countries is less than 3 miles. This is the reason why Helsingør was founded there and also the reason why it flourished from 1426 through 1857 by the collection of the "sound dues" from all merchant ships that passed.

If you are interested in maritime ferry operations, Helsingør is the place to observe it. Arrivals and departures take place almost endlessly throughout the day and into the night.

One of the tourist office's publications is *Helsingør Tourist Guide*. It describes, in great detail, Kronborg Castle, the churches of Saint Olai and Saint Mary, and the Carmelite monastery. These highlights of Helsingør are all nearby.

The **Kronborg Castle,** the city's most famous landmark, was built by Christian IV between 1574 and 1582. With this formidable fortress came the rapid development of the town under its protective shelter. For several centuries, Helsingør was the second largest city in Denmark. The castle is open May–September, 1030–1700. During April and October, hours are 1100–1600; November–March, 1100–1500 (closed Mondays).

Hamlet's residency in the castle was imaginary, but the play was performed there from 1916 until 1954, when performances were curtailed for financial reasons. It was again performed in 1979, but there are no definite plans for the future. In the castle the King's Chamber, the Queen's Chamber, and the Great Hall must be seen to appreciate the once great splendor of this fortress. Cannon still stand along the seawall.

While admiring the Great Hall, you'll probably note that there are no fireplaces or other heating devices. Apparently, they were overlooked by the royal architect. This created no problem for the royal occupants, however, when they wanted to lay on a royal midwinter bash; they merely marched several thousand men of the royal guard into the area and the troops' body heat sent the mercury soaring—along with a few other atmospheric additives, no doubt.

While in Helsingør, make certain that a part of your tour includes a stop at the **Raadhus** (town hall). In its council chamber, you can see a stained-glass window that depicts the history of the town. Outside of the town hall you will see a narrow street (Brostraede) leading to the sea. Follow it. The ice cream shop is there.

Copenhagen—Helsingør

FROM COPENHAGEN TO HELSINGØR:

Trains depart Monday–Friday every 20 minutes at 9 and 29 minutes past the hour, 0509–0029. Trains depart every 20 minutes 0649–0029 Saturday–Sunday. Journey time is approximately 55 minutes. Check with the train-information office in the København H. Terminal.

FROM HELSINGØR TO COPENHAGEN:

Trains depart daily every 20 minutes at 39 and 59 minutes past the hour, from 0439 through 2339 (service begins at 0539 on Sunday). Check with the train-information office in the Helsingør train station.

FERRIES BETWEEN HELSINGØR, DENMARK, AND HELSINGBORG, SWEDEN:

Most Copenhagen–Helsingør trains connect with ferries to Sweden. Eurail pass is accepted for passage. Several ferries depart every 20 to 40 minutes per hour beginning at 0510 and running until 2330; a few also depart between 0030 and 0430. Service in either direction takes about 20 minutes. If desired, you may combine a day excursion to Helsingør, Denmark, with a round trip ferry crossing to Helsingborg, Sweden. Return trips are similar, beginning at 0510 and returning until 2340.

Distance: 46 km

Day Excursion to

Hillerød

PICTURE-BOOK SCENERY

Depart from Copenhagen H. Station

Distance by Train: 19 miles (30 km)
Average Train Time: 40 minutes
No city code required
Hillerød Turistbureau: Slangerupgade 252, Postboks 5, DK–3400 Hillerød
Tel: 48 24 26 26; *Fax:* 48 24 26 65
E-mail: turistbureau@hillkomm.dk
Internet: www.hillerod.dk
Hours: June–August, 1000–1900 Monday–Friday; Saturday, 1000–1700.
    September–May, 1000–1700 Monday–Friday; Saturday, 1000–1300. Closed Sundays and holidays.
    To get there, follow the signs to the castle, starting just outside the station building. The tourist office is next to the castle on the left side of the pedestrian street. If

you like, you can obtain a brochure in the railway station that contains a city map to help guide your way. Or take bus No. 701 or 702 and ask the driver to let you off at the tourist information office. You can buy tickets on the bus for 11 DKK. However, your train ticket also includes the bus fare.

Hillerød can become the crowning touch to your visit to Denmark. The town has an atmosphere distinctly its own with beautiful woodlands surrounding it. A picture-book lake rests in the town's center, faced on one side by the old town and its market square and on another by the majestic **Frederiksborg Castle.** There are few places in the world where nature and culture blend together so perfectly.

No doubt the Frederiksborg Castle will be the first stopping point on your tour of Hillerød. A tour boat plies along the "most beautiful nautical mile in Denmark" between the castle and the marketplace from May through September, a delightful way of seeing both the city and the castle.

The castle actually spans three islands. The first of its structures, erected by Frederik II in 1560, occupied the largest island. The balance of this imposing castle complex was built by Christian IV between 1600 and 1620. Between 1570 and 1840, Danish monarchs were anointed in the castle chapel, and it was used for the wedding of Danish Prince Joachim and Alexandra Manley from Hong Kong in 1995.

In 1859, a disastrous fire destroyed the interior of the main building, and irreplaceable treasures were lost forever. The chapel and all of its valuable contents, however, remained relatively undamaged. Among those items was the celebrated chapel organ built by Esaias Compenius in 1610. The chapel organist plays every Thursday between 1330 and 1400. The castle has been restored, at first by royal contributions and public donations, and, more recently, by philanthropic support from J. C. Jacobsen, former owner of the Carlsberg Brewery and the Carlsberg Foundation. The museum is open daily 1000–1700 April–October; 1100–1500 November–March; (admission: 45 DKK, adults; children, 10) The castle gardens, water canals, and fountains are among the most exquisite. The Baroque Gardens escaped transformation (the only Danish garden to do so) probably due to the many line avenues and terraced grounds. There is an interesting museum of local and regional history known as the North Sealand Folk Museum by a small pond in a corner of the castle's gardens, and the castle itself now houses the Museum of Natural History.

In 1996, the reconstruction of the French baroque park was finished and inaugurated by Danish Queen Margrethe II; it resembles the original park from 1720. In another section of the castle garden, known as the *Indelukket*, you can inspect a charming little country house built in 1562 for the king to conduct informal entertainment. Several guided tours are offered of the sites, castles, museums, forest, and parklands of Hillerød. Contact the tourist center for arrangements.

Copenhagen (København)—Hillerød

DEPART COPENHAGEN H	TRAIN NUMBER	ARRIVE HILLERØD
0817	Local	0856
0917	Local	0956
1017	Local	1056
1117	Local	1156

Additional hourly service at 37 and 57 minutes past the hour through 0034

DEPART HILLERØD	TRAIN NUMBER	ARRIVE COPENHAGEN H
1508	Local	1546
1608	Local	1646
1708	Local	1746
1808	Local	1846

Additional hourly service at 08, 28, and 48 minutes past the hour through 0028

Daily, including holidays
Distance: 19 miles (30 km)

The shop-'til-you-drop group will enjoy Hillerød's shopping center, the **"SlotsArkaderne" (Castle Arcades)** with more than forty-seven specialty shops. It, too, is conveniently located on Slotsgade. When you are coming from the railway station, the glass-covered SlotsArkaderne shopping mall is on the left-hand side of Slotsgade.

The **Money Historical Museum** at No. 38 Slotsgade is on your way to the castle. It should attract coin collectors of all ages as it comprises a very fine collection of Danish and foreign coins as well as other means of payment used in ancient times. Illustrations tell the story of political, historical, and cultural aspects of money and coinage.

Just outside Hillerød, you may want to visit an exhibit of costumed dolls. You can reach it on bus No. 736. The display features seventy dolls with hand-made costumes that present the history of dress as well as the history of humankind. You'll see everything from Queen Victoria to the bustle that your great-grandmother used to wear.

Day Excursion to

Odense   HOME OF HANS CHRISTIAN ANDERSEN

Depart from Copenhagen H. Station

Distance by Train: 103 miles (165 km)
Average Travel Time: 1 hour, 40 minutes
No city code required
Internet: www.odenseturist.dk
Odense Turist Bureau: Radhuset (Town Hall), DK–5000 Odense C
Tel: 66 12 75 20; *Fax:* 66 12 75 86
Hours: June 15–August 31, Monday–Saturday 0900–1900; Sunday 1000–1700.
  September 1–June 14, Monday–Friday 0930–1630; Saturday 1000–1300.
    When you arrive in the Odense railway station, look for the train information
booth on the second floor. There you can obtain train information and a map of
Odense showing how to get to the Turist Bureau at the Radhuset (Town Hall).
Information booth hours: Monday–Saturday, 0600–2100; Sunday, 0700–2200.

    Hans Christian Andersen, Denmark's famous teller of fairy tales, was born
in a tiny yellow house in Odense on April 2, 1805. One hundred years later,
the city bought the house and turned it into a museum—probably the best
investment that the city ever made. Tourists of all ages still flock to this magic
point to see what his early life was like and to wonder what developed an
imagination that could captivate the entire world.
    Many of Andersen's stories were set in or near Odense. Most of the loca-
tions can be seen today. The small, half-timbered house where he was born,
now the nucleus of the **Hans Christian Andersen Museum,** is set in a cluster of other small houses from the same period. A visit there is like stepping
back into the nineteenth century.
    The Hans Christian Andersen house (near the tourist office, about a
10-minute walk from the rail station) is open daily June 16–August 31
0900–1900; September 1–June 15, 1000–1600. The area surrounding Hans
Christian Andersen's home, with its little colored houses and cobblestone
streets, is very attractive.
    If you are visiting the museum area at mealtime, we suggest that you eat in
a charming little restaurant across the lane, Under the Linden Tree. It's but one
of a score of excellent restaurants in Odense. The tourist office has a handy
pocket guide describing many of these eating establishments. You'll find an
interesting selection—including such names as *Jensen's Boefhus* and *Den
Grimme Ælling* (Ugly Duckling).
    The house of Hans Christian Andersen is not the only attraction in Odense.
With more than 185,000 inhabitants, the city is Denmark's third largest.
Industrial and vigorous in its lifestyle, Odense has smart shops, spacious parks,

Copenhagen (København)—Odense

At least two trains hourly depart København H on the hour and half-hour; journey time on IC trains is 1 hr 29 to 32 min (a few min faster on Sat–Sun). Lyntog trains take only 1 hr 17 min.

At least two trains depart Odense hourly at 15 and 47 min after the hour; journey time for IC trains is 1 hr 30 min. Lyntog trains (departing at 1510, 1610, 1710, and 1910) take 1 hr 17 min.

Note: Seat reservations are recommended on all IC and Lyntog trains in Denmark. Passengers may board the train without a reservation but are not guaranteed a seat.

Distance: 103 miles (165 km)

and sparkling residential areas. Situated in the center of Denmark's second largest island, the Isle of Funen, the city is the focal point for those wishing to explore the island's rolling countryside.

The German Emperor Otto III officially mentioned Odense for the first time in a letter dated 18 March 988. Although there were people living there at the time and a church had been previously erected, the present-day residents applied the emperor's date as a benchmark and declared 1988 as the "1,000th Anniversary of Odense."

A Hans Christian Andersen fairy tale is presented from mid-July through the first week in August at the **Open Air Theater** in Funen Village. The village is one of the largest open-air museums in Denmark, characterized by a coherent layout of landscape and a real village of seventeenth-century houses assembled from the Island of Funen and the surrounding islands. Here you will find farms with animals, a rectory, a school—even a brickyard and a forge. The theater seats 2,000 people.

Odense has a museum for every interest—from art to transportation. The **Brandts Klaedefabrik Art Gallery, Danish Museum of Printing, Danish Press Museum,** and **Museum of Photographic Art** are all located in Brandts Passage. The **Danish Railway Museum** is next to the railway station at Dannebrogsgade 24 (*Tel:* 6613–6630). Experience 150 years of train and ferry history. It is open daily from 1000 to 1600.

The **Odense Adventure Pass** will provide free public transport within the Odense area and either free or reduced-price admission to Odense's museums, sights, and the zoo. A 24-hour pass costs 50 DKK for adults and 25 for children, and the 48-hour pass costs 90 DKK for adults and 45 for children. The Adventure Pass can be purchased at the Odense Tourist Bureau. To reach the zoo, board one of Odense Aafart's covered cruise boats for a relaxing journey.

Day Excursion to

Roskilde   THE VIKING SHIP MUSEUM AND THE CATHEDRAL

Depart from Copenhagen H. Station

Distance by Train: 19 miles (31 km)
Average Train Time: 25 minutes
No city code required
Roskilde-Egnens Turistbureau: Gullandsstraede 15, DK–4000 Roskilde
Tel: 46 35 27 00; *Fax:* 46 35 14 74
Internet: www.destination-roskilde.dk
E-mail: info@destination-roskilde.dk
Hours: July–August, 0900–1800 Monday–Friday; 0900–1500 Saturday; 1000–1400 Sunday. September–June, 0900–1700 Monday–Friday; 0900–1300 Saturday.
    Ten-minute walk from the railway station, or take a taxi for about 50 DKK. If walking, exit the station and proceed downhill to the main street. Turn left at this point to the city square. The tourist office is only about 300 yards off the pedestrian street in Gullandsstraede.

Since Roskilde is so close to Copenhagen, you might think that it would be so much like Denmark's capital city that a day excursion there would be pointless. On the contrary, Roskilde is as different from Copenhagen as night is from day. Known as the "Town of Viking Ships and Royal Tombs," Roskilde warrants a definite visit. In fact, it is difficult to see all that you might want to see in Roskilde in just one day.

We recommend at least three things to do during your day excursion: (1) visit the cathedral, (2) take a guided tour, and (3) visit the Viking Ship Museum. If you decide to stay over, Roskilde offers one of the most beautiful campsites with waterfront and fjord views, plus 11 chalets available to rent. The area also has modern hotels and beautiful manor house accommodations. Consider contacting the tourist office prior to departure for the "Destination Roskilde" guide.

Roskilde's twin-spired, red brick **Domkirke (cathedral)** dominates the city's skyline. Its construction was begun in 1170 on the same site where King Harald Bluetooth erected a church in A.D. 960. Today it's considered Denmark's most important medieval building and is now inscribed on the World Heritage List. It is an international attraction primarily because it has been the burial place of Danish royalty for centuries. Thirty-eight kings and queens of Denmark are buried there, representing the longest reign of family monarchy in the world.

The cathedral is one of Denmark's first brick buildings, and it is said that it has as many tales to tell as it has bricks in its walls. Originally, a limestone edifice was erected on the foundation of Harald Bluetooth's church, only to be

Copenhagen (København)–Roskilde

Trains run about every 25 minutes from Copenhagen to Roskilde all day beginning at 0500 through 0004; a couple of trains also run during the middle of the night.

Distance: 19 miles (31 km)

---

torn down and replaced slowly by the present brick structure, which was completed in the year 1280.

Some less significant but nevertheless interesting features of the cathedral are its granite measuring column and a 500-year-old clock. The column was used to measure the height of royal visitors. The tallest, Peter the Great of Russia, checked in at 6 feet 10 inches! The clock features Saint George and the dragon. For nearly 500 years, Saint George has mounted his trusty horse each hour and attacked the dragon, which screams in pain before going off to dragon heaven to be refurbished for the next hour's performance. The cathedral is open (except when services are being conducted) April–October: 0900–1645 Monday–Friday, 0900-1200 Saturday, and 1230–1645 Sunday; October–April: 1000–1545 Tuesday–Friday, 1130–1545 Saturday, and 1230–1545 Sunday. Admission is 12 DKK for adults; 6 DKK for children. Guided tours offered by Roskilde-Egnens Turistbureau, *tel:* 46 35 27 00.

If you visit Roskilde on a Wednesday or a Saturday morning, you will find the city's **market** in full operation. The market is unique in that it isn't limited to the sale of meats, poultry, fish, and produce—the usual bill of fare that you find throughout Europe. The market activities include a flea market that could rival the best American garage sale ever held. All of this activity takes place in the town square, the Staendertorvet, fronting the Town Hall.

The **Viking Ship Museum** is an interesting addition to Roskilde's many attractions (open daily May–October, 0900–1700; October–May, 1000–1600). Admission is 50 DKK for adults, 28 DKK for children in summer; and 42 DKK for adults, 26 DKK for children in winter. Family tickets are 125 DKK in summer and 92 DKK in winter. Proceed downhill from the cathedral. Expansions since 1997 to the museum island include the Boat Yard, Visitor's and Archaeological Workshops, plus sailing trips from June–August are offered in Viking ship replicas for all Viking wanna-be's.

Viking ships, circa A.D. 1000 to 1050, have been restored piece by piece in this most modern of maritime museums on the banks of the Roskilde fjord. For centuries legend had it that a barrier at the fjord's narrowest point actually had a Viking vessel beneath it. The legend was only partially correct in that a cofferdam operation in 1962 revealed that not one but five vessels had been sunk there to protect Roskilde's harbor from enemy fleets.

Just 6 miles west of Roskilde is the **Prehistoric Village-Historical-Archaeological-Experimental Centre** at Lejre, representing one of the most profound studies of prehistoric housing. Ask the tourist office about bus connections from the small station in Lejre to the center.

And if you visit during June 29–30, July 1–2, be sure to check out the **Roskilde Festival,** the greatest rock-and-jazz fest in northern Europe. Visit www.roskilde-festival.dk to keep up with the latest news and ticket information. For those who want to plan ahead, 2001 festival dates are June 28–30, July 1.

All ages will enjoy "one of the most beautiful houses in Scandinavia." **Ledreborg Slot,** an impressive example from the Rococo period. Tours of the palace are 45 DKK for adults and 25 DKK for children. *Tel:* 46 48 00 38 or *Fax:* 46 48 04 80 for more details. Admire exquisite landscape, architecture, paintings and furnishings from over 250 years ago, see the home's servant quarters and even visit the dungeon. Don't forget your children (in the dungeon area, that is), as they will not want to miss the treasure hunt in and around the park or trying to find their way through one of Europe's most amazing mazes. Summers provide concerts on the green and winter visitors will want to experience "Fairy-tale Christmas in Ledreborg," every weekend in December.

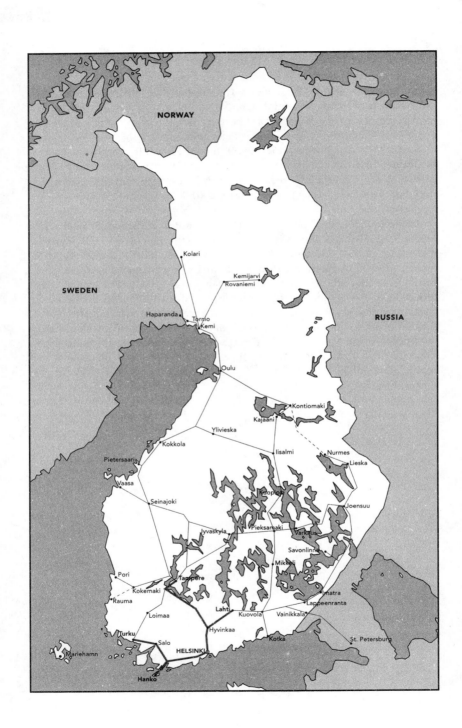

NORWAY

SWEDEN

RUSSIA

• Kolari

Kemijarvi
Rovaniemi

Haparanda •   •Tornio
                 •Kemi

Oulu

Kontiomaki
Kajaani

Ylivieska

•Kokkola   Iisalmi   Nurmes
                                       •Lieska
Pietersaari•

•Vaasa
                                       Kuopio
Seinajoki   •Joensuu

            Jyvaskyla   •Pieksamaki
                                       Varkaus

                         Savonlinna

                         Mikkeli

•Pori
        •Kokemaki   Tampere
                                              Imatra
•Rauma   Lappeenranta
        Loimaa   Kuovola   Vainikkala•
                         Lahti
                    Hyvinkaa
•Turku   Salo   Kotka   •St. Petersburg
                     HELSINKI
•Mariehamn

Hanko

Finland

Finland is well known for its unique natural beauty, including 188,000 lakes, 179,000 islands, and Europe's biggest archipelago. Known as the "Land of the Midnight Sun" in summer, it is an artistic array of color in autumn, dazzling white in winter, and swashed with green beauty in spring. Finland is a country for all seasons.

Finnish and Swedish are the two languages spoken most frequently. English is a second language for many Finns, particularly for those involved in tourism and transportation.

Since they share a common border, Finland has long been associated with Russia in one way or another. During the Napoleonic Wars, Russia invaded Finland and it became a Russian grand duchy in 1809. Finnish nationalism grew, however, and the Finns proclaimed their independence in 1917. The Finns were again defeated by Soviet troops in the beginning of World War II. In the late 1980s, the Soviet's political demise fostered development of closer relations with Western Europe, and in 1995, Finland joined the European Union.

Finland is still considered a gateway between East and West. If you've always wanted to visit Russia, now's your chance. There are daily rail connections from Helsinki to Vyborg, St. Petersburg, and Moscow.

For tourist information, contact the Finnish Tourist Board Offices in North America:

New York: P.O. Box 4649, Grand Central Station, New York, NY 10163-4649. *Tel:* (212) 885–9700; *Fax:* (212) 885–9710; *E-mail:* info@goscandinavia. com; *Internet:* **www.goscandinavia**.com or **www.mik.fi**

Ontario: P.O. Box 246, Station Q, Ontario, CAN M4T 2MI. *Tel:* 800–FININ-FO; *Fax:* (416) 964–1524

Banking

- **Currency:** Finish Markka (FIM)
- **Exchange rate at press time:** 5.54 FIM = $1.00 U.S.
- **Hours:** 0900–1600 Monday. Hours may vary regionally. Foreign currency

and traveler's checks can also be exchanged in the following currency exchange offices: Katajanokka harbor, Helsinki, open daily 0900–1899 and during the arrival and departure of ships and the Helsinki-Vantaa Airport, open daily 0630–2300.

Communications

* **Country Code:** 358
For telephone calls within Finland, dial a zero (0) preceding area code.
Direct dial: AT&T Direct: 98100–100–10

Rail Travel in Finland

The Finnish Railways (VR Ltd.) operate Finland's mass transportation system. High-speed Pendolino S220 trains and InterCity and express trains provide long-distance services, and local and commuter trains provide connections for shorter routes. **Eurailpass** is accepted on the national rail network of Finland and a 50 percent discount on the crossing by Finnjet from Helsinki to Rostock (Germany) is available when reservations are made 7 days before departure in Budget or Tourist IS class. Free transport is also offered on buses operating as train substitutes during certain hours. The national rail pass, **Finnrail Pass,** and the regional **Scanrailpass** are also accepted.

Finnrail Pass

Valid for any 3 days unlimited train travel within a 1-month period
First Class $180; Second Class $120; or any 5 days within one month First Class $244; Second Class $162. Children 6–16 years, half the adult fare; children under age 6 travel free.

ScanRail Pass

Unlimited train travel in Denmark, Finland, Norway, and Sweden for a specified number of days. Also includes 20–50 percent discounts on certain ferries and bus connections. The passes range from 5 days of travel within a 2-month period ($270 Adult First Class) up to 21 consecutive days of travel ($486 Adult First Class); special Senior (age 60 and over), Youth (age 12–25), and Child (age 4–11) rates.

See Appendix for a more detailed list of railpass types and prices.

Base City . . .

Helsinki

City Dialing Code: 9

Internet: www.hel.fi

Arriving by Air

Vantaa Airport: *Tel:* 9 8277 3315; *Fax:* 9 8277 3317

Location: 20 kilometers north of Helsinki, 25 kilometers northeast of Espoo.

Airport–City Links: By Bus—Finnair buses run between the airport, the Air Terminal, Toolonkatu 21 and the Finnair City Terminal, Asema-Aukio 3 next to the main railway station two to four times an hour; journey takes 35 minutes. Fare: 24 markkaa (FIM). Local bus service: operated by Sirolan Liikenne Oy, take bus No. 615 between the airport and the station square two to four times an hour; trip takes 40 minutes. Fare 15 FIM.

By Taxi—Airport to the Central Railway Station takes 20 minutes. Fare about 130 FIM. Yellow Taxi is a service requiring a minimum of three passengers to share the ride.

Passengers should check in at the airport a minimum of 45 minutes before departure time for overseas flights. Contact Finnair several hours before flight time to check weather conditions at the airport.

Duty-free shops in the departure lounge of the Vantaa Airport are loaded with gifts of Finnish origins.

Arriving by Train

Helsinki is served by a single train terminal, the **Central Terminal,** which is considered the most important work designed by Eliel Saarinen, the prominent Finnish-American architect. The terminal lies right in the heart of Helsinki and is close to everything. The train platforms have a total of fourteen tracks. The tracks are not covered, so an umbrella or a raincoat will come in handy if you are arriving in, or departing from, Helsinki during inclement weather.

- **Baggage storage** available on the far right of the main hall entering from the trains. Baggage lockers are scattered throughout the station. A standard charge is required for all lockers, regardless of size.
- **Money exchange** is located in the main hall. Hours: 0800–2100 daily. Banks are open 0915–1615 Monday through Friday.
- **Hotel reservations** at the hotel booking center in the main hall. *Tel:* 9 17 13 13, *Fax:* 9 17 55 24. Reservation fee 10 FIM for either a single- or

double-room reservation; 15 FIM for three; 18 FIM for four persons. This
is the only hotel-reservations office in Helsinki. Hours: 0900–1900
Monday–Saturday; 1000–1800 Sunday; September 1–May 30,
Monday–Friday, 0900–1700.
- **Train information** on the right side of the station's main hall (Tel: 9 82
27 66). Train-seat reservations can be made at window Nos. 1–9. **Railpass
validation** also can be accomplished at these windows. Hours: 0615–2200
daily. The charge for seat reservations on the "Rapido" trains is 25 FIM.
Reservations on these trains are obligatory.

A large cafeteria on the main level serves fast-food specialties for the hurried traveler. On the floor above, a modern *ravintola* (restaurant) serves
0900–0100 daily.

Similar to Munich's Hauptbahnhof, Helsinki's Central Terminal connects
with a vast underground system lined with shops and restaurants. This lively
underground shopping area is open until 2200 every day, including Sunday. It's
a great place when returning late from a day excursion to pick up a loaf of
crusty bread, tasty cheese, and a beer—but on the other hand, there's always
room service.

Arriving by Ship

The Silja Line ferries from Stockholm arrive at Helsinki's Eteläsatama dock.
Silja Finnjet and Viking Line ferries dock at Katajanokka Pier. Each ferry company maintains spacious passenger facilities complete with food services,
lounges, currency exchanges, and connections to public transportation.
Shipping activities in the harbor present many photographic opportunities. If
you are continuing your Eurail journey back aboard the Silja Line, a money-
exchange service is offered aboard by the ship's purser. The rates are governed
by the Swedish banks but have basically the same exchange rates as the onshore
facilities in Helsinki.
- Silja Line, Mannerheimintie 2, Helsinki Fin 00100. *Tel;* 9 180 41; *Fax:* 9
1804 279; *Internet:* www.silja.fi
- Viking Line, P.O. Box 35, Mariehamm, FIN 22101. *Tel;* 18 26001; *Fax;* 18
15811

Tourist Information/Hotel Reservations
- *Helsinki City Tourist Information Office:* Pohjoisesplanadi 19, 00100 Helsinki
- *Tel:* 9 16 93 757; *Fax:* 9 16 93 839
- *Internet:* tourist.infor@hel.fi
- *Hours:* Summer, 0900–1900 Monday–Friday; 0900–1500 Saturday and
Sunday. October–April, 0900–1700 Monday–Friday; 0900–1500 Saturday;
closed Sunday.

Located in the market square area of the harbor. To reach this office, board tram No. 3T immediately in front of the train station. The fare for adults is 10.00 FIM; for children, 5.00 FIM. In about 10 minutes, the tram will pass the Silja Line Terminal for Stockholm ferries. Disembark at the next stop, which is the market square on the harbor. Look for the green **i** sign.

Getting Around in Helsinki

The Helsinki Card is a veritable key to the city. This card not only grants you free travel on buses, trams, trains, and the Metro in the metropolitan area but also provides free entry to about fifty museums and other places of interest in and around Helsinki and includes a free guided sightseeing tour by bus. Showing the card in department stores brings you a free gift; it will spoil you in many of the city's restaurants, theaters, the opera, and concerts. A ninety-six-page brochure describing the scores of opportunities the Helsinki Card provides may be obtained from the Helsinki City Tourist Office or in the Hotel Booking Centre at the railway station, as well as at some travel agencies, hotels, and department stores. The cards are issued for periods covering 24 hours for 110 FIM, 48 hours for 140 FIM, and 72 hours for 170 FIM. Kids ages 7 to 16 pay reduced rates. It's a value you can't refuse.

Sights/Attractions/Tours

During the summer, Helsinki operates an unusual form of sightseeing—a tram (streetcar) named "3T." It circles the city and takes in most of its important sightseeing points. Board the tram and pay your fare to the driver. Pick up a pamphlet containing a map and descriptions of the sights you'll see on your tour from the city tourist information office. The round trip takes about forty-five minutes. Fare: 10.00 FIM; kids under 12, 5.00 FIM.

Another way to become acquainted with the city is to take a guided bus tour. City tours depart from the Station Square from June–August at 1100 and 1300 daily. The fare is 90 FIM (free for Helsinki Card holders), the duration is one and a half hours. The same tours are conducted on a more limited schedule throughout the year. Check with the Helsinki tourist information office for details.

For a more intimate way to get to know Helsinki, ask the tourist office for the brochure *See Helsinki on Foot.* Tour No. 5—Market Square–Kaivopuisto–Eira—interested us. Just follow the route on the map in the brochure. The sights are numbered and explained. If you begin at Market Square, one of the first sights will be the **Havis Amanda** (a beautiful mermaid) Fountain by the sculptor Ville Vallgren in 1908. Next you'll see the first public monument in Helsinki—the **Czarina's Stone**, designed by C. L. Engel to commemorate the Czarina

Alexandra's visit. About midway through your tour, you may want to stop at the **Ursula Seaside Café** (No. 33 on the map).

Other tours originate at the Silja Line or Viking Line terminals in the harbor area. These tours run two hours, and some schedules include lunch. Again, the tourist information office has the details.

Highlights of Helsinki

Helsinki is a city born of the sea, and it is from the sea that it draws its soul and nature. It is the beautiful daughter of the Baltic—a sparkling jewel with the blue sea as its setting. Helsinki is a modern city. Here the visitor does not come face to face with the past as he or she does in many other long-standing European capitals. Great fires destroyed the original Helsinki many times, but it was always rebuilt. The only original remains of the trade-and-seafaring town that Swedish King Gustav Vasa founded in 1550 at the mouth of the Vantaa River are the foundations of a church.

Helsinki did not become Finland's capital until 1812. It is very cosmopolitan, the heart of cultural and artistic experiences for the Finns. The city's colorful market square on the harbor is characterized by the glittering sea and an abundance of flowers and fruit, white seagulls, and busy salespeople. Helsinki has an ambience that is all its own, supported by a friendly population and the physical comforts to enable you to enjoy fully its many features.

Helsinki's market square, besides presenting flowers, fish, vegetables, fruits, and souvenirs, can also provide visitors with coffee and delicious sugared buns at the square's tent cafe. Market hours: 0700–1400 Monday–Saturday. From mid–May through August, the evening market hours are 1530–2000 Monday–Friday. Most shops in Helsinki are open 0900–1800 (or 2000) weekdays and 0900–1400 on Saturdays.

Surrounded as the city is by the sea, there is a lot of island hopping you can do while visiting Helsinki. A ride on a ferryboat will take you to **Korkeasaari Island**, Helsinki's zoo; by ferry you can also reach **Suomenlinna**, a fortress island started by the Swedes, captured by the Russians, and shelled by the British before being given to Finland, which used it as part of its sea defenses until 1973. Should you tire of all this activity, you can plan to relax in one of Helsinki's excellent saunas.

Day Excursions

When you have finally broken the fine Finnish spell Helsinki casts over its visitors, you will want to venture forth into the Finnish countryside. We have selected four such adventures for your pleasure. They are **Hanko, Lahti, Tampere,** and **Turku**. Hanko, Finland's southernmost city, is a very popular summer resort with miles of wide beaches, good fishing, sailing, and all types of amusements. Lahti, site of the 1978 World Ski Championships, is about 65 miles north of Helsinki and provides an opportunity to ride trains plying between Helsinki and Saint Petersburg. Also north of Helsinki lies Tampere, Finland's third largest city. Both industrial and recreational, Tampere has much to offer visitors year-round. Turku, Finland's gateway to the west, was its former capital and an important cultural center before Helsinki was founded. Wherever you go, the friendly Finns will make you feel right at home. Enjoy Finland as the Finns do.

Ferry Connections from Helsinki

There are two competing ferry services between Helsinki and Stockholm: Silja Line and Viking Line. The Eurailpass is valid on Silja Line ferries between Helsinki and Turku and Stockholm. Passholders pay a supplement for cabin space.

Silja Line
Main Office: Mannerheimintie 2
FIN-00100 Helsinki
Finland
Tel: 9 18 041
Fax: 9 18 04 279
Internet: www.silja.fi

Depart Helsinki Eteläsatama dock at 1800, arrive Stockholm Värtahamnen dock at 0830 the next day (arrive 0900 Jan 1–Mar 31); sails daily except May 3,5,7, Sept 13,15,17, Dec 24.

Bus service available from Värtahamnen dock to Ropsten Metro (underground/subway) station where there are trains to Stockholm Central station.

Viking Line
Main Office: P.O. Box 35
FIN-22101 Mariehamn
Finland
Tel: 18 26 011
Fax: 18 15 811
Internet: www.vikingline.fi

Depart Helsinki Katajanokka dock at 1800, arrive Stockholm Stadsgården dock at 0900 the next day; sails daily except May 5,7,9,11,13.

Bus connection to Stockholm Cityterminalen bus stop near the Stockholm Central station is available. In Helsinki, take Bus 13 from the Helsinki train station to the Viking Line terminal.

Ferry Connections from Helsinki to Stockholm*

A. Stockholm–Helsinki
   1. Silja Line ferries depart Stockholm at 1800 and arrive at Helsinki at 0830 the next day; sailings are daily except May 2,4,6, Sept 12,14,16, and Dec 24. Silja line docks are Stockholm Värtahamnen and Helsinki Eteläsatama.
   2. Viking Line ferries depart Stockholm at 1800 and arrive at Helsinki at 0900 the next day; sailings are daily except May 4,6,8,10, and 12. Viking Line docks are Stockholm Stadsgården and Helsinki Katajanokka.

B. Helsinki–Stockholm
   1. Silja Line ferries depart Helsinki at 1800 and arrive at Stockholm at 0830 the next day; sailings are daily except May 3,5,7, Sept 13,15,17, and Dec 24.
   2. Viking Line ferries depart Helsinki at 1800 and arrive at Stockholm at 0900 the next day; sailings are daily except May 5, 7, 9, 11, and 13.

C. Stockholm–Turku by Ferry; train from Turku–Helsinki
   1. Silja Line
      a. Silja Line ferries depart Stockholm at 0800 and arrive at Turku Harbor at 1900; sailings are daily from Jan 1–May 15 and from Aug 17–Dec 31 except not Dec 24–26.
      b. Silja Line ferries also depart Stockholm at 2000 and arrive at Turku Harbor at 0800 the next day; sailings are daily from Jan 1–May 15 and Aug 17–Dec 31 except Sept 7, 8, Nov 16, and Dec 23–25.
      c. Silja Line ferries also depart Stockholm at 0830 and arrive at Turku Harbor at 2045 daily from May 16–Aug 16 except June 1–2.
      d. Silja Line ferries also depart Stockholm at 2100 and arrive at Turku Harbor at 0800 the next day; sailings are daily from May 16–Aug 16. Silja Line docks are at Stockholm Värtahamnen and Turku Harbor.
   2. Viking Line
      a. Viking Line ferries depart Stockholm at 0800 and arrive at Turku at 2010 daily except Dec 24–25.
      b. Viking Line ferries also depart Stockholm at 2020 and arrive at Turku at 0715 the next day; sailings are daily except May 25–27 and Dec 24–25.
Viking Line docks are at Stockholm Stadsgården and at Turku Linnansatama.

3. Connecting Trains: Turku–Helsinki

DEPART TURKU HARBOR	TRAIN NUMBER	ARRIVE HELSINKI	NOTES
0820	130	1058	Departs from Turku Satama (harbor train station)
2110	148	2334	Departs from Turku Satama (harbor train station)

For other trains from Turku Station (in the city), see the separate tables for Helsinki–Turku.

D. Helsinki–Turku by train; ferry to Stockholm
1. Connecting trains

DEPART HELSINKI	TRAIN NUMBER	ARRIVE TURKU HARBOR	NOTES
0634	121	0842	Arrives at Turku Satama (harbor train station)
1834	139	2059	Arrives at Turku Satama (harbor train station)

2. Silja Line
   a. Silja Line ferries depart Turku at 1000 and arrive at Stockholm at 1900 daily from Jan 1–May 15 and Aug 17–Dec 31 except Sept 7, 8, Nov 16, and Dec 24–26.
   b. Silja Line ferries also depart Turku at 2000 and arrive at Stockholm at 0700 the next day; sailings are daily from Jan 1–May 15 and Aug 17–Dec 31 except Dec 23–25.
   c. Silja Line ferries also depart Turku at 0930 and arrive at Stockholm at 2000 daily from May 16–Aug 16.
   d. Silja Line ferries also depart Turku at 2145 and arrive at Stockholm at 0730 the next day; sailings are daily from May 16–Aug 16 except May 31 and June 1.

3. Viking Line
   a. Viking Line ferries depart from Turku at 0910 and arrive at Stockholm at 1915 daily except May 25–27 and Dec 24–25.
   b. Viking Line ferries also depart from Turku at 2130 and arrive at Stockholm at 0645 the next day; sailings are daily except June 7 and Dec 24–25.

★ 2000 sailing date exceptions unavailable at press time.

Day Excursion to

Hanko (Hangö)   SOUTHERNMOST CITY

Depart from Helsinki Station

Distance by Train: 85 miles (137 km)
Average Train Time: 2 hours, 15 minutes
City Dialing Code: 19
Tourist Information Office: 5 Raatihuoneentori, P.O. Box 14, 10901 Hanko
Tel: 2203 411; *Fax:* 2203 261
Internet: www.hanko.fi
E-mail: tourist.office@hanko.fi
Hours: 0900–1700 Monday–Friday year-round

To get to the Hanko tourist office, depart the station and proceed along the overpass crossing the railroad, which will be on your left as you arrive. Walk over the bridge and continue past the market square on your right. Turn left on Bulevardi Street. The tourist office is in the town hall on the corner of Bulevardi and Vuorikatu Streets.

Hanko (Hangö) is Finland's southernmost town. It is best known as a summer resort; but as the climate in this part of Finland often is very mild, you can visit Hanko in any season. In September, for example, the seawater is still warm enough for swimming. If you do not want to swim, you can lie on the beach, take a walk in the surrounding area, go for a bicycle tour, hire a horse, or just relax. Hanko in autumn is an unusually peaceful place. No matter when you go there, you will find clean water, lots of fresh air, and lots of things to do.

The peninsula where Hanko lies, known long ago among seafarers, was used for centuries as a harbor where sailing vessels could seek refuge from storms or winter ice packs. With time on their hands, many navigators, merchants, and soldiers kept themselves busy by carving their names or family coats of arms in the rocks along the shoreline of the harbor. More than 600 of these carvings have been found. Due to these inscriptions, the area gained the title "Guest Book of the Archipelago." You can inspect this handiwork during the sightseeing cruises available in the harbor area.

Hanko did not begin as a town until the 1870s. With the introduction of iron ships, winter navigation became possible, and Hanko's peninsula was found to be well suited as a year-round harbor. Both a railway and a harbor were constructed, and Hanko was well on its way to becoming an important part of the Finnish economy.

By the end of the nineteenth century, Hanko was a fashionable summer resort, especially among the Russians coming from the St. Petersburg area. The Russian influence is visible in the architecture of many wooden villas in Hanko, most of which are in the **Spa Park.** The peninsula on which Hanko

Helsinki—Hanko (Hangö)

DEPART HELSINKI	TRAIN NUMBER	ARRIVE HANKO	NOTES
0634	121/352	0828	
0906	123/354	1049	R
1106	127/356	1300	

DEPART HANKO	TRAIN NUMBER	ARRIVE HELSINKI	NOTES
1312	357/134	1458	R
1612	359/138	1802	
1844	361/142	2034	

Daily, including holidays
R This train is an S220 Pendolino train: reservations required, supplement required.
Change trains in Karjaa
Distance: 85 miles (137 km)

lies was ceded to the Soviet Union in 1940 but was regained in 1941.

Hanko is inseparably linked to the sea. There are about ninety islands just within its town limits! The town has four small boat harbors, including the largest harbor for visiting boats in all of Finland, two commercial harbors, four industrial harbors, and an important rail-ferry loading facility in Finland. None of this activity is detrimental to tourism; in fact, it attracts it. More than 200,000 tourists visit Hanko annually. They come not only for the long sandy beaches and aquatic sports but for the more than 1,000 events that take place every year.

The day excursion to Hanko requires a change of trains at **Karjaa,** which you reach in just over an hour from Helsinki. In Karjaa, you will transfer to a local train that makes an interesting trip through southern Finland's woods and quaint little rail stations before reaching Hanko. The Hanko station is the last stop on the line, so there's no chance of missing it.

Between the years 1880 and 1930, thousands of emigrants set off from Hanko for the United States, Canada, and Australia. In 1967, a statue commemorating this period was erected near the beach, a short distance from the tourist office. Depicting wild birds in free flight, this **"independence monument"** is well worth the time to visit. Also worthwhile is a visit to the **Fortress Museum** (*Tel:* 2203 223) in the Eastern Harbor and the **Municipal Art Gallery** (*Tel:* 2203 317), which features exhibitions from local, Finnish, and foreign artists.

To experience Hanko's spa history, visit the famous **Summer Restaurant Casino**, one of the largest summer restaurants in Finland. To get there, head down Bulevardi toward the sea. Turn left onto Appelgrenintie. As you enter the Spa Park, you will see the beaches on your right. The villas in the park once housed Russian nobles and their families as guests.

Hanko has several other interesting restaurants, some of which are open year-round in the Eastern Harbor area. You can find seafood, Italian-style entrees, or homemade Finnish fare.

Other tours of Hanko and its surroundings can be arranged through the city tourist office. Brochures, maps, and special information leaflets are available, and guides can be hired. Sea cruises operate every day from mid-June to the end of August. The sea tours start at the Eastern Harbor and last about two hours. Tickets are sold onboard. Fishing trips may also be arranged, but before angling off, check with the tourist office and obtain a general fishing permit from the town's post office. Hanko is packed with exciting as well as relaxing things to do.

Day Excursion to

Lahti   Ski, Skate, Sail, or Cycle

Depart from Helsinki Station

Distance by Train: 81 miles (130 km)
Average Train Time: 1 hour, 30 minutes
City Dialing Code: 3
Tourist Information Office: Aleksanterinkatu 16, PL/Box 175, SF–15111 Lahti
Tel: 814 4568; *Fax:* 814 4564
Internet: www.lahti.fi
E-mail: matkailu@lahti.fi
Hours: June–August 0800–1700 Monday–Friday; 0900–1400 Saturday. September–May 0900–1600 Monday–Friday.

When you arrive in Lahti from Helsinki, exit on the left side of the train. Use the underground exit and walk toward track No. 4 to the station. Exit the terminal and proceed along Rautatienkatu Street to Aleksanterinkatu Street, where you turn right. Walk straight on. Tourist office is located at the courtyard on the first floor. Some tourist information is available in the rail station, as well as in the Sports Centre and the Passenger Harbour, throughout the summer.

Lahti is the seventh largest city in Finland, with nearly 100,000 inhabitants. It is particularly noted for its timber and wooden furniture, brewers' products, and clothing and is equally famous as a winter sports center. Sporting events have always played a prominent role in Lahti's lifestyle. The **Salpausselkä Ski**

Games, as well as the **Finlandia** and other skiing events, have made Lahti world-famous.

Perhaps the most spectacular sight in Lahti is its 116-meter ski jump, located in the **Lahti Sports Centre.** The jump is about a 15-minute walk from the tourist information office and merits everyone's inspection. An observation platform on top of the jump can be reached by elevator and is accessible to visitors daily during summer months and on weekends during low season. In addition to the 116-meter ski jump, there are smaller ski jumps and practice areas nearby. The ski-jump area actually is a year-round attraction for tourists. In addition to the observation platform, there is an open-air, heated swimming pool at the foot of the ski-jump complex.

The Sports Centre is not the sole attraction in Lahti. In the 1920s and 1930s the city had the most powerful broadcasting station in Finland and now stands as a Radio and TV Museum. The museum contains more than a thousand items of great interest in the field of radio technology.

In Lahti, general fitness is a feature of everyday life. There are illuminated trails for walking, jogging, and skiing—about 40 kilometers of them—as well as nonilluminated trails. Summer weekly events include outdoor theater, concerts, a lively marketplace, and hiking.

The city is unique in that it is one of the few metropolitan areas where you can live in a one-family house in the center of the city on the shore of a lake. (We suggest that the city planners of America go to Lahti to pick up a few pointers.) Much of Lahti's housing is spread over a wide area, along the city's green hillsides and lakeshores. Many visitors are surprised to find Lahti so sophisticated and versatile. The infrastructure of quality department stores, good hotels, and good restaurants coupled with civic convention centers capable of handling large numbers of people are the elements of Lahti's success. Lahti is modern yet traditional.

Shopping for excellent Finnish glassware can be a full-time occupation. Numerous Lahti department stores, as well as specialty shops, feature fine Finnish glassware and other high-quality items. The city is well known for its ready-to-wear garments for both men and women. The Finnish furniture industry is centered here, and Lahti bread and beer are known all over Finland for their quality.

In summer, Lahti's cultural life includes performances in the **Kariranta open-air theater** and the open-air concerts at the **Mukkula Tourist Centre.** Lahti provides an interesting as well as relaxing day-excursion site; it's a year-round attraction you shouldn't miss.

Sights to see while in town include the **Historical Museum,** the **Museum of Military Medicine,** the **Ski Museum,** and the **Museum of Art.** The City Tourist and Marketing Bureau conducts a two-hour city tour every Wednesday starting at 1700 from mid-June through mid-August.

Helsinki—Lahti

DEPART HELSINKI	TRAIN NUMBER	ARRIVE LAHTI	NOTES
0802	71	0925	
0908	9747	1059	2nd class
1026	3	1151	
1118	73	1242	
1222	21	1348	except Sa
1324	5/867	1450	

DEPART LAHTI	TRAIN NUMBER	ARRIVE HELSINKI	NOTES
1500	862/8	1630	
1634	24	1806	except Sa
1736	10	1902	
1830	76	1956	
1927	9828	2102	Su only; 2nd class
2041	14	2206	
2130	80	2258	

Daily, unless otherwise noted
Distance: 81 miles (130 km)

Lahti has been described as Finland's most American city. Founded in 1905, Lahti is, historically speaking, a young city, but it has grown more rapidly than towns of similar age or older. One reason for its vigorous development is its geographic position in the center of southern Finland, at the junction of major traffic routes. Another, we might add, is its friendly, courteous people.

Day Excursion to

Tampere

CITY OF THEATERS

Depart from Helsinki Station

Distance by Train: 116 miles (187 km)
Average Train Time: 1 hour, 55 minutes
City Dialing Code: 3
Tourist Information Office: Verkatehtaankatu 2, Box 487, FI-33101 Tampere
Tel: 31466800; *Fax:* 31466463
Hours: June–August 0830–2000 Monday–Friday; 0830–1800 Saturday; 1100–1800 Sunday. September–May 0830–1700 Monday–Friday.

Internet: www.tampere.fi
E-mail: touristbureau@tampere.fi

To get there, walk from the rail station down Hämeenkatu Street, which lies directly in front of the station. After four blocks, just before the river, turn left to Hatanpaan Valtatie. The city tourist information office, housed in a red brick building beside a small park, will then be in front of you.

Known as "the cradle of Finnish industry," Tampere is the youngest of the "triangle towns" of Finland, the others being Helsinki and Turku. The reference to a triangle comes from the fact that all three cities are approximately 93 miles (150 kilometers) apart from each other. The town of Tampere was granted its charter in 1779 by Gustavus III, who was king of both Sweden and Finland at that time. From a modest start, Tampere developed into an industrial and resort center early in the nineteenth century. Today, with its 195,000 inhabitants, it is the third largest city in Finland.

Tampere is a city of lakes and parks. Its two major lakes are connected by rapids flowing over three waterfalls. Tampere is considered to be a "small" city. The city center is located on a narrow isthmus that is divided by the rapids. The "smallness" actually means that all shops, stores, restaurants, hotels, and other sights are within easy reach of each other, which makes Tampere an easy city to explore on foot.

Many tours are offered through the tourist office, such as the **Rapids Walk**, through the heart of the city, and the **Pispala Walk**, to the top of the ridge for a spectacular view, then to the bohemian historical district. Learn about Finland's Grand Duchy past during the **In the Footsteps of the Tsar** tour, or take the **Art Tour**, the **Guided Shopping Tour**, or the **Tour of Churches**. Visit the Web site of the tourist board for more listings. Many lake cruises are offered as well.

Among the noteworthy places to see and visit in Tampere is the **Sarkanniemi Theme Park**, an amusement area containing a dolphinarium, an amusement park, and a children's zoo, all of which are open daily in summer. An aquarium, a planetarium, an observation tower, and the **Sara Hilden Modern Art Museum** are also located in the complex. These attractions are open daily throughout the year.

In the Sarkanniemi aquarium, you will find some 2,000 fish of more than 200 species from all over the world. See Eevertti, the newest addition to the Dolphinarium. There is a seal tank, too. The seals are fed daily at 1100 and again at 1600. In the completely renovated multimedia planetarium, a veritable sea of 6,000 twinkling bodies will open up before you. Here you will see both past and future movements in space projected on the planetarium's dome ceiling in a thirty-minute space adventure. The new Orion space adventure has opened also.

The Sarkanniemi also offers a separate amusement park area complete with a roller coaster ride, big and small bumper cars, and many other attractions. The

Helsinki—Tampere

DEPART HELSINKI	TRAIN NUMBER	ARRIVE TAMPERE	NOTES
0658	49	0856	
0758	IC 91	0958	1
0858	163	1102	

and later service at hourly intervals.

DEPART TAMPERE	TRAIN NUMBER	ARRIVE HELSINKI	NOTES
1500	52	1702	
1558	172	1802	
1706	IC 94	1858	1
1800	54	2002	
1834	174	2034	
1919	46	2114	Sun only
1954	176	2154	
2014	56	2200	Fri, Sun, R
2058	58	2302	
2212	100	0008+1	

Daily, unless otherwise noted
R Reservations required
1. A supplemental fare is charged on all IC trains. If the supplemental fare is paid in advance of boarding the train, a seat reservation is included at no extra charge; the supplemental fare may be paid aboard the train, but such payments do not guarantee seat availability.
Distance: 116 miles (200 km)

new ultimate experience is the Rapids Ride, a 490-meter-long track excavated out of the rock. The little ones in the family will love getting to know all of the fluffy animals in the children's zoo.

Art lovers will enjoy the Sara Hilden Modern Art Museum, with its outstanding collection of contemporary art. The paddle-wheel steamboat *Finlandia Queen* starts its one and one-half hour cruises from the Sarkanniemi quay from June through August, running daily. Need we say more—except that the Sarkanniemi is the place to be?

Another place of interest in Tampere is the revolving auditorium of the **Pyynikki Summer Theater.** It is world renowned and was the first of its kind when it opened in 1959. Nearby Pyynikki Park and Pispala Ridge, with their old timbered houses, are also worth visiting.

The new **Museum Centre Vapriikki** is located in a former engineering plant by the Tammerkoski Rapids. Site of the 1999 preliminary European Union (EU) summit meeting, the collections of five formerly separate museums form the basic exhibition in addition to several international exhibitions. The basic exhibition will be fully opened in 2000–2001.

In Tampere, you can find a good cross section of Finnish architectural history. It ranges from charming wooden houses and Art Nouveau houses in the center of the city to the most modern designed office buildings and red brick factory buildings at the city's rapids. Tampere's oldest building is the **Messukyla stone church**, which dates back to the fifteenth century. The city's cathedral with its architecture and frescoes is an outstanding example of Finland's Art Nouveau period. A newer place of worship is the Kaleva Church, a strikingly modern construction completed in 1966. Another fine example of modern Finnish architecture is the city's main library, the City Library Metso. The Moomin-Valley Museum in the same building is also worth a visit. The Moomin collection includes over 1,000 fairy-tale sketches and illustrations by the author–artist Tove Jansson and is to be enjoyed by all ages. If you are interested in architectural design, Tampere can come up with a good serving of it.

In the center of Tampere, there is the **Verkaranta Arts and Crafts Center** with Finnish articles of high quality on exhibition. Close by, you can browse about in Tampere's colorful old market hall and the outside markets that surround it. If you happen to be in town during the summer (June–August), there's a concert at 1900 at the Old Library Park in the city center on Thursdays. Folk dance groups perform at 1830 on Wednesdays.

Major cultural festivals in the year 2000 include the Tampere Film Festival, March 8-12 (Tel: 3 2130 034); the International Theatre Festival, August 8–13 (Tel: 3 31466 958); and the Tampere Jazz Happening, November 3-5 (Tel: 3 31466 751).

Day Excursion to

Turku

FINLAND'S FIRST CAPITAL

Depart from Helsinki Station

Distance by Train: 124 miles (200 km)
Average Train Time: 2 hours
City Dialing Code: 2
Tourist Information Office: Aurakatu 4, Fin–20100
Tel: 262–7444; *Fax:* 233–6488
Internet: www.turku.fi
E-mail: touristinfo@turku.fi
Hours: 0830–1800 Monday–Friday and 0900–1600 Saturday and Sunday.

Turku's tourist information office can be reached by proceeding from the rail station down Humalistonkatu (Humlegardsgatan). Turn left at Eerikinkatu and proceed for two blocks, then turn right onto Aurakatu. The tourist information office will be at your right near the city hall. If arriving at the harbor from Stockholm, check with the Silja Line desk for city information and directions to the city.

Turku is a city of contrasts, where past and present meet and blend. Finland's oldest established town, Turku celebrated its 770th anniversary in 1999. Turku was never founded; it seems it was always there. It developed naturally at the crossing of the northern trade routes at the mouth of the Aura River. The present population of approximately 165,000 is hardworking, industrious, and friendly.

With a railpass, you can choose from two forms of traveling to Turku. You can go by train on a day excursion from Helsinki, or you can take the Silja ferry from Stockholm. Whether you go by train or ferry, Turku deserves an extended examination because it has many interesting sights to offer.

Turku has three rail stations. Arriving from Helsinki, your train will make a brief stop at the Kupittaa suburban station before arriving in the city's main station. Do not detrain at Kupittaa. If you arrive in Turku on a day excursion from Helsinki and your train is scheduled to terminate at the ferry port (the third stop), rather than getting off at the main station (second stop), stay aboard the train and ride to the end of the line. There you can, time permitting, visit the nearby **Great Castle of Turku,** and, if you return to the center of town on foot by the Aura River, visit the **museum ship *Sigyn.*** Farther along the river, by the Martinsilth Bridge, is the sailing ship *Suomen Joutsen* (the "Swan of Finland"), the best-known tourist attraction in Turku. If you prefer a taxi, the fare is approximately 30 FIM; the walk from the port to the station should take about twenty to thirty minutes, and there's a lot to see en route. Bus service is also available. Bus No. 1 plies between the town's marketplace and the port. The bus fare is 8.00 FIM.

Helsinki—Turku

DEPART HELSINKI	TRAIN NUMBER	ARRIVE TURKU	NOTES
0630	121	0830	continues to Turku Harbor, arriving 0839
0906	123	1056	R
1106	125	1306	
1306	127	1508	R, 1
1434	129	1632	
1538	131	1723	R
1602	133	1812	
1734	135	1934	continues to Turku Harbor, arriving 1957
1834	137	2042	
2004	139	2202	R
2130	141	2330	

DEPART TURKU	TRAIN NUMBER	ARRIVE HELSINKI	NOTES
0545	122	0750	
0640	124	0830	R
0730	126	0930	R, 1
0904	128	1102	departs from Turku Harbor at 0855
1100	130	1302	
1313	133	1458	R
1430	134	1630	
1550	136	1802	
1733	138	1930	R, 2
1830	140	2034	
2004	142	2202	
2125	144	2334	departs from Turku Harbor at 2045

Daily, unless otherwise noted
R S220 high-speed train, reservations mandatory, supplement payable
1. Daily except Sunday
2. Daily except Saturday
Distance: 116 miles (200 km)

Tours depart the Aurakatu tourist office Monday through Saturday from mid-June through August. Check with either of the city's tourist information offices for full details regarding sightseeing opportunities in and around Turku. The **Great Castle of Turku,** which is only a brief walk from the Silja

Line, was begun in the 1280s. It is the largest castle in Finland and once served as a prison, but now it provides a magnificent banquet hall for state and civic functions. Also of interest to visitors is the historical museum that is housed in the Great Castle. Its collection provides insight regarding 400 years of Finnish history. Hours of operation are 1000–1800 daily from April 16 to September 15; 1000–1500 from September 16 to April 15 (on Mondays 1400–1900 in winter).

An interesting museum combination is the **Aboa Vetus Museum** and the **Ars Nova Museum.** The Aboa Vetus tells of how life in Turku developed since the fourteenth century, while Ars Nova focuses on twentieth-century art. Multimedia programs help guide you through the museums. The museums are open daily 1000–1900 May 3–September 5 and Tuesday–Sunday 1100–1900 the rest of the year. The museum closes at 1600 from June 24–27.

The **Turku Cathedral**, another thirteenth-century structure, is open throughout the year. The Cathedral is open to visitors 0900–2000 daily from April 16 to September 15 and 0900–1900 daily from September 19 to April 15. Turku Cathedral, the major medieval ecclesiastical building in Finland, is regarded as the national shrine. You will see many interesting Neoclassical buildings surrounding the cathedral. Turku boasts two major universities—one Finnish and one Swedish—with a combined student body exceeding 15,000.

During the early hours of the day, the bustling marketplace is full of life. There you will see brisk bargaining amid a brilliant display of flowers, fruit, vegetables, and fresh fish. Fire destroyed a major part of Turku in 1827, but Cloister Hill, a neighborhood of carpenters and stonemasons, escaped damage. Today the area houses the unique **Luostarinmäki Handicrafts Museum,** with some thirty workshops that reflect the eighteenth and nineteenth centuries. It's open daily 1000–1800 April 16–September 15 and 1000–1500 Tuesday–Sunday, September 16–April 15.

The word *turku* means "marketplace." The city, born out of the needs of commerce, is still one of the largest commercial centers in Finland. **The Hansa Shopping Center,** the country's largest, is adjacent to the city's marketplace and features more than one hundred shops and boutiques—plus a supermarket. Also there are hotels, theaters for movies and live performances, more than one hundred restaurants, and four banks.

If you, too, are a rail travel enthusiast, be certain to stop at **The Blue Train Café** in the market center. Its decor originates from a wooden long-distance Finnish railway car built in 1952 and is typical of the Finnish passenger rail cars of the 1950s.

France

"*How can you be expected to govern a country that has 246 kinds of cheese?*"
—Charles de Gaulle, 1962

Now, France has 340 different kinds of cheese and more than 450 types of wines. France is Western Europe's largest and probably its most diverse country. Each of France's 22 regions has its own culture and scenery, its own style of architecture and art, its own gastronomy and lifestyle, and, in many cases, its own dialect. This delightful diversity makes travel in France so intriguing.

The primary language is, of course, French, but most tourism officials and rail personnel speak at least *un peu* (a bit) of English. The best way to obtain the most help and cooperation in France is to first of all smile and then ask *in French, "Excusez moi, parlez-vous Anglaise?"* Even if your pronunciation makes the French language unrecognizable, the idea that you at least attempted to ask in French makes a big impression.

For more information on France contact the French Government Tourist Offices. *Internet:* www.france-tourism.com; *Tel:* (900) 990–0040 in the United States (charge is 95 cents per minute); (410) 286–8310.

New York: 444 Madison Avenue, Sixteenth Floor, New York, NY, 10022-6903. *Tel:* (212) 838–7800. *Fax:* (212) 838–7855

Chicago: 676 N. Michigan Avenue, Suite 336, Chicago, IL 60611. *Tel:* (312) 751–7800. *Fax:* (312) 337–6339

Los Angeles: 9454 Wilshire Boulevard, Suite 715, Beverly Hills, CA 90212-2967. *Tel:* (310) 217–6665. *Fax:* (310) 276–2835

Montreal: 1981 McGill College Avenue, Suite 490, Montreal, Quebec PQH3A 2W9, Canada. *Fax:* (514) 845–4868

Toronto: 30 St. Patrick Street, Suite 700, Toronto, Ontario M5T 3A3, Canada. *Fax:* (416) 979–7587

Banking

- **Hours:** 0900–1400/1600 Monday–Friday (Some are open Saturday and closed Monday)
- **Currency:** French Franc (FRF). The franc is divided into 100 centimes.

Coins: 1, 2, 5, 10 francs; 5, 10, 20, and 50 centimes. Notes of 20, 50, 100, and 500 francs.
- **Exchange rate at press time:** 6.11 FRF = $1.00 U.S.

Communications

- **Country Code:** 33
  For telephone calls within France, dial the two-digit prefix applicable for the area as listed below, and then the 8-digit phone number:
  01– for Paris numbers
  02– for the northwest of France
  03– for the northeast of France
  04– for the southeast of France
  05– for the southwest of France
  All calls within France must use the full 10 digits. When placing calls to France from another country, use the country code 33 and drop the initial zero. (As an example, to call the Lyon Tourist Information Office from the United States, you would dial 011 + 33 + 4 + 72 77 69 69.)
- **Direct dial:** AT&T Direct: 0800 99 00 11
  Phone cards available (40 FRF).

Rail Travel in France

Seemingly, France has more varieties of trains than it has cheeses. The French lead the world in rail technology and their TGV (*train à grande vitesse*) trains hold the world's friction rail speed record at 320 mph.

French National Railroads (*Société Nationale des Chemins de Fer Français,* or SNCF) operates some 21,100 miles of rail lines, supplemented by SNCF buses in mountainous areas. For train information and reservations for all of France, call 08 36 35 35 39.

French National Railroads accepts Eurailpass, Europass, and their own France Pass. **Eurailpass bonuses** in France include:
- P&O European Ferries (ship)—30 percent discount
- Calais, France–Dover, England; Cherbourg/Le Havre, France–Portsmouth, England (ship)
- SeaFrance—50 percent discount on Calais-Dover crossing
- Chemins de Fer de la Provence—50 percent reduction on Digne–Nice
- Irish Ferries Cherbourg and Roscoff—Rosslare, Republic of Ireland
- Paris, France–London, England, via Eurostar thru the Chunnel—Special Fare

Europass includes a Special Fare for travel via Eurostar (Paris–London) trains through the Channel tunnel.

The **France Pass** provides any 3 days of unlimited rail travel in France within a 1-month period. Purchase additional travel days (up to a maximum of 6 extra days) for $30 per day. The First Class France Pass is $195; Second Class, $175. Children age 4–11 travel at half the adult fare, and children under age 4 travel free. The France Pass also provides discounts on the Paris metro and bus pass and discounted fares on the Thalys train supplements.

Base City . . .

Lyon

Internet: www.lyon-france.com

Lyon bustles with industry, trade fairs, and business. Its origins, however, go back to Roman times. Founded in A.D. 43, its old town stands on a hillside of volcanic soil containing some of the richest archaeological sites in France and still contains an unspoiled area of fourteenth- and fifteenth-century houses.

Lyon also claims to be the gastronomic capital of the world, and it has some impressive credentials to back its claim. The gastronomic tradition comes from its geographic position in the center of such great culinary areas as Bourgogne, Savoy, Beaujolais, and many others. With tongue in cheek, Lyon citizens say that the whole world cannot come from Lyon—there has to be at least a little from elsewhere. With our tongue in cheek, we note that Lyon also has several American-style fast-food establishments. Touché!

Although proud of its history and devoted to preserving its antiquity, Lyon forges ahead toward the twenty-first century with a continuous modernizing, building-and-expansion program that rivals even that of Paris. Part-Dieu, a complete and separate metropolis on the left bank of the Rhône, rises like a modern phoenix above the rest of Lyon, most of which was built during the eighteenth century. Lyon's contrasts are great. By virtue of these contrasts, Lyon is becoming one of the great cities of France and of Europe.

Arriving by Air

Satolas Airport, 15 miles (25 kilometers) to the east of Lyon. International air service between Lyon and New York is provided by Air France. Frequent air service to Paris, Frankfurt, Brussels, and Amsterdam provides additional connections for passengers with North American destinations.

- **Airport–City Links:** Airport bus (Satobus) service to Lyon's Perrache and Part-Dieu stations. Every 20 minutes 0500–2100 Monday–Friday; every 30

minutes Saturday–Sunday. Journey time: about 45 minutes; fare, 46 FRF.
- **Limousine** service is also available direct to most of the city's hotels. Journey time: about 45 minutes.
- **Taxis:** about 180 FRF (daytime) and 270 FRF (nighttime).
- Air France office closest to the station: 17 rue Victor Hugo. *Tel:* 04 72 56 22 20.

Arriving by Train

Most of the TGV Duplex trains (double-decker) from Paris to Lyon terminate at Part-Dieu, but a few continue on to terminate at Perrache.

The facilities provided by **Gare de Perrache** have been expanded by the ultramodern annex appended to the front of the present station building. This annex houses a bus terminal, the terminal for the city's metro system, and a bevy of offices, shops, snack bars, and restaurants. The terminal for the airport bus and local taxi services is also located in the annex.

Access to the annex is gained by escalators immediately in front of the station's main doors. Pedestrian traffic, moving from the station through the annex and into the city, uses another escalator system to exit into Lyon's Place Carnot. The square, with its statues, fountains, and waterfalls, is one of the city's showplaces and an excellent place to spend a few quiet moments.

Gare de Perrache, together with its annex, is a large and sprawling complex. Access to train platforms is through two underground passageways—SORTIE NORD and SORTIE SUD (north and south exits)—and escalators that descend from the ticket office and the waiting-room areas. Use of either passageway will take you to platform No. 1 and, in turn, to exits leading to the street side of the station. Fortunately, there's an abundance of pictographs throughout the station.

If you have baggage, be prepared to carry it. Baggage carts for passenger use are not available, probably due to the platform stairways. The escalators serve only the tracks reserved for express-train service.

Train-departure signs are displayed in the underground passageways at the bottom of the platform stairways. The north passageway, however, will not list a southbound departure, nor the south a northbound one, unless it is a train running through Lyon Perrache and not originating there. All train departures are displayed over the ticket windows in the main station hall.

Money exchange services are available at the Thomas Cook Bureau de Change in the Perrache station. Hours: 0800–2000 daily. From the train information area, follow the pictographs and proceed by either escalator or elevator to the station's TGV departure lounge on the second level.

To reach the **bank**, Société Générale, use the escalator on the side of the station annex facing Place Carnot, the city square immediately in front of the station. When you reach ground level, walk down the steps alongside the waterfall to the fountain at the bottom. At this point, turn to the right between the fountain and the waterfall, and then proceed across the square. The bank is at No. 12 Place Carnot. When you approach the first street, you will see the bank across the intersection to your left. This is the only bank in the vicinity of Place Carnot.

Train Information office is within the main building of the Perrache station. Use the main entrance, turn right once you have entered the hall, and proceed through an archway to the train information office. Hours: 0900–1900 Monday–Saturday; 0900–1830 Sunday/holidays.

The French National Railroads produces *Le Fiches Horaires* (minitimetables), which are free. A selection is normally kept immediately outside the train information office door and inside the office on the left-hand wall. These timetables may eliminate standing in line to make inquiries.

Train reservations may be made in the train information office at any one of the operating windows. We did not find the train information staff too adept at English. Consequently, we recommend submitting your reservation requests in writing.

Railpass validation is handled at any window in the train information office. Write the starting and ending dates on a piece of paper and obtain concurrence from the attendant before the entry is made on your railpass.

Transportation between Gare de Perrache and Gare Part-Dieu is facilitated by Lyon's ultramodern Metro (subway) system that serves both rail stations.

Tourist Information/Hotel Reservations

Lyon Tourist Information (central office), Pavillon du Tourisme, No. 25 Place Bellecour (two Metro stops from Gare de Perrache).
Tel: 04 72 77 69 69; *Fax:* 04 78 42 04 32
Hours: 1000–1900 Monday–Saturday; 1000–1800 Sunday/bank holidays

Hotel reservations for within the city of Lyon may be made at the tourist information office for a nominal fee.

Getting Around in Lyon

Lyon has an ultramodern Metro (subway) system. One of its main terminals is in Gare de Perrache; there's another in the rail terminal at Part-Dieu. Trains run every three to ten minutes from 0500 to 2400 daily. A single-ride ticket costs 8 FRF; a book of 10 tickets, 68 FRF; 1-day tourist tickets, 24 FRF.

Sightseeing/Attractions/Tours

Lyon Vision operates a 2-hour sightseeing bus tour of Lyon April 1–October 31. The buses are equipped with headsets providing explanations of the tour sights in five languages, including English. Fare for adults, 110 FRF; children under age 16 is 55 FRF. Buses depart daily at 0910, 1055, 1405, 1605, and 1805 from Place Bellecour No. 25. Ask for a folder at the tourist office.

Or, join the Lyon Tourist Office's guided tour, "A Stroll Through Old Lyon," which is conducted on foot over a 2-hour period. Departures are daily throughout the tourist season at a charge of 50 FRF. An evening tour is also available. Check with the tourist office for the daily schedule.

Le Vieux Lyon (Old Lyon) is a charming area to visit. For your convenience, use the *funiculaires* (funicular) to gain the summit. Take bus No. 44 from the station annex and ask the driver to let you off at the St. Jean bus stop. The funicular station is located at rue St. Jean and avenue Max, immediately to the left of **Place St. Jean.**

Old Lyon is said to be the most extensive Renaissance area in France. It covers about 1 mile along the right bank of the Saone River at the foot of **Fourviére Hill.**

While visiting the Fourviére Hill area, check out Lyon's answer to Paris' Eiffel Tower located behind the basilica. The Lyonese claim their tower is five feet higher than the Parisians', and it is—above sea level, that is.

Day Excursions

Contrasts continue in the selection of day excursions from Lyon, the third largest city in France. A scant 25 miles short of Geneva, the town of **Annecy** and its crystal-clear lake wait to charm you. Annecy's old quarter, lying back from the lake, has one of Europe's finest marketplaces.

Dijon vies with Lyon for gastronomic honors. During your visit to Dijon, you will want to shop for its world-renowned product, mustard. But that's not all it has to offer. The history of Burgundy breathes in Dijon, its capital, and you will want to catch its scent.

Grenoble is situated in the midst of a breathtaking panorama of mountains. A ride on its *téléphérique* will provide an even more remarkable view of the city and the countryside surrounding it.

Vienne, 20 miles to the south, is almost a suburb of Lyon, but it is very different. It has some of the best preserved Roman buildings and amphitheaters in all of Europe and one of the world's finest restaurants, La Pyramide.

Train Connections to Other Base Cities from Lyon Part Dieu

DEPART	TRAIN NUMBER	ARRIVE	NOTES
Amsterdam Centraal			
0912	TGV 9566	1640	R, 1
1439	TGV 9572	2240	R, 1
2000	TGV 632	0809+1	R, 2, Sleeper
Barcelona Sants			
1226	TGV 868/9	1958	R, 3
1403	5511/6140	2249	R, 3
2357	377/378	0925+1	4
Bern (Berne)			
0739	750/5751	1211	5
1223	756/5757	1611	5
1607	TGV 861	2101	R, 5
Brussels (Bruxelles) Midi/Zuid			
0618	TGV 9560	1025	R
0912	TGV 9566	1306	R
1437	TGV 9572	1836	R
1841	TGV 9584	2307	R
Madrid			
1600	TGV 861	0858+1	R, 6
Milan (Milano) Centrale			
0708	EC 142/3	1250	R, 7
1828	EC 138/9	2350	R
Nice Ville			
0917	TGV 821	1438	R
1339	TGV9532	1847	R
1409	6172/73	2004	
1713	6132/33	2314	
2357	none	0741+1	R, Sleeper, 9
Paris Gare de Lyon			
0630	TGV 642	0834	R, Mon–Fri
0700	TGV 619/0	0904	R
0712	TGV 644	0916	R
0800	TGV 610	1010	R
0900	TGV 693	1104	R, Mon–Sat
1000	TGV 614	1204	R

and then hourly service until 2000

Rome (Roma) Termini

| 0708 | EC 142/3 | 1755 | R, 8 |

Zürich Hauptbahnhof

0605	376/375	1154	5
0739	5750/5751	1326	5
1223	5756/5757	1726	5
1607	TGV 861	2126	R, 5
1720	5760/5761	2226	5

Daily, unless otherwise noted
R Reservations required
Thalys high-speed trains require supplement.
1. Change trains in Brussels Midi/Zuid.
2. Change in Paris to Nord station, train 289, sleeper, departing 2316
3. Change to Talgo train in Montpellier, reservations required.
4. Change trains in Portbou.
5. Change trains in Geneva.
6. Change in Paris to Est station, train 409 Fransisco de Goya departing 1947. Special hotel train fares applicable.
7. Change in Turin Porta Nuoca to IC 503 departing at 1115. Does not run Dec. 25, 26, or Jan. 1.
8. Change trains in Turin.
9. Change trains in Valence.

Day Excursion to

Annecy
ALPINE LAKE

Depart from Lyon Part-Dieu Station

Distance by Train: 99 miles (130 km)
Average Train Time: 2 hours, 25 minutes
Annecy Tourist Information, Bonlieu Center, 1 rue Jean Jaurés
Tel: 04 50 45 00 33; *Fax:* 04 50 51 87 20
Internet: www.lac-annecy.com
Hours: From April to November 0900–1830 daily, 0900–1200 and 1500–1800 on Sundays. If closed, go to the bureau of information in the city hall, which is open until 1900 daily, except Sundays and holidays.

Reach the information office via bus No. 1 from in front of the station to Place de la Liberation, where you'll find the office in the Bonlieu Center. On foot, use the underground pedestrian passageway to the left of the station as you exit. Continue to walk a block ahead to rue Vaugelas. Here, you turn left and walk four blocks to where rue Vaugelas ends at place de la Liberation (a large open area).

Annecy (pronounced "Ahn-see") still remains largely undiscovered by North Americans, although it has long been a retreat of the French themselves. A crystal-clear lake, a spectacular view of the Alps, foothills that touch the town, an old quarter where quaint canals cross arcaded lanes, an engaging market selling everything from apples to zinnias—these are Annecy.

Annecy is a health spa as well as a popular holiday center. It has innumerable hotels, casinos, and, best of all, the lake. The basin in which the lake lies is so protected against pollution that the latter is almost transparent in its purity. The Thiou River, flowing out of the lake and through the old quarter of Annecy, runs through canals and meanders around islands en route to the Rhône and the Mediterranean.

Tour-boat operators offer a wide variety of tours around the "sea" of Annecy. Rapid tours, lasting just over an hour, have frequent departures. The more vigorous traveler can opt to cycle around it. Either mode will provide a spectacular view of alpine meadows, rivers, waterfalls, and the bountiful natural riches surrounding the lake.

Visit the town hall, **Hôtel de Ville,** just a short walk along **quai Chappuis.** But exercise caution when crossing the street—the locals stage a "Grand Prix" on occasion.

The tourist information office has several brochures describing the city and its lake, including an illustrated booklet, *Through the Old Town.* The office also contains bulletin boards with numerous announcements of cultural events in Annecy.

From the bridge crossing the Thiou River, you will catch your first glimpse of the **Palais de l'Isle** sitting astride the river. As its name suggests, this curious palace was an island stronghold, and it remains one of the most arresting monuments of Annecy. Its oldest sections date from the twelfth century. At one time it housed Annecy's municipal offices, the high judges' private apartments, and it also served as a dungeon.

Beyond the Palais de l'Isle lies the enchanting marketplace of Annecy's **Old Quarter.** A network of narrow streets filled with every type of shop imaginable is augmented on market days by hundreds of stands erected in the streets, where only pedestrians are allowed to pass.

Along with the chic boutiques and appliance shops, the marketplace vends every imaginable food product, pastry, flower, and condiment. Lavender, picked in the Alps, and locally manufactured culinary wares are also available.

The picturesque medieval appeal of Annecy stems from both the French and Italian civilizations as a result of having changed sides several times during its 2,000-year existence. The area became a part of the French empire in 1792, although it reverted to the Italian Kingdom of Sardinia in 1815. It was not until 1860 that all of Savoy, where Annecy is situated, was again reunited with France as a reward to the French for helping Italy in its war with Austria.

Lyon—Annecy

DEPART LYON PART-DIEU	TRAIN NUMBER	ARRIVE ANNECY
0639	5400/5401	0905
0811	5403/5402	1022

DEPART ANNECY	TRAIN NUMBER	ARRIVE LYON PART-DIEU
1550	5424/5425	1812
1709	5426/5427	1927
1905	5428/5429	2104

Daily, including holidays
Distance: 99 miles (160 km)

Annecy slipped quietly into the twentieth century with the introduction of TGV train service directly from Paris. The distance from the Gare de Lyon station in Paris to Annecy is covered in just three and a half hours—a trip that formerly consumed at least eight hours. Currently, there are four trains daily, making the possibility of a day excursion to Annecy from Paris a reality.

Departing Paris Gare de Lyon station on a TGV at 0642, you would arrive in Annecy at 1032; boarding TGV 938 departing Annecy at 1908, you would be back in Paris by 2248. It's a full day but a fun-packed one, too.

Day Excursion to

Dijon

CUTTING THE MUSTARD

Depart from Lyon Gare de Perrache or Part-Dieu

Distance by Train: 119 miles (190 km)
Average Train Time: 1 hour, 30 minutes
Dijon Tourist Information: Place Darcy
Tel: 03 80 44 11 44
Hours: May 1–November 15: 0900–2100 daily; 0900–1300 and 1400–1900 daily the remainder of the year.

Exit through the main doors of the station and bear to the right onto Avenue Maréchal Foch. Average walking time: 5 minutes. Use the Hotel Climat de France as a landmark. Proceed along Avenue Foch for one block. As you approach Place Darcy, you will find the tourist information office on the left-hand side of the street.

Say "Dijon" to any American who likes to eat well and the response will be "mustard." Mention Dijon to any Frenchman, and his eyes will roll and his hands will fly as he describes the gastronomic wonders of the Burgundian city's pastry shops, restaurants, cassis (black-currant liquor), *and* mustard—but not necessarily in that order. Dijon, the ancient capital city of Burgundy, has something for everyone. It sets a fine table, lives its history, and preserves its art.

Dijon is the gateway to France's most famous wine region, the Cote d'Or. Important historically in 1015 when Robert I, Duke of Burgundy, made it the capital of his duchy, today it produces over 40 million bottles each year. The city's most brilliant era, however, was from the fourteenth through the eighteenth centuries, when it gained most of its art and beautiful monuments.

Dijon cannot be visited in a hurry. Actually, an entire day can easily be spent visiting its **Palace of Burgundy Dukes** and the **Museum of Fine Arts,** which is housed in the palace. The museum, founded in 1783, is the most important in France after the Louvre in Paris. Don't miss the huge banquet room of the palace. It is identified as the Guards Room, and the tombs of the dukes are located here. The tombs provide some descriptive background as to how the populace rated the four "Valois" Dukes of Burgundy: Philip the Bold, Jean the Fearless, Philip the Good, and Charles the Rash.

Modern art has made an entry in the palace in the form of a department housing an exhibition of Impressionist works from the Granville collection. There's also a gallery devoted completely to the works of local artists from the Burgundy area.

The city is particularly proud of its artists, among them François Pompon (1855–1933). Sculptor Pompon began his career as a Burgundy marble cutter. He attended Dijon's school of fine arts before further studies and apprenticeships in Paris. He sculpted 300-plus works, almost all depicting animals. His fresh, clear style has astonishing simplicity.

Engrossing as Dijon's works of art can be, don't forget to break for lunch—another Dijon work of art that can't be hurried. Whatever entree you select, we are certain that you will want to enhance it with a dab or so of Dijon mustard. A word of caution—make that dab a small one and determine first if it suits your palate. Dijon's favorite condiment has some varieties that exceed the fire power of any Mexican pepper.

Dijon's railway station is unique in that its main hall is circular. Train information is available in the area marked INFORMATION VOYAGEURS on the right as you enter the main hall of the station. Hours: 0830–1900 Monday–Friday; 0830–1830 Saturday. A map showing the location of the city's tourist information office in relation to the rail station is displayed prominently in the station's foyer.

The tourist office displays a room-availability list immediately outside the office entrance. This depicts the number of vacancies existing in the various hotels of Dijon and its surrounding areas. Within the tourist office, you will

Lyon—Dijon

DEPART LYON PART-DIEU	TRAIN NUMBER	ARRIVE DIJON	NOTES
0651	6606/6607	0833	
0738	none	0938	arrives 0942 Sat–Sun
0925	5070	1125	arrives 1106 Sat–Sun
1220	6634/6635	1421	Mon–Fri only
1224	6634/6635	1405	Sat–Sun only
1356	5052	1557	

DEPART DIJON	TRAIN NUMBER	ARRIVE LYON PART-DIEU	NOTES
1535	6132/6133	1707	arrives 1732 from Aug 20–Sept 30
1604	5053	1807	
1703	5009	1845	daily except Fri
1703	6134/6135	1845	Fri only
1821	none	2014	Mon–Fri
1927	5073	2137	except Sat
2001	none	2208	Sat only
2047	6106/6107	2230	except Sat

Daily, unless otherwise noted
Distance: 122 miles (197 km)

find hotel-reservations facilities and money-exchange services. There is a nominal fee for each call within Dijon to secure hotel reservations.

The **Saint Benigne Cathedral** probably holds the record for being destroyed and rebuilt more times than any other place of worship in France—four times since its origins back in the sixth century! The present church was built between 1281 and 1325.

Also constructed in the thirteenth century, the **Church of Notre Dame** in Dijon fared better over the centuries. Both edifices are typical Burgundian Gothic.

One of the newer attractions in Dijon includes the **University of Bourgogne.** The Centre International d'Etudes Françaises attracts students from all over the world to study the French language and culture.

Day Excursion to

Grenoble

Depart from Lyon Part-Dieu Station

Distance by Train: 80 miles (129 km)
Average Train Time: 1 hour, 30 minutes
Grenoble Tourist Information: 14, rue de la République
Tel: 04 76 42 41 41; *Fax:* 04 76 00 18 98
Hours: 0900–1900 (until 1800 during winter) Monday through Saturday. Also open on Sundays 1000–1300.

Located some distance from the railway station in a labyrinth of winding streets. Reach it by either of the tramways in the direction of Grand Place, Universités, or Auguste Delaune. Your stop is Hubert Dubedout/Maison du Tourisme. MAISON DU TOURISME signs are displayed at many intersections.

Grenoble will remind many North Americans of Denver, Colorado. Lodged on a wide plain, butted against the swift waters of the Isere River, and back-dropped by the French Alps, it is a breathtaking scene of man and nature in concert.

Known as "the capital of the French Alps," Grenoble lies at the feet of three majestic mountain ranges at the crossroads of a number of large valleys. Its Isere River was first bridged by Roman legion engineers in 43 B.C.; Napoleon employed the concealment of the area to move his armies into the Italian campaign; and modern mountaineering was born on its towering peaks.

Grenoble unfolds the past as well as the present in its monuments and art. The **musée de Grenoble** houses one of the finest collections of old and modern masters in France. The classics of Rubens and Watteau, along with those of Utrillo and Picasso, adorn its galleries. The **Cathedral of Grenoble** dates to the twelfth century. In the center of Grenoble, in the oldest part of the town, you will find the **Musée de l'Ancien Evêché**. Begin by exploring an area below the surface of the outside square to see the remains of the town wall and Grenoble's first baptistery then continue on to the old bishop's palace. The early **Renaissance Palace of Justice** was built in the sixteenth century.

The **University of Grenoble** was founded in 1339—making it one of the oldest in Europe—and is considered by many academics to be one of the best in France. Grenoble's student population exceeds 40,000, more than 8,000 of whom are foreigners from 150 different countries. With university students near snow-covered slopes, it was inevitable that winter sports should develop. The 1968 Winter Olympics were hosted by Grenoble, and many other sports gatherings, including the Davis Cup finals, have taken place in the city's magnificent Sports' Hall.

Lyon—Grenoble

DEPART LYON PART-DIEU	TRAIN NUMBER	ARRIVE GRENOBLE	NOTES
0611	5453	0739	Mon–Sat
0708	5451	0833	Mon–Fri
0819	5455	0943	Mon–Sat
0922	58573	1057	
1027	5457	1153	Mon–Sat
1120★	58583	1250	Mon–Sat
1234	5459	1404	

DEPART GRENOBLE	TRAIN NUMBER	ARRIVE LYON PART-DIEU	NOTES
1400	5464	1524	Mon–Sat
1556	5466	1726	
1700	5468	1821	
1723	none	1908★★	
1813	5470	1936	
1900	5472	2031	
2000	5474	2103	except Sat
2154	none	2334	

★Departs from Lyon Perrache Station
★★Arrives at Lyon Perrache Station
Daily, unless otherwise noted
Distance: 80 miles (129 km)

To ride the **Téléphérique de la Bastille**, wend your way to the banks of the Isere River and then to the Jardin de Ville (city garden). From practically any point on the riverfront, you can see the "bubbles" of the cableway flying up and down the hillside in groups of three. A photographic hint: Ride the rear "bubble" up and the front one down for better views of Grenoble and its environs.

The terminal at the top of **Guy Pape Park** provides a spectacular view of the city and its surrounding countryside. Dominating the heights is the **Bastille**, a nineteenth-century fortress housing a military museum and a restaurant featuring traditional, regional cuisine. On a suitable day, you may opt to descend on foot through the Guy Pape Park to the **Jardin des Dauphins** (Dauphins' garden) on the banks of the Isere. Contact the tourist office for bicycle rental information, then search for and explore the gardens, the fountains, or the famous "grey gold" (concrete) buildings of Grenoble.

TGV service makes a Grenoble day excursion from Paris practical.

Departing Paris Gare de Lyon at 0621 on TGV 901 places you in Grenoble at 0923; or depart Paris at 0836 and arrive at 1141. There are six TGVs departing from Paris Gare de Lyon Monday–Friday, four TGVs on Saturday and five on Sunday. The last daily TGV returning to Paris departs Grenoble at 1933 and arrives at Gare de Lyon in Paris at 2243. On Sunday, the latest TGV departs Grenoble at 2037 for arrival at 2346 in Paris.

Day Excursion to

Vienne   Of Roman Origin

Depart from Lyon Gare de Perrache or Part-Dieu

Distance by Train: 20 miles (32 km)
Average Train Time: 24 minutes
Vienne Tourist Information: No. 3 Cours Brillier
Tel: 04 74 85 12 62
Hours: Mid-June–mid-September, 0900–1230 and 1330–1900 Monday–Saturday; 1000–1200 and 1430–1800 Sunday
      About a 10-minute walk from the railway station. Depart from the statue in front of the rail station down Cours Brillier to the tourist pavilion on the left-hand side of the street.

Turn a corner in Vienne and you turn a page of history. Roman in origin, this charming city lies on the Rhône River to the south of Lyon but so close (20 miles) that it could be mistaken easily for a Lyon suburb. Such is not the case. Vienne is distinctly different.

Among the remains of this once great city of the Roman Empire, and dating from the first century B.C. to the end of the third century A.D., stand a temple, an amphitheater, and a pyramid that was once the center of a Roman circus. Roman Vienne spread to both sides of the Rhône River, where ruins of a warehouse and baths have been uncovered.

A statue to the fallen during 1914 and 1940 stands in the square fronting the railway station. Take a moment to pause and reflect here. Note, too, that many of the names have family extensions in North America.

Attendants at the tourist office will assist by marking a suggested walking tour on your map. The majority of the city's sights, concentrated in the old north quarter, allow visitors to move quickly from one attraction to another.

Collections of bronze, ceramics, and jewels are on display at the **Museum of Fine Arts.** Perhaps the most impressive Roman ruin of Vienne is the **Temple of Augustus and Livia,** which is perfectly preserved. One almost

Lyon—Vienne

DEPART LYON PART-DIEU	TRAIN NUMBER	ARRIVE VIENNE	NOTES
0757	none	0820	daily except Sun
0835	5357	0855	
0927	none	0955	
1204	none	1235	daily except Sun
1224	none	1245	

DEPART VIENNE	TRAIN NUMBER	ARRIVE LYON PART-DIEU	NOTES
1357	none	1421	arrives Perrache 1433
1658	none	1721	arrives Perrache
1747	none	1808	Mon–Fri; arrives Perrache
1816	5008	1838	
1827	none	1855	Mon–Fri; arrives Perrache
1827	none	1855	Sun only; arrives Perrache
1928	none	1950	
2011	none	2038	Except Sat; arrives Perrache
2144	none	2203	Sun only
2200	5356	2220	arrives Perrache

Daily, unless otherwise noted
Distance: 20 miles (32 km)

expects toga-clad senators to step through its portals and into a local pastry shop. The temple is surrounded by more modern structures in the center of the city. No doubt the proximity of other buildings has helped shield and preserve the temple through the ages.

The great **amphitheater of Vienne** was cleverly built into the slope of the hillside on which the town now stands. In its original state, it could hold 13,000 spectators. It was covered entirely by soil in the first century, but excavations between 1922 and 1938, when activities were curtailed by World War II, have brought to life some very beautiful remnants of statuary, coins, and jewels from the era.

The amphitheater, modernized with stage lighting, is now the scene of many fine theatrical presentations in Vienne for thousands of spectators throughout the summer season, including the Vienne Jazz Festival. Similar lighting of the Temple of Augustus and Livia makes an evening visit to the city a memorable one.

The pyramid was erected in the center of a Roman circus to guide the racing chariots, but it was never completed. For centuries it was believed to be the tomb of Pontius Pilate, who, according to a twelfth-century legend, had died in Vienne while living there in exile. Little else remains of the circus site, but it stirs your imagination.

The city's famous restaurant, **La Pyramide** (named for its location on Boulevard Fernand-Point at the former Roman circus), has been endorsed by many gourmets as the world's finest. Reservations are recommended at La Pyramide, which is closed every Wednesday and Thursday at noon in season and annually from November through mid-December. Call ahead at 04 74 53 01 96 or fax them at 04 74 85 69 73. It's expensive, but you only live once!

When departing from the main part of town, you can reach Vienne's pyramid and the restaurant La Pyramide by taking the main road running to the south, Cours de Verdun (RN 7), to Boulevard Fernand-Point, on your right. When proceeding from the tourist information office at Cours Brillier, head south on Quai Riondet and turn left onto Boulevard Fernand-Point.

Vienne also has its share of medieval buildings. Most of them are still being lived in and look very much as they probably did back in the fifteenth and sixteenth centuries.

Although its industrial history is not as well known, for more than 200 years Vienne was an important center for textiles, especially carded wool and a cloth called "Renaissance." The **Musée de la Draperie**, housed in the Saint Germain building, is worth a visit. Hours: April 1–September 30, 1430–1830; closed Mondays and May 1. Still a center of a lively wool trade, the town manufactures chemicals and flourishes from other industries, too. The people of Vienne are justly proud of their industrial endeavors set in the midst of a richly wooded countryside.

Base City . . .

Nice
and the French Riviera

Internet: www.nice-coteazur.org

Nice, "the gateway to southern Europe," has changed more in 50 years than it did over the past two centuries. According to Nice's Convention and Visitors' Bureau, Nice's "history advances, but its past remains."

In the days before World War I, the Riviera was a haven for rich Russian dukes and English lords seeking escape from the rigors of a more northerly winter. When such aristocracy, particularly the Russian version, began to fade from the scene, summer became the popular season, bringing with it hordes of Americans and others seeking the sun and all sorts of fun, including the nocturnal varieties.

The Riviera began to change. Towns and fishing villages that earlier visitors knew have grown together into an almost continuous resort town stretching from Saint-Raphael to the Italian border. Nice, the largest community in the area, lies about halfway between these two points and is our base city for numerous day excursions in either direction. However, because of the relatively short distances between points and excellent rail service, one could select any one of the day excursions (Cannes, Monte Carlo, or Saint-Raphael) as a base city.

Arriving by Air

Nice Côte d'Azur Airport, 4 miles west of the city.

The airport has a convenient *Rendezvous* (meeting place) just beyond the arrival gates and a Bureau des Change (**money exchange**) and **information** desk farther into the international terminal, Terminal 1. Terminal 2 is for flights within France. If you are not certain of your transportation mode to your final destination, inquiries at the airport's information desk or at one of the airline counters inside.

Airport-City Links: An **airport bus** and **limousine** service is available between the airport and the railway station. Bus fare: 20 FRF; departs every 20 minutes. It makes three stops between the airport and the station. Journey time is about 30 minutes. Connections can be made in the front-left section of the airport building as you exit.

Taxis are available at the exit from the airport terminals. Fare between airport and rail station: 140–180 FRF. Journey time: about 15 minutes. Taxi and intercity bus service between the airport in Nice and the resorts of Cannes and Monte Carlo is also available.

Several resort hotels offer free or reduced-rate transportation to their locations along the Riviera. Inquire at the airport information desk.

Arriving by Train

Nice Ville Station—Gare SNCF Centrale, avenue Thiers *Tel:* 04 36 35 35 39 (in English)

Nice is a major rail terminus for the Mediterranean region, with 30 daily connections from France's largest cities and 27 from other countries.

The exterior of the central station in Nice is deceptive. There is a lot more activity, more facilities than those you see. Although it is smaller than most major train terminals in Europe, it seems to function equally well, with the exception of long ticket lines. Here again, a rail pass will prove to be an invaluable convenience.

Manual lockers are available (*Tel:* 04 92 14 82 68)

If your luggage is lost or stolen, if you missed your train, or if you need help with a handicapped or elderly passenger, don't panic. The railway station provides a helpful service—the **SOS Voyageurs SNCF** (Travelers' SOS Service). *Tel:* 04 93 16 02 61 Monday–Friday, 0900–1200 and 1500–1800, for assistance.

Money-exchange office is outside the main station and on the right as you exit from the trains (*Tel:* 04 93 82 13 00). Hours: June–September, 0700–2300 daily; remainder of the year, 0800–2000 daily.

Train-information, reservations and railpass validation office is inside the main station on the extreme left side when exiting from the trains. The office is marked RESERVATION INFORMATION—RENSEIGNEMENTS. Hours: 0830–1830 Monday–Saturday; 0830–1115 and 1400–1730 Sunday/holidays.

Remember, when having your pass validated, write out the starting and ending dates on a piece of paper and get the railroad clerk to agree to the correctness of the dates before the validation information is entered onto your railpass.

Tourist Information and Hotel Reservations

- The **Office du Tourisme** (Tourist Bureau) has three offices in the city of Nice, plus one at the international terminal at the airport (*Tel:* 04 93 21 44 11). The one in the railway station can probably best serve all of your needs. It is located outside the station and beyond the train administration office on the left. Hours: 0730–2000 daily June–September; 0800–1900 October–May. If you need to call ahead to the tourist office in the rail station, the number is 04 93 87 07 07 (*Fax:* 04 93 16 85 16); or call or fax the tourist office on the Promenade des Anglais (*Tel:* 04 92 14 48 00; *Fax:* 04 92 14 48 03).

- **Hotel reservations** are handled by the tourist office on avenue Thiers. Room vacancies in Nice and throughout the Riviera are extremely hard to come by during the months of June, July, and August, as well as during the winter holiday period. If possible, reserve your accommodations well in advance by writing ahead.

  Hotel rates in Nice and the rest of the Riviera vary according to the season of the year, so be specific when requesting reservations. The most expensive time of the year is between late March and the end of October. If you are looking for bargain rates, late October through January is when the rates are lowest.

- **American Express,** 11 Promenade des Anglais (*Tel:* 04 93 16 53 53). Second bus stop en route from the rail station to the airport. Hours:

May–September, 0900–2050 daily; remainder of the year, Monday–Friday. 0900–1950; Saturday, 0900–1850, with a lunch break 1300–1400. (Sunday, 1000–1800). Bank holidays it is open from 1000–1800.

Getting Around in Nice

The best way to get around in Nice is on foot, by bicycle/scooter, or by bus. *Bus Services:*

- Agence Sunbus, 10, avenue Felix Faure
  (*Tel:* 04 93 16 52 10 [0715–1900 Monday–Friday; 0715–1800 Saturday; 1120-1815 Sunday])
- Eden Tour Minibus, 4 rue Veillor
  (*Tel:* 04 93 92 55 85; *Fax:* 04 93 92 56 20)
- Glaude Transport Service (GTS)
  (*Tel:* 04 92 29 50 19; *Fax:* 04 92 29 50 10)
- *Bikes:* Arnaud, 4 place Grimaldi
  (*Tel:* 04 93 87 88 55 [bikes, mopeds, scooters])
- Nice Location Rent, 9 avenue Thiers
  (*Tel:* 04 93 82 42 71; *Fax:* 04 93 87 76 36)

Sights/Attractions/Tours

Nice boasts more than 200 hotels and 1,000 restaurants. Most of these facilities are located in the modern section of Nice, west of the Paillon River, which divides the town in two.

The Riviera is noted for its spectacular scenery. Every proper ingredient of sea, shore, cliffs, and mountains is present. Grapes and flowers are the predominant crops of its highly cultivated farmlands. It is one of the great flower-growing areas of Europe and probably the most famous center in the world for perfume production.

The Riviera is also a center for modern art. The works of many twentieth-century artists can be found in its numerous museums and exhibition halls. Picasso spent the last years of his life in a villa overlooking the Mediterranean.

In selecting Nice as the base city for the day excursions in the Riviera area, we considered the variety of features and attractions that the city has to offer, and they are many.

In the maze of Old Nice's narrow streets, you will discover, in variations of light, shade, and fragrances, the **fish market,** the **Palais Lascaris,** the public squares of the city—each one different in function but all with an air of grace and function—and, in a sudden burst of sunlight, the beaches.

To the east, the old town and port offer many attractions to those who have a feeling for the past. At 300 feet above the **Old Town,** in a public park where once a fortress stood, the views are unforgettable. Streets and houses in the old town date from the seventeenth and eighteenth centuries.

The **Marché aux Fleurs** (Flower Market), one of the most beautiful and truly native sights in the Old Town of Nice, is held daily except Monday in the **Cours Saleya,** a block south of the **Prefecture Palace** near the opera. At Cours Saleya, you'll discover what makes Nice so fragrant and colorful. You will also discover what makes the cuisine of the area so appetizing: A fruit-and-vegetable market flourishes right in the midst of the floral beauty. Mondays are a bit different in the Cours Saleya, since that's when the market is reserved for antiques dealers. But here again is another opportunity to delve into the priceless things that make Nice so nice.

There are ten casinos within 40 miles of Nice and three international ski resorts only 2 hours away. The world-famous **Nice Carnival** takes place every February. Other festive events, however, are to be found in Nice throughout the year. The King Carnival takes place just before Lent and rivals New Orleans' Mardi Gras.

Turn from the sea in Nice and your eyes confront **Mont Alban** and its fortress overhanging the harbor. If you choose to go to the Alpine area behind the city, there's a charming private narrow-gauge railroad, **Chemin de Fer de Provence** (Railroad of Provence), that will transport you through rocky gorges and sheer cliffs and Lingostiere, on the invasion route used by Napoleon, to an exceptional panorama of the Alps and the Mediterranean Sea.

For another train ride, this one within the city, board the **Nice "little train"** at its station on the Promenade des Anglais for a scenic ride through the shady, narrow streets of the Old Town to **Castle Hill** for a vista of the *Baie des Anges* (Bay of Angels) and the Port of Nice.

Day Excursions

With Nice as their pivot point, four wonderful day excursions have been selected. **Cannes** was picked for its beaches and bikinis (or something even less); **Marseilles**, melting pot of the Mediterranean, because of its flair for bouillabaisse and its Bogart background; **Monaco (Monte Carlo)** for its coastline and casino; and **Saint-Raphael**—the resort on the Riviera with something for everyone—and at popular prices.

Train Connections to Other Base Cities from Nice

DEPARTURE	TRAIN NUMBER	ARRIVAL	NOTES
Amsterdam Centraal			
1540	TGV 848	0809+1	R, 1
Barcelona Sants			
1025	164/165	1924	2
1204	6950/6951	2220	2
Berlin Zoobahnhof			
1252	TGV 846	0916+1	3
Brussels (Bruxelles) Midi/Zuid			
0924	TGV 9572	1836	R
0945	TGV 844	1920	R, 4
1835	none	0950+1	Sleeper, 5
Luxembourg			
0952	TGV 844	2052	R, 6
Lyon Part-Dieu			
0814	6676/6677	1438	
0925	TGV 9572	1434	R
1125	6638/6639	1738	
1420	TGV 820	1942	R, Mon–Thu
1535	TGV 836	2046	
1654	TGV 810	2210	R, Mon–Thu
1730	TGV 810	2305	R, Sun
Milan (Milano) Centrale			
1004	IC 343	1450	
1827	347/348	2300	
Munich (München) Hauptbahnhof			
1004	IC 343	1450	
Paris Gare de Lyon			
0945	TGV 844	1625	R
1248	TGV 846	1922	R
1908	5058	0620+1	R, Sleeper
	and then hourly service until 1200		
Rome (Roma) Termini			
0820	6478/6479	1655	8
1004	IC 343	1955	9
2035	369	0646+1	R, Sleeper

Daily, unless otherwise noted
R Reservations required
1. In Paris, transfer to Nord station for sleeper train 289 departing 2316.
2. Change in Montpellier to Talgo train, reservations required.
3. In Paris, transfer to Nord station for sleeper train 243 departing 2046.
4. Transfer in Paris to Nord station, Thalys high-speed train, reservations required, supplement payable.
5. Runs May 30–September 26.
6. Transfer in Paris to Gare de l'Est, train EC 53/1834 departing at 1717.
7. Change trains in Milan.
8. Change trains in Ventimiglia.
9. Change trains in Genoa (Genova PP).

Day Excursion to

Cannes

TOP OF THE RIVIERA

Depart from Nice Ville Station

Distance by Train: 19 miles (31 km)
Average Train Time: 25 minutes
Cannes Tourist Information: Cannes Syndicat d'Initative in the rail station, Office de Tourisme, Place de la Gare, 06 400
Tel: 04 93 99 19 77; *Fax:* 04 93 39 40 19
Hours: 0900–1830 Monday–Saturday
    Reach it by turning left in the main station hall, then take the stairs located immediately outside. Elevator service is also available. Look for the sign that reads SERVICE DU TOURISME DE LA VILLE DE CANNES, SYNDICAT D'INITIATIVE ACCUEIL DE FRANCE, SYNDICATS DES HOTELIERS.

- **Cannes Bureau du Tourisme, Palais des Festivals,** blvd. de la Croisette, across from the Majestic Hotel
  Hours: 0900–1830 Monday–Saturday; during July–August, 0900–2000 daily
- **American Express,** 3 blvd. de la Croisette 06 400
  Hours: 0900–1800 Monday–Friday

Cannes has been described as a magnet that attracts the famous, the rich, and the dreamers. It also has a reputation of being impossibly expensive. No doubt this is true of **La Croisette**—the waterfront boulevard of Cannes lined with sandy beaches, extravagant restaurants, and elegant hotels. But this reputation does not apply to all of Cannes.
    Cannes is a large resort with an official list of more than 5,000 hotel rooms

within its city limits and that many again in its suburbs. A hundred yards or so back from the waterfront, hotels charge a fraction of the rates extracted from the famous, the rich—and the dreamers—who insist on living at the water's edge.

The Cannes railway station is modern and efficient. All services are grouped conveniently in or near its main hall. As you exit from the track area, you can reach the **train information and reservations office** via the escalator to your right. Summer hours: Monday–Saturday 0900–1230 and 1400–1830; winter hours: 0900–1900 Monday–Friday. Coin-operated baggage lockers are available on the main level at either end of the station.

Walking through Cannes is enjoyable and easy. Certainly no one would want to miss a stroll along the Promenade de la Croisette, one of the most beautiful and highly celebrated seaside walks on the Riviera. It borders the Bay of Cannes for about 2 miles until you reach its extreme eastern end at the Palm Beach Casino—with its gaming rooms and gala evenings—on place Franklin D. Roosevelt.

Along the way, you will see some of the world's finest yachts berthed close by magnificent rose gardens in the Port Pierre-Canto and the famous **Palais des Festivals et des Congrés,** home of the International Film Festival. Walk along the old port to the old part of town called **"Le Suquet,"** which over-looks the harbor and offers a marvelous view of the bay.

Except for the brief period in the late fall when the Mistral winds make things a bit uncomfortable, the climate of Cannes is wonderfully mild and temperate. Because of a few canes and reeds growing in the bay, the Romans named the spot "Castrum de Canois," and for centuries Cannes remained a small village inhabited only by fishermen.

History relates that in 1834, the Lord Chancellor of England, Lord Brougham, "whilst" en route to Nice, was prevented in reaching there due to a cholera quarantine and paused briefly in Cannes. Taken by the place, his lord-ship decided on the spur of the moment to build a house in Cannes and did so, straight away—the transaction in real estate taking a matter of only eight days. For the next 34 years, until the time of his death, Lord Brougham left the winter fogs of London for the sunshine of Cannes.

His lordship's example was quickly followed by other English aristocracy, and Cannes' population began to swell accordingly. Alluding to the eight days required to get Cannes under way, locals point out that God took only seven days to create the universe—so Cannes, necessarily, is a cut above all else in the universe.

The center of Cannes is ideal for strolling and shopping. Locals claim that you get more than what you pay for because the area has a theatrical atmos-phere about it, and the show is free. Not so on the Croisette, the waterfront. Here the most elegant of shops extol the virtues of high fashion at equally high prices. Window shopping, however, is free to all.

Excursion-boat services from the main port take you to the islands of **Sainte-Marguerite** and **Saint-Honorat.** Sainte-Marguerite's prison incarcerated the Man in the Iron Mask, and the island named after Saint Honorat has the remains of the monastery the saint started in the fourth century. Boats run daily throughout the year.

Another very delightful boat ride provides an unequaled panorama of the Mediterranean and the Alps each afternoon from June through September. This excursion departs at 1430, cruises the Bay of Cannes and the **Esterel Coast,** and returns at 1730. If you don't happen to be one of the millionaires with a yacht tied up in Port Pierre-Canto, now's your chance to enjoy the same exhilarating view that they enjoy—at a more reasonable price.

Nice—Cannes

There are at least 3 trains per hour in each direction throughout the day from 0500 to 2300; journey time, 25–30 min.

Distance: 19 miles (31 km)

Day Excursion to

Marseilles

CITY OF INTRIGUE

Depart from Nice Ville Station

Distance by Train: 140 miles (225 km)

Average Train Time: 2 hours, 15 minutes

Tourism Office: Maison du Tourisme Marseilles, No. 4 La Canebiere, 13000 Marseill Cedex 01

Tel: 04 91 13 89 00; *Fax:* 04 91 13 89 20

Hours: July–September, 0900–2000 daily; October–June, 0900–1900 Monday–Saturday; 1000–1700 Sunday/holidays.

Located adjacent to the municipal docks. You may taxi there just by showing the driver the address. To reach it on foot—about a 15-minute walk—leave the railway station by descending the steps to street level. Directly in front is the boulevard d'Athens (a promenade from the original settlers, no doubt). Follow this street to the third traffic signal, including the one at the foot of the train-station steps. Turn to the right onto the boulevard La Canebiere, and just beyond the second traffic light now in front of you, look for the tourist office in the last building on the left-hand side of the street just before the small boat harbor.

Also, there is a small tourist office in the train station on the track level that is open 1000–1800.

Nice—Marseilles

DEPART NICE VILLE	TRAIN NUMBER	ARRIVE MARSEILLE ST. CHARLES	NOTES
0550	6964/6965	0831	
0614	6634/6635	0848	
0814	6676/6677	1046	
0900	5682/5683	1124	
0925	TGV 9572	1145	R
1025	164/165	1245	
1128	6638/6639	1408	

DEPART MARSEILLE ST. CHARLES	TRAIN NUMBER	ARRIVE NICE VILLE	NOTES
1524	5680/5681	1754	
1555	6464/6465	1817	
1625	TGV 9532	1848	R
1628	6130/6131	1857	
1650	162/163	1908	
1737	6172/6173	2004	
1840	6452/6453	2123	
2215	59259	0050+1	except Fri

Daily, unless otherwise noted
R Reservations required
Distance: 140 miles (225

Marseilles, the great port of France, is second only to Paris in population and one of the oldest surviving towns in the world. Although French in character, Marseilles is distinctly Mediterranean, with an international flair. There is much to compare in the character of Marseilles to the contents of its epicurean delicacy, bouillabaisse, and the three ingredients so essential in its making.

Greeks, fleeing out of Asia Minor from the Persians, founded Massalia (Marseilles) in 600 B.C. Their enterprising nature disturbed the Ligurians, who came from Italy, as well as the Iberians coming from Spain, and a lot of head smashing took place until the Greeks appealed to Rome for help. Romans came by the legions and promptly named the area a Roman province. Hannibal and his elephants created some disturbance, but nothing like that of 360,000 Teutonic warriors in 102 B.C. who were seemingly bent on destroying the civilized world and all that was in it.

Rome, again to the rescue, dispatched Caius Marius to the province; he, in turn, disposed of 100,000 Teutons near Aix-en-Provence, just north of Marseilles, thus saving the day for the province and impacting the future of modern–day France. Even today, the most popular name for men in this region is Marius.

The French national anthem, *The Marseillaise*, was composed in Strasbourg by a young French military officer, Rouget de Lisle. The battle song was published and reached Marseilles just at the time when the city was giving a send-off banquet to 500 volunteers bound for Paris and the revolution. Someone sang the new song and immediately the banquet room picked it up in chorus.

The song was an immediate success, and the volunteers sang it in unison at every stopping place en route to Paris. By the time they reached Paris they had become somewhat of an accomplished choir, which electrified the Parisians as they marched through the streets of Paris singing the stirring words at the tops of their voices.

All the foregoing was given to set the mood for your arrival in Marseilles. Although the city is not famous as a tourist center, it is a very enjoyable place to visit. Its unusual character and mixture of peoples cannot be found anywhere else in the world.

Not far from the tourist office, you will find the **Vieux–Port** and its fish market, which defies description. This is one of the few places in the world where you can obtain those three essential ingredients for bouillabaisse: red gurnet, conger eel, and a Mediterranean fish known locally as *rascasse*. Nearby restaurants serve it to perfection.

Here in the Vieux-Port, from a pier known as the Quai des Belges (Belgian Wharf), you can take a ferry for the 15-minute crossing to the island of **Chateau d'If,** made famous in *The Count of Monte Cristo* by Alexandre Dumas. The castle is an interesting place to visit, and your guide will dramatically conclude your tour by showing you the opening through which the count was said to have made his escape. The visit to the island takes about 1½–2 hours, including the tour of the dungeons where the Man in the Iron Mask and many other political prisoners were imprisoned.

Day Excursion to

Monte Carlo ROULETTE AND RELAXATION

Depart from Nice Ville Station

Distance by Train: 9 miles (14 km)
Average Train Time: 20 minutes
Tourism Office: Monaco Government Tourist/Convention Bureau in North America: 565 Fifth Avenue, New York, NY 10017
Tel: (800) 753–9696 or (212) 286–3330; *Fax:* (212) 286–9890
Internet: www.tourism.org.mt

Tourism Office: Monte Carlo Tourist Information 2, blvd. des Moulins
Tel: 04 92 16 61 16
Hours: Monday–Saturday 0900–1900; Sunday 1000–1200
   The bus terminal is a short distance downhill from the railway station. Board bus No. 4 and ask the driver to let you off at the Office National du Tourisme (the National Tourist Office). From June 15 to September 30, there's a small tourist information kiosk in the station lobby open daily 0800–2000.

   The Principality of Monaco lies 4,092 miles east of Philadelphia—two cities inexorably linked by the memories of their princess, Grace Patricia Kelly, who died as the result of a tragic accident in 1982.
   Monaco consists of 0.7 square miles (453 acres) of rocky coastline along the Riviera. It has been ruled by members of the Grimaldi family for the past ten centuries. Its famous gambling casino is located in Monte Carlo, one of four sections that make up the principality. The other three are Monaco-Ville itself (the capital and site of the palace), La Condamine (a commercial and residential area), and Fontvieille (a residential and light-industries section).
   Monaco operates a highly efficient bus system consisting of five major lines: No. 1 (Red), No. 2 (Blue), No. 4 (Gold), No. 5 (Brown), and No. 6 (Green), which serves the Fontvieille-Larvotto (beach) area. These are augmented by Line No. 3, serving the beach area during the summer.
   French francs are the legal tender in Monaco, so there is no need to change your currency. Traveler's checks can be cashed at "Credit Lyonnais," a bank opposite the train station, 0845–1155 and 1330–1600 Monday through Friday. The American Express office is just to the west of the casino at 2, avenue de Monte Carlo.
   If cracking casinos is your cup of tea, Monte Carlo's public gambling rooms open at 1000 daily. You must be twenty-one to enter. Youngsters are not barred, however, at the National Museum and Collection of Dolls and Automats of Yesteryear, located at 17, avenue Princesse Grace. Hours: daily April–September, 1000–1830; October–March, daily, 1000–1215 and 1430-1830. Admission 26 FRF, adults; children age 6–14 and students, 15 FRF.
   Pomp and ceremony still prevail in Monte Carlo. The changing of the guard takes place daily in front of the **Place du Palais** exactly at 1155. The charge for visiting the Prince's **Palace State Apartments** is 30 FRF; children 8–14, 15 FRF. Tours are conducted daily June–September, 0930–1830, and during October, 1000–1700. One of Europe's greatest aquariums, the **Musée Oceanographique,** lies near the palace on the seaside. Hours: July–August 0900–2000; reduced hours during the rest of the year. Admission: adults, 60 FRF; children, 30 FRF.
   While at the Place du Palais, you should visit the **Museum of Napoleonic Souvenirs** and **Collections of the Palace Historic Archives**. Hours: 0930–1830 daily June–September; reduced hours during

Nice—Monte Carlo

There are at least two trains per hour—often 3 or 4—from 0604 throughout the day in both directions; journey time is about 20 min.
   Distance: 9 miles (14 km)

---

the balance of the year. Admission: adults, 20 FRF; children 8–14, 10 FRF.
   Other attractions include the **Wax Museum of the Princes of Monaco,**
the **Museum of Old Monaco,** and the **Museum of Prehistoric
Anthropology,** the last featuring the **Exotic Gardens** and the **Observatory
Cave.** The tourist office publishes a brochure listing all places of interest, opening times, and admission fees. Also available is a map showing the city's "semi-
pedestrianized" zone, 12 public lifts, and the bus system.
   The grandeur of the Monaco yacht harbor may be viewed from many vantage points. The view from the casino's restaurant **Le Prive** is impressive—
expensive, too. Probably the best site (at popular prices) is a canopy-covered
table at the **Portofino Restaurant,** which clings to the cliff just above the
quai President Kennedy.

Day Excursion to

Saint-Raphael   "IN" PLACE ON THE RIVIERA

Depart from Nice Ville Station

Distance by Train: 37 miles (59 km)
Average Train Time: 50 minutes
Saint-Raphael Tourist Information: Office de Tourisme, rue W. Rousseau, 83 700
Tel: 04 94 19 52 52; *Fax:* 04 94 83 85 40
Hours: Sunday 0830–1200 and Monday through Saturday 0830–1200 and 1400–1900.
From June 15 to September 15 it does not close for lunch.
   Located across the street and to the left of the main entrance to the railway sta-
tion. It is identified by a white i sign together with TOURISME in brown letters.
   If you arrive late there is also a tourist information stand available on the Veillat
Beach, one block from the main tourist information office. It is open 0200–2200.

Saint-Raphael is the Riviera resort that has something for everyone—and
at popular prices. Its primary asset is its delightful weather, which is mild in the
winter and moderate throughout the entire summer. Sports enthusiasts are

attracted by its 18-hole golf course, tennis clubs, riding academy, and well-protected bay. Its 16 miles of coastline fringe magnificent pine forests. Nearby mountainous peaks beckon hikers, while sandy beaches and a casino fill the needs of those seeking sun and fun.

Before leaving the railway station, check the departure schedules for trains returning to Nice. There is a train information office in the station on your right as you exit the train platform. Hours: Monday–Saturday 0800–1930. *Tel:* 36 35 35 35.

The fishing-boat dock in Saint-Raphael is not far from the railroad station. The tourist office can point the way. Here you will find some unusually fine local restaurants where, in the summer, you can dine at tables set under trees close to the boats. It is a relaxing atmosphere.

Saint-Raphael has an interesting history. Its modern origins stem from the era of the Roman Empire, when it was a fashionable suburb of the Roman port of Frejus. Napoleon passed through Saint-Raphael in both victory and defeat. In 1799, the emperor and his generals disembarked there upon returning from Egypt; a pyramid standing in the town still commemorates the event. In 1814, he sailed again from Saint-Raphael, this time for Elba and exile. On April 28, as Napoleon, overcome with emotion, was saying good-bye to the soil of France, the English frigate he was to sail in fired a salute of twenty-one guns.

The site where the present town of Saint-Raphael now stands has played an exciting part in the history of the Mediterranean. Because of its natural harbor, which is deep enough to accommodate even the deepest-draught warships, the Romans developed it first as a holiday center. The town's casino is built over the original foundations of the Roman baths and a fish-holding tank.

Villas of the rich Romans who had come to Saint-Raphael to "take the sea air" were destroyed by Saracen pirates. By the time the pirates were driven from the area in the tenth century, the land lay deserted.

Development was hindered by poor drainage and the diseases that accompanied this impairment. Even by the eighteenth century, when fishermen and peasants began to rehabilitate the area known today in Saint-Raphael as the "old quarter," they were so weakened by marsh fever that they became known in the region as "palefaces." The introduction of drainage and improved sanitation turned it into a pleasant land again.

Much of Saint-Raphael's modern development has been due in great part to the establishment of the cut-flower industry started there in 1880 by Alphonse Karr. Although its biggest revenues today are developed by the tourist industry, Saint-Raphael is still a large and prosperous center for cut flowers.

An excellent excursion-boat service operates from Saint-Raphael. The tourist information office will have to provide you with schedules and fares, as

Nice—Saint-Raphael

DEPART NICE VILLE	TRAIN NUMBER	ARRIVE SAINT-RAPHAEL
0550	6964/6965	0642
0614	6634/6635	0706
0703	none	0818
0805	none	0930
0814	6676/6677	0904

and continuing with 3 to 4 trains each hour

DEPART SAINT-RAPHAEL	TRAIN NUMBER	ARRIVE NICE VILLE
1448	5359	1541
1658	TGV 845	1745
1703	5680/5681	1754
1727	6464/6465	1817
1709	none	1835
1800	TGV 9532	1848
1805	6130/6131	1857
1821	162/163	1908
1914	6172/6173	2004
1936	TGV 847	2021
1944	none	2102
2028	6452/6453	2123

Daily, unless otherwise noted
Distance: 37 miles (59 km)

they are too varied to mention here. There are short cruises on the Mediterranean as well as full-day excursions to many ports of call on the Riviera.

Saint-Tropez, summer home of Brigitte Bardot and one of the better "topless" beaches of France, can be reached from Saint-Raphael by bus or boat. Journey time: 1 hour, 25 minutes in each direction, but connections can be made that allow almost 7 hours of visiting and sightseeing in this quaint resort town. For details on bus service between Saint-Raphael and Saint-Tropez, consult the rail information office in Nice or Saint-Raphael, or ask for assistance from the tourist office in Saint-Raphael. There is no rail service between Saint-Raphael and Saint-Tropez.

Base City . . .

Paris

Internet: www.paris-touristoffice.com

"Every traveler has two cities," wrote Edna St. Vincent Millay, "his own and Paris." Besides being one of the most beautiful and captivating cities in Europe, Paris is the center of one of the most interesting regions of France. Local people call the area around Paris the **Ile de France** (Island of France), for it is here that the nation began in the forested lands stretching out in all directions around Paris. The city is not only the political capital of France; it's the country's industrial and commercial center as well. To understand and appreciate it, follow the suggestion of British poet and novelist Lawrence Durrell and watch it "quite quietly over a glass of wine in a Paris bistro."

Arriving by Air

Charles de Gaulle Airport, 17 miles (23 km) north of the city center (Tel: 01 48 62 22 80)
- **Airport–City Links: Roissybus** departures every 15 minutes 0545–2300; journey time about 45 minutes. Fare, 49 FRF.
- **RER** (Regional Express Airway) Line B every 15 minutes from 0455–2355 to main stations: Gare du Nord, Châtelet-les-Halles, St. Michel, and Denfert-Rochereau.
- **Taxis** take about 45 minutes; average fare, 250 FRF.
- **Tourist information** is available 0700–2200.
- **Currency exchange** is open 0615–2300.
- **SNCF (French Rail) airport office** is open 0730–2015. You can immediately board a train to Lyon, Avignon, or Nice without having to transfer to Paris.

Orly Airport, 10 miles (14 km) south of Paris (Tel: 01 49 75 15 15)
- **Airport–City Links: Orlybus** buses run every 15 minutes 0600–2300, 30 minutes en route. Arrive/depart from Place Denfert-Rochereau. Fare, 32.50 FRF.
- **RER** (Regional Express Railway) Line C every 15 minutes from 0545–2315 to main stations: Gare d'Austerlitz, St. Michel, Invalides, and Porte Maillot.
- **Taxis:** average 150 FRF.
- **Tourist information** is available 0600–2330.
- **Currency exchange hours:** 0630–2300.

- **SNCF (French Rail) office hours:** 0800–2000 Monday–Saturday; 1000–1300 and 1500–1830 Sunday/holidays.

Arriving by Train

Paris has six major railway stations, but arriving there by train from one of the other base cities listed in this edition of *Europe by Eurail* will place you either in Gare du Nord (North), Gare de l'Est (East), Gare de Lyon, Gare d'Austerlitz or Gare Montparnasse. Details of these stations follow.

Transfers between rail stations in Paris may be made by bus, Metro, or taxi. If you have baggage, a taxi is your best bet. There are, however, inter-station buses that provide baggage storage. Rule out the Metro unless you are without baggage. Suggestion: Consult the conductor on your train at least 30 minutes prior to arrival. If you are transferring between stations to continue your journey, the railroad is obliged to assist you. For train information in France call 08 36 35 35 39.

The Railway Stations

Gare du Nord (North Station) 18, rue de Dunkerque, 75010 Paris

Gateway to the channel ports of Calais and Boulogne plus Belgium, Germany, The Netherlands, and London via Eurostar.

- **Money-exchange office:** in the station concourse area across from track No. 3. Hours: 0615–2230 daily, except holidays.
- **Train information:** displayed in digital format throughout the station. A rail information office is located across from track 1. Hours: 0600–2300 daily, including holidays.
- **Train reservations,** including TGV and sleeping cars, may be made in the train information office. A layout of the station can be seen on a chart across from track 5.
- **Eurostar** has its own terminal, reservations, and waiting room upstairs from the main part of the station. The well-marked signs will direct you to it.
- **Tourist information/hotel reservations:** in the Paris Convention and Visitors Bureau, opposite track 21. Hours: May–October, 0800–2000 Monday–Saturday. This is a branch of the central tourist office located on the Champs Elysées. Charge for hotel reservations varies.

Gare de l'Est (East Station), Place du 11 Novembre 1918, 75010 Paris

Gateway to eastern France, Germany, Luxembourg, and Switzerland. Located a short distance from Gare du Nord and can be reached on foot or by the Metro.

- **Money-exchange:** in the main reception hall area opposite tracks 25 and

26. Hours: 0645–2200 daily.

- **Train information:** displayed in digital format throughout the station. A rail information office is located on the left-hand side of the station coming from the trains, between tracks 6 and 7. Hours: 0845–2000 every day although on Sunday for information only (no reservations).
- **Train reservations:** may be made in the train information office.
- **Tourist information/hotel reservations** available in the branch office of the Paris Convention and Visitors Bureau across from track 27. Hours: May–October, 0800–2100 Monday–Saturday; November–April, closes at 2000.

Gare de Lyon (Lyon Station) 20, boulevard Diderot, 75012 Paris
Gateway to the Riviera, southeastern France, Italy, and western Switzerland. Located on the right bank of the Seine, some distance south of the north and east terminals.

- **Money exchange:** on the left side of Sortie (Exit) 1 as you enter the station and proceed toward track A. Hours: 0630–2300 daily.
- **Train information:** in digital format throughout the station. The office for train information, marked INFORMATION AND RESERVATIONS, is in the center of the station, to the left of the *Billets Grandes Lignes* area. Hours: 0800–2200 Monday–Saturday; 0800–1900 Sunday/holidays. **Train reservations** at the same office.
- **Tourist information/hotel reservations:** in the Paris Convention and Visitors Bureau located in the main ticket hall. Hours: 0800–2000 Monday–Saturday.
- **Restaurant le Train Bleu** is located on the mezzanine of Gare de Lyon. Without doubt, it is the most elegant restaurant of any train station in the world. Opened in 1901, it was originally called the *Buffet de la Gare de Lyon.* Quickly, however, it became the fashionable place for well-heeled passengers to partake of a late supper prior to boarding the *Train Bleu,* the stylish sleeper that traveled between Paris and the French Riviera, and so it was renamed. The food is good, and the decor is France at the turn of the century at its opulent best: crystal chandeliers, shimmering brass, and mahogany.

Gare d'Austerlitz (Austerlitz Station), 55, quai D'Austerlitz, 75013 Paris
Gateway to central and southern France as well as eastern Spain. Located on the left bank of the Seine, a short distance from Gare de Lyon, which may be reached on foot or by the Metro.

- **Money exchange** within the main hall of the station, close to the ticket windows. Hours: 0630–2300 daily.
- **Train information** is displayed in digital format throughout the station. A rail information office is located in the foyer of the station just before entering the main hall. It is open 0730–1945 Monday through Saturday.

- **Train reservations** may be made in the train information office.
- **Tourist information/hotel reservations** may be made in the Paris Convention and Visitors Bureau office located in the main hall of the station. Hours: 0800–1500 daily.

Other major railway stations in Paris include **Gare Saint-Lazare** (north and west of France) and **Gare Montparnasse** (west of France). There are four Métro stations (Routes 4, 6, 12, and 14) in or adjacent to the Montparnasse railway station. Consequently, it is easy to reach from other parts of the rail network. Route 4 connects directly with Gare du Nord (North Station) and the Gare de l'Est (East Station). Trains departing Paris for Chartres from Montparnasse also stop in Versailles, but this station is some distance from the Palace of Versailles and should not be used for that day excursion.

In these railway stations, the **reservation offices** are open 0800–2000 daily. Train information and reservations for all France: *Tel:* 08 36 35 35 39.

In addition to the six major railway stations of Paris, there are six smaller or suburban-type stations.

- **Gare des Invalides,** another station that begins underground with its trackage until well past the Eiffel Tower, is exclusive for trains running to the Palace of **Versailles.**
- **Gare Bercy** and **Gare Charolais** are two auxiliary stations serving the Gare de Lyon complex on the right bank of the Seine.
- On the Rive Gauche (Left Bank) side, **Gare Tolbiac** serves the Austerlitz station network, and **Gare Vaugirard** performs the same function for the extensive train trackage terminating in the Montparnasse station compound.

A system of buses connects the major Paris stations, Gare St. Lazare, Gare du Nord, Gare de l'Est, Gare de Lyon, Gare Montparnasse, and Gare d'Austerlitz. Operated privately, the system charges a fare slightly higher than that of the Métro, and it is much more convenient for passengers with luggage than the regular city buses.

Tourist Information/Hotel Reservations

Office de Tourisme de Paris, 127, avenue des Champs Elysées, 75008 Paris
Tel: 01 49 52 53 54 or 08 36 68 31 12; *Fax:* 01 49 52 53 00
Hours: 0900–2000 daily
Branch office at Eiffel Tower open May–September 1100–1800 daily
Tel: 4551–2215

Free maps of Paris are available at most hotels, or you can purchase one at tourist offices. You may also consult the Galeries Lafayette travel agency, 40, boulevard Haussman; hours: Monday–Saturday 0930–1900 (until 2100 on Thursdays). *Tel:* 01 42 85 21 20.

Getting Around in Paris

The mainstay of transportation within Paris is its subway system, the Metro. It has sixteen lines, several with rubber-tired coaches that sort of sneak up on you in the station. The system covers all of the city and much of its suburbs. You can reach all the railway stations in Paris via the Metro.

Obtain a map of the Metro system from one of the tourist offices and ask for a brief explanation of its operation or call (800) 722–7151 for a free city map of Paris, including Metro, Bus, and RER Lines. Many of the Metro stations have an illuminated map in their entrances, where, by pushing the button of your desired destination, the entire route will light up showing what line to take, in what direction, and, when necessary, where to make transfers.

The French refer to transfers as *correspondances*. Although the lines are numbered, the reference you should remember is the direction, which refers to the last station on the end of the line in the direction in which you are traveling. For example, Line No. 1 has two directions: Grande Arche de la Défense in the west, Château de Vincennes in the east. If you were visiting the Louvre and wanted to see the Place de la Concorde next, look for the direction Grande Arche de la Défense because your destination lies to the west.

At transfer points, watch for the orange CORRESPONDANCE sign, then disembark and look for the direction sign for the line you want to transfer to. Proceed to that platform and there determine from the line map how many stops to your destination.

Purchase a **Paris Visite** (tourist pass) valid for 1, 2, 3, or 5 consecutive days, which provides for travel on public transportation in Paris and surrounding areas using the Metro, bus, or RER and SNCF (French National Railways) lines within Ile-de-France as far as Disneyland, Versailles, Fountainebleau and the airports. The Paris Visite also includes discounts at many museums and monuments. Prices vary according to the number of zones selected.

Paris Visite Pass Prices in French Francs

	1–3 ZONES	1–5 ZONES	1–8 ZONES
1 Day	55	110	155
2 Days	90	175	225
3 Days	120	245	280
5 days	175	300	350

If you are staying in Paris for the prescribed number of days and plan to make more than three one-way trips on the Metro or bus systems per day, the pass will definitely save you money, and the convenience is invaluable. These passes may be purchased in all of the main metro and train stations in Paris, at the international airports, and from the Paris tourist offices.

Acquaint yourself with the **Paris RER** (Regional Express Railway), the high-speed, limited-stop rail service that runs *under*—that's right, *under*—the regular Paris Metro. If you need to get somewhere in a hurry, the RER's the way to go. For example, we have ridden from Gare de Lyon to the Arc de Triomphe (the Étoile) in less than ten minutes. Call 08 36 68 41 41 for information.

The RER consists of four lines. RER color-coded lines appear on maps as follows: Line A = Red Line, B = Blue Line, C = Yellow Line, and D = Green. *Line A* goes west to east from St. Germain-en Laye, La Défense, the Étoile, Auber, Châtelet, Gare de Lyon, and the Marne Valley. *Line B* goes north to south from Roissy-Charles de Gaulle Airport to Gare du Nord, Châtelet, Pont St. Michel, Luxembourg, and the Chevreuse Valley. *Line C* runs from Versailles and follows the Seine through Paris to the Orly airport. *Line D* runs from Orry-la-Ville Coye through Central Paris then splits at the Villeneuve-St-Georges to Meluri or around to Malesherbes.

Eurailpass and Europass are accepted on parts of the RER, but not all, so inquire at the tourist information office or any one of the major Metro stations for specific information. You may also ask at the train information office alongside platform 1 in the Gare du Nord for details of the RER.

- **Train information** (*Tel:* 01 36 35 35 39) and request an English-speaking operator. Available 0800–2000 daily.
- **Bus information** (*Tel:* 01 43 46 14 14)
- **Taxi** (*Tel:* 01 47 39 47 39, 01 45 85 85 85, 01 49 36 10 10, or 01 41 27 27 27. To reserve a taxi for the airport, call before 2100 the night before.

Sights/Attractions/Tours and Paris Potpourri

Musts during your stay in Paris include:
- A visit to the **Louvre** to view the *Mona Lisa* and *Venus de Milo*.
- A cable-car ride up to **Montmartre** for a view of the "City of Light" or by elevator up the **Eiffel Tower** to the highest point in Paris.
- Walk the **Champs Elysées** to the **Arc de Triomphe** and look deep into its "flame of remembrance" for the faces of France and its allies who fought and died in the two world wars.
- Lunch at a sidewalk cafe.
- Ride the **Seine** on a *bateau* (boat).
- Get a gargoyle's point of view from high atop **Notre Dame.**
- Dine at Maxim's (if your waistline and wallet can afford it).

Paris has triumphed once again in the arts—this time in a museum that served the city as a train station for nearly 40 years. **Gare du Quai d'Orsay** was inaugurated on Bastille Day 1900. Designed by architect Victor Laloux, it included a 400-room hotel in part to serve the nearby 1900 World's Fair. By 1939, the Gare d'Orsay was obsolete, its platforms too short to accommodate the longer, electrified trains of the day. In 1971, the city of Paris reluctantly scheduled the structure for demolition, creating an uproar from its citizens equal in furor to the march on the Bastille.

The history of the Gare d'Orsay, although short in time, had made impact. Charles de Gaulle made his announcement to return to power from the hotel in 1958; Orson Welles used the station in the filming of *The Trial* (1952). Under pressure, the government reversed itself and saved both the station and the hotel, which became the **Musée** (museum) **d'Orsay.**

Located at 1, rue de Bellechasse (at entry to Quai d'Orsay RER station and near Solferino Metro stop), Musée d'Orsay boasts a glorious collection of nineteenth-century French painting and sculpture. Hours mid-June to end of September 0900–1800 Tuesday–Saturday; 1000–2145 Thursday; closed Monday. Opens 1000 during winter. Entry fee, 40 FRF. It is usually most crowded on Thursday night and the weekend. Reduced price, 30 FRF, on Sundays.

An interesting mix of Egyptian and European art can be found at the **Musée du Louvre.** Its glass-pyramid entrance, designed by I. M. Pei, has sparked much controversy, similar to that brought about by Gustave Eiffel and his iron tower. Referred to by the writer Guy de Maupassant as the "disgraceful skeleton," the Eiffel Tower did, of course, become the city's most recognizable landmark. While you ponder Pei's pyramid, visit inside the museum. Hours: 0900–2145 Wednesday, 0900–1800 Thursday–Monday (*Tel:* 01 40 20 53 17). Entrance fee, 45 FRF. Reduced price (26 FRF) after 1500 and all day Sunday.

To avoid queueing up and having to purchase a separate ticket for each museum and monument, consider purchasing the **Carte Musées et Monuments,** which covers entrance fees to about 65 museums and monuments in Paris and Ile de France.

1-day pass	80 FRF
3-day pass	160 FRF
5-day pass	240 FRF

In France, you can purchase the pass at any of the museums, at more than 100 Metro stations, or at the tourist information offices.

The Champs-Elysées is the most famous thoroughfare in Paris, but you should also see Paris from its most beautiful avenue, the River Seine. Aboard a *bateau* (boat), sights such as The Louvre, Notre Dame, and the Eiffel Tower take on a different perspective—particularly at night, when the floodlights of the *bateaux* illuminate the passing scenes. Add a meal served in the tradition of French gastronomy and you will have the best that Paris can offer!

Bateaux Parisiens, Port de la Bourdonnais (at the foot of the Eiffel Tower). *Tel:* 01 44 11 33 55 for schedules, rates, and reservations. *Bon voyage!*

Train Connections to Other Base Cities from Paris

Depart from Paris Gare du Nord station, unless otherwise noted

DEPARTURE	TRAIN NUMBER	ARRIVAL	NOTES
Amsterdam Centraal			
0655	Thalys 9309★	1108	R
1055	Thalys 9325★	1508	R
1555	Thalys 9345★	2008	R
Barcelona Sants			
1030	TGV 853	1916	R, 1, 2
1330	TGV 857	2220	R, 1, 2
2047	477	0900+1	R, Sleeper
Berlin Zoobahnhof			
0855	Thalys 9417★	1850	R, 3
1055	Thalys 9425★	2050	R, 3
2046	243	0916+1	
Bern (Berne)			
0718	TGV EC 21	1213	R, 1, 4
1018	TGV EC 973	1611	R, 1, 5
1241	TGV EC 23	1811	R, 1, 6
1441	TGV EC 975	2011	R, 1, 5
1652	TGV EC 429	2122	R, 1
1752	TGV EC 27	2253	R, 1, 4
Brussels (Bruxelles) Midi/Zuid			
0655	Thalys 9309★	0820	R
0731	Thalys 9311★	0857	R, Mon–Fri
0755	Thalys 9313★	0920	R
0855	Thalys 9417★	1020	R
0955	Thalys 9321★	1120	R
1055	Thalys 9325★	1220	R
1155	Thalys 9329★	1320	R, Mon–Sat
1255	Thalys 9433★	1420	R
1455	Thalys 9441★	1620	R
1555	Thalys 9345★	1720	R
1655	Thalys 9449★	1820	R
1722	Thalys 9351★	1847	R, Exc. Sat
1755	Thalys 9353★	1920	R
1855	Thalys 9357★	2020	R
1955	Thalys 9321★	2120	R
2055	Thalys 9365★	2220	R
2155	Thalys 9369★	2320	R, Thu–Sun

Budapest Keleti

1749	263	1203+1	R, 7, Sleeper

Copenhagen (København) H

1655	Thalys 9449★	0840+1	R, 8

Hamburg Hauptbahnhof

0655	Thalys 9409★	1507	R, 3
0855	Thalys 9417★	1707	R, 3
1055	Thalys 9425★	1907	R, 3
1255	Thalys 9433★	2107	R, 3

Lisbon (Lisboa) Santa Apolonia

1600	TGV 8543	1026+1	R, 9

Luxembourg

0654	EC 203	1035	7, Exc. Sun
0854	EC 57/1832	1234	7, Sun
1054	EC 357	1435	7, Exc. Sun
1715	EC 53, 1834	2052	7
1820	EC 207	2202	7, Exc. Sat
1949	355/4	2345	7

Lyon Part-Dieu

0730	TGV 643	0940	R, 1
0800	TGV 605	1004	R, 1, Mon–Fri
0830	TGV 645	1034	R, 1, Mon–Fri
0900	TGV 647	1104	R, 1, Exc. Sun
1000	TGV 607	1204	R, 1
1100	TGV 609	1304	R, 1, Exc. Sun
1200	TGV 611	1404	R, 1
1300	TGV 685	1504	R, 1
1400	TGV 615	1604	R, 1
1500	TGV 627	1704	R, 1
1600	TGV 619	1804	R, 1, Mon–Fri
1700	TGV 623	1904	R, 1
1800	TGV 617	2010	R, 1
1900	TGV 629	2104	R, 1
2000	TGV 689	2204	R, 1

Madrid Chamartin

1600	TGV 8543	0805+1	R, 9
1947	409	0858+1	R, 10, Sleeper
2258	179	1455+1	R, 10, Sleeper

Milan (Milano) Centrale

0812	TGV EC 17	1450	R, 1
1112	TGV EC 19	1755	R, 1
2216	EN 217	0845+1	R, 1, Sleeper

Munich (München) Hauptbahnhof

0749	EC 65	1611	7
1348	EC 67	2211	7
2229	261	0849+1	R, 7, Sleeper

Nice Ville

1118	TGV 845	1745	R, 1
1354	TGV 847	2021	R, 1
2114	5059	0818+1	R, 1, Couchettes only
2153	183	0759+1	R, 1, Sleeper
2233	189	0958+1	R, 1, Sleeper

Rome (Roma) Termini

0812	TGV EC 17	2025	R, 1, 11
1112	TGV EC 19	2330	R, 1, 11
1933	EN 213	1005+1	R, 1, Sleeper
2216	EN 217	1333+1	R, 1, 11, Sleeper

Vienna (Wien) Westbahnhof

0749	EC 65	2118	7, 12
1749	263	0835+1	R, 7, Sleeper

Zürich Hauptbahnhof

0729	1741	1500	7, 13, except Sun
0838	1841	1603	7, 13
1312	1745	2000	7, 13
1442	1747	2122	7, 13
1652	TGV EC 429	2247	R, 1
2238	469	0643+1	R, 7, Sleeper

Daily, Unless otherwise noted
R Reservations required
★ Thalys high-speed train, supplement required
1. Depart from Paris Lyon station.
2. Change in Montpellier to Talgo train.
3. Change trains in Cologne (Köln).
4. Change trains in Frasne.
5. Change trains in Geneva.
6. Change trains in Lausanne.
7. Depart from Paris Gare de l'Est (East) station.
8. Change in Cologne (Köln) to sleeper train EN 233 departing 2127.
9. Depart Paris Montparnasse station. Change in Irun to sleeper train, sleeping accommodations reservations required; contact the rail reservations office in station for details.
10. Depart Paris Austerlitz station. Trains 409 and 179 convey different types of overnight sleeping accommodations; contact the rail reservations office in station for details.
11. Change trains in Milan.
12. Departs at 0719 on Saturday and Sunday.
13. Change trains in Basel, Switzerland.

Day Excursions

Three of the six Paris day excursions have been selected to introduce the traveler to Ile de France: **Chartres, Fontainebleau,** and **Versailles.** These places are every bit as important to what Paris is today as the Louvre, the Place de la Concorde, or the Eiffel Tower. The three remaining day excursions venture farther afield in express trains to visit **Caen and the Normandy Beaches, Rennes,** and **Rouen.**

Day Excursion to

Caen   AND THE NORMANDY BEACHES

Depart from Paris St. Lazare Station

Distance by Train: 148 miles (239 km)
Average Train Time: 2 hours, 20 minutes
Caen Tourist Information: Office de Tourisme et accveil de France, Place Saint-Pierre, 1400
Tel: 02 31 27 14 14; *Fax:* 02 31 27 14 18
Internet: www.normandy-tourism.org
E-mail: Tourisminfo@ville-caen.fr

Hours: Monday–Saturday 1000–1300 and 1400–1800; Sundays and bank holidays 1000–1300. In July/August: Monday–Saturday 0930–1900; Sunday 1000–1300 and 1400–1700.

More than five decades have passed since one of the greatest battles in history took place in Normandy. At dawn on June 6, 1944, American, British, and Canadian forces, together with elements of the Free French, assailed the Normandy beaches along a broad spectrum of the coastline at five preselected landing points, Utah, Omaha, Gold, Juno, and Sword. Preceded by the drop of three airborne divisions during the predawn hours, between 0630 and 0730, 120,000 soldiers and about 20,000 vehicles were landed from the sea. The assault upon Adolf Hitler's "Fortress Europe" had begun.

By the night of August 21, seventy-six days later, the **Battle of Normandy** was over. The German Seventh Army had been encircled and forced to surrender. It had cost the Germans 640,000 soldiers—killed, wounded, or taken prisoner. Allied losses were tallied at 367,000 dead or wounded. American losses were set at 127,000 casualties—31,000 of that number died in battle.

The town of Caen was the pivot of the battle and paid heavily for its part in the conflict. By the second day of the invasion, the whole of the town center had been flattened by Allied bombing. The German garrison fought fiercely. It wasn't until July 9 that the British and Canadian troops were able to take the town. The Germans, however, retreated to the right bank of the Orne River, where they continued to direct mortar fire into the ruined town. Caen was not completely liberated until August 9. The Battle of Caen lasted more than two months. Seventy-five percent of the town was destroyed.

For years following the war, Caen was one vast building site in which life was gradually beginning to return to normal. Reconstructed and restored, the town decrees that now is the time for all men of goodwill to be reconciled. To that purpose, the **Caen Memorial** has been established on the site of one of the bloodiest battles in history to take you on a compelling journey from the dark years of world wars to a vision of peace.

The memorial is unlike any other museum devoted to the theme of warfare. It employs audiovisual presentations to explain the sequence of events that led up to the outbreak of hostilities in 1939, the suffering of the people involved, the preparation for the invasion, and the strategies behind it. Peace can never be taken for granted; consequently, the memorial ends its presentation with a powerful and moving film emphasizing the need for vigilance if we are to have peace in our world in our own time and in our children's.

Allow one day for the Caen Memorial and sightseeing in Caen—a typical day excursion. If you want to tour the landing beaches and the memorial, consider purchasing a rail/drive package (see rail/drive package types and prices in the Appendix). Ask the tourist office for the brochure, "The D-Day Landings and the Battle of Normandy."

The **Hertz** office in Caen is directly across from the rail station. Reserve your first car rental on your rail/drive package at least seven days prior to your departure for Europe by calling Hertz at (800) 654–3001. Note that this Hertz office is closed on Sunday.

If you prefer not to drive, check with the Bus Verts office at the side of the Caen Railway station for Bus Verts' programs for visiting the D-Day landing areas. Or ask the tourist office about the guided tour with the combined "D-Day" ticket. (Advance booking required.)

This day excursion is a pilgrimage that every American should make. Arriving in Caen, you can proceed directly to the memorial on city bus No. 17 going in the direction of the memorial. It departs from the bus station outside the rail station on the right.

The memorial is open daily, 0900–1900 (until 2000 during July and August). A half-day tour time is recommended. Check at the information desk for the starting times of the English-language programs. A cafeteria is located on the second floor for refreshments.

Returning from the memorial to the station, take bus No. 17 in the direction of **Grace de Dieu.** The bus makes a stop in the center of the town at Tour Leroy near the tourist office (Office du Tourisme). Walk along **Boulevard des Allies** and proceed one block to where it intersects rue Saint-Jean. From this point, the tourist office sign may be seen across the street to the right. The tourist office can advise on accommodations in Caen and the Normandy towns close to the beaches. For each full-priced ticket purchased at one of the museums, you get reduced rates at all the other ones in the D-Day Landings and the Battle of Normandy region.

Tours of the invasion beaches start in Caen and proceed west through the Anglo-Canadian sectors of Sword, Juno, and Gold before arriving in the American sectors of Omaha and Utah. With a Hertz rental car, proceed west from Caen on Route 13 past Bayeux, LaCambe, and Carentan until reaching Ste.-Mere-Eglise, the first town in France to be liberated on D-Day, June 6, 1944. Visit the Airborne Museum with its CG4-A glider and a C-47 airplane and gaze in wonder at the Eighty-second Airborne paratrooper's predicament when his parachute caught on the church steeple opposite the museum.

Proceed from there to the **Utah Beach Landing Museum** at Ste.-Marie-Du-Mont. An audiovisual presentation explains how Utah beach was used to land about one million soldiers on its shores. Your next stop should be **Pointe-Du-Hoc,** which was captured by the Second Ranger Battalion in a spectacular assault on June 6, 1944, scaling 100-foot cliffs to destroy a German battery of coastal guns. The Rangers made it, but they paid a high price for their valor—seventy-seven dead, with an overall casualty rate of about 60 percent.

Leaving Pointe-Du-Hoc, head east to **Colleville-St.-Laurent,** where on a

Paris—Caen

DEPART PARIS ST. LAZARE	TRAIN NUMBER	ARRIVE CAEN	NOTES
0712	3303	0857	Mon–Fri
0810	3333	1020	Sat
0840	3337	1048	Mon–Fri
0908	3305	1056	Sat–Sun
1010	3339	1217	Sat–Sun
1043	3307	1227	Mon–Fri
1200	3343	1407	Sat
1225	3309	1409	Mon–Fri
1305	3309	1449	Sat

DEPART CAEN	TRAIN NUMBER	ARRIVE PARIS ST. LAZARE	NOTES
1321	3348	1529	Sat
1329	3350	1538	Sun
1424	3354	1633	Mon–Fri
1507	3308	1712	Sat
1516	3310	1702	Mon–Fri
1519	3312	1706	Sun
1632	3336	1836	1

and other frequent service until 2131 on Sundays, 2145 on Mon–Fri, 2152 on Sat

1. Sun from Aug 30
Distance: 148 miles (239 km)

summit overlooking Omaha beach, you enter the American cemetery. Pay your respects to the 10,000 Americans resting there. To paraphrase Sir Winston Churchill, "This part of a foreign field shall forever be American."

En route back to Caen, stop in Bayeux at the **Memorial Museum** that you passed earlier while en route to Ste.-Mere-Eglise—time permitting. Otherwise, plan to return there the following day and plan to visit the Anglo-Canadian sectors as well. Take advantage of your rail/drive package.

Day Excursion to

Chartres
CATHEDRAL COUNTRY

Depart from Paris Montparnasse Station

Distance by Train: 55 miles (88 km)
Average Train Time: 1 hour
Tourism Office: Chartres Office de Tourisme (tourist information), Place de la Cathedrale, B.P. 289, 28005 Chartres
Tel: 02 37 21 50 00; *Fax:* 02 37 21 51 91
Hours: April–September: 0900–1900 Monday–Saturday; 0930–1730 Sunday. October–March: 1000–1800 Monday–Saturday; 1000–1300 and 1430–1630 Sunday.

Exit the station, cross the street in the direction of the cathedral, and continue straight ahead until you come to a large square. Bear left at the square and follow the cathedral signs that you will begin to see from that point onward. The tourist information office is in a building at the far end of Cathedral Square. Its sign reads, OFFICE DE TOURISME.

Mention Chartres and anyone who has been there recalls their **Cathedral of Notre Dame** but not much more. But Chartres has many other attractions. To mention a few, we start with the town itself. Beguiling, gabled houses galore line the streets. Make it a point to stroll through the **old quarter** of town along streets with the appealing names of rue du Soleil d'Or (Street of the Golden Sun) or rue des Ecuyers (Street of the Horsemen). The tourist office has a special walking-tour program for the Old Town incorporating the rental of a headset and prerecorded audio cassette in English. The length of the recording is 60 minutes.

Food is another one of Chartres' attractions, so plan to dine there during your visit. There are many excellent restaurants—the one in the ancient **Inn of the Grand Monarque** at 22, place des Épars, for example, or we can highly recommend restaurant **La Truie qui File**, which is located in a fifteenth century house at the Place de la Poissonnerie. *Tel:* 02 37 21 53 90.

On arrival in the Chartres station, check the train departures for Paris on the posters displayed in the main hall near the ticket windows. The cathedral is illuminated at night, so if you would like to see this, check for a later train departure.

The **Cathedral of Notre Dame** in Chartres is in plain view from the railway station and will draw you like a magnet. It is said to be the most beautiful Gothic cathedral in Europe. To get there, just follow the directions above to the tourist office, which is located in the same area. The cathedral's stained-glass windows, the superb lines of its pillars and vaulting, and its interior are overwhelmingly beautiful. Fire destroyed the original eleventh-century building. The present cathedral was rebuilt between 1194 and 1220.

Paris—Chartres

DEPART PARIS MONTPARNASSE	TRAIN NUMBER	ARRIVE CHARTRES	NOTES
0701	13613	0755	Mon–Fri
0731	none	0841	except Sun
0801	none	0911	Sun
0830	none	0940	except Sun
0912	none	1015	Mon–Fri
0917	13611	1017	Sat
0926	none	1037	Sun
1114	none	1225	daily
1219	none	1332	from Aug 31 except Su

DEPART CHARTRES	TRAIN NUMBER	ARRIVE PARIS MONTPARNASSE	NOTES
1520	none	1630	Mon–Fri
1643	none	1748	Sun
1643	none	1757	except Sun
1710	none	1802	Mon–Fri from Aug 31
1723	none	1833	Mon–Fri
1751	none	1903	Sat–Sun
1819	none	1921	Mon–Fri

and other frequent service until 2130–2200

Distance: 55 miles (88 km)

It is interesting to note that the cathedral has two nonmatching spires. The plain one of simple architecture was built first; the elaborate spire in late Gothic followed later. On Sunday afternoons at 1645 during July and August, you can enjoy the organ recitals at the cathedral. Admission to these performances is free.

The district surrounding the cathedral is noted for its medieval houses. Time permitting, you should walk down to the river for a look at the old houses and bridges close to the restored Romanesque **Church of Saint André.**

The Cathedral of Chartres may be the most famous of the city's attractions. There is a lot more to this ancient town, however. In addition to the Church of Saint André, there are others that warrant your inspection. The **Church of Saint Pierre** is a Gothic masterpiece. Its stained-glass windows dating back to the fourteenth century, when added to those of the cathedral, make Chartres the metropolis of stained glass.

The **Episcopal Palace,** now the Museum of Fine Arts, has a lovely seventeenth-century facade in addition to its interesting contents. The exhibit includes a unique collection of harpsichords, painted wood carvings and art from Oceania, and many of French, Flemish, and Italian paintings.

Chartres is bountiful in its art and has many museums and galleries to enjoy, such as the **International Stained Glass Center, La Maison de l'Archeologie,** and the **Maison Picassiette,** as well as the **Natural History Museum** and the regional **School Museum.**

To assist visitors in seeing *all* of the city's attractions, hop aboard *Le petit train de Chartres* (The little train of Chartres). From April through October, the "train" departs daily on the hour from in front of the cathedral on a 35-minute tour of "Old Chartres." The first departure is at 1000; the last departure, at 1800. Adults, 30 FRF; children, 18 FRF. All aboard!

Day Excursion to

Fontainebleau

PALACE OF KINGS

Depart from Gare de Lyon

Distance by Train: 37 miles (60 km)
Average Train Time: 45 minutes
Fontainebleau Tourism Information: Office de Tourisme, 4 rue Royale, 77 300
Tel: 01 60 74 99 99; *Fax:* 01 60 74 99 98
Hours: 0800–dusk daily, except closed Tuesday; Royal Apartments tours conducted 0930–1700 in June; 0930–1800 July–August; 0930–1230/1400–1700 November–May.

To reach the palace from the railway station in Fontainebleau, take the No. 1 bus marked CHÂTEAU from the station to the palace. The ride takes 10 minutes. No admission charge to palace grounds; tour charge, 23 FRF.

The **Palace of Fontainebleau** is most famous today as the residence of Napoleon Bonaparte, but the site attracted the presence of the kings of France and other royalty as far back in history as the twelfth century. For many, Fontainebleau signifies the spirit of France more so than does Versailles.

In 1169, Louis VII had the chapel of his manor at Fontainebleau consecrated by Thomas à Becket, the famous English archbishop of Canterbury. The palace that stands today probably owes more to the imagination of Francis I of France than any other of its monarchs. In 1528, he had the remains of prior centuries torn down and rebuilt; he then filled the new structure with sumptuous jewels, weapons, statues, and pictures—among them the *Mona Lisa* (which graced the bathroom)—as a suitable reclining palace for his mistress, the Duchess d'Etampes. In 1539, with the place set in order, he received his great rival, Emperor Charles V, in the new digs.

The fortunes of Fontainebleau slumped under the reign of Louis XIV. He was giving more attention to his new project at Versailles and his dalliances

Paris—Fontainebleau

In addition to the trains listed below there is frequent commuter train service to and from Fontainebleu.

DEPART PARIS LYON	TRAIN NUMBER	ARRIVE FONTAINEBLEAU	NOTES
0827	none	0905	
1134	none	1212	
1342	5097	1420	

DEPART FONTAINEBLEAU	TRAIN NUMBER	ARRIVE PARIS LYON	NOTES
1504	none	1543	
1515	none	1554	Sat only
1719	5096	1802	
1933	none	2025	
2236	none	2316	

Daily, unless otherwise noted
Distance: 37 miles (60 km)

with Madame de Maintenon; but his successors, Louis XV and Louis XVI, were faithful to the palace as an autumn residence. Slowly, Versailles became the "in place" with French courtiers, and only the old retainers showed up to probe the forest surrounding the château for wild game. Fortunately, Fontainebleau survived the French Revolution much better than did Versailles and other royal residences closer to Paris. (Suburban living had its advantages even then.)

Fontainebleau has probably bedded more queens, court favorites, and royal mistresses than all other palaces in France. (Versailles had its headliners, like Pompadour and Du Barry, but Fontainebleau was more discreet.) Under the new management of Francis I, the Duchess d'Etampes was granted a chamber that later became known as the "King's Staircase" when Louis XV needed freer access to her apartments. Madame de Maintenon moved to Fontainebleau under the auspices of Louis XIV in 1686 and into a room that bears her name even today.

Since the beginning of the seventeenth century, every queen of France has slept in the queen's bed chamber within the palace. Marie Antoinette ordered the bed that now graces the chamber, but because of unfortunate developments, she never had the opportunity to lay her head upon its pillows.

When Napoleon Bonaparte became Emperor of France in 1804, he had Fontainebleau refurbished and refurnished to receive Pope Pius VII, who had come to crown him as Emperor of France. From 1812 to 1814, the pope was also in residence in Fontainebleau—only this time he was not an invited guest but Napoleon's prisoner.

Not all of Napoleon's residence at Fontainebleau was surrounded with the fringe benefits befitting an emperor of his stature; he had some bad days, too. He signed his abdication in a room known now as the "Abdication Chamber" (formerly a bathroom) on April 6, 1814. Nineteen days later, he bade farewell to his officers and bodyguard in the Court of the White Horse from the horse-shoe-shaped grand staircase that is now the main entrance to the palace.

Fontainebleau, unlike Versailles, possesses the secret of intimacy, no doubt due to the fact that each successive generation of kings or emperors added a wing of his own to the structure. The palace is full of nooks and crannies. There are back staircases and tapestries that pull aside to reveal secret hallways. Living in Fontainebleau, its occupants were surrounded by romance and intrigue. In a sense, it probably was the earliest version of the present "no-tell motel," but it had far more class!

The Germans used Fontainebleau as a military headquarters during World War II. Following the war, it served as a seat of the North Atlantic Treaty Organization (NATO) until 1965, when it became a public museum.

If you take the tour, and you should, your tour guide will lead you first through the Red Room, scene of Napoleon's abdication, then, in turn, through the Council Room, the Throne Room, and the Queen's Bedroom. From there, you pass through the Royal Apartments, then down the King's Staircase to the Oval Court, where the tour ends. It's intriguing.

The gardens and parks surrounding the palace are lovely throughout the year. You are invited to bring your own picnic lunch and spread it out on the royal grass as long as you don't litter the imperial landscape.

Day Excursion to

Rennes

CAPITAL OF BRITTANY

Depart from Paris Montparnasse Station

Distance by Train: 232 miles (374 km)
Average Train Time: 2 hours, 4 minutes
Rennes Tourist Office: 11 rue Saint-Yves in the center of the city:
Tel: 02 99 67 11 11; *Fax:* 02 99 67 11 10
Summer hours: 0900–1900 Monday–Saturday; 1100–1500 Sunday

From the rail station, take Avenue Janvier to the River Vilaine, where a left turn puts the office in view two blocks farther on.

There's an expression that has been making the rounds of the travel trade for some time now, "Half the fun is in the going." Rennes fully qualifies as such a day excursion, since you can go there on the TGV Atlantique, the pride of the French rail fleet and holder of the wheel-traction rail speed record.

Once outside of Paris and onto its special right-of-way, the TGV (*train à grande vitesse* or train of great speed) cruises at 186 mph and you will be experiencing the finest rail travel in the world. It's not a "seat belt" ride—it's smooth and totally enjoyable. Outbound in the morning, you can enjoy breakfast as the French countryside flashes by; inbound returning to Paris, you are in for a "Happy Hour" you'll never forget!

Be certain that you have a seat reservation. You can obtain seat reservations in Gare Montparnasse, the TGV Atlantique's home station in Paris, or at the time you purchase your railpass in the United States.

Rennes is unique in that it doesn't remind you so much of France as it does the area around Cornwall in Britain. As the cultural capital of the French province of Brittany, it has some strong ties to its Celtic origins in its architecture and gastronomy. Rennes stands at the confluence of the Ille and the Vilaine Rivers. This junction of waterways came to the attention of Julius Caesar, and in 56 B.C., his legions conquered its original Celtic settlers, the Riedones. After this flurry of activity, however, things settled down for the balance of the Middle Ages.

At the beginning of the eighteenth century, Rennes still looked as it had for several hundred years—with narrow alleys and houses constructed of lath and plaster and no running water for sanitation or firefighting. History records that in the evening of December 22, 1720, a drunken carpenter set fire to a pile of shavings, which, in turn, set fire to his house and then spread rapidly throughout much of the town, destroying over a thousand other buildings before it burned itself out.

The part of the wooden town destroyed by that fire was rebuilt with granite arches and stone along well-ordered lines. Gabriel, architect to the French King Louis XV, then designed a new Town Hall. Thus, Rennes developed its **"New Town"** that stands yet today and awaits your inspection following your arrival in its ultramodern train station designed specifically for the high-speed TGV Atlantique. Rennes's aesthetic value embraces its vibrant past, present, and future by offering visitors a wealth of architectural variety. It rightfully claims to be one of the prettiest cities in Brittany.

With a population of 200,000, Rennes describes itself as a youthful, well-established, and dynamic city that is striving to uphold the best interests of its citizens and the surrounding area as it moves toward the year 2000. Well equipped with prestigious theater and museum facilities and augmented with a city orchestra and the **National Centre for Dramatic Art**, the city plays a major role in the cultural activities of the region.

In the first week of July, during the *Tombées de la Nuit* (Summer Festival),

Paris—Rennes

DEPART PARIS MONTPARNASSE	TRAIN NUMBER	ARRIVE RENNES	NOTES
0745	TGV 9607	0948	Mon–Fri from Aug 31
0820	TGV 8709	1035	
0935	TGV 8713	1138	except Sun
0935	TGV 8615	1138	Sun from Aug 31
1020	TGV 8617	1223	Sat from Aug 31
1130	TGV 8619	1333	except Sat from Aug 31
1220	TGV 8623	1437	
DEPART PARIS MONTPARNASSE	TRAIN NUMBER	ARRIVE RENNES	NOTES
1559	TGV 8746	1815	
1604	TGV 8646	1820	Sun from Aug 31
1720	TGV 8654	1925	F only
1720	TGV 8754	1925	Mon–Thu and Sun from Aug 31
1751	TGV 8766	2010	except Sun from Aug 31
1751	TGV 8666	2010	Sun
1815	TGV 8768	2020	Sun
1935	TGV 8770	2140	except Sat
1956	TGV 8778	2215	Sun
2015	TGV 8784	2220	Sun
2045	TGV 8782	2250	except Sun
2045	TGV 8776	2255	Fri
2120	TGV 8614	2325	Sun
2130	TGV 8798	2335	Sun from Sept 6

Daily, unless otherwise noted
Distance: 232 miles (374 km)

Old Rennes is illuminated with spotlights while ballets, songs, plays, or visual arts presentations are performed. Daytime attractions include the contemporary architecture of the Law Courts, *Le Triangle*, and the cultural center. Saturday mornings are always special with the open-air market.

Guided tours depart from the main tourist information office at Pont de Nemous daily at 1030 (also at 2100 on Tuesday and Thursday only) and at 1500 July 1–August 31. City tours in English are offered Wednesdays at 1500 during summer months.

Evenings in Rennes are pleasant. The city is home to numerous eating places offering a wide range of local or exotic cuisine—each establishment exhibiting a character all its own. Located close to the Atlantic Ocean as well as the English Channel, Rennes offers a selection of seafood second to none. For fine seafood served in an authentic fifteenth-century house, dine at **l'Auberge St. Sauveur,** at 6, rue St. Sauveur (*Tel:* 02 99 79 32 56). As this is a university city, the bars in Rue Saint-Michel and Rue Saint-Malo attract the younger set, and there are plenty of concerts, plays, or films to keep the elders fully occupied, too.

TGV Atlantique service to Rennes opens up another day excursion opportunity, **Mont-Saint-Michel,** one of the great wonders of France. Operated by Les Courriers Breton, a special luxury bus runs between the rail station in Rennes to Mont-Saint-Michel, taking only one hour and ten minutes. The bus runs daily during summer and Friday through Sunday only during the balance of the year. For details, check with the House of Brittany in Paris, the Tourist Information Office in Rennes, or Les Courriers Breton in Saint Malo (*Tel:* 02 99 56 79 09).

Day Excursion to

Rouen   Joan of Arc Memorial

Depart Paris St. Lazare Station

Distance by Train: 87 miles (140 km)
Average Train Time: 1 hour, 15 minutes
Internet: www.mairie-rouen.fr
Rouen Tourist Information: Office de Tourisme et des Congres, 25 Place de la Cathédrale, 76 000
Tel: 02 32 08 32 40; *Fax:* 02 32 08 32 44
Hours: May–September, 0900–1900 Monday–Saturday; 0930–1230/1430–1800 Sunday; remainder of the year: Monday–Saturday, 0900–1830; Sunday 1000–1300

The office is 5 minutes away from the station by taxi; 10 minutes on the underground, which stops at the Théâtre des Arts, just two blocks away from the office.

Walking—and it's downhill all the way—takes about 20 minutes. Follow Rue Jeanne d'Arc from in front of the station, turning left at Rue du Gros Horloge (Big Clock). After walking under the clock, bear right at the Cathedral plaza for a few yards to the tourist office.

Rouen was established by the Romans, who selected the site as the first point from the sea where a bridge could be built across the Seine. Rouen became the capital of Normandy at the beginning of the Christian era, and, despite many thrashings in many wars, it still contains a number of lovely churches, towers, and other reminders of its colorful past, such as half-timbered houses and town clocks.

Rouen is steeped in history and is considered one of the capitals of stained glass. We told you Rouen was colorful! During the Hundred Years' War, the city was held by the English from 1419 to 1449. **Joan of Arc** was burned at the stake in Rouen by the English in 1431. Her memory is commemorated during the last week of May every year during the Joan of Arc Festival. Highlights include music and street entertainment, a medieval market, parade and fireworks.

Your train from Paris will arrive in Gare Rive Droite, the rail station in Rouen on the right bank of the Seine. Several hotels, restaurants, and bars are clustered about the station's plaza. The city abounds with eating and drinking establishments—even McDonald's—so finding refreshments in Rouen during your visit will be no problem.

The tourist office has prepared an English-language pamphlet describing a tour itinerary which takes about two hours. It starts at the tourist office and takes the visitor to the principal points of interest within the boundaries of the historical town center. The railway station appears on the map, so you need not worry about finding your way back to the station.

First stop on the tour is the city's **cathedral**, which stands as one of the most beautiful examples of French Gothic architecture. Construction began in the twelfth century. It was leveled by a devastating fire in 1200, however, and it was not until the fifteenth century that it began to take on its present appearance. The cast-iron spire atop the cathedral's central tower is a nineteenth-century addition. Heavily damaged during World War II, the cathedral's restoration work still continues.

In order to rebuild the cathedral, Rouen had to revive the medieval skills of its original creators. The cathedral's structure was said to have gained its name from the fact that it was built with money paid by the faithful members of the parish for the privilege of consuming butter during Lent.

Following the tour itinerary suggested by the tourist office, the midway point of the tour will be the **Palace of Justice**. Three short blocks beyond, you will enter Rouen's **old market area**, with its narrow streets and half-timbered houses. There are more than 800 structures in Rouen illustrating

Paris—Rouen

DEPART PARIS ST. LAZARE	TRAIN NUMBER	ARRIVE ROUEN RIVE-DROITE	NOTES
0732	3133	0838	exc. Sun
0806	13101	0933	Sun
0816	13103	0943	Mon–Fri
0839	13103	1010	Sat
0915	3135	1021	
1044	3193	1157	Sun
1051	3193	1157	except Sun
1204	13105	1334	except Sun
1240	3139	1345	except Sun

DEPART ROUEN RIVE-DROITE	TRAIN NUMBER	ARRIVE PARIS ST. LAZARE	NOTES
1424	3144	1532	Sun
1457	3146	1604	except Sun
1659	3192	1809	Mon–Fri from Aug 31
1718	3194	1843	Sat–Sun
1723	13116	1848	Mon–Fri from Aug 31
1736	3148	1846	Sun from Aug 30
1800	134	1907	
1820	none	2009	Mon–Fri
1823	13118	1950	Sun

and other frequent service until 2045 to 2223

Daily, unless otherwise noted
Distance: 87 miles (140 km)

the typical architecture of the city from the Middle Ages to the end of the eighteenth century. The houses were termed *half-timbered* because their external and internal walls were constructed of timber frames and the spaces between the structural members were filled with brick plaster or wattle—woven reeds covered and plastered with clay. You'll note that the upper stories of many half-timbered houses in Rouen project out over the ground level. This arrangement allows the lower part of the house to be protected against inclement weather.

Born a peasant in 1412, Joan of Arc believed she heard celestial voices. In 1429, during the Hundred Years' War when the English were about to capture Orleans, Joan convinced Charles VII (then Dauphine of France) of her divine mission and led the English at Compiegne in 1430. Subsequently, she underwent fourteen months of interrogation by her captors until burned at the stake in the Old Market Square at Rouen on May 30, 1431. The Maid of Orleans, national heroine and patron saint of France, by her valor decisively turned the Hundred Years' War in France's favor.

The place in the old market where Joan of Arc met her fate is marked by a huge cross of concrete and metal. Towering over it is a modern church, completed in 1979, its roof representing the flames of the stake. It blends masterfully into the scene against a background of black-and-white timbered houses. The impact of history can be felt here.

Last stop on the city tour is that huge clock you may have passed under en route to the tourist office. It was positioned at ground level until 1527, when the people of Rouen asked that it be raised so they could see it better. The city council obliged by housing it in the elegant Renaissance structure you see today. The clock is unique in that it has only one hand. The globe at the top, which is no longer functioning, used to indicate the phases of the moon. Although the clock was converted to electricity in 1928, the original mechanism is still in place.

Day Excursion to

Versailles CELEBRATED SITE OF FRANCE

Depart Paris for Versailles from any station on RER Line C

Distance by Train: 11 miles (18 km)
Average Train Time: 30 minutes
Versailles Tourist Information: Office de Tourisme, 7 rue de Reservoirs, 78000
Tel: 01 39 50 36 22; *Fax:* 01 39 50 68 07

Paris' RER Line C runs between Orly Airport and Versailles. Suggested stations are Austerlitz, Orsay, Pont St. Michel, or Invalides, the railway station close to the Hotel des Invalides, which was founded by Louis XIV to serve as a military hospital and home for veterans. Gare Invalides can be reached via Metro line 8 or 13. Get off at the "Invalides" Metro stop.

Trains for Versailles also run from Montparnasse station, but those should not be used. The station in Versailles to which this line connects is a considerable distance from the palace. Trains running from Gare Invalides, however, take you to within easy walking distance. Trains on RER Line C from Gare d'Austerlitz in Paris terminate in Versailles. Therefore, stay on the train until it reaches the end of the line. The main function of this station appears to be assisting visitors coming to Versailles to see **the palace**. Bilingual signs and voice announcements will assist you.

Turn right as you exit the rail station and walk about 100 yards to the next main intersection, the one at the traffic light. Turn left at this point and proceed to the palace, which is readily visible from the intersection.

The palace is open May 2–September 30, Tuesday–Sunday, 0900–1800. The hours for the remainder of the year are Tuesday through Friday 1000–1200 and 1400–1700; and on Saturdays and Sundays 1000–1700. You may take guided tours (25 FRF) inside the buildings and around the grounds, or you may purchase a small guidebook and conduct your own tour. Admission, 45 FRF; 35 FRF for 18- to 25-year-olds and seniors over 60; children under 18, free.

The only way to understand the powerful influence that France exerted during the centuries of monarch rule is to visit Versailles. Here, only at Versailles, can you come to appreciate the spiritual, artistic, and political renown of France and its lineage of kings.

In 1623, Louis XIII (1601–1643) ordered a hunting lodge built on a hill named Versailles in place of a windmill that had occupied the site until then. His orders were followed immediately because there was no arguing with kings in those days. The lodge was erected in 1624. Liking the spot so well, he then ordered the lodge replaced by a grand mansion, which was completed in 1634.

His son, Louis XIV (1638-1715), the Sun King, liked the spot, too, hated the crowds in Paris with equal vigor, and envied his finance minister's fine home at Vaux le Vicomte to the extent that he came up with an order that put his dad's to shame—"Build a palace at Versailles to surpass all palaces!" Orders being orders, before long 36,000 laborers aided by 6,000 horses were at work building palace walls, digging lakes with canals to connect them, and transplanting a forest when the king and his gardener decided that God had planted it in the wrong place to begin with. Work continued on **the Palace of Versailles** over a period of fifty years.

The Sun King made certain that nothing from the outside world would be imported for Versailles if it could be created or found in France. The result was an extraordinary showcase of French culture.

Urged on, first by Madame de Pompadour and then by Madame Du Barry, Louis XV (1710–1774) also ordered additions to the palace, including the Petit Trianon, which Louis XVI (1754–1793) gave to his wife, Marie Antoinette, when he came to the throne.

Despite the splendor of this edifice, Marie and her courtiers were drawn to the fantasies of a hamlet erected for her by her loving husband. There, among other rural objects, stood a dairy barn complete with cows, among which Marie and her companions would cavort—much to the consternation of the bovines, who had never observed such carefree antics before among the peasants of the land.

Versailles is an extraordinary complex of marvels where the kings of France stood in insulation against the distant horrors of the Revolution. Its restoration to the original is a marvel in itself—a testament to the heirs of its tradition.

Even with the crowds of visitors coming to Versailles on a weekend or a national holiday, it is difficult to realize how life on such a grandiose scale could take place. Let your imagination run by visualizing throngs of court favorites, courtiers, teams of prancing horses pulling royal carriages over the cobblestones of the courtyard, chambermaids scurrying about, valets rushing with the linens of the gentry, and butchers carving the roasts for the banquets under the surveillance of the king's hounds—all of this seventeenth-century tumult, cacophony, and frenzy taking place on a scale many times greater than that of any Cecil B. DeMille production.

It is impossible to see Versailles completely in one visit—three perhaps, but nothing less than that. Consequently, set priorities (and this may sound silly) by going there the first time and just wandering around. Go back the second time and take the tour. Return the third time to see the things you missed or wanted to see again from the times before.

Paris—Versailles

Note: In addition to the SNCF (French National Railroads) schedules shown below, there is frequent RER suburban train service to the Versailles Rive Gauche/Château de Versailles Station, which is significantly closer to the Château Versailles than the SNCF station, Versailles Rive Droite/Chantiers.

DEPART PARIS MONTPARNASSE	TRAIN NUMBER	ARRIVE CHANTIERS	NOTES
0735	none	0748	
0818	3057	0833	Sat–Sun
0917	none	0929	
0928	none	0941	Mon–Fri
1051	none	1005	except Sat

DEPARTS CHANTIERS	TRAIN NUMBER	ARRIVE PARIS MONTPARNASSE	NOTES
1406	none	1419	Sat
1412	none	1426	Mon–Fri
1634	none	1648	Mon–Fri
1810	none	1822	Mon–Fri
1858	none	1910	Sun
2110	none	2125	Sun
2236	none	2250	Sun

Daily, unless otherwise noted
Distance: 11 miles (18 km)

Germany

Germany's reunification, symbolized by the fall of the Berlin Wall in late 1989, had a great impact on the overall German economy and way of life; it also opened new doors to tourism. Unifying public transportation systems of the East and West did, of course, play a major role in the total reunification process.

Germany is a land based on a rich, complex history on track to a vibrant future. In recent years, Germany has seen an influx of refugees and foreigners that has fostered a political culture more tolerant of the customs and traditions of others.

Located in the heart of Europe, Germany makes a convenient starting point for travel, especially by rail, to nearly anywhere in Europe. Major   airports for North Americans are Berlin, Dusseldorf, Frankfurt, Hamburg, and Munich, each of which is connected by rapid transit (S-Bahn) to the city's center.

The Germans are famous for brewing some of the tastiest beer in the world, and they love celebrating dozens of national, regional, and local holidays, holy or otherwise, with great passion, beer and wine tents, pageants, beer and wine, parades, beer and wine, festivals, beer and wine, markets, and lots of beer and wine.

The most well-known festivals include the German Mardi Gras, also known as Fasching, Fastnacht, or Fastnet, which includes masked balls; Munich's Octoberfest, which attracts people from all over the world; and the Hamburg Dom, Nuremberg's Christ Child's Market at Christmas, the Passion Plays at Oberammergau, and the Onion Market in Weimar. Oberammergau hosts the Passion Play only every 10 years and it is geared up for the next performance in the year 2000.

Don't let the guttural German language frighten you; many Germans, particularly tourism and train personnel, are multilingual. It's the majority of Americans who are "unilingual."

For more information on delightful Germany, contact the German Tourist Offices in North America: Internet: **www.germany-tourism.de;** e-mail: gntony@aol.com

New York: 122 E. Forty-Second Street, Fifty-Second Floor, Chanin Bldg, New York, NY 10168–0072. *Tel:* (212) 661–7200; *Fax:* (212) 661–7174

Toronto: 175 Bloor Street East, North Tower, Suite 604, Toronto, Ontario M4W 3R8, Canada. *Tel:* (416) 968–1570; *Fax:* (416) 968–1986; E-mail: germanto@idirect.com

Banking

Hours are 0830–1300 and 1430–1600 Monday–Friday. Currency exchange offices are found at mainline railway stations, airports, and border crosspoints. They are generally open 0600–2200.

- **Currency:** Deutsche Mark (DEM)
- **Exchange rate at press time:** 1.82 DEM = $1.00 U.S.

Be aware that many establishments in Germany do not accept credit cards. Major hotels, restaurants, and department stores do; but have cash handy for the smaller establishments that do not.

Communications

- **Country Dialing Code:** 49
- **Direct Dial:** AT&T Direct: 0130–0010; MCI 0130–0012; Sprint 0130–0013

Rail Travel in Germany

Deutsche Bahn AG (GermanRail) operates more than 25,000 miles of the unified rail networks of the former East and West Germany. The service in the west is still better than in the east, and renovation and upgrades of the decrepit rail service in the east are requiring massive investments of money and ingenuity.

Germany's top-of-the-line, high-speed, long-distance **ICE (InterCity Express)** trains are big, bold, and beautiful, with an emphasis on passenger comfort and a wide range of services. ICEs, reaching speeds of up to 175 mph, depart hourly every day for major centers within Germany and into the Swiss cities of **Basel, Bern, Interlaken,** and **Zurich.** The network connects major cities in the north with the south and extends east to **Berlin** and **Dresden.**

Each train has a restaurant car, termed **BordRestaurant,** with two sections—a traditional-style dining car and a self-service bistro. They're big on other amenities, too, such as headphones, private lockers in which to stow purses, cameras, or other valuables while you visit the BordRestaurant car, and some have video systems.

German Rail Pass

| 4 days in 1 month | First Class | $252 |
| | Second Class | $174 |

Children age 7–11 travel at half the adult fare; under age 6 travel free.

German Rail Twin Pass

Price is total for 2 people traveling together

| 4 days in 1 month | First Class | $189 |
| | Second Class | $130.50 |

German Rail Youthpass

For travelers age 12–25, Second Class Rail Travel

| 5 days in 1 months | $138 |

Additional Rail Days on German Passes

up to a total of 10 days	First Class	$32
	Second Class	$22
	Youth Second Class	18
Twin Pass additional days	First Class	$48
	Second Class	$33

Changing trains in Germany is a snap. In many cities, platforms are designed in such a way that the train you need to transfer to may be standing immediately across the platform from the train in which you arrive. Since most GermanRail trains are often configured the same—first-class cars in the front, second–class cars in the rear, you merely cross the platform to find the same type of accommodation on the connecting train.

Train platforms are divided into sections A to E. If you are traveling on a long-distance train, consult the train configuration display to easily determine where you will be sitting.

Just when we thought porters went the way of the dinosaur, **porter service** is available in Dresden, Frankfurt am Main, Hamburg, Leipzig, Munich, Stuttgart, and Berlin Zoo stations. The porters wear blue uniforms and red caps. (DEM 5.00 for first 2 items of luggage; DEM 2.50 for each additional item.) Luggage requires a deposit of 1 or 2 DEM.

The new ICE2s have even more legroom, electronic destination indicators on the *outside* of the train cars, digital display seat reservation units above the seats, electronic 220V sockets for laptop computers, and increased facilities for the disabled, and one car has a family compartment. The third–generation ICE (NeiTec, or tilting) trains are even more high-tech and able to "tilt" to round curves at higher speeds.

Germany's **EuroCity (EC), InterCity (IC), D** and **InterRegio (IR)** trains round out the mainline service. Regional services are provided by trains designated RE, RB, and SE. The **S-Bahn** ("Schnell," or "fast") rapid-transit system provides service to and from the suburban areas of Berlin, Cologne (Köln), Frankfurt, Hamburg, Leipzig, Munich, Nuremberg, and Stuttgart. PAGE 186 GERMANY insert

Eurailpass, Europass and **German Railpass** are accepted on the above-mentioned trains. Bonuses include:

- Free transport on the Puttgarden–Rodby Faerge (Denmark) and Sassnitz –Trelleborg (Sweden) ferry crossings; the KD German Rhine Line boats between Cologne and Mainz, and Koblenz and Cochem (extra charge for hydrofoil transport)
- EUROPABUS, 75 percent discount on the following routes (reservations recommended highly in advance): EB 189 Burgentrasse (Castle Road): Mannheim–Heidelberg–Heilbronn–Rothenburg ob der Tauber–Ansbach–Nuremberg, *May to September.* EB 190/190A Romantische Strasse (Romantic Road): Frankfurt am Main–Rothenburg ob der Tauber–Augsburg–Munich/Füssen, *April to December*
- Ferry Crossings, 50 percent discount with TT-Line crossing Travemünde –Trelleborg (Sweden); TR-Line crossing Rostock–Trelleborg (Sweden); Finnjet crossing Rostock–Helsinki (Finland) in Budget or Tourist I S classes (must book 7 days in advance)
- Group/student rate for Finnjet crossing Rostock–Helsinki (Finland)
- Wurm & Köck boat day trips between Passau and Linz (Austria), 50 percent reduction
- Mountain railroad Garmisch Partenkirchen–Grainau–Zugspitzplatt and on same cable cars in the summit area, 25 percent discount; plus reduced fare on the Freiburg–Schauinsland rack railway

Base City . . .

Berlin

City Dialing Code: 30
Internet: www.berlin.de
E-mail: information@btm.de

Although eons apart, the modern city of Berlin and the ancient city of Jericho shared a common occurrence—their walls "came a tumblin' down." The Bible (Joshua 6) is a bit vague concerning the actual date of the occurrence in Jericho; but we do know the Berlin Wall "fell" on November 9, 1989, 28 years after it was built. Berlin became a whole city; Germany became one country; Berlin is the capital of the new Germany; and communism is on the wane worldwide.

For Berlin, World War II ended on the afternoon of May 2, 1945. Of the 245,000 buildings in Berlin before the war, 50,000 had been destroyed or rendered beyond repair. There was no electricity, no gas, no water. Before the war, Berlin had 4.3 million inhabitants; in May 1945, the remaining 2.8 million began the task of clearing away the debris.

In July of that year, Berlin became a four-power city with a joint Allied administration composed of Britain, France, Russia, and the United States. This division into zones turned the former German capital into an island of occupation surrounded completely by a sea of Soviets. East and West were in complete agreement about abolishing Nazism, but they had no common or precise answer as to what would replace it. Moreover, it quickly became evident that the Soviet intention was to gain complete control of the city.

On June 24, 1948, the Soviets sealed off the West's section of the city and, on the basis of "technical disorders," shut off their supply of electricity. They were left with a meager thirty-six-day food supply. A disaster appeared imminent, but two days later the largest airlift in history began. From July 1948 to May 1949, the Western Allies transported, in some 213,000 flights, more than 1.7 million tons of food and other supplies to the beleaguered city. While operating the airlift, seventy members of the Allied Air Forces lost their lives. On May 12, 1949, the siege was lifted. Berliners began demonstrating their political choice by moving en masse to the Western sectors.

By August 1961, faced with mass evacuation of their sector, the Soviets began erecting the Berlin Wall. In 1989, after twenty-eight years of division, the wall that Winston Churchill called the "Iron Curtain" was breached in one night. Before it "fell," more than one hundred people lost their lives while attempting to cross it. The eastern part of Berlin, including its historic center, is once again easily accessible to visitors. The infamous Checkpoint Charlie was dismantled. Its guardhouse is now a museum piece. Except for a small section that will stand as a mute reminder, every vestige of the Berlin Wall has been removed.

With the demise of the Wall, Berlin nearly doubled in size. The reunited metropolis rediscovered its traditional rhythm that made it famous throughout the world. Travelers from around the world are passing the word, "Berlin is worth the trip." Come to Berlin and stand in history.

Once again, Berlin is without boundaries. As it's been explained to us, "Berlin is more than the sum of two halves," and we agree.

Arriving by Air

Tegel (TXL), Tempelhof (THF), and Schönefeld (SXL). All three airports are connected with the city center by buses and trains. *Internet:* www.berlin-airport.de

- **Tegel Airport,** 5 miles northwest, is your most likely arrival airport. Exiting from Customs, you'll see an information office between two rows of ticket counters. Go there for transportation information. From that position, look over your right shoulder and you will see the money exchange office across the hall. ATMs are available near gates 4 and 10. *Tel:* 41 01 2306 from 0500–2300.

  Airport–City Links: Bus line 109, or X9, as well as the Airport Transport, takes you from Tegel Airport to Berlin Zoo rail station in about 20 minutes. If you have baggage, the Airport-Transport system is recommended.

- **Schönefeld** is served by many European airlines; you should check with the airline taking you into Berlin as to its landing airport. Tempelhof, which served as the Allies' airport during the Berlin Airlift (1948–1949), is in the southwest section of the city. Surrounded by a sea of buildings, it is used for regional flights.

  Airport–City Links: Airport-Transport or S-Bahn line S-9. Both connect with the Berlin Zoo rail station.

Arriving by Train

There are two major railway stations in Berlin: Zoologischer Garten (Zoo), or Ostbahnhof (formerly Hauptbahnhof or Hbf.). If you disembark at the Zoo Station, Berlin's main tourist information office is located nearby. There's ample time to get off the train, since it will stand in the station at least five minutes before proceeding on to the Ostbahnhof. The S-Bahn trains and the city's U-Bahn (subway) connect the two stations.

- **Rail Information** *Tel:* 19419
- **Berlin's Zoo Station** is centrally located in the former "West" sector of Berlin. The majority of the city's hotels, pensions, hostels, restaurants, shopping centers, and entertainment is also in this area.
- **Baggage Storage.** Berlin Zoo is not a baggage cart station, since ramps to the train level are nonexistent and elevators normally are not available for public use. Porters are available by prearrangement, but the best insurance for a no-hassle visit to Germany's capital is to observe the golden rule of rail travelers: Take one medium-size suitcase—nothing else.
- **Money Exchange** is available at the DVB Bank Zoo. Use the Kaiser-Wilhelm Gedachtniskirche exit. Bank hours 0730–2200 Monday through Saturday and 0800–1900 Sunday. There is a 7.50 DEM charge for cashing traveler's checks. An ATM is available outside the bank.

- **Train Information, Reservations, and RailPass Validation.** As you descend from the trains into the main hall of the Berlin Zoo Station, there's a train information office in the Reisezentrum (Travel Center) to the far left. Open daily 0600–2300. A rail schedule machine allows you to look up train schedules and receive a printout. Facing the Reisezentrum, you'll find lockers on the left-hand side. Train departure and arrival information is posted on boards above the stairway.
- **A EurAide Office** is located between the Reisezentrum and the station post office. During summer it is open daily; closed on Sundays and holidays during the remainder of the year. This office (like the one in Munich) is designed specifically to assist English-speaking travelers. Train tickets and reservations are also sold here.

Berlin Ostbahnhof (formerly Hauptbahnhof)

Deutsche Bahn AG (DB), or GermanRail, service counter is located in the center of the main hall. The personnel can give schedule information 24 hours a day, 7 days a week, but don't count on their speaking English.

- For detailed information and to make reservations, go to the **Reisezentrum (Travel Center),** located along the back wall of the station, opposite the street exit. Hours: 0600–2300 daily. Lockers are to the right of the Reisezentrum as you face it.
- **Money exchange** facilities can be found by ascending either flight of stairs and walking toward the back hall. Hours: Monday-Friday, 0700–2200; Saturday, 0700–1800; Sunday, 0800–1600. There's also an ATM behind the DB service center.

Tourist Information/Hotel Reservations

For written information in advance, write to Berlin Tourismus, Marketing GmbH, am Karlsbad 11, D–10785 Berlin.

Tel: (030) 25 00 25; *Fax:* (030) 25 00 24 24

Hours: Monday–Friday 0800–2000; Saturday–Sunday 0900–1800

The city's main tourist information office is within easy walking distance. To reach it, leave the Berlin Zoo Station via the **Kaiser-Wilhelm-Gedächtniskirche** (Kaiser Wilhelm Memorial Church) exit and walk toward the ruins of the church. Its jagged steeple is a stark reminder of war's destructive power. You will see the **Europa Center** and its globe fountain, which Berliners affectionately refer to as "the wet dumpling." Stay on the left side of the Europa Center. The tourist information office is on the street side of the center, just before the Palace Hotel. Open Mon–Sat 0800–2200; Sunday 0900–2100.

Another tourist information office is located at Brandenburg Gate and offers the same services as the one in the Europa Center. Hours: 0930–1800 daily. Both tourist offices can make hotel reservations (charge, 5 DEM).

For those interested in hostel-type economical accommodations, try **David's Home for Backpackers,** a privately owned hostel—no curfews, and you get your own key and a modest buffet breakfast. It's located about 7 minutes' walking time from the Berlin Zoo rail station (3 minutes by Metro, or U-Bahn). Cost is 35 DEM the first night; additional nights are only 30 DEM. Advance reservations are necessary. Telephone from outside Germany: (4930) 395–7788; within Berlin, just dial 395–7788; E-mail: David. Berlin@hotmail.com or Fabian.Berlin@mailcity.com.

Getting Around in Berlin

One of the first things visitors should do on arrival in Berlin is acquaint themselves with the city's phenomenal fast-train system—the S-Bahn ("S" is for *schnell*—fast) and the U-Bahn (underground train or subway). During rush hours, trains run every 3–5 minutes and approximately every 5–10 minutes at other times. The S- and U-Bahn systems are augmented by trams and buses. You can purchase an excellent city map for 1 DEM, and the map of the S-Bahn and U-Bahn system is free of charge

Standard tickets (*Einzelfahrschein*) for all forms of Berlin transportation cost 3.90 DEM.

The **Berlin Welcome Card** booklet of vouchers enables you to spend 3 days of free travel on all buses and trains operating within the A, B, and C fare zones of the Berlin-Brandenburg public transport network (VBB) for only 29 DEM. Purchase it at all VBB ticket offices, at tourist information offices, and at many Berlin hotels.

According to the tourist office, the city even operates an all-night bus system of buses and trams to gather "the barflies and the birds of paradise" from the disco scene on the Kurfürstendamm.

Sightseeing/Attractions/Tours

The Top Tour is an innovative tourist bus system that makes 20 stops within the city, ranging from the Zoological Gardens in the west to Alexanderplatz in the east. You are free to hop off the red double-decker bus whenever you fancy and hop back on another bus when you want. The operator, Berlin's public transport company (VBB), will provide you with a free street map and information describing the stops. In effect, you become your own tour guide. Purchase a ticket at the tourist office for 35 DEM.

Berlin is a fascinating city. Don't miss walking on the **Kurfürstendamm** and **Friedrichstrasse,** its shopping and entertainment streets. The **Berlin Zoo** is one of the finest in Europe, and there's no better place to relax than in the attractive **English Gardens**, dedicated by Sir Anthony Eden. Berliners call it the "Garden of Eden."

The **Berlin Welcome Card** includes vouchers for discounts of up to 50 percent to numerous museums, sightseeing tours, theaters, and other attractions in addition to the public transport tickets. Make use of it.

The **Friedrichstadtpalast** is Europe's largest light entertainment theater. Their program features gala performances, artistic displays, dancers and solo singers, and a live orchestra.

The **Berlin Teddy Museum** has a collection of some 3,000 teddy bears on display. It's located at No. 147 Kurfürstendamm. Hours: Wednesday–Friday, 1500–1800; donations welcome. *Tel:* 30 893 39 65.

Berliners claim they have more museums than they have rainy days. There are more than 170 museums housing collections of art, original artifacts, and other intriguing creations. Following Germany's reunification, the State Museums were restored and extended, and new buildings were built to create an outstanding cultural center.

The **Gemäldegalerie** (Painting Gallery) reunites an internationally renowned collection of more than 1300 paintings from the thirteenth to the eighteenth centuries that had been separated since the end of World War II. Part of the collection went to the United States and part to Russia.

Best of all, stand at the **Brandenburg Gate**—on either side—and feel democracy in action.

Day Excursions from Berlin

Three day excursions have been selected. All of them—**Dresden, Leipzig,** and **Potsdam**—are typical German cities in their own right. Since the end of World War II, and until the "Fall of the Wall," they had been a part of the then German Democratic Republic, more often referred to as "East Germany." Consequently, tourist and transportation facilities are still being improved.

Dresden is an important city in the historic German state of Saxony, and probably best known for its product Dresden china. **Leipzig** is also a part of Saxony and owes much of its prestige to its cultural accomplishments. **Potsdam** owes its appeal to Frederick the Great, who took the concept of *sans souci* (without care or worry) and transformed it into the reality of the delightful Sanssouci Palace. It was also the scene of the Potsdam Conference in 1945, where Harry (Truman) met "Old Joe" (Stalin) and got to like him—at least for a little while.

Train Connections to other Base Cities from Berlin

Many trains make stops at several Berlin train stations on arrival and departure from the city. The primary station used other than Berlin Zoobahnhof is the newly rebuilt Berlin Ostbahnhof that was named Berlin Hauptbahnhof by the German Democratic Republic government. After its reopening in 1998, the name reverted to the one used before 1945. Other stations used are Berlin Wannsee, Berlin Spandau, Berlin Lichtenberg, and Berlin Schönefeld. Consult the detailed timetables of the Deutsche Bahn (available on the Internet at http://hafas.bahn.de); www.railpass.com; or the *Thomas Cook European Timetable.*
Depart Berlin Zoo Station (Zoobahnhof) unless otherwise noted.

DEPARTURE	TRAIN NUMBER	ARRIVAL	NOTES
Amsterdam Centraal			
0742	IR 2344	1449	
1142	IR 2342	1849	
1542	IR 2340	2249	
2315	340	0659+1	R, Sleeper
Brussels (Bruxelles) Midi/Zuid			
0714	IC 942	1623	1, 2
0914	ICE 940	1806	1, 2
1114	ICE 848	2006	1, 2
2034	242/528	0706+1	R, 1, Couchettes
Budapest Kaleti			
0632	EC 171	1922	3
1032	EC 171	1922	3
1952	EN 229	1113+1	R, 3, Sleeper
Copenhagen (København) H			
0625	IC 918	1359	4
1031	EC 33	1759	4
1431	IC 910	2159	4
1631	IC 818	2359	4
2249	318	0945	5
Hamburg Hauptbahnhof			
0625	IC 918	0853	
0729	IC 878	0957	
0831	IC 916	1053	
0929	ICE 536	1154	
1031	IC 914	1253	
1129	IC 874	1357	
1231	IC 912	1453	

and continuing service (ICE, EC, and IC trains) at about 1 hr intervals until the last train at 2031.

Luxembourg

0914	ICE 946	1850	2

Munich (München) Hauptbahnhof

0532	EC 11	1307	
0732	IC 813	1508	
0932	IC 815	1710	
1132	IC 817	1907	
1332	IC 819	2107	
1532	IC 911	2307	
2233	ICN 1501	0645+1	R, Sleeper

Paris Gare du Nord

2035	242	0908+1	R, Sleeper

Stockhom Central

1318	316	0623+1	R, 6

Vienna (Wien) Südbahnhof

0832	EC 173	1848	

Zürich Hauptbahnhof

0932	IC 815	2223	7
2152	CNL 358	0934+1	R, Sleeper
2233	ICN 1501	1228+1	R, 8, Sleeper

Daily, unless otherwise noted
R Reservations required
Thalys high-speed trains require supplement

1. Depart Berlin Ostbahnhof station.
2. Change trains in Cologne (Köln).
3. Depart Berlin Lichtenberg station.
4. Change trains in Hamburg.
5. Arrive Malmö at 0838+1. Catamaran servicce between Copenhagen–Malmö is provided by two companies—Pilen and Flyvebådene. Sailings from Malmö use Malmö Skeppsbron dock. In Copenhagen, Havnegade dock is used by Pilen and Nyhavn by Flyvebådene. Sailings at hourly intervals throughout the day, 45-minute journey. These schedules are from Havnegade. Rail tickets are valid on catamaran sailings, with supplement payable on board. Connecting buses run between Havnegade dock and Copenhagen H. train station (15-minute journey). Malmö train station is about a 15-minute walk from Skeppsbron dock. Public transport and taxis are available at the train station.
6. Monday–Thursday and Sunday. Arrive Malmö 2242, transfer to sleeper train no. 2, reservations required.
7. Change in Munich to EC 98 departing at 1814, seat reservations recommended.
8. Change in Munich to EC 92 departing at 0814, seat reservations recommended.

Day Excursion to

Dresden

CHINA, CARILLONS, AND CULTURE

Depart from Berlin Zoobahnhof or Ostbahnhof

Distance by Train: 117 miles (189 km)
Average Train Time: 2 hours, 30 minute
City Dialing Code: 351
Dresden Tourist Information Office: Dresden Tourist Board, Goetheallee 18, D-01309
Tel: 49–1920; *Fax:* 310–5247
Internet: www.dresden-tourist.de
e-mail: info@dresden-tourist.de
Hours: 0900–2000, Monday–Friday; 0900–1600 Saturday; and 0900–1400 Sunday from April–October.

In the winter, the center is open on weekdays, but for fewer hours. Five-minute walk on Prager Strasse across the street from the rail station will take you there.

Dresden's name is derived from *Drezdzane*, the old Slavic word for "forest people," who were the early settlers in the area. Dresden is situated in the wide, gentle valley of the Elbe River, about 19 miles (30 kilometers) from the northwest border of the Czech Republic. Although the city's fame comes mainly from its past cultural achievements, Dresden is also economically important and is best known for its Dresden china.

Dresden has always enjoyed the delightful harmony of the river and nature in which to develop from its beginnings as a small Slavonic fishing village. As it grew, its scenic beauty was enhanced in the seventeenth and nineteenth centuries by builders who erected fine examples of Baroque and Rococo architecture. This, in turn, attracted a great number of artists and writers as Dresden grew into a modern, confident city of a half-million citizens. With its architectural landmarks and its art treasures of Dutch, Flemish, and Italian collections, Dresden gained the well-deserved title "Florence of the Elbe."

On February 13, 1945, more than a half-million bombs rained down on Dresden from Anglo-American aircraft. Thirty-five thousand citizens died and more than 15 square miles of the inner city were reduced to rubble. The air raid devastated nearly all of the city's cultural monuments. Dresden was declared dead.

But Dresden is rising like a Phoenix. Dust from the air raid scarcely settled before restoration began on the **Semper Opera House**. Forty years to the day, February 13, 1985, Dresden's population celebrated the reopening of this world-famous theater, and many other cultural and historic edifices have been rebuilt.

Dresden's *Altmarkt* (old market) is the historic center of the city. Between 1953 and 1956 it was rebuilt. The city's botanical gardens, completely

Berlin—Dresden

DEPART BERLIN ZOOBAHNHOF	DEPART BERLIN OSTBAHNHOF	TRAIN NUMBER	ARRIVE DRESDEN NEUSTADT	ARRIVE DRESDEN HAUPTBAHNHOF
0632	0645	EC 171	0843	0850
0832	0845	EC 173	1032	1041
	0936	IR 2371	1130	1139
1032	1045	EC 175	1232	1241
1232	1245	EC 177	1432	1441

DEPART DRESDEN HAUPTBAHNHOF	DEPART DRESDEN NEUSTADT	TRAIN NUMBER	ARRIVE BERLIN OSTBAHNHOF	ARRIVE BERLIN ZOOBAHNHOF
1515	1524	EC 176	1711	1729
1715	1724	EC 174	1911	1929
1906	1924	EC 172	2111	2125
2115	2124	EC 170	2311	2325

Daily, unless otherwise noted
Distance: 117 miles (189 km)

destroyed in 1945, were rebuilt in 1950. Only nine zoo animals survived the air attack, but in 1961 the zoo reopened with a stock of more than 2,000 animals representing nearly 500 species.

With typical Dresden determination, on February 13, 1992, the city announced that the **Frauenkirche** (Church of Our Lady)—decried by the communists to stand in ruin forever—would be rebuilt.

The church's dome dominates the scene. The Frauenkirche is the largest German Baroque and Protestant church and also the world's largest centrally planned Protestant church. It is undergoing archaeological reconstruction, that is, incorporating the remaining fragments in the reconstruction. Another feature is **Raffael's** *Sistine Madonna.*

The church's reconstruction site is near the **Albertinum Museum** at Brühlsche Terrace. The Albertinum houses the New Masters Picture Gallery, the "Green Vault," treasure chamber, and numismatic and sculpture collections. Hours: 1000–1800 daily, except Thursday.

Beginning with a group of only 55 dedicated members, the Society to Promote the Rebuilding of the Frauenkirche now numbers more than 5,000 members in Germany, with active supporters from more than twenty other countries. Out of the ruin long seen solely as an admonition against war, the

Frauenkirche is rising again as beautiful as ever—a symbol of the healing of war's wounds, with a resounding message of a strong desire for peace.

Obtain the *Tourist City Guide* from the tourist office. It contains a city map, places of interest, sightseeing tours, and just about everything you might ever want to know about Dresden. The **Old Town** is on the left bank of the Elbe and the **New Town** is across the river on its right bank. If you are an average sightseer, as we are, you can reach the Old Town area on foot from the city center in no more than 15 minutes.

Ask about the **Dresden Card** (27 DEM; valid for 48 hours), which provides for free transportation on all tram and bus lines plus ferries on the Elbe, free entrance to many museums, and discounts on city tours. In typical German fashion, the city's *Rathaus* (town hall) has a *Ratskeller* (restaurant) in its cellar where you may enjoy a cold draft and a sample of Saxon food before setting out to see Dresden.

One of the many magnificent edifices vying for your attention during your Dresden visit is the **Zwinger**. It is known as the most important Late Baroque building in Germany. The name "Zwinger" is a term used in the construction of fortresses and defines the space between the outer and inner ramparts. Heavily damaged in 1945, the Zwinger reconstruction was said to have begun "instantaneously" despite communist objections. It was restored to its present condition by 1963.

If you cross the Elbe, be sure to use Dresden's famous **Loschwitzer–Blasewitzer Bridge**. Opened in 1893, it was the only bridge to remain intact by 1945. The complex WWII German political and military organization known as the SS had the bridge set for destruction, but two Dresdeners, each unaware of the other's action, cut the wire to the explosives. The grateful populace of Dresden now refer to the bridge as the "Blue Miracle."

Make it a point to visit the **Old Masters Picture Gallery** in the Zwinger Semperbau and examine the famous views of the court painter, Bernardo Bellotto. They show the city at the peak of its splendor.

Day Excursion to

Leipzig
BACH AND MENDELSSOHN MEMORIES

Depart from Berlin Zoobahnhof

Distance by Train: 113 miles (186 km)
Average Train Time: 2 hours
City Dialing Code: 341
Leipzig Tourist Information: Richard-Wagner-Strasse 1, D–04109 Leipzig
Tel: 7104 260/265; *Fax:* 7104 271/276
Internet: www.leipzig.de

E-mail: lipsia@aol.com
Hours: 0900–2000 Monday–Friday; 0900–1600 Saturday; 0900–1400 Sunday;
1000–1600 holidays
  Located directly opposite the rail station—5-minute walk

Like many cities and towns in Europe, Leipzig has an old and a new section. Leipzig's old town is located between three rivers, the Parthe, the Elster,
and the Pleisse. No doubt the site selection had much to do with safety, and
the proximity to three navigable rivers also indicates an early interest in trade.
Leipzig has been known for its great trade fairs that date back to the Middle
Ages and still attract businesspeople from all over the world.

The city's name is derived from *Lipsk*, the original Slav settlement named
for the lime trees (*lipa*) growing there. Leipzig was built as a walled city in the
eleventh century; the walls surrounding the old town were replaced in the
eighteenth century by a ring of parks and promenades. Subsequently, Leipzig
expanded in all directions by gradually incorporating the suburbs that were
growing up around it—a tactic followed by many American cities.

Newly reconstructed from 1996 to 1998, Leipzig's main rail terminal
(Hauptbahnhof) has 23 platforms (plus 4 outside platforms) and is the largest
rail terminal in Europe. The three-level station houses restaurants, shops, cafes,
meeting rooms, travel agencies, money exchange, and other tourist facilities.
More than 800 trains move through the terminus daily, carrying an estimat-
ed 75,000 passengers. There's no need to worry about its size, since the
Hauptbahnhof comes well equipped with pictographs.

The **Leipzig Card** provides transport on trams and buses and on the city
railway to the **New Trade-Fair Centre.** There are also reductions on city
tours, museums, and concerts. 1-Day Card, 9.90 DEM; 1-Day Party Card (2
adults and up to 3 children under age 14), 21 DEM; 3-Day Card, 21 DEM;
3-Day Party Card, 34 DEM. Purchase at the tourist office, rail station, and
many hotels.

The main attraction on the old town's market square is the **Old Town
Hall.** It was built in the record time of nine months in 1556 by Hieronymus
Lotter. The building is one of the oldest Renaissance town halls still standing
on German soil. Although severely damaged by fire during the Allied air raid
on December 4, 1943, the building's facade remains almost unchanged from
the sixteenth century. The city was governed from here until 1905, when a
new town hall was erected in a more spacious area. Since 1909 the building
has been the **Museum of History of the City of Leipzig.** Its attractions
include the Old Council Chambers and special exhibits.

The **new town hall,** built between 1899 and 1905 on the foundations of
earlier buildings, will also attract your attention with its 115-meter tower. It
houses both the mayor and the city council.

Berlin—Leipzig

DEPART BERLIN ZOOBAHNHOF	TRAIN NUMBER	ARRIVE LEIPZIG HAUPTBAHNHOF
0725	IC 813	0939
0925	IC 815	1139
1125	IC 817	1339
1325	IC 819	1539

DEPART LEIPZIG HAUPTBAHNHOF	TRAIN NUMBER	ARRIVE BERLIN ZOOBAHNHOF
1421	IC 818	1626
1621	IC 816	1831
1821	IC 814	2031
2021	IC 812	2231
2221	EC 10	0017+1

Daily, unless otherwise noted.
Distance: 113 miles (182 km)

Within the rim of the old town, the spires of the **Church of Saint Nicholas** (Nikolaikirche) and the **Church of Saint Thomas** (Thomaskirche) stand as sentinels over the scene. The first mention of Saint Nicholas was made in 1017; Saint Thomas was erected between 1212 and 1222 as the collegiate church of the Augustinian Choir. Its Late Gothic hall was added at the end of the fifteenth century.

The stained-glass windows of Saint Thomas, dating from the end of the nineteenth century, depict four historical personalities closely associated with Leipzig: Johann Sebastian Bach, Felix Mendelssohn Bartholdy, Martin Luther, and King Gustav Adolf II of Sweden. Saint Thomas became world-famous from its association with Johann Sebastian Bach. The composer served as cantor of the church from 1723 to 1750. Since 1950, the remains of the great composer have lain in the church. For more information about the Leipzig Bach Festival July 21–30, 2000, contact Bach-Archiv Leipzig, Thomaskirchof 16, PF 10139, 04013 Leipzig; *Tel:* 964–4182 or *E-mail:* jsbach @rzaix530.rz.uni-leipzig.de. Contact the Tourist Office for a highlights list of 2000–2001 events in Leipzig.

The Church of Saint Nicholas, although containing some of the oldest building remains in Leipzig, recently played an important part in the reunification of Germany. From 1982, the prayers for peace held every Monday under the sheltering roof of the church "transmitted" loud and clear signals to the Leipzig demonstrators—impulses that, during the days of October and

November 1989, brought about the "gentle revolutions" that led to the downfall of the communist dictatorship.

Music lovers also will not want to miss the Mendelssohn House where the innovative composer Felix Mendelssohn Bartholdy lived and died. The Mendelssohn House has been restored to its original grandeur.

Outside Leipzig's old town you can visit the **Leipzig Zoo,** which was founded in 1878. The city information center will tell you it's "only a 15-minute walk," but perhaps a taxi would be better. The zoo is noted for its lions and tigers, including the breeding of some 2,500 purebred Berber lions. An unusual feature of the zoo is its "shop-window," whereby spectators are separated from the animals only by a moat—a *deep* moat.

At the end of World War II the city constructed a stadium, similar to the efforts in Munich, seating 100,000 spectators from the rubble left by the war. The stadium was the first major building project in Leipzig following the war. Three million cubic meters of rubble were used for the 23-meter-high terraces.

Day Excursion to

Potsdam

WHERE HARRY MET JOE

Depart from Berlin Zoobahnhof or Wannsee Station, or use S-Bahn

Distance by Train: 22 miles (36 km)
Average Train Time: 26 minutes
City Dialing Code: 331
Potsdam Tourist Information: 5, Friedrich-Ebert-Strasse
Tel: (0331) 27–5580 or (0331) 29–1100; *Fax:* (0331) 275–5899
Hours: April–October, 0900–2000 Monday–Friday; 0900–1800 Saturday; 0900–1600 Sunday. November–March, 1000–1800 Monday–Friday; 1000–1400 Saturday–Sunday.

Located in the old market, a 10-minute walk from the railway station. Turn right out of the station and walk across the Lange Brucke (Long Bridge) and up the Friedrich-Ebert-Strasse to the center, which is located on the right side of the street. Ask for the illustrated pamphlet *Info—Stadtplan Potsdam.*

Originally a small settlement of Slavs, Potsdam first appeared in German chronicles under the name *Poztupimi* (Under the Oak Trees) in a Deed of Gift dated July 3, 993. There are virtually no oak trees left in present-day Potsdam, but from days gone by you will find a large number of handsome oak mansions and palaces surrounded by beautiful parks.

After a period of almost total insignificance during the Middle Ages, Potsdam eventually entered the sphere of German history in the seventeenth century when Frederick William, the Elector of Brandenburg, decided to make Potsdam his place of residence.

In the eighteenth century, during the reigns of King Frederick William I and his son Frederick II, known as Frederick the Great, Potsdam grew to be a prestigious royal seat and garrison town. Frederick William I established a military orphanage where the boys "learned to work" in nearby factories and also drilled in "square bashing," which came in handy whenever the impoverished peasants could no longer stand their plight and chose to demonstrate in the town square.

Unlike many towns emerging from the Middle Ages, Potsdam was not surrounded by a wall until the eighteenth century. Oddly enough, the wall served not so much as a military protection as it did a device to prevent soldiers from deserting and dishonest folks from smuggling. Whether the wall contributed to the growth of the town is not known, but Potsdam did flourish under the Fredericks. The Alten Markt (old market), the Hollandisches Viertel (Dutch quarters), the **Brandenburger Strasse,** and the **Sans Souci Park and Palace** date to the era of their reign.

Frederick II was growing a bit "long-in-the-tooth" and decided he wanted to live "without cares" (*sans souci*). So, beginning in 1744 and during the following three decades, "Old Fritz" supervised the building of the palace and several other buildings, including his own tomb as a last resting place beside the palace.

The Rococo Sans Souci Palace was built from sketches by the king himself, together with designs by his architect, Knobelsdorff. With further additions made during the nineteenth century, Sans Souci stands today on a 717-acre complex as one of the largest and most significant parks in Europe.

But "Old Fritz" would not rest. After the Seven Years' War, in which he lost all the battles but won the war, he celebrated his "victory" by building another palace—the **Neues Palais** (New Palace).

The Potsdam Information Center conducts a bus tour from April to to October that includes a tour of the **Sans Souci Palace** and its gardens; the tour leaves the center at 1100 (3 hours). Cost: 39 DEM. Open year round and closed Mondays.

If you like palaces, you've come to the right place. **Charlottenhof Palace,** a part of the Sans Souci complex, comes complete with Roman baths. The baths, by the way, were not intended for the purpose of hygiene but formed a part of a museumlike dream world reflecting the romantic yearnings of Crown Prince Frederick William (Fat William).

The **Marble Palace** and the **New Garden**—called "new" in contrast with the "old" gardens at Sans Souci—were ordered built by "Fat William" when he was crowned in 1786. The Marble Palace is open to visitors on weekends only from May to October 1000-1700. Guided tours are 6 DEM; self-guided visits are 5 DEM. *Tel:* (0331) 969–4200 for more information.

Berlin—Potsdam

Berlin S-Bahn trains run frequently between many Berlin stations and Potsdam—4 or 5 trains each hour all day. In addition, Potsdam is a stop for many Deutsche Bahn mainline trains between Berlin and cities to the west—typically 3 or 4 trains each hour in both directions run from Berlin Ostbahnhof and from Berlin Zoobahnhof (many also stop at Berlin Wannsee Station). Journey time from/to Berlin Ostbahnhof is about 35 min, from/to Berlin Zoobahnhof about 20 min., and from/to Berlin Wannsee about 8 min.

Distance: 22 miles (36 km)

Potsdam's **old town** is a great place to browse. Right in the center of it you feel as though you've been transferred to Holland. To attract Dutch crafts-men to Potsdam, more than one hundred middle-class Dutch Baroque-style houses were built between 1734 and 1742. The project failed in that it did not attract Dutchmen in the number expected, but the houses were inhabit-ed, in turn, by Potsdam's craftsmen, artists, and military. Sometimes things just don't work out the way you want them to. Perhaps that is Potsdam's penchant—read on.

The son of Kaiser Wilhelm, Crown Prince William, built a second palace at the New Garden from 1913 to 1915. He named it **Cecilienhof** after his Crown Princess. Unlike his father, who never returned from his Dutch exile, the ex–Crown Prince did move back into Cecilienhof Palace in 1923 and stayed there until 1945, bringing a number of interesting guests.

From July 17 until August 2, 1945, Cecilienhof played host to the Potsdam Conference, the third and final meeting of Churchill, Stalin, and Truman. One of the conference aims was the unity of Germany, though what followed was actually its division. Harry Truman returned from the conference stating that he "liked old Joe." But just like the time when Harry met Sally, things didn't quite work out the way they wanted them to.

Base City . . .

Hamburg
City Dialing Code: 40
Internet: www.hamburg-tourism.de
E-mail:info@hamburg-tourism.de

The Free and Hanseatic City of Hamburg is an impressive title—for an equally impressive city. Its 1.7 million residents are intensely proud of their city and are most eager to show it. Hamburg is the largest in a league of "Hansa" cities in Germany that medieval merchants organized to secure greater safety and privileges in trading. For a long time, nobility was barred from entering this affluent city that sits poised between the Elbe River and Alster Lake.

Hamburg is full of surprises. It has more bridges than the combined total of Amsterdam and Venice. The city's harbor is one of the leading ports in Europe and ranks as one of the top ten largest ports in the world—notwithstanding the fact that it is 68 miles inland from the North Sea!

Chartered in 1189, Hamburg occupies a 288-square-mile area, 20 percent of which is covered by water. To the delight of residents and visitors alike, about 10 percent of the city's total area has been landscaped into public parks. Many of these areas date back to the eighteenth century, when landscaping was fostered by the city's wealthy residents as one of the arts.

Hamburgians have their port to thank for the development of their city to its present stature—an expansive metropolis of international business and culture. During the first weekend of May, the Hamburgians begin a three-day celebration to commemorate the year 1189, when Emperor Frederick Barbarossa granted Hamburg its "free port" status. The term *free port* means that transit cargo is exempt from custom duties. Not all of the harbor area, however, is classified as a free port.

In honor of the **World Expo 2000** in Hannover, Germany, Hamburg is staging a phenomenal millennium mega-event, **Carmen 2000**, from June 4 to October 1, 2000. *Carmen 2000* is a modern adaptation of George Bizet's *Carmen*, the most successful and popular opera of all time. Staged at the 2,000-seat dome at Hagenbeck's Zoo, this modern version has added circus features, including a big top, live animals, and international stars. Cord Garben, who has received the American "Grammy" recording award six times, ends the opera with a twist. It's a spectacular production you won't want to miss! Telephone 40 24 14 14 for more information.

Arriving by Air

Fuhlsbüttel International Airport, 8 miles north of the city center. Although the airport has four terminals, all international arrivals and departures utilize Terminal 4. Airport information: *Tel:* 50 75 10 10.

- **Airport–City Links**: Express bus service between the airport and a nearby U-Bahn station where frequent train service into Hamburg is available. If you are burdened with baggage, use the Airport–City bus; departures every 20 minutes, 0530–2300, for Hamburg's Hauptbahnhof (main rail station). Journey time: 25–30 minutes. Fare, 8 deutsche marks (DEM); round trip, 12 DEM. From city center to airport, service 0540–2120. For taxis (*Tel:* 66 66 66, 21 12 11, 61 11 22), follow the pictographs. Average taxi fare to the city center, 25 DEM.
- **Money exchange**: Deutsche Bank in the arrivals hall of Terminal 4, hours 0630–2030 daily. Icelandair, SAS, and Lufthansa operate transatlantic services to and from Hamburg.

Arriving by Train

The Hamburg **Hauptbahnhof** (main rail station) appears as though it was constructed to handle the dirigible *Hindenburg*. Its immensity is impressive. There are 14 *Gleise* (tracks). Gleise 1 to 4 serve the S-Bahn, the suburban rail service; Gleise 5 through 14 are for regular train service. Most InterCity Express (ICE) trains glide in and out of the Hauptbahnhof on Gleise 13 and 14.

For a full-service restaurant, visit the InterCity Restaurant, accessible by elevator, on the station's second floor front. The Gourmet Station on the main floor features national and international dishes. It's informal. Opposite the Gourmet Station are various boutiques in the "Wandelhalle."

- **Baggage storage** carts are scarce. The baggage room is the best source for a cart or a porter.
- **Money exchange** hours, 0730–2200 daily.
- **Post office** hours, Monday–Friday, 0700–2100; Saturday–Sunday, 0800–2000.
- **International telephones** are on the second floor of the post office.
- **Train information** is in the *Reisezentrum* (Travel Center). Hours: 0530–2300 daily.
- **Railpasses** can be validated at window 20 or any window marked AUS-LAND. Information windows are 21 to 24. If the attendant does not speak English, you will be referred to one who does.
- **Tourist office** in the main rail station open daily, 0700–2300 (*Tel:* 300 51 201 or 202).

Tourist Information/Hotel Reservations

The Hamburg Tourist Board has two information offices—one at St. Pauli Landungsbrücken (landing pier) facing the harbor and one in the main rail station.

For advance planning, contact

Hamburg Tourist Board
P.O. Box 10 22 49
D-20015 Hamburg, Germany
Tel: (40) 3005–1300; *Fax:* (40) 3005–1333

Hotline for **hotel reservations** (0800–2000): 40 3005–1300

In addition to general information, the board's information service can provide accommodation bookings; bookings for port tours and Alster cruises; arrangements for guides; and tips on sightseeing, dining, and shopping.

Visitors of Germanic origins will be interested in the **Historic Emigration Office** (*Tel:* (40) 3005–1282) of the Hamburg Tourist Board. It is Germany's only historic emigration office, based on the register of German emigrants kept by the municipal authorities from 1850 to 1934. The register has five million names of people who set sail via the Port of Hamburg for a new life overseas. Family-tree hunters need the emigrant's name and year of emigration. There is a charge of $30 for the search and a passenger list print-out.

Getting Around in Hamburg

Purchase a **Hamburg-CARD** at tourist information offices, from U-Bahn (metro) station vending machines, and at most hotels. The CARD is a real bargain. It entitles you to travel free on the city's bus and train systems, subways, and port ferries at any time within the card's period of validity. It also provides free admission to 11 museums and includes reductions up to 30 percent for such activities as the Alster tour, the Port tour, and many others.

The **Hamburg-CARD** is available as a daily card (12.50 DEM for 1 adult and up to 3 children age 12 or under or 24 DEM for up to 5 persons) or a 3-day card (26 DEM for 1 adult and 3 children or 42 DEM for up to 5 persons). The tourist information office will provide you with a brochure, *City Map and Tips from A to Z*, which explains the card's features.

Sightseeing/Attractions/Tours—Hamburg Highlights

A **tour of the harbor** by launch is available year-round. (The launches are heated in winter.) In summer, the tour operates every half-hour from 0900–1800; for winter tours contact the tourist information office. The launches sail from St. Pauli pier. From the Hauptbahnhof, take either the U-Bahn line U3, or S-Bahn lines S1 or S3 to the Landungsbrücken station. Tickets: 15 DEM adults; 7.50 DEM children. Hamburg-CARD holders pay 11 DEM and 6.50 DEM, respectively. The tour takes about one hour. Ask for a launch with an English-speaking captain.

From April through October, leisure cruise boats depart from the quay at Jungfernstieg—Hamburg's elegant shopping street—to **cruise on Lake Alster**. Actually, the Alster is not really a lake. It is a tributary of the Elbe River that has been widened into a lake just before it flows into the Elbe River. This 460-acre lake, an area larger than the entire principality of Monaco, was created when the Alster was dammed in the early thirteenth century.

There is a wide selection of tours available on the Alster boats, including a one-hour trip along its shoreline, a tour of the city's canal system, a bridge tour where you'll see a sampling of the city's 2,400 bridges, and a twilight tour. A guided tour of the **Inner and Outer Alster** operates every half-hour, 1000–1800; tour duration, about 50 minutes. Adults:15 DEM; children, 7.50 DEM; Hamburg-CARD holders receive a discount. Even in winter, the Alster boats cruise the lake for the popular "punch" cruises. To inquire, visit the **Alster-Touristik office** on the quay where the boats depart (*Tel:* 3574240). Brochures are also available in all of the Hamburg tourist offices.

Take a ride on the **Hamburger Hummelbahn.** Hamburg-CARD holders get a substantial discount. *Hummel* is German for "bumble bee," and this amazing form of transportation literally "buzzes" all over town. The train does not run on tracks. Its open platforms are ideal for photographing. It's a fun trip.

If you are in Hamburg on a Sunday, reserve a good part of the day for a visit to the **Fischmarkt** (fish market). Dating from about 1703, it is the oldest licensed market in Hamburg where just about everything that is movable is sold or traded. Fish? Well, fish have become incidental to the market's activities; freshly caught fish, however, are still sold any day of the week from fishing boats at the city's pier.

On Sunday mornings, the pubs scattered around the fish market area draw crowds of early risers and late-night revelers alike. Take in the Sunday-morning auction activities held in the **Fischauktionshalle** (fish auction hall). The auction hall opens promptly at 0500 (0700 in winter) and lasts only until 1000, so hurry. Following the auction, treat yourself to a jazz breakfast right in the Fischauktionshalle.

Shopping is an international pastime and Hamburg is a wonderful place to pursue such interests. No city on the Continent has so many covered shopping arcades. As a jumping-off place, start at the **Jungfernstieg** where the white ferries depart for water tours of the Alster Lake. Here, you will find covered arcades where shoppers may stroll regardless of the weather. For big department store shopping, head for **Monckebergstrasse** directly east from

Train Connections to Other Base Cities from Hamburg

Depart from Hamburg Hauptbahnhof, unless otherwise noted.

DEPARTURE	TRAIN NUMBER	ARRIVAL	NOTES
Amsterdam Centraal			
0553	EC 29	1049	1
0953	IC 505	1449	1
1353	IC 507	1849	1
1753 I	C 507	2249	1
Berlin Zoobahnhof			
0629	ICE 531	0845	
0802	EC 175	1032	
0905	IC 817	1128	
1002	EC 177	1232	
1105	IC 819	1328	
1202	IC 873	1432	

and continuing service with the same pattern (give or take a minute or so) until 2102.

DEPARTURE	TRAIN NUMBER	ARRIVAL	NOTES
Bern (Berne)			
0624	ICE 775	1412	2
1026	ICE 71	1812	2
1226	ICE 77	1855	2
1426	ICE 79	2212	2
Brussels (Bruxelles) Midi/Zuid			
0753	EC 109	1435	R★, 3
0853	IC 705	1617/1623	4
0953	IC 505	1635	R★, 3
1053	IC 701	1806	5
1153	IC 801	1835	R★, 3
1253	IC 601	2006	5
1353	IC 507	2035	R★, 3
1553	IC 803	2306	5
Budapest Keleti			
0801	ICE 91	2138	6
0802	EC 175	2322	
2026	EN 491	1203	R, 6, Sleeper
Copenhagen (København) H			
0729	EC 31	1159	
0929	EC 33	1359	
1337	EC 35	1759	
1737	EC 37	2159	
1937	EC 39	2359	

Milan (Milano) Centrale

0624	ICE 775	1835	2
0926	none	2245	7
2222	ICN 1589	1450	8

Munich (München) Hauptbahnhof

0503	ICE 581	1043	
0703	ICE 583	1243	
0903	ICE 585	1443	
1003	ICE 787	1606	

and continuing ICE service at hourly intervals until 1803, then

2222	ICN 1589	0704+1	R, Sleeper

Paris Gare du Nord

0735	EC 109	1605	R★, 3
0953	IC 505	1805	R★, 3
1153	IC 801	2005	R★, 3
1353	IC 507	2205	R★, 3
2242	234	0847+1	R, Sleeper

Rome (Roma) Termini

0047	EN 483	1950+1	R, 8, Sleeper
1426	ICE 79	0942+1	9

Stockhom Central

1737	EC 37	0741+1	10

Vienna (Wien) Südbahnhof

0801	ICE 91	1742	
1003	ICE 787	1945	11
1203	ICE 789	2145	11
2026	EN 491	0850+1	R, Sleeper

Zürich Hauptbahnhof

0624	ICE 775	1403	2
0926	none	1847	7
1026	ICE 71	1803	2
1226	ICE 77	2003	
1426	ICE 79	2203	
2107	CNL 471	0822+1	R, 2, Sleeper

Daily, unless otherwise noted
R Reservations required
★ Thalys high-speed train, supplement required
1. Change trains in Osnabruck
2. Change trains in Basel.
3. Change in Cologne (Köln) to high-speed Thalys train, reservations and supplement required.
4. Train 424 arrives Brussels Midi/Zuid station at 1617 Sat–Sun and at 1623 Mon–Fri.
5. Change trains in Cologne (Köln).
6. Change trains in Vienna Westbahnhof.

7. Change trains in Stuttgart.
8. Change trains in Munich.
9. Change to sleeper train (reservations) in Basel.
10. Change in Copenhagen to sleeper train 284 (reservations).
11. Change trains in Wurzburg.
Distance: 130 (214 km)

---

the **Rathaus,** Hamburg's city hall. Or, get off to a flying start right after arriving by train in Hamburg at the Wandelhalle, the covered mall above the train platforms in the Hauptbahnhof.

Hamburg abounds in museums. Its two museum ships are the *Rickmer Rickmers,* a reminder of bygone days when sailing ships ruled the waves, and the *Cap San Diego,* the "White Swan of the South Atlantic." Both offer discounts to Hamburg-CARD holders and are open daily starting at 1000.

At night, **St. Pauli,** the entertainment district, offers numerous pubs, restaurants, and discos along the (in)famous **Reeperbahn, Hans-Albers-Platz,** and **Grosse Freiheit.** Feeling erotic? Then, visit the **Erotic Art Museum,** located in the very heart of St. Pauli, at Nobistor 10. It contains masterpieces of erotic art from the Renaissance to the present. Hours: 1000–2400 daily.

Hamburg has no inhibitions and no curfew. See for yourself—there's a 4-hour bus tour, "Hamburg at Night," that departs from the Hauptbahnhof (Kirchenallee exit) at 2000 every evening except Sunday and Monday. The cost is 111 DEM and includes admission to selected bars and three free drinks. For reservations, telephone Hamburger Rundfahrten 227 10 60.

Day Excursions

Hamburg is situated in the center of a vast railway network. Consequently, the availability of day-excursion opportunities is virtually limitless.

Bremen, another great Hanseatic city of Germany, is quite a contrast to Hamburg, although jointly the two provide the largest operation of seaports within Germany today.

To the south of Hamburg, in the midst of the Weser Hills, stands the fascinating town of **Hameln,** where the tale of the legendary Pied Piper is reenacted every Sunday.

Ride the pride of the German fleet—the German ICE (InterCity Express)—to **Hannover** for a rewarding day of sightseeing amid the city's beautiful parks and gardens.

Lübeck is Germany's largest Hanseatic port on the Baltic and one of the oldest and most beautiful towns in Germany today. Go early and enjoy!

Day Excursion to

Bremen

AND THE TOWN MUSICIANS

Depart from Hamburg Hauptbahnhof

Distance by Train: 76 miles (120 km)
Average Train Time: 55 minutes
City Dialing Code: 421
Bremen Tourist Information: Findorffstrasse 105, D-28215
Tel: 30 80 00
Internet: www.bremen-tourism.de
E-mail: info@bremen-tourism.de
Hours: 0930–1830 Monday–Friday (until 2000 on Thursday and Friday); 0930–1600 Saturday–Sunday

Bremen is Germany's oldest maritime city. Bremen got its start as a port city in the tenth century when Emperor Otto I approved the construction of its docks.

It lies on the Weser River, 44 miles upstream from the mouth. Bremen is the second largest port in Germany. With so much to see and do in Bremen, we recommend that rail travelers visiting Bremen for the first time confine their sightseeing to the area in and around the city's market square, then follow up on a second visit with an inspection of the city's extensive harbor facilities. Certainly the charm of the market and its immediate surroundings will beckon the traveler to return again.

Finding your way from the Bremen railway station to the **market square** is an easy task. Attendants there can give you a considerable amount of information regarding Bremen. Particularly informative is a free brochure entitled *Bremen, Cosmopolitan and Historic.* The brochure contains background information on all aspects of Bremen.

The most direct route to the market square is down **Bahnhofstrasse,** which begins in front of the station. Proceed to where it intersects with Sogestrasse and crosses a former moat. A landmark at this point is a large windmill, seen in the distance on the right when crossing the bridge. Proceeding two blocks straight ahead on Sogestrasse brings you to the threshold of the old city center. A short walk through a shopping area and you are in the market square, where the **cathedral,** the **Rathaus** (city hall), and the **Liebfrauenkirche** are all clustered.

Bremen's oldest resident, the statue of ***Roland*** which was erected in 1404, is the center of attraction in the market square. Roland is a symbol of justice and freedom. Legend has it that Bremen will not pass away as long as the stone giant is still standing in the marketplace. Legend also has it that the city fathers have a replacement ready—just in case.

Hamburg—Bremen

IC trains depart Hamburg Hauptbahnhof hourly from 0453; journey time to Bremen Hbf is 1 hour 54 minutes.

IC trains depart Bremen Hbf hourly at 15 minutes after the hour until 2315; journey time is 1 hour 52 minutes.

Distance: 115 miles (183 km)

No one is quite certain as to Roland's origins. City history first mentions the existence of the knightly statue in the marketplace in 1366, but it was made of wood and went up in flames. So did its wooden replacement. The stone statue has fared better.

The seventeenth-century facade of the Rathaus makes it one of the most photographed public buildings in the world. Rising above the town hall are the twin towers of the eleventh-century **Saint Peter's Cathedral,** site of an ancient sand dune where the earliest Bremeners sought refuge from the surging tides of the Weser River.

Seek out the cellar of the town hall. It is said that the people of Bremen are most at their ease in a cellar—and this cellar is one of the best. It's a *Ratskeller* with more than 600 varieties of German wines to sample. Chances are if you find it, it may be a while before you see the light of day again.

The bronze statue of Bremen's **"Four Musicians"** (the donkey, dog, cat, and rooster) is stashed away in a cranny between the Rathaus (town hall) and the Liebfrauenkirche, the Church of Our Blessed Lady. Be certain you find and photograph it, or your kids will never forgive you. The "Four Musicians" is one of several statues erected in Bremen honoring the Brothers Grimm fairy tales. If you delve into the true origins of the odd assortment of these domestic animals, apparently they are symbolic of a peasants' revolt against aristocracy rather than the Grimms' version of frightening off robbers—but don't tell the kids. A free open-air stage performance at Liebfrauenkirchhof Square takes place on Sundays at noon and 1330.

The **Böttcherstrasse,** a narrow street leading off the market square, was redeveloped as a center for arts and crafts, with shops, workshops, art collections, and fine restaurants—even a casino. At the end of the street you will come to the Martini Church on the banks of the Weser. Boat tours of the Bremen harbor depart from the pier immediately in front of the church.

Another area that you can reach on foot by walking upstream along the banks of the Weser is the **Schnoor.** The oldest surviving residential area within the city of Bremen, it boasts quaint little houses, inns, and workshops dating back to the sixteenth, seventeenth, and eighteenth centuries.

City sightseeing tours depart daily from the bus station in front of the main railway station at 1030. Tickets (25 DEM adults; children up to age 12, 15 DEM) must be obtained beforehand at the tourist information office. Trips around the harbor depart the Martini Church jetty daily at frequent intervals from March through October. The trip lasts one and a quarter hours.

Anywhere in Bremen, the marketplace, the Bottcherstrasse, and the Schnoor included, you may come upon a chimney sweep garbed in traditional swallow-tailed coat and high, black hat. Reach out and touch him, for it is said that doing so brings good luck. Everyone does, and it's quite an exciting time when one passes through a crowd. Legends old and new abound in Bremen. Enjoy your visit.

Day Excursion to

Hameln

WHERE THE PIED PIPER PLAYED

Depart from Hamburg Hauptbahnhof

Distance by Train: 145 miles (218 km)
Average Train Time: 2 hours, 30 minutes
City Dialing Code: 5151
Hameln Tourist Information: Verkehrsverein Hameln, Deisterallee 3, D-31785 Hameln
Tel: 20 26 17; *Fax:* 20 25 00
Internet: www.hameln.de
E-mail: info@hameln.de
Hours: May–September, 0900–1300/1400–1800 Monday–Friday; 0930–1230/1400–1600 Saturday; 0930–1230 Sunday. October–April, 0900–1300/1400–1700 Monday–Friday.

A short walk from the Hameln railway station. Walk through the square in front of the station, turning right onto Bahnhofstrasse. At the first traffic light, turn left onto Deisterstrasse. When you note a tree-lined shopping plaza on the right of the main street, look for the tourist information office near the next main intersection on the right.

Hameln's Old Town will hold you spellbound with its cobblestone walks, ancient facades, and cozy eating places. If a time machine is ever invented, its first journey might well be to Hameln to confirm—or dispel—the *Legend of the Pied Piper.*

Fact or fable, the town's archives reflect that on June 26, 1284, an itinerant *Rattenfänger* (rat catcher) attired in a multicolored costume trilled his flute, and 130 children followed him out of town to an unknown fate. Only three children survived—one boy had returned for his coat and was left behind, a little blind lad lost his way, and a mute youngster returned but was unable to tell the story.

Hamburg—Hameln

DEPART HAMBURG	TRAIN NUMBER	ARRIVE HANNOVER	DEPART HANNOVER	ARRIVE HAMELN
0703	ICE 583	0820	0848	0935
0801	ICE 91	0920	0948	1035
0903	ICE 585	1025	1048	1135
1003	ICE 787	1125	1148	1235
1103	ICE 587	1225	1248	1335

DEPART HAMELN	ARRIVE HANNOVER	DEPART HANNOVER	TRAIN NUMBER	ARRIVE HAMBURG
1423	1508	1533	ICE 588	1652
1523	1608	1633	ICE 786	1752
1623	1708	1733	ICE 586	1852
1723	1808	1833	ICE 90	1952
1823	1908	1933	ICE 584	2052

and 4 later trains at hourly intervals

Change trains in Hannover. Train numbers apply only to the Hamburg–Hannover and Hannover–Hamburg portion.
Distance: 130 miles (214 km)

This most famous kidnapping supposedly happened in retribution for the town's elders' not paying the Pied Piper for his previous performance, when he trilled the town's burgeoning rat population to the Weser River, where they drowned. Moral of the story: You have to "pay the Piper."

The story of **Hameln's Pied Piper** is the most well known of all German folklore. It appeared in the Brothers Grimm German Legends and has been translated into at least thirty languages. There are probably as many theories as to what actually happened as there are children who disappeared—maybe more. The most probable explanation relates to the colonization of an area in the Czech Republic to which many citizens of Hameln migrated after being recruited by wealthy nobles during the same time in history. Peasants were referred to frequently as the children of towns, so it is quite possible that the tales became tangled. The present citizens, however, appear to be happy that it worked out the way the Brothers Grimm recorded it.

Every Sunday from mid-May through mid-September, a live reenactment of the event is staged in the town square. The colorful Piper, plus fifty or so of the town's children (attired in charming "rat" costumes) and another twenty adults representing the town mayor and citizens of Hameln, begin their performance promptly at noon.

You will have about 20 minutes to change trains in Hannover. You will realize you are approaching Hameln when you see the silhouette of the famous Piper on the railroad control tower.

If you plan to arrive in Hameln on the 1135 train for the performance at noon on Sunday, go directly to the town square. There is a tourist information office next to the stage in the town square that is open 1000–1400 during summer.

Adjacent to the main tourist office at Deisterallee on the right is a beautiful park, the **Burgergarten.** The park is readily identified by its pleasant green gate with the silhouette of the Pied Piper. The tourist information office conducts 1-hour guided walking tours (in German) every day from May through September at 1500 (cost 5 DEM per person). Ask the tourist office for prices of English-speaking tours. You can even arrange for a tour with the Piper himself!

If you're making your own walking tour, turn right when leaving the tourist information office and take the pedestrian underground route. Follow the signs reading ALTSTADT (Old City). When you leave the underground passageway, you will be on Osterstrasse. The **Gaststatte Rattenfangerhaus** (Pied Piper House), which is a charming cafe, will be to your immediate left. Either pause for refreshments here or proceed on Osterstrasse to the town hall, situated at the end of the street by the marketplace. En route, you will find several other attractive restaurants and cafes.

The Pied Piper isn't Hameln's only attraction—sightseeing in the Altstadt alone could fill your entire day. During the summer, it is possible to take a steamboat trip on the Weser River or stroll through the extensive woods surrounding Hameln. Visit **Museum Hameln** on Osterstrasse. Hours: 1000–1630 Tuesday–Sunday. It contains an extensive collection of civic art and culture dating back to the origins of Hameln, including the Pied Piper legend.

You can observe the 2000-year-old craft of glass-blowing and engraving in the historical **Pulverturm** (glassworks). The old and the new have been blended successfully in Hameln.

Day Excursion to

Hannover
FOLLOW THE RED THREAD

Depart from Hamburg Hauptbahnhof

Distance by Train: 111 miles (178 km)
Average Train Time: 1 hour, 30 minutes
City Dialing Code: 511

Hannover Tourist Information: Ernst-August-Platz 2, D-30159 Hannover, *Tel:* 30 14 12; for packages, *Tel:* 30–1422; *Fax:* 30–1414
Internet: www.hc.de
Hours: 0900–1900 Monday–Friday; 0930–1500 Saturday

Exit the station and turn to the right. The tourist office is on the right in the Hauptpost (main post office) building. Watch for the "Red Thread," a painted red line that runs directly to the information office.

Accommodations Service: Hannover Tourism Centre, Theodor-Heuss-Platz 1-3, D-30175 Hannover. *Tel:* 811–3500; *Fax:* 811–3541. Hours: 0800–2000 daily.

Hannover is known throughout the world as a commercial center dating back almost 1,000 years. Ideally located in the center of Europe, it is well served by rail and air. A world leader in hosting international events, Hannover has been chosen to host the first world's fair ever to be held in Germany—EXPO 2000: *Humankind–Nature–Technology.* More than 185 countries and organizations will participate. From June 1–October 21, 2000, Hannover is the place to be. Contact the German National Tourist Office listed in the Appendix for advance tickets.

The history of Hannover is interesting in that it produced the lineage of Britain's present royal family. George I of England was born in Hannover, as was his son and successor, George II. Thoroughly German in tastes and habits, both monarchs made frequent trips back to Hannover, where they also ruled under the title of "Elector." George III, who presided over the loss of Britain's American colonies, was the grandson of George II and the first English King George to be born on British soil.

Hannover's rail station, constructed initially between 1876 and 1879, has had numerous improvements, although it has retained its original nineteenth-century facade. Fourteen tracks serve passenger traffic from an elevated platform. A concourse at ground level connects all the tracks with the main station area. Running under the main station area and extending under the station's plaza and into the city is a shopping mall.

The **"Red Thread"** (the painted red line on the ground) is actually an unusual walking tour of the city. Follow the red line that runs through the city's sightseeing points, but do it with a *Red Thread* booklet that you can pick up at the tourist office for 4 DEM. The booklet fits easily in your hand—or it's small enough to slip into your pocket if you want to avoid looking like a tourist. It contains a map outlining the 2-hour walking tour and describes 36 points of interest you will pass while following the Red Thread. Take a camera with a wide-angle lens. Each point of interest has been numbered and the number placed so that if you stand on the number while photographing the scene, you'll have the best shot possible.

Highlights of the Red Thread walking tour include the **Passerelle,** a pedestrian shopping area, the city's **1852 Opera House,** the old city wall,

Hamburg—Hannover

Frequent service of at least two trains per hour in both directions from about 0700 to near midnight daily.

DEPART HAMBURG	TRAIN NUMBER	ARRIVE HANNOVER
0703	ICE 583	0825
0726	ICE 573	0841
0801	ICE 91	0920
0805	IC 781	0936
0826	ICE 773	0941
0903	ICE 85	1025
0926	ICE 575	1041
1003	ICE 787	1125
1026	ICE 71	1141
1103	ICE 587	1225
1126	ICE 577	1241

DEPART HANNOVER	TRAIN NUMBER	ARRIVE HAMBURG	NOTES
1606	IC 780	1759	
1616	ICE 772	1732	
1633	ICE 786	1752	
1716	ICE 576	1832	
1733	ICE 586	1852	
1811	ICE 1070	1927	Fri only
1833	ICE 90	1952	
1857	IR 2982	2028	
1916	ICE 574	2032	
1924	ICE 1084	2045	Sat only
1933	ICE 584	2052	
2016	ICE 774	2132	
2039	ICE 792	2159	
2116	ICE 572	2234	
2133	ICE 582	2252	
2224	ICE 570	2342	except Sat
2239	ICE 790	2358	

Distance: 111 miles (178 km)

and the new city hall. Hannover's oldest half-timbered building, dating from 1566, is also seen on the tour, which ends "under the stallion's tail"—unless you have succumbed on the tour route to the charm of the local *fräuleins* or *bierstube*.

Bus tours are conducted daily. The tour, which is described in English, takes two and one half hours; ticket, 20 DEM for adults and 15 DEM for children up to age 14 and college students.

Purchase a one-day **HannoverCard** at the tourist information office for 14 DEM (single) and receive a 50 percent reduction on the tour. Other benefits include free travel on all GVH buses and trams in fare zones 1 and 2 and a myriad of other sightseeing reduced fares, including a cruise on Hannover's downtown lake, Maschsee.

Hannover's **Zoo** is less than five minutes from the central station by U-Bahn Line 6 or by bus No. 128 from the central station. The stop is called **"Kröpke."** The zoo has the world's largest antelope collection, and all of the zoo's animals are exhibited in modern, fenceless enclosures.

The **Great Herrenhausen Garden and Garden Theater** is one of Europe's greatest tourist attractions (3 DEM entrance fee for people 14 years and older). In its 300-year-old landscaping, you will find the only example in Germany of early Baroque gardens that have survived in their original form. Herrenhausen Avenue, facing the gardens, is lined with 1,219 lime trees set in four rows; they link Hannover's inner city with the gardens of the former summer residence of the Royal House of Hannover in Herrenhausen. Many sections of the garden have remained unaltered through the centuries.

The garden is open 0800–1630 in winter and until 2000 in summer. Throughout the summer, the ornamental fountains of the garden operate from 1100–1200 and 1400–1600 daily. Either U-Bahn No. 4 or No. 5 will take you to the Herrenhausen Garden, or you will be able to see a portion of the gardens during a stop on the city bus tour.

Hannover has six major museums spanning 6,000 years of history. Entry to all is free, except the **Busch Museum** in the **Georgengarten,** a natural park developed in the eighteenth century. In sharp contrast to the baroque world of the Herrenhausen Garden, the Georgengarten is a mature example of English landscape gardening.

Many of Hannover's residents believe that a day in their city should have 48 hours. The refurbished city center alone—an ambler's paradise (reserved entirely for pedestrians) with shops, cascading fountains, and cafes—can captivate you. With the frequent train service between Hamburg and Hannover, you can easily extend your stay into evening.

Day Excursion to

Lübeck

RENAISSANCE AND ROTSPON

Depart from Hamburg Hauptbahnhof

Distance by Train: 39 miles (63 km)
Average Train Time: 38 minutes
City Dialing Code: 451
Lübeck Tourist Information: Lübeck and Travemünde Tourism Board, Beckergrube 95, D-23539
Tel: 122 1900; *Fax:* 122 1202
Internet: www.luebeck-tourismus.de
Hours: 0800–1600 Monday–Friday
  Tourist information: In the train station opposite track No. 1, Breite Strasse 62
Hours: 0930–1700 Monday–Friday; 1000–1400 Saturday–Sunday

The Hanseatic City of Lübeck extends its hospitality in a phrase, "Welcome, to yesterday, today, and tomorrow." The city's origins go back to the year 1000 when "Liubice" was established as a royal seat, artisan settlement, and trading center on the banks of the Trave River near the Baltic Sea. Today, parts of the old town of Lübeck have become a UNESCO World Heritage Site, and tomorrow is well in the hands of its energetic citizens who number more than 210,000.

Destroyed by fire in 1157, the city at present dates from 1159, when it was rebuilt. In 1358, it was chosen as the administrative headquarters for the Hanseatic League. Between 1806 and 1813, Napoleon I held Lübeck as a part of his empire. Until the turn of the twentieth century, when it began to build its own industries, Lübeck was known only as a Baltic port. Its industrial strengths and strategic maritime location, however, brought destruction to Lübeck during World War II, when most of Lübeck's industrial complex and some one-fifth of its Old Town were destroyed by Allied aerial bombardment. In 1949, the reconstruction of Lübeck, including the historic Old Town, began. As Germany's largest Baltic port, this proud city has once again become a center of economic, cultural, and commercial interests.

Lübeck is noted for two culinary specialties that you should sample during your visit—marzipan and *rotspon*. **Marzipan,** as a sweet specialty, is produced in a countless variety of forms. Try a piece of marzipan cake. The origins of marzipan are hidden in history. Lübeck's version is that during the famine of 1407, bakers produced a bread made from the stocks of almonds, since wheat flour was unavailable. Others believe that marzipan originated in Venice, and the recipe came to Lübeck through trade links.

In the early days, when salt was used to preserve fish, ships sailing from Lübeck began carrying salt mined in the Lübeck area to fishing ports along

Hamburg—Lübeck

DEPART HAMBURG	TRAIN NUMBER	ARRIVE LÜBECK
0715	RE 4008	0754
0729	EC 31	0806
0815	RE 4014	0854
0830	IR 2331	0910
0915	RE 4018	0954
0929	EC 33	1006
1015	RE 4024	1053
1040	IR 2333	1123
1115	RE 4028	1154

DEPART LÜBECK	TRAIN NUMBER	ARRIVE HAMBURG
earlier trains with about the same frequency as these:		
1803	RE 4067	1845
1903	RE 4075	1945
1941	EC 32	2015
2003	RE 4079	2045
2030	IR 2830	2114
2103	RE 4085	2144
2140	EC 30	2215
2203	RE 4089	2245
2247	2901/2903	2330
2303	RE 4091	2346

Distance: 38 miles (63 km)

the French coast of Biscay. Rather than return empty, the ships brought back casks of French wine to mature in Lübeck prior to bottling. A combination of sea climate and storage in Lübeck's wine cellars brought about an amazing improvement in the quality of the wine. This was first discovered in 1806 during Napoleon's occupation, when French officers found that the Bordeaux wine from Lübeck's wine cellars tasted considerably better than at home. Try a glass of *Lübeck er rotspon* and judge for yourself.

Lübeck's architecture ranges from Gothic to Neoclassical and you can find typical examples of these as well as Renaissance, Baroque, and Rococo in almost every part of the town's old section. Frequently, the various styles can be seen side by side. For example, starting with the College of Music at the head of Grosse Petersgrube you can see all five styles mixing in harmonic unity within one small block of the town.

With Lübeck's illustrated brochure in hand you can become your own tour guide, or you might want to opt for one of the town's regular guided walks that start from the tourist office in the marketplace. The guided walks take about two hours to complete. The tourist office in the train station can give you directions for finding the marketplace.

After you leave the train station, your point of reference will be the **Holstentor,** an imposing structure perched prominently at the head of the harbor just before the bridge leading over the Trave River into Old Town. Built between 1464 and 1478, more as a prestige symbol for the town than to protect its harbor, the unique design of its twin towers has become the symbol of Lübeck. The museum of city history housed in the Holstentor is very interesting and features a model of Lübeck in 1650.

After crossing the river, follow **Holsten Strasse,** which leads directly to Lübeck's *Rathaus* (town hall) in the marketplace. It is one of the oldest town halls built in Germany between the thirteenth and sixteenth centuries and certainly one of the most beautiful. The **Ratskeller Restaurant** in the basement of the Rathaus is a delightful place to pause for lunch or to sample a glass of *rotspon*. We can also recommend the **Schiffergesellschaft Restaurant** at No. 2 Breite Strasse, site of a meetinghouse built in 1535 for shipmasters and brimming with treasures from the world of shipping. Bring money—lots of it—the ambience and food are worth it. (Closed on Mondays.)

For an aerial view of Lübeck, cross Holsten Strasse from the marketplace to *Petrikirche* (St. Peter's Church). Destroyed in the war, the church no longer has its own parish since its restoration, but it serves as a popular center for meetings, concerts, and exhibitions. Here you can ride the elevator to a viewing platform 162 feet (50 meters) above the city.

Base City . . .

Munich (München)

City Dialing Code: 89
Internet: www.muenchen-tourist.de
E-mail: tourismus@muenchen.btl.de

Munich, the capital and heart of Bavaria, is situated in the center of a vast plain washed by the Isar River. The immaculate and astonishing beauty of its countryside is visible in any direction. Rimmed by the Alps to the south and dark green pine forests in all other quadrants, Munich becomes the gateway to day excursions galore. With a population of well over a million, Munich is Germany's third largest city, but it still retains its unmatched roisterous elegance.

Munich's mood is always festive, but twice a year the tempo soars even higher as the city observes Fasching and Oktoberfest. Fasching celebrations are held during January and February. The festivities could be compared to Mardi Gras, only Müncheners get a head start on everyone by cranking up just after New Year's Eve and never letting up until the sun sets on Ash Wednesday!

During this period of Fasching revelry, thousands of masked balls and parties are staged. Many are in fancy dress, and sometimes masks are worn because individuals don't wish to reveal their identities to their partners— who are seldom the ones they came in with. If they are, it's a complete surprise when the inevitable unmasking takes place.

The coming of Lent doesn't dampen Munich's spirits one drop, for it marks the beginning of the strong beer season. Munich's monks, limited to one meal a day throughout Lent (but with no limit on their drinking), started this ancient custom that still prevails today. They asked the brewmasters if, during Lent, they could increase the regular alcoholic content of their product; the brewmasters agreed—and everyone apparently has lived happily ever after. There are six major breweries in Munich.

Oktoberfest, instituted by a Bavarian King in 1810 on the occasion of the marriage between Princess Therese von Sachsen-Hildburgshausen and Prince Ludwig (later King Ludwig I), actually takes place during the latter part of September and ends the first weekend in October. About 660,000 gallons of beer are produced by the city's breweries and dispensed directly from huge, chilled barrels in enormous tents serving as beer halls. Bands play throughout the day and long into the night while drinkers wash down sausages, roast chicken, and oxen with five to six million liter-size drafts of the world's finest brews.

Colorful road signs on just about every highway entering Bavaria declare it to be FREISTAAT BAYERN, the Free State of Bavaria. Insurrection? Not really. It is the manifestation of the free and roisterous spirit of its citizens, who love their homeland and feel that there is no place quite like it anywhere else in the world.

Arriving by Air

Munich's Franz-Joseph Strauss International Airport is located 28 kilometers northeast of the city center. *Tel:* 9752–1313.

The airport features a system of passenger modules connected by a system of walkways, referred to as PTS (Passenger Transport System), that run the entire length of the terminal on level 03. The PTS also connects with the central area, where there is a 24-hour information area staffed by multilingual personnel.

- **Airport–City Links:** Munich's rapid transit rail system, S-Bahn No. 8 line, which stops at the Marienplatz (city center) and the Hauptbahnhof (main rail station). From the central area, descend to level 02. Trains depart every 20 minutes 0355–2455. Fare: 13.60 Deutsche Marks (DEM) for a one-way ticket, which you can purchase from machines at the airport (near the escalators leading to the S-Bahn). Eurailpasses, Europasses, and GermanRail passes are valid on the S-Bahn.
- **Lufthansa Airport Bus** departs every 20 minutes for Munich Hauptbahnhof 0750–2050 daily. From Munich Hauptbahnhof to airport, buses depart every 20 minutes, 0650–1950. Tickets: 15 DEM; round trip, 25 DEM. Travel time, about 45 minutes
- **Taxi stands** in front of modules A, B, C, D, and E. Due to traffic congestion, the time it takes to travel between the airport and the city by road can exceed 1 hour and can cost 100–120 DEM. Check at the taxi information desk in the central area of the airport. For advance taxi arrangements and information, *Tel:* 21610 or 19410 in Munich or *Fax:* 7470260.

Arriving by Train

Munich has several suburban stations, but most international trains stop only at the Hauptbahnhof.

Munich's Railway Station—The Hauptbahnhof is actually a city within a city. It even has its own hotel. In addition to the regular rail-station services, all you need do is descend one level on any one of the station's many escalators to discover a veritable city of shops, ranging from bakeries, *bier* (beer) *stube,* and fruit stands to supermarkets, as well as the subway entrances to many of Munich's department stores. This shopping colossus extends from the Hauptbahnhof all the way to Karlsplatz-Stachus—more than one-quarter of a mile. Most shops in the immediate Hauptbahnhof area are open late during the week as well as on weekends and holidays.

Money exchange (Geldwechsel-Exchange-Cambio): located in the far left corner (as you exit) of the main station hall next to the main entrance. Hours: 0600-2300 daily. This facility is operated by the Deutsche Verkehrs-Kredit-Bank (DVB) and offers a service not usually found in other exchanges. It will accept foreign coins (except coins from Eastern Europe). Most exchanges will only accept notes. If you have collected a variety of coins moving from country to country, here's your chance to unload if you're willing to accept 30 percent less than the total value.

An ATM (automated teller machine) is located on the left-hand side as you face the bank. A walk-up currency exchange office operated by DVB may be found by turning right when exiting the trains, by track 11 at the street exit.

Hours: 0730–1900 daily. There is also an ATM just before the Bayerstrasse exit.

The EurAide office is located in Room 3 next to track 11 in the Hauptbahnhof. It is open primarily during the summer months: 0730–1200 and 1300–1630 daily in May; 0730–1200 and 1300–1800 daily from June 1 to the end of September.

Tourist Information/Hotel Reservations may be made in the tourist information office. To reach it, exit through the Bahnhof Platz exit, and turn right. It is the second office on the right, next to the ABR Reisebüro. It is within the station complex, but can only be reached from the outside. A nominal charge is made for reservations. The attendants are very helpful in finding local reservations. Hours: 0900–2000 Monday–Saturday; 1000–1800 Sunday.

The **InterCity Hotel** is located conveniently in the train station. As you are exiting from the train-platform area, turn to the right just past the first main concourse shops and walk to the street entrance. The hotel will be on the left just before the doors leading to the street. It's convenient, but get reservations early—it's also popular. *Tel:* 54 55 60; *Fax:* 54 55 66 10.

Train reservations for EuroCity, InterCity, ICE, and express-train services can be made in the **Reisezentrum (Travel Center),** located in the center of the station in front of tracks 21 and 22. Hours: 0900–1800 Monday–Friday; 0900–1200 Saturday. It can be very crowded, particularly on weekends and during the summer tourist season. You must make train reservations at least one day in advance. They can also be made at counters with signs reading RESERVIERUNGENS.

Railpass validation and train information also can be obtained in the Reisezentrum. Use window 19, 20, or 47 for railpass validation. For train schedules only (international or domestic), use window 2 or 3 or the service counter in the middle of the station across from tracks 18 and 19. The sign reads DB SERVICE.

Prior to entering the train information office, prepare a list or an itinerary of the rail trips you intend to make. Too many people enter the office without a thought of where they want to go or when they want to arrive. This office can tell you what train to take and the time that it leaves the Munich Hauptbahnhof. They are not a travel agency, however, and you should not ask for suggestions of things to do.

Food services are available in several parts of the station. The most famous is the stand-up wiener-and-beer stube immediately to the right of the entrance into the main station concourse. Behind it, there are three full-service restaurants with posted prices and menus.

Luggage lockers are available in four areas of the station. Look for signs reading SCHLIESSFÄCHER. There is also a luggage-checking office on the main floor under the Burger King.

Another tourist information office is located in the New Town Hall in Marienplatz (same building as the glockenspiel). Hours are Monday–Friday

1000–2000; Saturday, 1000–1600; they are closed Sundays. This office also will make hotel reservations.

Getting Around in Munich

Munich's fine S-Bahn (rapid train) system is operated by Deutsche Bahn (DB). Eurailpass, Europass, Eurail Flexipass, and GermanRail Pass are accepted for travel throughout the entire S-Bahn system. The aforementioned rail-passes are *not* accepted on the U-Bahn (underground or subway system) or on the trams (*Strassenbahnen*).

The S-Bahn has eight main operating lines, S-1 through S-8. All of these lines converge on the Marienplatz and Hauptbahnhof. You can obtain maps and fare information at the tourist information office.

A U-Bahn (subway) station is located directly under the plaza in front of the railway station. The Munich Hauptbahnhof is the center of train, tram, bus, suburban train, and subway services for the entire city.

A great value is the MVV-Single (valid for one person) or Partner (valid for two adults) Tageskarte (Day Tickets). The Day Ticket provides unlimited travel on the S-Bahn (rapid transit line), U-Bahn (subway), streetcars, and buses on the date of validation until 0600 the following day. A Single Day Ticket for Munich's entire transport network costs 18 DEM; Partner Day Ticket, 26 DEM (5 adults). Remember to have your ticket "stamped/validated" by using any one of the machines near and in any station.

All of Munich's public transportation operates on the honor system. You must have a ticket for any conveyance you board, but you may not be asked to show it—then, again, you may. If you are apprehended without a valid ticket, you will be fined 60 DEM on the spot. The **München Welcome Card** is a great combination of city transport and sightseeing savings. Travel is free on all public transport with the card, and free or discounted entrance is offered for museums, cinemas, gardens, castles, horse-drawn carriage rides, walking and sightseeing tours. A Single Day Ticket costs 12 DEM; Single 3-Day Ticket costs 29 DEM; Partner 3-Day Ticket costs 42 DEM. The card is available at the Main Rail Station (Hauptbahnhof), Bahnhofplatz 2, the Town Hall, and at many hotels.

Sights/Attractions/Tours

Munich's heart pulsates at the Marienplatz, the city's central square. From the tower of the new town hall in the center of the Marienplatz, a glockenspiel chimes every morning at 1100 and 1200 (again in summer at 1700) and is followed by a performance of mechanical figures, including knights on horseback and a crowing rooster. You will have to see it to believe it.

Dallmayr's delicatessen is nearby. Facing the glockenspiel, walk around the right side of the town hall to the smaller square in the rear. Dallmayr's store will then be in plain view immediately across the street to your right, at 14 Dienerstrasse. You really don't have to buy a thing—the sights and the aromas are wonderful.

Munich has a great variety of things to see and do. There are approximately 100 historic buildings, 2 castles, 200 churches, 45 art collections and museums, and 56 performing theaters—all within the city limits and most of them within reasonable walking distance from the Marienplatz. An excellent illustrated folder containing a city map showing the exact location of each of the above points of interest is published by the Munich tourist information office.

There are 14 additional places of interest, including the 1972 **Olympic Park,** identified by color-coded circles. For admirers of the brewmaster's art, the map also pinpoints 12 of Munich's most famous beer gardens. The **Hofbrauhaus** (the state-owned beer hall) is a short walk from the Marienplatz via Dallmayr's delicatessen. (It would be un-American not to stop!)

The Hofbrauhaus dates back to 1591. It is no longer operated as a brewery but beer is drayed in to be consumed daily from one-liter (one-and-three-

Train Connections to Other Base Cities from Munich

DEPART	TRAIN NUMBER	ARRIVE	NOTES
Amsterdam Centraal			
1240	ICE 794	2054	1
1340	ICE 592	2154	1
2249	D 214	0940+1	
Berlin Zoobahnhof			
0651	IC 910	1425	
1251	IC 814	2025	
1451	IC 812	2225	
1651	EC 10	0025+1	
Bern (Berne)			
0814	EC 92	1346	2
1214	EC 94	1746	2
1356	EC 166	1936	2
1814	EC 98	0031+1	2
Brussels (Bruxelles) Midi/Zuid			
0646	IC 616	1617/1623	3, 4
0846	IC 614	1806	3
1046	EC 18	2006	3
1146	IC 118	2035	3-Thalys★, R

Budapest Keleti

0924EC 63	1720	
2319D 269	0723+1	R, Sleeper

Copenhagen (København) H

0712	ICE 682	1759	5
1115	ICE 588	2159	5
1928	EN 482	0958+1	R, Sleeper
2301	ICN 1588	1359+1	R, Sleeper

Hamburg Hauptbahnhof

0547	ICE 884	1152	
0712	ICE 682	1252	
0751	ICE 882	1352	
0912	ICE 680	1452	
0951	ICE 788	1552	
1115	ICE 588	1652	
1151	ICE 786	1752	
1315	ICE 586	1852	
1515	ICE 584	2052	
1715	ICE 582	2252	
2301	ICN 1588	0756+1	R, Sleeper

Luxembourg

1046	EC 18	1850	6
1146	IC 118	1922	6

Milan (Milano) Centrale

0729	EC 81	1450	
1214	EC 94	2135	2
1329	EC 13	2050	

Nice Ville

0729	EC 81	1958	7

Paris Gare de l'Est

0746	EC 66	1623	
1349	EC 64	2222	
2100	D 260	0807+1	R, Sleeper

Rome (Roma) Termini

0729	EC 81	1925	7
0929	EC 85	1950	
2030	D 287	0815+1	R, 8, Sleeper

Vienna (Wien) Südbahnhof

0924	EC 63	1418	
1124	EC 113	1635	9
1524	EC 115	2035	9

Vienna (Wien) Südbahnhof

1624	EC 65	2118
1824	EC 17	2315
2319	269	0647+1

Zürich Hauptbahnhof

0814	EC 92	1226
1214	EC 94	1626
1356	EC 166	1826
1814	EC 98	2223

Daily, unless otherwise noted
R Reservations required
* Thalys high-speed train, supplement required
1. Change trains in Mannheim.
2. Change trains in Zürich.
3. Change trains in Cologne (Köln).
4. Train 424 arrives Brussels Midi/Zuid at 1623 Mon–Fri and at 1617 on Sat–Sun.
5. Change trains in Hamburg.
6. Change trains in Koblenz.
7. Change trains in Milan.
8. Arrives Rome Tiburtina station.
9. Change trains in Salzburg.

---

quarter-pint) mugs while bands play lively tunes, often accompanied by the singing of the drinkers. There's a full-service restaurant on the second floor, where decorum is a bit more in evidence. **Planet Hollywood** is directly across the street from the Hofbrauhaus.

If you tire of city dining, take a southbound S-1 train on the S-Bahn from the main transfer station under the Marienplatz and get off in the **Village of Aying**—about a 40-minute ride. Walk four blocks toward the church steeple to the Aying Hotel, where you'll find the best Bavarian food, beer, and atmosphere.

Those visiting Munich for the first time probably will want to take a guided tour by bus. A 4-hour leisurely paced bicycle tour is also available for 28 DEM. For information call Mike's Bike Tours. *Tel:* 651–4275.

Munich also has the finest delicatessen in the world—it's **Dallmayr's** at 14–15 Dienerstrasse (*Tel:* 213–5100) Hours: Monday–Wednesday 0930–1900; Thursday–Friday 0930–2000; Saturday 0900–1600; closed Sunday. Extravagant beyond description, it demands to be seen. If for no other reason, go to Munich to savor the sights and scents of Dallmayr's! There are a restaurant specializing in seafood and a unique gift shop on the second floor. This is not your usual "deli"; you'll find rich German chocolates, caviar, lobster, fine wines—order a gourmet lunch "to go."

Day Excursions

South to the Alps and **Garmisch**. Into the Alps to **Berchtesgaden**. Through the Alps to Austria and its beautiful cities of **Innsbruck** and **Salzburg**. North to **Nuremberg, Ulm,** or **Rothenburg** and the **Romantic Road**. For a special adventure, ascend the peak of Germany's highest mountain, the **Zugspitze**. Take your choice—and go at your leisure.

Day Excursion to

Berchtesgaden ALPS, LAKES, AND SALT MINES

Depart from Munich Hauptbahnhof

Distance by Train: 112 miles (180 km)
Average Train Time: 2 hours, 40 minutes
City Dialing Code: 4
Berchtesgaden Tourist Information (Kurdirektion), Berchtesgadener Land, Köenigsseer Strasse 2, D-83471. Opposite the railway station.
Tel: (0) 8652–9670; *Fax:* (0) 8652–967400
Internet: www.berchtesgaden.de
E-mail: info@berchtesgaden.de
Hours: June 15–October 15: Monday–Friday, 0800–1800; Saturday, 0900–1700; Sunday, 0900–1500. October 16–June 14: Monday–Friday, 0800–1700; Saturday 0800–1200; closed Sunday.

To reach the tourist information office, cross the street in front of the station at the traffic light, incline to the left, following the KÖNIGSSEE sign. The office is located in a large cream-colored building on the right-hand side.

Don't let the train time to Berchtesgaden deter you from making this day excursion. The train follows a route that passes through some of the most beautiful countryside in the world, and the tours waiting for your arrival in Berchtesgaden are simply out of this world.

After Adolf Hitler seized power in 1934, he ordered the expansion of the facilities in **Obersalzberg,** an appendage to Berchtesgaden, with the intent of making it the equivalent of a summer White House. Der Führer's dream was destroyed, however, when the greater part of Obersalzberg was demolished by an air attack on April 25, 1945.

If possible, take the early train out of Munich to have ample time to select a tour and have a relaxing lunch in one of Berchtesgaden's charming inns. Current schedules are always posted in the main hall of the station.

Berchtesgaden Mini-Bus Tours (located in the tourist office) specializes in

Munich (München)—Berchtesgaden

DEPART MÜNCHEN HBF	TRAIN NUMBER	ARRIVE FREILASSING*	DEPART FREILASSING	TRAIN NUMBER	ARRIVE1 BERCHTESGADEN
0633	RE 31001	0818	0837	RB31909	0923
0741	IR 2095	0915	0930	RB31911	1021
0833	RE31008	1018	1022	RB31913	1113
0937	IC 717	1115	1130	RB31915	1221

DEPART BERCHTESGADEN	TRAIN NUMBER	ARRIVE FREILASSING*	DEPART FREILASSING	TRAIN NUMBER	ARRIVE MÜNCHEN HBF
1347	RB31918	1438	1443	IR2190	1622
1439	RB31920	1527	1540	RE31018	1728
1547	RB31922	1638	1643	IR2098	1821
1637	RB31924	1728	1740	RE31020	1927
1747	RB31926	1838	1843	IC716	2021
1839	RB31928	1927	1940	RE31022	2127
1947	RB31930	2038	2043	IR2094	2221
2039	RB31932	2127	2140	RE31024	2327

*Change trains in Freilassing
Distance: 112 miles (180 km)

English-speaking historical tours of Berchtesgaden's sights, including the Obersalzberg and **Eagle's Nest.**

The village of Berchtesgaden has many attractions. Among them is the Folk Museum housed in the **Adelsheim Castle** (Schloss Adelsheim), where you will find displays of wood carvings and the famous Berchtesgaden wood-shaving boxes.

For one of the most spectacular scenic views in the world, take the Jennerbahn two-person cable cars to the top of Mount Jenner above **Lake Königssee** (literally translated "Royal Lake"). Start from the valley station at Lake Königssee. Your breathtaking 20-minute ascent to 1,834 meters (6,017 feet) unveils vistas of mountain summits stretching as far as the eye can see. This wondrous landscape once caused Bavarian writer Ludwig Ganghofer to cry out: "Lord, if you love anyone, then set them down in this land!"

In addition to sightseeing in Berchtesgaden and its immediate surroundings, there are many interesting guided tours that can be taken outside of the village. The most popular ones for North Americans are visits to Obersalzberg, the Salt Mines, the Königssee, the Sound of Music/Salzburg Tour, and the Eagle's Nest. All tours are available year-round with the exception of the Eagle's Nest, which is open from mid–May to mid–October.

The **Obersalzberg tour** features a visit to the former location of the Berghof, Adolf Hitler's official home and the site of many pre–World War II conferences. Included on the tour is a trip through its air-raid shelters and bunkers, which provided protection to the conferees in the event that the Allied air forces wanted to disrupt the proceedings.

The **Salt Mines** are located a few miles outside the town of Berchtesgaden. If you have chronic respiratory problems, you may sigh a breath of relief in the specially treated air of the new curative salt mine tunnel. The guided tour is a thrilling experience. In miner's protective clothing, you ride a mine train, slide down chutes, and cross over subterranean lakes. What an adventure!

The **Königssee** is considered the pearl of Berchtesgaden and provides some of the most romantic scenery in Upper Bavaria. In order to preserve the quietness of the lake and the clearness of its waters, electric boats have been the only crafts permitted to navigate there since 1909. A tour aboard an electric boat runs daily whenever the lake is ice-free. Midpoint in the cruise, the captain shuts down the motor and, in the silence of the lake, lets go with a blast on a trumpet that resounds and resounds for as many as seven times off the alpine palisades surrounding the lake.

The **Eagle's Nest** tour begins in May and is conducted daily until winter snows block its access. A bus conveys you to a height of 5,600 feet, where an elevator lifts you the final 400 feet to a never-to-be-forgotten experience. Despite the publicity gained by the Eagle's Nest's connection with Adolf Hitler, Der Führer visited there only about five times. The road running to the elevator that takes you to the summit is beyond doubt a uniquely daring feat of road building. It's a white-knuckle ride all the way. The tour itself is far less strenuous than that of the Salt Mines, but the weather is all important.

Despite its ancient facade, Berchtesgaden is actually very modern in its tourist and recreational facilities. Should its charm overcome you—as it does many—consider an overnight stay. The Berchtesgadener Land tourist information office, opposite the rail station, can assist you in finding accommodations.

For lunchtime, try the **Gasthof Neuhaus,** opposite the fountain in the town square. Its selection of *Schmankerl* (Bavarian specialties) is a treat, and its ice cream specialties will make you forget all about Baskin-Robbins.

Day Excursion to

Garmisch-Partenkirchen BAVARIA AT ITS BEST

Depart from Munich Hauptbahnhof

Distance by Train: 63 miles (101 km)
Average Train Time: 1 hour, 30 minutes
City Dialing Code: 8821
Garmisch-Partenkirchen Tourist Information, Dr.–Richard–Strauss Platz, D82467
Tel: 1806; *Fax:* 18055
Internet: www.garmisch-partenkirchen.de
Hours: 0800–1800 Monday–Saturday and 1000–1200 Sunday

Reach the information office by turning left outside the station and walking downhill about 300 yards to Bahnhof Strasse. Turn left and walk about 150 yards to Richard Strauss Platz and the Kongresshaus (Congress Hall).

Bavaria's eccentric King Ludwig II spent lavishly, admired Wagner, and went mad—though not necessarily in that order. Two of his famous castles, **Neuschwanstein** and **Linderhof,** can be visited on tours from Garmisch-Partenkirchen, as well as the village of **Oberammergau** (home of the Passion Play) and the **Zugspitze,** Germany's highest mountain.

Tourism started in the area with the building of a railroad between Munich and Garmisch-Partenkirchen in 1889. Prior to that time, the area waned or prospered according to who was in town. The Romans occupied the area as far back as the first century B.C. At the beginning of the eighteenth century, the area was suppressed by the Spanish and then by the Austrians and the French. It wasn't until 1802 that the area was finally made a part of Bavaria. Because of its interest in winter sports, in 1966 the twin-city of Garmisch-Partenkirchen became the sister city of Aspen, Colorado, ski capital of the United States.

The U.S. Armed Forces maintain a recreation center in Garmisch and also conduct tours in the area. Tour participation, however, is limited to U.S. military personnel, their dependents, and retirees. Payment for these tours must be in U.S. dollars. If you qualify, to reach the recreation center, follow the ZUGSPITZBAHN signs to the cog railway station, where the U.S. facilities will be in plain view and just ahead.

ABR, a German tour agency, offers a wide selection of tours in the Garmisch-Partenkirchen area, including tours of King Ludwig's **Neuschwanstein Castle** and his **Linderhof Castle.** The ABR agency is immediately adjacent to the Garmisch-Partenkirchen rail station.

Proceed to track No. 1 by turning to the left at the bottom of the stairs leading from the arriving train platform. ABR is visible from the rail station lobby. Most tours are conducted daily.

Munich—Garmisch-Partenkirchen

DEPART MUNICH HBF	TRAIN NUMBER	ARRIVE GARMISCH
0800	RB 5407	0921
0900	RB 5409	1023
1000	RB 5411	1121
1100	RB 5413	1223
1200	RB 5415	1321

Zugspitze trains depart Garmisch thirty-five minutes past the hour from 0835 to 1435.

DEPART GARMISCH	TRAIN NUMBER	ARRIVE MUNICH HBF
1532	RB 5424	1653
1631	RB 5426	1754
1731	RB 5428	1854
1831	RB 5430	1955
1931	RB 5432	2052
2029	RB 5434	2153

Zugspitze trains arrive at Garmisch hourly from 1000 to 1600.
Depart Garmisch hourly 0835 to 1435 (80-minute journey; last train back at 1600).
All trains are daily, including holidays
Distance: 63 miles/101 km

Garmisch-Partenkirchen (actually two villages that united in 1935) hosted the 1936 Winter Olympics and the World Alpine-Ski Championship in 1978. Just visiting the Olympic facilities can consume an entire day. A downtown shopping spree can do the same, but with more injury to pocketbooks. In wintertime, the Winter Olympics ski jump provides spills and chills, and the Olympic Ice Stadium is open year-round.

The alpine ski runs extend 68 miles in length, and there are 93 miles of tracks for the growing sport of cross-country skiing. Two of the most popular alpine cable-car runs in summer are the **Eibsee-Zugspitze** system (9,678 feet) and the **Wank Bahn,** which takes you to the promontory of the Wank Alp (5,874 feet). There are others as well. One that is particularly convenient starts at the Olympic Ski Stadium on the fringe of Garmisch-Partenkirchen and scales the Eckbauer Alp to a height of 4,127 feet. From any of these points on a clear day, the view is extraordinary.

The **Zugspitze** is the highest mountain in Germany—9,718 feet, to be exact. A cog railway was completed in 1931 to the Zugspitzplatt, along with a cable car that scaled the last 2,000 feet to the top. Another cable car running from Eibsee, a station stop on the cog railway at the 3,500-foot level, was placed in operation during 1963. This system lifts passengers directly to the peak in a spectacular ten-minute ride.

These two systems make a circuitous routing possible—up one way and down another. The round-trip fare from Garmisch is 75 DEM (only 56 DEM for railpass holders). The ticket entitles you to ride on any part of the total system. When you arrive in the Garmisch-Partenkirchen station, walk about 100 yards to your right to the cog-railway station. The cog railway stops in Eibsee about 30 minutes after departing Garmisch. Transfer at this point to the Eibsee cable car.

The cable-car trip from Eibsee to the top of the Zugspitze takes about 10 breathtaking minutes. If you are in a hurry to return to Garmisch, you could retrace your trip by returning to Eibsee on the cable car, but we recommend that you proceed to the **Sonn Alpine Glacier Restaurant** via the "Gipfelbahn" cable car. At the Sonn Alpine, you join up with the cog railway, which terminates there in a huge vaulted hall blasted out of solid rock. Trains depart on the hour, and the trip back to Garmisch takes 1 hour and 10 minutes.

Day Excursion to

Innsbruck, Austria JEWEL OF THE ALPS

Depart from Munich Hauptbahnhof or Ostbahnhof

Distance by Train: 107 miles (172 km)
Average Train Time: 1 hour, 53 minutes
Austria Country Dialing Code: 43
City Dialing Code: 512
Innsbruck Tourist Information: Burggraben 3, A-6021
Tel: (0512) 59850; *Fax:* (0512) 598507
Internet: www.tiscover.com/innsbruck
E-mail: info@innsbruck.tvb.co.at
Hours: Monday–Friday, 0800–1800; Saturday, 0800–1200

Tourist information is available in the rail station at the "Hotel Information Office," which you can find by leaving the main station hall by the exit on the left-hand side and proceeding past the "Checked Baggage" area.

Munich (München)—Innsbruck

Note: There are two routes between Munich and Innsbruck; one is very scenic as it passes through/over the Bavarian Alps and the other is a less scenic lowland (valley) route.

Scenic Route

DEPART MUNICH HBF	ARRIVE INNSBRUCK	DEPART INNSBRUCK	TRAIN NUMBER	ARRIVE MUNICH HBF
0700	0947	1551	RB 5428	1854
0800	1058	1658	RB 5430	1955
1100	1357	1901	RB 5434	2153

Valley Route

DEPART MUNICH HBF	ARRIVE INNSBRUCK	DEPART INNSBRUCK	TRAIN NUMBER	ARRIVE MUNICH HBF
0729	0922	1437	EC 12	1630
0929	1122	1637	EC 84	1830
1129	1322	1837	EC 86	2030
1329	1522	2037	EC 80	2230

Daily, unless otherwise noted
Distance: 107 miles (172 km)

Theatrically surrounded by its mountains, Innsbruck is the cultural and tourist capital of the Austrian Tyrol. There is an exhilarating mountain view from nearly every street corner and every window in town. Looking northward from its main street, **Maria–Theresien Strasse,** you will confront the towering Alps, which seem to encroach upon the city. The scene is breathtaking. (American kids say it's "awesome!")

This day excursion from Munich to Innsbruck offers an opportunity to explore the **Tyrolean Alps** in the comfort of a cable car—plus a visit to one of the most picturesque "old towns" in Austria. To top it off, a circuitous return on the Mittenwald railroad is possible; it takes you on a fantastically scenic rail route straight through the heart of the Austrian and Bavarian Alps en route back to Munich via Garmisch-Partenkirchen.

You are in for an eye-filling day. Even the regular rail line running out of Munich is loaded with Alpine scenery. Take a seat on the right side of your coach outbound from Munich for the best views.

When you arrive in Innsbruck, you will note that train information is posted throughout the main station, and a train information office is immediately to the right of the exit from the trains.

Most of the shops and restaurants in Innsbruck accept German currency. If you want to change money into Austrian schillings, however, you may do so at a change booth located at your far left just as you exit from the trains. The **exchange office** hours are 0730–2000 daily. The local tourist-office branch office, also located in the station, is an official exchange, too.

Purchase a large guide map at the tourist office if you plan a walking tour of the city. Bus tours of the city are available throughout the year. Biking tours are a great way to see Innsbruck, too.

If you decide to become your own tour guide, check the map, then head west for a few blocks to Innsbruck's Arc de Triumph. From this point, turn north and wend your way slowly through the **Altstadt** (Old Town), which lines both sides of the street all the way to the **Goldenes Dachl** (Golden Roof) at the end of Herzog-Friedrich Strasse. It may come as a mild disappointment, but the so-called Golden Roof is actually made of heavy, gilded copper.

Eat lunch in the **Goldener Adler** (Golden Eagle), the oldest inn in the city. It was founded in 1390! It is around the corner on the left and can best be described as a delicious experience. If you go there for dinner, enjoy the Tyrolean music in the cellar restaurant. It will complete a perfect evening.

Mountain scaling via cable car? Railpass holders get a 20 percent reduction on the following private lines: Seegrube, Hafelekar, Patscherkofel, and Mutterer Alm. The Seegrube (6,287 feet) and the Hafelekar (7,700 feet) await your conquest, and scaling them by cable car makes mountaineering a sport for all ages.

Ready for that fantastic train trip back to Munich? Board the Express 5430, which *usually* departs from track 12-B in the Innsbruck Station at 1658 and returns to Munich via Mittenwald and Garmisch daily at 1955. (Check in the station for the proper departure platform.)

You start by crossing the Inn River, then the train begins climbing the steep valley walls that skirt the Inn. Approaching the Alpine station of **Hochzirl,** you will have a sheer, 1,500-foot vertical view of the river and the green valley through which it runs. Select train seats on the left-hand side for the best opportunity of seeing these sights.

Later, the train will stop in **Seefeld,** a delightful Alpine community, before continuing on to **Mittenwald** and Garmisch, where the Express 5430 cars are switched to another Munich train.

Day Excursion to

Nuremberg (Nürnberg)

BEER, GINGERBREAD, AND TOYS

Depart from Munich Hauptbahnhof or Pasing

Distance by Train: 125 miles (201 km)
Average Train Time: 1 hour, 36 minutes
City Dialing Code: 911
Nuremberg Tourist Information: Congress und Tourismus Zentrale, Frauentorgraben 3,
D-90443.
Tel: 233–6117; *Fax:* 233–6166
Internet: www.nuernberg.de
e-mail: tourismus@nuernberg.btl.de
Hours: Summer hours: 0900–1900 Monday–Saturday; 1000–1300/1400–1600 Sunday.
Winter hours: 0900–1900 Monday–Saturday; closed Sunday from October to April
(except during Christmas Market).
   Tourist information is in front of the main railway station.

   Although Nuremberg (Nürnberg) celebrates its 950th anniversary this
year, it is a lively modern city. A mecca for lovers of markets, music, and
museums, Nuremberg must have originated the "Day Excursion"!
   On December 7, 1835, the first German train chugged its way from
Nuremberg to Furth, a neighboring city, with honored guests *and* two barrels
of beer. But on this day excursion ICE trains average 76 miles per hour
between Munich and Nuremberg—considerably faster than in 1835—and
Nuremberg's brew is every bit the match for Munich's, for Nuremberg is a
part of Bavaria, too. Get ready for an enjoyable day out.
   When you arrive in Nuremberg, you will find the tourist office in front of
the railway station. Another tourist information office is on the main market
square at Hauptmarkt 18.
   Conducted tours of the city from May to October and in the Christmas
season depart daily at 1300. Individual tours may be arranged at any time; one
of the Tourist Board's experienced city guides will serve as escort *Tel:*
233–6123. Or put your own tour together with the **Nuremberg Cultour
Ticket**, available at the tourist office. This 2-day ticket offers entrance to
many museums and sites. If you decide to stay over, hotel guests get free public transport in Nuremberg, Fürth, and Stein with the card as well. Ask about
the Welcome Pack at the tourist office if you do book a hotel. You'll be in for
a nice surprise.
   Train schedules, posted in several prominent locations in the station, will
confirm the departure time and track location of your return train to
Munich, no matter how long you decide to stay.

Munich (München)—Nuremburg (Nürnberg)

DEPART MUNICH HBF	TRAIN NUMBER	ARRIVE NUREMBERG HBF
0751	ICE 882	0932
0834	IR 2882	1028
0838	RE 4604	1110
0851	IC 818	1032
0951	ICE 788	1132
1038	RE 4608	1310
1051	IC 816	1232
1151	ICE 786	1332
1234	IC 724	1427

DEPART NUREMBERG HBF	TRAIN NUMBER	ARRIVE MUNICH HBF	NOTES
1426	ICE 787	1606	
1526	IC 815	1710	
1626	ICE 789	1806	
1648	RE 4621	1914	
1726	IC 817	1907	
1731	IC 727	1928	daily except Sat
1826	ICE 881	2006	
1848	RE 4625	2114	
1926	IC 819	2107	
2026	ICE 883	2206	
2126	IC 911	2307	
2226	ICE 885	0006+1	

Daily, unless otherwise noted
Distance: 125 miles (201 km)

One of the main gates of the old walled city of Nuremberg, the **Kingsgate**, is directly across from the railway station. Picking up Königstrasse (King Street) at this point, you can follow it to the heart of the old walled area known as the Hauptmarkt (Central Market). Plan to be there at noon; a mechanical clock will entertain you at the stroke of twelve with its seven electors paying homage to the emperor. Now let's look for a nearby pub . . . shouldn't be too hard, as they seem to be everywhere.

What goes better with beer than an authentic "Three in One"? Famous for their sausages, these Nuremberg minnies may only be as big as your little finger, but they are spicy—and famous across Germany. Now, about that beer . . .

Connoisseurs of the brewer's art won't want to miss a visit to Nuremberg's **Museum Brewery** and **Medieval Cellars.** The museum is really the Altstadthof brewery, who's motto, "Beer like our Forefathers," is observed today by the use of only the finest materials and brewing methods, which date from the nineteenth century. The cellars, going down 85 feet through solid rock, form a labyrinth of tunnels dug in the fourteenth century for the storage of beer. A guided tour is available.

Nuremberg offers not only beer, but gingerbread and toys as well. The aroma of Nuremberg's special gingerbread, *Lebkuchen*, fills the Hauptmarkt every Christmas. At other times, including the pre-Christmas period (which starts in mid-August), the same aroma may be savored—and tasted—in the many pastry shops throughout the city. The traditional recipes of the original gingerbread are kept secret by the bakeries that produce it. Companies such as Lebkuchen Schmidt invite visitors to sample their products. Arrangements may be made by either of the tourist offices. Trying to save purchases can be tempting. To avoid teasing your tastebuds and have gifts for those left behind, we suggest having the bakery shop ship some home for you.

Toy shops are in profusion, and the **Toy Museum on Karl Street,** two blocks from the Hauptmarkt via Augustinerstrasse, has a splendid display of dolls, puppets, and tin soldiers. The museum also houses an interesting model-railway layout, featuring—of all things—the train station in Omaha, Nebraska.

Nuremberg's most famous citizen was Albrecht Dürer, a man who towered above his time. The stately home in which he lived, from 1509 until his death in 1529, is located two blocks north of the Toy Museum, past the Wine Market, on Albrecht Dürer Strasse. The house holds a collection of the famed artist's works. The area surrounding it is probably the most interesting section within the walled city. Unfortunately, Dürer's most famous work, *The Four Apostles*, now rests in Munich, but a number of his paintings are exhibited. A multilingual film presentation on his life and works, plus an acoustic tour are offered and narrated by Agnes Dürer. The New Museum features exhibits showing free form, applied arts, and modern design.

If you have any doubt about that first day excursion by train originating in Nuremberg, check in at the **Verkehrsmuseum (Transportation Museum),** three blocks to the right of the train station as you face it. The museum is open 0900–1700 Tuesday–Sunday. There you will find the *Adler* (Eagle), the first German locomotive, complete with the two beer barrels mounted on its tender.

If you are a model-railroad fan, you will be pleased to note that, in addition to the Toy Museum, two of Germany's largest manufacturers of HO- and N-gauge equipment, **Arnold and Fleischmann,** are located in Nuremberg. **E. P. Lehmann,** the manufacturer of G-scale equipment for the increasingly popular outdoor garden railways, is located at Sagnerstrasse 1–5 (*Tel:* 83 40

21). They have operating layouts, and visitors are welcome. The operating hours are seasonal, so check with one of the tourist information offices if you would like to visit.

Day Excursion to

The Romantic Road   DELIGHTFULLY MEDIEVAL

Depart from Munich Hauptbahnhof

Distance by Bus: 172 miles (276 km) and by Train: 173 miles (278 km)
Total Journey Time: 12 hours, 36 minutes
City Dialing Code for Rothenburg ob der Tauber: 9851
Rothenburg Tourist Information: Rothenburg o.d.T. Tourist Office, Markplatz 2, D-91541
Tel: 40492; *Fax:* 8 68 07
Internet: www.rothenburg.de
E-mail: info@rothenburg.de
The Romantic Road, Deutsche Touring GmbH, Am Romerhof 17, 60486 Frankfurt/Main
Tel: 69790–3256;   *Fax:* 69790–3219

Too long and too far? Not in the least. **The Romantic Road**, packed with superb scenery and delightful medieval villages, is worth every minute. The Deutsche Bahn (German Railroad) bus that takes you from Munich to **Würzburg** makes two stops en route: one in **Dinkelsbühl** for lunch and one in **Rothenburg** for sightseeing. After these pleasant interludes, plus a return trip to Munich on one of Germany's lightning-fast InterCity Express trains, you will wonder where the day has gone.

The Romantic Road bus carries an English-speaking guide. This trip has become so popular that seat reservations are necessary. Reservations can be made at the EurAide, Inc. office in the Munich railway station opposite track No. 11 in the main hall, three doors down from the line of four telephone booths. The office is open 0800–1600 Monday–Friday (*Tel:* 089 59 38 89). Seat reservations are 10 DEM, and the Eurailpass, Europass, and GermanRail Pass are accepted.

The Romantic Road bus has no special markings. Ask for its departure position (which is usually No. 20/21) when you make reservations. Your reservation ensures you a seat on the bus, but not a specified seat. Be at the bus station at about 0830, therefore, to ensure getting a window seat.

Rothenburg is one of the most frequently visited places in Germany. Every year thousands of visitors from all parts of the world come to this ancient walled city. You will see why Rothenburg is picturesque and photogenic. Be

Munich (München)—The Romantic Road

Romantic Road excursion by bus from München to Dinkelsbühl to Rothenburg ob der Tauber to Würzburg; return to München by train.

Schedule shown is valid from April 1 to October 27, 2000, but subject to change without notice.

BUS TRIP 190:

Depart München Hbf (near platforms 27–36)	0900
Arrive Dinkelsbühl	1245
Depart Dinkelsbühl	1400
Arrive Rothenburg ob der Tauber	1440
Depart Rothenburg ob der Tauber	1615
Arrive Würzburg Hbf	1830

DEPART WÜRZBURG HBF	TRAIN NUMBER	ARRIVE MUNICH HBF
1927	ICE 883	2206
2024	ICE 683	2246
2127	ICE 885	0006+1 (daily except Sat)

Distance: 172 miles (276 km) by bus, plus 173 miles (278 km) by train

For detailed information and registration, contact:
EurAide, Inc.
München Hauptbahnhof
Bahnhofplatz 2
D-80335 München Germany
Tel (089) 59 39 89
Fax (089) 550 3965
E-mail: euraide@compuserve.com

Note: Eurailpasses, Europasses, and GermanRail passes are valid for this excursion. Registration fee 10 DM. Credit cards accepted.

sure to take a camera. Probably more photographs have been taken of its **Kobolzeller Tor** and **Siebers Tower** than of any other scene in Germany.

The town is a museum piece of medieval character. Most of its 12,500 citizens living within or just outside the city's walls work to serve the tourist in some manner. This town has survived, even in the twentieth century, as the "Jewel of the Middle Ages."

Enjoy your visit in Rothenburg but keep your eye on the town clock, for the Romantic Road bus continues on its journey to Würzburg and its final destination, **Frankfurt,** promptly at 1615. If for some reason you do miss the 1615 bus departure, the German railroad also operates another bus line between Rothenburg and Steinach, where you can connect with train service back to Munich.

Arriving in Würzburg at 1830, you have the early opportunity of returning to Munich at 2206 aboard ICE 883; or, you might want to have dinner and linger as late as 2127, when the ICE 885 speeds back to Munich. The later departure would allow you to stay in Würzburg for several hours. There are several restaurants immediately across from the park fronting the east side of the Würzburg rail station where you could enjoy dinner.

Rothenburg is loaded with living legends. One concerns the salvation of the town from certain destruction by its wine-drinking mayor. In 1631, during the Thirty Years' War, the town was captured by imperial troops under the command of General Tilly. While the general toyed with the idea of destroying the town and executing its councilors, he was handed a tankard holding more than three quarts of heavy Franconian wine to aid his meditation.

The general promised mercy to Rothenburg if one of its councilors could drain the "bumper" in one mighty draft. Mayor Nusch did and thus saved the town. Although he slept for three days and nights following the mighty quaff, apparently he suffered no other effects, for he lived another 37 years and died at the age of 80—with a smile on his face. The historic deed is reenacted daily by a glockenspiel installed in the gable of the Councilors' Tavern at 1100, 1200, 1300, 1400, 1500, 2000, 2100, and 2200. Be there!

Day Excursion to

Ulm WORLD'S TALLEST CATHEDRAL

Depart from Munich Hauptbahnhof

Distance by Train: 92 miles (148 km)
Average Train Time: 1 hour, 13 minutes
City Dialing Code: 731
Ulm Tourist Information: Ulm/Neu-Ulm Tourismus Zentrale, Neue Strasse 45, D-89073. In the Stadthaus at Münsterplatz.
Tel: (0731) 161–2830; *Fax:* (0731) 161–1641
Internet: www.ulm.de
E-mail: unt@tourismus.ulm.de
Hours: 0900–1800 Monday–Friday; 0900–1300 Saturday; and 1100–1400 Sunday (May–October)

A display of tourist information is in the railway station to your left upon entering the station from the train platforms.

Silhouetted against a blue sky, the Gothic spire of the **Ulm Cathedral** is a scene you are not likely to forget. Poised on the banks of the swift-moving Danube, Ulm is a picturesque representation of a typical Swabian city. Birthplace of Albert Einstein, Ulm has withstood the onslaughts of many conflicts, including Napoleonic campaigns, with great dignity. Considered a miracle, its cathedral escaped damage throughout World War II, although serious damage was inflicted on the town by Allied bombing. All of Ulm's original façades have now been repaired or replaced.

With a skyward thrust of 528 feet, the spire of the cathedral is the tallest in the world. Although the foundation stone was laid in 1377, the two towers and the spire were not completed until 1890. When the central nave was completed in 1471, it could hold 20,000 people—twice as many as the town's population at that time. Truly, this was an ambitious undertaking right from the start.

The clear vertical lines and the lightness of the cathedral's architecture are beautiful. The interior is open 0900–1700 daily with extended summer hours, except when services are being conducted. There is no entrance fee, but there is a small admission charge to ascend the spire.

Speaking of the spire, a breathtaking panorama of Ulm, the Danube, and the surrounding area rewards those who climb its 768 steps. A word of caution—the climb is rigorous and should not be attempted unless you have good physical stamina. Back on the Münster square in front of the cathedral, you will notice the remarkable contrast of the old Gothic style and the contemporary architecture of the **Stadthaus** (Town House), built by Richard Meier in 1993. This modern building offers a variety of activities, including exhibitions, concerts, conferences, and tourist information, plus magnificent views of the Cathedral.

You will get a brief view of the Danube and the cathedral when crossing the railroad bridge entering Ulm. Watch on the right-hand side of the train immediately after passing the Neu-Ulm (New Ulm) station. The railroad bridge has a pedestrian crossing, so you may want to return to that vantage point again for a more prolonged observation. The bridge can be reached after leaving the station by walking to the right to an intersection where the trolleys swing farther right down an underpass. Continue straight ahead, not turning with the trolleys, on the promenade to the river's edge and the approach to the bridge. Cross onto the bridge to stand on the federal state borderline separating Bavaria and Baden-Württenberg right over the middle of the Danube.

Another route to the Danube is through the *Fischerviertel* (Fishermen's Quarter), which lies to the south of the cathedral. En route, you will pass the picturesque *Schiefes Haus* (Crooked House), which has settled over a canal.

Munich (München)–Ulm

DEPART MUNICH HBF	TRAIN NUMBER	ARRIVE ULM HBF
0736	ICE 598	0851
0746	EC 66	0903
0827	IR 2198	0944
0836	ICE 798	0949
0846	IC 614	1003
0936	ICE 596	1049
1026	IR 2196	1144
1040	ICE 796	1149
1046	EC 18	1203
1140	ICE 594	1249
1146	IC 118	1303

DEPART ULM HBF	TRAIN NUMBER	ARRIVE MUNICH HBF
1408	ICE 793	1519
1455	EC 65	1611
1508	ICE 593	1618
1608	ICE 795	1720
1611	IR 2199	1729
1655	IC 613	1811
1708	ICE 595	1819
1808	ICE 797	1921
1811	IR 2291	1929
1855	IC 615	2011

and continuing frequent service until 2208

Daily, unless otherwise noted
Distance: 92 miles (148 km)

If you walk downstream on the Danube's left bank, the river promenade will bring you to the **Metzgerturm** (Butcher's Tower), another Ulm landmark. Have a walk on the ancient city wall and see the old traditional Ulm river boat—the so-called *Ulmer Schachtel*—on the other bank of the Danube. If you plan on being in the area during July, do not miss the highlight event of Ulm, the **International Danube Festival** (July 8–15, 2000).

Walking to the city center from the Metzgerturm, you'll reach the **Rathaus** (Town Hall) from 1370, famous for its opulent frescoes and ornamental carved figures. On the east gable is a beautiful astronomer's clock (1520).

Visit the **Ulm Museum,** where you will find displays of art and culture ranging from the Middle Ages to modern times. Notable features are the collections of modern graphics and important examples of Late Gothic. There are also exhibits concerning some of Ulm's famous citizens, such as the physicist Albert Einstein and Albrecht Berblinger, the "tailor of Ulm," who in 1811 made man's first serious attempt to fly. A model of his hang glider is on exhibit in the covered courtyard of the Rathaus (Town Hall). A short visit merits the funny Einstein Fountain in front of the former Imperial city's arsenal ("Zeughaus") at the east of the old city center.

Although the cathedral dominates the scene, a stroll through Ulm will reveal its other aspects—exclusive shops, boutiques, and department stores. And for refreshment in between times, you will find traditional old taverns, pleasant restaurants, comfortable inns, and good hotels where you may enjoy Swabian specialty dishes accompanied by drafts of good Ulm beer.

Unique in the field of museums is Ulm's **German Bread Museum,** (Salzstadelgasse 10, D-89073 Ulm; *Tel:* 69955; *Fax:* 6021161) situated in the beautifully restored salt warehouse from 1592. It presents an impressive display of the major ingredient of our daily diet for the last 8,000 years. The museum is open 1000–1700 daily except Monday. It's only a 10 minute walk from the rail station. Not only does the museum effectively tell the story of breadmaking, it makes you aware of how serious hunger can be.

Very remarkable and to be noticed everywhere in Ulm and Neu-Ulm are the buildings and installations of the former Federal Fortification Ulm ("Bundesfestung"). Important landmarks of Europe's largest remaining nineteenth-century fortifications are the **Citadel Wilhelmsburg** on the "Michelsberg"—from where you have a splendid view of the city— Blaubeuren Gate or the "Glacis" bastion, now Neu-Ulm's municipal park.

Ulm University offers a unique Path of Art. More than 60 large works by artists of repute such as Niki de Saint-Phalle or Max Bill are presented along a 1.5-kilometer tour around the university and Science Park Ulm. To get there, take bus line 3 or 5 from the central station to James-Franck-Ring.

Wiblingen Monastery (founded in honor of St. Martin in 1093), with its Baroque basilica and splendid Rococo library, is only 5 kilometers away (bus line 9 from Rathaus [Town Hall] to Pranger). The famous library is open 1000–1200 and 1400–1700 except Monday (April to October). Church visit is free, but there is an admission charge for the library.

With so much to see and do the **Ulm Card** may be just the ticket for your visit. The card costs 9 DEM per person or 19 DEM per family. Prices include transport on buses and trams, benefits, and reduced prices for sites, eateries and a map of Ulm and Neu Ulm. The Ulm Card is available at the tourist office, along with the year's schedule of events. Highlights will include the International Danube Festival in July and the Ulm Christmas Fair from November 27–December 21.

Greece

Inasmuch as Greece is most famous for its archaeological finds and its significance in antiquity, many visitors to Greece are astounded to learn that this scenic, sun-drenched country also includes about 1,400 islands and more than 7,500 caves, many of which contain subterranean rivers, lakes, and waterfalls. Complementing this varied geographic wonder are the mountain ranges such as the Pindus and, of course, the waters of the Mediterranean, the Aegean, and the Saronic Gulf linking Attica (Athens area and its port Piraeus) to the Peloponnese.

CHAT Tours, a leading tour operator in Greece for more than 44 years, offers many delightful sightseeing tours and cruises to the Greek islands. The tour campus is located at 4, Stadiou Street, Athens, Greece (*Tel:* 323 0827, 322 2886, or 322 3137; *Fax:* 323 5270 or 323 1200).

For tourist information, contact the Hellenic Tourism Organization in North America:

New York: 645 Fifth Avenue, Olympic Tower, 5th Floor, New York, NY 10022. *Tel:* (212) 421–5777; *Fax:* (212) 826–6940; *Internet:* **www.gogreece.com** or **www.gnto.gr;** *E-mail:* gnto@greektourism.com or gnto@orama.com

Toronto: 1300 Bay Street, Upper Level, Toronto, Ontario M5R 3K8. *Tel:* (416) 968–2220; *Fax:* (416) 968–6533; *Internet:* **www.gogreece.com** or **www.aei.ca/~gntom;** *E-mail:* grnto.tor@sympatico.ca

Banking

- **Currency:** Greek Drachma (GRD)
- **Exchange rate at press time:** 306.35 GRD = $1.00 U.S.
- **Hours:** 0800–1400 Monday–Thursday; 0800–1300 Friday

Communications

- **Country Code:** 30
  Direct dial: AT&T: 00–800–1311; MCI: 00–800–1211; Sprint: 00–800–1411. Phone Cards may be purchased at most kiosks and Greek Telecommunications offices: 1,000 GRD for 100 units; also available for 500 and 1,000 units. All calls charged by units.

Public red phones operated with a 10-GRD coin and gray phones at kiosks are metered for long-distance calls. Pay the kiosk owner for number of units charged.

Rail Travel in Greece

The rail system of Greece is limited and presents a challenge to rail travelers. The trains can be too few and too slow. With a little perseverance, however, traveling by train in Greece can be charming, especially on overnight trains in first-class sleepers.

The line from Athens to Thessaloniki in the north has been modernized, but it still takes 5 hours, 40 minutes on the Greek Railways Organization (OSE) standard-gauge InterCity train *Hermes Express*. Narrow-gauge lines serve the Peloponnese, the southernmost part of Greece. Both networks serve Athens.

The OSE accepts a variety of multicountry railpasses, including **Eurailpass, Europass** (with purchase of the Greece add-on), the **Balkan Flexipass,** and the national railpass—the **Greek Flexipass,** for travel solely within Greece. (See the Appendix for prices and types of multicountry rail passes.)

Greek Flexipass
Provides unlimited first-class rail travel for any 3 or any 5 days within a 1-month period.

FIRST CLASS	ADULT	CHILD	YOUTH
3 days/1 month	$86	$58	$62
4 days/1 month	$110	$74	—
5 days/1 month	$120	$85	$89
6 days/1 month	$144	$101	—
Children age 2–11; under age 2 travels free. Youth age 12–25			

Greece to Italy via Ferry—Crossing the Mediterranean

The Eurailpass and Europass (with purchase of the Greece option) provide free deck passage on either **Hellenic Mediterranean Lines** (Greece) or **Adriatica Lines** (Italy) ferry crossing between Brindisi, Italy, and Patras, Greece. Some ships also stop at Corfu and Igoumenitsa—check with the Hellenic Mediterranean Lines office in Italy or in Greece or visit www.hml.it.

Having either type of railpass is quite a bargain considering that deck space for the crossing is about $110 U.S. first class, $90 second, plus there is a high-season surcharge (even for railpass holders) from June 1 to September 30 of $15. Cabins or reclining-type chairs do cost extra.

Patras–Brindisi Ferry Service

Ferry services between Brindisi and Patras are operated by three ferry companies:

1. **Adriatica di Navigazione S.p.a.**
   Zattere 1411
   30123 Venezia, Italy
   Phone: 39 41 781611
   Fax: 39 41 781894
2. **Hellenic Mediterranean Lines**
   HSAP Building
   P.O. Box 80057
   GR–185 10 Piraeus, Greece
   Phone: 30 1 4225341
   Fax: 30 1 4225317
   Internet: www.hml.it/indexen.htm
3. **Med Link Lines**
   49 Corso Garibaldi Str.
   72100 Brindisi, Italy
   Phone: 39 831 527 667
   Fax: 39 831 564 070

Sample schedules shown here are for Adriatica and Hellenic Mediterranean Lines (Eurailpasses are valid for deck passage on these ferries; Europass provides a discount—for details and fares, etc. contact the ferry company directly).

A. Adriatica

a. Depart Patras at 1900 and arrive Brindisi at 0900 the next day non-stop; sailings are on even dates from June 22–July 30 and Sept 2-20, and on uneven dates from Aug 1-31.

b. Depart Patras at 2200 and arrive Brindisi at 1700 the next day; stops at Igoumenitsa and Corfu; sails on even dates in Apr, May, Aug and on uneven dates Mar 11-31, June, July, Sept, and Oct, and on W, F, and Su from Nov 1–Dec 30, 1998.

c. Depart Brindisi at 2000 and arrive Patras at 1100 the next day non-stop; sails on uneven dates from June 21-July 31 and Sept 1-19, and on even dates from Aug 2-30.

d. Depart Brindisi at 2230 and arrive Patras at 1800 the next day; stops at Corfu and Igoumenitsa; sails on Mar 3,5,7 and on uneven dates in Apr, May, and Aug, and on even dates from Mar 10-30, June, July, Sept, and Oct, and on Tu, Th, and Sa from Nov 3-Dec 31, and on Oct 31.

B. Hellenic Mediterranean Lines

a. Depart Patras at 2200 and arrive Brindisi at 1330 the next day; sails on uneven dates from June 25–July 13 and daily from July 15 to Sept 6.

b. Depart Patras at 2200 and arrive Brindisi at 1530 the next day; sails on uneven dates in May and on even dates in June, from July 2-16, and from Sept 8-26.

c. Depart Brindisi at 1930 and arrive Patras at 1530 the next day; sails June 26, 28, and 30, July 2,4,6,10, and 12.

d. Depart Brindisi at 1900 and arrive Patras at 1300 the next day; sails Sept 6 and 7.

e. Depart Brindisi at 1930 and arrive Patras at 1700 the next day; sails on even dates from July 14-30, and on uneven dates from Aug 1-31, and on July 8, Sept 2 and 4.

f. Depart Brindisi at 2230 and arrive at Patras at 1730 the next day; sails on even dates in May, Aug, and on uneven dates in June, July, and Sept (but not Sept 29).

Advance reservations are recommended, especially during June through September, and they can be made through Hellenic Mediterranean Lines' agents online at **www.hml.it/indexen.htm.**

Arrivals and departures are shown in local times and are subject to cancellation or alteration without notice. Days of operation vary. Check with the Adriatica and Hellenic offices mentioned previously for other services between Corfu or Igoumenitsa and Brindisi.

To reach the **Patras Ferry Terminal** (*Tel:* 42 95 20 or 42 16 14) from the Patras rail station, turn left as you exit the station. Walk along the street side of the quay about 300 yards to the office marked CENTRAL AGENCY. Summer hours are 0900–2200 daily. Winter hours are 0900–1300 and 1700–2200. You report to the terminal on the day of embarkation only. No baggage checking is available. From mid-June to September, bus transportation is available between Patras and Athens or vice versa for about $15 (U.S.). For further information on ferries visit www.greekferries.com.

Base City . . .

Athens (Athinai)

City Dialing Code: 1

Arriving by Air

Athens Hellinikon Airport, East Terminal, *Tel:* 969 4111; West Terminal (or Olympic Terminal), *Tel:* 966 6666. Located 9 kilometers from Athens.

Airport–City Links: Express buses run between the airport and Syntagma (Constitution) Square at a fare of 250 GRD and a journey time of about 30 minutes. Express Bus No. 091 runs to/from Syntagma and Omonia Squares to/from the West Terminal and Bus No. 092 runs to/from the East Terminal to/from Omonia Square. Yellow, metered taxis are available opposite the arrivals exit at the East Terminal and outside the international arrivals exit at the West Terminal. Taxi journey time is about 20 minutes and cost is 2,000–2,500 GRD.

Money exchange: Branches of the National Bank of Greece, the Commercial Bank of Greece, and the Agricultural Bank in both terminals remain open until late in the evening every day.

Tourist information: in the arrivals hall of the East Terminal, *Tel:* 969 –500.

If you are departing Athens by air, the airport's tax-free shopping area offers a wide selection of Greek wearing apparel, liquors, and delicacies. Unlike many tax-free shopping facilities, the one in Athens' airport has some reasonable values, but you can't bargain with the salespeople—leave that for shopping in the city.

Arriving by Train

Arrivals from Eastern European countries and points in northern Greece terminate in Athens' Larissa Station, a standard-gauge facility. If you are traveling with a Eurailpass via the Adriatica Lines or Hellenic Mediterranean Lines ferries to the port of Patras, the Peloponnese Station (narrow gauge) will be your arrival point. The two stations lie parallel to each other, with a connecting, overhead footbridge. Each has a train-information booth with a limited amount of city information available.

Both stations have taxi stands and bus service, but we recommend that new arrivals use the taxi. The taxi fare from the station area to the tourist office on

Syntagma (Constitution) Square is inexpensive, about 500 GRD plus baggage charges, and well worth it.

Larissa Station serves the standard-gauge rail lines to the north.

Money exchange at the north end of the train platform. The sign reads BANK. Hours: 0800–1830 Monday–Friday; 0900–1400 Saturday; 0900–1300 Sunday.

Train information is in a booth to your immediate left when entering the station from the train platform area. Open daily, 0600–2330. *Tel.* 823–7741.

Baggage storage in room marked LEFT BAGGAGE OFFICE located to the left as you enter the station from the track-side of the station (open 0630–2300).

Train reservations are best obtained at the Greek Railways office at No. 1–3 Karolou Street or No. 6 Sina Street. Get taxi instructions from the tourist office on 2, Amerikis Street.

Railpass validation is also available at the Greek Railways' main office. Eurailpasses can also be validated at ticket windows in the stations, but only on your departure day.

Athens' Peloponnese Station serves the narrow-gauge lines to the south.

Money exchange is not available. Use the footbridge to cross to the Larissa Station Bank, or use the exchange services in the tourist information office on Syntagma Square.

Train information is in a booth to your immediate left when entering the station. Open 0730–1900 daily throughout the summer. The hours are split, 0730–1230 and 1630–1900, the rest of the year. *Tel:* 513–1601.

Train reservations are best obtained at the **Hellenic Railways'** office at No. 1-3 Karolou Street or No. 6 Sina Street. Get taxi or bus instructions from the tourist office on Syntagma Square.

Rail pass validation is available at ticket windows in the stations, or go to the aforementioned Hellenic Railways' office.

Tourist Information/Hotel Reservations

Hellenic Tourism Organization: No. 2 Amerikis Street, Box 1017, Syntagma, Athens 10110
Tel: 322 3111; *Fax:* 322 4148
Money exchange hours: 0800–1830 daily.
Tourist information hours: 0900–1900 Sunday–Friday; 1000–1600 Saturday.

Located in the vicinity of Syntagma Square. When you are facing the Parliament Building from the bottom of the square in the cafe area, the tourist information office is just across the street on the left. The tourist office also offers money exchange services.

Hotel and pension reservations: Hellenic Chamber of Hotels, located in the

National Bank at 2 Karagiorgi Servias Street, Syntagma Square. *Tel:* 323 7193 and 331 0022. For reservations by mail, the address is 24, Stadiou Street, Athens. *Tel:* 323 6962.

Getting Around in Athens

Transportation in Athens is inexpensive—120 GRD for a ticket covering one or two sections of Athens' subway system, the Athens-Piraeus Electric Railway (ISAP), and 100 GRD includes all three sections with 22 stations along the 14-mile route. Purchase tickets at ticket machines and ticket booths in the stations and validate them prior to boarding. ISAP now numbers 195 rail cars and carries more than 80 million passengers annually.

Sights/Attractions/Tours

Most of the tours being offered are bus tours that include some walking. Consequently, you should inquire as to the tour's duration and terrain before signing up, and don't forget to wear comfortable walking shoes. To avoid the daytime heat, select an evening tour when available. Most of the tourist attractions are illuminated.

The city tourist office is an excellent source for information concerning other areas of the country. Be certain to inform the attendant you speak with that you hold a Eurailpass. Otherwise you might find yourself signing up for a bus tour when a rail trip would suffice for the transportation to the site you want to see.

Although there is more to Athens than **the Acropolis,** it should be the first place to visit during your stay in the city. If you use the ISAP electric railway, detrain at Thission for the Acropolis. All else in and around Athens becomes secondary to this symbol of classic perfection that has stood majestically above Athens for about 2,500 years. Don't rush your visit or you will regret it. Plan to spend an entire day, and if you go there during the summer months, go prepared with some sunscreen, sun hats, bottled water, and comfortable walking shoes.

The Parthenon is the focal point of the Acropolis, but there is much more to see. Study the **Propylaea,** the impressive entrance to the sanctuary, along with the **Temple of Athena-Niki** and the elegant row of maidens along the facade of the Erechtheion. You can peer down on the Theater of Dionysius from the rim of the Acropolis, but go there later to feel its "presence."

During the tourist season, a light-and-sound show of the Acropolis is presented in several languages. Don't miss it. The program in English starts at 2100. The tourist office can provide you with more details. You view the show from an opposite hillside and it can cool down considerably. You may want to take a light sweater or pullover.

The Romans made their presence known in Athens, too. A group of ruins dating back to the days of Julius Caesar clusters about the **Roman Forum** at the beginning of Aeolou Street. There are so many other sights to be seen that we recommend a guided tour as the only means of possibly scratching the surface of this wonderful city where Western civilization began.

With an extensive history like Athens, expect to find a full retinue of museums. You won't be disappointed. Be aware that you may be required to check any bags, including purses, and that most museums charge a fee for videotaping within the museum. If your stay in the city is limited, visit the **Benaki Museum,** located on the corner of Vassilissis Sofias Avenue and Koumbari Street (*Tel:* 361–16178). In its twenty-eight chambers, you will see exhibits ranging from the Bronze Age to the beginning of the twentieth century. As you pass through the centuries of statuary development, take note of the style by which the sculptors slowly developed the technique of depicting fingers and toes.

The modern city of Athens also holds much interest for visitors. You must visit the **Tomb of the Unknown Warrior,** with its colorful guards. Go to a cafe on **Syntagma Square** for coffee and pastry. Climb the time-worn steps leading through the **Plaka Quarter,** which hugs the base of the Acropolis. Take the ISAP electric railway to Faliro Station and sample the fruits of the sea at one of Mikrolimano's charming seafood restaurants.

Despite being one of the easternmost cities in Europe, Athens has a distinct Western appearance. Modern Athens surrounds the splendor of its ancient Acropolis, which has a nobility that survives time and change. That first glimpse of the Parthenon from the window of the plane or train that brought you to Athens remains a once-in-a-lifetime experience.

Addendum to Athens

Select one of Athens's "tavernas" and enjoy its food, music, and dancing. To experience a popular form of Greek entertainment, visit a Bouzouki nightclub. Bouzouki music is similar to American blues in that the music reflects the pain and pathos often present in love and friendships. Before you participate in the traditional plate breaking, check with the management as to the cost per dozen. You could end up spending a lot of GRD.

Tourists are targets for ploys and pranks throughout the world. Athens is no exception. A waiter may suggest that you consume bottled water with your meal. After all, you may have been warned not to drink the regular water. Bottled water is a good idea, but insist that the waiter open the bottle at your table. Otherwise, you might receive an opened bottle of water that was just recently filled from the water tap in the kitchen. Or order a bottle of carbonated water. That's hard to bootleg!

Day Excursions

Riding a narrow-gauge train through areas steeped in the history of Western civilization is sufficiently stimulating to make the traveler overlook the lack of air conditioning, posh dining cars, and other amenities. Our day excursion to **Argos,** the oldest continuously inhabited town in Greece, is one such adventure. **Corinth,** both modern and ancient, is rich in Greek history, from Alexander the Great down through Roman rule. **Patras,** port city and scene of the most spectacular carnival in Greece, is still another place to see on the Peloponnese. **Piraeus,** main port of Athens, provides culinary delights from the surrounding sea.

An InterCity train between Athens and **Larissa** provides an opportunity to spend several hours in Larissa during a day excursion out of Athens. Depart

Train/Ferry Connections to Other Base Cities from Athens (Athinai)

Depart Athens Peloponnese Station by train to Patras (see rail schedule in "Day Excursion to Patras" section). Depart Patras by ferry to Brindisi, Italy (see previous section "Greece to Italy via Ferry—Crossing the Mediterranean"), and then depart Brindisi by train to the selected base city:

Brindisi—Rome Termini Trains

DEPART BRINDISI	TRAIN NUMBER	ARRIVE ROME TERMINI
0707	ES 9354	
1101	ES 9356	1655
1656	ES 9358	2255
2201	ICN 782	0630+1

Brindisi—Milan (Milano) Centrale Trains

DEPART BRINDISI	TRAIN NUMBER	ARRIVE MILAN CENTRALE
0827	IC 576	1755
1208	IC 586	2155
2124	IC 768	0835+1

Note: Although rail travel is possible on the Athens-(Athenai Larissa station) Thessaloniki-to-Budapest route, Eurailpass does not cover travel through Yugoslavia and other Eastern European countries (except Hungary). Also, travelers are warned of the hazards of traveling in politically unstable areas. The potential traveler choosing this route is urged to consult a European rail ticket agent for detailed schedule information and for information about procedures and visa requirements in Eastern European countries.

Athens at 0800, arrive in Larissa at 1203, and depart at 1810 to arrive back in Athens by 2214. Or, depart Larissa at 1910 for arrival in Athens at 2314. Although the IC 60 does not haul a restaurant car, there are beverages and some food available. Also you will find an abundance of cafes and patisseries on the town square. Larissa, the "citadel," is the capital of Thessaly, and for a time it was the home of Hippocrates, the Father of Medicine.

Day Excursion to

Argos (Arghos) OLDEST GREEK TOWN

Depart from Athens Peloponnese Station

Distance by Train: 89 miles (144 km)
Average Train Time: 2 hours, 30 minutes
City Dialing Code: 751

Argos does not have a tourist information office. Neither does it have a tourist police office such as one finds in many of the smaller towns throughout Greece. But these absences present no great hardship, for most of its sights are within the city limits. The area must be the birthplace of all Greeks who have ever worked in the United States as waiters. We met two of them by just standing on a corner and looking perplexed.

The railway station is about a kilometer from the town square in Argos. To reach the town square on foot, walk straight out of the station to the main road, where a road sign points to the right in the direction of town. Taxis are available for a nominal fare.

For sightseeing, orient yourself with the church in the town square. From its front door, you can reach the **Argos museum** by crossing the street, turning left, and proceeding to the first cross street, where you then turn right. The museum is half a block farther on the left-hand side of the street and is open daily, except Tuesdays. Admission is charged. It has an excellent collection of archaeological exhibits.

The ancient theater and Roman ruins lie on the outskirts of town, in the direction of the hillsides. They are a five-minute taxi ride or a fifteen-minute walk from the museum. On foot, turn left at the next street beyond the museum and walk until you reach the next main intersection. Turn right, and walk straight ahead to the site. If there is the slightest tinge of archaeology in your blood, you'll love this spot, for it is relatively unchanged and a perfect place to probe and peer for priceless treasures.

The theater has ninety tiers, which were cut into the hillside on rather a

Athens (Athenai)—Argos (Arghos)

DEPART ATHENS PELOPONNESE	TRAIN NUMBER	ARRIVE ARGOS
0724	1430	1017
1035	422	1326

DEPART ARGOS	TRAIN NUMBER	ARRIVE ATHENS PELOPONNESE
1511	423	1758
1852	1433	2142
2003	425	2248

Distance: 89 miles (144 km)

steep angle, making it possible for a perfect, uninterrupted view of the stage area from any seat in the house. Oddly enough, the 20,000 seating capacity of this amphitheater is more than adequate for the present 19,000 population of Argos.

History comes out to meet you on this day excursion. Argos lies in the plain of Argolis on the Peloponnese peninsula, land of myth and magic. Your mind can run rampant as you journey there. The *Iliad,* the *Odyssey,* and the beautiful Helen hover over all travelers who enter.

Modern history appears first as the train crosses the Isthmus of Corinth. Below the railroad bridge lies the canal connecting the Aegean and Ionian Seas. Alexander the Great, Caesar, and Nero all failed in their attempts to construct the waterway through 4 miles of solid rock. A French engineering firm finally succeeded in 1893. Watch for it about an hour and twenty minutes after leaving Athens. The best view is from the right side of the train. The railroad bridge is only 108 feet long; so if you intend taking pictures, have everything poised and ready to go, for it passes quickly.

Medieval history is next in line as you approach Argos, where the hillsides northwest of the city reveal at their highest point a Venetian fortress, which dominates the **White Chapel of the Prophet Elias** and **Our Lady of the Rocks Convent** lying below.

Ancient history unfolds in Argos itself, with the 20,000-seat theater, and 5 miles east of the town with the **Argive Heraeon** and the scattered remains of Greece's oldest recognizable temple (800 B.C.). **Tiryns,** legendary birthplace of Hercules, is also in the area. These last two sights are not on the rail line and are best visited by taxi from Argos.

Argos is the oldest continuously inhabited town in Greece. Many archaeologists suspect that it may be the oldest in all of Europe. Legends, many of them the basic stuff from which most of Greek mythology sprang, have their origins in Argos and the area surrounding it. In the legendary time of Danaus, storytellers relate how his fifty daughters slew their husbands on their wedding night and then tried to make amends with the devil by trying to fill a bottomless cask with water carried in sieves from the river Stykes. If this would happen in our times, no doubt Congress would investigate—taking equal time to determine the outcome.

The legend does, however, have a happy ending. One of Danaus's daughters, realizing that it could ruin her honeymoon, thought it over once or twice and then let her spouse escape the murderous nuptial-night activities. For this, she was rewarded by becoming the ancestral matriarch of a long line of mythological heroes.

The modern town of Argos was built up over ancient ruins from previous centuries of conflict. The last ethnic group to participate in that form of urban renewal was the Turks, who ravaged the town in 1397. As a result, Argos has scant visible remains of its ancient origins except the theater and the Roman baths.

Day Excursion to
Corinth (Korinthos) AND THE ISTHMIAN CANAL

Depart from Athens Peloponnese Station

Distance by Train: 57 miles (91 km)
Average Train Time: 1 hour, 32 minutes
City Dialing Code: 741

This day excursion runs from modern Greece back through the millennia to the Bronze Age. You have the opportunity to see modern Corinth, a typical "new" Greek city, and its port on the Peloponnese. You may delve as well into the hillside of ancient Corinth, where Saint Paul established a church, Nero fiddled around with a canal, and Julius Caesar implemented an earlier version of the Marshall Plan.

En route to Corinth, the railroad skirts the Aegean Sea and crosses the Isthmian Canal. Watch for the canal when the train is about one hour and twenty minutes out of Athens. The center of the canal runs 285 feet deep through solid rock. The railroad bridge passes 200 feet above the level of the water for a spectacular view.

Greek and Roman rulers (the infamous Nero included) periodically attempted to breach the Isthmus with a canal, but until a French company using modern methods succeeded in the years 1882–1893, all had failed. The ancients hauled their small ships across the Isthmus on rollers. Vestiges of the portage road are still visible just after the train crosses the bridge. Watch on the right side of the train for the best view. Have your camera poised and ready— the train traverses the area quickly.

The present "new" city of Corinth, moved to its site in 1858 after an earthquake destroyed "old" Corinth, was leveled by an equally devastating earthquake in 1928. The site has had its share of earth tremors; ancient scribes record devastation in A.D. 522 and 551. Called an "undistinguished town," new Corinth is interesting in that it represents a community rebuilt on antiseismic principles of low buildings that, paradoxically, give it an air of impermanence.

In fear of pirates, old Corinth was built well back from the sea. This strategic position served the city well. It prospered and became one of the three great city-states of Greece, along with Athens and Sparta. Things went reasonably well until Corinth led the Achaean League against the Romans in 146 B.C. The Romans won the ball game and, a la Carthage (as was the custom in those days), laid waste to Corinth. After the city withstood a hundred years of total desolation, Julius Caesar decided to rebuild Corinth, and it blossomed into one of the great trading cities of the Roman Empire.

During his eighteen-month sojourn in Corinth, Saint Paul became alarmed about the sinful ways of the Corinthians and frequently "read the riot act" to the city fathers. Because of his violent condemnation of moral laxity, he was charged with inciting a riot. Instead of dispensing punishment, the city fathers issued Saint Paul a reprimand—and the suggestion that he leave town as soon as possible, which he did.

Historians estimate that at one time the ancient city of Corinth had a population of more than 460,000; today, its citizens number about 21,000. Although termed a *citadel,* the old city was attacked repeatedly and conquered down through the ages. During their sweep through Greece, the Turks took over the city in 1458 and again in 1715. In 1458, the Turkish conquest ended when they retreated hastily in ships. The siege of the city in 1715 was described in prose by Lord Byron. There is little Turkish architecture visible in the Corinthian area, due mainly to the short time they were on the premises.

There is excellent bus service between the city and the **archaeological site**. Departures are daily on the hour from 0615 to 2100. The one-way fare is 160 GRD. Round-trip cab fare, including a reasonable wait, runs about 1,000 GRD. The bus terminal is on the south side of the city park. The sign over the terminal reads APXAIA. A taxi will take you there from the railway station for a nominal fare.

To reach the bus station on foot, turn left after leaving the station and then right onto Damaskinou Street and right again onto Ermou Street, just before the Hotel Belle Vue. Turn left at this point and, three blocks later, you'll arrive at the bus terminal on the far left-hand corner of the city park. For further information, check with the "**Tourist Police.**" Walk through the park past

Athens (Athinai)—Corinth (Korinthos)

DEPART ATHENS PELOPONNESE	TRAIN NUMBER	ARRIVE CORINTH
0724	1430	0919
0849	IC 20	1022
0937	302	1135
1035	422	1226
1207	IC 10	1339

DEPART CORINTH	TRAIN NUMBER	ARRIVE ATHENS PELOPONNESE
1417	IC 23	1549
1611	423	1758
1657	303	1858
1829	IC 11	2001
1954	1433	2142
2033	IC 25	2204
2103	425	2248
2224	305	0016+1

Distance: 57 miles (91 km)

another bus terminal to a pharmacy on the right-hand side. Turn right and find the police station half a block farther on the left-hand side.

Excavations have been in progress on the site of old Corinth for many years. Literature describing the excavations and the contents of the museum is available as you enter the site. Between 1925 and 1929, extensive excavations were made. Among the findings, an inscription was found that recorded the story of Androcles and the lion. According to Roman history, Androcles removed a thorn from a lion's paw. Later, when he was sentenced to death and thrown to the lions, the lion remembered Androcles' kindness and let him off without a scratch.

In ancient Corinth, you must pay for admission to the grounds and an additional fee to enter the museum. Hours: Monday–Friday, 0730–2100 (or sunset); Sundays, 1000–1300 and 1500–1900. Plan to spend a minimum of four hours at the site. There is a lot of walking. Several canteens serve refreshments outside the main entrance.

Day Excursion to

Patras
Port City

Depart from Athens Peloponnese Station

Distance by Train: 138 miles (222 km)
Average Train Time: 3 hours, 49 minutes
City Dialing Code: 61
Peloponnese and Western Greece Tourism Bureau Office: 110 Iroon Politehniou, Glifada, P.C.
  262 23 Patras
Tel: 65358–61; *Fax:* 423866
Hours: Daily, 0900–1400

Ask at the rail station or the ferry terminal for directions. Otherwise, turn right at the quay and walk well beyond the ferry terminal and look for the signs leading to the office. There also is an information office at the entrance of the port of Patras (at Glyfada)

The railway station in Patras lies on the quay, but it's about 500 yards from the pier where ferries depart for Brindisi. You'll spot the pier to the right as the train slows for its stop in the Patras station. A **tourist information** booth is located at the entrance to the ferry terminal. For complete information regarding Patras and its surroundings, visit the Peloponnese and Western Greece Tourism Bureau at the address listed above.

Patras is the fourth largest city in Greece. It is also the country's western gateway. Located at the entrance to the **Gulf of Corinth,** Patras has been a Greek seaport since the beginning of recorded history. Ships large and small are constantly arriving in, and departing from, its harbor. The ferry services of the Adriatica and Hellenic Mediterranean Lines ply between Patras and Brindisi, Italy. If you are traveling with a railpass, no doubt you will either enter or leave Greece through the Port of Patras.

Patras is the port where the majority of Greek emigrants sailed for the United States. It is interesting to note that in 1922, refugees fleeing Asia Minor arrived at the pier in Patras penniless. Many of them paid for their passage to America by selling their Oriental carpets, which they had carried from their homelands. Since the early 1960s, Patras has developed into a major Adriatic ferry port.

Eurailpass and Europass (if Greece option was purchased) holders are cautioned to use either the Adriatica or the Hellenic Mediterranean Line if they intend paying for their deck passage with the rail pass. Although other ferry companies operate between Greece and Italy, these lines are the only ones honoring the Eurailpass and Europass.

Spreading below its Venetian castle, Patras is where **Saint Andrew** taught Christianity and was crucified. The saint's head rests in a shrine following its return from Saint Peter's, Rome, in 1964. It was here in Patras in 1809 that Lord Byron first set foot on Greek soil.

Athens (Athinai)—Patras

DEPART ATHENS PELOPONNESE	TRAIN NUMBER	ARRIVE PATRAS
0629	300	1044
0849	IC 20	1215
0937	302	1418

DEPART PATRAS	TRAIN NUMBER	ARRIVE ATHENS PELOPONNESE
1354	303	1858
1635	IC 11	2001
1838	IC 25	2204
1959	305	0016+1

Distance: 143 miles (230 km)

The quay is an interesting part of Patras. The long mole, with its benches for resting, extends into the harbor and is a favorite place from which to watch the activity in the harbor. From it you can photograph the arrival of the ferryboats running between the ports of Patras and Brindisi. Patras is not just a busy harbor, however. Its eucalyptus-soaked shorelines, topaz waters, and vast sandy beach at Kilini have made it well known since antiquity for its spas.

Patras has two noteworthy celebrations: the stately procession of Saint Andrew on November 30 and a spectacular carnival during the last ten days before Lent. The city also conducts a classic-theater season during the summer. We suggest a walking tour of Patras starting at the **Trion Symmahon Square** across from the station and on the right. The long arcaded avenue leading off the park in the direction of the city's heights is studded with stores, restaurants, and specialty shops.

Continue walking on this avenue (Ayiou Nikolaou) to the foot of a broad flight of steps, which will bring you to the site of the ancient **Patras Acropolis.** Enjoy a wonderful view of the city, its harbor, and the surrounding hills and mountains from this point. Return to the base of the steps and proceed to the left on Yeoryiou Street, which will lead you to the **Odeum,** a characteristic Roman theater. It was discovered in 1889, but enterprising building contractors subsequently removed much of its marble, requiring the theater to be restored extensively in 1960.

Visitors seeking **Saint Andrews Church** should begin their quest at the Trion Symmahon Square and walk southwest along Andreou Avenue to the church, which stands by the sea at the avenue's end. A park dedicated to Andrew, the patron saint of Scotland, is across from the church.

To reach the city's museum, turn left at the Trion Fountain in Trion Symmahon Square and walk for two blocks, then turn right and walk for two more. The museum has an extensive collection of classic Greek and Roman statues plus a collection of prehistoric pottery. There is an admission charge.

The area surrounding Patras is steeped in history. Use Patras as a "base city" when visiting **Olympia,** original site of the Olympic Games. In Olympia, you can visit the site of the Olympic flame, which is carried by runners to any point in the world where the games are to be held. Also of interest is the arch commemorating Nero's "victory" in a chariot race staged in A.D. 67. The emperor's chariot was pulled by ten horses, while all other competitors had to make do with four—needless to say, Nero won.

Another interesting side trip can be made to the **Achaia Clauss Winery,** five miles outside Patras, to view the wine-making process and sample a bit of the product. If interested in either excursion, obtain information at the tourist office.

Culinary delights abound in Patras. A sea-bass dish, *tsipoures*, is a specialty of the area. This and other Greek dishes are available in the tavernas scattered throughout the upper part of town. An American-style restaurant lies just before the Hellenic Lines office on the quay. Customers may stow their suitcases and backpacks there free of charge while waiting for the ferry.

Day Excursion to

Piraeus SEAFOOD BY THE SEASIDE

Depart from Athens Peloponnese Station

Distance by Train: 5 miles (8 km)
Average Train Time: 20 minutes
City Dialing Code: 1
Tourist Information Office: East Central Greece Islands, Marina Zeas, 18504
Tel: 4135716; *Fax:* 4135730

Piraeus, main port of Greece, basks in the warm embrace of the Saronic Gulf just a few miles and minutes outside the heart of Athens. Piraeus today is one of the principal ports of the Mediterranean. It serves both commercial shipping and pleasure craft. Most tourists go to Piraeus not to view its remains of antiquity but, rather, to enjoy the picturesque atmosphere of its port and to indulge in some of the wonderful seafood served in its restaurants.

Throughout the centuries, Piraeus has had its successes and its failures. In 86 B.C., the Roman General Sulla destroyed the city and its docks, and for centuries Piraeus was considered an unimportant village. Its reconstruction began only in 1834, when Athens became the capital of Greece. Resettled by islanders, Piraeus grew rapidly throughout the nineteenth century and played a large part in the revival of Athens.

Between 1854 and 1859, Piraeus was occupied by an Anglo-French fleet to prevent Greek nationalists' forays against Turkey, an Allied power in the Crimean War. In World War II, the port was put out of action in April 1941 by a German air attack. The ammunition ship *Clan Fraser,* carrying 200 tons of TNT, together with two other ships loaded with ammunition exploded and destroyed the port.

You won't need your railpass for this day excursion. You'll be traveling on Athens' privately owned electric line—ISAP. The line is the "subway" for the city. A major portion of the rails running to Piraeus, however, are above ground.

Begin your journey from **Omonia Square** in the city. It connects with Syntagma (Constitution) Square via Stadhiou Street, which starts right outside the entrance to the tourist information office. The entrances to the underground terminal are clearly marked. Be certain to purchase and validate your tickets before boarding. The station uses a center platform for all trains, so check the directional signs for Piraeus before boarding.

Travel at off-peak hours to avoid the crowds. Service is frequent throughout the day. Train etiquette in Greece dictates that men relinquish their seats to the ladies and that the young do the same for elders. When in Greece, do as the Greeks do.

Leave the electric train at the end of the line in Piraeus. The terminal lies right at the harbor. To stroll along the quay, exit the station straight ahead, turning left at the side along the sea. Commercial ships and ferries to hundreds of island points occupy the piers along the waterfront of the main harbor. The railway station serving the Athens-Peloponnese Line is to the right of the subway terminal. Trains for Patras, Corinth, and Argos originate from there, but passengers are not accepted for the short ride between Piraeus and Athens.

In addition to its main harbor, Piraeus has two small-craft harbors, **Zea and Mikrolimano.** Zea shelters pleasure craft, and Mikrolimano features fishing craft and seafood restaurants, the latter rimming its waterfront like pickets of a fence. Bus No. 20 will take you to either of the smaller ports. Board it from the bus terminal on the left side of the train station. Bus No. 20 stands in the far line, facing away from the sea.

After skirting the main harbor, the bus passes through a built-up area before it again sides with the sea at Zea. If Mikrolimano is your destination, ride four stops beyond Zea and dismount. **The Castella Hotel** is on the left side at the bus stop. From there, walk down to the harbor. If you're going for lunch, try to arrive before 1230, when the area is invaded by a horde of tour buses packed with hungry tourists. At night the tables in the restaurants overlooking the sea groan under their loads of fresh fish, luscious lobsters, and opulent oysters. Top

Athens (Athinai)—Piraeus

DEPART ATHENS	TRAIN NUMBER	ARRIVE PIRAEUS
0917 Pel	1431	0945
1032 Pel	IC 21	1056
1355 Pel	421	1418
1238 Lar	1511	1319
1309 Lar	IC 53	1338

DEPART PIRAEUS	TRAIN NUMBER	ARRIVE ATHENS
1342	IC 22	1406 Pel
1454	304	1526 Pel
1536	432	1602 Pel
1751	IC 24	1820 Pel
2145	306	2219 Pel
2236	426	2310 Pel
2311	604	2355 Lar

Other frequent local trains run between Athinai Omonia station and Piraeus on the Athinai Electric Railway; journey time is approximately 20 minutes.

Note: Athens Larissa station is designated as Lar; Athens Peloponnese station is designated as Pel.

Distance: 5 miles (8 km)

off your evening by climbing the hill behind Mikrolimano for a magnificent view of the Mediterranean's Saronic Gulf.

Many restaurants employ solicitors to influence your selection of eating places. You can ignore them. We have found that the better places lie to the right of the harbor. **Kanaris 2** is one of the more expensive restaurants, but it is well worth it. While on the subject of price, a word of caution: Check menu prices carefully before ordering. Many menu prices are given for one kilo (2.2 pounds) of fish—a price that the government requires the restaurants to list. Certainly, your platter won't hold that much, but some places will try to charge you on that basis. *Caveat emptor*—let the buyer beware.

During the summer, Piraeus is considerably cooler than Athens. Should the temperatures soar during your stay in the Greek capital, take a quick trip on the Athens subway to the seaside at Piraeus. In the evening, the tavernas and nightclubs there provide a resort-type lifestyle. The city's night spots feature popular singers.

Lacking museums, Piraeus's archaeological discoveries are displayed in the Athens National Museum. Of particular interest is a collection of statuary stored and forgotten by General Sulla in 86 B.C. Perhaps the general lost his claim check.

Hungary

Hungary, the seventeenth member country to join the Eurail community, is a unique addition in that it is the first Eastern European nation to do so. Of the country's 10.7 million inhabitants, 2.1 million live in its capital city of Budapest.

Present-day Hungarians descended from the Magyars, a nomadic, horse-riding people who conquered the land in the ninth century. The Magyars spoke a language unlike any other language of Europe, except Finnish, and even today other Europeans have difficulty understanding it. English and/or German, however, are spoken by many Hungarians in the tourism industry, particularly in hotels and restaurants.

During World War II, the Hungarian government sided with the Axis powers. In April 1945 the country fell to Russian troops. Encouraged by the Polish defiance of the Soviet Union, Hungarians staged an uprising in 1956 that was quickly suppressed by Soviet troops and tanks. Hungary was under the "Iron Curtain" until 1989. The last Soviet troops left the country in June 1991. The Hungarian People's Republic became the Republic of Hungary with a newly elected democratic government—a coalition of six parties.

For more information on Hungary, visit **www.hungarytourism.hu,** E-mail tourinform@hungarytourism.com, or contact the Hungarian National Tourist Office in North America:

New York: c/o Embassy of the Republic of Hungary, 150 East 58th Street, 33rd Floor, New York, NY 10155-3398. *Tel:* (212) 355–0240; *Fax:* (212) 207–4103; *Internet:* **www.gotohungary.com;** *E-mail:* huntour@gramercy.ios.com

Banking

- **Currency:** Hungarian Forint (HUF)
- **Exchange rate at press time:** 241.02 HUF = $1.00 U.S.

Communications

- **Country Code:** 36
  For telephone calls within Hungary, dial a zero (0) preceding area code.
- **Direct dial:** first dial 00 and wait for second dial tone, then dial AT&T: 800–01111; MCI: 800–01411; Sprint: 800–01877.

Rail Travel in Hungary

The Hungarian State Railways (Magyar Allamvasutak, or MAV) includes more than 4,844 miles (7,750 kilometers) of rail lines with 1,423 miles (2,277 kilometers) electrified. Fifty-four international trains per day arrive in Budapest, including Euronight (EN) service from Zürich and Bucharest. All international trains have dining and sleeping facilities; however, many of the Hungarian intercity and express trains still do not afford all of the same amenities that can be found on the trains of Western Europe.

The **Hungarian State Railways** accepts **Eurailpass, Europass** (with purchase of the **Austria/Hungary Danube Zone**), the **European East Pass,** and its own national pass—the **Hungarian Flexipass.**

Hungarian Flexipass

5 days travel within 15-day period	$64.00 (U.S.)
10 days travel within 1-month period	$80.00 (U.S.)

Children age 5-14, half adult fare; children under age 5 travel free.

European East Pass

Valid for travel in Austria, Czech Republic, Hungary, Poland and Slovak Republic

	First Class
5 days travel in 1 month	$205 (U.S.)
Additional days	$23 (U.S.)

Up to 5 additional days may be added. Children age 4–11 half adult fare; under age 4 travel free.

For more detailed information on types and prices of other railpasses, please see RailPass Express' European RailPasses listed in the Appendix.

Base City . . .

Budapest

City Dialing Code: 1

Budapest's tree-lined boulevards and spacious public squares bordered by magnificent buildings make it one of the most beautiful capitals of Europe. Hungary welcomes more than 24 million visitors annually, the majority of whom pass through Budapest, pausing to enjoy its special charm and atmosphere.

The city is a combination of two ancient towns, Buda on the west bank of the Danube and the community of Pest on the east bank. Buda stands on a terraced plateau and contains relics of a Turkish occupation; Pest rises from a plain and is the site of the Houses of Parliament, the Palace of Justice, the Museum of Fine Arts, and the National Museum. Buda and Pest are linked by six bridges over the Danube, including the beautiful Stone Chain Bridge.

Budapest's origins date back to about 10 B.C. when the Romans established the colony of Aquincum on what is now Buda. The Vandals took it over from the Romans in A.D. 376, and, in turn, management changed hands frequently during invasions by the Tartars and the Turks until armies under Austrian leadership liberated what was left of the towns in 1686. Some Roman ruins withstood the assaults and may be seen even today.

Arriving by Air

Budapest's international airport, **Ferihegy,** consists of two terminals. Ferihegy 1 is about 20 kilometers southeast of the city center and Ferihegy 2 is 24 kilometers.

Terminal One	Telephone
Flight information (arrival, departure)	157–7155
Luggage location service	157–7690

Terminal Two	
Flight information	
Departures	157–7000
Arrivals	157–8000
Luggage location service	157–8108
Customs information	157–8306

Airport–City Links: **Bus Service** departs from either Terminal No. 1 or Terminal No. 2. The bus stop at the airport is located immediately to the right of the main exit.

Airport Minibus (fixed-route taxis); (*Tel:* 157–855), operates between the two terminals and any address in Budapest. Fare: 1,000 HUF.

Budapest Transport Enterprise (BKV) services, bus No. 93 between Terminals 1 and 2 and terminus of M3 metro line Kobanya-Kispest.

The airport **taxi** stand is farther to the right, about 200 feet beyond the bus stop. Taxi service is available twenty-four hours a day. All taxis in Hungary must have yellow license plates and meters that print out receipts. To reserve a taxi: City Taxi, *Tel:* 211–1111; Fotaxi, *Tel:* 222–2222; Palotaxi, *Tel:* 272–0616; Radiotaxi, *Tel:* 177–6766; or Tele 5 Taxi, *Tel:* 155–5555.

Tourist information: Terminal 1 at the airport. You will find it on your right as you approach the main exit. Hours: daily 0800–2300.

Customs control uses the red-green corridor system just like the Western European countries. If you have nothing to declare, you should use the green corridor.

Arriving by Train

Keleti (East) Station, *Tel:* 113–6835, is the terminus for most international express trains, with exception of the *Adriatica, Agram, Lehar* EuroCity, *Maestral,* and *Graz* trains, which terminate in Budapest Deli (South) Station. Although it has undergone extensive improvements and restoration since its original construction in 1884, the old charm is still evident. Statues of George Stephenson, the inventor of the locomotive, and James Watt, creator of the steam engine, grace its entrance. The modern touch is found in the digital departure boards displayed at the platform entrances.

Stairs at the front of the station take you to the city's Metro, a modern three-line subway system, but arrivals burdened with luggage should opt for the taxi queue immediately outside the station on the right. A word of caution: Be sure that the taxi you hail has a meter—and uses it. The best taxi service is City Taxi and most drivers speak English. Call them at 211–1111 and tell the English-speaking operator the telephone number you called from and a taxi will arrive in just a few minutes. Any "no-name" taxi is almost certainly a rip-off.

Keleti Station has all of the usual tourist services. For rail reservations, proceed to the sign FOREIGN RAILWAY TICKETS—SEAT RESERVATIONS on your right when exiting from the trains. Note that window 2 is for currency exchange, window 3 for hotels, and window 6 is where you request tickets and seat reservations. Pay for all services in cash (U.S. dollars; forints not accepted).

Deli (South), *Tel:* 175–6293, a modern concrete edifice on the Buda side of the Danube, features a huge supermarket on the ground level. Trains arrive overhead on uncovered platforms that lead to a covered concourse, with an enclosed waiting room and ticket office just beyond. The designation of Deli as Budapest's "south" station is a bit confusing in that it actually lies to the west of the city. A visit to the supermarket is a must. The products and produce selections offered may be fewer than those offered by even your local 7-Eleven store, but it's a great place to pick up the local flavor and mix with the citizens.

The Metro Line Z (or Red) terminates at the Deli Station, with direct connections to the other two rail stations, Keleti and Nyugati. To access, follow the "M" pictographs leading from the train level; same for taxis.

Nyugati (West), *Tel:* 149–0115, stands at the head of Terèz Boulevard just before Nyugati Square. Nyugati Station has a TOURINFORM office as well as the usual amenities found at Keleti and Deli.

Budapest Tourist Information/Hotel Reservations

Tourism information office: TOURINFORM, Main Hall, Nyugati (West) Rail
Station
Tel/Fax: 132–0597

The National Tourism Information Service has 754 travel offices in
Hungary and offers information about tourism office hours and services for
visitors, including money exchange, hotel reservations, travel reservations
(including rail and air), tour bookings, and general tourist information (*Tel:*
117–9800).

If you are interested in organized tours, TOURINFORM offers quite a
selection of sightseeing and tour activities. The "City Tour" is a three-hour
sightseeing adventure by bus to Budapest's famous spots, including Castle Hill
for a panoramic view. You may also want to take a two-hour sightseeing
cruise on the Danube.

For a night on the town, you have the option of a Goulash Party with wine
and a show, or you can pull out all the stops with the "Budapest by Night"
tour, which offers dinner, a floor show, dancing, and wine tasting accompanied by folk music. If visiting in August, plan ahead for the Buda-Fest by call-
in the tourist office for a list of highlights for this summer cultural event. If
you can work it in, the full-day Danube Bend bus tour on the right bank of
the Danube to the towns of **Esztergom, Visegrad,** and **Szentendre** is well
worth it. The area is not accessible by train, and the vistas along the river are
captivating.

Train Connections to other Base Cities from Budapest

Depart from Budapest Keleti station unless otherwise noted.

DEPART	TRAIN NUMBER	ARRIVE	NOTE
Amsterdam Centraal			
1525	344/EN 224	0940+1	R, 1, Sleeper
Berlin Zoobahnhof			
0650	EC 174	1931	R
1050	EC 170	2331	R
1745	EN 228	0830+1	R, Sleeper
Bern			
1745	EN 466/IC 908	0814+1	R, 2
Brussels Midi/Zuid			
1525	344/EN 224	0937+1	R,1, Sleeper

DEPART	TRAIN NUMBER	ARRIVE	NOTES
Copenhagen			
1745	EN 228/IC 876	1158+1	R, 3
1329	EC35	1759	R, 4
Hamburg Hauptbahnhof			
0650	EC 174	2158	R,
1745	EN 228/IC 876	1158+1	R, 3
Luxembourg			
1700	262/296	0859+1	R, 5,Sleeper
Lyon Part-Dieu			
1700	262/6171/6170	1137	R, 5, Sleeper, Mon-Sat
Munich (München) Hauptbahnhof			
1242	EC 62	2036	R
Paris (Est)			
1242	EC 62/D 260	0704+1	R, 6
1700	262	1022+1	R, Sleeper
2140	268/EC 66	1622	R, 6, Sleeper
Rome (Roma) Termini			
1525	344/EN 235	0922+1	R, 1, 7, Sleeper
Vienna (Wien) Westbahnhof			
0600	346	0900	R
0912	EC 24	1207	R
1050	342	1400	R
1242	EC 62	1530	R
1525	344	1830	R
1700	262	2100	R
1745	EN 228	2120	R, Sleeper
Zürich Hauptbahnhof			
0600	346/EC 162	1827	R, 1

Daily, unless otherwise noted
R Reservations mandatory
1. Change trains in Vienna (Wein).

2. Change trains in Zürich.
3. Change trains in Berlin (Zoobahnhof Station).
4. Change trains in Hamburg coming from Berlin.
5. Change trains in Strasborg.
6. Change trains in Munich (München).
7. Change from Wein Westbahnhof to Wein Sudbahnhof Station.

Day Excursions

Four day excursions have been selected for your Hungarian explorations. Two excursions explore **Balaton** and **Siofok,** resort towns along the shores of Lake Balaton, a large, long lake lying to the southwest of Budapest. The other two take you south through Hungary's Great Plain to the historic cities of **Kecskemét** and **Szeged.**

Note: Budapest Keleti station is designated as Klt and Budapest Deli station is designated as Del.

Budape—Balatonszentgyörgy

DEPART BUDAPEST	TRAIN NUMBER	ARRIVE BALATON	TRAIN NUMBER	DEPART BALATON	ARRIVE BUDAPEST
IC872/IC242	0615 Klt	0836	IC 855	1504	1726 Klt
862	0706 Del	1002	203	1556	1913 Klt
8502	0800 Del	1114	8503	1638	2010 Del
202	1005 Klt	1313	IC871/851	1704	1929 Klt
			861	1743	2034 Del
			243	2010	2246 Klt

Distance: 112 miles (180 km)

Budapest—Siofok

TRAIN NUMBER	DEPART BUDAPEST	ARRIVE SIOFÓK
269	0755 Klt	0935
8502	0800 Del	0950
202	1005 Klt	1200
415	1210 Klt	1354
IC 874	1245 Klt	1416

TRAIN NUMBER	DEPART SIOFÓK	ARRIVE BUDAPEST
414	1536	1738 Klt
IC 855	1555	1726 Klt
203	1720	1913 Klt
IC 871	1755	1929 Klt
8503	1819	2010 Del
861	1856	2034 Del
268	1934	2123 Klt
243	2110	2246 Klt

Distance: 72 miles (115 km)

Budapest—Kecskemét

TRAIN NUMBER	DEPART BUDAPEST NYUGATI	ARRIVE KECSKEMÉT	NOTES
IC 702	0715	0829	
752	0815	0950	
712	1025	1158	
IC 704	1115	1229	Su only
714	1225	1349	

TRAIN NUMBER	DEPART KECSKEMÉT	ARRIVE BUDAPEST NYUGATI	NOTES
713	1430	1554	
IC 703	1530	1643	
753	1629	1758	
711	1830	1954	
IC 701	1930	2043	
14701	2120	2306	M–F
17001	2151	2314	Sa–Su

Distance: 66 miles (106 km)

Budapest—Szeged

TRAIN NUMBER	DEPART BUDAPEST NYUGATI	ARRIVE SZEGED	NOTES
IC 702	0715	0927	
752	0815	1059	
712	1025	1308	
IC 704	1115	1327	Su only
714	1225	1459	

TRAIN NUMBER	DEPART0 SZEGED	ARRIVE BUDAPEST NYUGATI	NOTES
IC 703	1430	1643	
753	1520	1758	
711	1720	1954	
IC 701	1830	2043	
14701	1935	2306	M–F
17001	2015	2314	Sa–Su

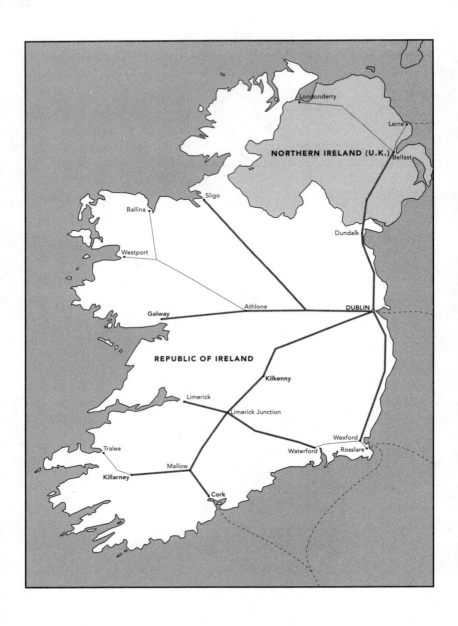

NORTHERN IRELAND (U.K.)

Londonderry

Larne

Belfast

Sligo

Ballina

Westport

Dundalk

Athlone

DUBLIN

Galway

REPUBLIC OF IRELAND

Kilkenny

Limerick

Limerick Junction

Tralee

Wexford

Waterford

Rosslare

Mallow

Killarney

Cork

Ireland

Known as "the Emerald Isle," Ireland is no doubt the greenest country of Europe. According to legend, a true Irishman can recognize at least forty shades of green. The breeze that blows across the seas to Ireland drops its moisture from the time it touches the Irish shoreline on the Atlantic Ocean until it's well out into the Irish Sea. A raincoat or an umbrella—or both—is essential equipment for your visit, and a sweater, even in summer. But the sun also shines a bountiful bit of the time, and most of the time showers disappear as quickly as they come.

Today's tourists to Ireland are discovering a new Ireland. Tourism to Ireland is growing rapidly, and Dublin is one of the most rapidly changing capitals in the 1990s. To accommodate these increases, Ireland has expanded all forms of its public transportation. Even Ireland's five international airports—Dublin, Shannon, Cork, Knock, and Belfast (in Northern Ireland) have undergone major expansions, reflecting the increase of air traffic from all parts of the world.

With all of the enhancements in Ireland, some things remain unchanged— Irish friendliness. Its citizens still seem to have the time to be genuinely interested in you and wondrously literate when discussing almost any subject. Even if scurrying for a bus, the Irish will stop to chat when they spy a friend—after all, there's always another bus. In Gaelic, *céad mile fáilte* means "one hundred thousand welcomes!" You'll hear it frequently.

For more information about Ireland, contact the Irish Tourist Board offices in North America:

New York: 345 Park Avenue, New York, NY 10154; *Tel:* (212) 418–0800; *Fax:* (212) 371–9052; *Internet:* **www.ireland.travel.ie**; *E-mail:* info@irish touristboard.com

Northern Ireland Tourist Board

New York: 551 Fifth Avenue, Suite 701, New York NY 10176; *Tel:* (800) 326–0036 or (212) 922–0101; *Fax:* (212) 922–0099

Toronto: 3 Bloor Street West, Suite 1501, Toronto, Ontario M4W 3E2. *Tel:* (800) 576-8174 or (416) 925-6368; *Fax:* (416) 925–6033; *Internet:* **www.northern ireland.tourism.com**

Republic of Ireland

- **Currency:** Irish punt (IEP)
- **Exchange rate at press time:** 0.73 Irish IEP = $1.00 U.S.

Communications

- **Country Code:** 353
- **Direct dial:** AT&T: 1–800–550–000; MCI: 1–800–551–001; Sprint: 1–800–552–001

Rail/Bus Travel in Ireland

Because the country is only about the size of the State of Pennsylvania in the United States, travelers can easily discover Ireland by using the rail and bus systems. **Irish Rail** (Iarnród Éireann)—a subsidiary of Coras Iompair Éireann (CIE), Ireland's transport company—has been upgrading its railroads and rail facilities as an essential part of Ireland's development plan, with the goal of reliable, convenient, and fast passenger travel throughout the country. Much of the equipment compares favorably with the EuroCity trains operated on the Continent.

If wishing to travel strictly within Ireland, then in North America contact **CIE Tours International,** P.O. Box 501, Cedar Knolls, NJ 07927–0501 (800–243–8687; *fax:* 800–338–3964). Visit their Web site at **www. irishrail.ia.** Otherwise, use your Eurailpass for rail travel on the Emerald Isle.

Ireland's high-speed trains are modeled after the futuristic TGV-style Eurostar trains and aptly dubbed "the trains of the future." *The Enterprise* is one of the high-tech trains that connects Dublin with Belfast in Northern Ireland. The air-conditioned carriages include digital displays and satellite route maps.

First class is referred to as "super-standard," and second class is known as "standard." First-class railpass holders are entitled to travel in super-standard coaches without payment of supplements. First class coaches are equipped with reclining seats and headphones, with a choice of listening to radio, cassette tape, or CD unit. A facsimile service is provided, as are "Silver Service" meals served at the seats.

Standard-class coaches include a "family room" at one end of the car for those with children. Light meals are available from the mobile food service cart and the buffet (pronounced "buffey" in Ireland) area of the coach.

Some trains operate with standard-class (second class) coaches only. Standard-class seats are not reservable for individuals, only groups (no seat reservations on bank holidays or weekends). You are required to show your ticket (or railpass) when entering the train platforms in Irish rail stations, so have it handy. Porters are usually tipped 1 £ per bag.

Food and beverages are served by Irish Rail's own catering service. The service varies according to the type of train. Full-service restaurant cars are hauled on main-line routes operating between Dublin–Cork, Dublin–Galway, Dublin–Limerick, Dublin–Tralee, and Dublin–Belfast, and then only on a few express trains. Most catering consists of buffet cars or snack-bar service. Food carts are used on some routes. When traveling on a train hauling a restaurant car, super-standard passengers are provided with in-seat catering. In buffet cars, you can obtain hot food, but trains equipped with snack-bar service offer only sandwiches and other prepared food. You may take your own food and beverages aboard. Take some candy treats with you—it's a good way to get acquainted with other passengers.

Service to the cities in the Republic slated for faster, more efficient service include Galway, Sligo, Westport, and Tralee.

Eurailpasses are accepted for rail travel in the Republic of Ireland, but not in Northern Ireland. Eurailpass bonuses include passage on the Irish Ferries between Ireland (Rosslare) and France v.v. (Cherbourg or Roscoff), at a 50 percent reduced rate. The **Bus Eireann "Rover Ticket,"** valid for 3 days of travel within an 8-day period on Bus Eireann Expressway, provincial buses, and city buses in Cork, Limerick, Galway, and Waterford, is offered at a discounted price of IR £25.

The **BritRail Plus Ireland Pass** is accepted in both the Republic of Ireland and Northern Ireland, as well as in England, Scotland, and Wales, and covers a round-trip connection on your choice of three **Stena Line** ferry routes: between Dun Laoghaire and Holyhead, Rosslare and Fishguard, or Belfast and Stranraer.

For more detailed information on travel in Britain, please read our other rail guidebook, *Britain by Britrail–How to Tour Britain by Train,* published by The Globe Pequot Press.

A variety of railpasses and rail/bus combination tickets are available to help in exploring the Emerald Isle. The Irish Rover Passes and the Emerald Cards cover both the Republic of Ireland and Northern Ireland.

The **Irish Rover Pass** (Republic of Ireland and Northern Ireland) offers 5 days of unlimited rail travel to be used within 15 consecutive days ($124, Adult; $62, Child) on Irish Rail, DART, Intercity, Suburban Rail, and Northern Ireland Rail.

The **Emerald Card** offers rail service throughout the Republic of Ireland and Northern Ireland, plus local rail in the Dublin area, combined with city bus services in Belfast, Cork, Dublin, Galway, Limerick, and Waterford.

Emerald Card

	Adult	Child
8-Day Ticket within 15 Consecutive Days	$174	$87
15-Day Ticket within 30 Consecutive Days	$300	$150

The **Irish Explorer** offers travelers 8 days of unlimited rail/bus transport or 5 days of purely rail travel. Both are valid only in the Republic of Ireland, plus local rail in the Dublin area.

Irish Explorer

	Adult	Child (under 12)
Rail Only 5-Day Ticket within 15 Consecutive Days	$100	$50
Rail/Bus 8-Day Ticket within 30 Consecutive Days	$150	$75

2000 prices unavailable at press time.
See the Appendix for a detailed list of multiple-country passes and the Ferry Crossings section therein for detailed information on sailing from Ireland to France and Britain.

Base City . . .

Dublin

City Dialing Code: 1
Internet: www.visit.ie/dublin or www.dublintourist.com

About one-third of the Republic of Ireland's population lives in or near Dublin. The city is as intoxicating as its national brew—Guinness—also lovingly referred to as Dublin's "water supply."

O'Connell Street is Dublin's somewhat tarnished "Main Street," the pulsating heart of the old city, and Ireland's broadest boulevard. A grand statue of the Irish patriot Daniel O'Connell, THE LIBERATOR, stands at the foot of O'Connell Street, where O'Connell Bridge crosses the River Liffey. A new sculpture of James Joyce's river spirit, *Anna Livia,* is one of the many statues of national heroes posed along the way to the Garden of Remembrance at Parnell Square.

Art galleries, museums, shopping areas such as the Powerscourt Townhouse Center and Grafton Street, famous cathedrals, and elegant cafes are within walking distance of O'Connell Street. The best-preserved examples of eighteenth-century houses are also found nearby. **St. Stephen's Green** at the top of Grafton Street is ringed with magnificently restored, stately Georgian residences, with solid-colored enameled doors and sparkling brass fixtures.

Arriving by Air

Ireland has two main gateways for air travelers: **Shannon International Airport,** on the west side of the Republic, and Dublin Airport, 6 miles northeast of the city's center. Aer Lingus, American Trans Air, Continental, and Delta service both Shannon and Dublin. Other air carriers stop only in Shannon, which has a world-famous, duty-free shopping area featuring items produced in Ireland. Shannon's major renovations are scheduled for completion by the year 2000.

Airport–City Links: Shannon connects with the rail station in Limerick by airport bus service. Journey time: 45 minutes; fare, £3.50 (£4.60 round trip).

Dublin Airport is near completion of its substantial (£95 million) redevelopment plan to increase its terminal building capacity to 15 million passengers per year.

Airport–City Links: bus to Dublin's central bus station. Journey time: 25 minutes; £3.50.

Arriving by Train

- **Connolly Station and DART,** 35 Lower Abbey Street, (*Tel:* 01 836–6222)

Connolly Station is the terminal in Dublin for trains arriving from Northern Ireland and for boat trains connecting with the Irish ferries that sail from the port of Rosslare, south of Dublin, to the French ports of Cherbourg and Le Havre.

Coming from London by train requires a transfer to either a Stena Line or Irish Ferries ferry at Holyhead. The Stena Line ferries serve the port of Dun Laoghaire, a suburb of Dublin, where passengers can transfer to the center of the city by the local rapid transit train service, DART.

The northwestern coastal city of Sligo is also reached by train service departing from Connolly Station, as are the towns of Wicklow and Wexford, located south of Dublin in the direction of Rosslare.

- **Heuston Station:** west of City Center on the River Liffey (*Tel*: 01-677–1871)

Heuston Station serves as the departure point for *Europe by Eurail* day excursions to Cork, Galway, Kilkenny, and Killarney.

City buses depart from the head of track No. 5 in Heuston Station and take passengers near the O'Connell Bridge. There is also a taxi stand on the opposite side of the station immediately beyond track No. 1 and outside the ticket-office entrance.

Heuston Station has eight main tracks. Ticket offices are located on the side of the station serving track Nos. 1 and 2. Train information and railpass validation are available at any of the ticket windows.

Advance seat reservations may be obtained from the CIE (Irish Rail) ticket office at Connolly and Heuston Stations and at the CIE Travel Centre at 35 Lower Abbey Street. Reservations are made up to 1700 on the preceding day. Without seat reservations, we suggest arriving in the station about a half-hour before your train's scheduled departure time just in case the travel is heavy on the day you have selected for your excursion.

Shopping for Waterford crystal? Depart Heuston Station via Kilkenny to the town where it's made—and take money, lots of it!

Tourist Information/Hotel Reservations

Tourist Information Office: Dublin Tourism Centre, Suffolk Street
Tel: 011–800-6686-6866, *Fax:* 011-353-6697-92116; *Internet:* www.visit.ie/dublin
E-mail: reservations@dublintourism.ie

Dublin is well equipped to offer a wide range of accommodations to visitors. Two exceptions, however, come during the Dublin Horse Show in early August and St. Patrick's Day in March. The principal sporting and social event of the year in Ireland, the horse show attracts thousands of visitors from all parts of the world. Don't plan to be in Dublin during the horse show unless you have confirmed reservations. The city is filled to overflowing at that time. If you are planning a visit to Dublin on St. Patrick's Day or during the summer months, it would be wise to check well in advance with the Irish Tourist Board in New York for accommodation arrangements.

Travelers looking for homelike accommodations can purchase the Irish Tourist Offices' *Self Catering* **services guide** describing apartments or houses for short-term rent (for a few days, a weekend, or a week). For reservations, contact the Dublin Tourism Centre.

Bed-and-breakfast establishments are also a viable alternative to large, expensive hotels. Again, the Irish Tourist Offices maintain current descriptions. Mary and Brian Bennett's extraordinary guest house **Number 31** at Leeson Close, Dublin 2 (*Tel:* 1–676 5011), is the former home of Sam Stephenson, one of Dublin's renowned architects.

For those who wish to experience the ambience of Dublin's newest landmark hotel, we suggest the Brooks Hotel, 59–62 Drury Street, Dublin 2 (*Tel:* 01670 4000; *Fax:* 01670 4455; *e-mail:* reservations@brookshotel.ie). Room rates range from standard to superior executive suites, and the location places you in the heart of the city, with Grafton Street, Temple Bar, and Trinity College only a short walk away.

Getting Around In and Outside Dublin

- **DART,** 35 Lower Abbey Street, *Tel:* (01) 836–6222
- **Bus Eireann,** Store Street, *Tel:* (01) 836–6111

DART, or Dublin Area Rapid Transit, is the electric commuter service running around Dublin Bay and provides the fastest way of getting around Dublin as well as convenient access to the many resorts and other attractions outside of Dublin.

Much of the route is coastal and gives many different views of the bay. It's excellent for short excursions to places such as the charming fishing village of Howth at its northern end or Dun Laoghaire, the busy harbor for the Stena Line ferry service to England via Holyhead. DART accepts Eurailpass, as well as the various Irish Rail and/or Bus combination passes.

Dublin's DART has expanded to include stations at Clontarf Road, Kilcock, and Drumcondra. They have also improved their public address system, electronic information displays, signs, and lighting, plus they have provided easier accessibility for the handicapped.

Service to the cities in the Republic slated for faster, more efficient service include Galway, Sligo, Westport, and Tralee.

Sights/Attractions/Tours—Discovering Dublin

Dublin, with a population of over one million people in its greater metropolitan area, offers the excitement of a vital city yet the ambience of an Old-World town.

Sightseeing on foot is easy. During your visit to the Dublin tourist information office, purchase the walking tour guide booklets that are of interest to you: **Heritage Trails,** or the **Rock 'n Stroll Trail** (significant sites in Dublin's music history), which is popular among the younger set. The success of bands like U2 and the Cranberries and singers like Sinead O'Connor, who began her career by singing traditional Irish songs, has made Dublin a rock music capital.

Each of these brochures describes specially selected, sign-posted walking tours through the center of Dublin and includes many points of interest. The tours are so designed that you can pick up the trails anywhere within the downtown area. The routes cover much of what is of interest historically and culturally to visitors and take about three hours.

If you plan to visit the **Dublin Writers Museum**, the **Joyce Tower, Shaw's Birthplace**, the **Viking Adventure, Malahide Castle, Newbridge House** and the **Fry Model Railway Museum,** purchase the **Dublin Super Saver Card** at the tourist office and save 25 percent off the total admission charges (£16 adults; £12.50 seniors and students; £8.60 children; and £37.50 families).

One of Dublin's sights to see is **O'Connell Street.** A block away on the river's south bank stands **Parliament House** (now the Bank of Ireland), which faces the entrance to Trinity College, founded in 1592. The **Book of Kells,** considered its greatest treasure, is housed in the Collonades. Tourist trails lead from that point to **St. Stephen's Green** at the top of Grafton Street, where its twenty-two acres are surrounded delightfully by splendid Georgian houses.

Most shops in these areas are open Monday–Saturday from 0900 to 1730 or 1800, with extended hours on Thursdays. Plus many shops are now open on Sundays from 1200 to 1800.

For an insight into Irish life, **visit a Dublin pub**. In general, the Irish treat their pubs as a second home. The French seem to spend a relatively short time in a cafe before heading off for lunch, dinner, or whatever. The English go to a pub for a chat with friends and the barmaid and perhaps a game of darts before heading homeward. But the Irish, when they have the time (and they generally seem to), are in the pub for the entire evening.

The main pub activities are drinking and talking, although many serve appetizing meals and snacks and provide entertainment in the form of traditional music and song. You are free to sit and watch or join in. To take the latter option, merely turn to your neighbor and mention the weather. With that, the ball's in play. What is revealed then is fascinating. You'll find that everyone has positive but sensible opinions about a myriad of subjects. Make certain that what you say about a topic is relevant, for unlike most bar conversationalists, the Irish listen when you speak. Listening is an art that can be developed to a fine degree in a Dublin pub. Unless you are a Scot, try not to match the Dubliners' drinking ability or verbal athletics.

If you have the luck of the Irish to be in Dublin for **New Year's Eve**, be sure to plan ahead for one of the many celebrations. A few choices include "Millennium Mania," offering musical time-zoned parties of the 70s, 80s, and 90s. Call 47 83 844 for details on the House of Fun, the 70s Experience, and the Bug Room themes. Perhaps the Mont Clare Hotel's "Music Through the Ages Party" with tunes from the 60s, 70s, and 80s or the premiere "Gala

Millennium Ball" at the Alexander Hotel are more your style. Call 60 73 900 for information on both hotel packages (both include 2 nights accommodations).

If you can keep up with the locals, then reserve tickets for the "Two Night Millennium Show Special" at the Red Cow Moran Hotel by calling 45 93 650. A Gala Ball will be held New Year's Eve and a semi-formal party on New Year's Night. Phhew!!

Suburban Dublin Day Excursions

Travelers can stay in Dublin, their "Base City," and easily make day excursions to visit other areas outside of Dublin. Or, they can use the "flip side" of the Base City–Day Excursion concept by taking advantage of less expensive accommodations outside the city and making day excursions into Dublin.

Some Dublin suburban-area day excursions include:

Dun Laoghaire, a charming, lovely port on the Irish Sea that can be reached in only 15 minutes by DART from Dublin's Connolly Station. The ferry terminal and DART station are much more convenient for travelers than the former underground facility. The Stena Line's HSS (High-speed Seacat Service) catamaran provides inexpensive passage to and from Great Britain in less than 2 hours. A variety of hotels, bed-and-breakfast establishments, hostels, and the new "self-catering" apartments and houses are available in Dun Laoghaire for those who prefer to stay just outside of Dublin.

For a high-standard hostel on a low-cost budget, consider **The Old Schoolhouse,** Eblana Avenue, Dun Laoghaire (*Tel:* (1) 280–8777; *Fax:* (1) 284–2266). It's a former Christian Brothers school that was renovated to create a modern, comfortable hostel that includes a laundry, a television room, and use of fully equipped kitchen facilities.

Other Dublin suburban areas within easy reach via DART, Suburban Rail and the Arrow lines include:

Bray, 30 minutes from Dublin, is where writer James Joyce and artist Neil Jordan once lived and where rock star Bono of U2 makes his home. Connecting buses can take you to the quaint little village of **Enniskerry,** with its delightful cafes, coffee shops, and comfortable bed-and-breakfast facilities.

Howth, only 25 minutes from Connolly Station via DART, is a charming fishing village on the northern side of Dublin Bay.

Naas, southwest of Dublin, can be reached by the Arrow train line departing from Heuston Station. Naas is famous as a center for horse breeding, and race horse owners from all over the world attend the October yearling sales held nearby.

Kildare, also famous with the equestrian set as a center for horse breeding and home of the Irish National Stud, is only 48 kilometers away and the last stop on the Arrow line trains departing from Dublin's Heuston Station. For luxurious resort-type accommodations (at resort-type prices, of course) the Kildare Hotel and Country Club is top notch. The transformation of the former fifth-century Straffan mansion into a luxury hotel took more than 2 years to complete. The clubhouse and 18-hole golf course were designed by Arnold Palmer.

Waterford, a twelfth-century Norman fortress positioned on the banks of the Suir, has been a significant port since the sixteenth century. The Dominican Blackfriars and ruins of the French Church are reminders of medieval times, as is the twelfth-century Reginald's Tower, where the city's museum is located. In 1170 Strongbow was married to Princess Aoife, daughter of the King of Leinster, in Christ Church Cathedral, where today an audio-visual presentation using the excellent acoustics of the nave re-creates a one-thousand-year-old history of the area. Hook Tower, one of the oldest lighthouses in Europe, stands proudly at Hook Head at the beginning of the estuary in Waterford Bay. Waterford is home to Waterford Crystal, the largest crystal factory in the world. From April through October, the **Waterford Crystal Visitor Centre** is open seven days a week from 0830 to 1800. Tours and audio-visual presentations are available April through October, and the gallery features some of the most unique and valuable crystal pieces ever created.

Waterford Castle (*Tel:* (05) 187–8203. In the U.S., *Tel:* (800) 221–1074), located on an island, began as a monastic settlement in the sixth century. It ultimately became one of the estates of the Fitzgeralds, who were the Kings of Ireland during the fifteenth and sixteenth centuries. Purchased by Eddie Kearns in 1987, it was developed into a luxurious hotel and country club. The castle's guest rooms are comfortable and bright, with beautiful views of the estate. Conference facilities are available, and special arrangements are made for business entertaining. The main dining room seats 65 guests and often hosts a resident pianist. Hunting and polo are available, as is deep-sea and freshwater fishing. Croquet is played on the Castle lawns. An excellent country club and championship golf course and luxurious leisure center also grace the island.

More Day Excursions

Other day excursions made conveniently with Irish Rail/Bus are **Cork, Galway, Killarney,** and **Kilkenny.** Cork provides a double treat when you tread its fascinating quays and kiss the renowned stone at nearby Blarney Castle. Galway, the western capital of Ireland, has all the charm of an ancient city, plus the vitality of expanding industries and popular holiday-resort attractions. The combination of Kilkenny Town and Kilkenny Castle offers a delightful variety of attractions, from cats and choir lofts to castle tours and witches' tales.

Train Connections to and from Port of Rosslare for Ferry Connections to Cherbourg

Dublin—Rosslare Harbour

DEPART DUBLIN CONNOLLY	ARRIVE ROSSLARE HARBOUR	NOTES	DEPART ROSSLARE HARBOUR	ARRIVE DUBLIN CONNOLLY	NOTES
0845	1200	except Sun	0720	1020	except Sun
1000	1259	Sun	0852	1156	Sun
1325	1630		1445	1758	
1830	2132		1825	2129	

Daily, unless otherwise noted
For more information, telephone (1) 836622
Standard class only on all trains
Distance: 95 miles (168 km)

Day Excursion to

Cork

AND THE BLARNEY STONE

Depart from Dublin Heuston Station

Distance by Train: 165 miles (266 km)
Average Train Time: 2 hours, 20 minutes
City Dialing Code: 21
Cork Tourist Information: Tourist House, Grand Parade
Tel: (021) 273251; *Fax:* (021) 273504
Internet: www.Ireland.travel.ie; *E-mail:* user@cktourism.ie
Hours: Monday–Saturday 0900–1900. In winter, 0915–1730 Monday–Saturday (closed for lunch 1300–1415). Guided tours of the city depart daily at 1100 and 1430. *Tel:* (021) 293822 to reserve your place on the tour.

To get to the tourist office on foot, exit the railway station to Railway Street and turn left to Penrose's Quay. Make a right onto Penrose's Quay to St. Patrick's Bridge. Turn left onto St. Patrick's Street until you come to Grand Parade on your left. Follow it past Oliver Plunkett Street and you will see the tourist office on your left. To get to the bus station from the tourist office, go back to Oliver Plunkett Street where you turn right. Turn left on Anglesea Street until you come to the bus station.

Dublin—Cork

DEPART DUBLIN HEUSTON	ARRIVE CORK	NOTES	DEPART CORK	ARRIVE DUBLIN HEUSTON	NOTES
0730	1010	daily except Sun	1445	1735	except Sun
1005	1320	Sun	1630	1910	Sun
1025	1255	Fri	1730	1950	Sun
1125	1407	daily except Sun	1730	2005	except Sun
1215	1505	Sun	1845	2125	Sun
1320	1615	daily except Sun	1900	2200	except Sun

Distance: 165 miles (266 km)

Cork, Ireland's second largest city (about 200,000 residents) and commercial and passenger port, is easily accessible from both Dublin and Shannon (via train from Limerick). From Dublin a special executive car called "City Gold" is available, with special amenities for doing business, including fax and phone.

Cork City, *Corcach* in Irish meaning "marshy place," was actually built upon the marshes and wetlands of the River Lee. **Saint Finbarr's Cathedral** is located where Cork's first settlement and monastery was founded by the missionary in the seventh century. The **Guinness International Jazz Festival,** held in October, attracts world-famous musicians, including famous American stars.

The village of **Blarney** is a short, 25-minute bus ride north of the city, where the "touristy" thing to do is visit **Blarney Castle** and kiss the legendary **Blarney Stone,** which promises the gift of eloquence to anyone believing enough to be lowered backward from the battlements on the roof of the castle to achieve it. You will, of course, be adding to the lip prints of thousands of other tourists who have attempted the same thing.

Board the bus marked BLARNEY in the city's bus terminal at Parnell Place. It's only a 10-minute walk down Glanmire Road to the river and the bus station. On Sunday buses depart Cork on the hour 0900–2300 and return at 35 minutes past the hour. During the week, buses run about every 15 minutes.

There are many legends regarding the origins of the Blarney Stone. According to one, it was brought to Ireland from the Holy Land during one of the crusades. Another theory has the Blarney Stone originating from half of the Stone of Scone, with Robert the Bruce giving the mystical rock to Cormac MacCarthy, Lord of Blarney, in 1314. Legend has it that the gift of eloquence would be bestowed upon anyone who kissed it. It was not until Cormac MacCarthy saved an elderly woman from drowning that he learned of this magical secret.

The moist, temperate climate of Cork makes for splendid gardens and wonderful parks. And shopping the maze of streets between Patrick Street and South Mall provides a plethora of fashions and fashionable cafes and eateries offering finely prepared foods at various prices.

Day Excursion to

Galway

ROUNDSTONE

Depart from Dublin Heuston Station

Distance by Train: 129 miles (208 km)
Average Train Time: 2 hours, 40 minutes
City Dialing Code: 91
Tourist Information Center: Victoria Place, Eyre Square (current location), Forster Street, across from City Hall (opening in late 2000)
Tel: 091 563081; *Fax:* 091 565201
Internet: www.galwaytourism.ie; *E-mail*: user@western-tourism.ie
Hours: Open daily May–June, September–October, 0900–1745; July–August, 0900–1945. Open November–April, Monday–Friday, 0900–1745; Saturday, 0900–1245.

Emerging from the railway station, you'll see Eyre Square with the Kennedy Park in its center. Turn left and left again at Victoria Place. The traditional green **i** signs will lead you to the tourist office. Fronting the square is the Great Southern Hotel. (Turn right and right again at Victoria Place, to find the new office.)

Like some other Irish cities, Galway was established initially by foreigners. Since medieval times, it has been a significant port dominated by an oligarchy of fourteen Norman and Welsh merchant families. As a thriving trade with Spain developed, the **Spanish Arch** was erected in 1594; it was created to protect the Spanish ships as they unloaded their cargo. It still remains below the Claddagh Bridge and has an adjacent museum. The avenue leading from the arch known as the "Long Walk," is where Spanish merchants supposedly strolled into Galway City. The area is still resplendent with Spanish architecture.

Galway has become Ireland's fastest-growing city. A university town since the fourteenth century, Galway still has a huge student population and is still a cultural center for writers and scholars. In October, March, and July, Galway (as in Dublin and Cork) hosts an **international film festival** to showcase new cinema.

Guided tours via double decker buses depart Eyre Square every 30 minutes. **Eyre Square,** given to the city by Edward Eyre in 1710, is the heart of Galway City activity and the site where the John F. Kennedy Memorial Park is located.

Dublin—Galway

DEPART DUBLIN HEUSTON	ARRIVE GALWAY	NOTES	DEPART GALWAY	ARRIVE DUBLIN HEUSTON	NOTES
0720	1000	except Sun	1525	1813	except Sun
0910	1155	Sun	1625	1921	Sun
1100	1350	except Sun	1805	2105	except Sun
			1810	2055	Sun

Distance: 129 miles (208 km)

Fronting the square is the **Great Southern Hotel,** a hostelry combining the charm of both old and new and an ideal place to halt for a libation or a luncheon. The shopping center west of the square is also where the last section of the old wall has been preserved, along with the Penrice and Shoemaker Towers.

At 19 Eyre Square, the Bank of Ireland displays the priceless **Silver Sword** and Great Mace, the finest examples of Irish silver work remaining in the Republic.

Galway is a ferry port for the Aran Islands, which lie 30 miles offshore, as are Doolin and Rossaveal. Air service is available via Connemara airport. The islands are a tribute to traditional Irish life and culture, and, as in Galway and Connemara, Gaelic is still proudly spoken among the natives.

The **Galway Bay Conference and Leisure Centre** (*Tel:* 091 520520) is a prime example of Galway City's growth. The new deluxe facility is located on Galway's promenade, just minutes from Eyre Square and the City Center. It includes a fitness center with swimming pool, sauna, and steam room. Restaurant, bar, and lounge each have panoramic views of Galway Bay. With its proximity to **Leisureland,** the hotel is one of the most extensive conference and leisure centers in the country.

Or, if you decide to base yourself in Galway for a night or two, try Jury's Galway Inn, a mere half-mile from Ceannt Station. The inn overlooks Galway Bay and is located in the heart of the city near the historic Spanish Arch. *Tel:* 3539–1566444; *Fax:* (353) 9156–8415.

Supposedly, the word *lynching* entered the English language through an act of Galway's chief magistrate, James Lynch-FitzStephen, elected to his post in 1493. According to a popular but dubious legend, his son, Walter, murdered a Spanish visitor and then confessed to the crime. He was condemned by his own father, but no one could be found to carry out the execution. So Judge Lynch, no doubt a firm believer in "spare the rod and spoil the child," hanged his own son and afterward retired into seclusion. **Lynch's Castle** stands today on Shop Street, and the Lynch Memorial attesting to this stern and unbending justice lies nearby, close to the **Church of St. Nicholas,** erected in 1320.

Legend has it that Columbus worshiped in the church before setting out on his voyage of discovery to America.

An unusual feature of Galway is its downtown salmon weir, where shoals of salmon swim in the clear river en route to spawning grounds. This unique sight may be viewed from the **Salmon Weir Bridge** crossing the Corrib River by the city's cathedral.

Roundstone is a picturesque fishing village on the southern shores of Connemara. Already well known for superb seafood and quaint bed-and-breakfast-style hotels, Roundstone is also "the home of the bodhran"—a one-sided framed drum made from goatskin—Ireland's oldest product made famous more recently when played by Christy Moore in *Riverdance*. A bus leaves daily during the summer from Foster Street in Galway City for Roundstone and Clifden.

If you have never seen *Riverdance* or heard the haunting tones of the bodhrans, you've missed one of the most exciting music and dance shows in the last 1,000 years. Visit master bodhran maker **Malachy Kearns'** (known locally as Malachy Bodhran) quaint craft and music shop. Malachy and artist-wife Anne are the only full-time bodhran makers in the world and they've been making them for 22 years.

You can purchase the handmade bodhrans with Celtic designs, family crests, or names. The shop is open daily 0900–1900. Malachy Kearns mixes the goatskins with secret ingredients and soaks them for 7–10 days before stretching them over a beech-wood frame. Mr. Kearns attributes the bodhran's haunting tones to the goatskins; we think his secret ingredients have something to do with achieving such extraordinary sound. It is truly fascinating!

Roundstone Music, Roundstone, Connemara, Co. Galway
Tel: 095 35808; *Fax:* 095 35980
E-mail: bodhran@iol.ie
Internet: www.musweb.com/kearns.htm

Day Excursion to

Kilkenny

<small>GHOSTS AND GIFTS GALORE</small>

Depart from Dublin Heuston Station

Distance by Train: 81 miles (130 km)
Average Train Time: 1 hour, 49 minutes
City Dialing Code: 56
Kilkenny Tourist Information: Shee Alms House, Rose Inn Street, Kilkenny
Tel: 056 51500; *Fax:* 056 63955
Hours: May–July, Monday–Saturday 0900–1800, Sunday 1100–1700

Dublin–Kilkenny

DEPART DUBLIN HEUSTON	ARRIVE KILKENNY	NOTES
0740	0937	except Sun
0955	1145	Sun
1145	1335	except Sun

DEPART KILKENNY	ARRIVE DUBLIN HEUSTON	NOTES
1520	1710	Sun
1540	1726	except Sun
1845	2040	Sun
1910	2058	except Fri, Sun
1920	2112	Fri
2055	2250	Fri

Distance: 81 miles (130 km)

To reach it, turn left onto John Street after leaving the station and walk to the bridge crossing the river. Cross the bridge and John Street then becomes Rose Inn Street. Continue walking up Rose Inn Street and you will find the office in the Shee Alms House on the right.

Kilkenny may be Ireland's smallest city, but it is one of the most popular destinations from Dublin. **Kilkenny Castle** (by guided tour only), a twelfth-century grand stone fortress on the River Nore, dominates the scene and sets the theme. It was the chief residence of the Butler family from 1391 until 1935—almost 550 years. Recently restored to the majesty of the 1820s, it is now home to the National Furniture collection and the modern Butler Gallery. The castle is impressive and reminiscent of the great bastions along the Rhine River.

Other sites include the thirteenth-century **St. Canice's Cathedral,** reputed to be one of the most beautiful in Ireland; **Rothe House,** home of the Kilkenny Archeological Society; and **Shee Alms House,** a restored sixteenth-century building that houses the Tourist Information Office.

Though small, Kilkenny is cosmopolitan, with a pub and club life that draws visitors from major cities. In fact, the **Paris Texas Bar & Restaurant** has to close its doors by 2100 because of the crowds. **Langtons,** a four-time winner of the National Pub of the Year award, is a traditional pub and restaurant in grand surroundings, with a disco club that stays open to the wee hours of the morning. (A hotel facility is adjacent to the disco; *Tel:* 056–65133).

Another interesting landmark is **Kytler's Inn,** which has the distinction of being the oldest residence in the city and, by tradition, the house of the witch Dame Alice Kytler, born there in 1280. Dame Alice seems to have been a very nice lady except that she acquired and disposed of husbands—four in all—in rapid succession. This aroused the curiosity of the local folks, and in 1324 she was charged by Bishop de Ledrede with witchcraft, heresy, and criminal assaults upon her husbands. Brought to trial and condemned to burn at the stake as a witch, Dame Alice eluded her accusers and escaped across the Irish Sea to Scotland. Her maid, Petronilla, was not as fortunate; the bishop had her burned at the stake as a suitable substitute. Locals claim that Petronilla's ghost still haunts the cellar of what is now the Kytler Inn on St. Kieran Street— possibly asking for back wages?

Day Excursion to

Killarney
LAKES AND JAUNTING CARS

Depart from Dublin Heuston Station

Distance by Train: 185 miles, 298 km
Average Train Time: 3 hours, 30 minutes
City Dialing Code: 64
Killarney Tourist Information: Town Hall,
Tel: 064 31633; *Fax:* 064 34506
Hours: July–August, Monday–Saturday 0900–1000, Sunday 1000-1300/1400–1800; June and September, Monday–Saturday 0900–1900; October–May, Monday–Saturday 0930–1830

To reach the tourist information office, turn left on Railway Road just after passing the Great Southern Hotel on your left as you leave the railway station. Railway Road crosses Muckross Road a short distance from the station and almost immediately ends as it runs into Main Street. The jaunting-car stand will be on your left at this point. The tourist information office is housed in the Town Hall just ahead on your left.

Killarney is the number-one tourist attraction in the Republic of Ireland. Horse-drawn carriages known as jaunting cars take tourists to feature sights including: **Muckross Abbey**, the ruins of a fifteenth-century Franciscan monastery; **Ross Castle,** on the banks of Lough Leane; and **Muckross House,** a nineteenth-century manor with a museum depicting local folk life, and housing various craft shops with blacksmiths, weavers, and potters. Jaunting-car rates are usually based on four passengers. If your party is fewer than four, the tourist office may be just the place to find other passengers

Dublin—Killarney

DEPART DUBLIN HEUSTON	ARRIVE KILLARNEY	NOTES
0730	1055	change at Mallow; daily except Sun
0830	1148	Sun
0905	1244	except Sun
1005	1358	change at Mallow, Sun

DEPART KILLARNEY	ARRIVE DUBLIN HEUSTON	NOTES
1437	1825	except Sun
1442	1810	Sun
1655	2015	Sun
1747	2200	change at Mallow; daily except Sun
1756	2105	Sun

Distance: 185 miles (298 km)

willing to share the cost. The central jaunting-car stand in Killarney is a stone's throw from the tourist office; so you won't have to return to the railway station.

Killarney's **St. Mary's Cathedral** is an impressive Neo-Gothic structure worthy of a visit. The **Great Southern Hotel,** opposite the railway station, is a fashionable hostelry of great beauty, and its amicable Punchbowl Bar is a good place to pause for a libation and friendly conversation.

There are many eating places to choose from. We found the food at the **Flesk Restaurant** to be tasty and satisfying. It's on Main Street, a few doors past the tourist office on the left-hand side. One of the favorite spots of the locals, too, the Flesk is known for its daily fresh fish specials, such as wild salmon, and its live Dingle Bay lobsters. Four-course menus range from £8 to £12.

A classic Killarney countryside excursion is by bus to **Kate Kearney's Cottage,** a coaching inn, where you are fortified with Irish coffee. Then, setting out by pony through the **Gap of Dunloe,** you are refreshed again at **Lord Brandon's Cottage** before returning by boat to Lough Leane and to Killarney by jaunting car. You can obtain information on prices from the tourist office.

Italy

Why do we find Italy so inviting? Just ask any Italian—it can be summed up in three little words: *La dolce vita*, the sweet life. Italy is pasta, Pavarotti, and the pope; it's fashion, Ferrari, and films; it's *vino* (wine), Venus, and villas—it's all of our favorite things that culminate in *La dolce vita*.

Perennially a tourist favorite, Italy's allure continues with the advent of the Holy Year, or Jubilee 2000. The Holy Year, founded in 1300 by Pope Boniface VIII, is a spiritual pilgrimage that is celebrated only every 25 years. At press time, the Italian Government Tourist Board (ENIT) is establishing a special office to assist those who plan to visit Italy during the Holy Year.

Most visitors are aware of Italy's predominantly Catholic heritage, but not many are aware that Italy also has a rich Jewish heritage dating as early as 140 B.C. Most Italian Jews are descendants of the group Sephardim, who were expelled from Spain and Portugal in the fifteenth and sixteenth centuries. Many outstanding synagogues and other Jewish sites are most evident in Florence, Rome, and Venice.

For more information about Italy, contact the Italian Government Tourist Boards (ENIT) in North America:

Internet: **www.entich.italiantourism.com**

Chicago: 401 North Michigan Avenue, Suite 3030, Chicago, IL 60611. *Tel:* (312) 644–9448; *Fax:* (312) 644–3019

New York: 630 Fifth Avenue, Suite 1565, New York, NY 10111. *Tel:* (212) 245–4822; *Fax:* (212) 586–9249

Los Angeles: 12400 Wilshire Boulevard, Suite 550, Los Angeles, CA 90025. *Tel:* (310) 820–009; *Fax:* (310) 820–6357

Montreal: 1 Place Ville Marie, Suite 1914, Montreal, Quebec, H3B 3M9. *Tel:* (514) 866–7667; *Fax:* (514) 392–1429; *E-mail:* initaly@ican.net

Banking

- **Currency:** Italian Lira (ITL)
  Coins are in 50, 100, 200, and 500 Lire. Banknotes are in 1,000, 2,000, 5,000, 10,000, 50,000, and 100,000 Lire.
- **Exchange rate at press time:** 1,804.19 ITL = $1.00 U.S.

Communications

- **Country Code:** 39

For telephone calls within Italy, dial a zero (0) preceding area code.

Direct dial: AT&T: 172–1011; MCI: 172–1022; Sprint: 172–1877 in Bologna, Brindisi, Catania, Cozena, Florence, Formia, Genoa, Latina, Milan, Naples, Olbia, Padua, Palermo, Perugia, Pescara, Pisa, Pordenone, Trieste, Turin, and Venice. Buy telephone cards at any tobacco or newsstand for 2,000, 5,000, or 10,000 lire. Within the city, it costs 200 lire for the first 9 minutes. It's also possible to use 200- or 500-lire coins for calls. Public phones are available in rail stations, post offices, and most bars and restaurants.

Rail Travel in Italy

The **Italian State Railways** (*Ente Ferrovie Italiane dello Stato, or FS*) provides excellent and frequent train services linking all of Italy, including Sicily and Sardinia via train ferries, with Austria, France, and Switzerland. All main lines and many minor lines are electrified. Italy's principal express train service, the Eurostar *Italia* (not to be confused with the cross-Channel Eurostar trains and formerly referred to as the ETR Pendolino and ETR 500 trains), are among the best in Europe.

Keep in mind that Italian trains are not just for tourists; the Italians are heavily dependent upon their rail system and 2nd class rail cars are often crowded. We recommend traveling in 1st class when in Italy.

The Italian State Railways accepts **Eurailpass, Europass, Italy RailCard, Italy Flexi RailCard,** and the **Italian Kilometric Ticket.** The Eurailpass and Europass bonus includes the ferries operated by FS between Civitavecchia and Golfo Aranci (Sardinia) and between Villa S. Giovanni and Messina (Sicily). Ferries operated by Adriatica Lines and Hellenic Mediterranean Lines between Brindisi, Italy, and Corfu/Igoumenitsa/Patras, Greece, are also included (high-season surcharge applicable) with the Europass plus/Greece zone.

The Italy RailCard provides for unlimited rail travel for the specified number of days consecutively, or for more flexibility, choose the Flexi RailCard for traveling the specified number of days within a 1-month period.

Italy RailCard

2000 RATES	VALIDITY	1ST CLASS	2ND CLASS
	8-Day	$299	$199
	15-Day	$373	$249
	21-Day	$433	$289
	30-Day	$522	$348

Italy Flexi RailCard

2000 RATES	VALIDITY	1ST CLASS	2ND CLASS
	4–Day within 1 month	$239	$159
	8–Day within 1 month	$334	$223
	12–Day within 1 month	$429	$286

Italy RailCard and Flexi RailCard are valid for unlimited travel on the entire Italian State Railways network, including InterCity, EuroCity, and Rapido trains, with no surcharge. **Supplement required for Eurostar *Italia* trains.** Children under 12 years of age pay half adult fare; under 4 years of age, free.

The Italian Kilometric Pass (1st Class $289; 2nd Class $181 U.S.) provides up to 3,000 kilometers (1,875 miles) of rail travel within a 2–month period, with a maximum of 20 single train trips. The pass may be used by as many as 5 persons, but each trip is calculated by multiplying the distance by the number of persons traveling. It also requires a supplement for traveling on *all* high-speed trains (and Italy has a lot of them), such as InterCity, EuroCity, Rapido, and Eurostar *Italia*. A "single trip" means boarding a single train by a single person. This pass is inconvenient in that it deviates from the general concept of a railpass because travelers must show the pass at ticket windows before each train trip.

Base City . . .

Milan (Milano)

City Dialing Code: 2

Milan is fashionable and futuristic—as evidenced by the growing number of high-rise structures and the accelerating pace of its population. At the same time, Milan is ancient and respectful of its glorious past. For instance, the **Duomo** (cathedral) is the second largest church in Italy, a beautiful example of Gothic stonework begun in 1386. *The Last Supper*, Leonardo da Vinci's famous painting, may be seen in the refectory of the **Santa Maria delle Grazie** convent. It was painted between 1495 and 1498. Like a typical Milanese, Leonardo was concerned with the future, and his drawings of machines in flight, together with some of his futuristic inventions, are exhibited in the **Leonardo da Vinci National Museum of Science and Technology.**

To promote its future, Milan created one of the most extensive fairgrounds in Europe; each year, thousands of businesses display or investigate products there. Milan does not live up to the stereotype of the Italian town. Lunches tend to be shorter, conversations seem more direct and to the point, and the Milanese appear to be in a bit of a hurry.

Unlike the case in many Italian cities, transportation in Milan is abundant and unusually dependable. Several decades ago, the five o'clock train never left Milano Centrale on time; today, the five o'clock train leaves at five o'clock. Milan has an excellent underground transportation system (Metropolitan). A ticket costs 1,500 lire and is valid for 75 minutes on buses and trams, or for one underground (metro) trip. There is also a day ticket available for 5,000 lire and a two-day ticket for 9,000 lire. Hotel services rival the finest in Europe; shops are sophisticated and efficient. In a word, Milan "works."

There is one crucial thing about Milan. It is virtually impossible to get a hotel room in the city during those periods when the major fairs and fall and spring fashion shows are in progress—September, October, and early March. Forget about August. That's when the Milanese go on vacation and the majority of the hotels are closed.

Arriving by Air

Milan has two airports serving international travelers. Milan's main international airport, **Malpensa,** is 30 miles northwest of the city, and 50 to 60 minutes is required to reach the downtown air terminal. Closer in, Milan's **Linate Airport** is located slightly more than six miles to the east of Milan. Check with your airline regarding which airport will be used for your flight.

Airport–City Links: Malpensa Airport Bus service connects Malpensa Airport with Linate Airport (travel time of 110 minutes) and Malpensa Airport with the Central Station (travel time of 60 minutes). Malpensa Express Train Service to the city departs every 30 minutes; journey time is 39 minutes. Fare: 13,000 lire. For schedules or information for both bus services *Tel:* (026) 698–4509.

Buses run every 20 minutes between Linate Airport and the bus terminal at the side of Central Station at Piazza Luigi d' Savoia from 0540 to 2100. Purchase tickets on board the bus (4,500 lire).

Bus, limousine, and taxi services are available at both air terminals. The taxi services are quite expensive.

Arriving by Train

Milan has seven railway stations, but luckily, readers need be concerned with only one, the Milan Central Station (**Milano Centrale**). Milan's central station is enormous.

Money exchange offices can be reached by going through the archway leading off *binari* (tracks) Nos. 10–15. Once through the archway and into the main hall of the station, you will see several exchange offices, two of which have hours daily from 0700 to 2300. Avoid the so-called money changers who frequent this area. Like the gypsies in the Paris Metro, their main purpose is to relieve you of your money. The gypsies do it by picking your pocket; the "money changers" are much more gentle in their approach—they just short-change you. You will find the best rates inside the official exchange office at the counter.

Tourist information is across from the exact change office in the main hall. Maps and tour information are available. This office is not equipped to assist in locating hotel accommodations but they can give you directions to the central tourist office at Piazza del Duomo. Summertime hours: 0830–2000 Monday–Friday; Saturday 0900–1300 and 1400–1700; Sunday and holidays, 0900–1300 and 1400–1700 (*Tel:* (027) 252–4360). A hallway on the left side of the tourist office will lead you to a public telephone.

Train information office is marked with a black **i** sign, located at the extreme right end of the station as you come from the trains. Illuminated flags indicate what language is spoken at the windows. The British flag means English is spoken. Hours: 0700–2100.

Train reservations for ETR 450 Pendolino, EuroCity, InterCity, and Rapido express-train services are made in an office separate from the one dispensing train information. To reach it, go through the main station hall and descend to the station foyer on the lower (street) level. Turn left and look for a huge door marked BIGLIETTERIA EST (ticket office east). Go through the door, and take a number from the ticket machine to wait your turn. You will see counter Nos. 49–53, labeled PRENOTAZIONI (Reservations). Hours: 0800–2200 Monday through Friday and 0800–1300 on Saturday and Sunday.

Railpass validation requires that you descend to the street level via the escalator in the middle of the station, make a right turn, and look for a sign, BIGLIETTERIA OVEST. Then proceed to window 20 or 22, marked INTERNA-TIONAL TICKETS.

Food services range from trackside vendors to a full-service restaurant. The restaurant, with a large and efficient self-service cafeteria next to it, is located on the far-left side of the main hall as you exit from the trains. A snack bar is also there. Downstairs near the BIGLIETTERIA OVEST sign you will find an excellent cafeteria that serves traditional Italian hot entrees and sandwiches. Just behind the cafeteria is a supermarket.

In this snack bar, as in the various smaller ones scattered throughout the main hall and track area, you need to purchase tickets for the particular food or beverage you desire from a cashier, then give the tickets to a counter attendant. The system works, but now you know how confused the Italian immigrant felt when ordering an American hamburger especially if asked "would you like that with mustard, catsup, lettuce, tomato, pickles—and was that to go?"

If this is your first rail trip into Italy, this will probably be your first acquaintance with the trackside vendors. Similar to the pushcarts that grace many of
the streets in New York City, they offer a convenient variety of refreshments—
and the price is right.

Baggage-checking facilities may be reached by taking the exit at the end
of tracks 6 and 7. Across the main hall and to the right, you'll see a sign in red
letters, DEPOSITO BAGAGLI. Rates vary according to what you store. The facility is open all the time. To store one bag costs 5,000 lire per 12 hours.

The main baggage room, located on the street level of the station, can be
reached either from the plaza facing the Michelangelo Hotel or from the bottom of the main escalator, between the street level and the train concourse.
Hours: 0700–2230 daily. Through experience, we have learned that you should
check items to be forwarded at least one day in advance, and then only to other
major points in Italy. We would not advise forwarding anything to France or
Switzerland.

There is a checkroom in the restaurant-and-cafeteria entrance that is convenient and safe to use for temporarily storing suitcases and wearing apparel
while you are eating or searching for a place to stay. If you check your baggage
here, it is most important that you find out when the attendant plans to leave.
Otherwise, you could return to collect your duds only to learn they have been
moved to a safe area until the operation starts again in the morning. The hours
of operation are posted as 0700–2400, but it appears to be an individual enterprise rather than one under the supervision of management.

Station miscellany. Milan's railway station has many other services. There
is a large and rather comfortable first-class lounge leading off the street side of
the main hall. Its entrance is just to the left of the tourist information office.
Inside the lounge you will find a computer that can give you train information.

Milano Centrale is a multilevel station, but elevator service from the train
level to the street level is available. The entrance on the train level is inside the
first-class lounge. If you have a first-class railpass, you have full access to the passenger lounge and elevator service.

Taxi service is available at both side entrances and the front, and **bus service** is in the Piazza Duca d'Aosta in front of the station. Pictographs of the
station's facilities are located conveniently at the end of many tracks.

Double-check your departing train number and platform location. For
example, when departing Milan for Munich aboard EuroCity 12 *Leonardo Da
Vinci*, you will note that signs in the station indicate the train's destination as
MONACO. In Italian, this means "Monk," and Munich (in German) is the "City
of Monks." So, you are on the right train and you are not bound for Monaco,
which, in French, means "Monte Carlo." InterCity 341/2 *Ligure* is the proper
train to board if you are in fact going to Monaco and Monte Carlo via Genoa.

Emerging from the train platforms, if you detect the aroma of an American-style hamburger, it's coming from Wendy's. To get there, turn right in the station hall and take the escalator at the far end to the street level. Skirt the tram terminal to the left then look for the WENDY'S sign.

Tourist Information/Hotel Reservations

Tourist Information Office: A.P.T., Via Marconi I, just off Piazza del Duomo
Tel: 02-72524300; *Fax:* 02-72524350
Internet: www.regione.lombardia.it
Hours: Summertime 0830–2000 Monday–Friday; 0900–1300/1400–1700 Saturday; until 1300 on Sunday.

To reach the central tourist information office, take bus No. 60 in front of the station to Piazza del Duomo, site of Milan's cathedral. You can also take line 3 of the metro to the Duomo stop. Attendants in the railway station information office will direct you.

The friendly Milanese devised the "Milano for You" *Welcome Card* kit to make your stay in Milan more convenient and enjoyable. The kit includes access to art tours, cultural theme dinners, the Giuseppe Verdi Symphonic Orchestra tickets, a 24-hour public transportation ticket, city map, and an opera music compact disc. It's available at the tourist information office.

There are times when Milan reaches the visitor saturation point and no-vacancy signs go up all over town. Should you arrive in Milan without hotel reservations and this is the situation you encounter, you have two alternatives to consider.

If there is no housing in Milan, you can leave town. A EuroCity train can have you in Como in 30 minutes, where hotel rooms probably will be more plentiful. In fact, you may be taken with the idea of residing in this lovely lake location throughout your stay in the area. There is express-train service back to Milan every morning.

Another alternative is a fast but systematic search of the concentrated hotel area adjacent to the railway station. There is a covey of luxury and first-class hotels to the left of it. Dominating the scene is the 17-story Michelangelo, with the Bristol, the Anderson, the Andreola, and the Splendido close by.

For lower cost but comfortable lodgings, walk two blocks on Via Roberto Lepetit, beginning at the Michelangelo, to Piazza San Camillo. Within this distance, you pass the Florida, the Colombia, and the Boston hotels. No luck? Turn right at the Plaza onto Via Napo Torriani. Between this point and Piazza Duca d'Aosta three short blocks ahead (where you can again see the station), you pass on your right the hotels Berna, Atlantic, and San Carlo; on your left, the Canova, Garda, Flora, Bernina, and Augustus.

If you have not found a room by this time, head back to Milano Centrale and one of the EuroCities. By this time, you'll be sure to fall in love with Lake Como.

The main tourist office charges a nominal fee for making accommodations reservations, but they are not authorized to accept deposits to guarantee that your reservation will be honored on your arrival at the hotel or pension. If you have made a room reservation through the tourist office, proceed immediately to your hotel to confirm your reservation in person. Many Italian hoteliers operate on a "first–come, first–housed" basis, and even though you have a reservation, someone else may end up with your room.

Day Excursions

A total of four day excursions have been selected from Milan. The first two take you south of Milan into the Italian peninsula to Italy's gastronomic capital, **Bologna,** and the birthplace of Christopher Columbus, **Genoa.** Another day excursion will take you to where Switzerland meets Italy, **Lugano,** the Swiss city with an Italian flair. The remaining day excursion will take you east to "the Queen of the Adriatic," **Venice,** and the romance of its gondoliers and grand canals. You'll enjoy each of them.

Train Connections to Other Base Cities from Milan (Milano)

Depart from Milan (Milano) Centrale

	DEPART	TRAIN NUMBER	ARRIVE	NOTES
Amsterdam	0725	IC 250	2054	1
Centraal	1715	CIS 46	0857+1	1, R, Sleeper
Barcelona	2000	EN 372	0913+1	2, R, Hotel Train
Sants				
Berlin	1525	IC 344	0801+1	2, R, Sleeper
Zoobahnhof				
Berne (Berne)	0715	CIS 32	1134	3
	0815	IC 332	1202	
	1025	EC 90	1434	
	1115	CIS 44	1425	
	1525	IC 888	1934	
	1715	CIS 46	2026	
	1815	CIS 38	2200	3
	1905	E 328	2331	3

	DEPART	TRAIN NUMBER	ARRIVE	NOTES
Brussels	0725	IC 250	1945	1
(Bruxelles)	1025	EC 90	2246	R
Midi/Zuid	2135	298	0929+1	R, Sleeper
Copenhagen	1125	EC 4	0958+1	5
(København) H				
Hamburg	0715	CIS 156	1932	4
Hauptbahnhof	0725	IC 250	1932	1
	0925	EC 8	2132	1
	1715	CIS 46	0838+1	5
Luxembourg	0725	IC 250	1650	1
	1025	EC 90	1956	
	2135	298	0632+1	R, Sleeper
Lyon	0700	EC 136	1222	R
Part-Dieu	1110	IC 615	1638	6
	1710	IC 622	2245	6
Munich	0910	EC 15/EC 12	1630	
(München)	1510	EC 83/EC 80	2230	
Hauptbahnhof	2215	2117/288	0635+1	R, Sleeper
Nice Ville	0710	IC 341/IC 342	1146	
	1610	IC 345/IC 346	1958	
Paris	0910	TGV EC 16	1551	
Gare de Lyon	1610	TGV EC 18	2252	
	2155	EN 216	0838+1	1, R, Sleeper
Roma (Roma)	0540	ES 9405	1025	
Termini	0700	ES 9407	1125	
	0800	ES 9409	1225	
	0900	ES 9411	1333	
	0915	IC 549	1450	
	1000	ES 9413	1425	
	1100	ES 9415	1525	
	1115	IC 551	1710	
	1200	ES 9417	1635	
	1300	ES 9419	1725	

DEPART	TRAIN NUMBER	ARRIVE	NOTES
1315	IC 555	1850	
1400	ES 9421	1825	
1500	ES 9423	1925	
1515	IC 557	2050	
1645	ES 9427	2125	
1800	ES 9429	2230	
1900	ES 9431	2325	
2325	E 1911	0833+1	R, Sleeper

Vienna (Wien) Westbahnhof

	0910	EC 15/EC 12	2045	7

Zürich Hauptbahnhof

DEPART	TRAIN NUMBER	ARRIVE
0715	CIS 156	1053
0825	IC 386	1253
1025	IC 388	1453
1225	IC 380	1653
1425	IC 382	1853
1625	IC 354	2053
1815	CIS 152	2153
1925	IC 358	2334

Daily unless otherwise noted
R Reservations required
*Thalys high-speed trains require supplement
2. Salvador Dali, Trenhotel (hotel train), special fares required.
3. Change trains in Brig.
4. Change trains in Zürich.
5. Change to sleeper train in Basel (R).
6. Change trains in Turin Porta Nuova station to an EC train (R).
7. Change trains in Innsbruck.

Day Excursion to

Bologna

Depart Milan Centrale

Distance by Train: 136 miles (219 km)
Average Train Time: 2 hours
City Dialing Code: 51
Tourist Information Office: Piazza Medaglie d'Oro
Tel: 24–6541; *Fax:* 25–1947
Hours: Monday–Saturday 0900–1230 and 1430–1900
  Piazza Medaglie d'Oro lies directly in front of the station. To reach the tourist office in the station you must first exit the main entrance of the station. Incline to the right and enter the station hallway at that exit.
Tourist Information Office: No. 6, west side of Piazza Maggiore
Tel: 239660; *Fax:* 231454
Hours: Monday–Saturday 0900–1900; Sunday and midweek holidays 0900–1400
  To reach it, turn left when exiting the rail station and walk two blocks to Via Dell'Independenza, one of Bologna's main avenues. Turn right onto the avenue, and a delightful 15-minute walk will bring you to Neptune's Fountain. Then continue your walk in the same direction a short distance into Piazza Maggiore.

  Bologna specializes in two areas—thinking and eating. When you think about it, you'll probably conclude, as we did, that it is not too bad a lifestyle to follow.
  Bologna stands out historically and architecturally. Tourists can walk under the porticoes of the city while visiting the many monuments. If lined up, the porticoes would cover 40 kilometers!
  Bologna's university, the oldest in Europe, was founded in 1088. By the 13th century, its student body numbered 10,000. One of its more recent students, Guglielmo Marconi (1874–1937), studied wireless telegraphy there. The university was noted for employing women professors. One professor, Novella d'Andrea, was said to be so beautiful in face and body that she had to give her lectures from behind a screen to avoid distracting her students.
  Bologna is the capital of **Emilia-Romagna,** a northwest-to-southeast slice of the Italian peninsula just below its juncture with the European Continent. It is here that the "cultura villanoviana," better known as the Iron Age, began over 4,000 years ago. After the fall of the Roman Empire, the city did not flourish again until after the eleventh century. Marvelous Etruscan and Roman examples of history can be seen at the **Civic Archaeology Museum.**

Milan (Milano)—Bologna

DEPART MILAN CENTRALE	TRAIN NUMBER	ARRIVE BOLOGNA CENTRALE
0700	ES 9407	0842
0800	ES 9409	0942
0900	ES 9411	1042
and hourly	other non-ES	
until 1600	trains are	
0915	IC 549	1122
1115	IC 551	1322
1315	IC 555	1522

DEPART BOLOGNA CENTRALE	TRAIN NUMBER	ARRIVE MILAN CENTRALE	NOTES
1428	ES 9412	1610	
1535	ES 9414	1750	
1618	ES 9416	1800	
and then hourly	other non-ES		
until 2218	trains are		
1535	IC 550	1750	
1745	IC 552	1955	
1910	IC 1566	2115	Sun
1935	IC 558	2150	

Daily, unless otherwise noted
Distance: 136 miles (219 km)

An economically strong region, with the nation's highest employment rate, Emilia-Romagna holds the uncontested title of the "richest gastronomic region in Italy." Endless strings of sausages and thousands of cheese varieties adorn the windows of its delicatessen shops. Restaurants line the city's arcaded streets, filled with people devouring delicacies to the accompaniment of fine wines. Many of them are in the luxury class, but you can also dine very well in the less expensive restaurants. Many maintain an "open kitchen," which you're welcome to inspect and where you may chat with the cooks.

The famous prosciutto of Parma is absolutely unlike any American prosciutto—and, like most Italian meat products, it cannot be sold in the United States.

Bologna is an ideal base for exploring the Emilia-Romagna area. Among the towns to visit are **Faenza,** for its ceramics; **Ferrara,** for its fortress; **Ravenna,** for its early Christian art; **Rimini,** for its Adriatic beach; and, of course, **Parma,** for its ham and Parmesan cheese. All are about one hour or less by rail from Bologna. All of these cities may be visited out of Milan, too. Consult the schedules in Milan's Central Station.

Bologna also has much to offer architecturally. An ensemble of rare Italian beauty is concentrated in its two enjoining squares, the **Piazza Maggiore** and the **Piazza del Nettuno.** Combined with the **Piazza di Porta Ravegnana,** the heart of Bologna even today reflects its Renaissance greatness.

Neptune's Fountain (Fontana del Nettuno) is the focal point of its piazza. Completed in 1566, it aptly depicts Bologna's vigorous nature. Saint Petronius Basilica, facing the Piazza Maggiore, was begun in 1390, but remains unfinished even today.

The Piazza Ravegnana contains not just one leaning tower, but two. The taller, built by the Asinelli family between 1109 and 1119, stands 330 feet with a tilt exceeding 7½ feet. The other, the Garisenda Tower, is only 165 feet high, but it leans out 10 feet over its foundation. If you're in good physical condition and feel like climbing 498 steps, there's a fine view from the top of the Asinelli Tower.

And if you would like to experience more of the "culta Bononia" (the Latin name for Bologna), call the tourist office for the *Not Just for the Weekend* brochure. Rates and special offers on over 50 hotels and inns, city and "pilgrim" tours, plus events year-round are listed.

Day Excursion to

Genoa (Genova) GREAT PORT OF ITALY

Depart Milan Centrale Station

Distance by Train: 93 miles (150 km)
Average Train Time: 1 hour, 25 minutes
City Dialing Code: 10
Internet: www.apt.genova.it
E-mail: aptgenova@apt.genova.it
Tourist Information Office: on the right-hand side of the station foyer after the second escalator coming from the trains
Tel: (010) 2462633
Hours: 0800–2000 Monday–Saturday; 0900–1200 Sunday
Tourist Information Office: Porto Antico-Palazzina Santa Maria (old harbor-aquarium area).
Tel: (010) 24871; *Fax:* (010) 2467658
Hours: 0900–1830 Monday–Saturday; 0900–1830 Sunday

Richard Wagner wrote, "I have never seen anything like this Genoa! It is

Milan (Milano)—Genoa (Genova)

DEPART MILAN CENTRALE	TRAIN NUMBER	ARRIVE GENOA PIAZZA PRINCIPE
0710	IC 341	0842
0715	IR 2181	0903
0815	IR 2183	1005
0845	IR 2185	1035
0910	IC 653	1040
1110	IC 659	1240
1215	IR 2187	1405
1310	IC 617	1440

DEPART GENOA PIAZZA PRINCIPE	TRAIN NUMBER	ARRIVE MILAN CENTRALE
1521	IC 630	1650
1555	IR 2164	1745
1721	IC 668	1850
1755	IR 2166	1945
1849	IR 2168	2040
1921	IC 648	2050
1933	IR 2170	2125
1955	IR 2172	2145
2055	IR 2174	2245
2131	IC 348	2300
2155	IR 2176	2345

Daily, unless otherwise noted
Distance: 93 miles (150 km)

something indescribably beautiful, grandiose, characteristic." According to its tourist office, Genoa is "a town that you have to know how to love . . . there can be no half measures." Genoa is a merchant town, a vertical city, a major Mediterranean port. It is a city of contrasts, mixing the ancient with the new.

To experience a taste of this interesting city ride the InterCity *Ligure* out of Milan to Genoa in the morning. Enjoy a leisurely walk along Genoa's avenues. Lunch in full view of the city's great harbor—largest in all of Italy. Board an InterCity late in the afternoon and be back in Milan for dinner that same day. Or, fall in love with Genoa by lunchtime and return to Milan on the InterCity *Ligure* on its return run to Milan just before midnight. The relatively short time en route between these cities makes a "set your own pace" schedule ideal.

Be mindful that Genoa has two major railway stations, **Piazza Principe** and **Brignole.** If you come from Milan, Piazza Principe is the first stop after the train emerges from a tunnel. Digital schedule boards in both stations advise what time the next connecting train departs for the other station. To be certain, board your returning train to Milan from Piazza Principe because many through-trains do not call at Brignole. You can, however, ride any shuttle train from Brignole north to the next stop, which is Piazza Principe.

A boat tour of the city's harbor is an excellent way for visitors to acquaint themselves with Genoa. Tours by boat leave from the aquarium, in the old port area, daily at 1515. Organized boat trips from the Maritime Building may be arranged ahead of time. The tour runs every hour starting at 1000 and ending at 1900, when a minimum of 15 persons is present. To reach the quay, turn right leaving the station, then make another right turn as you pass the bank on the corner. Walk downhill to the pedestrian crossing. Cross, and continue to walk downhill until the harbor is sighted to the left. After turning left and passing through Piazza Principe, you'll arrive at the Maritime Building. The tour boats are berthed on its right side.

Most visitors link Genoa with Christopher Columbus (1451–1505). This association begins as you leave the Piazza Principe Station fronted by **Piazza Acquaverde,** where a statue stands in honor of Columbus. A part of the city bus tour takes you to the Church of San Stefano, where Columbus was baptized, and into the Piazza della Vittoria—a vast expanse of lawns where the three ships of his fleet, the *Niña, Pinta,* and *Santa Maria,* are depicted in grass and flowers.

Plan a walking tour of Genoa. Depart Genova Piazza Principe Station and follow Via Balbi to Via Cairoli, which connects with "the street of Kings"—Via Garibaldi. At the end of Via Garibaldi, turn right (south) and proceed to the city's center, Piazza de Ferrari. From this point, you can continue along Via XX Settembre to the park in front of the Brignole Station or return on foot to the Piazza Principe Station by turning south and walking along the harbor. Both tourist information offices have maps to assist you in the walking tour. Be certain to include Genoa's great aquarium. The **Aquarium,** built in 1992 for the Columbus celebrations, is one of the biggest in Europe and should not be missed.

The city of Genoa lies beside a fine natural harbor at the foot of a pass in the Italian Apennines. It rivals Marseilles as the leading European port on the Mediterranean. Genoa's harbor facilities, which were damaged heavily during World War II, have been expanded and modernized. Shipbuilding is the leading industry of Genoa.

Ever since its birth, Genoa's calling has been the sea. Genoese ships transported Crusaders to the Middle East and returned laden with booty. Genoese merchants, profiting from the newly created demand in Europe for goods from the Middle East, expanded their operations throughout the Christian world. Genoese forts and trading posts soon spread throughout the Mediterranean and Aegean seas, creating a rivalry between Genoese and Venetians. Ask the tourist office for hours and information on the new sea and navigation museum called **Padiglione del mare e della Navigazione** in the Porto Antico Area.

Genoa is proud of its **Lanterna,** the lighthouse that has become the international symbol of the city. Built on the site of an ancient tower in the first half of the sixteenth century, it has guided mariners to its safe harbor for more than four centuries.

In the time of Christopher Columbus, another son of Genoa, Andrea Doria (1468–1560), did much to promote the development of the city's maritime power. Serving as captain-general of Genoa's navy until defeated by Spanish forces in 1522, he served the French briefly before restoring the republic of Genoa as an ally of the Holy Roman Emperor Charles V. Andrea Doria's palace can be seen during the city tour.

Those traveling with children will not want to skip the **La Citta dei Bambini.** This children's town is fascinating to young ones and to the curious of any age who want to learn how scientific things work.

Day Excursion to

Lake Lugano

THE SWISS RIVIERA

Depart Milan Centrale Station

Distance by Train: 48 miles (77 km)
Average Train Time: 1 hour, 15 minutes
Switzerland Dialing Code: 41
City Dialing Code: 91
Tourist Information Office: Palazzo Civico
Tel: 913–32 32; *Fax:* 922–76 53
Internet: www.lugano-tourism.ch
E-mail: info@lugano-tourism.ch

To reach the official tourist office of Lake Lugano, ride the *funicolare* (cable railway) to Piazza Cioccaro and proceed on foot downhill to the center of Lugano, Piazza Riforma. As you continue downhill toward the lake, stop at the town hall where the tourist office is located.

Holders of Eurailpass or Europass need not purchase separate rail tickets to make excursions from Milan into Switzerland, since both Italy and Switzerland are included on these passes.

Milan (Milano)—Lake Lugano

DEPART MILAN CENTRALE	TRAIN NUMBER	ARRIVE LUGANO
0725	IC 250	0854
0825	IC 386	0954
0925	EC8	1054
and hourly until 1625		

DEPART LUGANO	TRAIN NUMBER	ARRIVE MILANO CENTRALE
1506	IC 253	1635
1606	IC 385	1735
and hourly until 2106, and then		
2148	CIS 157	2245

Daily, unless otherwise noted
Distance: 48 miles (77 km)

Lake Lugano, known as the Swiss Riviera, is sheltered from the north by the Lepontine Alps. It is favored with a climate that is exceptionally mild, and purportedly the sunniest of all central European resorts. Considered a year-round resort, the city of Lugano sponsors a multitude of events to attract visitors of all ages.

Although Lugano is a very short distance from Milan, you will be crossing the Swiss border on this day excursion. Don't forget your passport. There is a currency-exchange desk in the railway station (open daily, 0515–2230), and the town abounds in banks and *cambio* (exchange) offices that offer official rates.

There is a **hotel-reservations-and-information office** to your immediate right as you leave the station. Train information may be obtained in the office bearing the **i** sign to the left of the main exit.

When the lake beckons, there is a choice of nine round trips by boat, each offering an opportunity for a special vista. If the mountains attract you, ascent is possible by cableways and funiculars in many different directions. Two funiculars, one at each end of Lugano, carry you swiftly up 3,000 feet to breathtaking views of either **Monte Bre** or **Monte San Salvatore.**

The list of things to do and see doesn't stop there. Take a motor coach to either **Sonvico** or **Tesserete**—typical Swiss mountain villages—even a journey to the world-renowned resort of **St. Moritz** is possible. In fact, anything's possible—just ask at the Lugano tourist information office.

For a relaxing day on the lake, select the cruise to the **Swiss Miniature Village,** a unique exhibition of towns, hamlets, castles, mountains, and railways—all on a scale of 1:25. The model railway is centrally controlled and has a length of 186 miles! Realize that this is an all-day outing, but it has wooed millions of other visitors—why not you? The village is open from mid-March through October, 0900–1800. *Tel:* 91640 1060 or *e-mail:* info@swissminatur.ch.

The tourist information office will gladly mark out a walking tour of the city and its interesting areas, or opt for a free guided walking tour every Monday morning from April until October.

For lunch in Lugano, you can make it a stand-up affair by selecting from a vendor's cart at lakeside or perhaps aboard a lake steamer. For an enjoyable sit-down meal, we recommend these quality restaurants: **Olimpia, Trani, Casino Kursaal, Orologio, La Tinera, Parco Saroli, Cantinone,** and **Da Armando.** All of these are in the center of Lugano.

Shopping in Lugano is a pleasant experience. The place to do this is concentrated in the market area stretching from the bottom of the *funicolare* to the city square fronting the lake. Mouthwatering food vies for your attention along with a wide selection of Swiss products and crafts. We have yet to see a visitor enter the market area around lunchtime and not emerge a few minutes later with a sandwich in hand rivaling anything that Dagwood could concoct.

Shopping in this market area is, for the most part, in the shelter of overhead arcades. If you have been looking for specialty items of the **Ticino** area of Switzerland, you will find them here. Although firmly Swiss, the market in Lugano does have that piquant touch of Italy.

If you are longing for a Swiss-made watch, stop by **Bucherer's** in Lugano at via Nassa 56. They are open Monday–Friday from 0900 to 1830 and Saturday until 1800 and carry their own styles as well as the other top Swiss names.

For a special treat, be certain to visit our "secret hang-out" **Gandria,** a small cliffside village that clings precariously to the mountains descending from the east into Lake Lugano. Gandria has no streets, but there is a bus stop on the mountainside above. The best, and more romantic, access is by lake steamer. If you want to share in our secret, inquire at any steamer pier regarding schedules to Gandria. You will want to take the Lugano–Porlezza line and plan to have an early dinner at one of Gandria's superb restaurants.

Day Excursion to

Venice (Venezia) GRAND CANALS AND GONDOLAS

Depart Milan Centrale Station

Distance by Train: 166 miles (267 km)
Average Train Time: 2 hours, 45 minutes
City Dialing Code: 41
Tourist Information Office: in Santa Lucia rail station.
  Proceed to the head of the train platform. Enter the main hall of the station. The train information office is on the immediate left. No tourist information is available at this office. Beyond that, you'll see a sign directing you to a self-service buffet. Digital train information is prominently displayed above the buffet sign. Telephones, ticket windows, newspaper stands, and specialty shops are on the right-hand side of the station hall. Just prior to exiting the station, you'll see tourist information.

  Upon arrival in Venice (Venezia), the American humorist Robert Benchley telegraphed his publisher, "Streets are flooded, please advise." Things have changed little since. Venice is situated on 120 islands surrounded by 177 canals in a lagoon between the Po and Piave Rivers at the northern extremity of the Adriatic Sea. The islands on which the city is built are connected by 400 or so bridges. Not only by its site but also by its architecture and history, Venice is known as "the Queen of the Adriatic."
  Venice was founded in A.D. 452 when the inhabitants of several northern Italian cities sought refuge there from the Teutonic tribes invading Italy during the fifth century. The Venetians improved their fortifications and erected bulwarks of masonry to protect their growing city from the sea and from their enemies.
  During the Crusades, Venice developed trade with the Orient and quickly became the center for commerce with the East. Venice became the leading wartime power of the Christian world by the end of the fifteenth century. In 1797, Napoleon Bonaparte conquered Venice and turned its government over to Austria. Through subsequent political maneuvers, Venice became part of the newly established kingdom of Italy in 1866.
  Be sure to obtain full details regarding the canal transportation system. Water taxis are extremely expensive; the public water buses are far more affordable. Also, ask for a map of Venice. You'll need it. Venetian addresses are somewhat peculiar in that they consist of a number and the name of a small area which could include several streets, thus making a particular restaurant or shop difficult to find. The canal navigation services (*Linee di Navigazione Lagunare*) are described in full detail on the reverse side of the map. If in Venice on a day excursion, purchase a one-way rather than a round-trip water-bus ticket from the rail station to **San Marco** on Line 1 and return to the station on foot.

Milan (Milano)–Venice (Venezia)

DEPART MILAN CENTRALE	TRAIN NUMBER	ARRIVE VENICE SANTA LUCIA
0705	IC 605	0955
0805	ES 9437	1055
0905	IC 609	1155

and hourly until 2105 (the 1005 and 1805 trains run Su only)
and IR trains departing at 0715 and 1115; journey time 3 hr 22 min.

DEPART VENICE SANTA LUCIA	TRAIN NUMBER	ARRIVE MILAN CENTRALE	NOTES
1458	IC 626	1755	
1558	IC 632	1855	
1643	IC 638	1955	
1758	IC 644	2055	
1858	Exp438	2155	
1958	IC 650	2255	
2058	IC 1508	2355	Sun only

Daily, unless otherwise noted
Distance: 166 miles (267 km)

Ticket in hand, board Line 1–Accelerata at Station 2 in front of the rail station. The dock and vessels are marked PIAZZALE ROMA–FERROVIA–LIDO, and the boat should be moving to your left as you come from the station. Boats proceeding to the right terminate at Station 1, Piazzale Roma, where you're required to disembark and purchase another ticket to get back on course!

Line 1 moves along the Grand Canal until emerging into open water from the canal at **Piazza San Marco** (St. Mark's), the center and most frequented part of Venice. The **Grand Canal** is Venice's principal traffic artery. It is lined with churches, museums, palaces—even a fish market—so keep your guidebook open so you can recognize these landmarks as you glide by.

Go ashore at St. Mark's and revel in the staggering sights before you. St. Mark's Bell Tower dominates the scene, but it won't be long before you'll find yourself standing in front of the Cathedral. If time permits, take the elevator to the top of the Bell Tower for a spectacular view of vibrant Venice.

With so much to see, be mindful of the time or you will miss the train back to Milan. You can't hail a taxi at the last minute, since there are none, so allow at least 45 minutes for the return trip from St. Mark's to Santa Lucia Station by water bus. Or start ambling through Venice by following the signs, ALLA FERROVIA (to the rail station). They are posted everywhere and easy to follow. Allow 2 hours to reach the station on foot, although a reasonable pace should get you there about 30 minutes sooner.

En route, you will cross the **Rialto Bridge**—the best place to view the Grand Canal and a good place to shop, too. There are 24 shops right on the bridge and a variety of vendors selling their wares along both sides of the canal. Farther on, you will cross the **Ponte Degli Scalzi** (**Station Bridge**) and arrive at the rail station where you started.

We're sure you will return to Venice, but heed the plight of tourists burdened with too many bags on the water buses—come back with minimum luggage or stow it in the lockers at the Venice Mestre Station.

Base City . . .

Rome (Roma)

City Dialing Code: 6

Italians refer lovingly to Rome as the "Eternal City." In the days of the Caesars, all roads led to Rome. Today, the same may be said of Italian State Railways.

No one knows exactly when people first started living along the Tiber River where Rome developed. Archaeologists continue to find evidence of still earlier civilizations than that of the Romans buried under those remains they have already identified. Etruscans ruled the area long before the Romans. Remains of that earlier Mediterranean civilization continue to be discovered in and around Rome.

Rome has already had two periods of greatness in the civilized world, each of which had a significant impact. Two thousand years ago, Rome ruled a good part of Europe and the Middle East. Rome contributed roads, architecture, art, law, literature, and political experience to the entire area.

Conquered by barbarians during the fifth century A.D., the city managed to remain the home of the popes, and through them and their armies, political power was regained. During the Renaissance, Rome again became a great center of art and learning. Since 1870, when Italian troops captured the city from Pope Pius IX, Rome has been the capital of Italy.

Readers considering "open jaw" (arrive in one European city, depart from another) air transportation to and from Europe should give serious consideration to Rome as either their entry or exit point. For example, in the spring, enter Europe through Rome and wend your way northward as the weather improves. Leave from Amsterdam. In autumn, reverse the procedure. Follow those lingering fall days southward from Amsterdam to Rome. By planning a rail vacation itinerary in this manner, you can assure yourself of having more moderate weather.

As a matter of fact, the average daily temperatures of Amsterdam and Rome vary by 10 to 12 degrees Fahrenheit—Rome's, of course, being the higher. So, when in Rome, do as the Romans do—move north as the mercury soars in the summer, south again when it begins to sink.

Arriving by Air

Rome has two airports, but because Ciampino Airport is small and deals mainly with charter flights, we focus on the main **airport Leonardo da Vinci,** also called **Fiumincino. Fiumincino Airport** is 22 miles southwest of Rome.

Airport–City Links: Direct train service from Fiumincino Airport to Rome's Stazione Termini (Central Station) in Rome runs 0700–2205. Journey time: 30 minutes; fare: 13,000 lire. It leaves and arrives at track No. 22 in Roma Termini.

There is also another train service from Fiumincino Airport to Tiburtina Station (total travel time, 45 minutes) with stops at local stations **Trastevere** and **Ostiense.** The train runs every 20 minutes 0615–0015; fare, 7,000 lire. If you arrive at night there is the No. 42 night bus service between Fiumincino Airport and Tiburtina Station. A taxi from Fiumincino Airport to the center runs about 70,000 lire (or at least $40), but we caution against using taxis unless your airline representative arranges it and determines the fare beforehand.

Arriving by Train

When you arrive at the railway station in Rome, beware of the many willing "helpers" eager to carry your luggage and find you a cab. If you need a taxi, carry your own bag and get in the regular taxi line.

Roma Termini. Rome has several suburban stations, but the InterCity and express trains stop only in the main station—Roma Termini. It is like a city within a city. In its main concourse, the section separating the train platforms from the main hall, you will find a bar and restaurant. On the lower level of the station you will find services you normally associate only with the most modern airports—barbershops, hairdressers, showers, and lounges.

Money-exchange facilities are located throughout the railway station. In the main concourse, there is an office just to the left of *binari* (track) 12, between gateways 2 and 3. Hours: daily, 0830–1930, and 0830–1400 and

1400–1930 on holidays. In the main hall, another currency exchange, including an ATM, is operated by the Bank of Rome. Turn left when entering the hall from the concourse and walk past all the ticket windows to the bank. Hours: Monday–Friday 0825–1335 and 1440–1600; holidays, 0825–1155; Saturday, 0830–1130.

Hotel reservations. Hotel reservations in Rome and other Italian cities can be made Monday through Sunday 0700–2200 directly across from track No. 10. You are required to leave a deposit and arrive at the hotel within one hour. We found that the line was always very long. If this is the case, telephone Rome's free hotel reservation service *Tel:* 06 699–1000.

Train information may be obtained from three free-standing computer touch-tone screens from which you can gather schedule information for your destinations. The computers are located across from the tracks in the center and sides of the station, across from tracks Nos. 1, 9, and 22.

Train reservations can be made at ticket windows 30 through 45. There are 45 ticket windows with their services indicated in Italian. Windows Nos. 7–29, labeled BIGLIETTI ORDINARI E RIDOTTI, sells tickets. At windows Nos. 30–38, labeled PRENOTAZIONI POSTI-WL-CUCCETTE-PENDOLINO, you can make reservations, including couchette and sleeper reservations. Finally, at windows Nos. 42–45 labeled PRENOTAZIONI, PENDOLINO, PARTENZA IN GIORNATA you can make reservations for trains leaving today. The cost of the reservation varies depending on destination. To ensure that you receive the proper reservation, determine the day and date of your travel, the number and departure time of your train, and its arrival time at your destination. This information can be taken from any of the train schedules posted throughout the station.

Print this information on a plain piece of paper, starting with the date, the train number, and the departure time. Draw a short arrow, then add the arrival time of the train and, finally, the name of the destination. Indicate the number of reservations required, then present the information to the attendant together with the rail pass you will use for the trip. Submission of this information may draw a small grin from the attendant making the reservations, but it will save time and lessen the possibilities of errors in completing your train reservations.

Railpass validation may be made at a window labeled in English located in the center of the train station near the main entrance facing the bus station. It is rather hidden away and there are not any signs directing you. Just follow the signs for taxi and bus service, and right before you exit the station behind several tobacco shops you will see several windows, including the Eurail window and other windows that can provide you with information.

If you plan an early morning departure on the first day you use your railpass, either allow an extra hour at the station that morning or inquire at one of the validating windows midevening the night before about the possibility of predating the validation.

Tourist Information/Hotel Reservations

- **Ente Provinciale Per Turismo-Rome**, 5 Via Parigi, 11
  Tel: (06) 4889–9253 or 4889–9255, *Fax:* 4889–9228.
  Hours: 0815–1915 Monday–Saturday; closed Sundays/holidays.
    To visit this office, exit the main entrance of Roma Termini, skirt the left side of the city square in front of the station, and proceed past Museo Nazionale Romano (the National Roman Museum) to Via Parigi. Turn right at that point, then look for the office on the left-hand side of the street.
- **"Enjoy Rome,"** a very helpful tourist office especially designed for English speakers, very close to the station at 39 Via Varese.
    To get there, cross Via Marsala adjacent to the station on the right as you exit the train terminal. After two more blocks, turn right onto Via Varese. Number 39 is at the end of this one-way street.
- **National Tourist Office, ENIT,** at 2 Via Marghera, one block east of the railway station (*Tel:* 4971282).
- For tours in Rome and vicinity, the Sesante office in the main hall of the railway station will be happy to oblige.

Rome abounds with tourist facilities. Every resident seems to know the exact location of everything and seems to be eager to direct you. But Rome has more than three million citizens, and each has a different opinion regarding the best way to get there—even if it's only around the corner.

Consequently, depend on the official tourist office staff, hotel staff, or city policemen, not the man on the street, for reasonably correct information. Above all, watch out for the "cab-and-coin" man. He'd be more than glad to take you where you want to go but probably at three times the regular rate. The legitimate taxicab service in Rome is moderate in price and equipped with meters. Ask your hotel personnel to hail one for you or telephone. Telephone numbers to call in Rome for radio-dispatched cabs are 3570, 4994, and 6645.

American Express has a convenient location in Rome near the Spanish Steps at 38 Piazza de Spagna (*Tel:* 67641). American Express can assist in making train or hotel reservations in Rome or any other of the base cities. They also conduct excellent tours, in English, of Rome and its surroundings.

Sights/Attractions/Tours

Rome is a great walking city. First, get a map from your hotel or the tourist office, then find your way to the **Spanish Steps** and walk down Via Condotti—with detours down some of the side streets—to the Tiber. Sightseeing musts during an initial visit include the **Pantheon,** the

Coliseum, and, close by, the **Forum.** Set aside at least a few hours for a visit to the **Sistine Chapel** and **St. Peter's.**

Roaming around Rome is like moving through history. Columns that looked down on the mighty Caesars, walls that saw Saint Peter and Saint Paul passing, statues sculpted by Michelangelo—these are Rome, where present-day life flourishes in the midst of monuments from past civilizations. Throw a coin in the **Trevi Fountain** as a down payment on your return trip, because you will certainly want to return.

When walking in Rome, keep pocketbooks, camera bags, and so on away from the curb side of the street and on a short leash. Motor-scooter thieves find them easy targets.

So vast is the city that it is essential to take some of the organized tours in order to see all of it. We recommend the tours conducted by the CIT (Compagnia Italiano Turismo). It is the general passenger agent for the Italian State Railways, and its tours can be booked through most hotels and pensions.

To dine differently, try **Da Meo Patacca** at 30 Piazza Mercanti (*Tel:* 58161198)—excellent food and entertainment. For that once-in-a-lifetime splurge, dine in the rooftop restaurant of the **Hassler Hotel,** Rome's finest hostelry; it overlooks the Spanish Steps. The view of the city from there on a summer's evening is unmatched. (*Tel:* 679–2651 for reservations.) Ignore the cost. You only live once!

Day Excursions

Four interesting day excursions from Rome await your visit: **Anzio,** scene of an Allied beachhead during World War II; **Florence,** one of the most prominent art centers of the world; **Naples,** with its world-renowned **Isle of Capri;** and **Pisa,** where the tower really tilts.

Train connections to Other Base Cities from Rome

Depart from Rome Termini station unless otherwise noted.

DEPART	TRAIN NUMBER	ARRIVE	NOTES
Amsterdam Centraal			
1630	ES9422/200	1137+1	R,1,Sleeper
1905	EN212/9329	1608+1	R,2, Sleeper
Bern			
0630	ES9422/IR3322	1756+1	R,1
1947	EN314	0749+1	R, Sleeper
Brussels (Bruxelles) Midi/Zuid			
1500	IC712/200	0929+1	R,3,Sleeper
1905	EN212/9425	1220+1	R,5,Sleeper

DEPART	TRAIN NUMBER	ARRIVE	NOTES
Budapest Keleti			
1907	EN234/345	1303+1	R,5,Sleeper
Copenhagen			
0805	EC84/EN482	0959+1	R,6,Sleeper
Luxembourg			
1612	1294	0836+1	R7
Lyon Part-Dieu			
2245	ICN752/	EC1361157+1	R,1
Milan (Milano) Centrale			
0930	ES9408	1400	R
1005	IC548	1550	R
1205	IC548	1550	R
1530	ES9420	2000	R
1830	ES9426	2325	R
Munich (München) Hauptbahnhof			
0805	EC84	1830	R
2115	286	0831+1	R, Sleeper
Nice Ville			
1005	IC518/IC345	1958	R, 9
2315	368	0950+1	R, Sleeper
Paris Gare de Lyon			
1005	IC548/EC18	2254	R
1905	EN212	0952+1	R, Sleeper
Vienna (Wien) Sudbahnhof			
0703	EC30	2032	R
1907	EN234	0853+1	R, Sleeper
Zürich Hauptbahnhof			
1005	IC548/IC354	2053	R, 1
2112	EN306	0853+1	R, Sleeper

Daily, unless otherwise noted
R Reservations mandatory
Thalys high-speed trains require supplement
1. Change trains in Milan (Milano).
2. Change from Paris Gare de Lyon station to Paris Nord station.
3. Change trains in Florence (Firenze), runs Saturdays
4. Change from Vienna (Wein) Sudbahnhof station to Wein Westbahnhof.
5. Change trains in Innsbruck.
6. Runs Mondays June 7–September 27.
7. Change trains in Torino, Porta Nuova station, supplement payable.
8. Change trains in Genova.

Day Excursion to

Anzio

Depart Rome Termini Station

Distance by Train: 35 miles (57 km)
Average Train Time: 1 hour
City Dialing Code: 06
Tourist Information Office: Regione Lazio Azienda Autonoma, Soggiorno e Turismo, Piazzo 19
Tel: 9845147; *Fax:* 9848135
Hours: June–September 0830–1230 and 1700–2000 daily. Off–season hours 0830–1230 and 1530–1800 Monday–Saturday. If the office is closed, directions will be posted on how to reach another office in the area.

To get to the tourist office on Pia Square: When leaving the Anzio railway station, walk downhill along the palm-lined avenue to Cesare Battisti Square. Then continuing on via dei Fabbri, you will be in the main square of Anzio, Pia Square, where you will find the city's tourist information office to the left, just near the church.

"Nothing more beautiful, nothing more agreeable, nothing more peaceful," wrote Cicero about Anzio. The Roman emperor Nero was born in Anzio. The villa where he spent his childhood and studied music still stands. Anzio's sandy beach attracted many important leaders over the centuries, which made it a VIP sanctuary, so to speak. Roman emperors such as Tiberius, Hadrian, Antoninus, and Commodus found escape from Rome and their affairs of state in Anzio.

American and British forces stormed ashore at Anzio and nearby Nettuno on January 22, 1944, to establish a beachhead, which they held until the taking of Rome on June 4, 1944. The devastated town that endured both the crossfire of the Germans and the bombardment of the Allied fleet offshore during that time has been restored completely, but row upon row of white crosses mark the graves in nearby military cemeteries, where lie 7,862 American and more than 6,000 British troops killed between Sicily and Rome. Those missing in action, 3,194 of them, sleep in unknown graves. A visit to these cemeteries is a sobering event.

If you, like the Roman emperors, want to escape the rigors of Rome or, on the other hand, wish to pay tribute to fallen comrades, Anzio extends a warm and pleasant welcome to all.

Because of the city's proximity to Rome and frequent train connections, rail travelers might consider accommodations in the area during their visit. Anzio, together with the neighboring sea resorts stretching southward to it from **Lida dei Pini,** can offer a wide selection of housing amenities and accommodations. If interested, telephone Anzio's tourist information office at (06) 9845147 or 9846119 (*Fax:* 9848–135) for details and rates. For a longer stay,

Rome (Roma)—Anzio

Depart Rome Termini at 0755 (except Sun), 0825, 0925 (Sun), 1025 (except Sun), 1125 (except Sun), 1154 (Sun), 1225 (except Sun), and 1325 (except Sun); journey time 60–65 min.

Depart Anzio at 1509 (except Sun), 1534 (Sun), 1554 (except Sun), 1654 (except Sun), 1719 (Sun), 1754 (except Sun), 1854 (except Sun), 1859 (Sun), 1954 (except Sun), 2005 (Sun), and 2159 (daily).

Distance: 35 miles (57 km)

villas and apartments are available for rent at moderate rates.

Commuter trains depart the Roma Termini frequently for Anzio. For complete information regarding train service, check the *Partenze* (departure) information board in the main hall of Roma Termini.

Anzio is listed in the **Roma–Nettuno** section. It is one stop before Nettuno and the end of the line. Nettuno is where the American beachhead was established in World War II. Tell the train conductor about your destination, who will be glad to alert you to the correct stop.

Upon arrival in Anzio, you will find directions for reaching Nettuno and the American Military Cemetery posted inside the train station; but before proceeding, check with the Anzio tourist office and obtain the details on the bus service running between Anzio and Nettuno.

Places to visit in Anzio are, of course, the beach area and the harbor, where the Allied forces landed. The beach is now lined with cabanas, and the sand is excellent and the surf usually moderate. Be certain to visit the beachhead museum on **Via di Villa Adele** near the rail station.

The harbor holds many interesting places to investigate. Watercraft of all types are moored there, and the waterfront is lined with seafood restaurants to which fishermen sell their catch right from the dock. Deciding where to have lunch can be difficult—they all look inviting. On the street side of the harbor you will find a number of smart shops with eye-catching selections of nautical clothing.

Aside from the beach and the port area, places of particular interest are **Nero's Grottoes,** those ancient warehouses of the port located at the northern end of the Riviera Mallozzi. Beyond Anzio's western harbor wall lie the remains and mosaics of Nero's villa, which runs from the beach up to the level of Via Fanciulla d'Anzio. It's an impressive sight.

At the foot of the **Innocenzio wharf** in Anzio you can examine the remains of an eighteenth-century fort, and from the wharf itself, there is a view of the gulf with the Astura Tower and Circeo visible in the distance. The monument commemorating the Allied landings in 1944 is situated nearby on the western shore.

Nettuno, a seaside town of Saracen origins, is less than 3 miles distant. The American Military Cemetery is located there. The two British cemeteries are in Anzio. En route to Nettuno, you'll pass the Villa Colonna on the right and the **Villa Borghese,** with its magnificent gardens, on the left.

Anzio's involvement with the sea is reflected in its festivals. One such festival, the "Festa del Mare" (Feast of the Sea), is held in June in honor of Saint Antony of Padua, patron saint of the town.

Day Excursion to

Florence (Firenze) CITY OF BEAUTY

Depart Rome Termini Station

Distance by Train: 197 miles (317 km)
Average Train Time: 2 hours
City Dialing Code: 55
Tourist Information Office: 1R, Via Cavour
Tel: (05) 529–0832; *Fax:* 276–0383.
Hours: Summer: 0800–1915 Monday–Saturday; 0800–1330 Sunday; Winter:
0800–1330 daily
Take a taxi there or board bus No. 1, 6, or 17. Tourist Information also available in the rail station concourse at the end of track 16 (in front of the pharmacy).

Florence as a day excursion is suggested for the traveler on a time-icompressed itinerary. It is impossible to see all the beauty of Florence in one day. A week—or even a lifetime—could easily be devoted to such a pursuit. No other city in the world pays better homage to human genius and creativity and, in turn, beauty appreciation than does Florence.

Aside from its buildings, art galleries, museums, and parks, Florence has had an interesting and rather hectic development as a municipality and seat of government. It was ruled by the Medici family until 1737, when the family died out and its leadership was assumed by Grand Duke Ferdinand III (1769–1824). Driven out by the French in 1799, the duke made several abortive attempts to resume power. He wasn't successful, however, until 1814.

Ferdinand's successor, Leopold II (1797–1870), held on until he was expelled in 1849. Florence was the capital of Italy under King Victor Emmanuel from 1865 to 1871, when the seat of government became Rome.

Although a part of Italian history since 200 B.C., it wasn't until the turn of the eleventh century that Florence began to develop power and influence. Coincident with this growth came the development of the city's powerful guilds.

Rome (Roma)—Florence (Firenze)

DEPART ROME TERMINI	TRAIN NUMBER	ARRIVE FLORENCE SMN	NOTES
0735	ES 9404	0911	R, Mon–Fri
0810	EC 84	1020	
0835	ES 9406	1011	R
0935	ES 9408	1111	R
1010	IC 548	1222	
1035	ES 9410	1211	R
1100	ES 9442	1236	R
1135	ES 9412	1321	R

DEPART FLORENCE SMN	TRAIN NUMBER	ARRIVE ROME TERMINI	NOTES
1458	ES 9417	1635	R
1447	IC 551	1710	
1524	ES 9443	1700	R
1548	ES 9419	1725	R
1637	IC 555	1850	
1648	ES 9421	1825	R
1724	ES 9445	1900	R
1748	ES 9423	1925	R
1756	EC 85	1950	
1837	IC 557	2050	

and later frequent service until 2148

Daily, unless otherwise noted
R Reservations required
Distance: 197 miles (317 km)

Florence was established on those banks of the Arno River spanned by the bridge of the Roman road Via Flaminia and where the Ponte Vecchio (old bridge) still stands today. With the single exception of Ponte Vecchio, all of the city's bridges were destroyed in 1944 during World War II. In 1966, a major flood damaged numerous art treasures in Florence, but many have been restored in succeeding years by the use of sophisticated techniques.

Hotel reservations can also be arranged at the ITA tourist office in the railway station. The one at Via Cavour cannot make hotel reservations, but gives the booking centers of Florence, which are Coopal, *Tel:* (05) 521–9525; Top Quark, *Tel:* (055) 462–0080; and Promothotels, *Tel:* (05) 557–0481. Maps are available at the tourist offices, the CIT office (the Gray Line office) outside the station, or purchase the illustrated book ***Florence, Pisa and Siena*** at the newsstand inside the main hall of the station. An excellent map of Florence is contained in this informative book.

A **train-reservations** office (hours 0700–2000 daily) and **money**

exchange (open 0820–1920 Monday–Saturday) are located inside the main station hall.

You can see most of the city's highlights by walking and, when needed, by taxi. Start by walking or taking a taxi to **Il Duomo** (the cathedral square) in the center of Florence. Here you can examine the three huge bronze doors of the **Battistero** (baptistery), enjoy the view from the top of the cathedral's dome, and enter the **Museo dell'Opera del Duomo** (cathedral museum), where you will find the priceless Altar of Saint John the Baptist displayed.

The **Galleria dell'Accademia** (Academy Gallery) is next. Hours: Closed Mondays; open 0900–1900 Tuesday–Saturday; 0900–1400 Sunday. Admission: 12,000 lire. Walk three blocks on Via Ricasoli, off Piazza Duomo's north side, to Piazza St. Marco. Michelangelo's original *David* is displayed here.

Taxi from here to **Piazza della Signoria,** which lies on the opposite side of the cathedral near the Arno River. (A brisk walk and some expert map reading will get you there in about 20 minutes.) This is the former center of Florence. The concentration of art treasures here is immense. The building with the tower is Palazzo della Signoria (Palace of the Lords), also known as **Palazzo Vecchio** (the Old Palace). Among its wealth of treasures is the little chapel of Eleonora of Toledo, with its magnificent frescoes by Bronzino (1503–1572). Closed Thursdays; open other weekdays 0900–1900 and 0800–1300 Sunday. Admission: 10,000 lire.

On the south side of the square, you will see the **Loggia dei Lanzi,** which picked up a few other names, such as "Loggia dei Priori" and "Loggia della Signoria," since it was built in 1376. Statuary such as *Hercules and the Centaur* (1599) and *Rape of the Sabine Women* (1583), both by Giambologna, surround Cellini's *Perseus* (1545).

The **Galleria degli Uffizi** (Office Gallery) is, in fact, a converted office containing the priceless works of art acquired by the Medici family. Located on the right flank of Palazzo della Signoria, it has forty-five exhibit rooms. Its vast collection includes the ancient sculpture *Medici Venus* from 300 B.C., Botticelli's *Primavera* and *Birth of Venus,* Leonardo da Vinci's *Adoration of the Magi,* and Michelangelo's *Holy Family,* plus an entire roomful of Rembrandts. Closed Mondays; open other weekdays 0900–1900, and 0900–1400 on Sunday. Admission: 12,000 lire.

This concludes your "quick" tour of the world-famous "City of Art, Florence," and it's time to taxi back to the rail station for the train back to Rome—unless, of course, you have succumbed to Florence's charms. It's a difficult decision to make. If you are still ambulatory, the walk back to the station will take about 20 minutes.

Day Excursion to

Naples (Napoli)

CITY BY THE BAY

Depart Rome Termini Station

Distance by Train: 134 miles (216 km)
Average Train Time: 2 hours
City Dialing Code: 81
Tourist Information Office: Main Hall of Napoli Centrale Rail Station (English-speaking staff)
Tel: 268779 or 206666; *Fax:* 401961
Hours: 0815–2000 Monday–Saturday; 0900–1400 Sunday

Naples is a world apart. There is no other place in Italy quite like it. In fact, there's no place that we have visited in the rest of the world quite like Naples. When you go there, you don't really see Naples—you feel it, hear it, and taste it. After you've been to Naples, you come away either loving it or hating it. You alone must be the judge.

Naples itself is a coalescing of gaiety and sadness. Its inhabitants, the Neapolitans, are expressive, noisy, and vivacious. They are imaginative, superstitious, and (about a third of them) unemployed, either by choice or by circumstance—it's difficult to determine which. But as a consequence, crime is rampant, so watch your wallets, pocketbooks, cameras, and other valuables.

But don't go to Naples in fear for your life; just be cautious. The Neapolitans don't want to harm you; they are only interested in your valuables. They want you to enjoy yourself and come back again—with more valuables. Deal only with official agencies. If you plan to take a city tour or sign up for a trip to **Vesuvius** and **Pompeii,** do it in an office, not on the street. Ignore the uniformed people who approach you on the street or in the rail station wearing badges proclaiming they are "official guides." There are several small shops on the square facing the station where you can buy one of those badges yourself.

Now for the fun part. Spaghetti was invented in Naples, as well as Neapolitan-style ice cream. Pizza first saw the light of day in Naples. If you can, enjoy a pizza in one of the pizzerias located in the old quarter of Naples. If you do, you'll probably not patronize your local pizza parlor for at least thirty days following your return home. The Neapolitan version of a Cajun fish-fry, *frittura di pesci,* is also well worth sampling. So much for tasting Naples.

You can't avoid hearing Naples. The musical style of Bel Canto is exclusively that of the Neapolitans. *Santa Lucia, Funiculi-Funicula,* and *O Sole Mio!* are but part of the repertory you will hear being played by hurdy-gurdies, all of it mixed in with the constant background noise of the crowded streets. Dray animals such as mules wear bells so that their presence can be acknowledged in the crowd.

Rome (Roma)—Naples (Napoli)

DEPART ROME TERMINI	TRAIN NUMBER	ARRIVE NAPLES CENTRALE	NOTES
0810	IC 725	1000	
0845	ES 9401	1030	R
0945	IC 1645	1142	1, Mon–Sat
1045	ES 9405	1230	R, Mon–Sat
1045	ES 9455	1230	R, Sun
1145	IC 731	1330	

DEPART NAPLES CENTRALE	TRAIN NUMBER	ARRIVE ROME TERMINI	NOTES
1530	ES 9424	1715	R
1600	IC 726	1750	
1646	IC 724	1850	2
1730	ES 9428	1915	R
1748	IC 1646	1950	2
1930	ES 9432	2115	R
2000	IC 732	2155	
2052	ES 9398	2245	R

Daily, unless otherwise noted
R Reservations required
1. Arrives Napoli Piazza Garibaldi Station
2. Departs Napoli Piazza Garibaldi Station
Distance: 134 miles (216 km)

If you haven't developed a feel for Naples after exposure to some or all of the above, you can take an early train back to Rome.

You will find the **Napoli Centrale** and **Napoli Piazza Garibaldi** terminals side by side in the city center and flanked by the two narrow-gauge railway stations serving the **Circumvesuviana Line** from Naples to **Pompeii** and **Sorrento.**

Money-exchange, train information, and food services are all housed within the Napoli Centrale terminal. A train-information-and-reservations office is located to the side of the main hall (open daily, 0700–2115).

Naples, a city with a population well over one million, is just large enough so that unguided sightseeing can become difficult. Several reputable tour operators provide excellent service such as the **Tourcar Travel Agency,** *Tel:* (081) 552 0429. The American Express Office located at Piazza Municipio 5/6 also provides tours under its travel agency. *Tel:* (081) 5518564; *Fax:* (081) 722242.

Local trains leave the Napoli Circumvesuviana railway station for **Pompeii** and **Sorrento**. To reach this station, walk in the direction of the Garibaldi statue in the center of Piazza Garibaldi. Just before reaching the statue, turn left on Corso Garibaldi and proceed to the station, which is close by. The train time from Naples to Pompeii averages about 25 minutes. To Sorrento, the average time is 60 minutes. Pompeii is 15 miles from Naples; Sorrento is 28. Check at the rail station for complete schedules. Eurailpasses and Europasses are not accepted on this line.

Day Excursion to

Pisa

NEW SLANT ON AN OLD SCENE

Depart Rome Termini Station

Distance by Train: 208 miles (335 km)
Average Train Time: 3 hours
City Dialing Code: 50
Tourist Information Office: in the station plaza
Tel: 42291
Tourist Information Office: Piazza del Duomo
Tel: 560464
Take bus No. 1 from rail station plaza to Piazza del Duomo.

Many consider Pisa to be the most beautiful city in Italy. Pisa possesses one of the loveliest architectural groupings in Europe. Known either as **Piazza dei Miracoli** (Square of the Miracles) or **Piazza del Duomo** (Cathedral Square), it contains, in addition to the famous **Leaning Tower** and the cathedral, the **Baptistery** and the **Campo Santo** (burial ground), each in its own stead a masterpiece of sculpture and architecture.

If you have never been to Pisa and actually stood and looked at the Leaning Tower, you are in for a surprise. Forget any photograph, painting, or motion picture you may have seen of the tower prior to your personal encounter. It is not an optical illusion—it *really* leans.

Ride bus No. 1 from Pisa's station plaza to Piazza dei Miracoli. Dismount from the bus on the southern end of the square—the direction in which the tower is leaning. You will have no doubt whatsoever that (1) the tower leans; (2) it's leaning in your direction; and (3) you had better get out of its way before it topples on you. No other work of art provokes the instinct of self-preservation like this one. You can spend hours gazing at it, but there is never a moment when you are not consciously aware of the trajectory it will take if it topples.

Rome (Roma)—Pisa

DEPART ROME TERMINI	TRAIN NUMBER	ARRIVE PISA CENTRALE
0705	ES 9302	1002
0805	IC 516	1113
1005	IC 518	1313
1205	IC 520	1513

DEPART PISA CENTRALE	TRAIN NUMBER	ARRIVE ROME TERMINI
1249	IC 519	1555
1349	IC 525	1655
1449	IC 527	1755
1728	ES 9311	2025
1849	IC 533	2155
2033	ES 9315	2330

Daily, unless otherwise noted
Distance: 208 miles (335 km)

Bonanno Pisano began construction of the tower in 1174, but the project was not completed until 1350. The primary reason for the delay in its completion was that the tower began to tilt when it reached its fourth level. With an annual increase of about 1 millimeter per year, the tower was closed to public access in 1990.

By using sonar soundings of the ground, the foundation of an ancient village was discovered under the north side of the Leaning Tower. This explains why the north side has remained relatively stable, while the south side has sunk almost three-quarters of a meter. Various plans have been proposed to stabilize the tower. One plan is to use sonic waves to break up the ancient foundation under the north side so that it will sink at the same rate as the south. Another proposal requires a ring of steel to be inserted into the base of the landmark. Perhaps the Italian Public Works Ministry should expedite its plans. Studies reveal that the tower is nearly 17 feet off plumb.

For a spectacular meal, visit the **Ristorante Antonietta,** a delightful Tuscan-Italian restaurant at 179 Via Santa Maria, immediately south of the square. It serves excellent food, and the location can't be beat. According to our best high school geometry, if the tower topples, it will fall some thirty feet short of the first table at Antonietta's.

When at last you can turn your attention away from the tower, you will realize that Piazza dei Miracoli holds some other fantastic sights that warrant your inspection. Among them is the cathedral, on which construction was initiated in 1063. The first work of art to catch your eye is the splendid bronze doors of its entrance. Inside the cathedral and opposite the pulpit, Lorenzi (according to legend) hung a bronze lamp on a chain so long that Galileo figured that it must be the first pendulum and proceeded to work out the theory of isochronism—one of the better "isms" existing today.

The astronomer and physicist Galileo (1564–1642) lived in Pisa and used the buildings of the **Piazza del Duomo** to conduct studies concerning the laws of gravity, the acceleration of falling bodies, and the movement of the pendulum. He used the Leaning Tower to work out his theories on gravity and acceleration and the cathedral for the accurate measurement of time. Galileo was said to have quarreled with his scholars over his theory of the rotation of the universe. During the Inquisition, when compelled to renounce his theory that the world turned, not the universe—because the Pope thought otherwise—in despair he whispered, "Nevertheless it does turn."

Last of the edifices within the confines of the Piazza dei Miracoli is the building known as the **Compo Santo** (cemetery). It began when fifty-three shiploads of earth were transported from Calvary in the Holy Lands to the site and then surrounded by the building, which, after completion in 1283 by Giovanni Pisano, was frescoed by local Tuscan artists. The structure suffered damage during World War II bombings, but repairs have all but removed those scars.

During its days of prominence, Pisa was in close touch with the Orient. As a result, you'll note an Eastern flavor in its architecture. In the ninth century, the city was a naval power of considerable proportion. Pisa and its ally, Genoa, drove the Saracens out of Sardinia and Corsica in the eleventh century. Pisa's powers, however, then went on the wane. No longer allied with Genoa, the city was taken by Florence in 1406, proving that, as is so often the case, your allies are not there when you really need them.

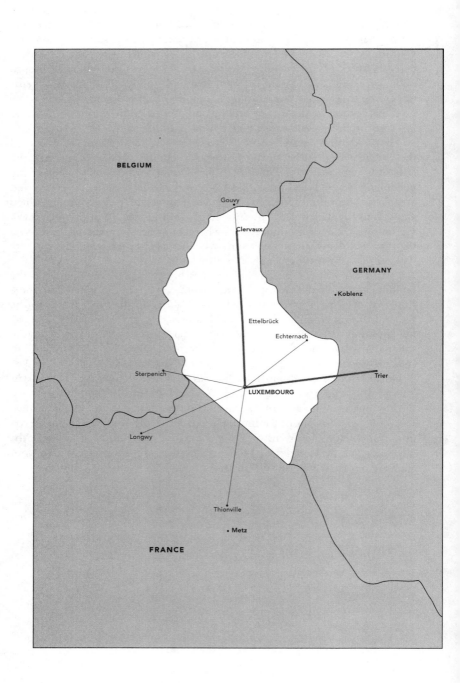

BELGIUM

Gouvy

Clervaux

GERMANY

• Koblenz

Ettelbrück

Echternach

Sterpenich

Trier

LUXEMBOURG

Longwy

Thionville

• Metz

FRANCE

Luxembourg

The Grand Duchy of Luxembourg is one of Europe's small countries—51 miles (82 kilometers) long and 32 miles (57 kilometers) wide, encompassing 999 square miles (2,586 square kilometers)—a little smaller than the State of Rhode Island. It is a constitutional monarchy with a population of about 400,000. Germany borders it to the east, France to the south, and Belgium adjoins it on the north and west. Luxembourg vies with Switzerland in the field of international banking. A substantial number of corporations doing business in the European community maintain accounts there.

The Grand Duchy once dominated an area nearly 300 times its present size. In more recent times, as well as in the past, Luxembourg's fate and fortunes have been linked with those of Belgium. The forces of French King Louis XIV conquered the city of Luxembourg in the middle seventeenth century. Subsequent fortifications built by the French and succeeding conquerors earned the city the title "Gibraltar of the North."

Luxembourg was overrun by the Germans during World War I, but its independence was restored by the Treaty of Versailles. It was occupied again by German forces during World War II. During the Battle of the Bulge in December 1944, the tides of war surged around Luxembourg. Liberated earlier by U.S. forces, the city was recaptured by the Germans, who executed many members of the Belgian and Luxembourgese underground before Luxembourg was again taken by the Allied Forces.

Luxembourg's monetary unit, the franc, has the same value as the Belgian franc. Belgian money is circulated freely throughout the Grand Duchy, but Luxembourg francs are not accepted in Belgium. If you cash a traveler's check in Luxembourg and plan to leave immediately, insist that you receive Belgian francs or the currency of the country where you are going.

For more information on Luxembourg, contact the Luxembourg National Tourist office in North America:

Internet: **www.visitluxemburg.com**; *E-mail:* luxnto@aol.com

New York: 17 Beekman Place, New York, NY 10022; *Tel:* (212) 935–8888; *Fax:* (212) 935–5896

Banking

- **Currency:** Luxembourg Franc (LUF)
- **Exchange rate at press time:** 37.59 LUF = $1.00 U.S.

Communications:

- **Country Code:** 352
- City codes are not used when dialing within Luxembourg
- Direct dial: AT&T: 0800–0111; MCI: 0800–0112; Sprint: 0800–0115

Rail Travel in Luxembourg

The information service of **CFL, the Luxembourg national railways** (also gives country bus information), can be contacted by *Tel:* (+352) 4990–4990 or (+352) 4990–5571 (every day GMT: 0600–2000) and by *Fax:* (+352) 4990–4470.

From the capital, Luxembourg City, you are no more than 1 hour away from anywhere within the Grand Duchy of Luxembourg. The **Oeko–Pass** is available at rail stations throughout the country and at Findel airport. It covers unlimited travel on all forms of public transport (city buses, trains, and country coaches) for 1 day (which is considered to last until 0800 the following morning) throughout the Grand Duchy. It is not valid on sightseeing buses, however. You can purchase a single ticket for 160 LUF or a block of 5 tickets for 540 LUF.

The CFL also accepts the multicountry passes of **Eurailpass** and **Europass,** with purchase of the Benelux—Belgium, the Netherlands, Luxembourg—add-on. (See the Appendix for a detailed list of multiple-country and regional rail passes and prices.) If your travels are confined only to the Benelux countries, consider the **Benelux Tourrail Pass** for unlimited rail travel throughout Belgium, the Netherlands, and Luxembourg:

Benelux Tourrail Pass

	1ST CLASS	2ND CLASS
5-day within 1 month	$ 217	$155
Youth: 5-day within 1 month	—	$104

Benelux Tourrail for Two Pass

2 PEOPLE TRAVELING TOGETHER	1ST CLASS	2ND CLASS
5-day within 1 month	$326	$233

Day Excursions

Four day excursions have been selected for the Grand Duchy and its surrounding countries. Each is distinctly different in its points of interest. The day excursion to **Clervaux** takes you through the rugged north country of the Grand Duchy, where the World War II Ardennes campaign was contested bitterly in 1944. The day excursion to **Koblenz** is saturated with scenic views along the Moselle and Rhine Rivers and the charm of Koblenz, one of the oldest cities in Germany. **Metz** measures up to a most interesting day excursion into France. The German city of **Trier,** founded by Augustus Caesar, provides an exciting opportunity to explore many Roman ruins and to titillate your taste buds with the most delectable Moselle wines.

Base City . . .

Luxembourg City

Internet: www.luxembourg-city.lu/touristinfo/
E-mail: touristinfo@luxembourg-city.lu

Arriving by Air

Findel International Airport is about 4 miles (6 kilometers) from the city center. Luxembourg, because of its central European location and convenient rail connections, attracts an increasing number of visitors from North America.

Airport–City Links: Bus service from the airport terminates at the Luxembourg rail station and Luxair downtown air terminal. Municipal buses (bus No. 9) depart every half-hour Monday–Friday, every 20 minutes on Saturday and hourly on Sunday from a platform about 50 feet outside the air terminal. Journey time: 25 minutes; fare 40 LUF, plus 35 LUF for each suitcase. At present there is no underground or train service link, but there are very interesting plans proposed to link the airport to the railway station via a direct connection.

Luxair Coach to the rail station: 150 LUF; children under 12 years, 50 percent. No charge for luggage.

Taxis: from 650–700 LUF (supplements for nights, Sundays, and extra luggage). All taxis are equipped with meters. No tips are expected.

Tourist information at Findel Airport: *Tél:* 42 82 82 21. Hours: Open daily 0945–1400 and 1515–1830, closed Saturday at 1330. Closed on Sundays November 1–March 31.

Arriving by Train

The city of Luxembourg is served by a single railway station located conveniently in the city center. Connections can be made directly to Belgium, France, Germany, Italy, the Netherlands, and Switzerland from the station. The downtown air terminal and the city bus terminal are clustered conveniently about the railway station, which, like the airport, has been modernized to handle an increasing number of passengers.

Luxembourg Central Station is actually located in what historians call the "new city." From 1855 to 1866, when the first rails were laid, the gorge of the Alzette River remained too wide to be bridged. Consequently, the rail station was established on the far side of the gorge opposite the city as it existed then, and the new section of the city began to develop around it.

The station has three platforms (quais) serving five tracks. Track 1 is served by platform 1, which is directly connected to the station with level access to the platform. Trains arriving on the other tracks, however, require passengers to utilize an underground tunnel to reach the main station hall.

A system of elevators serves the outer train platforms. To access them, take the hallway off to the right of the main hall until you arrive at the entrance to the elevator service tunnel just beyond the last ticket window and before reaching the baggage room.

The entrances to the elevators serving the train platforms are marked clearly, although it seems a bit confusing when you first use them. You descend from the train platform to a tunnel. There, you walk a short distance to another elevator, which you ascend to the station level; you then take another short tunnel into the main hallway.

Money exchange is on the right side of the main station hall as you enter from the train-platform area. Hours: 0900–2100 daily. An additional exchange facility is located in the nearby air terminus, which also houses the Luxembourg tourist information office. Hours: 0830–1200 and 1330–1600 Monday–Friday.

Train information is to your immediate left when exiting from the train platform area. Hours: 0700–2000 daily. A free mini-timetable describing the best train connections between Luxembourg and other major European cities is available.

Train seat reservations for EuroCity, InterCity, and regular express trains can be made in the train information office. Sleeper reservations and railpass validation may also be made here.

Luxembourg Tourist Information/Hotel Reservations

Office National du Tourisme, Luxembourg Air Terminal, Place de la Gare. *Tel:* 4282–8220. Hours: July–mid-September: 0900–1200 and 1400–1830 daily.

The office stands in the air terminal to the right of the railway station as you leave the main exit. It is easily identified by its AIR TERMINUS sign and the usual **i**. Tourist information is on your left. In addition to making hotel reservations, they can also provide information on youth hostels, camping grounds, and holiday flats and chalets available to tourists.

Luxembourg City Tourist Office, Place d'Armes (Syndicat d'Initiative et de Tourisme, Ville de Luxembourg), PO Box 181, L-2011

Tel: 22 28 09; *Fax:* 47 48 18

Internet: www.luxembourg-city.lu/touristinfo

E-mail: touristinfo@luxembourg-city.lu

Hours: January–March: 0900–1800 Monday–Saturday; closed Sunday. April–September: 0900–1900 Monday–Saturday; 1000–1800 Sunday. October–December: 0900–1800 Monday–Saturday; 1000–1800 Sunday.

Hotel reservations can be made by the tourist information offices. Also, there are numerous hotels on the side streets near the station in addition to some charming smaller hotels within reasonable taxi or city-bus distances. The four-star **Hotel International** is across the street from the rail station. For those who prefer an American-style hotel with all the amenities, the **Sheraton Aerogolf** is located near the Findel Airport.

Our choice is a small, quaint hotel with European-style charm and service—**Hôtel Italia** (20 rooms). Located at 15–17 rue d'Anvers, Hôtel Italia is near the rail station and features an excellent Italian restaurant. *Tel:* 48 66 26/27 or *Fax:* 48 08 07. Rates range from 2,625–2,940 LUF for a single and 2,940–3,255 LUF for a double, and major credit cards are accepted.

Getting Around in Luxembourg City

The city center is condensed and most sights are accessible on foot, despite the cliffs and ramparts that characterize this fortress city. For longer distances, use Luxembourg's efficient network of buses (single fare, 40 LUF). Taxis are metered.

The most practical way of getting around Luxembourg on your own is to purchase a **LuxembourgCard**. You get free admission to 32 tourist attractions, free use of public transportation and a 32-page guidebook to go along with it. Cost for 1 person: 1-Day Card, 350 LUF; 2-Day Card, 600 LUF; or a 3-Day Card, 850 LUF. A family of 2–5 persons is 500, 1,200 or 1,700 LUF, respectively. The LuxembourgCard is valid from Easter to October 31.

Sights/Attractions/Tours

A basic city sightseeing tour by bus departs from Platform No. 5 at the downtown bus terminal next to the rail station. The 2–hour tour departs at 1415 daily. It includes the Old Town, the rail station district, the fortress ruins, the casemates (underground outside fortifications), European Center, and Luxembourg's version of Wall Street—the banking district. The tour fee for adults, 450 LUF; children ages 6–12, 250 LUF.

The **Bock and Pétrusse Casemates** are two unique networks of underground rooms, one of the most interesting being the archaeological crypt. This room presents an audiovisual show relating the history of the Casemates (open March 1–October 31, 1000–1700). Admission: 70 LUF adults; 40 LUF children. The Pétrusse Casemates are open from Easter, Whitsunday, and during school holidays. Guided tours are daily from 1100–1600.

From April to October, you can rent the tape tour "City Walk" and a Walkman for 190 LUF (between the hours of 1000 and 1700 daily).

The **"City Promenade"** is a guided tour on foot and encompasses Place d'Armes, City Palace, the outside Casemates, Place de la Constitution, the Government District, the Holy Ghost Plateau, the Corniche, the Monument of the Millenium, the Old Town, Place Guillaume, and the exterior of the Grand Ducal Palace.

The **"Wenzel Circular Walk"** is an interesting historical and cultural tour that can be done either on your own or as a guided tour by making reservations through the Luxembourg City Tourist Office. Touted as "1000 Years in 100 Minutes," this tour takes you through the oldest quarters of the city.

There are other tours by bus that take you through the Ardennes, or opt to see much of the area on your own during day excursions to Clervaux, Metz, and Trier.

"The soldier, above all other people," said Douglas MacArthur, "prays for peace, for he must suffer and bear the deepest wounds and scars of war." Such is the drama of 5,100 grave sites in **The American Military Cemetery** near the village of Hamm, 3 miles outside the city of Luxembourg. Among the crosses standing row upon row, you will see one marked GEORGE S. PATTON, JR., GENERAL, THIRD ARMY, CALIFORNIA, DECEMBER 21, 1945. Solemn in its simplicity, beautiful in the manner in which it attests to the American spirit, this cemetery must be seen. It is a moving, memorable moment. Guided bus tours from Luxembourg City will take you there as a part of their tour program, or you can taxi there for about the same price as the airport-to-rail-station fare. Telephone for a return taxi.

Luxembourg's low value added tax (VAT) of 13 percent makes it a bargain base city in comparison to some other European cities. Even residents of Luxembourg's neighboring countries make purchases of tobacco, alcohol, and fuel in the Grand Duchy because the taxes are lower.

Train Connections to Other Base Cities from Luxembourg

	DEPART	TRAIN NUMBER	ARRIVE	NOTES
Amsterdam Centraal				
	0627	2129	1240	1
	0727	2130	1340	1
	1027	2133	1640	1
	1127	2134	1740	1
	1427	2137	2040	1
	1527	2138	2140	1
	1627	2139	2240	1
	1708	96	2308	2
	1727	2140	2340	1
Berlin Zoobahnhof				
	0939	D 1272	1850	3
Bern (Berne)				
	1002	EC 91	1825	
	1502	97	2012	4

Brussels (Bruxelles) Midi/Zuid

Service is hourly from 0527 to 2027. Journey time is 2 hr 57 min.

	DEPART	TRAIN NUMBER	ARRIVE	NOTES
Hamburg Hauptbahnhof				
	0939	D 1272	1707	3
	1033	IR 2431	1807	3
	1433	IR 2433	2207	3
Lyon Part-Dieu				
	0526	EC 209/8	1204	5, Mon–Sat
	0726	351/350	1404	5, Sun
	0802	353/352	1504	5, Mon–Sat
	1308	1835/EC 54	2010	5
Milan (Milano) Centrale				
	1002	EC 91	1925	
	2202	299	0710+1	R, Sleeper

Munich (München) Hauptbahnhof

1033	IR 2431	1811	6
1502	97	2211	7

Nice Ville

1002	EC 91	2247	8

Paris Gare de l'Est

0526	EC 209/8	0915
0726	351/350	1103
0802	353/352	1138
1308	1835/EC 54	1710
1634	EC 204/5	2013
1721	1839/EC 56	2104

Rome Termini

2202	299	0710+1	R, Sleeper, 9

Vienna (Wien) Westbahnhof

1502	97	0805+1	10
1912	295	0835+1	11

Zürich Hauptbahnhof

1002	EC 91	1500	4
1502	97	2000	

Daily, unless otherwise noted
R Reservations required
Thalys high-speed trains require supplement
  1. Change trains in Brussels.
  2. Change in Brussels to Thalys★ train 9357 (R).
  3. Change trains in Cologne (Köln).
  4. Change trains in Basel.
  5. Via Paris. Arrive Paris Gare de l'Est. Change to Paris Lyon station.
  6. Change trains in Koblenz.
  7. Change trains in Strasbourg.
  8. Change trains in Metz.
  9. Change trains in Milan.
  10. Change trains in Zürich.
  11. Change to sleeper train 263 in Strasbourg, departing at 2202.

Although hotel rates and restaurant prices are lower than those of most other European cities, the quality is not. Some Luxembourgers actually believe "the way to a man's heart is through his stomach," and they've made believers out of us. Try the smoked pork with broad beans or the delicate Ardennes ham cut paper-thin. For a real taste treat, try trout from the Moselle accompanied by a fine Luxembourg wine—all at popular prices.

Luxembourg abounds in international cuisine. One of our favorites is the **L'Hotel-Restaurant Italia** at 15–17 rue d'Anvers, (*Tel:* 48 66 26/27), which offers excellent Italian specialties. Phone ahead for reservations—it's popular with the local folks, too.

Day Excursion to

Clervaux   Grand Duchy's Medieval Charm

Depart from Luxembourg City Central Station

Distance by Train: 38 miles (61 km)
Average Train Time: 54 minutes
Clervaux Tourist Information Office: Clervaux Castle, B.P. 53, L-9701 Grand Duchy of Luxembourg
Tel: 92 00 72; *Fax:* 92 93 12
Hours: April–June, 1400–1700; July–September, 0945–1145/1400–1800; September–October, 1300–1700 Monday–Saturday (Also open Sundays July 1–August 28.)

Start at the station by walking along the main street in the direction from which the train came. When you reach the town square, turn right and follow the paths and steps leading up to Clervaux Castle. The Clervaux tourist information office is located at the entrance to the castle in a towerlike structure on the right-hand side.

Clervaux is a medieval town nestled in the valley of the Clerf River deep in the Ardennes of northern Luxembourg, through which runs the scenic rail route from Luxembourg through Liege in Belgium to Amsterdam in The Netherlands.

The scenic beauty of the train ride begins the moment you leave the Luxembourg station and the train crosses a viaduct high above the Alzette River. Take a seat on the left side of the carriage to enjoy best a spectacular view of the city of Luxembourg from the viaduct. Have your camera ready and start shooting a moment after the train clears a short tunnel just beyond the rail station. The morning departure is best for photographing the ramparts of Luxembourg because the sun will be shining directly upon them at a rather low level at that time. You will pass the same scene on later departures; how-

Luxembourg—Clervaux

DEPART LUXEMBOURG	TRAIN NUMBER	ARRIVE CLERVAUX
0813	110	0905
1013	112	1105
1213	114	1305

DEPART CLERVAUX	TRAIN NUMBER	ARRIVE LUXEMBOURG
1456	117	1547
1656	119	1747
1856	121	1947
2056	123	2147
2256	125	2347

Daily, unless otherwise noted
Distance: 38 miles (61 km)

ever, the sun will be at a higher angle and the shadows will be less dramatic.

Clervaux is the fourth express-train stop en route after stops at **Mersch, Ettelbruck,** and **Kautenbach.** Beyond Ettelbruck, you enter the hilly and heavily wooded Ardennes, where the Battle of the Bulge was fought during World War II in December 1944. Some of the buildings along the right-of-way still bear the scars of this engagement. Don't be alarmed if you should spot a German or an American tank at a road intersection en route. The locals have intentionally placed it there.

The Clervaux railway station is a fifteen-minute walk from the town's main square. It's a delightful stroll along the river and easy to do with the aid of several maps posted along the way with "you are here" arrows to assist you.

Clervaux is packed with points of interest. Three of the most prominent ones are the **DeLannoi Castle,** the **Benedictine Abbey of St. Maurice and St. Maur,** and the **parish church.** All three tower over the town and its surrounding countryside.

The DeLannoi family are some of Franklin Delano Roosevelt's maternal descendants. The DeLannoi Castle has so much to offer that we recommend you concentrate on it first and see the rest of Clervaux's sites in the time remaining at the end of your visit. It houses the "Battle of the Bulge" museum, an exhibition of ancient Luxembourg castle models, and the world-famous **"Family of Man"** photo exhibition of Edward Steichen, an American citizen born in Luxembourg.

No one is quite certain about the castle's origins. There are several hypotheses; some historians believe that it was built on top of an ancient Roman citadel, while others speak of Celtic origins. In any event, it has been established that the oldest part of the castle dates back to the twelfth century.

There's an immediate impact upon entering the castle's outer courtyard. One of General Patton's tanks is parked there, along with its chief antagonist, a German Army 88-millimeter cannon. History buffs of all ages will enjoy climbing aboard the tank to inspect its armor and speculate as to the role it played during the liberation of Clervaux and the Battle of the Bulge. Bear in mind that by December 1944, the castle you see now was reduced to a burned-out hulk. The authentic restoration that has been accomplished by the townspeople of Clervaux and the Duchy of Luxembourg is laudatory.

The "Family of Man" exhibit and the castle model exhibit are immediately inside the first gate leading off the courtyard (open 1000–1800 daily except Monday; closed January–February). The "Bulge" museum is located farther along toward the center of the castle off an inner courtyard.

Steichen considered the Clervaux castle an ideal location for his exhibition. The collection was given to the Grand Duchy of Luxembourg by the U.S. government in 1975, three years after Steichen's death.

Enjoy lunch in the castle. The **Café du Vieux Chateau,** dating from 1671, is a part of the castle's outer courtyard. During the summer, the café provides tables and chairs in the courtyard. You will find the café just inside the tower gate on the left. It was constructed originally as a dwelling for the guardian of the castle. Today, it would be a good place to launch hang gliders.

Day Excursion to

Koblenz

HEART OF THE RHINELAND

Depart from Luxembourg City Central Station

Distance by Train: 101 miles (163 km)
Average Train Time: 1 hour, 14 minutes
Germany Dialing Code: 49
City Dialing Code: 261
Koblenz Tourist Information: Löhrstrasse 14
Tel: 261-31304; *Fax:* 261-1004388
Internet: www.koblenz.de: *E-mail:* touristik@koblenz.de
Hours: May–September: 0900–2000 Monday–Friday; 1000–2000 Saturday, Sunday, and holidays. Easter–end of April and October: 0900–1800 Monday–Friday; 1000–1800 Saturday, Sunday, and holidays. November–beginning of April, 0900–1700 Monday–Friday.

To reach the tourist office, turn left as you exit the rail station and use the pedestrian crossing. (If you need to convert from Belgian or Luxembourgese francs to German marks, stop by Exchange-Geldwechsel-Cambio on your left as you exit the track area.)

The Koblenz railway station is just far enough away from the meeting of the Moselle and Rhine Rivers and the city's major tourist attractions to cause a "walk or ride" decision soon after arrival. If you decide to ride into the city center, the tourist office can help you hail a cab or provide you with the city's bus schedule and fare information. If you are planning to stay in Koblenz, they can make hotel reservations at no charge. Be sure to pick up a map and the brochure "Koblenz . . . Tour of The Town's Heritage" before setting out.

Just as there is a subtle difference between Rhine and Moselle wines, so is there a difference between the scenic beauty of the two great rivers from which the wines take their names. At the rivers' confluence you will be able to enjoy both. Koblenz claims that it offers more than 2,000 years of history to its visitors—and all within the span of a few hours. The historical background of this city in the very center of Germany's Rhineland makes this no idle boast as its claim to Germany's most beautiful corner.

The area around Koblenz was settled originally by the Celts. Julius Caesar, dividing and conquering as he went, arrived with his legions and established domain along the Rhine's western banks. Roman tranquillity thrived until the fifth century, when Rome's power weakened and the Franks took over.

Napoleon's "memorable campaign against the Russians" was inscribed on **St. Castor's fountain** in the city during 1812. In 1814, the tables were turned when the Russians captured the town and added a postscript, "SEEN AND APPROVED," beneath the original inscription. At the **Deutsches Eck,** a monument erected at the confluence of the Rhine and the Moselle in 1897, the statue of the German emperor Wilhelm I was toppled into the Rhine by the U.S. Army Corps of Engineers in 1945. The base of the monument was made as a memorial to German unity in 1953 by President Theodor Heuss. Since September 1993, Wilhelm I is back— in mini-model form on top of the monument.

If you choose to see Koblenz under your own foot power guided by the city map, a ten-minute walk down the **Markenbildchenweg** brings you to the Rhine, and a left turn at that point sends you in the direction of the Deutsches Eck, where the Rhine meets the Moselle. The riverside gardens along the Rhine join up with those on the Moselle to provide a delightful 5-mile promenade along their banks.

If you plan to whiz around the city on wheels, bus No. 1, marked RHINE (DEUTSCHES ECK) will deposit you on the promenade at a point opposite the **Rheinkran,** an antique building that once housed the harbor crane. The bus route takes you through the narrow streets of the old city along the Moselle

Luxembourg—Koblenz

DEPART LUXEMBOURG	TRAIN NUMBER	ARRIVE KOBLENZ	NOTES
0822	none	1039	change to train IR 2337 in Trier
0939	D 1272	1146	
1033	IR 2431	1239	

DEPART KOBLENZ	TRAIN NUMBER	ARRIVE LUXEMBOURG	NOTES
1614	D 1273	1850	
1715	IR 2430	1922	
2218	RE 3987	0022+1	daily except Sat; also runs on May 1, Oct 3, and Dec 26, but not on Dec 24 and 31

OR, returning to Luxembourg from Koblenz via Trier (change trains in Trier or spend several hours in Germany's oldest town and board a later train to Luxembourg):

DEPART KOBLENZ	TRAIN NUMBER	ARRIVE TRIER	DEPART TRIER	ARRIVE LUXEMBOURG
1418	RE 3979	1537	1547	1633
1515	IR 2336	1638	1647	1733
1618	RE 3981	1737	1747	1833
1818	RE 3983	1937	1840	1922
1915	IR 2334	2038	2047	2129
2018	RE 3985	2137	2147	2229

Daily, unless otherwise noted
Distance: 101 miles (163 km)

and past the Deutsches Eck before reaching its final stop on the Rhine. Returning to the train station, the bus follows a more direct (and less interesting) route through the town's shopping areas. If your "walk or ride" decision is still up for grabs, we suggest you compromise by taking the bus outbound and returning on foot. From the river to the station, the bus is bannered HAUPTBAHNHOF. The bus ride takes about fifteen minutes. Allow a little more time if you're walking.

Make the **Koblenz Weindorf** (Wine Village) a must stop during your visit. It consists of four taverns clustered around a village square that, in turn, is enclosed within a real vineyard along the Rhine. The taverns are actual copies of half-timbered houses found in the notable German wine areas. Six hundred or more guests can be accommodated in the taverns and more than 1,000 outside when the weather is good—as it usually is.

The wine village was built on the occasion of the 1925 German Wine Exhibition. Since then, it has achieved fame for its products and romantic atmosphere. The village offers an excellent menu and wine list daily from 1100 to 2400. From November through March, an advance booking is required.

Day Excursion to

Metz

MOSELLE STRONGHOLD

Departs from Luxembourg Station

Distance by Train: 39 miles (63 km)
Average Train Time: 53 minutes
France Dialing Code: 33
City Dialing Code: 87
Internet: www.mairie-metz.fr:8080
Metz Tourist Information: Office de Tourisme, Place d'Armes, BP 67002, 57030 Metz, France
Tel: 8755–5376/78; *Fax:* 8736–5943
Hours: Mid-July–September, Monday–Saturday 0900–2100, Sunday 1000–1300/1400–1700; remainder of the year, Monday–Saturday 0900–1900; Sunday 1000–1300/1500–1700.

To get there, turn right leaving the arrival gate and walk the length of the station hall to the departure gate (served by the northern underground passageway). The station's north end houses the train information office and faces the General de Gaulle Square. Money can be changed in the post office, the huge red building in front of the station. Board either minibus line A or B at the bus terminal directly in front of the rail station. Get off at the Hotel de Ville (town hall) stop in front of the cathedral. The tourist office will be on the right in Place d'Armes.

Throughout its 3,000-year history, Metz has been a great Roman city, a religious center of the Carolingian Empire, an independent republic, a part of Germany, and a bastion of France. Throughout the ages, various cultures have left their marks in the form of various architectural styles throughout the city.

Poised at the confluence of the Moselle and Seille Rivers, Metz claims one of the oldest churches in France, the fourth-century **St. Pierre-aux-Nonnains.** The center of attraction, however, is its Gothic cathedral of **Saint Etienne** (thirteenth–sixteenth centuries). The cathedral has been described as the "apotheosis of light" due to the luminescent quality of its stained-glass windows—two of the largest surface stained-glass windows in the world. Its 300-foot-high nave is among the highest in France.

Luxembourg—Metz

DEPART LUXEMBOURG	TRAIN NUMBER	ARRIVE METZ	NOTES
0750	none	0841	
0802	353/352	0845	
1002	EC 91	1024	
1129	none	1212	
1308	EC 54	1355	

DEPART METZ	TRAIN NUMBER	ARRIVE LUXEMBOURG	NOTES
1348	EC 357	1435	
1606	96	1650	
1702	none	1753	Mon–Fri
1736	none	1822	Sat from Sept 5
1806	none	1853	Mon–Fri from Aug 31
1902	none	1948	Mon–Fri
1911	EC 90	1956	
2004	EC 53/1834	2052	
2016	none	2102	Sun from Sept 8
2112	EC 207	2202	daily except Sat
2300	355/354	2345	

Daily, unless otherwise noted
Distance: 39 miles (63 km)

Metz further claims the largest railway station in eastern France. Due to its size, visitors arriving by rail may find the facilities somewhat confusing. When arriving from Luxembourg in the north, take the southern stairway rather than the northern one when transiting from the arrival platform to the main station hall via the underground passageway.

Obtain a map of Metz and a copy of *Transports Par Minibus* describing the two minibus lines from the tourist office. The two lines cover the city's major sights and shopping areas and terminate at the main railway station. The minibus stops throughout the city are marked with devices very similar in appearance to barber poles, to which are attached maps showing the course of the bus making that particular stop. Each pole is marked with the name of the stop, and inside the bus is a circular chart showing all of the stops that the bus makes. By noting first the name on the pole stop and then relating it to the map inside the bus, you can easily identify your position. Both minibus lines operate 0730–1930 daily except Sundays and holidays. A bus leaves the main railway station approximately every six minutes. Tickets are available in the bus.

Metz has many other interesting sights, such as the fourteenth-century **St. Louis market square** with its Italian influence. Its majestic buildings are constructed of yellow limestone, which seems to give them an aspect of light. The city's eighteenth-century theater, **Place de la Comédie,** is another typical example of this "brightness."

From the end of August and into early September, Metz goes "plum crazy." The golden mirabelle plum is celebrated in various deliciously edible forms—perhaps on a tasty tart or in a luscious, languid liqueur. Other gastonomic specialties include frog-legs pie, freshwater fish, and traditional stews, as well as not-so-traditional stews—snail stew.

Want to try a different type of city tour? Take a tour via Metz's **"Petit (little) Tourist Train"** (*Tel:* 87 73 03 08). It has departures at 1030, 1145, 1330, 1445, 1600, 1715, and 1830. Fare, 35 French francs; children, 20 francs.

The Metz tourist office proposes an audio-guided walking tour that covers the highlights of the city with an English narration. If you are sightseeing on your own in Metz, you should include the city's museum with its Gallo-Roman collections and impressive display of seventeenth-century paintings by Dutch masters and artists of the French School. Top off your visit with a stroll along the city's Esplanade on the banks of the Moselle River.

Day Excursion to

Trier

GERMANY'S OLDEST TOWN

Depart from Luxembourg Station

Distance by Train: 32 miles (51 km)
Average Train Time: 41 minutes
Germany Dialing Code: 49
City Dialing Code: 651
Trier Tourist Information: An der Porta Nigra, D-54290
Tel: 978–080; *Fax:* 44759
Internet: www.trier.de; *E-mail:* info@tit.de
Hours: April–October 0900–1830 Monday–Saturday; 0900–1530 Sunday. Shorter hours in the winter months.

Money exchange available in rail station. The tourist office is about a ten-minute walk from the rail station or there is a taxi stand at the right-hand front of the station. On foot, proceed down Bahnhofstrasse, which runs from the station into Theodor-Heuss-Allee leading to the Porta Nigra. Located immediately in back of the Porta Nigra monument. Walking tip: Avoid the din of traffic by using the park pathways on the left of the main thoroughfare for a relaxing stroll.

Welcome to Germany's oldest city!

"Before Rome, there was Trier." Although this is legend, it is also a historical fact. Evidence of human settlements as early as the third century B.C. have been discovered in and around the city of Trier. Further legend attributes the founding of Trier in 2000 B.C. to the Assyrians. But history more soberly attributes its roots to the Emperor Augustus, who founded (or refounded) Trier in 18 B.C., thereby beginning Trier's role in Roman history.

In A.D. 293, Trier became the capital of Rome's province of Belgica Prima and the seat of the emperor's court. History records that no less than six Roman emperors held court here. The city's population swelled to about 80,000 citizens, and its cultural growth kept pace with its expanding population. Many magnificent edifices and archaeological finds attest to this growth today.

Trier came to be known as the second Rome. By the end of the third century A.D., it had become a capital of the western part of the Roman Empire. Its many monuments from that time attest to its greatness. The fourth-century Roman cathedral has among its treasures the "Holy Robe," said to have belonged to Christ. In ancient Roman records, Trier was among the first places north of the Alps to bear the name of "city."

Trier's pedestrian zone begins at the town's northern edge with its prize possession—the Roman gateway building, the **Porta Nigra** (Black Gate), built in A.D. 200. Known as the "northern gate of the Roman Empire," it takes its name from the dark patina that formed over its sandstone facade. It was transformed into a church during the eleventh century, but Napoleon restored the building to its original appearance in 1804. Other Roman ruins still remaining are the **Barbara Baths** (A.D. 150), the **Imperial Baths** (A.D. 300), the **Forum Baths** (A.D. 100), the core of the **Cathedral** (A.D. 330/380). The **Amphitheater** (A.D. 100), and a bridge crossing the Moselle River.

Trier fell to the Franks in the fifth century, but the city's life did not end. During the thousand years that followed, churches, monasteries, convents, and mansions were built literally on top of, and around, its ancient structures. A cross, erected in A.D. 958 to signify Trier's right to conduct a market, marks the **Hauptmarkt** (Main Market) of today's city. On the other side of the coin, in 1818 a man was born in Trier whose ideas were in opposition to the free market concept; his name was Karl Marx.

Walks between the area of the Porta Nigra and beyond the Main Market will find you amongst stores galore. Ranging from the quaint antique shop to the eclectic gift emporium to the modern department store, one can easily find Himmel figurines at Antik Baser, wines in several locations (tasings offered, of course, prior to purchase), and rare Roman coins at the shop Haubrich. In 1993, Trier claimed the largest antique coin discovery with a find of over 2,500 Roman gold pieces.

Trier is an appealing city. It probably can attribute much of this appeal to the fact that it has been an imperial residence since the days of the Caesars. Strolling through Trier, you will see examples of Renaissance, Baroque, and Rococo architecture standing side by side. More recently, during the nineteenth century, several impressive citizens' houses of outstanding architectural beauty were built along with many museums including the Archaeological Museum, Bishop's Museum, Cathedral Treasury, the Karl Marx Museum, and the new favorite, the Toy Museum.

Sprechen Sie Deutsch? German speaking walking and bus tours are offered daily. City tours in English run Saturday and Sunday in April and daily from May to October at 1330. Tours last 2 hours and include entrance to Roman monuments. Arrangements may be made for private guides during the rest of the year as well. Walking tours: Adults 10 DEM, children 3 DEM. Bus tours: Adults 17 DEM, children 8.50 DEM. For more tour information, including summer boat trips down the Moselle, visit the tourist office Web site: www.trier.de.

Not all of Trier's attributes are readily visible, for beneath the city in the storage cellars of its wineries there are vats and casks capable of holding more than three million gallons of the Moselle, Saar, and Ruwer wines produced annually in the area surrounding the city. If you would like to enjoy a gourmet meal with a glass of the grape, settle into the **Doprint Hotel** or the **Pfeffermühle restaurants,** or taste the Mosel-Saar-Ruwer region wines and sparking wines at the new Mediterranean-style eatery, **Welcome at Simeonstiftplatz.** Wine tasting is also offered at the area's five wineries and at the vintners in Olewig.

Trier is abundant in festivals throughout the year. Celebrations include the Olewig Wine Festival, Trier Sparkling Wine Gala, Trier Wine Market, and the

Luxembourg—Trier

DEPART LUXEMBOURG	ARRIVE TRIER	DEPART TRIER	ARRIVE LUXEMBOURG
0721	0807	1447	1533
0822	0908	1547	1633
0922	1007	1647	1733
0939	1024	1747	1833
1033	1115	1804	1850
1122	1209	1840	1922
1222	1312	1947	2029
1322	1407	2047	2129
		2147	2229

Daily, including holidays
Distance: 32 miles (51 km)

Wine Forum, plus the Trier Summer Festival, Music Festival, and Christmas Market. Schedules available from the tourist information office.

A small street to the side of the great cathedral in Trier is named Sieh um Dich (Look Around You)—an expression that depicts the city's greatness, for you can see 2,000 years of history in just about as many steps. In fact, one of the tours conducted by the city bears the title "Trier—2,000 steps—2,000 years." Perhaps this tour should be taken before tasting the local nectar or maybe you would prefer to ride the bus. Trier 24-hour bus tickets may be purchased for 1 or 2 adults and up to 4 children under the age of 15. The tourist office also offers the Trier Card (adult, 17 DEM; family, 32 DEM) and the Trier Card Plus (adult, 25 DEM; family, 44 DEM). Both offer free or discounted entrance fees to museums, monuments, theaters, and more; the Plus Card includes free transport on the city buses. Both cards are valid for 3 consecutive days.

The Netherlands

Traditionally, when we think of Holland, windmills, wooden shoes, and wondrous flowers come to mind. While these things probably will always be a part of Dutch traditions and landscape, there is another not-as-well known facet to the Netherlands and its people—its important and enviable economic position in Europe.

Dutch innovation and know-how are responsible for making the computer software Windows accessible for blind users through the use of a cordless mouse that utilizes sound instead of visual images.

Developments in agribusiness include cattle comfort (how about bovine water beds?). Developed by the Dutch Dunlop-Enerka company, the water bed for cattle is more hygienic and safer than customary straw beds.

The Dutch seem to have an idea or an answer for just about everything. One Dutch company had an answer to automobile congestion and pollution problems by developing a new concept in public transport—People Movers—a combination of ski-lift design and the already existing airport-style people movers.

Another Dutch firm, Spectrum Buoca, has targeted another type of pollution—the acrid urine odor that plagues public facilities (particularly during hot weather). Biological Urine Odour Control Agent (Buoca) is a mixture of natural enzymes and bacteria that "eats" the smelly problem.

It doesn't take too long to discover that the Netherlanders are not only multitalented; they're also multilingual. The Dutch laughingly refer to their own language as "more of a throat condition than anything else" and readily join you in *your* native tongue. English is the primary second language spoken in the Netherlands, but French, Spanish, German, and many others are heard daily.

Although the Dutch are seemingly inventing the future, they are not forgetting their traditions. There are still about 1,000 working **windmills** that are functioning the same way they did more than a hundred years ago. A group of 19 windmills may be found at **Kinderdijk** in the province of South Holland, some of which you may tour inside. It's amazing—mills that were built in 1740 are still running.

Wooden shoes may not be worn very often anymore, but thanks to tourists, their production has continued. Now, almost any Dutch souvenir shops sells them and a few farmers in some rural areas still don their wooden clogs when they work in the fields or stalls.

Wondrous flowers are, of course, still in generous supply in Holland. Spanning about 70 acres, the **Keukenhof in Lisse,** accessible from Haarlem and Amsterdam via the *Keukenhof-Express*; (*Tel:* (25) 246–5555, *Fax:* (25) 246–5565) is the most famous and biggest bulb show in the world. It is open to the public from 0800 to 1930 daily in the spring from March through the end of May, welcoming more than 800,000 visitors to gaze upon some six million bulbs. Admission: 18 guilders, adults; 9.00 children age 4–12; 15.75 guilders age 65 and over. Ask for the savings certificate booklet for access to free gifts and discounts on air, hotel and more from the Netherlands Board of Tourism.

For more information on the Netherlands, contact the Netherlands Board of Tourism in North America:

Chicago: P.O. Box 220079, Chicago, IL 60622-0079. *Tel:* (312) 455–1601; *Fax:* (312) 455–1602; *Internet:* www.holland.com

Banking

- **Currency:** Netherlands Guilder (NLG)
- **Exchange rate at press time:** 2.05 NLG = $1.00 U.S.

Communications

- **Country Code:** 31
  For telephone calls within the Netherlands, dial a zero (0) preceding area code.
  Direct dial: AT&T: 0 (800) 022–9111; MCI: 0 (800) 022–9122; Sprint: 0 (800) 022–9119

Rail Travel in the Netherlands

The Netherlands Railways (Nederlandse Spoorwegen, or NS) has many of its own day excursions. Because Holland is a very compact country, it is possible to take any one of the day excursions from any railway station within the country and return to your point of departure the same day (a strategy similar to that outlined in *Europe by Eurail).*

Frequent trains run to every part of Holland and most of the stations are linked with bus services and train taxis. The Dutch **Rail Idee** program offers the day excursionist the convenience of a one-stop shop before hitting the rails. Travelers may purchase day passes directly from the rail station that include not only their transportation (train, bus, taxi, even bicycle rental), but also their admission to a variety of sightseeing attractions in the Netherlands. Rail Idee ticket packages range in price according to destination and offer a choice of over 200 attractions to visit. On average, one can save around 20 percent compared to separately buying transportation and admission tickets. The day pass also offers bonus discounts at various shops and restaurants.

To find out more about these day excursions, ask at the train information office in the Amsterdam Central Station. Or contact the Netherlands Board of Tourism for the brochure *Exploring Holland by Train*.

Many Dutch cities, such as **The Hague, Rotterdam,** and **Utrecht,** are less than an hour away from Amsterdam. In just two hours, you could be in Antwerp, Belgium, shopping for diamonds. Add another thirty minutes and you could hop on the fast Thalys train and have lunch in Brussels and then shop for lace. Continue your spree—the quaint town of **Delft,** where the world-renowned Delft blue pottery is made, is only fifty minutes' train time from Amsterdam.

Holland Railpass

3 Days/1 month	Adult	Child	Senior	Youth
1st Class	$98	$50	$78	—
2nd Class	$65	$33	$52	$52
5 Days/1 month				
1st Class	$147	$74	$119	—
2nd Class	$98	$49	$79	$79

Valid for travel throughout Holland; travel on bus lines not included. Senior fares valid for ages 60+. Youth fares for ages 12–25, second class travel only: child fares, ages 4–11.

Holland Rail Twinpass

3 Days/1 month	Adult	Child	Senior	Youth
1st Class	$147	$75	$117	—
2nd Class	$98	$50	$78	$78
5 Days/1 month				
1st Class	$221	$111	$179	—
2nd Class	$147	$74	$119	$119

Prices are total for two persons traveling together. Valid for travel throughout Holland; travel on bus lines not included. Senior fares valid for ages 60+. Youth fares for ages 12–25, second class only; child fares, ages 4–11.

Benelux Tourrail Pass

	1st Class	2nd Class
5-day within 1 month	$217	$155
Youth: 5-day within 1 month	—	$104

Benelux Tourrail for Two Pass

2 people traveling together	1st Class	2nd Class
5-days within 1 month	$326	$233

The Netherlands Railways accepts **Eurailpass, Europass plus Benelux option,** the **Benelux Tourrail Pass,** and the **Holland Railpass.** A bonus for Eurailpass and Europass plus Benelux option holders is a 30 percent discount on Stena Line high-speed ships (HSS) crossing from Hoek van Holland to Harwich, England.

Base City . . .

Amsterdam

City Dialing Code: 20
Internet: www.amsterdam.nl

One of the most unusual cities in Europe, Amsterdam is a "fun city"—fun to see, fun to be in. It is a pleasant, human city where handsome houses stand on quiet canals, shoppers walk uninterrupted on streets without vehicles, and street organs play in the parks (even on rainy afternoons). It is the kind of city that, when you are lost, sends a smiling old gentleman on his bicycle or a bevy of flaxen-haired schoolgirls to your rescue. Amsterdam is a patient city whose people listen as you attempt to read Dutch expressions from a phrase book—then respond in perfect English. Amsterdam is a city to fall in love with.

Though picturesque, by European standards Amsterdam is not an ancient city. In the thirteenth century it was a small fishing village tucked behind a protecting dam on the Zuider Zee. It wasn't until the seventeenth century that it emerged as northern Europe's most prosperous port. Dutch influence declined at the end of the seventeenth century, but Amsterdam survived in style, having been built on 90 islands linked by more than 1,000 bridges arching 160 canals.

Although their interiors have been altered many times, the fronts of seventeenth-century houses along the canals remain unaltered.

As the Netherlands Board of Tourism states: "Amsterdam is to Holland what New York is to the United States. It is the cuckoo in the Dutch nest, the strange bird with the big mouth, New York with a more easygoing nature. But that shouldn't be surprising. After all, New York was founded by Amsterdammers. Now you are invited to discover our Amsterdam."

Arriving by Air

Schiphol Airport, PO Box 7501, 1118 ZG Schiphol Airport, The Netherlands; Hello Port Schiphol Information *Tel:* (31) 900–0141; *Tel:* (20) 601–9111; *Fax:* (20) 604–1475; *Internet:* www.schiphol.nl

Amsterdam's **Schiphol Airport,** which ranks fourth in Europe after airports in London, Paris, and Frankfurt, is one of the most modern and efficient air terminals in the world. Schiphol handles over 25.4 million passengers per year and has some of the best tax-free shopping in Europe. It was built to be convenient. At last count, the airport provides flights to more than 220 destinations in 85 countries by more than 80 international airlines. After you have cleared customs, proceed to Schiphol Plaza to the **Holland Tourist Information (HTI)** center (open daily 0700–2200). There you can obtain all the information you may need for getting into downtown Amsterdam.

Airport–City Links: Rail service between the airport and Amsterdam's Central Station takes about 20 minutes and costs 10.75 NLG for a round trip. Trains run approximately every 15 minutes from 0600 to midnight. If your destination is in the southern part of the city, you can board a train for the Zuid (South) Station as well. In fact, direct train service from Schiphol Airport to many other points in the Netherlands, such as The Hague, Rotterdam, and Delft, is available. Within Holland (*Tel:* 0900–9292) for bus, tram, subway, and rail connections (75 cents per minute), or for international train information, *Tel:* 0–0900–9296, 50 cents per minute.

KLM Airport Hotel Shuttle operates a bus service between Schiphol Airport and the major hotels of Amsterdam. The bus stops at the Luchthaven Schiphol, Hilton Amsterdam, Barbizon Centre, Hotel Pulitzer, Krasnapolsky, Holiday Inn, Renaissance, and Barbizon Palace hotels. The one-way fare is 17.50 NLG, and tickets may be purchased on the bus. If your hotel is not listed above, ask at the HTI desk for the listed hotel nearest to yours and get off there—first checking that your hotel is only a short distance away.

Otherwise, a **taxi** may better serve your needs. A taxi takes about 30–45 minutes and costs about 55–65 NLG. Again, the HTI desk will be helpful. Taxis can be found just outside the Arrivals Hall.

Money-exchange machine is available in the South Lounge. It changes 17 different currencies into guilders. The West Lounge has an ATM (bank cards only). The tourist office will also exchange money with no commission charge, as opposed to the post offices and banks.

Duty-Free Shopping. Amsterdam's Schiphol Airport Shopping Centre is actually three centers. The Plaza totals over 50 shops with more than 120,000 different items. The shops are open from first to last flight departure. Duty-free shopping is available only to passengers departing Schiphol to destinations outside The European Union.

Schiphol Plaza shopping is available to everyone, but normal VAT is payable. Hours: 0700–2200 daily.

Arriving by Train

The **Amsterdam Centraal Station** is the focal point of all rail, tram (trolley), bus, and Metro (subway) traffic within the city. All train service for the listed day excursions depart from, and arrive in, this station. Trams, buses, and the Metro (entrance) are available immediately in front of the station, the hub of Amsterdam's city-transportation network; practically everything in Amsterdam begins and ends here.

Amsterdam's Centraal Station has managed to preserve its Old-World charm, but it is not a sparkling example of chrome and polished marble, as many rail terminals in Europe have become. The station's facade is unchanged. Its ability to handle incoming and outgoing passengers alike, however, has improved.

Although it abounds in digital train-information displays, the station still provides the standard train-departure posters with their yellow background giving train-departure information by separate directions. Rail service throughout The Netherlands is so dense—departures approximately every half-hour—that these sectional timetables to Rotterdam, Utrecht, and other cities are most helpful.

Amsterdam's Centraal Station is virtually a city within a city, with many restaurants and shops operating over extended hours—a good place to stock up for a trip. A word of caution regarding the station: It's an originating point for long-distance express trains, including the Thalys train connections to Brussels and Eurostar to London, as well as the EuroCity network. This means lots of tourists—and tourists attract pickpockets. Watch when boarding the trains, particularly for people who are apparently traveling without luggage and are following you closely with only an empty shopping bag in hand. Chances are that they are "shopping" for your wallet and they plan to leave the train before it departs.

Money-exchange office "GWK" is on the street side of the station foyer. It is open daily, 24 hours per day. Money exchange is also possible at the VVV Amsterdam offices.

Tourist information for all of Holland, including Amsterdam, is available from the VVV Amsterdam Tourist Offices located inside Centraal Station at Stationsplein 15, platform 2 (Spoor 2) or in front of the rail station; offices also located at tram stops Leidesplein and Stadionplein. Tourist information offices open from 0900–1700 daily.

Train information may be obtained in the office of the Netherlands Railways (information for trains within Holland [*Tel:* 0900–9292]), located on the far right of the main station hall as you exit from the trains. This office has the familiar **i** sign. Open daily 0630–2230. Take a number as you enter.

Seat reservations as well as **railpass validation** may be made in this office. Complete information regarding The Netherlands Railways day-excursion program is also available. Remember, when having your pass validated, write out the starting and ending dates on a piece of paper and have the railroad representative agree to the correctness of the dates before the information is entered on your pass.

Tourist Information/Hotel Reservations

VVV Amsterdam Tourist Office: P.O. Box 3901, 1001 AS, Amsterdam
Tel: 0900 400 40 40, 1 NLG per minute
Fax: 20 625 28 69
Hours: 0900–1700 daily
    Located immediately in front and slightly to the left as you exit Amsterdam's Centraal Station, in the Noord-Zuidhollands (NZH) Koffiehuis.

This office can provide complete city and national information for all of the Netherlands. Hotel, hostel, camping, and apartment bookings can be made here. Maps of Amsterdam are available at a vending machine for 3.50 NLG. You can also call 0900–400 40 40, Monday–Friday, 0900–1700, for information. Other VVV offices are located at Leidesplein, Stadionplein, and in the Centraal Station at Platform (Spoor) 2. A Holland Tourist Information center is located at Schiphol Airport Plaza.

Hotel reservations can be made at the Holland Tourist Information (HTI) office at Schiphol Airport, at the VVV Amsterdam Tourist Office (above) in the Noord-Zuidhollands Koffiehuis (NZH coffeehouse), in the VVV office in the Central Station at Platform 2, or at the Leidesplein and Stadionplein VVV offices. Hotel reservations may also be made over the phone by calling 31 777 000 888 or the Amsterdam Reservation Services at 31 6 340 340 66.

For convenience, comfort, and cuisine all in one place, we recommend the **Victoria Hotel,** one of the Park Plaza Hotels Benelux.
• *Convenience*—centrally located in Amsterdam and across the street from

```
┌─────────────────────────────────────────────────────┐
│         Europe by Eurail Special Offer                │
│                    from                               │
│          The Park Plaza Hotels Benelux                │
│                                                       │
│ Discount: 20 percent off rack rates!                  │
│ Offer valid in the following hotels:                  │
│  • Victoria Hotel Amsterdam, opposite central rail station │
│  • Park Plaza Utrecht, next to the central rail station │
│  • Mandarin Park Plaza in Eindhoven, near the central rail station │
│  • Astrid Park Plaza in Antwerp, Belgium, opposite the central │
│    rail station                                       │
│                                                       │
│ Offer valid until December 31, 2000, upon rate availability and only by using │
│ this discount coupon.                                 │
└─────────────────────────────────────────────────────┘
```

Amsterdam Centraal Station. The hotel will even send someone to help with your luggage.

- *Comfort*—the stately Victoria Hotel, built in 1890, offers all of the modern "creature comforts" such as deluxe rooms, indoor heated swimming pool, Turkish steam baths, beauty salon, and fitness room—even a free first class train ticket to and from Schiphol Airport.
- *Cuisine*—fine French and international dinners in the Seasons Garden Restaurant.

Park Plaza Hotels Benelux are located either opposite from, next to, or very close to the central rail stations in Amsterdam, Utrecht, and Eindhoven in The Netherlands, as well as in Antwerp, Belgium. In addition, they **offer *Europe by Eurail* readers a 20 percent discount** off their normal rack rates.

Just mention *Europe by Eurail* when you make your reservation and present the coupon on the following page upon check-in to receive your 20 percent discount. For reservations, *Tel:* 3120–6271 166; *Fax:* (31) 2062–74 259.

Getting Around in Amsterdam

GVB: located on square opposite Centraal Station
Tel: 06 9292 or 460 5840; *Reservations:* 0900 92 92
Hours: Monday–Friday 0700–2100; Saturday–Sunday 0800–2100

Amsterdam's public transportation system encompasses 17 tram lines, over 30 bus lines, and 3 underground systems/light rail lines, plus ferries, and canal boats. The transport office, GVB (Gemeentevervoerbedrijf), is located in front and slightly to the left as you exit Amsterdam's Centraal Station. Check with this office for up-to-date information, for public transportation maps, and to purchase transport tickets.

There are a variety of one-day or multiple-day transportation passes that have to be stamped only with the first use; strip tickets (strippenkaart) are also available but they require stamping with each use. The tourist transportation tickets are accepted on all trams, express trams, buses, and subways. Single day 12 NLG, two days 16 NLG, and 3.75 NLG per additional day up to a nine-day maximum. For transportation information, *Tel:* 0900 92 92. For **boat services** contact the tourist information office for details on the Canal Bus, Water taxi, Artis Express Rederij Lovers, and the Museum Boat. Bicycle and water bike rentals also available or contact European Vacation Tours and Groups for pre-planned walking or cycling tours, *Tel:* (888) TOUR–404 or visit www.europeanvacation.com.

Circle Tram 20 provides flexible access to sights and attractions, museums, hotels, and restaurants—30 different stops—in Amsterdam. Hop on and off when and where you please. Circle Tram 20 operates 0900–1900 daily and departs every 10 minutes in two directions. Purchase 1-, 2-, 3-, or 4-day tickets at the VVV Information offices, at the GVB transport offices, from the conductor at the back of the tram, or from tobacco shops and large hotels. The tickets are valid on all public transport everywhere in Amsterdam. With Circle Tram 20, a helpful conductor is onboard. If you have an Amsterdam Paspoort, you can purchase a 2-day Circle Tram 20 ticket for the price of a 1-day ticket.

The **Amsterdam Culture and Leisure Pass** costs 39.50 NLG with a value of over 160 NLG and offers substantial discounts or free entry for various museums, including the Rijksmuseum, the Stedelijk Museum of Modern Art, The Netherlands Maritime Museum, and the new Metropolis Museum with its focus on science, technology, and art. The Pass also includes discounts on other attractions, excursions and guided tours, a two-day public transportation ticket for the price of a 1-day ticket, a 25 percent discount on Holland International's romantic Candlelight and Wine Cruises—even a free canal boat cruise and discounts on the Museum Boat and the Canal Bus.

The Amsterdam Culture and Leisure Pass is available from the U.S. by calling (800) 722–7151 or visiting www.railpass.com. Once abroad you may purchase the Pass in 1 of 6 languages at any of the VVV Amsterdam Tourist offices, the Holland Tourist Information center at Schiphol Airport Plaza, or inquire at your hotel. After purchasing the Pass take advantage of the 50 percent discount on an Amsterdam city map and "What's On" magazine at the tourist office.

Sights/Attractions/Tours

If you'd like to see Amsterdam on foot, the VVV's color-coded signboards and map will guide you along six walking routes. More than thirty attractions are incorporated into the walking routes.

A boat trip on Amsterdam's canals and other waterways is, undoubtedly, the most relaxing way to see the city. Canal-boat terminals line the city's pier-studded canals, many of which may be found immediately outside the station. The closest of these is the **Holland International** pier (*Tel:* 622–7788). It is just across the bridge on the right. A canal tour costs 15 NLG for adults and 7.50 NLG for children age 4–12 and senior citizens over age 65. Other tour-boat terminals are scattered throughout Amsterdam.

There are several canal cruise companies to choose from—all are excellent. During summer evenings, when the buildings along the canals are illuminated and the canal bridges are outlined by tiny lights, Holland International offers a Candlelight and Wine Cruise (50 guilders)—the perfect way to end your day. (Receive a 25 percent discount if you've purchased an Amsterdam Paspoort.)

Amsterdam's old "inner city" is famous for its compactness. Most museums, markets, monuments, shopping streets, and other attractions are all within walking distance—or a short tram ride—from your hotel. Several of the city-center shops are open on Sundays—somewhat unusual when compared to the shopping hours for the rest of Europe. Amsterdam boasts the largest historical inner city in Europe, with more than 6,800 National Trust buildings.

The city has more than 60 museums, including the famous **Rijksmuseum** (open daily 1000–1700), where you can view Rembrandt's renowned *Night Watch*, along with an extensive collection of his other dazzling works. The South Wing is devoted to a wide-ranging overview of eighteenth- and nineteenth-century Dutch Impressionist art. All the paintings now have explanations in English, and for 7.50 NLG you can rent a CD-ROM player that describes in English, German, or French the 200 most significant paintings in the collection.

The **Van Gogh Museum** is underwent a 30-million NLG ($15.5 million U.S.) renovation and construction of a new wing and reopened in June 1999.

One of the newest of Amsterdam's museums is appropriately named **"newMetropolis" Museum**. It is an interesting attraction designed by Italian architect Renzo Piano, due to its location on top of one of the major tunnels leading into and out of Amsterdam. Plus its roof offers a spectacular view of the city. The building appears to arise from the water of the Oosterdok as a bow of a ship. A twenty-first-century public center for science and technology, this new museum fits with our earlier statement, "The Dutch are inventing the future," by using up-to-date hands-on techniques.

"Diamonds are a girl's best friend," and Amsterdam is a good place to see how a glassy little piece of stone can become the most beautiful, desirable

Train Connections to Other Base Cities from Amsterdam Centraal

DEPART	TRAIN NUMBER	ARRIVE	NOTES
Berlin Zoobahnhof			
0713	IR 2341	1430	
0913	IR 2343	1630	
1313	IR 2345	2030	
2213	341	0703+1	
Bern (Berne)			
1824	641/499	0709+1	1
Brussels (Bruxelles) Midi/Zuid			
0624	629	0920	
0724	630	1020	
0754	Thalys 9320★	1032	R
0824	631	1120	
0924	632	1220	
0954	Thalys 9328★	1232	R
1024	633	1320	
(and hourly until 2224)			
1354	Thalys 9344★	1632	R
1754	Thalys 9360★	2032	R
Copenhagen (København) H			
0713	IR 2341	1759	2
0913	IR 2343	2159	2
1313	IR 2345	2359	2
1904	EC 153	0840+1	3
Hamburg			
0713	IR 2341	1207	4
0913	IR 2343	1407	4
1313	IR 2345	1807	4
1713	IR 2347	2207	4
1904	EC 153	0223+1	5
Luxembourg			
0624	629	1233	6
0724	630	1333	6
0824	631	1433	6
0924	632	1533	6
(and hourly)			
1724	640	2343	6
1924	642	0110+1	6

Lyon Part-Dieu

0754	Thalys 9320★	1504	R, 7
0954	Thalys 9328★	1705	R, 7
1124	634	1914	8
1354	Thalys 9344★	2054	R, 8

Milan (Milano) Centrale

1655	EC 151	0745+1	R, 9

Munich (München) Hauptbahnhof

0755	EC 3	1618	10
1005	EC 105	1819	10

Nice Ville

0754	Thalys 9324★	2025	7

Paris Gare du Nord

0754	Thalys 9320★	1205	R
0954	Thalys 9328★	1405	R
1124	634	1605	11
1224	635	1705	11
1354	Thalys 9344★	1805	R
1754	Thalys 9360★	2205	R
2224	288	0629+1	Sleeper

Vienna (Wien) Westbahnhof

1925	EN 225	0945+1	Sleeper

Zürich Hauptbahnhof

0755	EC 3	1700	
2005	203/1203	0753+1	12

Daily, unless otherwise noted
R Reservations required
★ Thalys high-speed train, supplement required
1. Change to sleeper train 499 in Brussels Midi/Zuid departing 2233.
2. Via Germany. Change trains in Osnabruck and Hamburg.
3. Via Germany. Change to EN 233 Nord Express overnight train in
   Duisburg departing at 2218. 1st and 2nd class sleepers; couchettes.
4. Change trains in Osnabruck.
5. Change trains in Duisburg.
6. Change trains in Brussels Nord Station.
7. Change in Paris to Gare de Lyon Station.
8. Change trains in Brussels Midi/Zuid.
9. Change in Cologne (Köln) to train 201, 1st and 2nd class sleepers, 2nd
   class couchettes.
10. Change trains in Mannheim.
11. Change in Brussels Midi to Thalys★ train, reservations required.
12. Arrives Zürich Altstetten

gemstone in the world. With 7 diamond factories to tempt you, we suggest taking a tour of the **Amsterdam Diamond Center,** located at Rokin 1–5 (*Tel:* 624–5787; *Fax:* 625–1220). Hours: 0930–1800 Monday–Saturday, Thursday 1030–2030, and 1030–1800 Sunday. Although free samples are not available, a diamond sure makes a great souvenir!

Dining in Amsterdam is an exercise in international cuisine. The expression "You can eat there in any language" is no exaggeration. First decide what type of food you want—Hungarian, German, Italian, Greek, Scandinavian, Japanese, or Indonesian—then select from among the many restaurants offering such dishes. Our favorite for Indonesian food is **Restaurant Indonesia**, at 18 Korte Leidsedwarsstraat (*Tel:* 420–3300). Take tram 1, 2, or 5 from the Central Station to the Leidesplein area, about a twelve-minute ride. Their specialty is an eighteen-dish *rijstafel* (ricetable). Go there hungry—we guarantee you won't go home that way.

For more traditional Dutch bill-of-fare, try another favorite—**Haesje Claes** at Spuistraat 275 (*Tel:* (20) 624–9998; *Fax:* (20) 627–4817). Named after Lady Haesje Claes, this restaurant has as its slogan "From canapes to caviar." The eel and salmon with lobster is excellent. Born in 1520 into a prosperous merchant family, Lady Haesje Claes was the founder and patron of the Public Orphanage, now the Amsterdam Historical Museum. Have a typical Dutch lunch or dinner in one of the eight chambers, each with its own special atmosphere.

Visitors from the United States who are hankerin' for a good U.S. steak should not miss the **Three Sisters Restaurant.** The beef is USDA Prime. A porterhouse steak for two is 69.75 NLG. There's quite a story about how the restaurant got its name. Ask the waiter for the menu with the complete version of the story of the three sisters and their New York connections.

Day Excursions

The *Europe by Eurail* day excursions described in this chapter are to **Alkmaar,** home of the world-famous cheese market; **Enkhuizen,** for its open-air Zuider Zee Museum, which depicts what Dutch life was like before the Zuider Zee was sealed off from the North Sea; **Haarlem,** for the Frans Hals Museum and more aspects of life in The Netherlands; and **Hoorn,** for browsing in a medieval market. These day excursions present a cross section of the Netherlands, from its rural to its sophisticated side.

Day Excursion to

Alkmaar

WORLD-FAMOUS CHEESE MARKET

Depart from Amsterdam Centraal Station

Distance by Train: 24 miles (39 km)
Average Train Time: 30 minutes
City Dialing Code: 72
Tourist Information Office: Waagplein 2-3, 1811 SP Alkmaar
Tel: (72) 511–4284
Fax: (72) 511–7513
Hours: 0900–1730 Monday–Wednesday, 0900–1800 Thursday–Friday, and 0900–1700 Saturday

An easy route to the town square is to follow the street, Geesterweg, running perpendicular to the front of the station and the VVV signs leading you across a bridge toward a large church (Church of St. Laurens). Pass the church on its left side and pick up Lange Straat, still walking in the same direction. Pass the Town Hall, which will be on your right; four blocks farther, at a canal, turn left to the Weigh House, where the cheese market is held. The VVV office is located in the front of the Weigh House.

There is a cheese market in Alkmaar every Friday from mid-April to mid-September. But Alkmaar is such a picturesque town that it deserves a visit any day of the week at any time of the year. Trains run between Amsterdam and Alkmaar about every 15 minutes.

Alkmaar is famous not only for its cheese; it is steeped in Dutch history as well. It was at Alkmaar in 1573 that the Spanish were first compelled to retreat their occupying forces; hence, the Dutch expression "victory begins at Alkmaar." A festival is held annually on October 8 to commemorate the breaking of the Spanish siege.

Ask at the tourist office about seeing Alkmaar by canal, a popular way to see the town. Boats depart from Mient (near Waaggebouw). Adult fare, 7 NLG; children under age 12, 4.50 NLG. During the cheese market on Fridays, boats sail every 20 minutes from 0930. During May, June, July, and August, they depart daily on the hour from 1100. In April, September, and October, they sail Monday–Saturday, every hour on the hour, from 1100, depending on the weather. The canal trip takes about 45 minutes (*Tel:* 511–7750).

The **cheese auction** is *the* thing to see in Alkmaar. The square explodes into a frenzy of color and activity as cheese porters trot across the square wearing red, blue, green, or yellow hats according to the group they represent. This auction has continued for more than 375 years and attracts thousands of tourists. It is not, however, merely a tourist attraction. It is a genuine auction, at which cheese merchants sample the product, bargain for the best price, and

Amsterdam—Alkmaar

Daily departures from Amsterdam Centraal Station every 30 minutes at 22 and 52 minutes after the hour from 0722 throughout the day; journey time 35 minutes.

Daily departures from Alkmaar Station at 5 and 36 minutes after the hour throughout the day; journey time 35 minutes.

Distance: 24 miles (39 km)

conclude the sale "on hand clap." From there the porters move the cheese to the Weigh House, where the weigh master checks the weight and calls it out in a loud voice; then the porters take the cheese from there to the buyers' warehouses.

Alkmaar's cheese makers founded their guild in 1622, only two years after the Pilgrims landed on Plymouth Rock. Unique in the curatorial world, Alkmaar's **Cheese Museum** attracts visitors from far and wide (open April–October, Monday–Saturday 1000–1600; opens at 0900 on Fridays). Entrance fee, 3 NLG, but a **Dutch Museumpass** will get you in for free.

Another unique museum is dedicated to the history of beer production. Featuring the fine skills of brewmasters and covering 5,000 years of beer-making history, the city's **National Beer Museum De Boom** deals with all aspects down through the ages that have determined the various characteristics of beer, including the current Dutch favorite, pale lager. It is interesting to note that despite the complicated brewing equipment used today, the art of brewing has remained a natural process relatively unchanged from earlier times.

Both the Cheese Museum and the Beer Museum (April–September, open 1000–1600 Tuesday–Friday; 1300–1700 Saturday–Sunday; November–March, 1300–1600 Tuesday–Sunday) are but a few steps from the city square, where the cheese auction takes place.

Alkmaar is a charming town. It is crisscrossed by canals that, in turn, are spanned by humped stone bridges. The shining red roofs of its old houses are guarded by the towering vaults of the aged **St. Laurens Church,** constructed in 1520. Four blocks south of St. Laurens stands **Molen van Piet,** a windmill built in 1769.

There are an amazing number of things to do and see, among them a visit to the Municipal Museum, the Dutch Stove Museum, and the Hans Brinker Museum; on a Friday, take a look at the stately wooden gabled house complete with an embedded cannonball as a memoir of a war now past. Sample the famous Edam cheese at either lunch or dinner. Time moves slower in Alkmaar.

Day Excursion to

Enkhuizen

ZUIDER ZEE MUSEUM

Depart from Amsterdam Centraal Station

Distance by Train: 37 miles (60 km)

Average Train Time: 1 hour

City Dialing Code: 228

Tourist Information Office: VVV-Enkhuizen e.o., Tussen Twee Havens 1, 1601 Em Enkhuizen

Tel: 31 228 31 31 64

Fax: 31 228 31 55 31

Hours: April–mid-October, daily 0900–1700; mid-October–March, Monday–Friday 0900–1700, Saturday 0900–1400

    After disembarking from the train, bear left approaching the railway station. As you round the station, you will see the VVV tourist office. The route is well marked; just follow the signs.

    This day excursion from Amsterdam was made possible by the opening of the **Zuider Zee Open Air Museum** in Enkhuizen, east of Hoorn. Purchase museum tickets at museum's ticket office. Admission: adults, 17.50 NLG; children age 4-12, 12.50 NLG; adults age 65 and over, 12.50 NLG; children under 4 are admitted free. A visit to the Zuider Zee Museum begins with a 15-minute boat ride. After stopping at the VVV tourist office, walk along the right side of the boat yard in front of the rail station to its far end and board the launch at the pier.

    The museum was opened formally by Queen Beatrix on May 6, 1983 after 18 years of construction. It consists of 135 houses and workshops to depict the Zuider Zee culture before it was closed off from the North Sea in 1932 by the Afsluitdijk barrier dam. You will see a foundry, a steam laundry, a sail loft, and a smokehouse, to name but just a few items. There are a fishing village on the quay and a town center complete with a church and a general store, where postcards and wooden shoes and other souvenirs are for sale.

    Snacks and various Dutch food specialties are also available, as are tours led by English-speaking guides. Check at the museum office for information. You will pass it just after the foundry. The open-air museum is open April to October, 1000–1700 daily. The indoor portion, known as the **Binnen Museum,** is open throughout the year (except December 25 and January 1). Reduced entrance fees when the outdoor museum is closed.

    Enkhuizen has succeeded in preserving its seventeenth-century character. The old center of the city contains a picturesque fisherman's quarter and a corresponding essential from those days (a farmer's corner). Within the old seawall, which was constructed to protect the city from storms on the Zuider

Amsterdam—Enkhuizen

Daily departures from Amsterdam Centraal station at 19 and 49 minutes after the hour from early morning until late in the day; journey time about 75 minutes.

Daily departures from Enkhuizen station at 7 and 37 minutes after the hour from mid-morning until 2107, then hourly until 0007; journey time 1 hr 7 minutes.

Distance: 37 miles (60 km)

Zee, you will find a shopping center, sidewalk cafes, and restaurants.

Ever wonder how artisans build those beautifully detailed ship models inside glass bottles? A visit to the **Bottle Ship Museum** will reveal the secrets of this ancient sailors' handicraft. The world's largest collection of ships-in-a-bottle is housed in an early seventeenth-century building—the "Spuihuisje"—within easy walking distance of the Zuider Zee Museum. More than 500 models are contained in bottles ranging in size from small perfume bottles to a 30-liter wine flagon. Tickets may be purchased at the VVV office (adults, 5 NLG; children 4 to 12, 3.50 NLG).

For the small-fry, Enkhuizen offers **Sprookjeswonderland (Fairyland).** Situated in a park setting, it contains a children's zoo with a deer park, a farm, and a "hugging" barn. (Open daily, mid-April to mid-October, Monday–Saturday 1000–1730; Sunday 1000–1730.)

The town of Enkhuizen is a living museum in itself. The Zuiderkerk church, with its spiraling tower and copper-clad roof, dominates the skyline of the city, assisted by the wooden bell tower of Enkhuizen's other church, the "Wester." Together with the ramparts and fortress walls, Enkhuizen ensures its future by preserving its rich past.

Day Excursion to

Haarlem

AND THE FRANS HALS MUSEUM

Depart from Amsterdam Centraal Station

Distance by Train: 12 miles (19 km)
Average Train Time: 15 minutes
City Dialing Code: 23
Tourist Information Office: Stationsplein 1
Tel: 0900 6161600; *Fax:* 23 534 0537

Hours: Monday–Friday 0930–1700, Saturday 1000–1400, closed Sunday.

The **VVV tourist information office** is situated on the south right-hand corner of the railway station as you exit. (The train bringing you to Haarlem is headed in a westerly direction as it enters the station.) The office is marked with an ample sign reading VVV HAARLEM and cannot be missed

Haarlem is close to Amsterdam, and this trip has the shortest travel time of any day excursion described in this edition of *Europe by Eurail*. It is also one of the most interesting.

Haarlem remained relatively undamaged by both world wars. What you find there in the **Grote Markt** (Great Market), the old center of the town, has authentic origins dating from the thirteenth century. Haarlem was put to the sword in July 1573, when it fell to its Spanish besiegers and its citizens were butchered. Its devastation, however, was not on the scale that modern weapons could perpetrate.

With the release in 1976 of the motion picture ***The Hiding Place***, the attention of the world was drawn to a quaint little watchmaker's shop established in 1837 at 19 Barteljorisstraat in the heart of Haarlem. It was here in the shop and home of a Christian, Opa ten Boom, and his family that Jewish refugees fleeing the wrath of Nazi Germany were hidden for a time during World War II. A hiding place was built in a bedroom where the refugees could go in case the Germans made a surprise inspection. The ten Boom family operated the refuge for more than 18 months, until they were betrayed on February 28, 1944.

At the time of the betrayal, six persons were concealed in the hiding place. They escaped while the Gestapo was still in the house. The ten Boom family, however, was imprisoned in a concentration camp for their acts of mercy. The ten Boom house is now a museum. It is open for visits 1000–1600 Tuesday through Saturday from April 1 through October 31. It is open 1100–1500 the rest of the year. Entrance is free, but a donation is always graciously appreciated. Check with the VVV for directions and details.

The old center of Haarlem is not so large as to require transportation to its points of interest, but the city bus system is available to assist if necessary. You will want to visit the Great Market and see the town hall and the **Church of Saint Bavo,** then proceed to the world-famous **Frans Hals Museum** and from there to the **Teylers Museum** before returning to the railway station.

The Great Market is actually the central square of Haarlem, in which the nobles of Holland staged their tournaments during the Middle Ages. Today, it is traditionally the social gathering place of the townspeople. A part of the town hall was once a hunting club. The Church of Saint Bavo houses a pipe organ that was once played by the eleven-year-old Mozart.

On foot, head south from the station, crossing the Nieuwe Gracht (New Canal), and proceed to the city's central square, using the tower of the great

Amsterdam—Haarlem

Daily departures from Amsterdam Centraal station at 12 and 42 minutes after the hour throughout the day; journey time 16 minutes.

Daily departures from Haarlem station at 7 and 37 minutes after the hour throughout the day; journey time 15 minutes.

Distance: 12 miles (19 km)

church as your point of destination. As you enter the square, the church stands on your left, the town hall on your right. This square has been termed the most beautiful in Holland. A pause here in one of the many restaurants, outdoor cafes, or ice cream shops is recommended.

Time permitting, before leaving the Great Market, you may wish to visit the **Meat Hall** and the **Fish Hall.** No longer functioning by their descriptive names, both structures are now employed in the exhibition of modern visual art. The seventeenth-century architect Lieven de Key designed the Meat Hall, which is said to be one of the finest examples of Renaissance architecture in the Netherlands.

From the western end of the church, follow the street running south from the square to the **Frans Hals Museum,** just before the canal. This street has several names—Warmoesstraat, Schagchelstraat, and Groot Heiligland—appearing in that order as you move to the museum through some of the most heady seventeenth-century atmosphere to be found anywhere in Europe.

The Frans Hals Museum is a moving experience. It's open Monday through Saturday, 1100–1700, and Sunday, 1200–1700. Perhaps nowhere else can you find such a perfect combination of setting and display. The building is a gorgeous sight—its inner courtyard is a magnificent example of seventeenth-century architecture. The versatility of the museum's collections is unusual. In one section, the peak achievements of Haarlem's seventeenth-century painters may be viewed; in another wing of the museum, visitors may view an exhibition of modern Dutch art. Admission for adults is 10 NLG.

A left turn at the canal below the museum takes you to the **Turf Markt** on the Spaarne River, where another left turn takes you winding along the river to Holland's oldest museum, the **Teylers Museum,** just beyond Damstraat (Dam Street). Here you will be treated to a rich collection of drawings and paintings by Michelangelo, Raphael, Titian, and Rembrandt. The Coin and Medal Room displays Dutch coins and medals from the sixteenth to the twentieth centuries. The museum also includes a collection of fossils and minerals.

Day Excursion to

Hoorn
OLD DUTCH MARKET

Depart from Amsterdam Centraal Station

Distance by Train: 26 miles (42 km)
Average Train Time: 40 minutes
City Dialing Code: 299
Tourist Information Office: Veemarkt 4
Tel: 06–34031055
Hours: In summer, 1300–1800 Monday; 0930–1800 Tuesday–Friday (until 2100 Thursday); 0930–1700 Saturday
    Cross the main street in front of the railway station, bear right to the first street, then turn left to the next intersection. Here, you turn left, then take the second street on your right. Green signposts scattered along this route indicate the location.

Ever since its harbor slowly silted in the eighteenth century, the city of Hoorn has taken to relaxing—except on Wednesdays from July to August, when it awakens with colorful markets and fun events.

In stalls grouped around the statue of Admiral Jan Pieterszoon Coen (founder of the East India Company) in the square the town calls **Rode Steen,** Hoorn's seventeenth-century crafts of clog making, net mending, basket weaving, and many others come to life while groups of folk dancers perform with musical ensembles. If you are not particularly fond of mingling with the crowd, this colorful spectacle may be viewed from the comfort of the **Old Dutch Tavern** on Rode Steen Square.

Although the Zuiderzee has been landlocked since the strait to the North Sea was sealed off in May 1932, Hoorn has managed to maintain its status of a port by establishing four harbor areas with more than 1,100 moorings for commercial and recreational watercraft. The pursuit of water sports, including windsurfing and waterskiing, may be observed—or participated in—throughout the season in Hoorn.

Steam-engine buffs will find interest in Hoorn, too. You can travel on a genuine **steam train** from Hoorn to Medemblik and back in old-fashioned coaches. The Netherlands Railways operates a day excursion, "Historical Triangle," during spring, summer, and fall. Starting either in Hoorn or Enkhuizen, a steam train plies between Hoorn and Medemblik and a boat between Medemblik and Enkhuizen. The VVV office in Amsterdam or the train information office in Amsterdam's Central Station can provide details for this triangle trip. Information for finding Rode Steen Square, as well as the departure point and tickets for the steam train to Medemblik, is also available in the Hoorn railway station.

On Wednesdays, you'll find the market area merely by following the crowd. At other times, follow the directions to the VVV tourist office (above).

Day excursions by train to Hoorn are popular trips out of Amsterdam in the summer. Local trains bear special markings (on Wednesday) from July through August, when the market is staged. Take these trains for a festive mood; but regular train service between Amsterdam and Hoorn runs about every half-hour throughout the day, so you have the option of going and returning whenever you feel like it.

The steam train operates every day but Monday from April through the end of October; so Hoorn stages this market plus many other attractions on days other than Wednesday. In fact, the steam train continues to operate through September and October from Tuesday through Sunday. (For more complete details, check The Netherlands Railways day-excursion brochure.)

Wednesdays during the summer are, of course, the times of high activity in Hoorn, but you may go there at any time throughout the year and spend an enjoyable day in this ancient town on the **Ysselmeer,** a freshwater lake that was once part of the Zuiderzee. It is one of Holland's loveliest cities. As an important fourteenth-century fishing harbor, it grew in stature until the seventeenth-century East Indies trade made it rich. The warehouses and mansions of the East India merchants that still line its streets make exploring the town on foot a sheer delight. You can obtain a street map with a recommended walking tour from either the VVV office or the ticket office in the railway station.

At Rode Steen Square you may inspect the seventeenth-century **Weigh House** and the **Westfries Museum,** which houses a collection of antiques, paintings, and objects associated with the city and its surroundings. The museum is crammed with beautiful paintings of Hoorn's citizen soldiers and other memories of Hoorn's "golden age" during the seventeenth century.

Stop at the fifteenth-century calligrapher's workshop. Here is where Hoorn's wealthy merchants had their contracts and correspondence penned prior to the invention of the printing press later in the century.

Take time to smell the flowers. It took Hoorn many centuries to become what it is today. Relax and enjoy it.

Amsterdam—Hoorn

Daily departures from Amsterdam Centraal Station at 19 and 49 minutes after the hour throughout the day; journey time to Hoorn is 41 minutes.

Daily departures from Hoorn station at 4 and 34 minutes after the hour throughout the day; journey time is 40 minutes.

Distance: 26 miles (42 km)

Norway

"See, darling, how the departing day
On a scarlet pillow is laid away;
How the sun has set
In clouds of gold and violet."
From the poem "Beautiful Clouds" (1839), by Henrik Wergeland

Norway—Land of the Midnight Sun. In the upper reaches of Norway during the summer, the sun never fully sets, generating extraordinary hues of scarlet, gold, and violet in the northern skies. The Norwegian Tourist Board succinctly describes a visit to Norway as "A nature so incredibly beautiful one can't help but feel spiritual. Overall, a vacation in Norway feels like a spa treatment. Norway will capture your heart and renew your spirit."

More than 30 percent of Norway's 155,000 square miles are covered by forests, rivers, and lakes, creating majestic landscapes and mystic fjords. Norwegian beauty and charm are not confined to its landscapes—they are reflected in its people.

Norwegian is the official language, but most Norwegians speak English and some also speak French or German. Norwegians are friendly and fun and eager to make visitors feel welcome.

Norway is a constitutional monarchy with a Parliament, known as "Stortinget," and has been a member of NATO (North Atlantic Treaty Organization) since 1949. Oil and gas are the cornerstone of its economy, and its people have one of the world's highest per capita incomes.

From art, beauty, and culture to hiking, skiing, and whale watching, Norway has something for everyone.

For more information on Norway, contact the Norwegian Tourist Board in North America:

New York: Scandinavian Tourist Board P.O. Box 4649, Grand Central Station, New York, NY 10163–4649. *Tel:* (212) 885–9700; *Fax:* (212) 885–9710; *Internet:* **www.goscandinavia.com** or **www.norway.org**; E-mail: info@goscandinavia.com or usa@nortra.no

Banking

- **Currency:** Norwegian Kroner (NOK)
- **Exchange rate at press time:** 7.67 NOK = $1.00 U.S.
- **Hours:** 0815–1500 (1530 in winter) Monday–Friday, closing at 1800 on Thursday. Some banks are open longer than regular hours in larger cities. Most shorten hours during summer.

Communications

- **Country Code:** 47
  City codes are not used when dialing within Norway
  Direct dial: AT&T: 800–19–011; MCI: 800–19–912; Sprint: 800–19–877

Rail Travel in Norway

The **Norwegian State Railways (NSB)** successfully combines a comprehensive system (4,044 kilometers) of express and local rail service with bus and boat services.

The **NSB** cleverly designed **"Norway in a Nutshell"** comprises package tours that incorporate various transportation modes to create a great way to see Norway. These packages include hotel, breakfast, and a Norway Railpass. *Tel:* (800) 722–7151, (888) TOUR–404, *Fax:* (614) 764–0711 for a free *Norway in a Nutshell* brochure; or visit www.europeanvacation.com for further information.

Norway's trains traverse difficult geography; consequently, train speeds are limited to a maximum speed of 160 km/h. The rail connection between Gardermoen Airport and Oslo on the *Gardermoen Express*, however, is built for 200 km/h and takes only 19 minutes. Norwegian trains are known for cleanliness and comfort.

On the night trains, sleeper cars contain 1, 2, or 3 beds per compartment, and couchettes and/or reclining seats are available on some trains.

NSB accepts the 17-country **Eurailpass,** the **ScanRail Pass** (for rail travel in Denmark, Finland, Norway, and Sweden), and the **Norway Railpass.** Eurailpass holders receive a 30 percent discount on the Color Line steamship fare between Norway and Denmark.

Crossings:
Kristiansand–Hirtshals, Moss–Hirtshals, Moss–Frederikshavn, Larvik–Frederikshavn, Larvik–Skagen.
- Scandinavian Seaways–50 percent discount between Oslo and Copenhagen.

• Ferry reduction of 50 percent on Flaggruten ANS: Bergen–Haugesund–Stavenger and on Stena Line between Oslo and Frederikshavn.

Seat reservations are compulsory (20 NOK) on InterCity (ICE) trains and most other express trains. Supplement is charged for use of the ICE's "Bureau car," and for the "Saloon car," which includes a meal.

In June 2000, Norway's new "Signatur-trains" begin operating on the Bergen Line.

Norway Railpass

	ADULT		SENIOR	
	First Class	Second Class	First Class	Second class
3 days within 1 month	$181	$139	$144	$111
4 days within 1 month	$224	$172	$179	$139
5 days within 1 month	$250	$192	$200	$154

Children age 4–4 travel at half the adult fare. Children under age 4 travel free; maximum of 2 children travel free per adult. Senior age 60+.

Travel on the Flam Railway Line no longer included with the Norway Pass, ScanRail Pass, or Eurailpass. Beginning May 1, 2000, a discount of 30 percent will be offered on the Flam Line.

New "Signatur" Expresstrains run on the Southern Line and Dovreline; Bergen Line added beginning June 2000. Supplement required, includes meals and refreshments.

Base City . . .

Oslo

No city dialing code required.
Internet: www.oslo.no

Oslo, known as "the Viking Capital," is unique. If you love to bask in the sun, go to Oslo sometime between May and October, when more sunbeams fall on Oslo than on any other capital city in Europe north of the Alps. About half a million of Norway's 4 million people live in Oslo, and soaking up the sun is *the* thing to do in town during the summer. Sauna baths, of course, become the rage for the balance of the year.

Oslo is also Norway's business, cultural, and fun capital. Frequently referred to as the "Nightclub of the North," Oslo is Scandinavia's center for entertainment and night life. Artists and performers entertain into the wee hours of the morning.

Arriving by Air

Touted as "Europe's safest and most efficient airport," Oslo's newly opened (October 1998) international airport at Gardermoen is a beautiful example of contemporary Norwegian architecture. Located some 47 kilometers north of Oslo, the new airport has the capacity to handle 16-17 million passengers per year. There are daily direct flights to more than 30 European cities and hourly flights to Copenhagen and Stockholm.

Airport–City Links: High-speed rail connections into Oslo take only 19 minutes. The rail station is located in the air terminal. Follow the pictographs. Long-distance train service provides connections to all parts of Norway and Scandinavia.

The taxi stand at Gardermoen is on your right as you exit from the arrivals hall. If you ask for a shared taxi, expect to pay 450 NOK for 1–2 persons; 3 persons, 200 NOK each; 4 persons, 175 NOK each; and 5 or more, 150 NOK each. Taxi fares should be negotiated with the taxi driver, but you can expect to pay more if traveling alone in a cab. All taxis are equipped with meters and accept all major credit cards. Oslo Taxi service (information in Norwegian): *Tel:* 22 38 80 90; *Fax:* 22 38 85 80.

NOR-WAY Bussekspress (Internet: www.nor-way.no) or SAS Flybussen (Internet: www.sol.no/trafikanten) provide airport-to-city coach service.

Arriving by Train

Oslo has several suburban rail stations, but all international trains stop only at the **Oslo Sentralstasjon (Oslo Central Station).** You will see the station name frequently abbreviated as "Oslo S," or shortened to "Oslo Sentral."

Within the station, rail travelers can take advantage of a mini-market area amid a variety of kiosks (small shops) selling everything from apples to zircons. The nostalgic market area stands on what was once known as the East Station. The East Station was devoted to steel rails, nail-spiked wooden platforms, and tiles bearing the patina of wear from countless passengers' feet as they hurried to and from the steam-hauled trains.

Oslo Sentral Station is a model of efficiency. Access from the train platforms to the station's main hall is by ramps. A new shopping mall, Byporten

("City Gate"), is connected to Oslo Sentral and has over 65 shops, 10 restaurants, and a hotel.

Baggage carts are available for a 10-NOK coin. The coin is refunded if you return it to a rack when you are finished. Although the carts may be used on the ramps, they cannot be used on the station's escalators. You can, however, use the large passenger elevators located at either end of the main hall when moving from one level to another. The elevators are marked *heis*, which comes close to the word *hoist* in English.

Follow the pictographs and you will find every service you might need.

Baggage storage lockers are located on a balcony to the right of the station's main exit. Access to the locker area is open 0700–2300 daily.

Money exchange facilities are located on the mezzanine level of the station, directly across from the ticket windows. Follow the currency exchange pictographs. Hours: June–September, Monday–Friday 0700–1800; Saturday 0900–1500. When the money exchange is closed, you can change money in the post office or at the tourist information office in Oslo opposite the City Hall.

Ticket offices are on the left-hand side of the station. Domestic tickets are available 0600–2300 Monday–Saturday; 0630–2330 Sunday. The international ticket office is located next to the domestic ticket windows (open daily 0630–2300).

Tourist information office is open from 0800–2300 daily and is located next to the money exchange office. It provides tourist information covering Oslo, hotel reservations, guest house and private accommodations, sales of the Oslo Card, and sightseeing tours. To request information/accommodations in advance, write to Tourist Information, Oslo Sentralstasjon, Jernbanetorget 1, N-0154, Oslo.

Train information is located in Oslo Sentral's main concourse area on the left-hand side just prior to the moving walkways. Hours: Monday–Saturday 0700–2300; Sunday 0700–2330. If possible, get the information you need from the regular arrival and departure digital bulletin boards installed throughout the station. Departures carry the heading AVGAENDE TOG, and arrivals are labeled ANKOMMENDE TOG.

Train reservations and railpass validation are handled at window No. 4 in the ticket office of the main lobby. The ticket windows are marked BILLETTER, and any of the other windows can assist you if No. 4 is closed. This office can also make sleeping-car reservations.

Tourist Information/Hotel Reservations

Tourist Information Office: Brynjulf Bulls plass 1, N0250 Oslo
Tel: 47 23 11 78 80; *Fax:* 47 22 83 81 50
Guide Service: Tel: 22 42 70 20

Hours: October–March 0900–1600 Monday–Friday; April–May 0900–1700 Monday–Saturday; June–August 0900–1900 Monday–Sunday; September 0900–1700 Monday–Saturday.

The tourist Information Centre is located opposite Oslo's City Hall in the old railway station building "Vestbanen."

The attitude of the personnel at the Centre is, "If we can't tell you what you need to know, we can tell you who does and where to go to get it."

The Centre provides details on Oslo and its surrounding regions plus selected destinations throughout Norway. The Centre houses a nice cafe and interesting gallery and giftshop, a newspaper kiosk, and it neighbors a restaurant serving "Norway's best food in a contemporary setting at an attractive price" are also available.

Hotel reservations can be made in the tourist information office across from City Hall or in the one next door to the money-exchange office in Oslo Sentral Station. This service is operated by Oslo Promotion. It will make reservations for you in hotels, pensions, and private homes (20-NOK fee per booking). Oslo Promotion has an exceptional track record. Few, if any, are ever turned away though the entire town is "fully booked." Oslo is one of the few European cities where you can arrive without an advance reservation and still be reasonably certain of lodgings that night.

Ask for the *Oslo Package* brochure. This package combines your hotel (choose from thirty selected hotels) and the Oslo Card. Prices start from 399 NOK per person, per night, double occupancy.

Tourist information and hotel bookings for Oslo are also available from the tourist information office in the Sentral Station.

Be certain to ask for *The Official Guide for Oslo,* since it will aid you in seeing the various attractions in and around Oslo.

USE IT–Youth Information: Mollergata 3

Tel: 22 41 51 32

Internet: www.unginfo.oslo.no

Hours: Monday–Friday 1100–1900 with extended hours during summer months.

Getting Around in Oslo

Both tourist offices plus most Oslo hotels sell the **"Oslo Card,"** which provides unlimited use of city transportation by bus, train, tram, suburban railway, and ferry within Oslo's boundaries as well as up to four fare-stages within **Akershus.** The Card includes free admission to over 30 attractions and museums, various sightseeing discounts, a free tour by boat (May through mid-August), discounts at local eateries such as Restaurant Dan Turell and Tryvannstua, and a surprise on the menu at Holmenkollen Restaurant and

Train Connections to Other Base Cities from Oslo

Depart from Oslo Sentral Station

DEPART	TRAIN NUMBER	ARRIVE	NOTES
Copenhagen (København) H			
2253	393	0741+1	R, Sleeper
Hamburg			
2253	393	1215+1	R, 1, Sleeper
Helsinki			
0930	55	0830+1	R, 2
Stockholm Central			
0930	55	1529	R, 2
1620	59	2235	Sun–Fri

Daily, unless otherwise noted
R Reservations required

1. Via Copenhagen. Change trains in Copenhagen H. to EC 38 departing at 0755.
2. Arrives Karlstad 1238. Change trains to X2000/466 (R) for Stockholm departing at 1250. Arrive Stockholm 1529.

Brasserie 45. Reductions are also available at several shops (don't leave town without an authentic Norwegian sweater), ski lift tickets, theme parks and even Oslo by Horse.

The Oslo Card can be valid for 24, 48, or 72 hours and may be purchased at the following NOK rates: 24 hours, 150; 48 hours, 220; 72 hours, 250. Children's cards are 50, 60, and 70 NOK and family rates are 350 NOK.

Sightseeing/Attractions/Tours

Visitors desiring personal-guide services can contact Guideservice or *Tel:* 22–427020 for reservations and tariffs. Students, taxi drivers, and couriers are not permitted to arrange paid guided tours in Oslo and the museums.

A variety of tours in and around the city are available. For details, call at the tourist information office or consult your hotel. You may book the standard sightseeing bus tours, which normally take 3 hours to complete, or you may want to opt for one of the more specialized tours combining bus and boat transportation. You will find them listed in *What's On in Oslo* and *The Official Guide for Oslo and Surrounding Area.*

With so much good weather on hand, it is only natural that the majority of Oslo's sightseeing services concentrate their schedules into the summer months. In the period beginning with April and ending with October, a myriad of sightseeing opportunities are available to visitors. Fjord cruises from 50 minutes' duration to several hours are available. Likewise, there are land-and-water combinations to select from that include (among other attractions) a visit to the **Kon-Tiki Raft Museum,** a cruise on the **Oslofjord,** and a view from the top of the famous **Holmenkollen ski jump.**

The usual types of city bus tours are also available, along with a wide selection of things to be seen. There's an old adage that when the weather is nice, you will never find anyone home in Oslo. That is true. Chances are, you will find that many of the passengers on your tour bus or boat are townspeople enjoying the view along with you.

Information describing **Bygdoy** and many other attractions in Oslo is available at the tourist information office at the Oslo Sentral Station or from the Tourist Information Centre.

Visit Oslo's famous **Vigeland Park** while you are in town. Among the 193 granite and bronze statues by sculptor Gustav Vigeland, you will be able to examine *The Monolith*, the world's largest granite sculpture.

All members of the family will enjoy a visit to **Akershus,** a medieval castle built in the twelfth century and reconstructed as a fortress during the seventeenth century. Standing at the front of Oslo's City Hall, you can see the fort off to your left. Arkershus's military atmosphere is aided by the presence of two military museums. The **Norwegian Resistance Museum** chronicles Norway's struggle against the Nazis, and the **Norwegian Armed Forces Museum** traces the country's military history from the Vikings to World War II. The fort maintains a garrison of armed sentries who patrol the grounds in dress uniform and plumed headdress.

During your stay in Scandinavia's oldest capital—Oslo was established in 1050 by Harald Hardrade—you should plan to visit the world-famous *Kon-Tiki* raft, the polar vessel *Fram,* and the collection of viking ships on exhibition at Bygdoy, across the harbor from the city hall. Each vessel bears a proud history in nautical accomplishments.

Day Excursions

When you consider that Norway is larger than the British Isles, you can readily appreciate why we deviate from our usual Base City–Day Excursion™ format for Oslo. An "out-and-back" excursion between Oslo and **Bergen** offers an almost limitless variety of travel modes and a visit to the fjord at **Flam.**

Within our usual Base City–Day Excursion™ concept, we selected a variety of daytime trips that will permit you to see the beautiful fjords, lakes, and mountains without daily packing and unpacking.

A day excursion to the towns of **Larvik** and **Skien** takes you into Norway's seacoast towns for a look at some breathtaking scenery as well as a close look at the country's ports.

Hamar lies to the north of Oslo. Its day excursion affords inspection of the countryside surrounding the town and its extensive railroad museum.

The northernmost day excursion takes you to **Lillehammer,** site of the 1994 Winter Olympics and one of Norway's best known summer-and-winter resorts.

Day Excursion to

Bergen

AND THE FJORD AT FLAM

Depart from Oslo Sentral Station

Distance by Train: 293 miles (471 km)
Average Train Time: 6 hours, 40 minutes
No city code required
Tourist Information Office: Vågsallmenningen 1
Tel: 55 31 38 60; *Fax:* 55 31 56 82
Internet: www.bergen-travel.com
E-mail: bergen@bergen-travel.com
Hours: June–August, 0830–2200 daily; May and September, 0900–2000. Rest of year
   0900–1600 Monday–Saturday
      Located by the fish market harbor. There is a map in the station that will point
   the way. When you exit the main door of the rail station, continue straight ahead for
   about 600–700 meters. There is also a tourist information office at the rail station
   during June, July, and August, 0715–2300, that can provide the same services.

Bergen is Norway's second largest city. It is beautifully framed by seven mountains. One cable car and one funicular terminate at mountaintop restaurants overlooking the city. Bergen has a fish market that also has live fish, a sixteenth-century town hall, and a twelfth-century cathedral. **Troldhaugen** is the home of Edvard Grieg (1843–1907), the most distinguished Norwegian composer of the nineteenth century. The city has a 300-year-old wooden village **("Old Bergen"),** a symphony orchestra founded in 1765, and the oldest performing theater in Norway. Inseparable from the sea, Bergen also has the largest aquarium in northern Europe.

Founded in 1070 by King Olaf Kyrre, Bergen grew quickly as a commercial center, and during the twelfth and thirteenth centuries, it was the capital of Norway. Built mainly of wood, the buildings were highly susceptible to fire, and the city suffered severe fires in 1702, 1855, and 1916. Bergen was badly damaged during World War II, when it was occupied by the Germans.

This excursion has more route options than a cat has lives. The variations are such that we can list only a few. The daily train service between Oslo and Bergen has three daytime trains and one overnight train in each direction. During summer, a fourth train operates daily except Saturday. The overnight trains haul sleeping cars between Oslo and Bergen.

Express boats cruise between Bergen and Flam from mid-May to mid-September. As a result, many options are available in both time and mode. Before examining some of the options, let's look at the destinations and some of the reasons for going.

Flam is the terminus of a spectacular railway—the **Flamsbanen**. It climbs 2,845 feet from Flam in only 12.4 miles, and between mid-May and the end of September, it stops for you to take pictures. Until May 1, 2000, the Flam Line is included on railpasses; after May 1, railpass holders receive a 30 percent discount only with the Norway pass and the Scanrail Pass.

Option 1 Oslo–Bergen:	**January 1–December 30**
Train from Oslo	0811★
To Myrdal	1250
Change trains and depart from Myrdal	1255
To Flam	1346
Boat from Flam	1445
To Gudvangen	1645
Bus from Gudvangen	1715
To Voss	1830
Train from Voss	1900
To Bergen	2018

Option 2 Bergen–Oslo:	**September 22–December 30**
Train from Bergen	0830
To Voss	0943
Bus from Voss	1000
To Gudvangen	1125
Boat from Gudvangen	1130
To Flam	1340
Train from Flam	1520
To Myrdal	1610
Train from Myrdal	1733★
To Oslo	2221

★ $10 (U.S.) seat reservation required per person.

Notes on Oslo–Bergen railway "*New Express*": About 30 minutes after stopping at Drammen, the railway travels above the timberline. When you reach Finse, you'll see the looming Hardanger Glacier. Farther west, you enter the Finse Tunnel, the highest point on your way to Myrdal. As you descend toward Bergen, you pass through the longest tunnel on this route—the 5-mile Ulriken Tunnel.

To see **"Norway in a Nutshell"** with the Norwegian State Railways' Combination Tours, *Tel:* (800) 722–7151 or (888) TOUR–404, *Fax:* (614) 764–0711. For a comprehensive brochure visit www.europeanvacation.com.

Day Excursion to

Hamar

HEART OF NORWAY'S LAKE COUNTRY

Depart from Oslo Sentral Station

Distance by Train: 78 miles (126 km)
Average Train Time: 1 hour, 45 minutes
No city code required
Tourist Information Office: Parkgata.2, 2300 Hamar
Tel: 6252–1217; *Fax:* 6253–3565
E-mail: nehamkom@online.no
Hours: June 16–July 29, weekdays 0800–1800; Saturday 1000–1800; Sunday 1200–1800; June 30–August 3, weekdays 0800–2000; Saturday–Sunday 1000–1800; August 4–10, weekdays 0800–1800; Saturday 1000–1800; Sunday 1200–1800; and for the rest of the year, weekdays 0900–1500.
Located to the left just outside the railway station.

On September 17, 1976, en route to Hamar for the first time, we wrote, "This train passes through some of God's most beautiful countryside along one of His most beautiful lakes." That has not changed.

The countryside is the rich farmland of **Hedemarken,** and the lake is Norway's largest, **Lake Mjosa.** The lake is 75 miles long, and every foot of it is beautiful.

For a special treat, cruise Lake Mjosa on the oldest operating paddle steamer in the world, the *Skibladner.* It was built in 1856. Ask the tourist office for excursion timetables and fares. For information in advance, e-mail: skibladn@sn.no, or visit the internet address: www.skibladner.no.

Hamar is situated on the eastern side of Lake Mjosa at its widest point. The train from Oslo traverses the river Vorma from Eidsvoll to Mirucsund and then continues along the eastern shore of Lake Mjosa to Hamar. Watch for the bridge that the train crosses about an hour and ten minutes out of Oslo. Station

Oslo—Hamar

DEPART OSLO SENTRAL	TRAIN NUMBER	ARRIVE HAMAR	NOTES
0805	ET41	0939	R
0900	IC 313	1045	
1035	401	1223	
1305	IC 317	1446	

DEPART HAMAR	TRAIN NUMBER	ARRIVE OSLO SENTRAL	NOTES
1507	IC 318	1656	
1709	IC 320	1855	
1918	404	2102	
2028	348	2210	Sun, except May 31
2053	ET 44	2225	R

Daily, unless otherwise noted
R Reservations required
Distance: 78 miles (126 km)

yourself on the right side of the coach for a spectacular view down the lake from the vantage point of the bridge as the train crosses.

It seems that you have hardly settled in your seat when the train glides to a stop in Hamar. Time will pass even more quickly here, for there is much to see and do in this most pleasant city. Two of its feature attractions are the **Hedmark Museum** and the **Norwegian State Railways Museum.** These are not stuffy old buildings crowded with relics. Both are spacious, outdoor areas with fascinating displays of what rural and railroad life was like in Norway's earlier times.

Check with the tourist office regarding transportation to the museums. Both can be reached by public bus. If you prefer a taxi, you will find a taxi stand on your right when leaving the station. Fares by taxi to either museum are about 40–50 NOK one-way for a maximum of four persons.

Within the Hedmark Museum boundaries is the **Hamardomen** enclosing the remains of a medieval cathedral built in 1152. Designed by architect Kjell Lund of Lund & Slaatto Arkitekter, Ltd., and completed in 1998, the glass and steel protective enclosure is a unique architectural and technical masterpiece. It is climate controlled to prevent any further deterioration of the cathedral's remains. The ruins reveal that it was one of the most magnificent churches in Scandinavia. History proves that the town of Hamar suffered along with the demise of the stately church. Years of civil strife and the Reformation practically wiped out what was once a thriving city.

It was not until 1849 that Hamar once again enjoyed the status and charter of a town. Marking this return to status, the present Hamar Cathedral, replacing its medieval predecessor, was built in 1886.

The museum area also includes forty buildings from the County of Hedmark. Most of them date back from the fifteenth to the eighteenth centuries. One unusual building, the house of a Norwegian emigrant, was built in North Dakota in 1871 and moved to the museum in 1973.

The **Odden Restaurant** on the museum grounds is open for business from mid-May to mid-September each year. From mid-June through mid-August, the museum is open from 1000 to 1800 daily. During the balance of the year, it is open for groups by appointment only.

The railway museum rivals anything the Disney folks have come up with to date. If you are a railroad buff, don't miss this stop. Included in its collection of rolling stock are the old royal train, several "stagecoach" types, and even an old fourth-class (or, shall we say, no-class) wagon—without seats.

Norway's first railway station is among the many buildings found on the seven-and-a-half-acre tract covered by the museum. It is open daily from mid-May through mid-September, 1000–1600, and during July 1000–1800. From October through April, it's closed on Sundays and holidays but in operation on weekdays with the same schedule.

When the Norwegian government closed the Aurskog-Hoeland railway in 1960, two steam locomotives and a selection of rolling stock from the narrow-gauge line were given to the railway museum together with many structures from this private railway that began operation in 1896. In addition to the two locomotives from the Aurskog-Hoeland line, the museum has eleven standard-gauge and four narrow-gauge engines—all in operating condition.

Hamar's railway museum is the oldest in Scandinavia, and it is also the oldest technical museum in Norway. No doubt it will still be in full operation during the Norwegian Railway Bicentennial in 2054.

Hamar is also a sporting town, and its Olympic halls can attest to that. Visit Hamar's **Olympia Hall,** the "Viking Ship," and the **Hamar Olympic Amphi Hall (**or the "Northern Lights Hall"). The Viking Ship is one of the largest sports halls in the world and the architectural symbol of the 1994 Winter Olympics. The Northern Lights Hall is the world's largest wooden building. Check with the tourist office for opening times.

Day Excursion to

Larvik and Skien

FJORD COUNTRY

Depart from Oslo Sentral Station

Distance by Train: 120 miles (193 km)
Average Train Time: 2 hours, 30 minutes
No city code required
Tourist Information Office:
Larvik: Larvick OgOfoten Reiseliv AS, Post Boks 318, 8501
*Tel:*47 3590–5520; *Fax:* 47 3590–5530.
Skien: Skien Turist Kontor, Nedre Hjellegat 18, 3724 Skien
Tel: 47 3590–5520; *Fax:* 47 3590–5530
Hours: Monday–Friday, 0830–1600; summer (May–August) Monday–Friday
0830–1900; Saturday–Sunday 0900–1600
Internet: www.grenland.no; *E-mail:* info@grenland.no

If there's a fjord in your future, you'll probably find it on this day excursion. The greater part of that huge seaway known as the Oslofjord unfolds its grandeur as the train wends its way to Larvik and Skien. The sight of huge tankers and ocean liners miles from the ocean, plying between tree-covered mountains, is a breathtaking sight. You are certain to enjoy this outing.

As the train leaves Larvik en route to Skien, you'll also leave the fjords but begin to travel in an area of beautiful lakes connected by streams running through a wooded countryside. This, too, is fascinating and well worth the trip.

Because a train departs the Oslo Sentral Station on the Oslo–Drammen–Larvik–Skien line every two hours throughout the day, you might consider leaving the train at any point that catches your interest and returning to board the train that follows to continue your journey. It's a nice option to take.

There is a need to seek out the local tourist information office in some of the places you elect to stop, and the train gives you an excellent preview of what each town has to offer as you approach. Basically, the route through Larvik takes you to typical Norwegian seafaring towns, and each seems to offer a different type of land- and seascape. In a sense, you'll be window shopping, so be prepared to leave the train on impulse.

A summary of the cities the train passes follows. Be sure to take along a copy of the Norwegian State Railways schedule for this line in order to plan the follow-on portion of your trip as you go.

Drammen (40 kilometers from Oslo): Important center of Norway's timber and paper industries. There are many attractive buildings in town dating back to the seventeenth century. Have your camera handy—the city covers the headwaters of the Drammensfjorden, where it joins the river, and the docks teem with seafaring activities.

A. Oslo—Larvik—Skien—Oslo

DEPART OSLO SENTRAL	TRAIN NUMBER	DEPART LARVIK	ARRIVE SKIEN	NOTES
0621	IC 801	0840	0922	daily except Mon–Sat
0909	IC 807	1118	1206	
1109	IC 811	1318	1402	
1309	IC 815	1522	1610	

DEPART SKIEN	TRAIN NUMBER	DEPART LARVIK	ARRIVE OSLO SENTRAL	NOTES
1346	IC 824	1430	1651	
1542	IC 828	1628	1851	
1750	IC 832	1840	2051	
1850	IC 834	1934	2151	Sun only
1955	IC 838	2042	2250	
2042	IC 840	2144	2348	Sun–Fri

B. Oslo–Skien–Larvik–Oslo (circuitous route via Nordagutu)

DEPART OSLO SENTRAL	TRAIN NUMBER	ARRIVE NORDAGUTU	DEPART NORDAGUTU	TRAIN NUMBER	ARRIVE SKIEN	NOTES
0709	711	0902	0906	575	0938	except Sun
0839	701	1052	1056	577	1129	R

DEPART SKIEN	TRAIN NUMBER	ARRIVE NORDAGUTU	DEPART NORDAGUTU	TRAIN NUMBER	ARRIVE OSLO SENTRAL
1601	582	1633	1638	710	1842
1833	584	1906	1934	702	2139

See tables in section A above for return from Skien via Larvik to Oslo
Sentral.

Daily, unless otherwise noted
R Reservations required
Distance: 120 miles (193 km) to Skien

Tonsberg (103 kilometers from Oslo): The oldest town in Norway and the seat for centuries of its Viking kings. The Oseberg Viking ship now resting in the Oslo Viking Museum was found in a nearby burial mound. The ruins of a Viking castle overlook the town.

Sandefjord (127 kilometers from Oslo): Home of the Norwegian whaling fleet. Regardless of your opinions about this industry, there's a whaling museum in town, and there's a spectacular whaling monument in the center of the town square. The coastline around Sandefjord is spotted with many islands and inlets, making it very photogenic.

Larvik (146 kilometers from Oslo): The city has its own fjord, which connects to the Lagen River. The beautiful lake country we mentioned begins immediately beyond its city limits. An interesting museum is housed in **Herregarden,** a seventeenth-century manor house built for the counts of Larvik. The building is one of Norway's best-preserved wooden structures. A world-famous mineral water, Farris, originates here. Many of the small fishing harbors along the coast are accessible by bus. For ferry service from Larvik to **Frederikshavn** and **Skagen,** Denmark, *Tel:* (625) 810–00811.

Prior to your visit, write to the Tourist Office, Storgatae, 48, Box 200, 3251 Larrvick, Norway, for interesting booklets describing the Larvik district tourist attractions. Otherwise, when in Larvik visit the tourist office at Storgata, 48, across from the rail station.

Skien (193 kilometers from Oslo): Situated where the Skien River and Lake Hjelle meet, this city has been an active trading center since A.D. 900 Sawmills were an important part of its industry. The first began here in the sixteenth century. Skien is the birthplace of Henrik Ibsen (1828–1906), famous Norwegian playwright. Ibsen's well-constructed plays dealing realistically with psychological and social problems won him recognition as the Father of Modern Drama.

Brekke Park, which looks out over the river and town of Skien, warrants a visit. There you will find the **Museum of Telemark and Grenland.** (Skien is the administrative center for the District of Telemark.) In the park there are a number of old houses from different parts of the district, including a reconstruction of Ibsen's childhood home, **Venstøp.** The **Telemark Canal** starts in Skien and stretches 105 km into the country. Canal boats sail daily in the summer. For more information, contact Skien Tourist Office.

Rather than return to Oslo by retracing your route back through Larvik and the other coastal towns, you might want to return to Oslo via the main rail line running from Stavanger on the North Sea. Board train 582, which departs from Skien at 1600 to Nordagutu, where you'll arrive at 1632. Look around Nordagutu, then board train 702 at 1934 bound for Oslo. You will arrive in the Oslo Sentral Station promptly at 2142.

Day Excursion to

Lillehammer

NORWAY'S VACATION CENTER

Depart from Oslo Sentral Station

Distance by Train: 114 miles (184 km)
Average Train Time: 2 hours, 35 minutes
No city code required
Tourist Information Office: 19 Elvegata
Tel: 61 25 92 99; *Fax* 61 25 65 85
Internet: www.lillehammerturist.no
E-mail: post@lillehammerturist.no
Hours: Summer: 0900–1900 Monday–Saturday; 1100–1800 Sunday. The office remains
   open a few extra hours during late June, July, and early August. The remainder of the
   year, the office is open 0900–1600 Monday–Saturday.

   The office is only about a 5-minute walk from the rail station. Just follow the signs.
   This day excursion is one of the most northerly of any appearing in ***Europe
by Eurail***. Thanks to its latitude, Lillehammer is a famous summer resort and
an important winter-sports center as well with over 300 miles of prepared ski
runs. Snow conditions for skiing are good from December until April, and the
long summer evenings are perfect for enjoying the town's beautiful parks and
recreation areas. No matter what the season, outdoors is how to enjoy
Lillehammer.

   If you have succumbed to the charm of Hamar, then you have already been
introduced to the beauty of its Lake Mjosa. The train ride to Lillehammer will
permit you to see the balance of the lake because Lillehammer lies 35 miles to
the north of Hamar. Here, Lake Mjosa narrows to the Lagen River and, in
doing so, provides a scenic blend of green forestlands and the special green
color of the river. If you have ever wondered what most of the world was like
before pollution, here is your answer.

   Lillehammer served as the site for the 1994 Olympic Winter Games. The ski-
jumps tower, with a view of the entire town, is open 0900–2000 in the summer, and 1100–1600 in the winter. For those of us not in attendance at the 1994
Games, the **Norwegian Olympic Museum** in Håkons Hall offers a chance
to revisit the XVII Winter Olympic Games. History of both summer and winter Games plus the relevance of sport in society are highlighted from the beginning of the Olympics to present day. The exhibit is translated into 4 languages,
including English; the entrance fee includes a ticket for Maihangen Museum
(referenced below). For more details contact: olmuseum@maihangen.
museum.no or visit www.ol.museum.no.

   Among the city's attractions, the **Museum of Historical Vehicles** opens
at 1000 from mid-June through mid-August and at 1100 the remainder of the
year. Just north of Lillehammer you may visit **Lilleputhammer,** a scale model

Oslo–Lillehammer

DEPART OSLO SENTRAL	TRAIN NUMBER	ARRIVE LILLEHAMMER	NOTES
0805	ET 41	1021	R
0900	IC 313	1135	
1035	401	1313	
1305	IC 317	1541	

DEPART LILLEHAMMER	TRAIN NUMBER	ARRIVE OSLO SENTRAL	NOTES
1419	IC 318	1656	
1620	IC 320	1855	
1821	404	2102	
1833	322	2125	Fri only
1939	348	2210	Sun except May 31
2011	ET 44	2225	R

Daily, unless otherwise noted
R Reservations required
Distance: 114 miles (184 km)

town of 62 miniature houses, where kids can romp at **Hunderfossen Family Park.** Ask the tourist office for details.

The city's stellar attraction is a one-hundred-acre open-air museum known as **Maihaugen.** It is within easy walking distance of the tourist information office. The office can provide you with a city map as well as several brochures describing the Maihaugen Museum. The museum area is divided into three sections. Each depicts a different mode of Norwegian life. Its origins spring from the private collection of a dentist, Dr. Anders Sandvig.

As a young dentist just out of school, Dr. Sandvig came to Lillehammer in 1885. He soon learned that many of his patients preferred to pay him in kind. Sometimes it was a farm implement or a piece of furniture. Dr. Sandvig's practice grew, and so did his collection. Eventually, he laid out the museum area and began filling it with old buildings, which he acquired and transported to Lillehammer. Apparently, the museum business was more rewarding than dentistry, for Dr. Sandvig retired from the profession to run the museum personally, which he did until 1946, when he died at the age of eighty-four.

The museum was founded in 1887. There are 175 old buildings in the museum with handicrafts sections of sixty workshops demonstrating skills of the local artisans. The museum is open from October through May 16 (closed Mondays) 1100–1600. From June through mid-August, the peak season, it is open 0900–1800. For more information e-mail post@maihaugen.museum.no or visit the website www.maihaugen.museum.no. One of the most interesting objects of Norway's past on exhibit in the museum is the **Garmo Stave Church,** which was built in the Ottadal Valley area in the eleventh century and reassembled at the museum in 1920. Another interesting exhibit is "Slowly We Conquered Our Country," Norwegian history from the Ice Age until tomorrow.

In the dock area of the city from mid-June to mid-August, you can see the *Skibladner*, a paddle-wheel steamer launched in 1856 and still in service today. Its nickname is *White Swan*. True to tradition, salmon and strawberries are served onboard. It is really difficult to accept the fact that the vessel is now more than 130 years old and is in as good a condition now as the day it was launched. Some things do get better with age!

Art lovers will not want to miss the **Lillehammer Art Museum**, one of the leading visual art centers of Norway. Exhibits alternate between international and Norwegian art from the 1800s through today, with the core of the permanent collection composed of works by artists such as Dahl, Gude, and Munch. Guided tours run Saturday and Sunday from 1400–1500 or by prearrangement with the museum. Open Tuesday through Sunday 1100–1600, closed Monday. Tickets are adults 40 NOK; children under 12 free; and group rate 30 NOK. E-mail: kunstmus@online.no for further information.

After visiting Lillehammer, if you would like to return to Oslo via a different route, board the bus to **Gjovik** in front of the railway station at 1550. You arrive in Gjovik at 1650. Board the train for Oslo that departs at 1934. This train returns to Oslo by a different route and arrives in the Oslo Sentral Station at 2127. The train service is one-class only, but it's always clean and neat.

The bus fare from Lillehammer to Gjovik is 73 NOK. You will have time to do some fast sightseeing in this charming little town on the west shore of Lake Mjosa before departing on the 1934 train to Oslo.

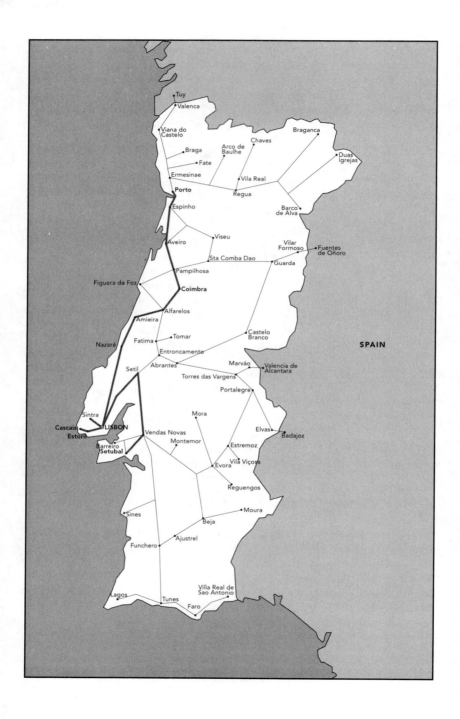

Portugal

Visitors to Portugal will find the Old World traditions, charm, and culture well preserved. Each province retains its own heritage and individual characteristics, and its history can be traced through its medieval cities and ancient palaces, castles, and cathedrals.

Being an independent kingdom since 1143, Portugal is one of the oldest nations in Europe. In fact, 10,000-year-old cave paintings have been uncovered in the northern reaches of Portugal and are said to be Europe's greatest outdoor gallery of Stone Age art. Their museums contain some of the finest collections in the world, reflecting their exposure to rich cultures explored by courageous Portuguese navigators of the fifteenth and sixteenth centuries.

But Portugal is more than antiquity. Its geography is diverse, making it a popular holiday destination for travelers from all over the world. You will find wonderful white-sand beaches, crystal-clear mountain streams, and some of the finest golf courses in all of Europe. You'll even find fun and games at glamorous casinos and discos.

Portuguese is the national language, with English and French being the second languages. Though some words are similar to the Spanish language, Portuguese is its own language, and not a Spanish dialect. According to the Portuguese National Tourist Office, Portugal is "a vision for the future." Portugal had the honor of hosting the last World Exposition of this century—Expo '98—in Lisbon. (See Hannover, Germany, for the 2000 world's fair.) For more information about Portugal, contact the Portuguese National Tourist Office of North America:

New York: 590 Fifth Avenue, 4th Floor, New York, NY 10036. *Tel:* (212) 719–3985 or (800) PORTUGAL; *Fax:* (212) 719–4091

Montreal: 500 Sherbrooke Street West, Suite 940, Montreal QC H3A 3C6. *Tel:* (514) 282–1264; *Fax:* (514) 499–1450

Toronto: 60 Bloor Street, Suite 1005, Toronto, Ontario M4W 3B8. *Tel:* (416) 921–7376; *Fax:* (416) 921–1353

Internet: **www.portugalinsite.pt**; *E-mail:* aavila@portugal.org

Banking

- **Currency:** Portugese Escudo (PTE) and centavos; the symbol "$" is used as a decimal point (2$50 means 2 escudos and 50 centavos). 1,000 escudos is usually referred to as 1 conto
- **Exchange rate at press time:** 186.84 PTE = $1.00 U.S.
- **Hours:** Open Monday–Friday 0830–1500.

Communications

- **Country Code:** 351

Portugal Telecom operates the public telephones, including pay, Credifone, and TLP Card telephones. Coin values of 10, 20, 50, or 100 PTE are used in pay telephones.

Use 00 before the country code to dial internationally from Portugal.

Rail Travel in Portugal

Portugal's rail system, **Caminhos de Ferro Portugueses (CP)** offers rail information by telephone. CP Information: *Tel:* (01) 888–4025, available 0800–2300 for Alfa and Intercity Lines: *Tel:* (01) 888–5092, available 0800–2300 or *Tel:* (01) 790–1004, 24 hours.

The CP accepts **Eurailpass, Europass** the **Iberic Flexipass,** and the **Portuguese RailPass.** The **Portuguese RailPass** is valid in First or Second Class trains: 7 days, 18,000 PTE; 14 days, 30,000 PTE; or 21 days, 42,000 PTE. Children age 4–11 are half fare. The Iberic Flexipass is valid for unlimited rail travel for 3 days within 2 months in Portugal and Spain. 1st Class, $205; additional days are $45 each (a maximum of 7 extra days may be purchased). Supplements are required on the AVE and Talgo high-speed trains. Children 4–11 travel at half the adult fare and children under age 4 travel free.

Interregional trains commute through the various regions of Portugal, while CP's **Intercity** service links about 60 Portuguese cities to Lisbon or Porto. The express **Alfa** service connects Lisbon, Porto, and Braga with four trains in each direction conveying both first and second class service. Alfa and Intercity should be reserved at least 24 hours in advance.

Two other international train connections are available between Porto and Vigo (Spain) and between Lisbon and Badajoz (Spain).

Base City ...

Lisbon (Lisboa)

City Dialing Code: 1

Lisbon, Portugal's largest city, is the capital and primary gateway for visitors from North America. It's also the center of the country's rail network and the major industrial and commercial area.

Built on the terraced sides of the hills overlooking the harbor, languid Lisbon is an excellent gateway to the Iberian peninsula and base for rail travel thoughout Portugal.

Arriving by Air

Lisbon International Airport (Portela), 5 miles north of Lisbon. *Tel:* 841–6990.

Airport–City Links: Passengers connect to Lisbon's Cais Sodre railway station via the shuttle Aerobus 91 every 20 minutes, from 0700–2100. Fare 430 PTE (1-day ticket).

Taxi fare from the airport to the city center averages about 1,200–2,000 PTE, depending on your destination and how much luggage you have. Taxis are metered; a tip is appreciated.

Tourist information at the airport, *Tel:* 844–6473. Open 0600–2400 daily.

Arriving by Train

Lisbon has four stations and a ferryboat terminal and is the main gateway to other cities in Portugal. **Santa Apolonia** station is Lisbon's international link and the western terminus of most European rail traffic. However, you can also arrive in Lisbon at the "Terreiro do Paço" south railway station, with the train departing from Vila Real St. Antónia to Barreiro (and then the ferry connection) if you come from Seville (Spain).

- **Money exchange** is on the left side as you exit from the trains, beyond Porta (Gate) 47.
- **Rail Information (CP) and Tourist Information:** Turn to the right as you exit from the trains and walk past ticket window No. 1. Hours: 0900–2200.
- **RailPass Validation:** Porta (Gate) 47. Hours 1000–1800 daily. Buses No. 9, 39, and 46 run from Santa Apolónia Station to the **Rossio** Station in downtown Lisbon. The fare may be minimal, but buses frequently are

crowded, making it rather difficult for you and your suitcase to board the same bus at the same time. Because taxi fares are reasonable and metered, leave your forays on Lisbon's public transportation system for when your luggage is safely stowed in your hotel room.

- **Rossio Station,** at Praça do Rossio (Rossio Square), is located in the heart of Lisbon in a lovely nineteenth-century Neo-Gothic building. It is on the immediate left of the Teatro Nacional D. Maria II (National Theater). Rossio Station serves as the commuter station to locations west of Lisbon (from Cacem Station to Figueira da Foz). Trains depart for Sintra on tracks Nos. 4 and 5 every 16 minutes.
- **Campolide Station,** the first station past Rossio, is the stop for the Alcantara commuter to Cascais or for travel to Azambuja.
- **Cais do Sodre Station** is where trains from Estoril and Cascais terminate.
- **Terreiro do Paco Station** is the ferryboat terminal for crossings to Barreiro Station on the east bank of the Tagus River. From Barreiro trains depart for cities in the Algarve.

Lisbon Tourist Information/Hotel Reservations

Available in rail stations, at Praça dos Restauradores in the Palácio Foz building (*Tel:* 346–6307; Hours: 0900–2000 daily); or at the Lisbon Card office in the same building. (*Tel:* 343–3314; Hours: 0900–1800)

To reach it, take a taxi or bus No. 9, 46, or 39 to Praça dos Restauradores. It is opposite the post office, near Rossio Station. The building, Palácio Foz (Foz Palace), has three main doors. Enter the one on the left marked TURISMO. Hours: 0930–1800.

Hotel reservations can be made at the rail stations' combined train and tourist information offices.

Getting Around in Lisbon

Electric, cable-car-like trams provide inexpensive and enjoyable transport to many parts of the city. Historic Belem, for instance, can be reached via tram 15—an alternative to taking the train from Cais do Sodre station.

Of super value is the **Lisboa Card,** which provides unlimited travel on the public transportation system (CARRIS), including buses, trams, and the metro (underground) system; free entry to 26 museums, monuments, and other attractions that normally charge admission; and discounts at certain shops. It is truly your "password" to the city.

The Lisboa Card is available at the Central Office, at Palácio Foz; at Jeronimos Monastery, Praca do Imperio; at the National Museum of Ancient Art, Rua das Janelas Verdes; and at various CARRIS offices.

1-Day Lisboa Card, 1,900 PTE; 2-Day, 3,100 PTE; 3-Day, 4,000 PTE; children age 5–11 pay 750, 1100, and 1,550 PTE, respectively.

Attractions/Tours

Tourist offices or your hotel can arrange for a sightseeing tour of Lisbon. Or, ask the tourist office for the guide booklet, "Lisboa Step by Step," purchase a Lisboa Card, and conduct your own tour. Highlights of any tour will include the sixteenth-century **Jerónimos Monastery** and the **Tower of Belém** in the Belém district. Lisbon's more modern side can be seen by visiting the **Discoveries Monument** (Centro Cultural das Descobertas), inaugurated in 1960. Another symbol of Lisbon is the **25 de April Bridge** spanning the Tagus River, which is equal to the Golden Gate Bridge of San Fransisco in its structural beauty.

Completed for Expo '98, Lisbon's **Vasco da Gama bridge** is a massive engineering feat. The bridge is 17 kilometers long—making it the longest bridge in Europe—1 kilometer longer than the one between Sweden and Denmark. Besides providing another modern symbol of Lisbon, it provides much-needed relief of traffic congestion crossing the Tagus River, especially during the summers. The new Vasco de Gama Steel Tower (the tallest building in Portugal) and the impressive Lisboa Oceanarium contribute to the Eastside's modern attractions.

Lisbon has three distinct districts—the shopping areas clustered around **Rossio, Baixa, and Chiado;** the more ancient areas such as the Moorish quarter **Alfama and Castelo;** and the "new Lisbon" with postmodern high-rise structures, **Amoreiras,** stretching out to the airport and to the north. Just 5 minutes from the airport is the new Gare Intermodal de Lisboa multistation complex known also as Oriental Station which serves long-distance and suburban trains, the underground railway system, a bus and motorcoach terminal, and a taxi stop. A day can easily be spent in any one of its districts.

Of particular interest to Western visitors is the Alfama district, which suffered the least damage during the earthquake and has thereby been able to preserve much of its old facade and narrow, winding cobblestone streets. **St. George's Castle** offers a splendid view of the city. The tourist office has several excellent illustrated brochures describing Lisbon, one of which lists walking tours *From the Castle to Alfama via Mouraria,* where examples of Moorish and medieval architecture prevail. A city map is also available.

Spend at least one evening in Lisbon's famous nightlife district—**Bairro Alto.** It can be reached via the Elevador da Gloria, which operates from the west side of the Praça dos Restauradores at Calcada da Gloria. Dine in a typical Portuguese restaurant/music bar called "Fado houses" and listen to *Fado* (meaning "fate")—the plaintive, nostalgic, dramatic music of the fadista (Fado singer) that is unique to the Portuguese. Lisbon has its own type of Fado, which is considered to be more emotional and dramatic than that performed elsewhere.

Such Fado establishments are abundant in Lisbon, particularly in the Alfama and Bairro Alto districts. One of our favorites is **Adega Mesquita** at Rua do Diário Noticias, No. 107. Phone ahead for reservations: (*Tel:* 321–9280).

In Alfama on Largo do Chafariz de Dentro, visit Lisbon's newest museum—the **Casa do Fado e da Guitarra Portuguesa**, the fado museum. According to the tourist office, "It gives an insight and enables one to better understand the development, identity, and soul of this incomparable form of urban musical expression that was born in Lisbon in the 19th century." It's open Tuesday–Sunday 1000–1300 and 1430–1700; entrance fee, 450 PTE. *Tel:* 01 886 7922.

Day Excursions

Cascais and **Estoril,** resort towns along the beautiful beaches of Costa do Estoril, are frequented by celebrities, royalty, and just plain folk. **Coimbra** reveals Portugal's academic nature. This fine old university town was at one time the capital of Portugal. **Setubal** is a city of beautiful beaches, hillside castles, and excellent seafood. Castle buffs and romantics will enjoy **Sintra,** with its ancient castles and nearby Cape Roca, the westernmost point of Europe.

Train Connections to Other Base Cities from Lisbon (Lisboa)

DEPART	TRAIN NUMBER	ARRIVE	NOTES
Madrid Chamartin			
2200	335	0835+1	R, Sleeper
Paris Gare Montparnasse			
1803	311/310	0910+1	R, Sleeper

Daily, unless otherwise noted
R Reservations required

Day Excursion to

Cascais and Estoril   Lisbon's Riviera

Depart from Lisbon Cais do Sodre Station

Distance by Train: 16 miles (26 km)
Average Train Time: 30 minutes
City Dialing Code: 1
Costa do Estoril Tourist Information Office: Arcadas do Parque, 2765 Estoril
Hours: 0900–2000
Tel: 466 38 13; *Fax* 467 22 80

> Tourist office is near the rail station. Use the underpass from the ocean side (the trains run on the left) to the city side.

Portugal boasts miles and miles of sun-drenched, white-sand beaches. Probably the most famous stretch lies just to the west of Lisbon along the Costa do Estoril. Here the two resort towns of Cascais and Estoril offer a wide variety of scenes to suit everyone's tastes.

We recommend you make **Estoril** your first stop on your visit to this coastal area because Estoril is two stops before Cascais, which is the end of the rail line. Estoril has long been famous as a chic resort for royalty and a playground for the rich and famous. Besides the white-sand beach with its excellent facilities, the beautifully landscaped **Casino complex** of gaming rooms, restaurants, bars, and movie theater is a major attraction. But new, moderately priced hotels now make Estoril a major attraction for everyone.

Those who are sports minded can enjoy championship 18-hole golf courses that offer temporary memberships. **The Estoril Golf Course,** with its splendid seascape, has been home to the Portuguese Open. Tennis, horseback riding, and sailing are also available.

Cascais, which is only 4 minutes beyond Estoril, maintains a slightly lower-key atmosphere than its chic neighbor. Its beaches are smaller, but more intimate. Reflecting the traditions of its fishing village past, Cascais's Wednesday-morning market is well worth the trip from Lisbon. Locals in their traditional garb hawk everything imaginable. Farmers' wives, suspicious of supermarket packaging, can be seen scrutinizing their chickens while they are still alive and squawking loudly.

To reach the marketplace, bear to the right around the plaza in front of the rail station and continue to the right onto Avenue 25 de April. Two short blocks farther and you will see the market—probably hear it, too. Bring your own market basket.

On Sundays during the summer, locals and visitors alike flock to the **Monumental de Cascais,** the bull ring. Bullfights in Portugal are different from those in Spain in that the bull is not killed but taken by the horns (literally) and forced to a standstill. The proceedings often end more on a comic note than the tragic one at the end of a Spanish bullfight.

Some rail travelers base themselves in a local resort hotel in or near Cascais or Estoril, and then make day excursions into Lisbon for sightseeing or for continuing on with other day excursions. The fast and frequent rail service and the abundance of hotels to fit any budget make this concept a feasible on

Lisbon–Estorial–Cascais

Trains depart daily every 20 minutes from Lisbon's Cais do Sodre Station, and trains run to Estoril in 29 minutes. Cascais is 3 minutes beyond Estoril. All trains are one class only.

Distance: 16 miles/26 km

Day Excursion to

Coimbra   University Town

Depart from Lisbon Santa Apolonia Station

Distance by Train: 135 miles (218 km)
Average Train Time: 2 hours
City Dailing Code: 39
Coimbra Tourist Information Office: Largo da Portagem
Tel: 39 33019 or 33028; *Fax:* 39 25576
Hours: Monday–Friday 0900–1900; Saturday–Sunday 1400–1730

Trains from Lisbon stop at the Coimbra B. Station, a short distance north of the city center. Either take a taxi to Largo da Portagem or take a shuttle train into the main station. The tourist office is at the approach to the great bridge spanning the Mondego River. If you take the shuttle to the main station, walk four blocks away from the station, upstream along the river, until you come to the bridge approach.

Coimbra is one of Portugal's most charming cities, uniquely blending the old and the new. Site of the oldest university in Portugal, its ancient buildings seem to blend perfectly with the modern spirit of its students. Founded in 1290 in Lisbon, the university was transferred to its present site in 1537 to compensate for moving Portugal's capital from Coimbra to Lisbon.

Coimbra University sits on a hilltop overlooking the river. In keeping with tradition, many students wear black suits and capes, marked with ribbons in tones that denote their scholarship.

There is an air of antiquity surrounding Coimbra. It is the scene of the largest Roman archaeological site in Portugal. Coimbra's cathedral is said to

Lisbon–Coimbra

DEPART LISBON SANTA APOLONIA	TRAINS NUMBER	ARRIVE COIMBRA B (JUNCTION)	NOTES
0703	IC 511	0924	1, 2
0800	IC 531	1007	1, 2
0806	IR 811	1033	2, 3
0905	IR 823	1141	2, 3
1100	IC 521	1307	1, 2
1205	IR 825	1441	2, 3

DEPART COIMBRA B (JUNCTION)	TRAIN NUMBER	ARRIVE LISBON SANTA APOLONIA	NOTES
1354	IR 824	1625	2, 3
1526	Alfa 122	1730	2, 4
1706	IC 512	1925	1, 2
1754	IR 826	2025	2, 3
1826	Alfa 124	2030	2, 4
1855	IR 810	2130	2, 3
1954	IR 828	2225	2, 3
2026 Sun–Fri	Alfa 126	2230	2, 4,
2050	IR 812	2321	2, 3
2125	IC 532	2330	1, 2

1. Reservations required on all IC trains in Portugal
2. Connecting shuttle trains run between Coimbra B station and Coimbra city station
3. Reservations are recommended on all IR trains in Portugal
4. Reservations are required on all Alfa trains; supplemental fares are charged between Lisboa and Porto (including Coimbra service shown above)

be the finest Romanesque building in Portugal. Gothic tombs and art collection are housed in this twelfth-century monument.

An unusual attraction for "children" of all ages is the **Portugal dos Pequeninos** (Portugal of the Little Ones), in which you will find a miniaturized version of architectural styles of continental Portugal, Coimbra, Portuguese monuments, insular Portugal, and its overseas territories.

In the city center, you can visit the **monastery of the Holy Cross, Santa Cruz,** constructed in the twelfth century. Later additions include a charming Renaissance sacristy and a magnificently carved facade. A pictorial record of the explorer Vasco da Gama's voyages adorns the choir loft.

Day Excursion to

Setubal

SEASIDE AND CASTLES

Depart from Lisbon Terreiro do Paço Ferry Terminal and Barreiro Station

Distance by Train: 18 miles (29 km)

Average Train Time: 35 minutes

City Dialing Code: 65

Tourist Information Offices: Regiao de Turismo de Setubal, Travessa Frei Gaspar, 10, 2900-388 Setubal

Tel: (65) 53 91 20;   *Fax: (*65) 53 91 27

Internet: www.costa-azul.rts.pt

E-mail: costa.azul@mail.telepac.pt

Hours: 0900–1230/1400–1900 Monday and Saturday; 0900–1900 Tuesday–Friday; 0900–1230 Sunday

Town Hall Tourist Information: Praca do Quebedo *Tel:* 534 222

Hours: 0900–1230/1400–1730 Monday–Friday.

Take a taxi from the station to the regional tourist office (Regiao de Turismo de Setubal) or to the tourist office in the Town Hall, located across from the park, Praca do Quebedo.

A day excursion to **Setubal** begins at Lisbon's Terreiro do Paço ferry terminal and a 25-minute ferryboat ride across the Tagus River to Barreiro Station, where you board a southbound train to Setubal. At press time, plans are for trains to cross the Tagus River on the 25 de April Bridge after Lisbon's new **Vasco da Gama bridge** opened for Expo '98.

Although Setubal is Portugal's third largest city, its location on the estuary of the Sado River provides a more restful, rural-type atmosphere. It can best be enjoyed from **Saint Philip's Castle,** which overlooks Setubal from its highest point. The sixteenth-century castle was converted into a *pousada* (inn, or resting place), and it commands an impressive view of both land and sea. A local taxi can take you there. It's a perfect spot for a lunch in its fine restaurant or for an overnight stay.

Setubal has a remarkable assemblage of monuments and grand old buildings. The **Church of Jesus** is said to be one of the most beautiful small churches ever built. Next door, the Town Museum displays a priceless collection of old masters. There are also a Maritime Museum and the Bocage Monument, which honors the city's great poet.

About 5 or 6 miles from Setubal at the nearby seaport Sesimbra, the **Pousada do Castelo de Palmela** (Palmela Castle) offers a fantastic view of the surrounding countryside from high atop a hillside. Again, the best way to get there is via taxi.

Lisbon—Setubal

FERRY FROM LISBON TERREIRO DO PAÇO DOCK	ARRIVE BARREIRO PIER	DEPART BARREIRO STATION	TRAIN NUMBER	ARRIVE SETUBAL STATION	NOTES
0755	0825	0835	IR 871	0903	1
1540	1610	1635	3801	1707	

DEPART SETUBAL STATION	TRAIN NUMBER	ARRIVE BARREIRO STATION	FERRY BARREIRO PIER	ARRIVE LISBON TERREIRO DO PAÇO DOCK	NOTES
2123	2123	2153	2210	2240	
2206	IC 570	2229	2245	2315	1

Daily, unless otherwise noted
1. Reservations required on all IC trains in Portugal and recommended on all IR trains.
Distance: 18 miles (28 km) from Barreiro

Day Excursion to

Sintra
MOUNTAIN PEAKS AND PALACES

Depart from Lisbon Rossio Station

Distance by Train: 17 miles (28 km)
Average Train Time: 45 minutes
City Dialing Code: 1
Tourist Information Office: Praca da Republica
Tel: 923 11 57 or 924 17 00
Hours: open daily (except January 1, Easter, May 1 and Christmas) 0900–2000 June–September; 0900-1900 October–May
The main tourist office is about 1 kilometer from the rail station. Reach it by taxi or by boarding the bus marked S. PEDRO, which leaves from near the station (at Correnteza). The bus stops a short distance from the National Palace of Sintra and the main tourist office. On foot, it is an interesting 15-minute walk.

According to the Sintra Tourist information office, "Sintra is a location which is not to be talked about, its history discussed or its countryside described—it is a location to be felt." **Sintra** with its ancient castles and palaces towering above the countryside is the former home of Portuguese kings. It is surrounded by mountains and close by **Cape Roca,** the western-most point of Continental Europe "where the land ends and the sea begins." This is the place Lord Byron termed "a glorious Eden," and it's all only 45 minutes from Lisbon by train.

There is no public transportation to most of the places of tourist interest. Taxis and horse-drawn carriages take you there. Since the taxis do not have meters, the fare usually includes up to four passengers plus a fixed amount of time for you to complete your sightseeing. You should also ask the tourist office about the half-day tour, which includes **Pena Palace,** the **Convent of Capuchos** (the Cork Convent), **Cape Roca,** the **Gardens of Monserrate**, and other sights.

Of all the sights in the area, you'll probably want to visit the exquisite **Sintra National Palace** (Paço Real or Palácio da Vila) first. It is closed on Wednesdays and there are no guides. There is a nominal admission charge to the palace grounds. Inside, it possesses the most extensive collection of *Mudejar azulejos*—colored glazed tiles—in the world.

Pena Palace's commanding position from the highest peak in the area makes it well worth the visit. It is closed on Mondays.

The **Queluz Palace** captures the style of Versailles, but on a smaller scale. It houses a gourmet restaurant in its former kitchen area. This palace is closed on Tuesdays.

For a different experience, visit the Sintra Toy Museum (open Tues–Sun 1000–1800). Joao Arbués Moreira believed one could better understand the history of humankind through toys. He began his toy collection at the age of 14 with toys from his grandparents, parents, and others. As he acquired money, he began purchasing more toys. He spent a lifetime researching their manu-facture and history and collected more than 20,000 different toys. You, too, can view this extraordinary collection at the Museu do Brinquedo, the Toy Museum, located in the old Sintra Fireman's Headquarters (tel: 924 21 71). There's a toy restoration workshop and the gift shop is a great place to pur-chase that special memento.

Lisbon—Sintra

Frequent suburban trains run between Lisbon's Rossio Station and Sintra. The journey takes 45 minutes.

All trains are one class only. Trains for Sintra depart approximately every 15 minutes. Ride the train to the end of the line.

Distance: 17 miles/28 km

Spain

Spain is a delightful dichotomy—futuristic in many ways yet respectful of its rich history and tradition. Spain is the second most popular tourist destination in the world.

From the *delicato* music of Flamenco to swashbuckling matadors, Spain's culture and tradition are as widely varied as its geography. Flamenco is a genuine Southern Spanish art form influenced by diverse cultures throughout Spain's history, including the Gypsies, the legendary Tartessos, and the Muslims.

Spain shares the Iberian Peninsula with its neighbor to the west, Portugal. France and the tiny country of Andorra lie to the north. The Castilian Spanish is spoken throughout Spain, but Catalan, Valencian, Basque, and Galician Spanish are still spoken in their respective autonomous regions.

One social custom that visitors will notice immediately is that Spaniards get up later in the morning and usually stay out later at night than other Europeans. If you want to dance until dawn, you're visiting the right country. The nightlife in Spain is intensely zealous, with bars and discotheques remaining open until the wee hours of the morning, especially in the larger more cosmopolitan cities of Barcelona and Madrid.

Arriving from North America, our Base City Madrid is the primary gateway, with Barcelona being second. During summer, however, there are some direct flights to Malaga on the Mediterranean Sea.

For more information about Spain, contact the Tourist Offices of Spain in North America:

Toll-free Tel: 888 OK SPAIN; *Internet:* **www.okspain.org;** *E-mail:* oetny@okspain.org

Chicago: 845 North Michigan Avenue, Suite 915 East, Water Tower Place, Chicago, IL 60611. *Tel:* (312) 642–1992; *Fax:* (312) 642–9817

Los Angeles: San Vicente Plaza Building, 8383 Wilshire Boulevard, Suite 960, Beverly Hills, CA 90211. *Tel:* (213) 658–7188; *Fax:* (213) 658–1061

New York: 666 Fifth Avenue, 35th Floor, New York, NY 10103. *Tel:* (212) 265–8822; *Fax:* (212)265–8864

Toronto: 2 Bloor Street West, 34th Floor, Toronto, Ontario M4W 3E2. *Tel:* (416) 961–3131; *Fax:* (416) 961–1992

Miami: 1221 Brickell Avenue, Miami, FL 33131 *Tel:* (305) 358–1992; *Fax:* (305) 358–8223.

Banking

- **Currency:** Spanish Pesetas (ESP)
- **Exchange rate at press time:** 155.07 ESP = $1.00 U.S.
- **Hours:** Open Monday–Friday 0900–1400, with some open Saturday 0900–1430.

Credit and ATM transfers at machines are the best exchange rate, since no commission is charged.

Communications

- **Country Code: 34**
- **Direct Dial:** AT&T: 900 99 00 11; MCI: 900 99 00 14; Sprint: 900 99 00 13

Public telephones are available most everywhere in Spain; they offer instructions in English and may be used to call most parts of the world. Use primarily 25- and 100-peseta coins. Some phones are equipped to take credit cards. Since calling from Spain to America is about 10 times more expensive than calling from America to Spain, it is advisable to access your American Calling Card Connection.

When in Spain, dial 07 to telephone outside of Spain. When calling Spain from abroad, include Spain's country code. It is then necessary to dial the provincial codes for each province. If calling within Spain, you must dial 9 before the provincial code.

Some provincial codes include Alicante 6; Avila 20; Barcelona 3; Burgos 47; Cordoba 57; Madrid 1; Malaga 5; Seville 5; Toledo 25; and Valencia 6.

Rail Travel in Spain

With **RENFE** (Red Nacional de los Ferrocarriles Espanoles, or Spanish National Railways), the trains in Spain run mainly on time—98 percent on time. RENFE accepts **Eurailpass, Europass, the Iberic Flexipass,** and **Spain Flexipass,** but it deviates from the basic railpass concept in that certain trains such as Trens Hotel, AVE ("Alta Velocidad Espanola," or Spanish High Speed) trains, and Talgos operating on high-speed lines are *not* included, but railpass holders do receive substantial discounts. (Please see the Appendix for Iberic Flexipass, Eurailpass, and Europass types and costs.) Special sightseeing/tour trains such as *Al Andalus* and the narrow-gauge *FEVE* are not included on the railpasses either, but tickets may be purchased separately.

The Eurailpass bonus for Spain includes a 20 percent discount on the Transmediterranea Line ships between Barcelona–Palma de Mallorca and Valencia–Palma de Mallorca.

The Spain Flexipass may be purchased for a minimum of 3 days of unlimited rail travel in Spain within a 2-month period.

Spain Flexipass

	1ST CLASS	2ND CLASS
3 days in 2 months	$200	$155
Additional days	$35	$30

Seven-day maximum additional rail days. The AVE and Talgo 200 trains require additional supplements. Children ages 4–11 travel half-price.

Not to be outdone by French high-speed TGVs and Germany's ICEs, RENFE's sleek **AVEs** are derivations of the French TGV (*Train a Grand Vitesse*, or Train of Great Speed) *Atlantique*. Dynamic RENFE has been "on the move" since the first AVEs cruised into service as the main rail link between Madrid and Seville due to the opening of the International Exposition of Seville—Expo 1992. Via AVE, the Madrid-Seville trip can be done in just under 3 hours.

Reservations for AVE trains are required. Choose Turista, Preferente, or Club class. All three classes include television sets with individual earphones and four music channels, family areas with games for kids, facilities for the disabled, telephones, cafeteria, and a beverage machine. Club and Preferente Classes also include access to AVE club lounges, newspapers, and magazines. In-seat food/beverage service is provided only in Club Class.

For AVE telephone information in

Madrid: Tel: (91) 534 05 05

Córdoba: Tel: (957) 49 02 02

Ciudad Real: Tel: (926) 22 02 02

Puertollano: Tel: (926) 41 02 02

Seville: Tel: (95) 454 02 02

Ultramodern Talgo 200 trains link Madrid and Malaga in a little more than 4 hours. These gauge-changing high-speed trains have also significantly reduced the travel time between Madrid and Cadiz/Huelva.

The attractive blue and white **Euromed** (*Velocidad Alta Mediterranea* or Mediterranean High Speed) trains provide services to **Alicante, Valencia, Castellon, Tarragona,** and **Barcelona** with a cruising speed of 200 km/hour. These trains offer two classes of service—"Preferente" and "Turista."

Base City . . .

Barcelona

City Dialing Code: 3

Internet: www.barcelona.es

Barcelona as it is formed today, the **New Barcelona,** was created only in 1874 by joining 27 separate municipalities. It has become Spain's most prosperous port and has developed a thriving industrial complex as well. The center of this new metropolitan area is the **Plaça de Catalunya,** a square rimmed with trees and highlighted by sculptures and fountains—and an abundance of pigeons. This square is where the old and the new Barcelona meet.

Founded in ancient times by the Phoenicians and occupied by the Romans, **Old Barcelona** is composed of three sections: Barcelona Antigua or Barrio Gotico (the Gothic Quarter), Ribera, and El Raval. A visit to the History Museum in Plaça del Rei square provides insight to Barcelona's rich and ancient past.

At the other end of the spectrum, the new World Trade Center (WTC) complex provides insidght to Barcelona's promising future. According to the Tourist Office of Spain, the WTC association (including 300 centers in 97 countries) was created "to stimulate world trade and to increase cultural exchange and the development of nations." This stunning waterfront complex solidifies Barcelona's position as a major portal to European and Mediterranean markets.

Arriving by Air

Barcelona has one of the most modern international airports in Europe, having been improved immensely for the 1992 Olympic games. About 8 miles from the city, transportation to and from is easily available and inexpensive.

Airport–City Links: Cercanias/Rodalie local line No. 1 **trains** connect travelers to Barcelona Sants Station in 18 minutes, and depart every half-hour from the airport between 0612 and 2242. Trains depart from track No. 1 in Sants Station every half-hour to the airport, Fare 300 ESP.

Buses connect to the airport from the Placa de Catalunya every 15 minutes Monday–Friday 0530–2315.; every 20 minutes Saturday, Sunday, and holidays 0600–2320. Time en route is 15-20 minutes Fare 435 ESP.

There are 3- and 5-day packages that include round trip airport bus service and unlimited travel on the buses and subway system.

Approximate **taxi** fare from the airport to city center is 2,000–3,000 ESP.

Arriving by Train

National Renfe (Spanish National Railroads) train information available daily 0730–2230. *Tel:* 93 490 02 02. *International train information:* 93 490 11 22 Monday–Friday 1000–1400 and 1600–2000; www.renfe.es. *Passengers' assistance:* 93 490 38 51 daily 0600–2300.

Estacio de Sants, or Barcelona Sants Station, Placa Paisos Catalans, is the central Barcelona rail station and the center of Barcelona's transportation system, including rail, metro (subway), bus, and airport train service. The entrance to the metro system is to the right of the station's arrival-departure board leading down from the station's ground level and marked with a capital **M** inside a diamond shape.

The Sants station provides access to all long-distance Spanish trains, including the new high-speed Euromed trains to Tarragonna, Castellon, Valencia, and Alicante; trains to the French border towns Cerbere and La Tour de Carol; trains to the beaches to the south of Catalonia and to the northern coast; trains to the airport; and direct rail service on the Catalan Talgo train to Montpellier for connections to Paris and Geneva on the high-speed French TGV.

Seat reservations are mandatory on all express trains in Spain. Reservations can be made in Barcelona Sants at the ticket counter in the access area. If you are making reservations for advance travel, report to the section marked VENTA ANTICIPADA. For same-day departures, report to the section marked VENTA IMMEDIATA. This section handles reservations only for travel on the current date. Since reservations can be made up to two months in advance of the departure date, it is sensible to makde all of your reservations with one visit to the ANTICIPADA section when possible. Waiting until the day of departure to get a seat reservation could be very time consuming.

The Sants station has 12 track platforms running beneath its ground level, which are accessible by escalators or elevators. Be certain to check the platform and track numbers on the departure board before descending to the train level.

Station facilities and services:

•Hotel reservations service adjoins the Hertz facilities. *Hours:* Monday–Friday 0800–2200 and Sunday 0800–1400/1600–2200. Also, Vetraemar Express Travel Agency, *tel:* 93 491 44 63, open daily 0800–2200, and Julia-Via Internacional (Eurolines) *tel:* 93 490 40 00.

•Luggage storage: Near track 12, open 0530–2300.

•Money-exchange located in the center of the station at ground level. *Hours:* 0800–2200 daily. Official bank rates and ATM services.

•Sala Club Euromed, Renfe's version of an airline-style passengers' lounge, is located in the center island between elevators for tracks 10 and 11. First-

class tickets or railpasses are required for entrance. Free juice, coffee, soft drinks. Magazines and television are also available.
• Tourist information office.

Estacio de Franca, Avenida Marques de l'Argentera, provides long-distance national services and direct international trains to Paris, Geneva, Zurich, and Milan. Train information and ticket sales office is open 0730–2200 daily. *Passengers' assistance:* 93 319 64 16 or 93 496 30 07 daily 0600–2330. Money exchange services, ATMs, and lockers also are available at Franca Station.

Barcelona Tourist Information/Hotel Reservations

Turisme de Barcelona Tourist Information Offices:
Plaça Catalunya, 17-S.
National calls: *Tel:* 906 30 12 82
International calls: *Tel:* 93 304 34 21
Hours: 0900–2100 daily; closed January 1 and December 25

Plaça Sant Jaume, 1.
Hours: 1000–2000 Monday–Saturday; 1000–1400 Sunday/holidays.

Sants Railway Station, Plaça Paisos Catalans (center of station).
Hours: 0800–2000 daily in the summer. Winter: 0800–2000 Monday–Friday; 0800–1400 Saturday–Sunday/holidays. *Tel:* 93 490 4000.

Also, the Cassaques Vermelles, tourism officials in red coats, patrol the Rambles and Barri Gotic areas, providing maps and information in summer.

Getting Around in Barcelona

The Barcelona Metro has 5 separate lines and runs Monday–Thursday 0500–2300; Fridays and Saturdays 0500–0200; and Sundays 0600–2400. Stations are marked by signs with red diamonds. Single tickets, 145 ESP; 10 ticket cards, 790 ESP (metro only) or 795 ESP (metro and bus). A 3-day metro/bus card is 1450 ESP; a 5-day card, 2150 ESP.

Sights/Attractions/Tours

Ramble along **La Rambla,** one of Europe's most delightful areas originally engineered by nature. It began as an ancient path carved out by mountain streams rushing to the sea and is the best way of getting to know Barcelona. The plural form "Las Ramblas" is often used, since this tree-lined

Train Connections to Other Base Cities from Barcelona

Depart Barcelona Sants Station

DEPART	TRAIN NUMBER	ARRIVE	NOTES
Brussels (Bruxelles) Midi/Zuid			
2010	475	1020+1	R, 1, Sleeper
Lisbon (Lisboa) Santa Apolonia			
1533	TAL 379	0840+1	R, 2, 3
Madrid Chamartin			
0830	TAL 41	1450	R
1030	IC 179	1735	Not April 2–13
1533	TAL 379	2200	R
2300	Hotel 875	0800+1	R, 3
Nice Ville			
0845	TAL 73	1817	R, 4
1139	TAL 72	2123	R, 4
1838	IC 182	0745+1	5
Paris Gare de Lyon			
0845	TAL 73	1828	R, 6
1139	TAL 72	2122	R, 6
2010	475	0814+1	R, Sleeper, 7

Daily, unless otherwise noted

R Reservations required

Thalys high-speed trains require supplement

1. Via Paris. Arrive Paris Austerlitz station 0814+1; transfer to Paris Nord station for Thalys• 9417 departing at 0855.
2. Via Madrid. Arrive Madrid Chamartin station 2200. Transfer to Spanish TrenHotel train.
3. Spanish TrenHotel train. Deluxe sleeping accommodations (including toilet and shower in the compartment) are available. Special fares applicable.
4. Change trains in Narbonne.
5. Change trains in Cerbere to sleeper train (R).
6. Change trains in Montpellier.
7. Arrive Paris Austerlitz.

boulevard is actually a collection of five different ramblas and two squares. It stretches 2 kilometers between the Plaça de Catalunya and the port. It is the very pulse of Barcelona.

Located at the end of Las Ramblas on the Moll de Barcelona is the magnificent new **World Trade Center** waterfront complex designed by architects Pei, Cobb, and Freed, the same designers of the Glass Pyramid at the Louvre in Paris. Three of the four buildings house offices; the fourth is a 225-room hotel. For more information, visit the Web site: **www.wtcbarcelona.com**.

Rambla de Canalete, with its refreshing fountain, is a picturesque square surrounded by eating establishments and alive with people.

Rambla dels Estudis derives its name from the fact that it was at one time the site of a university and it is the present location of the Academia de Ciencies (Science Academy). It is also referred to as *Rambla dells Ocells* (birds) because of its animal market offering a variety of birds, fish, dogs, and other animals for sale. Here, you will also find the Poliorama Theatre, Capitol Cinema, Gothic and Baroque architecture, and the recently restored **Moya Palace,** which hosts visiting art collections.

Rambla de Sant Josep is the site of the busiest and probably the finest market in all of Barcelona—**La Boqueria** market, located in the arcaded Placa Real with its huge iron and glass roof. Also known as Rambla de les Flors, the flower market and stalls selling vegetables, meats, and fish produce aromatic scents and colorful sights, making this rambla one of the most pleasant. **Plaça de la Boqueria** is the square that once was the center of the city and contains an area paving designed by the famous painter Joan Miró.

The **Rambla de Caputxins** or **del Centre** is lined with stylish cafes and streetside bars such as La Opera or Los Italianos. It is also the location of **El Liceau,** Barcelona's opera house, a large, impressive building that hosts concerts, ballet, plays, and carnival festivities.

A convent once stood at the 150-year-old **Plaça Reial.** Today, it is home to many local artists, bars and pubs, shops, and the Herbolario del Rei (the King's Herbalist), where "Los Tarantos" flamenco dancing is performed.

Plaça del Teatre, the small square separating the Rambla del Centre and Rambla de Santa Monica, is the beginning of the "red light" districts of Barrio Chino and Escudellers and site of the Principal Theatre.

Rambla de Santa Monica is typified by flea markets, souvenir shops, jazz clubs, and the site of Santa Monica Church. Beyond this rambla is the port.

Other interesting sites include the **Olympic Stadium,** the **Museum of Catalonian Art,** the **Miró Foundation,** and the **Picasso Museum.**

Barcelona conforms to the Spanish tradition of late dinners. In theory, restaurants begin serving the evening meal at 2030. If you arrive earlier than 2130, however, you will probably have the restaurant all to yourself. Don't be alarmed by the increase in traffic at this hour. Barcelona's citizens are not evacuating the city—they're just going out for dinner.

Day Excursions from Barcelona

A visit to **Blanes,** north of Barcelona, along the **Costa Brava (Wild Coast),** provides the breathtaking beauty of the Mediterranean coast and an opportunity to sample culinary delights from the sea. The citadel city of **Lerida,** stormed by Caesar's legions and conquered by the Moors, carries visitors far back into Spanish history. South of Barcelona along the beaches of Spain's Coasta Dorada (Gold Coast), picturesque **Sitges** attracts sun worshippers, gourmets, and wine connoisseurs alike. Farther south, the ancient city of **Tarragona's** first-century Roman ruins stir the imagination.

Day Excursion to

Blanes
BEACHES, BOATS, AND BIKINIS

Depart from Barcelona Sants (suburban section) station

Distance by Train: 38 miles (61 km)
Average Train Time: 1 hour, 10 minutes
City Dialing Code: 72
Oficina de Turismo: Plaça Catalunya, 21 *Tel:* 972 330 348; *Fax:* 972 33 46 86
Internet: www.blanes.net
E-mail: otblandes@ddgi.es
Hours: Open June–September, Monday–Saturday 0900–2000; including/ July and August Sundays 0930–1400; May–October, Monday–Friday 0900–1400/1600–1900, Saturday 0930–1330. Winter hours: Monday–Friday 0900–1400; Saturday 0930–1330.

To get there from the rail station, board buses marked *"Estacion-Blanes."* They will take you into town to the bus terminal at Plaça Catalunya. The tourist office is just a few steps from the bus terminal.

The **Costa Brava** is a breathtaking, 90-mile stretch of rugged coastline blessed with fantastic beaches and hidden coves. And it all begins at Blanes. **Blanes** is best described as a typical Spanish coastal village, where fishing is still the primary industry. Blanes curves around the Mediterranean much like Cannes on the French Riviera, but it is not a "resort" in the usual, more commercialized sense. As with most Spanish fishing villages, the pace is slow and the people friendly.

The rail station serving Blanes is perched on a hill about a half-mile from the center of the village and the sea. Buses marked ESTACION-BLANES will take you into town to the bus terminal at Plaça Catalunya near the sea.

A stroll along the beach is a delightful experience. It is fronted by fishermen's houses and dotted with boats lying at anchor in the curve of the bay. There is an auction of the day's catch each weekday evening at about 1700 at the breakwater. Blanes has plenty of fun-in-the-sun beaches, too.

Other diversions include a delightful botanical garden located near the breakwater where the fish auctions are held. Founded in 1924 by Karl Faust, the garden exhibits more than 4,000 species of regional and international flora. Hours: 0900–1800 daily April to mid-October (reduced hours in winter).

From Blanes, other ports along this rugged and beautiful coast can be accessed by local buses, cars, or cruise boats. The Crucerus Line, which identifies its vessels with a blue whale at each bow, operates from June to September. Boats sail north from Blanes to call at places like **Lloret de Mar,** famous for its new hotels and exciting nightlife; **Tossa**; and **San Feliu de Guixols**. Obtain details and schedules from the tourist office.

Barcelona–Blanes

Trains depart Barcelona Sants daily, including holidays, from 0610, 0642, and every 30 minutes until 2042 and then at 2118, 2148, and 2218.

Trains depart Blanes to Barcelona Sants daily every 30 mintues until 2139. (Second class only).

Distance: 38 miles/61 km

Day Excursion to

Lleida (Lerida)   FROM THE COAST TO THE MOUNTAINS

Depart Barcelona Sants Station

Distance by Train: 114 miles (184 km)
Average Train Time: 3 hours
City Dialing Code: 73
Oficina de Turismo: 36 Madrid Avenue, 25002 Lleida
Tel: 973 270997; *Fax:* (97) 327–0949
Internet: www.lleidatur.es
E-mail: lleidatur@llediatur.es
Hours: Open June–September, Monday–Friday 0900–2000; Saturday 0900–1400. October–May, Monday–Friday 0900–1900; Saturday 0900–1400.

It's about a 15-minute walk from the rail station to the tourist information office. Exit the station and walk along Rambla de Ferran and Blondel Avenue to Madrice Avenue. The tourist office is in front of the University Bridge. A taxi can get you there in about 5 minutes.

A fast-moving ELT (electrotren) diesel train takes passengers in comfort through the spectacular scenery of the rugged, steep slopes of Sierra de Montserrat in the Pyrenees to the Roman fortress city Lleida. The train ride alone is worth the experience.

Be certain to make seat reservations well in advance of your day excursion date, since the train's early-morning departure does not allow sufficient time to make same-day reservations.

Your train stops briefly in Manresa, after which the scenery becomes more mountainous. Watch from the left side of the train as it approaches Lleida. The sight is unforgettable. Lleida's brooding **Seu Vella cathedral** stands as a sentinel atop a hill on the banks of the Segre River. The original cathedral makes Lleida's skyline very impressive.

Lleida served as an important Roman military outpost where Caesar's legions gathered to pursue their conquests. The Moors left a more lasting impression, which is reflected in the discernibly Mediterranean flavor of the city's marketplaces. Lleida's stormy history continued with Napoleon's attempts to annex it to France, and with artillery fire during the Spanish Civil War.

Constructed in the thirteenth century on the former site of a mosque, Seu Vella was converted from a church to a military fortress in 1707 by Philip V and then burned and pillaged in the wars that followed. It was restored and reconsecrated in 1950. The **Seu Nova** (new cathedral) stands on Carrer Major, the main street of the old town. The ancient fifteenth-sixteenth-century **Hospital de Santa Maria** is just opposite and houses many fine Iberian and Roman archaeological excavation exhibits. If you are up to it, scale the tower for a panoramic view of the plain surrounding Lleida.

Lleida's picturesque "Old Quarter" teems with interesting pedestrian streets of shops with colorful awnings and generally lower prices than you'll find in Barcelona. Take time out to enjoy the simple yet high-quality cuisine of the region. Many dishes are flavored with olive oil of the Garrigues area—considered to be the best in the world. The **Agricultural Fair of Sant Miguel,** usually held at the end of September, shows off the best produce of the area annually. Top off your visit with a toast of one of the Costers del Segre wines.

Festival buffs will enjoy many of the other time-traditioned celebrations of Lleida, including "Els Tres Tombs" (Feast of Saint Anthony) in mid-January, when the horses and cattle are led in procession through the streets of the city to be blessed; the "Aplec del Cargol" (Snail Feast), held on the first Sunday of May; and the Festival of the White Virgin, held in the beginning of October, when the city celebrates their patroness, the Madonna.

Barcelona–Lleida (Lerida)

DEPART BARCELONA SANTS	TRAIN NUMBER	ARRIVE LLEIDA	NOTES
0730	623	0924	1
0830	TAL 41	1016	1, 2
0906	none	1406	2nd class only
1003	11533	1218	1, Sat only, 2nd class
1200	TAL 377	1407	1, 2
1203	none	1438	2nd class

DEPART LLEIDA	TRAIN NUMBER	ARRIVE BARCELONA SANTS	NOTES
1305	none	1600	2nd class
1545	TAL 374	1800	1, 2
1644	530	1930	1, 2nd class
1755	none	2003	3, Catalunya Express
1837	TAL 42	2030	1, 2
2035	TAL 378	2235	1, 2
2118	620	2305	1

Daily, unless otherwise noted

1. A reservation is required for *all* trains that have numbers. A reservation purchased on board the train costs more than one purchased in advance.
2. Higher fares incorporating a supplement are payable for travel by Talgo and InterCity trains.
3. This train arrives at Barcelona Sants station 4-6 min later on Sundays. Advance seat reservations are possible on Catalunya Exprés trains.

Distance: 114 miles (184 km)

Day Excursion to

Sitges

JEWEL ON THE MEDITERRANEAN

Depart from Barcelona Sants Station

Distance by Train: 25 miles (36 km)
Average Train Time: 30 minutes
City Dialing Code: 3
Patronat Municpal de Turisme: Carrer Sínia Morera, 08870 Sitges (Barcelona)
Tel: 93 894 50 04 or 93 894 42 51; *Fax:* (93) 894–4305

Internet: www.sitgestur.com
E-mail: info@sitgestur.com
Hours: 0900–2100 daily in summer; remainder of the year: Monday–Friday 0930–1400/1600–1830; Saturday 1000–1300

Only 25 miles (40 km) south of Barcelona, **Sitges** can be accessed by train from several stations in Barcelona, but Sants and Passeig de Gracia stations are the most centralized. Sitges is one of the most cosmopolitan seaside resorts in Europe and a pleasant escape from Barcelona's summer heat.

Sitges, a member of the prestigious Jewels of European Tourism Club, boasts 17 golden beaches that stretch over 4 kilometers. It is also located in an important wine and "cava" champagne production area known as the Penedés region. Ask the tourist office about visiting the wine cellars in Vilafranca del Penedés and the Cava Cellars in Sant Sadurni de Noia.

Annually, Sitges hosts the national carnation show in June, when the town is awash with the brilliantly colored flowers. It coincides with the procession of Corpus Christi, one of the most renowned festivals in Spain, when streets are adorned with splendid carnation carpets, bands perform, and parades glide along narrow streets.

Fresh seafood is Sitges' specialty, but there are excellent meat and chicken dishes available as well at a multitude of fine restaurants. Typical Sitges dishes include *xato*, a salad of endive, tuna fish, salt-cod, anchovies, and olives, dressed with *nyora* peppers, roasted almonds, chilis, garlic, olive oil, more anchovies, and salt and vinegar. Or, try *arros a la sitgetana*—rice with a delicious mixture of shellfish, sausage, pork, peas, and peppers, seasoned with saffron and almonds. Follow it all with a glass of delicious Sitges' dessert wine, *Malvasia de Sitges.*

The February carnival, **June International Theater,** and the **October Film Festival** attract a varied mixture of participants and spectators, including international celebrities.

Other Sitges attractions include **Museo de Casa Llopis,** an outstanding exhibit of antique dolls housed in a refurbished eighteenth-century mansion; **Cau Ferrat**, the magnificent home of twentieth-century artist Santiago Rusinol, which displays Rusinol's best work as well as art by El Greco, Casas, and Picasso; and the **Maricel del Mar Museum.**

Barcelona—Sitges

Second class local service trains depart daily from Barcelona Sants station at 6 and 36 min after the hour from 0606 until 2236; journey time to Sitges is 30 min.

Second class local service trains depart daily from Sitges at 29 and 59 min after the hour throughout the day until 2059, then at 2159; journey time to Barcelona Sants station is 30 min.

Distance: 25 miles (36 km)

Day Excursion to

Tarragona

CITY OF ROMAN SPAIN

Depart from Barcelona Sants Station

Distance by Train: 55 miles (89 km)
Average Train Time: 1 hour
City Dialing Code: 77
Oficina de Turismo: 39 Carrer Major
Tel: 245 203
Hours: Open Monday–Friday 1000–2000.

To reach it, board a No. 2 bus across from the rail station. Get off at the Roman Wall, where you will see signs directing you to the tourist information office.

Tarragona can be reached via Barcelona's single-class suburban train system or by the more stylish and comfortable "Rapido" trains, which require seat reservations.

Tarragona is rich in antiquity. It was once considered a jewel in the crown of the Roman Empire, with more than one-quarter of a million inhabitants (more than twice the present population) enjoying all the privileges of Rome. Tarragona's enormous stone walls were constructed in the first century B.C. As with the great pyramids of Egypt, modern engineers still wonder how the ancient Iberians could position such massive blocks of stone. Its attractive seascape of azure blue water, gold-colored beaches, and flower-laden cliffs has attracted visitors for centuries.

St. Paul supposedly preached at the site of Tarragona's twelfth-century cathedral, where a Roman temple to Jupiter once stood. Illustrations of his life are exhibited in the altar area.

A visit to the **Archeological Museum** is a journey into Tarragona's rich past, from Roman remains and reflecting the peoples who followed, including Visigoths, Moors, and Catalans. The penetrating stare of Medusa's eyes, cornices from the **Temple of Jupiter** (where the cathedral now stands), and age-old ceramics are on view. The museum operates on seasonal hours. Check with the tourist information office.

Hungry? While you're in the tourist office, ask for directions to the **Bufet el Tiberi Restaurant** at 5, Marti d'Ardenya or the **Restaurant el Celler** and **Restaurant el Trull.** All feature local specialties.

Barcelona—Tarragona

DEPART BARCELONA SANTS	TRAIN NUMBER	ARRIVE TARRAGONA	NOTES
0700	Em 1071	0749	1, 2
0800	IC 697	0851	1, 2
0803	none	0903	
0900	Em 1091	0949	1, 2; Mon–Sat
1000	IC 185	1052	1, 2
1103	none	1203	
1230	TAL 463	1322	1, 2

DEPART TARRAGONA	TRAIN NUMBER	ARRIVE BARCELONA SANTS	NOTES
1537	TAL 460	1630	1, 2
1600	Em 1142	1703	1, 2; Sun–Fri
1659	none	1805	
1735	IC 182	1833	1, 2
1803	Em 1162	1903	1, 2
1928	TAL 264	2035	1, 2
1955	none	2100	3
2022	IC 694	2135	1, 2
2054	none	2208	2nd class
2100	Em 1192	2203	1, 2
2224	IC 266	2317	1, 2

Daily, unless otherwise noted

1. A reservation is required for *all* journeys by services for which a train number is given in the tables. A reservation fee paid to the conductor on board the train costs more than one purchased in advance.
2. Higher fares incorporating a supplement are payable for travel by Talgo (TAL) and InterCity (IC) trains. A special fare structure may apply for travel by Em trains (Euromed–200 km/hr high-speed trains similar to AVE trains). Passengers wishing to travel on Em trains are advised to inquire at the Barcelona Sants station before boarding Em trains.
3. This train conveys 2nd class only on Sundays

Distance: 57 miles (92 km)

Base City . . .

Madrid

City Dialing Code: 1
Internet: www.madrid.es

Madrid's central location in the very heart of Spain makes it a convenient Base City and a major point of entry for Spain. Madrid, the capital of Spain, at first glance appears typical of any other modern capital that serves as a center for government and finance. But it is atypical of a busy metropolis in that the Spanish seem to move at a slower pace. They make time for friends and conversation, and as one Spanish writer noted, "Madrid is a city where no one is a stranger."

The Madrilenos are apparently connoisseurs of a variety of nightlife activities, and have a flair for Flamenco—the sensual, Gypsy-influenced form of singing and dancing. There are numerous specialized Flamenco clubs in Madrid, including the Corral de la Moreria, Los Canasteros, and Torres Bermejas. It would appear that the Madrilenos never sleep!

According to the Spanish National Tourist Office, "Madrid has turned into the fable of Europe. It is called the capital of joy and of contentment. Describing our city in such terms means that it is welcoming, cordial, free, peaceful and universal."

Arriving by Air

Madrid's Barajas International Airport, about 9 miles (12 kilometers) northeast of the city.

- **Airport Information:** *Tel:* (91) 305–8343; 305–83 44; 305–8345, and 305–8346; *Fax:* (91) 393–6200
- **Flight Reservations:** *Tel:* (91) 401–9900
- **INFORIBERIA:** *Tel:* (91) 329–5767

Airport–City Links: Airport Bus (*Tel:* 431–6192), a yellow bus service, runs to and from Barajas Airport and Serrano in La Plaza de Colon (Columbus Square) every 5 minutes daily during peak hours until 0200. Journey time: about 30-60 minutes; fare, 360 ESP.

The Atocha metro line is a link to metro-Madrid; and numerous buses carry travelers to and from many locations in the city.

Taxi fare from the airport to city center is about 2,400–2,800 ESP and the trip takes 30-60 minutes depending on traffic.

Arriving by Train

RENFE (Spanish National Railways)—For information on fares, schedules and destinations: *Tel:* 328–9020; *Internet:* www.renfe.es.

Madrid's two main railway stations, **Chamartin** and **Atocha,** are connected by underground trackage via Madrid's Metro system and by "Apeadero Cercanias" (local) trains or any through-trains scheduled to stop at both stations. The Metro stop for Atocha Station is marked ATOCHA RENFE. Apeadero Cercanias stations also include **Nuevos Ministerios** in the government buildings area and **Recoletos** at the main post office. Rail passes are accepted on Apeadero Cercanias trains, but not on Madrid's Metro.

Chamartin Station, San Agustin de Foxa St., is Madrid's international station connecting with most European capitals, as well as the north, northeast, and south of Spain. The station is near the Chamartin metro stop and buses Nos. 5 and 80 connect from the city and this railway station. High-speed AVE trains shuttle passengers quickly to and from **Seville** (2½ hours), with stops at **Cordoba** and **Ciudad Real.** Other fast trains depart to and arrive from various southern and southeastern Spanish destinations and from Portugal. There are 21 tracks.

- **Money exchange:** opposite track Nos. 17 and 18. The sign reads CAJA ESPANA. Hours: 0830–1400 Monday–Friday. Banco Bilbao Vizcaya, across from track 12. Hours: 0800–2200 daily (closed for lunch 1415–1500). ATM located next door.
- **Hotel reservations,** opposite track Nos. 7 and 8. Hours: 0730–2300 daily. Nominal reservation fee. Be certain to ask for accommodations near one of the rail stations or close to public transportation. The check-in counter for Hotel Chamartin is near the luggage locker area.
- **Luggage lockers** available 0730–2330 daily. Follow the sign CONSIGNA AUTOMATICA.
- **Sala Club Intercity:** First-class lounge between entrances to track Nos. 13 and 14.
- **Tourist information:** opposite track No. 19 (*Tel:* 315 99 76). Hours: 0800–2000 Monday–Friday; 0900–1300 Saturday.
- **Train information, seat reservations,** and **railpass validation**: in the center of the station between track Nos. 11 and 12. Hours: 0830–2000. Take a number from the machine labeled RECOJA SU TURNO to reserve a place in line. Make certain the date (*fecha*) and departure time (*hora salida*) are correct on your reservation. **Seat reservations are mandatory on all express and international trains**.

Puerta de Atocha Station—High-speed AVE and Talgo 200 trains connect Madrid with Andalusia from this station. A pleasant tropical garden and cafe provide a respite from the heat and noise. The local/suburban Cercanias trains depart from the lower level and connect with Chamartin Station.

Sala Club Intercity: First-class lounge on the mezzanine level.

Principe Pio or Norte, near the Royal Palace on the west side of the city, links Madrid to cities in the north and northeast of Spain via the Cercanias, or suburban, trains. Other stations where you can board the suburban-type Cercanias trains include **Nuevos Ministerios** and **Recoletos.** Eurailpass, Europass, and the national Spain railpasses are accepted on these trains. Although considered "local" trains, they do extend to the surrounding countryside to our day excursions **Aranjuez** (Line C-3) and **El Escorial** (Line C-8a).

Tourist Information/Hotel Reservations

Offinas de Informacion de Turismo (Tourist Information Centers): Opposite track No. 19 operated by the Madrid province and can provide information about Madrid or nearby cities. Brochures describing all of the day-excursion points are usually available in English. Hours: Monday through Friday 0800–2000 and Saturday 0900–1300. *Tel:* 315–9976. When closed, the hotel office opposite track Nos. 6 and 7 will assist you.

Hotel reservations can be made for a nominal charge under the INFOR-MATCIO Y RESERVA HOTELERA sign opposite track Nos. 6 and 7. The office is open 0730–2300 daily. Madrid is a large city, so be certain that you ask for lodging near one of the rail terminals or close to public transportation.

Getting Around in Madrid

Madrid has an excellent Metro and bus system. Purchase reduced-fare 10-trip tickets, called "Bonobus," at newspaper stands, tobacco stores, and all main bus stops. The tickets are magnetically encoded.

Although Madrid has no Spanish National Tourist offices, the following Provincial and Municipal offices provide general information about Spain. And while most of the tourist and rail personnel speak English, it's always polite to ask: *"¿Habla Ingles, por favor?"* (Do you speak English, please?).
- **Chamartin Railway Station** (*Tel:* 315 99 76). Hours: Monday–Friday 0900–1900; Saturday 0930–1330.
- **Barajas Airport** (*Tel:* 305–8656) (international arrivals). Hours: Monday–Friday 0800–2000; Saturday 0800–1300.
- **Torre de Madrid in Plaza de Espana** (*Tel:* 541–2325).
- **Metro station: Plaza de Espana,** Duque de Medinaceli.
- **Outside the Palace Hotel** (*Tel:* 429–4951). Hours: Monday–Friday 0900–1900; Saturday 0930–1330.
- **Metro station: Banco de Espana.** Hours: Monday–Friday. 1000–1400/1600–1900; Saturday 1000–1330.
- **Metro station: Sol,** below Puerta del Sol.

- **Travelers' Hotline** (*Tel:* 90220–2202) provides tourists with the latest information about accommodations. A wide variety of accommodations are available in Madrid, including the Palace Hotel, across the square from the Prado Museum. As the name implies, the hotel is on the site of a former palace (*tel:* 360–8000). The Hotel Chamartin at Chamartin Station is convenient for those businesspersons and tourists traveling by train *Tel:* 323–3087; *Fax:* 733–0214.

Sights/Attractions/Tours

A convenient way to see the sights is on **Madrid Visions Touristic Bus.** For 1,800 ESP, you can jump on and off the bus at more than 14 various sights, museums, and churches.

Some "don't-miss" sights include **Puerta del Sol** (Gate of the Sun), the center of the old town and the terminus for the city's metro lines and many of the buses. Six of Spain's national freeways radiate from Kilometer Zero, a stone slab buried in the pavement from which all distances are measured in Spain. **El Oso y el Madrono,** the bush and the bear statue, is Madrid's emblem.

Proceed southwest along **Calle Mayor** to **Plaza de la Villa,** with two stunning buildings dating from the fifteenth century—the **Casa** (house) and the **Torre (tower) de los Lujanes.** Continuing to the right of Calle Mayor and beyond the Plaza de la Villa, turn into the alleyway leading to **San Nicolas de los Servitas,** to visit Madrid's oldest church

Going north along the **Calle del Arenal,** one can view a famous El Greco at the Church of San Gines or visit Joy Enslava, the city's trendy disco. Farther on are the Royal Palace and the Opera House.

Other significant landmarks include the **Palacio Real** (*Tel:* 541–0876; hours 0900–1800 Monday–Saturday; 1000–1430 Sunday)—one of the best-conserved palaces in Europe. It's filled with paintings, frescoes, clocks, furniture, and porcelain. **Plaza Mayor** behind Calle Mayor is an exquisite seventeenth-century arcaded square

A **Museum Pass,** which costs 1,050 ESP, is a bargain for visiting Madrid's fine museums. The incomparable **Prado Museum** at Paseo del Prado (*Tel:* 330 2800; hours 0900–1900 Tuesday–Saturday; 0900–1400 Sunday) houses more than 3,000 of the world's most precious works of art, including fine collections of the Spanish masters—Goya, Velazquez, El Greco, Murillo, and Zurbaran.

The **Thyssen–Bornemisza Museum** (*Tel:* 369 01 51; hours 1000–1900 Tuesday–Sunday.), in the Villahermosa Palace, features one of the world's most extensive private art collections now open to the public. The **Reina Sofia National Art Museum** has a fantastic collection of twentieth-century

Train Connections to Other Base Cities from Madrid

Depart from Madrid Chamartin Station unless otherwise noted

DEPART	TRAIN NUMBER	ARRIVE	NOTES
Barcelona Sants			
0700	IC 178	1403	R
1100	TAL 374	1800	R
1400	TAL 42	2030	R
1600	TAL 378	2235	R
2200	370	0700+1	R, Sleeper
2300	Hotel 847	0800+1	R, 1, Sun–Fri
Lisbon (Lisboa) Santa Apolonia			
2235	Hotel 332	0840+1	R, 1
Paris Montparnasse Austerlitz			
1000	IC 203	2305	R, 2
1545	TAL 251	0714+1	R, 2, Sleeper
1900	Hotel 407	0829+1	R, 1
2245	205	1500+1	R, 2, Sleeper

Daily, unless otherwise noted

R Reservations required

1. Spanish TrenHotel train. Deluxe sleeping accommodations (including toilet and shower in the compartment) are available. Special fares applicable.

2. Change trains in Hendaye.

Spanish art, and the **National Chalcography Institute** includes 221 original copper and brass engraved plates by Goya.

If you plan to attend a bullfight in Madrid, remember what Ernest Hemingway wrote: "It is a tragedy; the death of the bull, which is played, more or less well by the bull and the man involved and in which there is danger for the man but certain death for the bull."

For people watching, visit several of Madrid's *chiringuitos*, a combination German-style beer garden and discotheque, and cafes that line the **Paseo de la Castellana** (which becomes Paseo del Prado as it nears the Prado Museum).

In the cuisine category, Madrid has some very old and very famous restaurants. The **Casa Botin** (*Tel:* 366–4217) is in the *Guinness Book of Records* as the oldest continuously operated restaurant and Hemingway's favorite for suckling pig and baby lamb. The **Zalacain** at Alvarez de Baena 4 (*Tel:* 561 59 35) features Basque seafood and game.

Day Excursions

Aranjuez, Avila, El Escorial, and Toledo are four very different Spanish destinations easily accessed by train from Madrid.

Aranjuez and **El Escorial** are particularly picturesque. Aranjuez, on the fertile banks of the Tagus River, is set in a forested valley less than 1 hour's train journey south of Madrid. El Escorial is a village at the base of the Sierra de Guadarrama, 1 hour north of Madrid. Favorites of the royalty for centuries, they are now popular retreats for Madrilenos.

Avila and **Toledo** are cities with such different styles that they exemplify the diversity of this ancient land. Both are worth more than a day's visit to more thoroughly explore and enjoy.

Burgos, home of El Cid, is about 3 hours' journey time from Madrid.

Day Excursion to

Aranjuez   SPANISH ROYAL RETREAT

Depart from Madrid Atocha Station

Distance by Train: 30 miles (49 km)
Average Train Time: 50 minutes
City Dialing Code: 1
Oficina de Turismo: No. 9, Plaza de San Antonio (*Tel:* 891–0427)

We recommend taking a taxi from the station to the tourist office, located near Palacio Real.

In the eighteenth and nineteenth centuries, **Aranjuez** was a favorite hangout for Spanish royalty. Now, it's a popular place for "regular" Madrilenos to gather on weekends. You may want to make this day excursion during the week to avoid the weekend crowds.

Aranjuez has often been described as the "Oasis of Castille," in part because it nestles on the banks of the Tagus River that nurses dense groves of poplars and rich vegetation. Apparently, the jade green waters of the river favorably foster the growth of trees, as evidenced by the city's Circus of the Twelve Streets, a square from which twelve beautifully shaded avenues radiate.

The **Palacio Real** (Royal Palace) is a lavish palace that would vie with Versailles in extravagance. Its 18 magnificent rooms include the Porcelain

Madrid—Aranjuez

DEPART CHAMARTÍN	TRAIN NUMBER	DEPART ATOCHA CERCANÍAS	DEPART PUERTA DE ATOCHA	ARRIVE ARANJUEZ	NOTES
0835	none	0850	—	0922	1
0905	TAL 228	0920	—	0948	R, Sat
1030	TAL 222	1045	—	1113	R, Sun–Fri
—	IC 80	—	1315	1341	R
1335	none	1350	—	1421	1

DEPART ARANJUEZ	TRAIN NUMBER	ARRIVE PUERTA DE ATOCHA	ARRIVE ATOCHA CERCANÍAS	ARRIVE CHAMARTÍN	NOTES
1326	TAL 223	—	1358	1413	R
1524	TAL 77	—	1558	1611	R
1618	none	—	1650	1703	1
1719	TAL 23	—	1719	1749	R
1815	IC 85	1848	—	—	R
1917	none	—	1951	2004	1
2011	none	2048	—	—	
2046	none	—	2119	2133	1, Sun
2201	none	—	2236	2249	Sun

Daily, unless otherwise noted
R Reservations required
— Train does not stop in or depart from this station.
1. These trains are *Andalucia Exprés* trains; reservations are possible.
Reservation is required for *all* journeys by services for which a train number appears. A reservation fee purchased on board the train costs more than one bought in advance. Higher fares incorporating a supplement are payable for travel by Talgo (TAL) and InterCity (IC) trains.
Distance: 0 miles (49 km)

Salon, the Throne Room, and The Museum of Royal Robes, which displays the court dress of sovereigns up to the nineteenth century. Another highlight is the grand staircase built during the reign of Philip V. During spring and summer, the palace is open 1000–1830 Tuesday–Sunday. It closes one hour earlier in autumn and winter.

The Farmer's Cottage with its resplendent furnishings can be reached through the Prince's Garden. The Casa de Marinos, the sailor's house that holds the royal vessels, displays Spain's dominant maritime history. And among the gardens, the Parterre Garden and the Jardinde la Isla (Island Garden) are most memorable.

You can purchase a combination ticket that includes a guided tour of the Royal Palace. The tours operate 1000–1815 April through August; 1000–1715 September through March. Note that all of the museums are closed on Mondays.

Trains to Aranjuez depart every 30 minutes from Madrid's Attocha station.

Day Excursion to

Avila
WALLED CITY

Depart from Madrid Chamartin Station or Principe Pio

Distance by Train: 70 miles (112 km)
Average Train Time: 1 hour, 15 minutes
City Dialing Code: 1
Oficina de Turismo: No.4 Plaza de la Catedral
Tel: (92) 021–1387; *Fax:* (92) 025–3717
Hours: Monday–Friday 1000–1400/1700–2000; Saturday 0930–1430/1600–1900; Sunday 0930–1400/1600–1830.
RENFE at Avila Railway Station: *Tel:* 22–0188
     Taxis to the far right of the rail station as you exit. Rail station is about 1 mile from city center.

Avila is the capital of the province of Avila, and at 1,127 meters it is the highest provincial capital in Spain and the best-preserved walled city in the world. The city is completely enclosed by 1.2 miles (2.5 kilometers) of century walls averaging 33 feet high and 10 feet thick, with 90 towers and 9 gateways. The enormousness of this project becomes apparent when you realize it was constructed in 1085.

Viewed from **Los Cuatro Postes,** an observation post on the Salamanca Road outside the city, Avila is a breathtaking sight nestled on the Adaja River against the mountains. From here, the walled city appears to be a fascinating giant stage all set for a medieval drama.

Avila is most remembered for Saint Teresa. Her presence is most evident in the convent **Nuestra Senora de Gracia,** built at the site of her parents' home; the Monastery de la Encarnacion, which depicts her lifestyle; and "Las Madres" (Monastery de San Jose), her first foundation.

Across the street from the tourist office is the Gran Hotel Palacio Valderrabonos. This former noble's residence is an excellent place to have lunch. Its door dates from the fifteenth century.

Madrid—Avila

DEPART MADRID CHAMARTIN	TRAIN NUMBER	ARRIVE AVILA	NOTES
0800	IC 131	0925	R
0830	none	0953	1
0900	TAL 61	1021	R
1000	IC 203	1121	R, 2nd class only
1130	none	1253	1, 2
1330	none	1453	1, 2nd class only
1400	TAL 151	1521	R, Mon–Sat
1400	TAL 129	1521	R, Sun only

DEPART AVILA	TRAIN NUMBER	ARRIVE MADRID CHAMARTIN	NOTES
1326	IC 202	1455	R, 2nd class
1410	TAL 78	1540	R
1605	TAL 74	1735	R
1730	none	1910	1
1835	none	2025	2nd class
1935	none	2110	1
1950	TAL 60	2120	1
2003	TAL 152	2130	R, Sun–Fri
2038	none	2213	2nd class, Sun, 3
2045	IC 130	2220	R
2110	500	2240	R, 2nd class, Sat only
2150	none	2320	1, 3, Sun
2216	none	2349	3, 2nd class, Sun

Notes:
Daily, unless otherwise noted
R Reservations required
Reservation is required for *all* journeys by services for trains with numbers.
A reservation fee paid to the conductor on board the train costs more than
one purchased in advance. Higher fares incorporating a supplement are
payable for travel by Talgo (TAL) and InterCity (IC) trains.
1. This train is a Castilla y León Exprés train; reservations are available.
2. This train departs from Atocha Cercanías station 15 min earlier
3. This train arrives at Atocha Cercanías station 15 min later.
Distance: 70 miles (112 km)

Other sights in Avila include the Cathedral, which forms a part of the great wall, thus giving it the distinctive look of a fortress rather than a church. Its somewhat austere exterior is in contrast to its interior, which has many beautiful details. In the Cathedral's museum, you may view a portrait painted by El Greco and a colossal silver monstrance, weighing nearly 200 pounds, made by Juan de Arfe in 1571.

The Cathedral was begun in the twelfth century in Romanesque style and finished in the fifteenth century with a facade of Gothic Towers, the Palacio de Polention, the Mansion de los Deanes, Mansion de Davila—all magnificent with art and architecture.

The cuisine of this area is fit for a king's palate. Trout from the Tormes River is renowned for its distinctive flavor; the roast suckling pig, lamb, or veal dishes are equally excellent and served with a hearty accompaniment of vegetables, followed by *yemas de Santa Teresa,* small sweets made of egg yolks.

Nearby Paradors offer unique accommodations for those who prefer to "base" themselves here. *Paradors* are historic buildings and palaces that the Spanish government has converted into hotels.

Day Excursion to

Burgos

HOME OF EL CID

Depart from Madrid Chamartin Station

Distance by Train: 211 miles (340 km)
Average Train Time: 3 hours
City Dialing Code: 47
Oficina de Turismo: 7, Plaza Alonso Martinez Square,
Tel: (947) 20–3125 or 20–1846; *Fax:* (947) 27–6529
Hours: 0900–1400/1700–1900 Monday–Friday; 1000–1400/1700–2000
Saturday–Sunday and holidays.

To reach the office on foot (about a 15-minute walk), exit the station and go straight ahead until you cross the Arlanzon River. Turn right and proceed along General Franco Avenue to the arch where the walkway Paseo del Espolon begins. Or, take a taxi.

Burgos is north of Madrid, approaching France, and on the crossroads to Portugal. Birthplace of the warrior El Cid, Burgos is the capital of Burgos province, one of the nine provinces of Castile and Leon.

El Cid and his wife, Ximena, are entombed in the **thirteenth century cathedral,** one of the world's outstanding examples of Gothic architecture. Its twin spires rise to greet you long before your Talgo train comes to a halt in the Burgos Station.

Madrid—Burgos

DEPART MADRID CHAMARTIN	TRAIN NUMBER	ARRIVE BURGOS	NOTES
0830	none	1208	Sat
0830	none	1226	1
1000	IC 203	1326	R, 2nd class
1330	none	1726	1, 2nd class

DEPART BURGOS	TRAIN NUMBER	ARRIVE MADRID CHAMARTIN	NOTES
1635	none	2020	Sun, 2nd class
1903	TAL 200	2205	R, except Sun–Fri
1903	500	2240	R, 2nd class, Sat only
1921	none	2320	1, 2, 2nd class

Daily, unless otherwise noted
R Reservations required
Reservation required for *all* trains with numbers. A reservation fee paid to the conductor on board the train costs more than one purchased in advance. Higher fares incorporating a supplement are payable for travel by Talgo (TAL) and InterCity (IC) trains.
1. This train is a Castilla y León Exprés train; reservations are available.
2. This train arrives at Atocha Cercanías station 15 min later.
Distance: 211 miles (340 km)

The nave of the cathedral and the ambulatory and portals of El Sarmental and Coroneria date from its beginnings in 1221. The latest additions, dating from the sixteenth century, include Diego de Siloe's *Golden Stairs*; the chapels of La Consolation, Santiago, and Navidad; and Juan de Vallejo's exquisite lantern.

Burgos was the site where the Castilians initiated their campaigns against the Muslims to reclaim Madrid in 1083 and Toledo in 1085. In this century, Generalissimo Franco used Burgos as his headquarters during the Spanish Civil War, and here declared the cease-fire in 1939.

The **Casa del Cordon,** a fifteenth-century house so named from the huge cord of rope carved in stone fronting its entrance, forms the backdrop for **El Cid's statue.** It was here that Christopher Columbus was received in formal audience by the Spanish monarchs on his return from his second voyage to the Americas.

For lunch, we suggest the **Ojeda Restaurant** at Calle Vitoria No. 5. It is quite pleasant to have a light snack or even a full meal at its outdoor tables in the summer.

Day Excursion to

El Escorial WORLD'S EIGHTH WONDER

Depart from Madrid Atocha or Charmartin Stations

Distance by Train: 32 miles (52 km)
Average Train Time: 60 minutes
City Dialing Code: 1
Oficina de Turismo, No.10 Calle Floridablanca,
Tel: (91) 890–1554
Hours: 1000–1400/1500–1700 Monday–Friday; 1000–1400 Saturday
    The rail station is about 1 mile from town. Taxis are to the left of the station exit. A taxi ride to the town square or the tourist office costs about 350 ESP. Buses are also available that will take you to the town square.

El Escorial names the village and the immense palace-monastery, both havens of Phillip II, who personally supervised construction of the monumental structure to commemorate his victory over France at St. Quentin in 1557. Part monastery, part palace, part cathedral—El Escorial reflects its builder's vanity. The monastery and palace are open 1000–1800 in summer, until 1700 in winter, and closed on Mondays.

El Escorial encompasses 8 acres, 9 towers, 16 courtyards, 86 staircases, 1,200 doors, and 2,673 leaded-glass windows. A force of 1,500 laborers worked 21 years to complete it. Wear your best pair of walking shoes—you'll need them.

The **Hall of Battles** epitomizes Spain's aggressive history in paintings by Italian artists Castello, Grenello, and Tavorone. Priceless artworks by Borsch, Rembrandt, Tintoretto, and Titian are also displayed throughout the palace. Tapestries of Spanish country life woven over sketches drawn by Goya also hang on the walls.

Prior to mounting the Armada against England, King Phillip tried to bring England into the Spanish Empire by marrying Mary Tudor, known as "Bloody Mary" for her overzealous persecution of English Protestants. By forty years later, just before his death, Phillip had become a religious fanatic. He returned to the palace to live as though in poverty in a sparse second-floor apartment, which provides stark contrast to its surroundings—one of the grandest palaces in Europe.

Two other attractions of interest are the **Casita del Principe** (the Prince's

Madrid—El Escorial

DEPART MADRID ATOCHA	DEPART MADRID CHAMARTIN	ARRIVE EL ESCORIAL	NOTES
0703	0717	0808	R
0833	0847	0938	R
1032	1046	1137	R
1232	1246	1337	R

DEPART EL ESCORIAL	ARRIVE MADRID CHAMARTIN	ARRIVE MADRID ATOCHA	NOTES
1617	1708	1721	R
1817	1908	1921	R
2017	2108	2121	R
2217	2308	2321	R

Daily, including holidays
R Reservations required
Distance: 32 miles/52 km

Cottage), which you pass en route to the station, and **Casita de Arriba,** a hunting lodge 2 miles farther on. Both are open 1000–1800 (1700 in winter); closed Mondays. Both were constructed by Charles III (1759–1788). His friendship with France and hostility toward Great Britain led to the alliance in support of the American Revolution.

Day Excursion to

Toledo

CITY OF HISTORY

Depart from Madrid Atocha Station

Distance by Train: 57 miles (91 km)
Average Train Time: 1 hour, 15 minutes
City Dialing Code: 25
Oficina de Turismo: Puerta Nueva de Bisagra
Tel: (92) 522–0843
Hours: 0900–1800 Monday–Friday; 0900–1900 Saturday; 0900–1500 Sunday

Public bus service from rail station into town. Buses depart every 15 minutes. Bus stops first at the tourist information office at Puerta de la Bisagra before terminating in the main square, Plaza de Zocodover (Marketplace). There is also an information office at the city hall, in front of the cathedral.

Toledo is (as is Avila) capital of a province with the same name. Toledo province is defined by mountain ranges, rivers, and rich rolling valleys; it abounds with game, aromatic plants, and delicate white-leafed rock roses—all of which distinguishes Toledo from the other provinces of La Mancha with their monotonous, flat expanses.

Divided by the River Tagus, Toledo has the rich and varied history of most river towns, and in Europe's south that means conquests by Romans, Visigoths, Moors, and ultimately Christians, who declared it Spain's Imperial City. It was ruled by the legendary El Cid. The impact of such a diverse history earned Toledo the UNESCO "Heritage of Mankind" status, defining it as one of the richest historically, culturally, and monumentally endowed cities in Spain.

A Cretan named Domenico Teotocopulo arrived in Toledo in 1577. His arrival might have gone unnoticed, except that Señor Teotocopulo, better known as El Greco, happened to be a painter of some renown. El Greco painted and bequeathed his best to Toledo. The **Museum of Santa Cruz** and the **El Greco** museum as well as the cathedral honor the achievements of one of Spain's most creative artists.

Although Toledo's history may be complicated, its charm is definitely not. Wander the city's narrow cobblestone streets; visit its friendly cafes, which remain open late into the night; and taste its fresh fruits from the open market in the morning.

In 1226, King Ferdinand III laid the first stone in the **Cathedral of Toledo,** and today it is renowned for its art and architecture. The thirteenth-century fortress **Alcazar** was in the third century a Roman Pretorian Palace.

Toledo also is well known for its crafters who work steel into some of the finest blades for knives and swords. The distinctive black-on-gold designs embellishing the handles of blades have been carried over to jewelry and other accessories available in shops throughout the city.

Although there are numerous eateries, most visitors seem to gather in the main square, **Plaza de Zocodover** (Marketplace). Here, you will find cafes and bars to sample local sandwiches and *tapas* (appetizers).

The **Parador Conde Orgaz** and the **Hotel Alfonso VI** are exceptional accommodations in Toledo, if you choose to stay.

Madrid—Toledo

All train service to Toledo is 2nd class and departs from and returns to Madrid Atocha Cercanías station; departure times are 0705 weekdays, and 0820, 1025, and 1225 daily; journey time is 72–82 min. Departures from Toledo are daily at 1430, 1630, 1830, and 2100.

Distance: 57 miles (91 km)

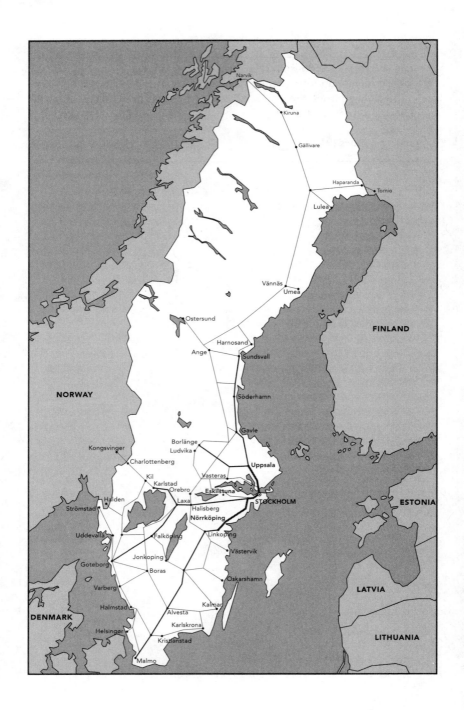

Sweden

In size, Sweden is about the same size as the State of California or the country of Spain. It is half covered by forests, dotted with nearly 100,000 lakes, and thousands of islands line its coastline. It is one of the largest and most prosperous countries in Europe and supports a large and efficient industrial complex. With a population of only 8.7 million inhabitants, however, it is not crowded and its citizens enjoy a superb quality of life and one of the highest standards of living in the world.

Although Swedish, a Germanic language, is the language of the majority, Finland was a part of Sweden until 1809 and Finnish-speaking natives still occupy the northeastern area along with another minority group, the Sami (Lapp). Fortunately for English-speaking tourists, English is spoken by most Swedes who are involved in tourism, transportation, and international business.

From 1846 to 1930, approximately 1.3 million Swedes immigrated to North America. Thousands of visitors, including North Americans, trace their Swedish ancestry at the Swedish Emigrant Institute in Växjö, which houses and records memorabilia from that time period.

It is difficult to realize that only about a century ago, Sweden was one of the most backward countries in Europe. Today, Sweden is forward thinking—spending a large percentage of national output on industrial research and development. Since 1995, Sweden has played an important role as a member of the European Union. Sweden's strategic geographic location between the North Atlantic and Russia has affected its foreign policies and security strategies for all of Europe.

For more information about Sweden, visit **www. visit-sweden.com** or **www.gosweden.se,** e-mail info@gosweden.rg or contact the Swedish Travel and Tourism Council in New York:

New York: P.O. Box 4649, Grand Central Station, New York, NY 10163–4649. *Tel:* (212) 885–9700; *Fax:* (212) 885–9764

Banking

- **Currency:** Swedish Krona (SEK)
- **Exchange Rate at Press Time:** 8.13 SEK = $1.00 U.S.
- **Hours:** 0900–1700 Monday–Friday Closes at 1500 on the day before a holiday, which the Swedes refer to as a *halvdag* (half-day).

Communications

- **Country Dialing Code:** 46
  For telephone calls within Sweden, dial zero (0) preceding area code.
  Direct dial: AT&T: 020–795–611; MCI: 020–795–922; Sprint: 020–799–011

Rail Travel in Sweden

Swedish State Railways: Central Station, S-105 50 Stockholm
For calls within Sweden, call toll-free *Tel:* 020–757575. From outside of Sweden call 46–8 696 7540; Internet site: www.sj.se

The Swedish State Railways (SJ) operates about 7,000 miles of rail lines. Its **X 2000 trains** are Sweden's modern high-speed "tilting" trains, which travel at 125 miles per hour and serve most of the major cities in Sweden. In business first class, meals are served at travelers' seats. There is also a bistro car, which serves hot and cold meals, plus beverages at traveler's seats.

July 1, 2000, will begin the combined rail and motorway connection via the 16 km Øresund Bridge. This major infrastructure will bring the cities of Malmö, Sweden, and Copenhagen, Denmark together to create the largest Northern European market.

InterCity trains operate between all of Sweden's major cities and between Stockholm and Oslo. These trains often have a bistro car where you can purchase food, refreshments or games for the kids and a "family car" with play areas available for children. **InterRegio** trains operate between regions. These trains have radio sockets at all seats and refreshments available. **Night trains** in Sweden offer several different types of accommodations ranging from exclusive compartments with two beds, shower, and toilet to six-bedded couchettes with toilet and washing facilities in the corridor.

Train platforms are referred to in Sweden as *spoors*. On most trains operated by the Scandinavian countries, drinking water is supplied at no charge. Train reservations are mandatory for trips of more than 90 miles.

SJ accepts **Eurailpass, ScanRail Pass** and the **Sweden RailPass** (see list of European RailPasses in the Appendix for prices and ordering information for the multicountry passes, Eurailpass, and ScanRail Pass). Pass prices do not include reservation fees, but a point-to-point ticket does. Eurailpass, ScanRail Pass, and Sweden Rail Pass holders do pay a reservation fee of SEK 50 to ride X 2000 trains. Ferry crossing between Helsingborg and Helsingor (Denmark) and between Trelleborg to Sassnitz (Germany) are included.

Bonuses for passholders include 50 percent reductions on the ferry crossings of Stena Line between Göteborg and Frederikshavn (Denmark), TR line between Trelleborg and Rostock (Germany), and the TT Line crossing between Trelleborg to Travemünde (Germany). The Flyvebådene company offers 25 percent discount on the catamaran crossing between Malmö and Copenhagen (Denmark).

Sweden RailPass

Unlimited travel on all routes operated by the Swedish Railways. Up to 2 children under 15 years of age travel free when accompanied by an adult. For additional children there are reduced prices available. Prices do *not* include reservation fees or supplement fees for sleepers or couchettes. The Sweden RailPass will be valid on the night trains between Gothenburg/Stockholm-Umea/Boden/Kiruna/Vassijaure, which from January 10, 2000, will be operated by Tagkompaniet, a private company. (Night train supplements are excluded.)

| | ADULT | | ADDITIONAL CHILD | |
	1ST CLASS	2ND CLASS	1ST CLASS	2ND CLASS
3 days within 1 month	$211	$156	$148	$111
4 days within 1 month	$239	$177	$168	$124
5 days within 1 month	$268	$198	$188	$129

Special: Two children under age 16 travel free together per adult.

Base City ...

Stockholm

City Dialing Code: 8
Internet: www.stoinfo.se

Stockholm declares intentions of retaining the old, then in the same breath states great love of progress and things modern. Voted the Cultural Capital of Europe in 1998 by the European Union, Stockholm provides visitors with the opportunity to experience Sweden's modern culture and to celebrate its ancient traditions.

Stockholm's **Gamla Stan** (Old Town) is located on a small island in the city center. Its narrow cobblestone streets wind their crooked ways over paths unchanged since the Middle Ages past houses bearing the same facades they had when they were built. But behind these old facades you find the most modern of business establishments and apartments whose decors rival those of similar dwellings anywhere in the world. With a delicate touch, Stockholm has made this dualism work in every way.

Another example is **Sergels Torg,** Stockholm's space-age city center. It exists comfortably surrounded by other structures centuries older. Call it what you will, but most people call Stockholm absolutely beautiful.

Arriving by Air

Arlanda Airport lies 24 miles (40 kilometers) northwest of the city.

Airport–City Links: Airport coach. Departures every 10 minutes; time en route, 35-45 minutes. Coach terminates in Stockholm at the World Trade Centre next to the Central Station. Fare for a single trip is 60 SEK for adults; reduced rates for children. For information *Tel:* 600–1000; *Fax:* 686–1362.

SAS Limousine service (*Tel:* 797–3700; *Fax:* 797–4198) is available 24 hours per day (about $75 U.S./car) to Stockholm Central Station.

Taxis are available 24 hours daily. The taxi stand is located just outside the arrivals hall of the airport. Taxi fare is 400–500 SEK.

Arriving by Train

Stockholm has several suburban stations, but international trains stop only at the main rail station in the center of the city, Stockholm Central. All of the day excursions out of Stockholm depart from Stockholm Central Station.

Stockholm's Central Station is modern, well organized, and easy to move about in. International trains usually arrive on track No. 17 or 18.

Luggage carts: Insert a 5-SEK coin in the lock which will be refunded upon returning the cart to a rack.

The Central Station is close to several major hotels and directly connected to the Stockholm subway (the Tunnelbanan). The main taxi stand is across the street from the railway station.

The station does an excellent job of moving its passengers to and from the trains. It also provides a full complement of services for the traveler. An arcade of shops, on the lower station level in the proximity of the exits from track Nos. 17 and 18, provides all types of foodstuffs, beverages, tobacco, newspapers, and so forth.

The *Konsum*—Sweden's answer to the American supermarket—is a good place to restock your larder. It is located in the same area within the station. There are also shops in the main station-concourse area where you may purchase food and soft drinks.

The station's food-service facilities range from a cafeteria to a restaurant with its own gambling casino. The cafeteria is located on the main level of the station to the far right as you stand looking into the station from the train exit. It can be identified by its sign, CAFE OASEN. Cafeteria service is continuous Monday through Saturday 0630–2330 and Sunday 0700–2330; it is a good place to have breakfast, lunch, or dinner.

The **Centralens Restaurang (restaurant) Orientexpressen** has the previously mentioned casino. You'll see its sign on the right side of the station as you exit from the track area. In addition to the casino, the complex includes a pub and a restaurant with good food at reasonable prices. The "all you can eat" breakfast in the restaurant section is a real bargain. The restaurant has an expansive but relatively inexpensive luncheon-and-dinner menu featuring many Swedish specialties (closed during July).

Across the street from Central Station, along the street Vasagatan, you can find a number of excellent food facilities ranging from fast to fancy.

Train information is displayed on bulletins following the usual format. Departures are printed on yellow paper; arrivals appear on white. Train information is readily available throughout the station, including key positions just inside the main entrance and again in the corridors leading to the track areas. The office is in the main concourse to the left of the main exit. Hours: 0600–2300 Monday–Saturday; 0700–2300 Sunday.

Local train information, usually for commuter trains, is displayed by a bank of large-screen, closed-circuit television sets.

Train reservations can be made in a large ticket office located in the main hall to the right as you proceed from the track area. A sign, FARDBILJETTER PLATSBILJETTER, identifies it. Take a queue number for seat reservations and sleeping-car accommodations. Hours: Monday-Friday 0545–2100; Saturday 0545–1900; Sunday 0800–2100.

Railpass validation should be completed before making your first train trip. Operating personnel aboard the trains can validate the pass, but they are required to charge for the service. Validation is free in any regular railway station. In Stockholm's Central Station, use the window marked INTERNATIONAL TICKETS to the right of the main exit.

Money exchange is located in the main station concourse and to the right of the main exit as you proceed from the track area. The office displays the regular pictograph sign plus one reading FOREX (exchange office). Hours: daily 0700–2100.

Hotel reservations at Stockholm Information Service, located in the main station concourse next to the post office. Look for the sign HOTELLCENTRAL TURISTINFORMATION. Hours: June–August 0700–2100 daily; September–May, 0800–1900 daily. Small charges are made for obtaining hotel rooms and space in youth hostels. Advance payment is accepted to assure that the hotel or pension will hold your room until your arrival. If your accommodations are located some distance from the train station, this can be a welcomed service.

Tourist information is available in the rail station at the same office, HOTELLCENTRAL TURISTINFORMATION, or in the main tourist center at Sweden House.

Tourist Information/Hotel Reservations

Stockholm Tourist Information Center: Sweden House; Kungsträdgården; *Tel:* (08) 789–24–90, *Fax:* 789 24 50
E-mail: info@stoinfo.se
Hours: May: 0900–1800 Monday–Friday; 0900–1500 Saturday–Sunday; June–August: 0800–1800 Monday–Friday; 0900–1700 Saturday–Sunday; September: 0900–1800 Monday–Friday; 0900–1500 Saturday–Sunday

Inquiries about the "Sweden at Home" plan of meeting Swedes with similar interests should be made at this information office. An excellent publication is the *Stockholm Guide*.

Getting Around in Stockholm

The city has excellent transportation facilities for sightseeing in Stockholm. The extensive network of bus and subway systems makes it easy to reach practically any point in the city from any other point.

Your key to the use of these city transportation facilities is **The Stockholm Card**, which provides free admission to 70 of the city's museums and sights, as well as free sightseeing and transportation throughout the Stockholm area.

Adult prices are 199 SEK for 24 hours, 398 for 48 hours, and 490 for 72 hours. Child rates are 35 SEK for 24 hours; 70 SEK for 48 hours; and 105 SEK for 72 hours. For additional children there are reduced rates available. The card is on sale at the tourist center in Sweden House and at the central station. It is sold undated and is stamped with the date and hour the first time you use it. With the card, you will be given a folder explaining its use and validation procedure.

Sights/Attractions/Tours

Gamla Stan—The Old Town dates back to 1290 and is Stockholm's oldest and most enchanting area. Besides containing many historical sights such as the world's oldest existing bank (since 1656), the Royal Palace, and Parliament, you'll also find unusual shops, art galleries, antiques stores, and more than 30 restaurants.

With The Stockholm Card in your pocket, you can expand your day-excursion itinerary to include places of interest in and near Stockholm. For example, you can make a day excursion to **Norrtalje,** with its quaint port, and have lunch aboard a vintage steamer permanently moored there. You can also ride one of the Stockholm Transit Authority (SL) buses to **Furusund,** a narrow passage for ships entering and leaving the city's harbor. You can have lunch in a quaint Inn at Furusund. During high season, from May–August, sightseeing boats can take you to the outer archipelago.

Yet another alternative use for the card would be to take a bus ride to historic **Vaxholm** for a great Swedish lunch at the waterfront hotel overlooking the old fortress and shopping there at leisure. Stockholm has many museums to explore, so it is difficult to single out but a few recommendations. There is one, however, that we are sure you won't want to miss: the *Vasa* **Museum.**

In 1628, Sweden proudly launched what was then the world's largest warship and pride of the nation, the *Vasa* carrying the name of the royal family, along with sixty-four cannon, and this ship was presumed to be unconquerable. But the nation's joy was short-lived. The *Vasa* capsized in the harbor during its maiden voyage. Raised in 1961, painstakingly restored, and now resting in a museum especially constructed for its preservation, the warship is enthroned in the middle of a great hall, displaying the *Vasa* in all her grandeur. The cobblestone ground floor suggests a quay, and the restored warship can be viewed from various perspectives from four levels.

Vasa is unique since it is the oldest fully preserved warship in the world. Films of the raising and the restoration of the *Vasa* are shown hourly in the museum, and guided tours following the film are conducted during the summer. The Vasa Museum will participate in the big Millennium celebration Stockholm 2000, from December 27, 1999–January 6, 2000, with salutes from

Train Connections to Other Base Cities from Stockholm

Depart from Stockholm Central Station

DEPARTURE	TRAIN NUMBER	ARRIVAL	NOTES
Berlin Zoobahnhof			
2312	1	1621+1	R, 1, Sleeper
1612	X2000/541	0638+1	R, 1, Sleeper
Copenhagen (København) H via Malmö catamaran			
0606	X2000/521	1245	R, 2, Mon–Fri
0712	IC 287	1617	R
0812	X2000.525	1445	R, 2
1012	X2020/529	1645	R, 2
1118	IC 31	1958	R, 2
1412	X2000/537	2045	R, 2
1512	IC 39	2245	R, 2
2312	1	0845+1	R, 2, Sleeper
Helsinki			
1800	Silja Line Ferry	0830+1	R, 3
1800	Viking Line Ferry	0900+1	R, 4
Oslo Sentral			
0706	61	1325	
1542	57	2205	Sat
1642	X2000/8463	2228	Sun–Fri, 5

Daily, unless otherwise noted

R Reservations required. Seat reservaions required on Swedish trains for journeys longer than 150 kilometers.

Schedules will change when the Øresund Bridge opens July 1, 2000, connecting Sweden and Denmark via rail.

1. Change trains in Malmö.
2. Change in Malmö to catamaran service provided by two companies: Pilen and Flyvedabene. Sailings from Malmö use Skeppsbron dock and two different docks are used in Copenhagen. Havnegade is used by Pilen; Nyhavn by Flyvebådene. Sailings at hourly intervals throughout the day. Journey time 45 minutes. The schedules used here are from Havnegade. Rail tickets are valid on catamaran sailings, with supplemental payment on board. Connecting buses run between Havnegade dock and Copenhagen H. rail station (15-minute journey). Malmö rail station is about a 15-minute walk from Skeppsbron Dock. Public transport/taxis available at the station.

3. Silja Line ferries depart daily except May 2, 4, 6, September 12, 14, 16, and December 24. Silja Line docks are Stockholm Värtahamnen and Helsinki Eteläsatama.

4. Viking Line ferries depart daily except May 4, 6, 8, 10 and 12. Viking Line docks are Stockholm Stadsgarden and Helsinki Katajanokka.

5. Change trains in Arvika.

---

a replica of the ship's cannons and be serving soup from a large cauldron in the ship's galley. For details: *Tel:* 519 548 00; *Fax:* 08 789 2450.

Winter travelers plan ahead to experience Stockholm 2000, a huge city festival. Set to become an annual winter festival, events and activities run from December 27, 1999–January 9, 2000, and include several parties on New Year's Eve. *Tel:* 08 442 8000 or watch it on TV in your hotel room. For information on the party of the century set to include international artists, dance, games, stories, food and drink on seven floors call, *Tel:* 08 506 20 200. For more information visit www.event.stoinfo.se or *E-mail:* info@stoinfo.se.

Day Excursions

We have selected a group of day excursions that will give you an excellent cross section of life in Sweden. **Eskilstuna** is often referred to as "Sweden's Sheffield," although it bears little resemblance to its English counterpart. Next is a trip southward through Ostergotland, where the city of **Norrkoping** will unfold its industrial lifestyles.

Uppsala brings another contrast, that of a university town. Admittedly, planning day excursions in Sweden is made somewhat difficult by the distances involved between the centers of population, but all of these are within reasonable travel times and well worth the visit.

Day Excursion to

Eskilstuna

SWEDEN'S STEEL CENTER

Depart from Stockholm Central Station

Distance by Train: 73 miles (117 km)
Average Train Time: 1 hour
City Dialing Code: 16
Tourist Information Office: Företagens Hus at Munktellstorget
Tel: (01) 610–7000; *Fax:* (01) 614–9500

E-mail: info@turism.eskilstuna.se

Hours: June–August 0900–1800 Monday–Friday; 1000–1600 Saturday–Sunday;
September–May 0900–1700 Monday–Friday

Exit by the front of the station and follow Drottninggatan Street all the way down to Hamngatan. Turn left onto Hamngatan and walk two blocks to Tullgatan. Turn right and cross two small bridges. During summer only (June through August), the tourist office *in* the rail station is open 1000–1800.

Eskilstuna is unique in that it has preserved its industrial birthplace in the midst of a great industrial expansion. In a quiet section in the center of Sweden's "steel town," the well-preserved **Rademacher Forges** stand today just as they have for the last 300 years. Be certain to include a visit to this area during your day excursion.

The Rademacher Forges are the scene of many entertainment programs for visitors to Eskilstuna. In spring and late summer, the "Eskilstuna Guards" present concerts there. Folk dancing and theater performances may be seen in this locale throughout July. Descendants of the "smiths" are still at work forming gold, copper, and iron into colorful trinkets for sale.

The forges were erected in 1658 under the supervision of Reinhold Rademacher. Originally twenty in number, six have been preserved as a tribute to the heritage of modern Eskilstuna. The entire area surrounding the forges was restored in 1959 to commemorate the city's tricentennial. The **Faktorimuseet** is a museum of technology and industrial and cultural history situated in the old Musket Factory.

To expedite your arrival and orientation in the Eskilstuna station, look for

Stockholm—Eskilstuna

DEPART STOCKHOLM CENTRAL	TRAIN NUMBER	ARRIVE ESKILSTUNA STATION	NOTES
0654	3909	0800	Mon–Sat
0854	3915	1000	
1054	3921	1200	
1254	3927	1400	

DEPART ESKILSTUNA	TRAIN NUMBER	ARRIVE STOCKHOLM CENTRAL	
1405	3926	1505	
1605	3932	1705	
1805	3938	1905	
2005	3944	2105	
2205	3950	2305	

Daily, unless otherwise noted
Distance: 73 miles (117 km)

a RESTAURANG sign in red with white letters and a VANTSAL sign in blue with white letters. Enter the station at this point. Inside the station, look for an UPPLYSNING sign on the left just beyond the ticket windows. Ask here for a map of the city and instructions for reaching the main tourist office at Munktellstorget (Företagens Hus).

Eskilstuna is situated in the most populous part of Sweden. Named after the eleventh-century English missionary Saint Eskil, Eskilstuna is the center of the Swedish steel industry. Its parks and squares, combined with its sparkling charm, do seem, however, to make it unlike any steel town visited previously.

A statue of Saint Eskil stands in the churchyard of the **Fors Kyrka.** Both the statue and the church are worthy of a visit. The church and statue are marked as No. 6 on the Eskilstuna map. It can be one of your stops when you are en route back to the railway station, which is No. 24 on the map.

Eskilstuna's town charter dates from 1659. In 1971, five surrounding rural communities, and the town of Torshälla, merged with Eskilstuna. Torshälla is more than 650 years old. Its name was derived from the Nordic god, Thor, who was worshiped by offertory gatherings of the barbarians occupying Torshälla.

Some 50 prehistoric monuments are in the immediate area surrounding Eskilstuna, the best known being the **Sigurd Rock** carving—Scandinavia's first "strip cartoon." The tourist information office can help in finding transportation to the carvings.

The **Park Zoo** (Parken Zoo) in Eskilstuna ranks as one of Scandinavia's most visited tourist attractions. Hours: May–September at 1000 daily. In addition to the zoological gardens, there are an amusement park known as the **Tivoli,** a heated swimming pool with water slides, and **Phantom Land,** a popular play area for children. For the younger set, the zoological garden offers its famous Flamingo Valley and a petting zoo in its animal park. The zoo is noted for its collection of animals that are unique and rare to Sweden, including a dwarf panda, walruses, and a family of white tigers. In the wild, the white tiger is thought to be extinct. To our knowledge, Eskilstuna's Park Zoo and the Mirage Hotel in Las Vegas, Nevada, are the only places in the world where one can still see these animals in any number.

The city is well endowed with works of art. The **art museum** (open daily, except Monday, 1200–1600) is particularly proud of its collection of Swedish art from the seventeenth century to the present. Exhibitions of contemporary art succeed each other at intervals of between three and four weeks throughout the year.

Eskilstuna's **Djurgård open-air museum** of cultural history is centered on **Sörmlandsgården,** a typical nineteenth-century farm commune, and Herrgärden, a manor house from the same period. The farm is complete with a hay barn, stables, a storage shed, and a curious apparatus used for shoeing oxen. The manor house includes a number of rooms furnished in different periods of history.

Eight miles outside Eskilstuna by public bus lines is **Sundbyholm Castle.** Built by an illegitimate son of a Swedish king, it has been restored to its original splendor, and a restaurant has been added.

Day Excursion to

Norrköping   THE NORTHERN CACTUS CENTER

Depart from Stockholm Central Station

Distance by Train: 101 miles (163 km)
Average Train Time: 2 hours
City Dialing Code: 11
Tourist Information Office: Tradgardsgatan & Drottninggatan
Tel: (461) 115–1500
Hours: 0900–1900 Monday–Friday; 0900–1500 Saturday–Sunday in summer. September–May, 1000–1700 daily.

Norrkoping's tourist information office is located conveniently near the railway station. You will find it on the corner of Tradgardsgatan and Drottninggatan, 200 meters from the station.

Believe it or not, Ripley's *Believe It or Not* featured Norrkoping many years ago. People would not believe that 25,000 cactus plants were growing in Sweden. It's true. They are growing there even today. The cactus plantation is in **Karl Johans Park** in front of and at the opposite end from the railway station. Approximately 25,000 cactus plants are rearranged annually according to a new theme by the city's gardeners. The motifs vary from year to year, reflecting important events within the community.

The **Karl Johans Park** must be the best-kept park of its kind in the world. Its appearance can only be described as "manicured." From its fountain to its floral arrangements, it reflects a quiet blending of nature's most beautiful assets into an atmosphere of contentment and relaxation. Its tranquillity is broken pleasantly at intervals by the chattering of countless parakeets housed in an aviary near the fountain. Perhaps a primary reason for the high quality of the cactus and floral displays is the presence of Sweden's National School of Gardening and the Flower School.

If roses are your favorites, go to the **Himmelstalundsparken** (Himmelstalund Park) and visit its rose gardens. You can combine this visit with an inspection of the 3,000-year-old Bronze Age rock carvings, also a part of this park, that are to the right of the railway station.

The city is one of Sweden's most important industrial cities. Take a walk in

Stockholm—Norrköping

DEPART STOCKHOLM CENTRAL	TRAIN NUMBER	ARRIVE NORRKÖPING	NOTES
0606	X2000/8521	0730	R, 1
0812	X2000/525	0936	R
0712	IC 287	0827	2
1012	X2000/529	1135	R
1118	IC 31	1305	2
1200	X2000/8533	1335	R

DEPART NORRKÖPING	TRAIN NUMBER	ARRIVE STOCKHOLM CENTRAL	NOTES
1425	X2000/8534	1553	R
1450	IR 8336	1635	2
1520	X2000/536	1647	R, Fri
1620	X2000/8538	1747	R, Sun–Fri
1650	IC 286	1841	2
1820	X2000/542	1947	R
2020	X2000/8546	2147	R, Sun–Fri
2055	IC 48	2247	2

Daily, unless otherwise noted
R Reservations are required on all X2000 trains and for all journeys of more than 150 km on other trains. Special supplements are payable on X2000 trains.
1. This train runs M-F only.
2. Seat reservations presumably not needed since this trips is only 103 km, but passengers should check at the Stockholm Central Station to be sure before boarding this train.
Distance: 101 miles (163 km)

---

the old industrial section. You'll find industrial buildings dating from the nineteenth century.

The town hall has a carillon that is prized by its citizens. It helps create the ambience of the town that has been referred to often by visitors as the Paris of the North. The time to hear the carillon is at 0955, 1155, 1455, or 1655. Following the carillon performance, it might be a good time to stroll along the banks of the nearby **Motala Ström River** in the old city center. You can follow the river down to the old **Dyer's House** to see how wool was made and dyed in the old days. There's also a cafe where you can relax and have a snack.

While at the tourist information office, inquire about the **Kolmarden–Norrkoping Card.** It's a special ticket that gives you a multitude of visitor admissions and discounts. To mention just a few: sightseeing by boat; entrance to the **Lofstad Castle;** a complimentary ride on the **old No. 1 tram,** restored from circa 1902; and free admission to the animal and nature park, **Kolmarden.**

The ruins of the **Johannisborg Fort** lie on the left of the rail station. All that remain of the Johannisborg Fort now are the gate tower and its ramparts, but these are enough to convey a mental image of how this magnificent construction (started in 1613) must have looked.

Other sights near the railway station are the **Gamla Torget** (Old Square), the Concert and Congress Hall **Louis de Geer**, the **Radhus** (town hall), and the **Hedvigs Kyrka** (German Church). All are clustered in the city's center.

Twenty-five kilometers north of Norrkoping is the largest animal and nature park in Europe—the **Kolmarden Zoo.** There are no bars or cages, and the animals thrive in large outdoor pens. Check with the tourist office for transportation details.

Day Excursion to

Uppsala UNIVERSITY CITY

Depart from Stockholm Central Station

Distance by Train: 40 miles (66 km)
Average Train Time: 43 minutes
City Dialing Code: 18
Tourist Information Office: 8 Fyristorg, 75310 Uppsala
Tel: (018) 27 48 00; *Fax:* (018) 13 28 95
Internet: www.res.till.uppland.nu
E-mail: info@utkab.se
Hours: July–August: 1000–1800 Monday–Friday; 1000–1500 Saturday; 1200–1600 Sunday. September–June: 1000–1800 Monday–Friday; 1000–1500 Saturday.
    Five-minute walk from the railway station. Exit the station and walk diagonally through the small park in front to the main street, Kungsgatan. Turn right, then turn left on Vaksalagatan (the next crossing). Walk until you reach the square (Stora Torget) where all the city buses meet. Follow the street Drottninggatan from the square and cross the small river Fyrisan. Turn right immediately after the bridge, and the tourist office is identified by the traditional i sign.

No other town in Sweden has such a long recorded history as Uppsala. This is where Sweden began. As far back as the sixth century, it was the political and religious center of the expanding Swedish kingdom. According to the ancient legends, pagans from all reaches of the kingdom came to Uppsala every ninth year to feast and offer up sacrifices until the eleventh century, when Christianity began to take over. Legend has it that one of the kings of the period, King Aun, got all wrapped up in the nine-year cycle by sacrificing one of his sons each cycle. His tenth and last son put an end to old dad—and to the cycle, too!

Stockholm–Uppsala

Note: In addition to trains shown here, there is local train service between Stockholm and Uppsala; get information at Stockholm Central station.

DEPART STOCKHOLM CENTRAL	TRAIN NUMBER	ARRIVE UPPSALA	NOTES
0825	IR 958	0904	
0945	IC 842	1024	Sat–Sun
1025	IC 882	1104	
1340	IC 844	1419	Sun–Fri

DEPART UPPSALA	TRAIN NUMBER	ARRIVE STOCKHOLM CENTRAL	NOTES
1536	IC 845	1615	Sat–Sun
1659	IC 963	1735	Mon–Fri
1759	IR 965	1835	Mon–Fri
1842	IC 827	1920	Mon–Fri
1941	IC 847	2020	Sat–Sun only
2059	IC 885	2135	
2137	IC 849	2215	Sun–Fri

Daily, unless otherwise noted
Seat reservations presumably not needed since this trip is only 66 km, but passengers should check at the Stockholm Central station to be sure before boarding these trains.
Distance: 40 miles (66 km)

Modern Uppsala won't remind you of Oxford or Heidelberg—or Bryn Mawr, for that matter. Uppsala is a university town but with an academic environment distinctly its own. The city and the area surrounding it enshrine a great deal of Swedish history encompassing religion (pagan and Christian alike), academe, and politics. This composite results in a city of multifaceted interests, architecture, and customs.

Gamla Uppsala (Old Uppsala) lies 3 miles north of the present city center. Here, the graves of the sixth-century Ynglinga Dynasty kings are found. The pagan religion of the Vikings persisted here well into the eleventh century. A twelfth-century church, heralding the advent of Christianity, then replaced the pagan temple. The area is now an open-air museum, accessible to visitors daily during June, July, and August.

Uppsala Castle stands on a hill overlooking the city. Begun in the 1540s by King Gustav Vasa as a symbol of his power over the church, it was completed during the reign of Queen Christina. The king had cannon mounted on the castle pointing at the church. They still point that way today. Partially destroyed by fire in 1702, the castle has been restored. After the extensive renovation in 1994, you can now visit new parts of the castle on a 45-minute guided tour conducted in English at 1200, 1330, and 1530 from June 18 through August 8 and at 1100 and 1500 August 9–22. You'll see the Hall of State and the castle church's uncovered altar wall.

The great **Hall of State** is frequently the scene of historic events. Both the coronation banquet for Gustavus Adolphus and Queen Christina's abdication took place within the castle's walls. The castle is open 1100–1600 daily from May 1–August 22. A more restricted schedule is followed during the remainder of the year.

Three-quarters of Uppsala was destroyed by fire in 1702. It was in the subsequent period of reconstruction that the character of the city changed. The university and its scholars began to dominate, and the reputation of the university spread throughout the civilized world. The present university building was opened in 1887.

Among the collections in Exhibition Hall of The Uppsala University Library (located on Dag Hammarskjolds vag 1) are the Silver Bible from the sixth century, medieval manuscripts, and musical notations by Mozart. Take Bus No. 6, 7, 22, 26, or 52. *Tel:* 018 471 39 00. *Internet:* www.ub.uu.se. Open: 0900–1800 Monday–Friday, 1000–1800 Saturday, 1100–1600 Sunday (May 16–Sept. 12).

In Uppsala, Saint Erik, Saint Olof, and Saint Lars' church is usually referred to as **The Cathedral**. Two of its patron saints, Erik and Olof, were Christian kings in Scandinavia during the eleventh and twelfth centuries, when the Christians finally had the pagans on the run. Lars died a martyr's death in Rome in A.D. 258. Building of the cathedral started in the late thirteenth century, and it took a century and a half to complete. It has been ravaged by fires, and its towers collapsed, but with Swedish determination it was restored. English-language tours of the Uppsala Cathedral are conducted during the summer months.

Switzerland

Switzerland is a year-round wonderland of astonishing beauty and one of the most multilingual countries in Europe. You can experience several different cultures encompassing four national languages—all within one neat little country. The German-speaking Swiss make up 65 percent of the population; French, 18 percent; Italian, 10 percent; and Romansch, 1 percent; and 70-plus dialects lend a special charisma to tiny villages and hamlets. And many Swiss can speak all four languages and English, too.

The diversity doesn't end there—from majestic snow-capped mountains to languid palm-fringed lakes, from cowbells and yodeling to craftsmanship and incredible feats of railroad engineering—Switzerland is surprising.

For more information about Switzerland, contact the Switzerland Tourism Offices of North America:

Internet: **www.switzerlandtourism.com;** *E-mail:* stnewyork@switzerland tourism.com

Chicago: 150 North Michigan Avenue, Suite 2930, Chicago. IL 60601. *Tel:* (312) 630-5840

Los Angeles: 222 North Sepulveda Boulevard, Suite 1570, El Segundo, CA 90245. *Tel:* (310) 335-5980; *Fax:* (310) 335-5982

New York: 608 Fifth Avenue, New York, NY 10020. *Tel:* (212) 262-2090; *Fax:* (212) 262-6116

Toronto: 926 The East Mall, Etobicoke, Ontario M9B 6K1. *Tel:* (416) 695-2090; *Fax:* (416) 695-2774

Banking

- **Currency:** Swiss Franc (CHF)
- **Exchange rate at time of press:** 1.48 CHF = $1.00 U.S.
- **Hours:** 0830-1630 Monday-Friday

Communications

- **Country Dialing Code:** 41
  For telephone calls within Switzerland, dial zero (0) preceding area code. You can buy a Calling Card for calls within Switzerland at any Swiss post office. International calls can be placed from public phones at the post office and some major railway stations.
- **Direct dial:** AT&T: 0-800-890011; MCI: 0-800-890222; Sprint: 0-800-899777

Rail Travel in Switzerland

The Swiss are well known for their excellence in clock production, and they know how to run a railroad with the same finesse—on time. Rail travelers from North America may take advantage of the "Fly Rail Baggage Service" program by checking their luggage through from all airports and all airline companies to one of the 116 railway stations offering the service. When returning to North America, they can also check their luggage through to their destination airport (20 CHF per bag).

According to the Swiss, only the "Man in the Moon" knows how dense the network of railroads in Switzerland *really* is. Although Switzerland is only 216 miles from north to south and 137 miles from east to west, more than 3,000 miles of rail lines run through it. Even mountains don't stop the Swiss. They either tunnel through them or scale their heights with funiculars or cog railways. Switzerland has one of the longest railroad tunnels, the highest railroad, plus more bridges, tunnels, and other engineering works per square mile than any other country in the world.

The Swiss Federal Railways (CFF/SBB) accepts the following railpasses that can be purchased in advance of your departure for Europe: the 17-country **Eurailpass,** the 5-country **Europass,** the **Swiss Pass,** and **Swiss Card.**

The **Swiss Pass** provides unlimited travel on Swiss Federal Railways, private railways, lake steamers, and city and bus lines. The second adult pass purchased is 40 percent off the price of the first adult pass. Children age 6-15 are 50 percent adult fare; children under age 6 travel free.

Swiss Pass

CONSECUTIVE DAYS	1ST CLASS	2ND CLASS
4 days	$264	$188
8 days	$316	$238
15 days	$368	$288
21 days	$403	$320
1 month	$508	$400

Flexipass

3 days of travel within a 1-month period	$264	$176
Additional days	$30	$24

Swiss for Two

Prices are per person when 2 people are traveling together, includes 40 percent companion discount. Children under age 16 travel free with a parent.

	1ST CLASS	2ND CLASS
4 days	$211	$150
8 days	$253	$190
15 days	$294	$230
21 days	$322	$256
1 month	$406	$320
3 days in 15	$221	$141
Additional days	$24	$19

The **Swiss Card** is a good buy for skiers—it provides one round trip rail journey within a 1-month period for $166 (U.S.) First Class or $128 Second Class. Children under age 16 are free if traveling with a parent; otherwise, children age 6-15 pay half adult fare in Second Class and 40 percent of the adult fare in First Class.

The **Swiss Family Card** provides for children under age 16 to travel free when traveling with an adult. This card is *free* when you purchase any Swiss Pass.

Swiss Federal Railways provide the following bonuses to holders of a **Eurailpass or Europass:**
- Biel–Solothurn (on the Aare River)—ship free
- Schaffhausen–Kreuzlingen (on the Rhine River)—ship free
- Steamer services on lakes of Biel, Brienz, Geneva, Lucerne, Murten, Neuchâtel, Thun, and Zürich—free
- Alpnachstad–Mont Pilatus (see Lucerne section)—cable railway 35 percent discount
- Burgenstock cable railway—50 percent discount
- Jungfrau Region Railways—25 percent discount
- Kriens–Mont Pilatus (near Lucerne)—cable railway—35 percent discount
- Lake Constance (Bodensee)
    Romanshorn–Friedrichhafen (Germany)—ship 50 percent discount
    Rorschach–Lindau (Germany)—ship 50 percent discount
    Rorschach–Romanshorn (Germany)—ship 35 percent discount

- Transportation Museum in Lucerne—35 percent off entrance fee
- Vitznau Rigi Railways—25 percent discount

Some of Switzerland's most scenic railroads (below) also accept Eurailpass or Europass; most private railroads, however, do not, although some offer discounts (above). Reservations are mandatory and cost extra. Remember to take along your passport for border crossings.

- *Bernina Express*–Chur–St. Moritz–Bernina Pass–Poschiavo–Tirano. Runs daily in the summer and only to and from Tirano in the winter. Trip is 2½ hours from St. Moritz or 4 hours from Chur.
- *Centovalli Railway*—Locarno–S. Maria Maggiore–Domodossola. Runs all year long.
- *Glacier Express*—Zermatt–Brig–Andermatt–Chur–Davos/St. Moritz. Journey runs daily in summer and winter. Trip is 7½ hours and passes through 91 tunnels and over 291 bridges. Eurailpass/Europass valid only between Davos/St. Moritz and Disentis. You must purchase an additional point-to-point ticket for the portion from Disentis to Zermatt.
- *Golden Pass*—Lucerne–Brünig Panoramic Express–Interlaken—Jungfraujoch—Salon bleu–Crystal Panoramic Express–Montreux–Genève. Runs daily all year.
- *William Tell Express*—Lucerne–Fluelen–St. Gotthard–Locarno/Lugano. Combination steamer and rail journey; includes gourmet Swiss lunch. Reservations compulsory; includes seats on the boat, train, journey documentation, and souvenir. Runs daily May–October.

RAIL TRAVEL NOTE: A timetable bookshop is operated by the Swiss Federal Railways in St. Gallen, Switzerland, where you may purchase the current offical timetables of many European countries, as well as a wide range of rail travel literature and rail maps. St. Gallen is one hour by train from Zürich in the direction of Austria and Germany. Call at Room 224 in the St. Gallen rail station or telephone ahead on 071–222–1021, extension 208, for details.

For an in-depth look at Switzerland's incredible rail system, *Switzerland by Train* (40 minutes) presents the adventure of some of the area's classic rail journeys. This video excites the novice and the expert alike. To order visit www.railpass.com or call (800) 722–7151.

Base City . . .

Bern (Berne)

City Dialing Code: 31
Internet: www.berntourism.ch

Bern has the unique distinction of being the only city in Europe joined by all three of Europe's high-speed trains—the TGV from Paris, the ICE from Berlin, and the Cisalpino from Milan.

Bern, the federal capital of Switzerland, was built between the twelfth and eighteenth centuries. According to legend, it was named after the first animal caught in the area, a bear, and bears have played a part in its history ever since. The city's bear pits, where the animals are raised and displayed, are a "must" stop on any tour.

The most striking thing about Bern is its medieval appearance. Some of the buildings in the city's old town date from the thirteenth and fourteenth centuries. The low silhouette of its roof lines appears to be different from those of most of Europe's other cities with origins in the same era—and indeed it is, for there is a medieval ordinance still in effect today that mandates each roof line be at a different level from adjoining structures. This ancient architectural asset is most visible when you view the city from the Nydeggbrücke Bridge crossing the Aare en route to the bear pits. If you miss it, you'll have another opportunity when you view the city from the location of its rose gardens on the high bluff of the Aare's right bank.

Bern is a medieval city, yet it is a new city as well. Over the centuries, Bern's citizens have developed a remarkable means of combining modern living with the centuries-old facades of their surroundings. It is cosmopolitan, with a wide selection of restaurants, hotels, museums, and concert halls. Modern Bern has grown well beyond the curve of the Aare and into the surrounding foothills. The main commercial, cultural, and political activities of the city, however, still take place in its old sector.

The Aare River embraces Bern in a great natural bend. Like the river, you too will embrace this ancient Swiss city, once you have trod its cobblestone streets.

In summer, Bern leads you to believe it is the geranium capital of the world as well as being the federal capital of Switzerland. These flowers bloom everywhere in an eye-dazzling display of color. Bern was once voted Europe's most beautiful city of flowers. You will be bewitched by Bern, beguiled by its bears, and satisfied with its sights.

Arriving by Air

Switzerland's international airports, Basel, Geneva, and Zürich connect incoming flights with trains to Bern. Bern is only 1 hour and 29 minutes away from Zürich's airport and under two hours from Geneva's by comfortable passenger trains that depart daily from the airports every 30 minutes. In Zürich, the rail station lies immediately beneath the airport's terminal. In Geneva, the rail station and the airport terminal are connected by a plaza. At the Bern-Belp Airport (9 kilometers south of the City Centre), direct connections can be made to and from many European cities, as well as shuttle bus service directly to Bern's railway station.

Arriving by Train

Bern's modern rail station is a small city within a city, with an impressive array of facilities, including a spacious underground arcade that connects at its surface entrances with the city's fabled, arcaded shopping walkways. Direct rail transport from Bern to Amsterdam, Berlin, Brussels, Luxembourg, Milan, Paris, Rome, Venice, and Zürich is available.

Fifty-four trains a day depart Bern for Zürich Hauptbahnhof with no change of trains required; 34 of these continue on to the Zürich airport following the city stop. Forty-four trains a day depart Bern for Geneva. Upon arrival in Geneva, stay aboard, and 8 minutes later you will be at the Geneva airport.

Bern's Railway Station. Bern's railway station is a model of efficiency and functionalism. Trains are reached from its ground level via ramps, thus making the use of baggage carts practical.

With your baggage stacked in one of the station's baggage carts, leave the train platform by descending the ramp, then turn in the direction of track No. 1 and walk to the end of the passageway, where you will emerge into the station's underground arcade, with its myriad of shops and services. You'll see the escalators directly ahead.

Escalators take you to the other levels of the station. Elevator service is also available. If you have your luggage on a cart, use the elevators. At street level you will find the **train information** and **Bern Tourismus** information offices, plus additional facilities such as shops and restaurants. Snack bars and fruit stands prevail on the ground level; more extensive food-service facilities are on the upper levels, ending at the top of the escalators with a full-service restaurant.

Baggage storage. Visitors burdened with baggage may want to use the coin lockers on the ground (train) level or find the area marked FLY BAGGAGE (baggage room) on the street level. Taxi service is available from the street level—follow the pictographs—but check with Bern Tourismus before attempting to use the public-bus and streetcar services. Their access ramps, fares, ticket machines, and so forth can be confusing.

A suburban train station is located on the underground arcade level. To reach it, continue past the escalators that run to the street level and watch for its entrance on the left side of the passageway. This system is operated by a private Swiss railroad. Swiss Passes are accepted and Eurailpasses and Europasses are accepted by *some* private Swiss railroads such as RBS. Check prior to boarding the train.

The Bern station, like most of the major rail terminals in Switzerland, will accept your baggage and check it through the Zürich or Geneva airports directly to your U.S. port of entry. Trains for both airports depart the Bern station every 30 minutes throughout the day. Place your baggage on a train an hour or so in advance of your departure for the airport.

- **Money-exchange** facilities, two of them, are located on the ground level of the station. Both may be reached by turning right, just before the elevators, as you come out of the passageway leading from the trains. Both will be on your right as you proceed into the station's arcade. The first office, marked CHANGE SBB, is operated by the Swiss railroads. Opening hours: June–October 15, 0615–2145 daily; October 16–May 31, 0615–2045. There is also an ATM.

    There are several banks in the plaza surrounding the station. The rates of exchange are standard throughout the city each day, however, and the rail-station money-exchange facilities are the most convenient. There is also a money-exchange machine available 24 hours a day near the station at Schwanengasse 4.

- **Train information, reservations, and railpass validations** can be obtained from the rail-reservations center immediately across the passageway from the tourist information office. Look for the blue **i** sign. Hours: 0800–1900 Monday–Friday; 0800–1700 Saturday. The center dispenses rail information, reservations, and other services, including validation of rail passes. Keep in mind that your Eurailpass is accepted on all of the Swiss federal railways and lake steamers; on the other hand, it is accepted only on a few of the private railroads. To be certain, check your day excursions plans with the train information office. For example, if you plan to ascend the **Jungfrau**, a Eurailpass or Europass will take you to **Interlaken**, where you must purchase a ticket for the private railroads leading out of **Interlaken** to **Grindelwald** or **Lauterbrunnen** and **Wengen** en route to the **Jungfrau.**

- **Tourist information** and **hotel reservations** are available at **Bern Tourismus,** one of the most complete information centers in Europe. Turn left coming off the escalator from the ground level, then right at the passageway leading to the street. The office will be a few steps farther on your right. It is identified by a green **i** sign. Hours during summer (June–September): 0900–2030 daily; remainder of the year, 0900–1830 Monday–Saturday; 1000–1700 Sunday. There is no fee for hotel reservations.

Ask here for the booklets *Bern Information* and *Bern Excursions*, the latter being an informative publication listing more day excursions from Bern by rail, lake steamer, and postal buses.

- **Hotel Reservations** can also be made by using an automatic telephone system located beside Bern Tourismus. The automatic telephone system makes finding and booking a hotel an easy task. There is a lighted board showing the locations of the hotels along with pictures of the hotels and their room rates. Press the button for your choice, and you'll be immediately connected with the hotel by telephone to discuss vacancies.

Sights/Attractions/Tours

There are two excellent means of sightseeing in Bern: on foot or by comfortable motor coach escorted by a multilingual guide. From June through September the bus departs from in front of the railway station at 1400 daily; from April 1–May 31 and October at 1400 Monday through Saturday; January–March and November–December on Saturdays only at 1400. The bus tour takes 2 hours and tickets may be purchased at the tourist office for 23 CHF (half fare for children).

If interested in the walking tour, ask at the tourist office for the *Short City Sightseeing Map.* It leads you right through the heart of Bern's ancient walled city to its famed **bear pits** (open daily 0900–1700 June–September and 1000–1600 October–March remainder of the year 1000–1600) Friday–Sunday only. From there you return to your point of departure by a different route. According to the map, the entire route can be covered in approximately 1 hour, but without any stops en route. Plan for a minimum of 2 hours and consider yourself lucky if you make it in 3. (According to the tourist office, no one has ever returned within the hour.)

Be certain to see the *Zeitglockenturm,* the city's famous clock tower. It first began ticking in the year 1250, and it is still the city's official timepiece today. The clock's glockenspiel starts promptly at 4 minutes before the hour as accompaniment to a parade of armed bear figures following a rooster. It's quite a show. What makes it tick? Take the fascinating 45-minute guided tour, held at 1630 daily from May through October, *inside* the clock tower. Purchase your ticket (6 CHF) at Bern Tourismus from the tour guide, or at your hotel. Another option is the stroll through the old town, which includes visits to the cathedral and the clock tower. Tours depart daily at 1100 from the station and at 1115 from the Clock Tower, June–September. During July and August, an identical tour departs from the bear pits and cost 12 CHF.

Another unusual feature of Bern is its **shopping arcades**—nearly 4 miles of them. They line the route of the walking tour suggested by Bern Tourismus and offer one of the finest selections of wares and food to be found anywhere

Train Connections to Other Base Cities from Bern (Berne)

DEPART	TRAIN NUMBER	ARRIVE	NOTES
Amsterdam Centraal			
1148	EC 104	2054	
1248	IC 870	2154	1
2148	IC 996	0857+1	2
Berlin Zoobahnhof			
0948	ICE 72	1907	R
1047	EC 108	2006	3
1148	EC 104	2106	3
1948	IC 886	0801+1	2
Brussels (Bruxelles) Midi/Zuid			
0648	IC 952	1445	1
1048	EC 108	2006	4
1148	EC 104	1945	1
1448	EC 90	2248	
2219	498	0645+1	R, Sleeper
Budapest Keleti			
1945	IC 941	1213+1	5
Hamburg Hauptbahnhof			
0748	IC 854	1532	1
0948	ICE 72	1752	6
1148	EC 104	1932	1
1348	IC 972	2132	1
2032	CIS 46	0838+1	R, 2
Copenhagen (København) H			
1548	IC 878	0958+1	2
Luxembourg			
0648	IC 952	1159	1
1148	EC 104	1650	1
1448	EC 90	1956	
Lyon Part-Dieu			
0832	TGV EC 420	1404	R, 7

Milan (Milano)

0734	CIS 41	1045	
0850	IC 863	1245	
1258	IC 333	1645	
1526	EC 91	1925	
1734	CIS4 5	2045	

Munich (München)

0610	IC 705	1153	8
0814	IC 711	1358	8
1214	IC 721	1748	8
1614	IC 729	2155	8

Paris Gare de Lyon

0645	422	1127	9
0832	TGV EC 420	1309	R
1049	IC 716	1631	10
1649	426	2150	9

Rome (Roma)

0734	CIS 41	1635	R, 11
0850	IC 863	1825	11
2226	EN 313	0940+1	R, Sleeper

Vienna (Wien)

0814	IC 711	1845	8
1214	IC 721	2245	8
2114	IC 743	0805+1	5

Zürich Hauptbahnhof

InterCity (IC) depart at 14 and 45 minutes past the hour. Journey time 1 hour 12 minutes; local trains depart at 50 minutes past the hour. Journey time 1 hour 41 minutes.

Daily, unless otherwise noted
R Reservations required
Thalys high-speed trains require supplement
1. Change trains to Basel.
2. Change to sleeper (R) train in Basel.
3. Change trains in Mannheim.
4. Change trains in Cologne (Koln).
5. Change in Zürich to Sleeper (R) train.
6. Change trains in Kassel.

7. Change trains in Dijon.
8. Change trains in Zürich.
9. Change in Frasne to a TGV(R) train.
10. Change in Lausanne to a TGV(R) train.
11. Change to Italian Eurostar train (R) in Milan.

---

in the world. The shopping arcades are completely covered, so they are weatherproof as well as traffic-free and totally delightful. On Tuesday and Saturday mornings, there are markets where Swiss farmers sell their meat and produce. Shop the city's arcades Monday–Friday 0900–1830 (until 2100 on Thursday), and 0815–1600 Saturday. Pick up a shopping guide at the tourist offices.

Or, if museums appeal to you, Bern has plenty to choose from, including the **Swiss Alpine Museum,** the **Museum of Communication,** and the **Einstein House**—even a **Museum of Psychiatry.**

For a view of Bern from an unusual perspective, take the **city tour by raft** on the river Aare (tickets cost 30 CHF, 20 CHF for children). The 1½-hour rafting tour departs at 1700 daily, June–September, from Schwellenmätteli (indicated on the city map) and includes a ten-passenger raft, life jackets, paddles, and, of course, a guide.

Day Excursions

Bern is an ideal base for day excursions to almost any point in Switzerland. Geneva is 1 hour and 40 train minutes to the west; you can reach Zürich to the east by rail in only 1 hour and 10 minutes. Travel north and, in the same amount of time, your train will set you down in Basel on the banks of the Rhine.

The five day excursions that we have selected for this edition reveal the natural grandeur of the country. The **Golden Pass** adventure takes you through Alpine surroundings, in the comfort of a vista-dome rail car, to Lake Geneva and a cruise on the lake before returning to Bern. The outing to **Interlaken** unfolds a panorama of towering peaks along the shore of the Lake of Thun, where again you have the opportunity of a lake cruise to conclude a memorable day.

Picture-postcard perfect, **Lucerne** will charm you with its scenery, cuisine, and ambience. Promenade along its ancient walkways, scale nearby Mount Pilatus, or cruise the Lake of Lucerne during your visit.

For a peek at a Disney-type setting that has been going strong since the eleventh century, journey to **Rheinfelden,** where the mighty Rhine River swirls past a medieval setting that stirs the imagination. Or travel to Brig to catch the *Glacier Express* to **Zermatt** to view the magnificent Matterhorn.

Day Excursion to

The Golden Pass
THE ALPS A LA TRAIN

Depart from Bern

Distance by Train: 65 miles (104 km) to Montreux
Average Train Time: 10 hours, 25 minutes
Montreux Tourist Information: Place du Debarcadere, 1820
Tel: 962–8484; *Fax:* 963–7895
Internet: www.montreux.ch
Hours: October 1–March 1 open Monday–Friday, 0900–1800. April 1–September 30 open Monday–Saturday, 0900–1800; Sunday 0900–1200.

Dollar for dollar, or franc for franc, this day excursion is one of the best train-travel values in Europe. The Lucerne-Interlaken-Montreux rail route provides an exciting variety of landscapes and cultures. The Montreux-Bernese-Oberland Railroad (MOB) operates the **Crystal Panoramic Express,** the **Golden Panoramic Express,** and the **Panoramic Express.** These trains offer an unobstructed view of the breathtaking scenery between Zweisimmen and Montreux.

Before departure, check with Bern Tourismus. Inform them you are going on the Golden Pass trip and pick up the booklet *Bern Excursions.* (The booklet is usually available in the train information office as well.) Trains run through the Golden Pass rather frequently, and you may want to follow a different schedule. We selected the **Crystal Panoramic Express,** a luxury first-class train with panoramic-view windows and bar car on the portion of the route from Zweisimmen to Montreux and vice versa.

There is ample time for a leisurely lunch at the Majestic Hotel (located between the rail station and the city pier) in Montreux before boarding a lake steamer to Chillon. Disembark and go ashore to visit its famous castle. **Chateau de Chillon** is a beautifully restored eleventh-century castle that was made famous by Lord Byron in his poetic story of the imprisonment of Francois de Bonivard. After touring the castle, board another lake steamer back to Montreux. Then, ride the funicular adjacent to the steamer dock to the **Lausanne** train station, and board your train back to Bern. Whew! It's a day loaded with extras.

Check the weather report the night before embarking on this day excursion. The clearer the day, the better. You will be viewing some of the Alps' most spectacular scenery, and if it's shrouded in clouds, it just might spoil your day. To get the weather report in English, dial 162 on any Swiss telephone.

InterCity trains usually depart from the Bern railway station on track 6, but double-check just to be sure. The destination of this train is **Brig,** and it makes a stop at **Thun** (pronounced "tune") before it arrives at **Spiez.** At

Bern—The Golden Pass

Depart Bern 0922	Train IC 910	Arrive Spiez 0954
Depart Spiez 1003	Train 2346	Arrive Zweisimmen 1039
Depart Zweisimmen 1044	Train 2	Arrive Montreux 1225

Lake steamers depart Montreux pier at 1235 and 1350; stop at Château-de-Chillon is 10 to 13 min after leaving Montreux. (Summer schedules.)

Lake steamers depart Château-de-Chillon for Lausanne-Ouchy dock at 1538, 1628, and 1714; journey time to Lausanne-Ouchy is 1 hr 27 to 46 min; steamers also stop at Montreux 12 to 17 min after departing Château pier.

Mainline trains depart Montreux station for Lausanne at 10 and 35 min after the hour throughout the day; journey time to Lausanne is 21 min. There are other local trains that make several stops and take longer.

DEPART LAUSANNE STATION	TRAIN NUMBER	ARRIVE BERN HBF
1502	IC 729	1611
1602	IC 735	1711
1625	2737	1739
1702	IC 737	1811
1725	2739	1839
1802	IC 739	1911
1825	2741	1939
1902	IC 741	2011
1925	2743	2039

Thun, the beautiful Lake of Thun comes into view. As you approach Spiez, you'll see Mount Niesen (7,750 feet) towering over this quiet town on the southwestern shore of the lake.

In Spiez you have 11 minutes to cross a platform to board the next train—time enough to enjoy the breathtaking view. **Zweisimmen,** the next stop and transfer point, lies almost halfway between Spiez and Montreux. When you depart Spiez, you will enter the Golden Pass.

The transfer at Zweisimmen places you aboard MOB's *Crystal Panoramic Express* on a narrow-gauge railroad, with Montreux as its destination. The best instruction here is to "follow the crowd" as you move between the standard- and narrow-gauge trains. The *Panoramic Express* narrow-gauge train will make two stops before reaching Montreux (three from mid-December through March, when it calls at **Saanenmose**r during the skiing season).

The first regular stop is **Gstaad,** which, you may recall, is the alpine-resort retreat of many famous movie stars, including Elizabeth Taylor and Roger Moore. During his lifetime, Richard Burton frequented the area, and the late David Niven maintained a chalet there on a mountainside for many years. **Chateau d'Oex** (pronounced "day") is an alpine resort, too, but more at the family level, frequented by the Genevese when they grow tired of viewing beautiful Lake Geneva—possibly because it's flat.

Our "wood pile theory" can be tested—at least two-thirds of it—because you will be passing from a German-speaking area into one of French habitation. Based on research we have made during several decades of European rail travel, the theory is this: the Germans pile wood with precision, the Italians pile it artistically, and the French stack theirs with an air of independence. The two regular stops are Gstaad and Chateau d'Oex. Watch what happens to the wood piles between these two points. Gstaad, as the name may imply, is German; Chateau d'Oex lies in the French-speaking district.

Approaching Montreux, the train descends 2,000 feet to Lake Geneva in much the same manner as a jet airliner does when entering a landing pattern. It whirls through a series of hairpin curves for almost a half-hour before coming to rest beside the main Montreux railway station. Have your camera handy, for you are going to see some sensational scenery during the descent.

You have several options while visiting Montreux. You can extend your shopping and sightseeing in the city for 1 hour and 50 minutes if you forgo Chillon and yet board the same steamer for Lausanne and not miss any of your friends who may have elected to see the castle made famous by Lord Byron. If it's stormy on Lake Geneva, you can still keep to the schedule by proceeding to Lausanne by rail.

Chillon-bound passengers should scurry to the castle as quickly as possible after the lake steamer docks to ensure maximum use of the time ashore. The steamer proceeds on to the French port of St. Gingolph and then returns to Chillon. Check at the Chillon dock for its return time. Should you miss the boat, you still have another option. Hail a cab back to Montreux, then entrain for Lausanne to join your friends in the dining car en route back to Bern.

Day Excursion to

Interlaken

LAKE OF THUN CRUISE

Depart from Bern

Distance by Train: 37 miles (59 km)
Average Train Time: 50 minutes
City Dialing Code: 33
Tourism Office: Interlaken Tourism office is on the left side of the Höheweg, about a 5-minute walk from the station (the grand promenade), which starts at the West station and ends at Interlacken Ost (East) Station.
Tel: (33) 822–2121; *Fax:* (33) 826–5390
Internet: www.interlakentourism.ch
E-mail: mail@interlakentourism.ch
Hours: July–August, 0800–1830 Monday–Friday; 0800–1700 Saturday; 1700–1900 Sunday. Hours are shorter the rest of the year, and the office is closed Sunday.

Interlaken can best be described as the cultural and social focal point of Switzerland's Alpine areas. The English poet Lord Byron is said to have exclaimed, "It's a dream!" at his first sighting of Interlaken and its surroundings. Nestled between the **Lake of Thun** and the **Lake of Brienz,** Interlaken (Latin for "between the lakes") began in the twelfth century as a small cluster of buildings surrounding a monastery, traces of which can still be seen today.

The town's main thoroughfare, **Höheweg,** is lined with great hotels, shops, and even a grand casino that is set back from the main promenade and banked with such beautiful flowers that one might think it is a retirement home.

For Interlaken, the Höheweg plays the same part as does the Champs-Elysées for Paris or the Via Veneto for Rome—it is *the boulevard,* with the ambience for which the Swiss are famous. Just as in its larger counterparts, you'll find strollers on foot or aboard horse-drawn carriages taking in the sights along with those relaxing over coffee and pastries at the sidewalk cafes. Towering over this entire scene is the **Jungfrau,** a massive mountain that tops out at 13,642 feet above sea level, a mere 11 miles south of Interlaken. On a clear day the view is dazzling.

Believe it or not, the Jungfrau can be scaled by train. Beginning in Interlaken at the Ost (East) rail station, a private cog railroad terminates at the Jungfraujoch station, at 11,333 feet, the highest rail terminal in Europe. The round trip takes the better half of a day, and it should be made only in ideal weather. Furthermore, the round-trip fare is just as steep as the ascent, 169.40 Swiss francs per person first class and 159 francs for second class. Eurailpass or Europass does, however, provide a 25 percent discount. Plan your "assault" on

Bern—Interlaken

There is hourly InterCity (IC) train service from Bern Hauptbahnhof to Interlaken West and Interlaken Ost (East) stations; departures are at 22 min after the hour from 0722; journey time to Interlaken West is 50 min and time to Interlaken Ost is 53 min.

Return hourly IC service departs Interlaken Ost at 45 min after the hour and departs Interlaken West at 50 min after the hour; journey time to Bern from Interlaken West is 48 min.

Distance: 37 miles (59 km)

Lake of Thun Cruise

DEPART INTERLAKEN PIER	ARRIVE THUN DOCK	DEPART THUN STATION	TRAIN NUMBER	ARRIVE BERN HBF
1455	1659	1714	IC 837	1734
1555	1804	1814	IC 884	1834
1655	1907	1914	IC 886	1934

Note: Interlaken Pier is approximately 100 meters from Interlaken West station. Thun Dock is approximately 50 meters from Thun Station.

the Jungfrau for a separate day after you have checked the weather—and your wallet.

If you *must* scale a mountain while in Interlaken, take the funicular running up to **Harderkulm,** which overlooks Interlaken to the south from 4,337 feet above sea level. On a clear day you can see both lakes surrounding Interlaken, as well as the Jungfrau. This can be done in about an hour for only 20 Swiss francs per person. The Harderkulm station is only a short walk from Interlaken's Ost (East) station. Ask for directions at the tourist office.

Interlaken has two railway stations, west and east. Coming from Bern, you arrive first in the west station. Disembark here rather than riding another 5 minutes to the east station. Remember, however, if you are closer to the east station as your visit draws to a close, you can catch the same train from that point, too—but 5 minutes ahead of the west-station schedule.

An extra bonus offered with the Swiss Card is a 50 percent discount (25 percent with a Swiss Pass) on the **Brienz Rothorn Bahn**—Switzerland's oldest steam cog railway. Since 1892, it has climbed the 7,710 feet above sea level for a spectacular view from Rothorn Kulm. For further information, *Tel:* (33) 952–2222 or *Fax:* (33) 952–2210.

The Höheweg starts at the west station, and the grand promenade extends to the east station. With a city map in hand, courtesy of the tourist office, you are all set to tour the town. If walking isn't your forte, you may prefer to see the sights from a surrey. These horse-drawn vehicles are available just outside the west station. Rates vary and must be arranged with the driver.

There are more than one hundred restaurants in Interlaken. We do have a favorite, although it's a bit off the beaten path—the **Hotel Roessli,** No. 43 on the city map. It is run by a friendly gentleman who worked in New York City restaurants for many years before he moved to the German district of Switzerland. The result is German-Swiss food served with a French flair and an American accent—rather unusual.

Interlaken is a good base for explorations of the entire **Jungfrau Region.** We suggest that you devote one day to Interlaken and its immediate area and check with the tourist office regarding other day-excursion possibilities. In addition to the rail ascent to the Jungfrau, you can reach the **Schilthorn** and lunch in the restaurant **Piz Gloria** (at 10,000 feet), where James Bond escaped the murderous intents of the opposition by skiing down the world's longest ski slope in the film *On Her Majesty's Secret Service.*

Wearers of pacemakers should be wary of the higher altitudes, but there's no reason to miss out on the fun around Interlaken. The **Swiss Open-Air Museum** at nearby **Ballenberg** is an ideal alternative and easy to reach by either train or lake steamer departing from the city's east station. Ask for details at the tourist information office.

If the weather is agreeable, a cruise on the **Lake of Thun** before returning from Interlaken is a must. The ships depart from a pier that can be reached from either the west station by tunnel or the Bahnhofstrasse, where it intersects with the Höheweg alongside the station.

Day Excursion to

Lucerne (Luzern) And Mount Pilatus

Depart from Bern

Distance by Train: 59 miles (95 km)
Average Train Time: 1 hour, 20 minutes
City Dialing Code: 41
Lucerne Tourist Information: Zentralstrasse 5, 6002
Tel: (41) 4107171; *Fax:* (41) 410–7334
Internet: www.luzern. org
E-mail: Luzern@Luzern.org
Hours: May 1–October 31, 0830–2030 daily; November 1–April 30, 0830–1800 Monday–Saturday and 0900–1300 Sunday.

Located immediately outside on the left-hand side of the railway station as you exit from the trains.

This day excursion is weatherproof. Rain or shine, Lucerne has much to offer. So much, in fact, that you may want to return again and again until you have seen it all—an impossible but challenging task.

Lucerne is in its glory on a bright, sunny day, when the city and its surroundings sparkle with a brilliance that defies description. At the northwestern end of Lake Lucerne, where the Reuss River resumes its swift quest for the Rhine, Lucerne's lakefront, rimmed by the mighty Alps, is an unforgettable sight. But a rainy day in Lucerne (and that sort of thing does happen occasionally) won't dampen your spirits one bit, for there are many things to see that are under cover.

The *Kapellbrücke* covered bridge is one example. A symbol of Lucerne, the bridge was built at the beginning of the fourteenth century, together with the *Wasserturm* (water tower) at its side. During the seventeenth century, artists painted a total of 112 pictures under its eaves, depicting Swiss history, particularly that of Lucerne and its patron saints. The bridge was destroyed by fire in 1993, but the bridge and the artwork were re-created and reopened to the public in April 1994.

The **Swiss Museum of Transport and Communications** in Lucerne is open daily April–October, 0900–1800; November–March, 1000–1700 daily. It is the largest and most modern museum in Europe—also one of the most visited. The museum is reached easily from the center of Lucerne by bus No. 6 or 8, which departs from the rail station every 6 minutes for the 10-minute trip, or by lake steamer to the Lido dock (Eurailpass, Europass, and Swiss Pass accepted).

Its special attraction is the **Longines Planetarium** at Sternenplatz 3, and the museum also traces vividly the development of Swiss transportation, including rail, road, aeronautical, and water navigation. Tourism since the nineteenth century is also highlighted. Kids from 7 to 77 will be fascinated by the operating scale model of the Gotthard tunnel railroad, and everyone will end up breathless following a visit to the museum's spectacular Swissorama and IMAX Filmtheater. With three restaurants to choose from, you can really plan to spend an entire day.

If you don't mind mixing fondue with frivolity, by all means eat at the **Stadtkeller Restaurant** at Sternenplatz 3, just two blocks north of the *Kapellbrücke's* right-bank entrance. It may be a bit "touristy," but if you like yodeling, alphorn blowing, cowbell ringing, beer drinking, and flag throwing, this is the place. At lunchtime, you should be there no later than 1130. It's a tour-bus lunch stop and fills up rapidly. Telephone 041–410 7433 for reservations. You can watch those poor, tired bus passengers try to determine what country they are seeing today.

For a sobering experience, follow up lunch with a visit to *The Dying Lion of Lucerne*. It is one of the world's most famous monuments. It was hewn from natural rock in commemoration of the heroic, fatal defense by Swiss

Bern (Berne)—Lucerne (Luzern)

DEPART BERN	TRAIN NUMBER	ARRIVE LUZERN HBF
0730	IR 2807	0847
0930	IR 2813	1047
1130	IR 2817	1247

and continuing daily at 2 hr intervals.
Other service at 2 hr intervals from 0650 requires a change of trains at Olten, with arrival at Luzern Hauptbahnhof in 1 hr 29 min.

DEPART LUZERN HBF	TRAIN NUMBER	ARRIVE BERN
1312	IR 2826	1430
1512	IR 2830	1630

and continuing daily at 1712, 1812, 1912, then 2056 and 2156. Other service requiring a change of trains at Olten departs at 1341 and every 2 hr until 1941, then 2254 and 2334; journey time to Bern Hauptbahnhof is 1 hr 29 min.

Distance: 59 miles (95 km)

Luzern–Pilatus

Via Pilatus cogwheel railway May–October. Discount for railpass holders on Pilatus railway. Pilatus is 7,000 feet (2,132 meters) above sea level.
Train service from Luzern Hbf to Alpnachstad throughout the day; departures at 0630, 0700, 0824, 0924, 0954, 1024, 1124, 1154, 1224, 1324, 1424, 1524, and others later in the day; journey time is 15-20 min.
Trains depart Alpnachstad for Luzern Hbf at 1417, 1444, 1513, 1617, 1644, 1713, 1817, 1844, 1913, 2119, 2209, and 2309; journey time is 18 to 22 min.
Alpnachstad—Pilatus Kulm rack railway—operates daily, weather permitting.
Depart Alpnachstad at 0850, 0930, 1010, 1050, 1130, 1210, 1310 and continuing until 18-1900. Journey time to Pilatus Kulm is 30 min.
Depart Pilatus Kulm at 1215, 1305, 1345, 1425, 1505, 1545, 1625, 1705, 1745, and—Th F Sa only July 2—Sept 12 at 1830, 2005, and 2120; journey time to Alpnachstad is 40 min.
Distance: 3 miles (5 km) Pilatus cogwheel railway

guards of Louis XVI at the Tuileries in Paris at the beginning of the French Revolution in 1792. Mark Twain described the Lion of Lucerne as "the saddest and most poignant piece of rock in the world."

Next door, you will find Lucerne's **Glacier Garden Museum,** which contains remnants of Lucerne's prehistoric past that were discovered in 1872. Twenty million years ago, Lucerne was a subtropical palm beach on the ocean; twenty thousand years ago, Lucerne was covered by more than a mile of glacier ice. Don't miss it.

On your way to the Lion Monument and the Glacier Garden Museum, you will pass one of Switzerland's most outstanding and attractive restaurants, the **Old Swiss House.** Built in 1859, the restaurant contains an antique collection of rare beauty. The oil paintings are all originals. The food's superb, too! Call ahead for reservations (*Tel:* 410 61 71), because the Old Swiss House is frequented by the locals. Meals are served from 1100–2300 Tuesday–Sunday.

Visit **Mount Pilatus** as a side adventure during your Lucerne day excursion. Be certain to go on a clear day, for there is nothing more disappointing than a fog-shrouded peak. The world-famous Pilatus electric railway, with its maximum gradient of 48 percent, is the steepest cog railway in the world. Discounts are available for Eurailpass and Europass holders. It's best to purchase tickets at the tourist information office at Frankenstrasse 1. If you have a lot of time, you can take a lake steamer to **Alpnachstad.** For a breathtaking view and a beautiful way to end your day in Lucerne, descend Mount Pilatus in a cable car to **Kriens** and catch the bus to Lucerne. Check with the tourist information office for details and discounts available to railpass holders.

Day Excursion to

Rheinfelden
WALLED CITY ON THE RHINE

Depart from Bern

Distance by Train: 76 miles (122 km)
Average Train Time: 1 hour, 30 minutes
City Dialing Code: 61
Rheinfelden Tourist Information, 61 Marktgasse
Tel: 831–5520; *Fax:* 831–5570
Hours: 0800–1200 and 1330–1730 Monday–Friday

To reach the tourist information office, proceed downhill on Bahnhofstrasse (Station Street) to the bottom of the hill, where it meets Marktgasse, the pedestrian shopping area. Turn left and walk a short block to the office at 61 Marktgasse, near the Swiss Customs station at the bridge leading to Germany. Look for the sign identifying the office: TOURISMUS RHEINFELDEN (Official Tourist Bureau).

A medieval jewel set on the banks of the swift-moving Rhine River just above Basel, Rheinfelden stirs the imagination. Much of its wall and many of its watch towers are still standing, and they were erected back in the eleventh century. An island on the Swiss side of the river's channel forms an important part of a bridge linking Switzerland to Germany. In the thirteenth century, it was the site of the famed "Emperor's Palace" described by Schiller in the tale of William Tell. The castle is gone now, and the island serves mainly as a city park; but the swirls and eddies of the mighty Rhine continue to stimulate one's sense of the centuries of history that have unfolded there.

During World War II, the bridge over the Rhine was the center of intrigue and mystery. Many downed, but uncaptured American and British aviators seeking the sanctuary of Switzerland attempted to flee Nazi Germany from there. Some made it; some were apprehended. We have talked with residents who still remember those days and the risks that were taken. One person recalled for us her perilous escape across the Rhine's waters in a rowboat.

Be certain to pick up a city map during your stop at the tourist office. Armed with the map, you can easily wind your way through the labyrinth-like streets to any point of interest and still find your way back to the train station in time for your return to Bern.

Check out the shops lining the Rhine. Here you can find bargains in jewelry, clothing, and sporting equipment. Most shops and restaurants are closed on Monday.

When your stomach (or your watch) tells you it's lunchtime, you have several excellent eating places to choose from in Rheinfelden. Our favorites are the **Hotel Schiff** and the **Café Rheineck** close to the river.

Rheinfelden is home for two of Switzerland's largest breweries, **Cardinal** and **Feldschlösschen.** Tours are available on an irregular basis. Excellent restaurants and beer stubes are located at each brewery.

Clustered about the bridge entrance are several eating places offering menus ranging from light snacks to full-course meals. Want to picnic by the Rhine? Pick up some cheese, bread, and wine at one of the market stalls and have your repast on the island as the Rhine provides the background accompaniment.

Saline deposits were discovered under the town in 1844, and Rheinfelden quickly developed into an international spa. Its natural brine, which is one of the strongest in Europe, is piped from a depth of more than 600 feet to several bathing facilities in town, including the **largest saltwater swimming pool** in Switzerland. The tourist office can provide full details. The structures housing the pumps that bring the brine to the surface from the deep wells bear a striking resemblance to the original oil fields of western Pennsylvania, where oil refining first began in North America.

There is an unusual inside-outside saltwater swimming pool that you should see. You can reach it on foot by walking along the Rhine in an upstream direction. The brine-well structures may be seen nearby.

River steamers ply between Rheinfelden and **Basel.** Returning to Bern via Basel and a boat trip on the Rhine becomes an attractive option between May

Bern–Basel–Rheinfelden

DEPART BERN	TRAIN NUMBER	ARRIVE BASEL	DEPART BASEL	CHANGE TO TRAIN NUMBER	ARRIVE RHEINFELDEN
0649	IC 952	0756	0851	IR 1763	0903
0749	IC 854	0856	0951	IR 1765	1003
0849	IC 864	0956	1051	IR 1767	1103

DEPART FROM RHEINFELDEN	TRAIN NUMBER	ARRIVE BASEL	DEPART BASEL	CHANGE TO TRAIN NUMBER	ARRIVE BERN
1456	IR 1776	1508	1604	IC 887	1711
1656	IR 1782	1708	1804	EC 109	1911
1756	IR 1784	1808	1904	EC 105	2011

and continuing at hourly intervals until 2256

Alternative Route via Brugg:

DEPART BERN	TRAIN NUMBER	ARRIVE BRUGG	DEPART BRUGG	CHANGE TO TRAIN NUMBER	ARRIVE RHEINFELDEN
0652	2709	0806	0825	1756	0856
0752	2711	0906	0925	1760	0956
0852	2713	1006	1025	IR 1762	1056
0952	2715	1106	1125	IR 1764	1156

Alternative return route:

DEPART RHEINFELDEN	TRAIN NUMBER	ARRIVE BRUGG	DEPART BRUGG	CHANGE TO TRAIN NUMBER	ARRIVE BERN
1503	IR 1777	1534	1555	2730	1710
1703	1783	1734	1755	2734	1910
1803	1787	1834	1855	2736	2010
1903	EC 97	1934	1955	2738	2110
2003	IR 1791	2034	2055	2742	2210
2203	1795	2235	2255	2746	0006+1

Distance: 76 miles (122 km)

and September, when the service is in operation. Schedules are posted at the *Schifflande* (boat landing) opposite the island. Information on the steamer service to Basel, as well as cruises on the Rhine, is also available in the Rheinfelden tourist information office. Rhine steamers, unlike the lake steamers, do not accept Eurailpass or Europass, but the rates to Basel are nominal.

Day Excursion to

Zermatt

Depart from Bern

How about a cheese fondue luncheon in Zermatt while viewing the **Matterhorn?** It can be done very easily as a day excursion during your stay in Bern. Board the 0720 or 0820 express from Bern to Brig. There, you connect with the *Glacier Express* private railroad to Zermatt. The earlier train from Bern will have you in Zermatt at 1042; the later one will still get you there in time for that luncheon at 1142. In fact, you could stay in Zermatt for an early dinner, too. Leaving there on the express at 2015 and changing in Brig, you would still be back in Bern at the respectful hour of 2325—all in the same day!

Eurail and Europass holders can travel to Brig, but from there, a round-trip ticket must be purchased to Zermatt. Swiss Pass holders can ride the entire route at no additional charge. Interested? Check with Bern Tourismus for Zermatt information and the rail information office across the hallway.

Advance reservations can be made through

RailPass Express, Inc.
2737 Sawbury Boulevard
Columbus OH 43235
Tel: (614) 793–7650
Fax: (614) 764–0711

Base City . . .

Zürich

City Dialing Code: 1
Internet: www.zurichtourism.ch

Some describe it as a garden city by a lake. Others picture it as one of the most elegant cities in Europe. Statisticians term it the largest in Switzerland, and anyone engaged in international business knows it is a world center for industry and commerce. Bankers seem content in knowing that it all begins and ends right there. Zürich can be all things to all people.

Zürich is packed with surprising contrasts. A tree-shaded avenue named Bahnhofstrasse runs charmingly from the railway station to Lake Zürich, yet houses the headquarters of the great world banks and some of the most elegant shops to be found in Europe. A few short blocks away, the scene yields to the Middle Ages around St. Peter's Church near the Limmat River, and the bridge that crosses the river leads into Niederdorfstrasse, the city's roistering nightclub area.

Zürich is a hub for rail transportation. Trains between Milan in the south, Munich in the east, and the great trunk line crossing Switzerland glide in and out of its Hauptbahnhof (Central Train Station) in a never-ending procession.

Arriving by Air

Zürich's Kloten International Airport lies 10 miles northeast of the city. **Airport-City Links:** direct rail connections at the airport for Zürich, Bern, and Geneva. Shuttle train service to the main station in Zürich takes 10 minutes and runs every 15 minutes 0526–2345 from Zürich and 0611–0020 from the airport.

- Limousine service between the city and the airport is also available.
- Taxi queues are found by heading straight out of the international arrivals baggage claim area. Journey time 25-35 minutes. Approximately 45 CHF
- Train information, railpass validation, and money exchange can be obtained on the main shopping level before descending to the train platforms located beneath the air terminal.

Arriving by Train

The **Hauptbahnhof** is Zürich's central railway station. All EuroCity, InterCity, and express trains stop only in this station, even though there are three suburban terminals within the city. Train departures are displayed by electrically operated digital bulletin boards.

- **Money exchange** office (open 0630–2245) is located in a logical spot—on the left side of the main arrival hall. If you don't have Swiss francs in your possession on arrival, stock up on them. Not only is Zürich expensive, but the Swiss prefer their francs.
- **Hotel bookings** may be made through an automatic telephone system located in the center of the station forecourt or through the tourist service on the left side of the main arrival hall. The automatic system operates like clockwork—Swiss, that is. There is a lighted board showing the locations of the hotels (and pensions), together with pictures of the establishments and a list of their room charges. Press the button for the one of your choice, and you'll be connected with the hotel by telephone to discuss vacancies. The only disadvantage of this system is that your reservation cannot be confirmed until you arrive at the hotel to register, whereas the

tourist office will ensure that the reservation is held or will refund its service charge. Be sure to obtain directions to the hotel when connected with the reservation staff.

- **Train information** can be obtained from the office located on the left side of the main arrival hall. You will find one of the attendants there fluent in English. In addition to train information, this office (open daily 0700–2045) can assist you in obtaining **seat reservations** and the validation of your **rail pass** if you are starting your European rail trip from Zürich.

Tourist information/Hotel Reservations

Zürich Tourist Information: Hauptbahnhof 8023
Tel: 215–4000; *Fax:* 215–4044
Hours: April–October: 0830–2030 Monday–Friday; 0830–1830 Saturday–Sunday. November–March: 0830–1930 Monday–Friday; 0830–1830 Saturday–Sunday.

To reach the Zürich tourist office, exit from the trains, turning right at the end of the tracks, and proceed directly through the main hall. The office will be on your left. The tourist office can also make hotel reservations (5 CHF fee). Reservations are held for 1 hour. A city map and a brochure describing the Zürich public transportation system are available.

Getting Around in Zürich

The *Ride with Us* brochure is particularly helpful because it explains how to use the self-service facilities of the city's transportation system, including rail (S-Bahn), trams, buses, and funiculars. The Swiss Pass includes travel on the city network, but Eurailpass or Europass is accepted only on the S-Bahn network. If you have a Eurailpass or Europass we recommend that you purchase a 1-day or multiple-day pass to cover the remaining public transport network in Zürich. Ask about the **Zürich Night Card** which offers reductions at most of Zürich's attractive restaurants, bars, and nightclubs, and also gives free transport after 1700 on Zürich's buses and trams.

Sights/Attractions/Tours

Obtain a copy of the brochure *Zürich City Tours and Excursions* from the tourist office. This brochure describes city sightseeing, and excursions by motor coach or by trolley, cruises on the Limmat River as well as those on Lake Zürich, ascension of Mount Uetliberg for a panoramic view of the city and Alps, and how to see Zürich by night.

Train Connections to Other Base Cities from Zürich

DEPART	TRAIN NUMBER	ARRIVE	NOTES
Amsterdam Centraal			
0757	ICE 76	1657	1
1000	IR 1762	1857	1
1200	IR 1770	2054	4, R
1257	EC 2	2154	
1500	EC 96	2354	1
2200	IR 1794	0857+1	2, R, Sleeper
Berlin Zoobahnhof			
0757	ICE 76	1616	3
0957	EC 102	1816	3
1157	ICE 70	2016	3
1257	EC 2	2217	3
1945	CNL 478	0725+1	R, Sleeper

Bern

Approx. 35 direct trains daily; most depart at 03 and 34 min. past the hour; average journey time, 1 hr 10 min.

DEPART	TRAIN NUMBER	ARRIVE	NOTES
Brussels (Bruxelles) Midi/Zuid			
1200	IR 1770	1945	4
1500	EC 96	2246	
2200	1794/498	0645+1	2, R, Sleeper
Budapest Keleti			
0933	EC 163	2304	5
2233	EN 467	1133+1	R, Sleeper, 5
Copenhagen (København)			
0757	ICE 76	2159	6
0957	EC 102	2359	4, 6
2043	CNL 470	1359+1	2, R, Sleeper
Hamburg			
0757	ICE 76	1532	
1157	ICE 70	1932	
2043	CNL 470	0904+1	R, Sleeper

DEPART	TRAIN NUMBER	ARRIVE	NOTES
Luxembourg			
1200	IR 1770	1650	4
1500	EC 96	1959	
Lyon Part-Dieu			
0734	IC 710	1220	7
0934	IC 716	1442	7
1034	IC 718	1543	7
1234	IC 724	1812	7
1434	IC 728	2006	7
1834	IC 736	2346	7
Milan (Milano) Centrale			
0633	CIS 151	1015	R
0704	CIS 153	1045	R
0830	IC 357	1245	
0907	IC 355	1335	
1107	IC 383	1535	
1307	CIS 155	1635	R
1507	IC 387	1935	
1707	IC 381	2135	
1907	CIS 157	2245	R
Munich (München)			
0733	EC 99	1155	
0933	EC 167	1359	
1333	EC 95	1748	
1733	EC 93	2156	
Nice Ville			
1107	IC 383	2218	10
Paris Gare de l'Est			
0637	IR 1854	1310	4
0715	TGV EC 420	1309	R, 8
1037	IR 1864	1718	4
1500	EC 96	2140	4, Mon-Fri
1700	1784	2344	4
2300	468	0645+1	R, Sleeper

DEPART	TRAIN NUMBER	ARRIVE	NOTES
Rome (Roma) Termini			
0633	CIS 151	1530	R, 9
0704	CIS 153	1530	R, 9
0830	IC 357	1730	R, 9
0907	IC 355	1830	R, 9
1107	IC 383	2030	R, 9
1307	CIS 155	2238	R, 9
2207	EN 303	0910+1	R, Sleeper
Vienna (Wien)			
0933	EC 163	1850	
1333	EC 161	2250	
2233	EN 467	0808+1	R, Sleeper

Daily, unless otherwise noted
R Reservations required
+1 Next day
1. Change trains in Basel and Cologne (Köln)
2. Change to sleeper train in Basel
3. Change at Mannheim
4. Change in Basel
5. Change in Vienna (Wien)
6. Change in Hamburg
7. Change in Geneva (Genève)
8. Arrives Paris Gare de Lyon station
9. Change in Milan (Milano) to Eurostar Italia train
10. Change in Genoa (Genova)

Escorted and unescorted tours are available at various times throughout the week during certain seasons of the year; so be sure to check with the train-information office or the tourist office. Some of these excursions will require Eurailpass or Europass holders to pay supplemental charges. Payment of these charges, along with reservations for the excursions, can be made at these offices.

Lake steamers at the far end of the Bahnhofstrasse at the Schiffstation (boat station) offer several interesting cruises, including one to the eastern end of the lake to an interesting old Swiss town, **Rapperswil.**

Zürich has its share of cathedrals. The **Grossmunster Cathedral** stands brooding on the east bank of the Limmat River. The cathedral has a statue of Charlemagne, who is said to have built the original church. Almost opposite on the other side of the river stands the **Fraumunster Cathedral,** reached by crossing the Munsterbrucke (Cathedral Bridge). Alongside the central station is the **Swiss National Museum**. On exhibition are authentic rooms of the sixteenth and seventeenth centuries, removed from their original sites and rebuilt within the museum. Zürich is not totally old in face. Its **Kunsthaus** (Fine Arts Museum) is an attractive modern building with a magnificent collection of modern art.

Day Excursions

Zürich provides an alternative Base City to Bern for those arriving via the Zürich Kloten International Airport. The city's proximity to Lucerne and Rheinfelden decreases travel time for these day excursions when compared to Bern, but this time saving comes at a price. Zürich maintains a reputation for being one of Europe's most expensive cities. Budget-minded travelers may do well to use Bern as their Base City and save Zürich for a day excursion and as a gateway city.

Appendix

RAIL–TOUR ITINERARIES

Three sample rail-tour itineraries are presented in response to readers' requests for sample itineraries combining several base cities and day excursions into a rail-tour package. These itineraries are similar to those used in previous tour programs and are considered "route-tested."

All of the base cities and day excursions in the following rail-tour itineraries are described elsewhere in this edition. Each itinerary may be completed with a 15-day Eurailpass, or a 15-day in 2 months, Eurail Flexipass or Saverpass.

Gateway cities are an important pre-trip consideration. Discuss them with your travel agent before buying air tickets or before purchasing them yourselves online. We have included airport information in Base City descriptions for your assistance. When suggested gateways are cities other than the rail-tour base cities, we have included rail schedules to assist in your planning, but as stated previously in this edition, our rail schedules are for planning purposes only. *Europe by Eurail* and its publisher cannot be held responsible for the consequences of either schedule or train changes occuring after press time or for inadvertent inaccuracies.

The following rail-tour schedules have been compiled on the basis of what we consider to be the best trains running at the best times; but in almost every case, there are several other trains departing at other times that may be more convenient for your purposes. For this reason, you may want to contact the Rail Information Department (*Tel:* 614–793–7650) or visit the Point-to-Point section for scheduling at www.railpass.com.

Hotels suggested for the itineraries have been selected for their convenient locations near the railway stations and/or close to public transportation. Hotel price ranges are quoted in local currencies for planning purposes only and are subject to change without prior notice. To convert the rates to U.S. dollars, consult the Foreign Exchange listing in the financial section of your hometown newspaper, contact your bank, or visit **www.oanda.com** and go to the cheat sheet for travelers page; (you can print the rates for the countries on your itinerary and carry them with your other travel papers); another great site is

www.xe.net for universal currency exchanges.

Confirm hotel rates either through your travel agent or directly with the hotel. Most of the hotels listed have U.S. representatives through whom your travel agent can make reservations at no additional cost to you. We also suggest contacting European Vacation Tours & Groups at 888–TOUR–404 or **www.europeanvacation.com** for further tour ideas and/or hotel arrangements. Hotel ratings are based on government standards.

Europe à la Carte

A rail tour using *Europe by Eurail* base cities Munich, Bern, and Paris in an adventure through the heart of Europe.

Base Cities

Munich: Germany's fun capital. Plan ample time for shopping and sightseeing before beginning your exciting rail adventure. Allow for jet lag, too.

Bern: Medieval elegance in the heart of Switzerland. An all-weather shopping center. Save the sunny days for Bern's eye-filling day excursions.

Paris: The City of Light and everyone's "second" city is the only one of its kind. Mix Paris' pleasures with its unusual array of day excursions.

Gateways

Open Jaw: Munich inbound, Paris outbound. Discuss with your travel agent for professional advice. Other gateways include:

Frankfurt: ICE 797 to Munich departs 1550 and arrives 1922 or ICE 799 departs 1750 and arrives 2122. Return to Frankfurt on ICE 990 departing 0633 and arriving 0951 or ICE 796, 1039–1410.

Amsterdam: EC 3 to Munich departs at 0755; arrives in Mannheim at 1325. Change to ICE 593 departing 1331 and arriving Munich 1621. Return to Amsterdam on ICE 794 departing Munich at 1239; arrive Mannheim 1529. Change to EC 104 Mannheim to Amsterdam, 1531–2054.

Paris: Depart Paris Est on EC 65 *Mozart* to Munich at 0749; arrive Munich 1616. Return to Paris on EC 66 *Maurice Ravel,* at 0742; arrive Paris Est 1622.

Base-City Hotels

Munich: The InterCity Hotel, located in the station, is first choice. Quiet, good restaurant, but usually booked up months in advance. Drei Lowen, one block from the station, is convenient. Balance of those hotels listed are clustered nearby. Hilton and Sheraton properties in suburbs have easy tram connections to city center.

Bern: Schweizerhof, on the station plaza, is tops in location, restaurant—and price. Hotel Baeren and Hotel Bristol are more economical and 3 minutes walk to station. Other hotels listed are also within a short walk of station and maintain highest Swiss standards.

Paris: For economy and excellent location, choose Rèsidence Elyssées Maubourg, one block from Maubourg Metro stop. Hotel Lyon-Palace-Paris, one short block away from Gare de Lyon's rail, Metro, and RER connections, has excellent neighborhood-restaurant section.

Europe à la Carte 15-Day Rail Itinerary

Day 1   Munich–Salzburg: Visit Mozart's birthplace and listen to Salzburg's sound of music.

Day 2   Munich–Garmisch–Partenkirchen: Home of the Winter Olympic Park and gateway to ascent of the mighty Zugspitze.

Day 3   Munich–Berchtesgaden: Explore salt mines, then soar to Hitler's ill-famed Eagle's Nest.

Day 4   Munich–Innsbruck: World famous for winter Olympics, with year-round exhilarating scenery.

Day 5   Munich–Nuremberg: Germany's leading toy producers spice activities with fresh gingerbread.

Day 6   Munich–Bern: Base-city transfer via Zürich.

Day 7   Bern–Interlaken: A day in Alpine splendor; return to Bern by Lake of Thun steamer.

Day 8   Bern–Lucerne: A rain-or-shine outing with Mount Pilatus and Swiss cheese fondue.

Day 9   Bern–Milan: A change of pace, a change of place to Italy's bustling northern capital.

Day 10   Bern–Paris: Base-city transfer via Geneva.

Day 11   Paris–Rouen: Visit historic site of France's Joan of Arc.

Day 12   Paris–Rennes: Half-timbered houses and a ride on the TGV Atlantique.

Day 13   Paris–Fontainebleau: Visit the scene where Napoleon ruled and later was vanquished.

Day 14   Lyon–Annecy: Breathtaking scenery, sparkling water, and a charming medieval marketplace.

Day 15   Paris–Lyon: City of contrast visited after exciting journey aboard TGV, one of the world's fastest trains.

Tour Tips: Make seat reservations immediately on arrival in Munich. At minimum, reserve all base-city legs. Reservations are obligatory on TGV and many EuroCity trains. Don't overlook the Romantic Road and the Golden Pass day excursion possibilities.

European Escapade

A more than passing acquaintance with some of Europe's most fascinating sights and cities. From gateway Luxembourg, you travel to Bern, Amsterdam, and Paris, with shopping in Brussels.

EUROPE À LA CARTE BASE-CITY TRANSFER SCHEDULE

FROM	TO	DEPART	TRAIN #	ARRIVE	NOTES
Munich	**Zürich**	0814	EC 92	1226	R
Zürich	**Bern**	1234	IC 724	1344	R
or		1303	IC 924	1414	R
Bern	**Paris Lyon**	0832	TGV EC420	1309	R

EUROPE À LA CARTE DAY—EXCURSION SUGGESTIONS

BASE CITY	EXCURSION	DEPART	ARRIVE	RETURN	ARRIVE	NOTES
Munich	Berchtesgaden	0741	1021	1747	2021	1
	Garmisch–Partenkirchen	0800	0921	1831	1955	
	Innsbruck	0729	0922	1837	2030	
	Nuremberg	0748	0930	1830	2011	
	Salzburg	0725	0855	1905	2036	
Bern	Interlaken	0826	0917	1944	2034	
	Lucerne	0743	0903	1857	2017	
	Milan	0734	1050	1710	2026	
Paris	Annecy	0642	1032	1908	2248	
	Rennes	0820	1035	1835	2040	
	Fontainebleau	0827	0904	1719	1802	
	Lyon	0700	0904	1830	2034	
	Rouen	0915	1021	1911	2016	

Note: All trains are daily.   R = Reservations required or recommended

1. Change trains in Freilassing

Base Cities

Luxembourg: Fortress city, steeped in European and American history. Virtually a tax-free city; save some of your dollars for Luxembourg shops.

Bern: Medieval settings in the heart of the Swiss Alps. Bern's arcaded walkways make shopping and sightseeing easy no matter what the weather may be.

Amsterdam: Canals, cheese shops, diamond cutters, and Rembrandt's finest masterpieces await you.

Paris: City of Light. Mix Paris' pleasures with an array of action-packed day excursions.

Gateways

Discuss all gateway possibilities with your travel agent, because the tour's circular itinerary provides a wide selection, including all of the base cities in this itinerary plus Brussels. Depart Brussels Midi for Luxembourg at 0715 for a 2½-hour EuroCity trip; same service returns you to Brussels at end of tour.

Base City Hotels

Luxembourg: Pick a price. Most of the hotels listed are near the station. Book well in advance, particularly in summer tour season.

Bern: Schweizerhof for luxury, but the other listed hotels offer only a shade less at varying prices. All are within walking distance of the station.

Amsterdam: Victoria Park Plaza Hotel, a scant block from the station, is most convenient and highly recommended. Grand Hotel Krasnapolsky is just another stone's throw away but posh, with prices to match.

Paris: Best bargain and good location is Rèsidence Elysées Maubourg on the Left Bank. Same for independent Lyon-Palace-Paris Hotel, close to Gare de Lyon.

European Escapade 15–Day Rail Itinerary

Day 1   Luxembourg–Clervaux: An opportunity to visit site of World War II Battle of the Bulge.

Day 2   Luxembourg–Koblenz: A rail excursion along the Mosel to the Rhine in German wine country.

Day 3   Luxembourg–Bern: Base-city transfer via France.

Day 4   Bern–Interlaken: View of mighty Jungfrau and cruise on Lake of Thun highlight exciting rail tour.

Day 5   Bern–Lucerne: Sparkling highlights of Switzerland's lake city plus Mount Pilatus ascent.

Day 6   Bern–Milan: Cross into Italy for a delightful day of sightseeing in fascinating Milan.

Day 7   Bern–Amsterdam: Base-city transfer via Rhine.

Day 8   Amsterdam–Enkhuizen: Visit the Zuider Zee museum, depicting the Dutch battle with the sea.

Day 9   Amsterdam–Hoorn: Steam-engine ride from Hoorn to Medemblik; the old Dutch Market on Wednesdays.

EUROPEAN ESCAPADE BASE-CITY TRANSFER SCHEDULE

FROM	TO	DEPART	NUMBER	ARRIVE	NOTES
Luxembourg	Bern	1002	EC 91	1511	R
Bern	Amsterdam	1148	EC 104	2054	R
Amsterdam	Paris Nord	0954	Thalys 9320	1405	R
Paris Est	Luxembourg	1054	EC 357	1435	R

EUROPEAN ESCAPADE DAY-EXCURSION SUGGESTIONS*

BASE CITY	EXCURSION	DEPART	ARRIVE	DEPART	ARRIVE	NOTES
Luxembourg	Clervaux	0813	0904	1856	1947	
	Koblenz	0822	1039	1715	1922	1
Bern	Interlaken	0826	0917	1944	2034	
	Lucerne	0743	0903	1857	2017	
	Milan	0734	1050	1710	2026	
Amsterdam	Alkmaar	0822	0853	1737	1811	
	Enkhuizen	0819	0923	1737	1844	
	Hoorn	0819	0858	1734	1814	
Paris	Annecy	0642	1032	1908	2248	
	Rennes	0820	1035	1835	2040	
	Chartres	0830	0940	1643	1757	
	Fontainebleau	0827	0904	1719	1802	
	Lyon	0700	0904	1830	2034	

Note: All trains are daily.   R Reservations required or recommended

(1) Change trains in Trier

Day 10   Amsterdam–Alkmaar: World-famous cheese market and site of Dutch revolt against Spanish rule.

Day 11   Amsterdam–Paris: Base-city transfer via Brussels.

Day 12   Paris–Chartres: Palaces and castles abound along with Gothic Cathedral of Notre Dame.

Day 13   Paris–Rennes: Experience TGV Atlantique at 186 miles per hour.

Day 14   Paris–Fontainebleau: Visit palace where Napoleon relaxed with Josephine—and a few others.

Day 15   Paris–Lyon: "Newest" city of France, with Roman history, visited aboard one of the world's fastest trains, a TGV.

Tour Tips: Book all seat reservations when you arrive in Luxembourg. Depart Luxembourg (Day 2) at 0822, arriving Koblenz at 1039 (transfer in Trier required during winter months). In Koblenz, board EC9 at 1054 for Mainz, arriving there at 1146. You'll get a great view of the Rhine from the train. Lunch in the Mainz station restaurant and depart at 1253 in the direction of Koblenz, but get off in Bingen at 1310. Board the steamer ship from the Bingen pier at 1415. Then relax on the Rhine until reaching Koblenz at 1800. Service operates April–October. Have dinner at the Weindorf. Catch RE 3985 at 2018 back to Luxembourg (transfer in Trier).

En route to Amsterdam from Bern (Day 7), after departing Mainz, watch on the right-hand side of the train for spectacular Rhine scenery to Koblenz.

Scandinavian Splendor

Tour Scandinavian capitals of Copenhagen, Helsinki, Oslo, and Stockholm and board the Silja Line's finest cruise ship for adventure on the Baltic.

Base Cities

Copenhagen: Jovial, entertaining, the fun capital of Scandinavia. Save it for the grand finale.

Helsinki: Daughter of the Baltic. A glittering gem set in a picture-book harbor. Make the best of your "shore leave" by enjoying every moment.

Oslo: Friendly, pleasant, and compact. Take the Bergen-Flam excursion option if time permits.

Stockholm: Striking harbor skyline, a city of islands and waterways. Sightseeing must include a visit to Old Town, where it all began centuries ago.

Gateways

All the base cities have direct U.S. air service, even Helsinki. The circular nature of the tour's itinerary makes it possible to select any one of the above base cities as both the inbound and outbound gateway. Our choice would be Copenhagen; which is yours?

SCANDINAVIAN SPLENDOR BASE-CITY TRANSFER SCHEDULE

FROM	TO	DEPART	NUMBER	ARRIVE	NOTES
Copenhagen	Oslo	2205	392	0707+1	R, Sleeper
Oslo	Stockholm	0930	55/466	1529	June 14–Aug 21
Stockholm	Helsinki	1800	Silja ferry	0900+1	R
Helsinki	Stockholm	1800	Silja ferry	0900+1	R
Stockholm	Copenhagen	0818	X2 525/363	1533	R, 1
	or	2230	281	0705	R, Sleeper

SCANDINAVIAN SPLENDOR DAY-EXCURSION SUGGESTIONS*

BASE CITY	EXCURSION	DEPART	ARRIVE	NUMBER	DEPART	ARRIVE	NOTES
Copenhagen	Aarhus	0751	1035		1738	2027	Mon–Fri, R
	Helsingør	0829	0925		1639	1735	
	Odense	0800	0929		1752	1922	
	Roskilde	0830	0850		1825	1848	
Oslo	Hamar	0805	0934		1921	2102	R
	Larvik	0933	1143		1945	2151	Mon–Sat
	Lillehammer	0805	1019		2014	2225	R
Stockholm	Eskilstuna	0854	0954		1703	1803	
	Norrkoping	0818	0935		1620	1741	R
	Uppsala	0825	0901		1901	1935	R

★ See appropriate base city chapters for additional day excursion suggestions.

Note: All trains are daily unless otherwise noted.
R Reservations required
1. Change trains in Hassleholm

Base-City Hotels

Copenhagen: Palace Hotel gets the tourists' nod for convenient location, midrange rates, and so on. The Plaza, facing the station, is great but difficult to book in high season.

Helsinki: No listing, because we recommend using the Silja Line's accommodations for this tour's out-and-back day excursion, but we can recommend the Presidenti if you elect to extend your stay in Helsinki.

Oslo: The Grand Hotel features Old World elegance with modern conveniences—with the exception of price. The Hotel Nobel, with a wider rate range, is near the Grand Hotel.

Stockholm: Take your pick. All three hotels listed face Central Station. Price is probably the deciding factor. All have acceptable restaurants and are clean and well managed.

Scandinavian Splendor 15–Day Rail Itinerary

If Copenhagen is selected as the in-out gateway, spend jet-lag adjustment time there before validating your Eurailpass or Scanrailpass and leaving for Oslo.

Day 1   Copenhagen–Oslo: Scenic base-city transfer.

Day 2   Oslo–Larvik: Put a fjord in your future with an excursion to Larvik and on to Skien.

Day 3   Oslo–Hamar: Drink in the beauty of Lake Mjosa before exploring the rail museum in Hamar.

Day 4   Oslo–Lillehammer: Lillehammer can provide an insight into Norway's culture.

Day 5   Oslo–Stockholm: Colorful base-city transfer.

Day 6   Stockholm–Uppsala: Spend an interesting day in a city that dates from pagan times.

Day 7   Stockholm–Eskilstuna: See Sweden's "steel city" and visit 300-year-old Rademacher Forges.

Day 8   Stockholm–Norrkoping: Surprises such as cacti growing in Sweden await your arrival here.

Day 9   Stockholm–Silja Line cruise to Helsinki: Cruise the Baltic in luxury to Finland.

Day 10 Helsinki–Stockholm: Set sail again for Sweden ·after an exciting day ashore in Helsinki.

Day 11 Stockholm–Copenhagen: Arrive in Denmark's capital after overland rail through Sweden.

Day 12 Copenhagen–Aarhus: Ferry and rail transportation join to make an exciting day excursion.

Day 13 Copenhagen–Helsingør (Elsinore): A rail visit to north Zealand to inspect Hamlet's castle.

Day 14 Copenhagen–Odense: A rail visit to the birthplace of Hans Christian Andersen.

Day 15   Copenhagen–Roskilde: Five Viking ships await your inspection in Roskilde's museum.

Tour Tips: Make the Silja Line cruise to Helsinki and back a highlight of your tour. Book a round-trip cabin and spend a carefree day ashore in Helsinki sans luggage. In Helsinki, ride tram 3T for a quick view of this remarkable city. The Silja Line can also arrange extended shore leave in Helsinki if desired.

BASE CITY HOTELS AND INFORMATION

All hotel rates, given in local currencies applicable at press time, are subject to change. Rates range from the price of a single to double occupancy. The hotels listed are close to the railway stations and/or public transport facilities. The hotel's street location is below the hotel name. European Vacation Tours & Groups may also arrange hotel accommodations before departing for Europe. *Tel:* **888–TOUR–404** or visit **www.europeanvacation.com**.

Amsterdam Hotels (rates in Dutch Guilders)

Victoria Park Plaza	★★★★	*Tel:* (20)5240621
Damrak 1-5	475–510	*Fax:* (20)6274259
1012 LG		
Breakfast	32.50	

Grand Hotel Krasnapolsky	★★★★	*Tel:* (20)5549111
Dam 9	545–680	*Fax:* (20)6228607
1012 JS		

Internet: www.krasnapolsky.nl; E-mail: book@krasnapolsky.nl
Breakfast 37.50; Lunch 52.50–72.50; Dinner 67.50

Damrak	★★★★	*Tel:* (20)6262498
Damrak 49	165-350•	*Fax:* (20)6250997
1012 LL		
•Breakfast included in rates		

Tulip Inn Dam Square	★★★	*Tel:* (20)6233716
Gravenstraat 14-16	200-220	*Fax:* (20)6381156
1012NM		

To telephone or fax the Amsterdam hotels listed above from the United States, dial 011-31, then the number listed above.

When writing, the postal code and country name should follow the hotel name and street address; for example, 1012 JS Amsterdam, The Netherlands.

Bern Hotels (rates in Swiss Francs)

Gauer Schweizerhof	★★★★★	*Tel:* (31)3114501
Bahnhofplatz 11	240–410	*Fax:* (31)3122119
CH–3001		

Bern-Hotel	★★★★	*Tel:* (31)3121021
Zeughausgasse 9	175–275	*Fax:* (31)3121147
CH–3011		

Best Western Bristol	★★★★	*Tel:* (31)311101
Schauplatzgasse 10	165–270	*Fax:* (31)1311479
CH–3011		

City Am Bahnhof	★★★	*Tel:* (31)3115377
Bahnhofplatz	111–203	*Fax:* (31)3110636
CH–3011		

E-mail: ambassador@mail.pingnet.ch
Buffet breakfast 16; Continental breakfast 8

Metropole	★★★	*Tel:* (31)3115021
Zeughausgasse 26/28	100–220	*Fax:* (31)3121153
CH–3011		

To telephone or fax the Bern hotels from the United States, dial 011–41, then the number listed.

Copenhagen Hotels (rates in Danish Kroner)

Best Western Webers Hotel	★★★★	*Tel:* (31)311432
Vesterbrogade 11	850–1,250	*Fax:* (31)311441
DK–1620		

Best Western Mayfair	★★★★	*Tel:* (31)314801
Helgolandsgade 3	650–825	*Fax:* (31)239686
DK–1653		

The Palace Hotel	★★★★	*Tel:* (33)144050
Rådhuspladsen 57	1525–2495•	*Fax:* (33)145279
DK–1550		

•Some 5★ rooms available; rates include VAT, service charge and breakfast
Internet: www.palace-hotel.dk; E-mail: booking@principle.dk

Plaza	★★★★	*Tel:* (33)149262
Bernstorffsgade 4	1,450–2,050	*Fax:* (33)939362
DK–1577		

To telephone or fax hotels in Copenhagen from the United States, dial 011–45 then the number as listed.

Luxembourg Hotels (rates in Belgian Francs)

Golden Tulip Central Molitor Hotel		Tel: 489911
28 Avenue de la Liberte	3800–6200*	Fax: 483382
L-1930		

Internet: www.hotelmolitor; E-mail: molitor@pt.lu

Nobilis Hotel		Tel: 494971
47 Avenue de la Gare	3350–4050	Fax: 403101
L-1611		

President Hotel	★★★★	Tel: 486161
32 Place de la Gare	4600–7000*	Fax: 486180
L-1024		

Internet: www.president.lu; E-mail: info@president.lu

Note: Government of Luxembourg does not usually rate hotels.

To telephone or fax Luxembourg hotels from the United States, dial 011–352, then the numbers as listed.

*Rates include buffet breakfast and taxes

Munich Hotels (rates in Deutsche Marks)

InterCity	★★★★	Tel: (89)545560
Bayerstrasse 10	195–400	Fax: (89)5456610
D–80335		

Located in Munich Hauptbahnhof (rail station)

Drei Löwen	★★★★	Tel: (89)551040
Schillerstrasse 8	195–365*	Fax: (89)55104905
D–80336		

*Breakfast included; lunch 28; dinner 28

Germania	★★★★	Tel: (89)51680
Schwanthalerstrasse 28	120–260	Fax: (89)598491
D–80336		

Atrium	★★★★	Tel: (89)514190
Landwehrstrasse 59	219–450	Fax: (89)535066
D–80336		

Cristal	★★★★	Tel: (89)551110
Schwanthalerstrasse 36	140–230	Fax: (89)55111992
D–80336		

Internet: www.bestwestern.com/de/hotelcristal
Email: info@cristal.bestwestern.de

To telephone or fax Munich hotels from the United States, dial 011–49, then the numbers as listed.

Oslo Hotels (rates in Norwegian Kroner)

Grand Karl Johansgate 31 N–0101	★★★★ 1,450–3,050	Tel: (22)429390 Fax: (22)421225
Hotell Bondeheimen Rosenkrantz gate 8 0159 •Breakfast included in rates	★★★ 575–1075•	Tel: (23)214100 Fax: (23)419437
Best Western Hotel Nobel Karl Johansgate 33 N–0162	★★★★ 990–1,125	Tel: (22)427480 Fax: (22)420519

To telephone or fax Oslo hotels from the United States, dial 011–47, then the numbers as listed.

Paris Hotels (rates in French Francs)

Hotel Ambassador 16, Blvd. Haussmann F–75009	★★★ 1210–1710	Tel: (1)42469263 Fax: (1)40220874
Concorde St. Lazare 108, rue St. Lazare F–75008 Internet: www.concorde-hotels.com E-mail: stlazare-sales@concorde-hotels.com	★★★★ 1800–2200	Tel: (1)40084444 Fax: (1)42930120
Plaza Haussmann 177, Blvd.Hausmann F–75008	★★★ 620–790	Tel: (1)45639383 Fax: (1)45611430
Best Western Anjou–Lafayette 4, rue Riboutte F–75009 •Buffet breakfast 50	★★★ 520–795•	Tel: (1)42468344 Fax: (1)48000897
Lyon-Palace-Paris 11, rue de Lyon F–75012	★★★ 525–545	Tel: (1)43072949 Fax: (1)46289155

Maine Atlantique	★★★	*Tel:* (1)45428143
55, rue des Plaisance	450–570	*Fax:* (1)45429787
F–75014		

To telephone or fax the above-listed Paris hotels from the United States, dial 011-33, then the numbers as listed.

Stockholm Hotels (rates in Swedish Kronor)

Sheraton	★★★★	*Tel:* (8)142600
Tegelbacken 6, Box 289	1,400–2,300	*Fax:* (8)217026
S–10123		
Scandic Hotel Continental	★★★	*Tel:* (8)244020
Vasagatan/Vattugrand 4	1,175–1,725	*Fax:* (8)4113695
S–10122		
Best Western Terminus	★★★★	*Tel:* (8)222640
Vasagatan 20	540–750	*Fax:* (8)248295
S–10125		

To telephone or fax the above-listed Stockholm hotels from the United States, dial 011–46, then the numbers as listed.

FERRY CROSSINGS

In addition to unlimited rail travel and other conveniences, a Eurailpass, Eurail Flexipass, or Eurail Youthpass provides holders with passage on ferries conveying train passengers within the Eurailpass countries. In some instances, passengers must detrain and board the ferries; but on most major rail lines, the passenger coaches are loaded directly onto the ferry. In either case, the ferries are equipped with amenities such as restaurants, bars, boutiques, and, when traveling between countries, money exchanges and tax-free shops.

Three major international ferry crossings exist; they are between Italy and Greece, Finland and Sweden, and Ireland and France. The distances are considerable and usually involve overnight travel. Details, including schedules and services available, appear on the following pages.

Other ferry crossings of international importance to railpass travelers include the lines between Ireland to Britain, the major route which lies between Germany (Puttgarden) and Denmark (Rodby), and several crossings connecting the Scandinavian countries.

Italy–Greece Via Eurailpass/Europass

The Eurailpass or Europass covers travel via ferry facilities operated by the Hellenic Mediterranean Lines and the Adriatica Line between Brindisi, Italy, and Patras, Greece. Departing either Greece or Italy, you must present your railpass to the shipping-company office in the port and have a ticket and a boarding pass issued before boarding.

Railpass holders are granted free deck passage, but the reservation fee, meals, reclining chairs, or sleeping accommodations are not included. (Reclining chairs, by the way, are similar to those found in commercial airlines and are a great bargain for the budget-minded traveler.) Reclining seats are approximately $22; cabin rates range from $31 to $98 per berth.

Reservations for departure dates and cabin accommodations may be reserved in advance by contacting: *Adriatica Line directly by calling* 011 39 41 781 861; fax 011 39 41 781 864. Or you may visit the website of Hellenic Mediterranean Lines at **www.hml.it**.

Patras Ferry Terminal: To reach the office from the railway station, turn left as you exit the station. Walk along the street side of the quay approximately 300 yards to the office marked "Central Agency." Summer hours are 0900–2200 daily. Winter hours are 0900–1300 and 1700–2200. Report on day of embarkation only. No baggage checking is available. Useful telephone numbers for information: 429520 or 421614.

Brindisi Ferry Terminal: A 15-minute walk downhill to the Seno di Levante pier at the foot of Corso (Umberto), Corso Garibaldi, and Via del Mera, the streets leading to the waterfront. The terminal is on the right, just before the pier. It opens daily two hours prior to departure times. With *stet peton* (a telephone token) and a lot of patience, call ahead to the pier on 22861.

Attenzione (That's "attention" in Italian): From the time you arrive in Brindisi until you are safely aboard the ferry, beware of "entrepreneurs" approaching you with offers to help. Many are garbed in official-looking uniforms or are wearing "Official Guide" headgear. They bear alarming messages such as, "I have bad news. All of the deck space for tonight's sailing has been sold out." Then he relates the good news: "You are fortunate in meeting me, for I can take you to an agency where a few cabins are still available." With that, he'll reach for your baggage unless, by now, you have interrupted his presentation with a firm, "No, thank you." If he insists, *Polizia* (police) is another good word to inject into the conversation.

Mediterranean (Italy-Greece) Ferry Crossing

Between Brindisi, Italy and Patras, Greece
Ferry Service Provided by Hellenic Mediterranean Lines

Reservation fee: $3.00 (all year). Advanced reservations recommended during July and August. During high season (June through September), a surcharge (U.S. $15.00) must be paid. Check with Hellenic Mediterranean Lines on actual crossing dates as ferries do not run daily nor year-round. When operating, there are usually two crossing per day. Both depart in the evening and arrive approximately 16-18 hours later. Times may vary from day to day. For specific day depatures, visit **www.hml.it**.

Before boarding, all passengers must check in at the pier office of the ferry line issuing the reservation.

Deck passage is free for Eurailpass holders (but a reservation fee is payable). Meals and port charges are not included. "Deck passage" allows you to board the ferry. Aboard, you are limited to the public areas and facilities of the vessel unless you book accommodations.

Author's suggestion: The port cities of Brindisi and Patras are interesting, charming, and steeped in history. Why not take a day to see them at a leisurely pace? Plan to arrive a day before your scheduled ferry departure. Ask your concierge to call ahead for a hotel reservation. Also ask him/her to check on your ferry reservation. The address and telephone numbers of the city tourist information offices are posted in the arrival halls of the rail stations.

Note: Schedules and prices provided by Hellenic Mediterranean Lines are subject to change without notice.

Finland–Sweden Via Eurailpass/ScanRail Pass

The Silja Line has modern passenger terminals in Stockholm, Turku, Helsinki, and Travemünde that rival any airport for convenience. Eurailpass, Eurail Flexipass, and ScanRail Pass holders are entitled to discounted rates on Silja Line and may use the food services and rest rooms aboard. They will be provided with sleeping accommodations after cabin space is reserved and paid for. Schedules are shown on the opposite page. Cabins may be reserved in advance by contacting Silja Line's U.S. agent:

> *Bergen Line, Inc.*
> Park Avenue
> New York, NY 10022
> Telephone: (800) 323–7436; (212) 319–1300
> *Fax:* (212) 319–1390

Crossing between Sweden and Finland, you may select between two routes: Stockholm-Helsinki direct, or Stockholm-Turku with train connections or the Silja Line express bus service between Turku and Helsinki. Our preference is the direct route between the two capital cities because it gives you a few more hours aboard ship to enjoy the scenery, which is spectacular. Both routes traverse the breathtaking archipelago between the two countries.

Although your Eurailpass entitles you to travel the Silja Line, you also need to obtain a boarding pass before embarking. If you need a boarding pass, you should be at the ferry terminal one and one-half to two hours before ship departure; pass holders do pay for cabin space. All terminals have cafeterias, waiting rooms, and baggage lockers.

Silja Terminals:

—Stockholm: Reached by underground line No. 13 or 14, both running from the city's Central Station to the end of the line—Ropsten. The fare is 12 Swedish kronor. Taxi fare from the train station to the Silja Line terminal is approximately 75 kronor and takes about 15 minutes.

—Helsinki: Reached by tram No. 3T from the central railway station. Fare is 8.00 Finnish markkaa; journey takes 15 minutes. The taxi between the rail station and Silja terminal costs approximately 35 markkaa and takes 10 minutes.

—Turku: Reached from Turku central station by train to harbor station (most through trains terminate at harbor). Taxi from central station costs about 30 markkaa and takes about 10 minutes.

Baltic Ferry Crossings

Silja Line Between Finland and Sweden

STOCKHOLM—HELSINKI V.V.

Stockholm	Depart daily	1800
Helsinki	Arrive following day	0900
Helsinki	Depart daily	1800
Stockholm	Arrive following day	0900

STOCKHOLM—TURKU V.V.

Depart Stockholm	Arrive Turku
0800	2020
2015	0800 following morning
Depart Turku	Arrive Stockholm
0915	1915
2115	0700 following morning

Ireland–France

Eurailpass holders may travel between the Continent and the Republic of Ireland aboard the vessels of the Irish Ferries line. Service from the French port of Cherbourg to the Irish port of Rosslare is available April 1 through September 27, 2000. Limited service begins the last week in February through the third week in March, then daily service through the end of September. There is no winter service.

Ferry service is provided by the line's two ships, the *Saint Killian II* and the *Saint Patrick II*. The *Saint Killian* is a 10,256–ton vessel with a capacity of 2,000 passengers and 380 cars; the *Saint Patrick* can carry 1,630 passengers and 300 cars.

Eurailpass travelers are entitled to 50% reduction on the Irish Ferries. Meals and cabin accommodations are not included. For cabin rates, availability, and reservations, call Irish Ferries' 24-hour information line in Ireland (011 44 01 6610715) or visit their Web site at www.irishferries.ie.

All passages are overnight. Cabin accommodations may also be booked at the ports when presenting your Eurailpass for a boarding pass. The check-in points are usually open two hours prior to sailing times. Passengers are requested to check in not less than one hour before the sailing time.

Rosslare Ferry Terminal: Trains from Dublin and Limerick connect with the Irish Continental ferries on the Rosslare harbor pier. There are no transfer costs.

Cherbourg Ferry Terminal: Bus transfer service from the SNCF rail station is not available. Alternatively, a taxi service is available for about 20 francs. Inquiries should be made because bus-transfer service may be implemented.

Connolly Station: Trains connecting Dublin with the Rosslare ferry terminal use this station. A sign directing visitors to the nearby tourist information office on O'Connell Street is located to the right of the station's cloakroom in the concourse. The train information office is just beyond the cloakroom on the right-hand side. Use the side escalator to the street exit. A taxi stand is located at the station front.

Connolly station is the terminal in Dublin for trains arriving from Northern Ireland. It is also the terminal for boat trains connecting with the Irish Ferries that sail from the port of Rosslare, south of Dublin, to the French port of Cherbourg.

Irish Ferries Sailing Schedule in 2000

Service runs April 1–September 27

IRELAND TO FRANCE
Rosslare/Cherbourg
Departs at 1600   April even dates
                       May even dates
                       June uneven dates
                       July 5 + uneven dates
                       August even dates
                       September uneven dates
                       No winter dates

FRANCE TO IRELAND
Cherbourgh to Rosslare
Departs at 1800

April uneven dates
May 3 + uneven dates
June even dates
July 6 + 12 + even dates (no travel on 22, 24)
August uneven dates
September 2–20 even dates + 27 and 29
No winter dates

Sailing From Ireland to Britain

Stena Line, the world's largest international ferry company, operates on 16 routes in northwestern Europe, including the Irish Sea and the English Channel. Stena's HSS (High–speed Sea Service) ships cruise between Belfast in Northern Ireland and Stranraer in Scotland in only 105 minutes. Stena Line's Superferry service offers leisurely crossings with duty-free shopping, meals and even a movie (on some routes). The Superferry *Koningin Beatrix* on the Rosslare-Fishguard route, capable of carrying 2,100 passengers and 500 automobiles, is the largest and most luxurious ferry to operate on the southern Irish Sea.

Irish Ferries can take you from Dublin to Holyhead and P&O European Ferries serve on the Larne-Cairnryan route.

Coming from London by train requires a transfer to either a Stena Line or Irish Ferries ferry at Holyhead. The Stena Line ferries serve the port of Dun Laoghaire, a suburb of Dublin, where passengers can transfer to the center of the city by the local train service, DART.

IRELAND TO GREAT BRITAIN
Stena Line to Britain

ROUTE	JOURNEY
Rosslare-Fishguard	three hours twenty minutes Superferry or ninety-nine minutes Stena Lynx
Dublin-Holyhead	three hours fifteen minutes Superferry
Dun Läoghaire-Holyhead	ninety-nine minutes HSS
Belfast-Stranraer	three hours Superferry or 105 minutes HSS

Irish Ferries Sailing Schedule: Service
January 1–December 31, 2000

	DEPART	ARRIVE
Dublin to Holyhead	0945	1300
	2145	0100
Holyhead to Dublin	1545	1900
	0345	0700
	(Crossing time: three hours and fifteen minutes)	
Rosslare to Pembroke	0915	1300
	2130	0115
Pembroke to Rosslare	1500	1845
	0315	07.00
	(Crossing time: three hours and fourty-five minutes)	

INTERNATIONAL CALLING

The following chart provides the country codes and city codes you will need when calling from one country to another. The country codes should be used when dialing to that country from another country. In most cases you will also need to dial a city or area code prior to the local number.

Calling Europe from North America

To use these codes from within North America, dial 011 + country code, city code, and the local number you wish to reach.

Calling North America from Europe with a calling card:

Your local long-distance phone company will have a number for you to dial while in Europe (either a toll-free or a local call) to connect to an operator in your home country. For more information call one of the following:

AT&T Direct Service: (800) 331–1140; from abroad (412) 553–7458; www.att.com/traveler

MCI WorldPhone: (800) 996–7535; www.mci.com

SprintExpress: (800) 877–4646; www.sprint.com

Canada Primus: (800) 565–4708

	Country/City Code	AT&T	MCI	Sprint
AUSTRIA	43	022-903-011	022-903-012	022-903-014
Vienna	1			
Baden	2252			
Innsbruck	512			
Melk	27			
Salzburg	662			
BELGIUM	32	0–800-100-10	0800-10012	0800-100-14
Brussels	2			
Antwerp	3			
Bruges	50			
Ghent	9			
Namur	81			
DENMARK	45	8001-0010	8001-0022	800-10-877
City codes not required. All points are 8 digits or 45 plus 121				
FINLAND	358	9800-100-10	08001-102-80	0800-110-284
Helsinki	9			
Hanko	19			
Lahti	3			
Tampere	3			
Turku	2			
FRANCE	33	0800 99 00 11	0800 99 00 19	0800 99 00 87
City codes not required; regional codes are included.				
GERMANY	49	0800–2255–288	0800–888–8000	0800–888–0013
Berlin	30			
Dresden	351			
Leipzig	341			
Potsdam	331			
Hamburg	40			
Bremen	421			
Hameln	5151			
Hannover	511			
Lübeck	451			
Munich	89			
Berchtesgaden	8652			
Garmisch-Partenkirchen	8821			
Nuremberg	911			
Rothenburg (Romantic Road)	9851			
Ulm	731			
Koblenz	261			
Trier	651			

	Country/City Code	AT&T	MCI	Sprint
GREECE	30	00-800-1311	00-800-1211	008–001411
Athens	1			
Argos	751			
Corinth	741			
Patras	61			
Piraeus	1			
HUNGARY	36	00★★ 800-01111	00★★800-01411	00★★800-01-877
Budapest	1			
Key: ★★ = wait for second dial tone				
IRELAND	353	1–800–550–000	1–800–551–001	1–800–552–001
Dublin	1			
Cork	21			
Galway	91			
Kilkenny	56			
Killarney	64			
ITALY	39	172-1011	172-1022	172-1877
Milan	2			
Bologna	51			
Genoa	10			
Venice	41			
Rome	6			
Anzio	06			
Florence	55			
Naples	81			
Pisa	50			
LUXEMBOURG	352	0-800-0111	0800-0112	0800-0115
City codes not required.				
MONACO	377	800-90-288	800-90-019	800-90-087
Monte Carlo	no code required			
THE NETHERLANDS	31	0800-022-9111	0800-022-9122	0800-022-9119
Amsterdam	20			
Alkmaar	72			
Enkhuizen	228			
Haarlem	23			
Hoorn	299			
NORWAY	47	800-190-11	800-19912	800-19-877
City codes not required.				
PORTUGAL	351	0800-800-128	050-17-1234	0800-800-187
Lisbon	1			
Cascais and Estoril	1			
Coimbra	39			
Setubal	65			
Sintra	1			

Country/City Code		AT&T	MCI	Sprint
SPAIN	34	900-99-0011	900-99-0014	900-99-0013
When calling in Spain, use 9 before dialing city codes.				
Barcelona	3			
Blanes	72			
Lleida	73			
Sitges	3			
Tarragona	77			
Madrid	1			
Aranjuez	1			
Avila	20			
Burgos	47			
El Escorial	1			
Toledo	25			
SWEDEN	46	020-795-611	020-795-922	020-799-011
Stockholm	8			
Eskilstuna	16			
Norrkoping	11			
Uppsala	18			
SWITZERLAND	41	0-800-89-0011	0-800-89-0222	0800-89-9777
Bern	31			
Interlaken	33			
Lucerne	41			
Lake Lugano	91			
Rheinfelden	61			
Zürich	1			

TRAIN TRAVEL TERMINOLOGY

English	French	Italian	German	Spanish
On the train:				
aisle	couloir	corridoio	gang	pasillo
car	compartement	vettura	wagen	vagón
couchette	couchette	cuccetta	liegeplatz	couchette
restaurant car	voiture–restaurant	carrozza-restaurante	speisewagen	coche-restaurante
seat	place	posto	sitzplatz	asiento
sleeper	wagon-lit	cabina	bettplätz	cama
sleeping car	voiture-lit	vagone letto	schlafwagen	coche-cama
smoking	fumeur	per fumatori	raucher	fumadores
nonsmoking	non fumeur	non fumatori	nichtraucher	no fumadores
table	table	tavolo	tisch	mesa
toilets	toilettes	tolette	toiletten	servicios
window	fenêtre	finestrino	fenster	ventana
In the station:				
entrance	entrée	entrata	eingang	entrada
exit	sortie	uscita	ausgang	salida
Gentlemen	Hommes	Signori	Herren	Caballeros
Information	renseignements	informazioni	information	información
Ladies	Femmes	Signore	Damen	Señoras
left luggage	consigne	bagaglio depositato	gepäckauf-bewahrung	consigna
lost and found	objets trouvés	oggetti smarriti	fundbüro	oficina de objeto/perdidos
luggage	bagages	bagagli	gepäck	equipaje
luggage lockers	consigne automatique	armadietti per bagagli	schließfächer	consigna automática
station	gare	stazione	bahnhof	estación
subway/underground	Métro	Metropolitana	die U-bahn	Metro
track/platform	quai	binario	bahnsteig	andén
telephone	téléphone	telefono	telefon	teléfono
ticket office	guichet	biglietteria	fahrkarten-sshalter	despacho de billetes
train	train	treno	zug	tren

English	French	Italian	German	Spanish
At the ticket window:				
arrival	arrivée	arrivo	ankunft	llegada
arrives	arrive	arriva	kommt an	llega
change at	correspondance	cambiare a	umsteigen in	cambiar en
first class	première classe	prima classe	erste klasse	primera clase
second class	seconde classe	seconda classe	zweite klasse	segunda clase
connection	correspondance	coincidenza	anschluß	conexión
departure	départ	partenza	abfhart	salida
departs	part	parte	fährt ab	sale
domestic tickets	billets	biglietti nazionali	fahrkarten inland	billetes nacionales
earlier	plus tôt	più presto	früher	más temprano
express	express	espresso	schnellzug	expreso
fast	rapid	rapido	schnell	rápido
from Rennes	(en provenance) de Rennes	(proviene) da Rennes	von Rennes	(procede) de Rennes
international tickets	billets internationaux	biglietti internazionali	fahrkarten ausland	billetes internacionales
not available	non disponible	non disponibile	nicht erhältlich	no disponible
later	plus tard	più tardi	später	más tarde
local service	service local	servizio locale	personenzug	servicio local
next train	prochain train	prossimo treno	nächst zug	próximo tren
reservation	reservation	prenotazione	reservierung	reservación
schedule/ timetable	horaires	orario	fahrplan	horari
supplement payable	avec supplément	con pagamento di supplemento	zuschlagp-flichtig	con pago de suplemento
to *Oslo*	vers Oslo, à destination de Oslo	a Oslo	nach Oslo	a Oslo
via	via	via	über	via

RAIL FARES BETWEEN BASE CITIES

First Class one-way fares (*without* a railpass) between Base Cities are listed in U.S. dollars, but do not include seat reservation fees or sleeping car accommodation charges. Rates applicable as of press time and subject to change without notice. Second Class fares are approximately one-third less than First Class.

	AMS	ATH	BAR	BAS	BER	BRN	BRU	BUD	COL	CPH	FLO	FRA	GEN	HAM	LIS	LUX	LYN	MAD	MIL	MUC	NCE	OSL	PAR	PRA	ROM	STK	VCE	VEN
Amsterdam																												
Athens	585																											
Barcelona	272	441																										
Basel	179	399	190																									
Berlin	153	551	403	236																								
Bern	290	370	167	37	293																							
Brussels	49	543	236	95	198	132																						
Budapest	317	184	316	204	247	241	304																					
Cologne	62	527	264	130	155	167	50	255																				
Copenhagen	203	708	466	332	148	369	250	303	202																			
Florence	332	278	188	145	266	117	241	200	270	478																		
Frankfurt	115	528	295	105	158	142	104	202	54	241	248																	
Geneva	227	382	112	78	314	55	173	282	208	410	130	231																
Hamburg	110	614	370	238	85	275	156	349	108	94	383	159	316															
Lisbon	338	656	141	291	469	329	302	457	306	506	282	333	254	412														
Luxembourg	67	458	214	59	206	96	37	263	56	265	204	72	137	171	280													
Lyon	220	364	98	60	296	126	138	224	188	388	96	166	41	298	239	78												
Madrid	210	510	74	254	435	295	268	390	283	485	234	299	282	391	67	246	172											
Milan	296	289	152	110	346	81	205	164	238	442	36	213	93	325	293	169	75	226										
Munich	224	382	287	119	162	156	216	131	166	310	104	110	197	223	392	217	179	325	99									
Nice	253	341	110	162	398	133	217	216	290	494	63	265	99	377	251	134	80	184	52	151								
Oslo	388	881	453	505	261	542	435	487	375	185	628	426	583	267	689	438	565	663	592	490	594							
Paris	124	442	148	74	115	88	314	116	207	316	119	103	222	214	477	66	96	186	151	183	129	477						
Prague	236	190	416	185	222	252	85	175	224	193	121	281	161	477	289	313	485	363	99	213	343	204	238					
Rome	362	252	182	174	300	269	198	308	384	495	194	277	159	416	323	239	145	258	70	138	87	603	204	198				
Stockholm	402	890	604	514	551	551	432	496	384	194	684	435	592	271	688	447	570	654	648	427	603	683	474	344	689			
Venice	321	315	183	140	305	112	290	140	269	390	31	244	125	356	324	200	106	257	31	99	78	151	202	184	65	598		
Vienna	387	415	276	159	132	196	301	49	215	361	124	162	284	309	417	218	219	350	124	90	176	623	273	60	158	398	100	

PASSPORT INFORMATION

The phone numbers of the passport office call centers listed below provide a recorded message that describes the documents you need and the application process for obtaining a passport as well as reporting the loss or theft of your passport. The call centers also explain how to obtain a copy of the report of the birth or death of a U.S. citizen abroad. The message will direct you to the proper agencies for information regarding naturalization, travel advisories, customs regulations, and shots required by various countries.

Applying several months in advance is advised. Passport forms are available not only from official passport offices, but also through many post offices, clerks of court, and local municipal offices.

The National Passport Information Center at 1–900–CALLNPIC provides telephone operators for prompt and accurate response to any questions you may have. You can access more passport and travel information via the Internet at http://travel.state.gov.

The regional offices are as follows:

Boston: Thomas P. O'Neill Federal Building, 10 Causeway Street, Suite 247, Boston, Massachusetts 02222–1094; (617) 565–6990.

Chicago: Kluczynski Office Building, 230 South Dearborn Street, Room 380, Chicago, Illinois 60604–1564; (312) 353–7155. ★

Honolulu: First Hawaii Tower, 1132 Bishop Street, Suite 500, Honolulu, Hawaii 96813–2309; (808) 522–8283 or (808) 522–8286.

Houston: Mickey Leland Federal Building, 1919 Smith Street, Suite 1100, Houston, Texas 77002–8049; (713) 209–3153. ★

Los Angeles: Federal Building, 11000 Wilshire Boulevard, Room 11000, Los Angeles, California 90024–3615; (310) 575–5700. ★

Miami: Claude Pepper Federal Office Building, 51 Southwest First Avenue, Third Floor, Miami, Florida 33130–1680; (305) 539–3600. ★

New Orleans: Postal Services Building, 701 Loyal Avenue, T-12005, New Orleans, Louisiana 70113–1931; (504) 589–6728 or (504) 589–6161.

New York: Greater Manhattan Federal Building, 367 Hudson Street, New York, New York 10014; (212) 206–3500. ★

Philadelphia: U.S. Customs House, 200 Chestnut Street, Room 103, Philadelphia, Pennsylvania 19106–2970; (215) 597–7480.

San Francisco: 95 Hawthorne Street, 5th Floor, San Francisco, California 94105–3901; (415) 744–4010 or (415) 744–4444.

Seattle: Federal Building, 915 Second Avenue, Room 992, Seattle, Washington 98174–1091; (206) 220–7788.

Stamford: One Landmark Square, Broad and Atlantic Streets, Stamford, Connecticut 06901–2667; (203) 325–3530. ★

Washington, D.C.: 1111 19th Street NW, Washington, D.C. 20524–1705; (202) 647–0518.

★ These offices use an appointment system.

EUROPEAN TOURIST OFFICES IN NORTH AMERICA

**Austrian National Tourist Office—www.anto.com;
E-mail: antonyc@ibm.net**
New York: P.O. Box 1142, 500 Fifth Avenue, #800, New York, NY 10110. *Tel:* (212) 944–6880. *Fax:* (212) 730–4568.
Montreal: Office National Autrichien du Tourisme, 1010 Ouest Rue Sherbrooke, Suite 1410, Montreal, Quebec H3A 2R7, Canada. *Tel:* (514) 849–3709. *Fax:* (514) 849–9577.
Toronto: 2 Bloor Street East, Suite 3330, Toronto, Ontario M4W 1A8, Canada. *Tel:* (416) 967–3381. *Fax:* (416) 967–4101.
Vancouver: 200 Granville Street, Suite 1380, Granville Square, Vancouver, BC V6C 1S4, Canada. *Tel:* (604) 683–5808. *Fax:* (604) 662–8528.

**Belgium Tourist Office— www.visitbelgium.com;
E-mail: belinfo@nyxfer.blythe.org**
New York: 780 Third Avenue, Suite 1501, New York, NY 10017–7076. *Tel:* (212) 758–8130. *Fax:* (212) 355–7675.

British Tourist Authority—www.visitbritain.com
New York: 551 Fifth Avenue, Suite 701, New York, NY 10176–0799. *Tel:* (800) 462–2748 or (212) 986–2200. *Fax:* (212) 986–1188.
Chicago: 625 North Michigan Avenue, Suite 1510, Chicago, IL 60611. *Tel:* (312) 787–0464. *Fax:* (312) 787–7746.
Montreal: P.O. Box 760, Succursale NDG Montreal, Quebec H4A 3S2 Canada. *Tel:* (514) 484–3594. *Fax:* (514) 489–8965.

Czech Service Center—www.czech.cz
New York: 1109 Madison Avenue, New York, NY 10028. *Tel:* (212) 288–0330; *Fax:* (212) 288–0971.

French Government Tourist Office—www.fgtousa.org or www.francetourism.com; E-mail: info@francetourism.com
For information on France by telephone, dial (900) 990–0040 in the United States (charge is 95 cents per minute). Or call (410) 286–8310 for information requests.
New York: 444 Madison Avenue, Sixteenth Floor, New York, NY, 10022–6903. *Tel:* (212) 838–7800. *Fax:* (212) 838–7855.
Chicago: 676 N. Michigan Avenue, Suite 336, Chicago, IL 60611. *Tel:* (312) 751–7800. *Fax:* (312) 337–6339.
Los Angeles: 9454 Wilshire Boulevard, Suite 715, Beverly Hills, CA 90212–2967. *Tel:* (310) 271–6665. *Fax:* (310) 276–2835.

Montreal: 1981 McGill College Avenue, Suite 490, Montreal, Quebec PQH3A 2W9, Canada. *Fax:* (514) 845–4868.

Toronto: 30 St. Patrick Street, Suite 700, Toronto, Ontario M5T 3A3, Canada. *Fax:* (416) 979–7587.

German National Tourist Office—www.germanytourisim.de; E-mail: gnotony@aol.com

New York: 122 East Forty-Second Street, Fifty-Second Floor, Chanin Building, New York, NY 10168–0072. *Tel:* (212) 661–7200. *Fax:* (212) 661–7174.

Toronto: 175 Bloor Street, East, North Tower, Suite 604, Toronto, Ontario M4W 3R8, Canada. *Tel:* (416) 968–1570. *Fax:* (416) 968–1986. *E-mail:* germanto@idirect.com

Greek National Tourist Organization—www.gogreece.com; E-mail: gnto@orama.com

New York: 645 Fifth Avenue, Olympic Tower, Fifth Floor, New York, NY 10022. *Tel:* (212) 421–5777. *Fax:* (212) 826–6940. E-mail: gnto@aurora.eexi.gr.

Hungarian National Tourist Office—www.gotohungary.com; E-mail: huntour@ldt.com

New York: c/o Embassy of the Republic of Hungary, 150 East Fifty-Eighth Street, Thirty-Third Floor, New York, NY 10155–3398. *Tel:* (212) 355–0240. *Fax:* (212) 207–4103.

Irish Tourist Board—www.ireland.travel.ie; E-mail: info@irishtouristboard.com

New York: 345 Park Avenue, New York, NY 10154. *Tel:* (212) 418–0800, (800) 223–6470. *Fax:* (212) 371–9052.

Toronto: 160 Bloor Street East, Suite 1150, Toronto, Ontario M4W 1B9, Canada. *Tel:* (416) 929–2777. *Fax:* (416) 929–6783.

Italian Government Tourist Board—www.italiantourism.com

New York: 630 Fifth Avenue, Suite 1565, New York, NY, 10111. *Tel:* (212) 245–4822. *Fax:* (212) 586–9249.

Chicago: 401 North Michigan Avenue, Suite 3030, Chicago, IL 60611. *Tel:* (312) 644–9448. *Fax:* (312) 644–3019.

Los Angeles: 12400 Wilshire Boulevard, Suite 550, Los Angeles, CA 90025. *Tel:* (310) 820–0098. *Fax:* (310) 820–6357.

Montreal: 1 Place Ville Marie, Suite 1914, Montreal, Quebec, H3B 3M9, Canada. *Tel:* (514) 866–7667. *Fax:* (514) 392–1429.

Luxembourg National Tourist Office— www.visitluxembourg.com; E-mail: luxnto@aol.com

New York: 17 Beekman Place, New York, NY 10022. *Tel:* (212) 935–8888. *Fax:* (212) 935–5896.

Malta National Tourist Office—www.visitmalta.com; E-mail: 104452.2005@compuserve.com

New York: Empire State Building, 350 Fifth Avenue, Suite 4412, New York, NY 10118. *Tel:* (212) 695–9520. *Fax:* (212) 695–8229.

Monaco Government Tourist/Convention Bureau— www.monaco.mc/usa

New York: 565 Fifth Avenue, New York, NY 10017. *Tel:* (800) 753–9696 or (212) 286–3330. *Fax:* (212) 286–9890.

Netherlands Board of Tourism—www.goholland.com; E-mail: go2holland@aol.com

Chicago: P.O. Box 220079, Chicago, IL 60622–0079. *Tel:* (312) 455–1601. *Fax:* (312) 455–1602. *Internet:* www.holland.com.

Northern Ireland Tourist Board— www.northernireland.tourism.com

New York: 551 Fifth Avenue, Suite 701, New York, NY 10176. *Tel:* (800) 326–0036 or (212) 922–0101. *Fax:* (212) 922–0099.

Toronto: 3 Bloor Street West, Suite 1501, Toronto, Ontario M4W 3E2. *Tel:* (800) 576–8174 or (416) 925–6368; *Fax:* (416) 925–6033.

Portuguese National Tourist Office—www.portugal.org

New York: 590 Fifth Avenue, 4th Floor, New York, NY 10036–4704. *Tel:* (212) 719–3985 or (800) PORTUGAL. *Fax:* (212) 719–4019.

Montreal: 500 Sherbrooke Street West, Suite 940, Montreal, Canada, QC H3A 3C6. *Tel:* (514) 282–1264; *Fax:* (514) 499–1450.

Toronto: 60 Bloor Street, Suite 1005, Toronto, Ontario M4W 3B8, Canada. *Tel:* (416) 921–7376; *Fax:* (416) 921–1353.

Scandinavian Tourist Boards of Denmark, Finland, Iceland, Norway, and Sweden—www.goscandinavia.com; E-mail: info@goscandinavia.com

New York: P.O. Box 4649, Grand Central Station, New York, NY 10163–4649. *Tel:* (212) 885–9700. *Fax:* (212) 885–9710.

Tourist Office of Spain—www.okspain.org; E-mail: oetny@okspain.org

New York: 666 Fifth Avenue, Thirty-Fifth Floor, New York, NY 10103. *Tel:* (888) OK SPAIN or (212) 265–8822. *Fax:* (212) 265–8864.

Chicago: 845 N. Michigan Avenue, Water Tower Place Suite 915 E, Chicago, IL 60611. *Tel:* (312) 642–1992. *Fax:* (312) 642–9817.

Los Angeles: San Vicente Plaza Building, 8383 Wilshire Boulevard, Suite 960, Beverly Hills, CA 90211. *Tel:* (213) 658–7188. *Fax:* (213) 658–1061.

Toronto: 2 Bloor Street West, Thirty-Fourth Floor, Toronto, Ontario M4W 3E2, Canada. *Tel:* (416) 961–3131. *Fax:* (416) 961–1992.

Miami: 1221 Brickell Avenue, Miami, FL 33131. *Tel:* (305) 358–1992. *Fax:* (305) 358–8223.

Switzerland Tourism—switzerlandtourism.com; E-mail: stnewyork@switzerlandtourism.com

New York: 608 Fifth Avenue, New York, NY 10020. *Tel:* (212) 757–5944. *Fax:* (212) 262–6116.

Chicago: 150 North Michigan Avenue, Suite 2930, Chicago, IL 60601. *Tel:* (312) 630–5840.

Los Angeles: 222 North Sepulveda Boulevard, Suite 1570, El Segundo, CA 90245. *Tel:* (310) 335–5980. *Fax:* (310) 335–5982.

Toronto: 926 The East Mall, Etobicoke, Ontario M9B 6K1, Canada. *Tel:* (416) 695–2090. *Fax:* (416) 695–2774.

AIRLINE NUMBERS AND WEB SITES
(Dialing from U.S.)

Aer Lingus (EI) 800–771–1466/223–6537
www.aerlingus.ie

Air Canada (AC) 800–776–3000
www.aircanada.ca

Air France (AF)........................ 800–237–2747
www.airfrance.com

American Airlines, Inc. (AA) 800–433–7300
www.aa.com

Austrian Airlines (OS) 800–843–0002
www.aua.com

British Airways (BA) 800–AIRWAYS
www.britishairways.com

Continental Airlines (CO)........ 800–525–0280
www.continental.com

CSA Czechoslovak
Airlines (OK)....................800–628–6107
www.csa.cz

Delta Air Lines, Inc. (DL) 800–241–4141
www.delta-air.com

Finnair (AY) 800–950–5000
www.us.finnair.com

Icelandair (FI) 800–223–5500
www.icelandair.com

KLM Royal Dutch Airlines (KL) 800–374–7747
klm.com

Lufthansa German
Airlines (LH) 800–645–3880
www.lufthansa-usa.com

Northwest Airlines,
Inc. (NW)........................ 800–447-4747
www.nwa.com

Olympic Airlines (OA) 800–223–1226
www.olympic-airways.com

Sabena Belgian World
Airlines (SN) 800–955–2000
www.sabena.com

Scandinavian Airlines
System (SK) 800–221–2350
www.flysas.com

Swissair (SR) 800–221–4750
www.swissair.com

TAP Air Portugal (TO) 800–221–7370
www.tap.pt.com

Tower Air (FF) 800–221–2500
www.towerair.com

Trans World Airlines, Inc.
(TWA)............................800–221–2000
www.twa.com

United Air Lines, Inc. (UA) 800–241–6522
www.ual.com

USAirways (US) 800–428–4322
www.usairways.com

Virgin Atlantic Airways
Ltd. (VS) 800-862-8621
www.virgin-atlantic.com

HOTEL RESERVATIONS NUMBERS
(Dialing from United States)

Best Western International 800–528–1234
www.bestwestern.com

Choice Hotels
International, Inc. 800–4–CHOICE
www.hotelchoice.com

Consort Hotels Ltd 800–55–CONSORT
www.consorthotels.com

Forte & Meridian Hotels.......... 800–225–5843
www.forte-hotels.com

Golden Tulip International........ 800–344–1212
www.goldentulips.com

Hilton Reservations
Worldwide 800–HILTONS
www.hilton.com

Holiday Inns Worldwide 800–HOLIDAY
www.basshotels.com

Hyatt Worldwide
Reservation Centres 800–233–1234
www.hyatt.com

Inter-Continental
Hotels Corp 800–327–0200
www.interconti.com

Inter-Europe Hotels 800–221–6509

ITT Sheraton Corporation 800–325–3535
www.sheraton.com

International B&B 800–722–3679

Kempinski International 800–426-3135
www.kempinski.com

Leading Hotels of the World 800–223–6800
www.lhw.com

Loews Representation Int'l........800–223–0888
www.loewshotel.com

Marriott Corporation 800–228–9290
www.marriott.com

MinOtels Int'l 800–336–4668

Movenpick Hotels Int'l 800–34–HOTEL

Nikko Hotels International 800–645–5687
www.nikkohotels.com

Preferred Hotels & Resorts
Worldwide 800–323–7500
www.preferredhotels.com

Radisson Hotels, Int'l 800–333–3333
www.radisson.com

Ramada International Hotels
& Resorts 800–854–7854
www.ramada.com

SRS Steinberger Reservation
Service 800–223–5652

Swisshotel 800–63–SWISS
www.swisshotel.com

AIRPORT CITY CONNECTIONS

Those arriving in many popular European cities will find direct rail service between central stations and airports at a growing number of European airports. Service includes:

CITY	AIRPORT	DISTANCE	TRANSPORT TYPE	BUS #	CITY TERMINAL
Alacant	Alicante	12 km	Bus services daily	13/14	Plaza Chapi
Amsterdam	Schiphol	14 km	Train every 15 min.	—	Centraal Station
Athens (Athinai)	Ellinikon	14 km	Bus every 30 min.	A&B	Syndagma Square/ Amalias Avenue
Barcelona	Barcelona	10 km	Train every 30 min.	—	Barcelona Sants
Basel	Basel/Mulhouse/ Freiburg	9 km	Bus every 20-30 min.	50	SBB Station/ Kannenfeldplatz
Belfast	Belfast International	26 km	Bus every 30 min.	300 (airbus) Sundays #60	Europa Buscentre, Glengall Street
Berlin	Schönefeld	18 km	S-bahn train every 30 min.	—	Bahnhof Zoo/Ost Hbf
Berlin	Tegel	7 km	Bus every 10 min.	X9 & 109	Bahnhof Zoo
Bonn	Köln/Bonn	20 km	Bus every 20 min.	670	Hauptbahnhof
Bordeaux	Merignac	12 km	Bus 15 services daily	—	Gare St. Jean
Bristol	Bristol	13 km	Bus 10 services daily	331	Bus station, also Temple Meads Station
Brussels	Nationaal	12 km	Train every 20 min.	—	Midi/Zuid Station also calls at Central and Nord
Budapest	Ferihegy	16 km	Bus every 30 min.	—	Bus Station, Erzébet tér
Dublin	Dublin	11 km	Bus "Airlink" every 15–25 min.	—	Heuston Station/ Busaras
Düsseldorf	Düsseldorf	7 km	Train (S-Bahn) every 20 min	—	Hauptbahnhof

STATION	AIRPORT	DISTANCE	TRANSPORT	BUS #	CITY TERMINAL
Florence (Firenze)	Firenze Peretola	7 km	Bus every 25 min.	ATAF 62	Stazione FS
Frankfurt am Main	Frankfurt/Main	10 km	Train (S-Bahn) 4–5 hourly	—	Hauptbahnhof
Gèneve	Cointrin	4 km	Train, 4 times hourly	—	Cornavin Station
Genova (Genoa)	Cristoforo Colombo	7 km	"Volabus" 12–14 services daily	—	Brignole and Principe stations; Piazza de Ferrari
Göteburg	Landvetter	25 km	Bus every 15 min. Mon–Fri; every 20–30 min. Saturday, Sunday, and holidays	—	City Air Terminal/ Central Station
Grenoble	Lyon Satolas	85 km	Bus (Cars Faure) 9–13/day 0500–1915	—	Gare routière (bus station)
Hamburg	Fuhlsbüttel	11 km	Bus (Jasper) every 20 min.	—	Hauptbahnhof/ Kirchenallee
Hannover	Langenhagen	13 km	Bus every 30 min.	60	Bus station at Hauptbahnhof
Helsinki	Vantaa	19 km	Bus every 15–20 min.	—	City Air Terminal/ Rail Station
Copenhagen (Kobenhavn)	Kastrup	9 km	Train every 20 min.	—	Central Station
Cologne (Koln)	Koln/Bonn	20 km	Bus every 20 min.	670	Hauptbahnhof
Lisbon (Lisboa)	Portela	7 km	Bus every 20 min. 0700–2100	AeroBus 91	Cais do Sodré
London	City	10 km	Bus every 10 min. 0650–2050 Mon–Fri, exc. holidays; 0710–1150 Sat; 1100–2050 Sun	—	Liverpool Street Station
London	Gatwick	44 km	Train every 15 min.	—	Victoria Station
London	Heathrow	24 km	LT train, every 5–10 min.	—	London Underground/ Paddington Station

STATION	AIRPORT	DISTANCE	TRANSPORT	BUS #	CITY TERMINAL
Luxembourg	Findel	7 km	Bus every 15-30 min.	9	Gare Centrale
Lyon	Satolas	25 km	Bus (Navette Aéroport) every 20 min.	—	Perrache Station, via Part Dieu Station
Madrid	Barajas	12 km	Bus approx. every 10 min.	—	Plaza Colón
Málaga	Málaga	7 km	Train, every 30 min.	—	Málaga Station Centre-Alameda & RENFE Stations
Marseille	Marseille/Provence	28 km	Bus every 20 min.	—	Gare St. Charles
Milan (Milano)	Linate	9 km	Bus approx. every 30 min.	—	Piazza S. Babila/Milano Centrale Station
Milan (Milano)	Milano-Malpensa	45 km	Train "Malpensa Express" (FNM) every 30 minutes	—	Cadorna rail Stations
Münich (Munchen)	Strauss	28 km	Train S-Bahn , every 20 min.	—	Hauptbahnhof
Naples (Napoli)	Capodichino	7 km	Bus every 20 min.	14	Piazza Garibaldi (Central Station)
Nice	Nice-Côte d'Azur	7 km	Bus every 20 min. Bus every 20 min.	23 20	Gare Routière Départmentale/SNCF rail station
Oslo	Gardermoen	49 km	Airport Express Trains every ten minutes	—	Central Station
Palma de Mallorca	Palma	11 km	Bus every 30 min.	—	Plaça España
Paris	Charles de Gaulle	25 km	RER train (Line B) every 7–15 min.	—	Gare du Nord/ Châtelet les Halles & St. Michel
Paris	Orly	15 km	RER train every 15 min. (Line C)	—	Austerlitz, St. Michel, Musée d'Orsay and Invalides
Piraeus	Hellinkon	20 km	Bus every 50-60 min.	—	Central Passenger Terminal and Akti

STATION	AIRPORT	DISTANCE	TRANSPORT	BUS #	CITY TERMINAL
Pisa	Pisa (Galilei)	2 km	Train 11 Daily Bus	— 7	Pisa Centrale (trains continue to/from Firenze)
Porto	Pedras Rubras	17 km	Bus every 15–30 min.	—	Praça do Carmo
Prague (Praha)	Ruzyne	17 km	Bus (CSA) every 30 min.	—	CSA office, Vcelnici (100 m from Masarykovo rail station)
Rome (Roma)	Leonardo da Vinci (Fiumicino)	26 km	Train every 20–30 min.	—	Roma Tiburtina/ Ostiense/Termini
Salzburg	Maxglan	5 km	Bus every 15 min.	77	Salzburg Bahnhof
Stavanger	Sola	14 km	Bus every 15–20 min.	—	Sentrum/Hotel Atlantic
Stockholm	Arlanda	44 km	Bus every 10–15 min.	Flygbuss	Cityterminalen (close to Central Station)
Strasbourg	Entzheim	12 km	Bus every 15–30 min.	—	Etoile Hommede Fer/ Central Rail Station
Stuttgart	Echterdingen	14 km	Train SBahn every 20–30 min.	—	Hauptbahnhof
Turin (Torino)	Caselle	16 km	Bus every 45 min.	—	Corso Inghilterra 3
Toulouse	Blagnac	8 km	Bus every 20 min. while airport open	—	Gare Routière/ Place Jeanne d'Arc
València	Manises	9 km	Train every 30–60 mins.	—	Nord Rail Station
Venice (Venezia)	Marco Polo	13 km	Bus every 30/60 min. (summer/winter)	5	Pizzale Roma
Vienna (Wien)	Schwechat	17 km	Train every 30 min. Bus every 20–30 mins.	—	Wien Mitte and Wien Nord Stations
Zürich	Zürich (Kloten)	12 km	Train 7 times per hour	—	Zürich Hauptbahnhof

In addition, rail service to other cities via the Airport Station may be available.

To order, call (800) 722–7151 or (614) 793–7651 or visit the secure Web site of Rail Pass Express at www.railpass.com.

EURAIL PASSES

Eurail Passes entitle you to unlimited travel on Europe's extensive 100,000–mile rail network in 17 countries of Europe (England, Scotland, and Wales not included) as follows:

Austria • Belgium • Denmark • Finland • France • Germany • Greece
Hungary • Ireland (Rep.) • Italy • Luxembourg • Netherlands • Norway
Portugal • Spain • Sweden • Switzerland

Eurail Pass
Travel on any or all days
for the duration of the pass.
1ST CLASS

15 days	$554
21 days	$718
1 month	$890
2 months	$1260
3 months	$1558

Children 4-11, half adult fare. Under age 4 travel free.

Eurail Saverpass
Rail travel for 2-5 people
traveling together at all times.
Price is per person.

$470
$610
$756
$1072
$1324

Eurail Flexipass
Choose your travel days and
use them within 60 days.
1ST CLASS

10 days in 2 months	$654
15 days in 2 months	$862

Children 4-11, half adult fare. Under age 4 travel free.

Eurail Saver Flexipass
Rail travel for 2-5 people
traveling together at all times.
Price is per person.

$556
$732

Eurail Youth Pass*
2ND CLASS

15 days	$388
21 days	$499
1 month	$623
2 months	$882
3 months	$1089

*Available for passengers 12–25 on their first date of travel.

Eurail Youth Flexipass*
2ND CLASS

10 days in 2 months	$458
15 days in 2 months	$599

*Available for passengers 12–25 on their first date of travel.

EUROPASS

The Europass features unlimited travel in the 5 most frequently visited countries of Europe: France, Germany, Italy, Spain, and Switzerland.

You determine the number of travel days from 5, 6, 8, 10, or 15 travel days needed in a 2-month period, making the Europass the most flexible rail pass available. In addition you may add up to 2 of the following zones to extend the geographic area of the pass (additional zones do not extend the pass length in days):

Benelux	Belgium, Luxembourg, & the Netherlands
Danube	Austria & Hungary
Greece Plus	Greece & Ferry Crossing to Italy
Portugal	

Europass
Valid for rail travel in: France, Germany, Italy, Spain, and Switzerland.

	ADULT 1ST CLASS	YOUTH* 2ND CLASS
5 days in 2 months	$348	$233
6 days in 2 months	$368	$253
8 days in 2 months	$448	$313
10 days in 2 months	$528	$363
15 days in 2 months	$728	$513

*Youth price available for passengers 12–25. Children 4-11, half adult fare; under age 4 travel free.

Associate Zones
May add up to 2 of the following zones to extend the geographic area of the Europass: Benelux, Danube, Greece, and Portugal.

	ADULT 1ST CLASS	YOUTH* 2ND CLASS
1 Add-on Zone	$60	$45
2 Add-on Zones	$100	$78

Children 5–11, half adult fare; under age 4 travel free.

Europass SaverPass
Valid for First Class rail travel for 2–5 people traveling together at all times in the countries of: France, Germany, Italy, Spain, and Switzerland. Prices are per person.

	ADULT 1ST CLASS
5 days in 2 months	$296
6 days in 2 months	$314
8 days in 2 months	$382
10 days in 2 months	$450
15 days in 2 months	$620

Children 4-11, half adult fare; under age 4 travel free. Rates are per person.

Europass SaverPass Associate Zones
May add up to 2 of the following zones to extend the geographic area of the Europass SaverPass: Benelux, Danube, Greece, and Portugal.

	ADULT 1ST CLASS
1 Add-on Zone	$52
2 Add-on Zones	$86

Children 4–11, half adult fare; under age 4 travel free.

COUNTRY AND REGIONAL PASSES

Amsterdam Culture & Leisure Pass

ADULT
$25

Contains over 30 vouchers for free entrance and discounts to Amsterdam's sites and museums including the Van Gogh Museum, the Rijksmuseum, Holland Casino. Receive substantial savings on canal cruises, meals, and entertainment.

Austrian Railpass

	ADULT	
	1ST CLASS	2ND CLASS
3 days in 15	$154	$104
Additional Days	$22	$16

Children 4–12, half adult fare; 4 and under travel free. 5 day maximum additional rail days. Bonuses include discounts on steamers, local trains, and bicycle rentals.

Balkan Flexipass

Valid for rail travel in Bulgaria, Greece, Former Yugoslav Republic of Macedonia, Montenegro, Romania, Serbia, and Turkey.

	1ST CLASS	
	ADULT	YOUTH
5 days in 1 month	$152	$90
10 days in 1 month	$264	$156
15 days in 1 month	$317	$190

Children 4-12, half adult fare. Youth 13–25.

Benelux Tourrail Pass

Valid for rail travel in Belguim, Luxembourg and the Netherlands.

5 days in 1 month	1ST CLASS	2ND CLASS
Adult	$217	$155
Youth	—	$104

Benelux Tourrail for Two

Valid for rail travel in Belgium, Luxembourg and the Netherlands. Prices are for two people traveling together at all times.

	1ST CLASS		2ND CLASS	
	1ST PERSON	2ND PERSON	1ST PERSON	2ND PERSON
5 days in 1 month	$217	$109	$155	$78

Youth 4-25; under age 4 travel free.

Czech FlexiPass

	1ST CLASS
5 days in 15 days	$69

Children 4–11, half adult fare; under age 4 travel free.

European East Pass
Valid for rail travel in Austria, Czech Republic, Hungary, Poland, and Slovak Republic.

	1ST CLASS
5 days in 1 month	$205
Additional Days	$23

Up to 5 additional days can be added. Children 4–11, half adult fare; under 4 free.

FinnRail Pass

	1ST CLASS	2ND CLASS
3 days in 1 month	$180	$120
5 days in 1 month	$244	$162

Children 6–16, half adult fare; under age 6 travel free..

France Pass

	ADULT		2 ADULTS*	
	1ST CLASS	2ND CLASS	1ST CLASS	2ND CLASS
3 days in 15	$164	$140	$205	$175
Additional days	$30	$30	$30	$30

	YOUTH
4 days in 2 months	$158
Additional days	$26

Maximum of 6 extra days. Youth 12–25; children 4–11, half adult fare; under age 4 travel free.

*Price per person based on 2 people traveling together at all times, includes 40% companion discount.

German Railpass

	ADULT		YOUTH
	1ST CLASS	2ND CLASS	2ND CLASS
4 days in 1 month	$252	$174	$138
Additional rail days	$32	$22	$18

Maximum of 6 extra days may be added. Bonuses for passholders include free travel on KD River Steamers on certain Rhine, Main, and Moselle River sections and free travel on selected bus lines operated by Deutsche Touring/Europabus. Youth 12–25. Children 7-11, Half adult fare; under age 6 travel free.

German Twinpass
Valid for 2 adults traveling together at all times.

	ADULT	
	1ST CLASS	2ND CLASS
4 days in 1 month	$378	$261
Additional rail days	$48	$33

Same extra day maximum and bonuses as German Railpass.

Greek Flexipass
Valid for 1st class rail travel in Greece.

	ADULT	YOUTH	CHILD
3 days in 1 month	$86	$62	$58
4 days in 1 month	$110	—	$74
5 days in 1 month	$120	$89	$85
6 days in 1 month	$144	—	$101

Youth 12–25. Children 2–11; under age 2 travel free.

Holland Railpass

| | ADULT | | YOUTH |
	1ST CLASS	2ND CLASS	2ND CLASS
3 days in 1 month	$98	$65	$52
5 days in 1 month	$147	$98	$79

| | SENIOR | | CHILD | |
	1ST CLASS	2ND CLASS	1ST CLASS	2ND CLASS
3 days in 1 month	$78	$52	$50	$33
5 days in 1 month	$119	$79	$74	$49

Youth 12–25. Seniors 60+. Children 4–11; under age 4 travel free.

Holland Rail TwinPass

| | ADULT | | YOUTH |
	1ST CLASS	2ND CLASS	2ND CLASS
3 days in 1 month	$147	$98	$78
5 days in 1 month	$221	$147	$119

| | SENIOR | | CHILD | |
	1ST CLASS	2ND CLASS	1ST CLASS	2ND CLASS
3 days in 1 month	$117	$78	$75	$50
5 days in 1 month	$179	$119	$111	$74

Youth 4–25. Children age 4–11; under age 4 travel free.

Hungarian Flexipass

	1ST CLASS
5 days in 15 days	$64
10 days in 1 month	$80

Children 5–14, half adult fare; under age 5 travel free.

Iberic Flexipass

Valid for unlimited rail travel in Spain and Portugal.

	1ST CLASS
3 days in 2 months	$205
Additional days	$45

Supplements required for travel on the AVE and Talgo high-speed trains. Maximum of 7 extra days may be added. Children 4–11, half adult fare. Under age 4 travel free.

Irish Rail & Bus Passes

Contact CIE Tours International to order Irish products: (800) 243-8687.

Irish Explorer—Rail

Unlimited rail travel on standard class Irish Rail in Republic of Ireland and local rail services in Dublin area.

	ADULT	CHILDREN
5 days in 15 days	$106	$53

Irish Explorer—Rail and Bus

Unlimited rail and bus travel on standard class Irish Rail in Republic of Ireland and local rail services in Dublin area; plus city bus services in Cork, Limerick, Galway, and Waterford.

	ADULT	CHILDREN
8 days in 15 days	$158	$79

Irish Rover—Rail
Unlimited rail travel on Irish Rail, Northern Ireland Rail and Suburban rail services in Northern Ireland plus local rail services in Dublin area.

	ADULT	CHILDREN
5 days in 15 days	$132	$66

Irish Rover—Rail and Bus
Unlimited rail travel on Irish Rail, Northern Ireland Rail, and suburban rail services in Northern Ireland plus local rail services in Dublin area plus bus services.

	ADULT	CHILDREN
5 days in 15 days	$316	$158

Emerald Card—Rail and Bus
Unlimited rail travel on standard class Irish Rail, Northen Ireland Rail, Irish Bus, Ulsterbus, local rail and bus services in Dublin; plus bus services in Belfast, Cork, Limerick, Galway, and Waterford.

	ADULT	CHILDREN
5 days	$316	$158
8 days	$182	$91

Italian Kilometric Ticket
The Kilometric Ticket is good for 20 trips on the entire Italian Rail Network—limited to 3,000 kilometers (1,875 miles) within 60 days and used by as many as five persons traveling together. When used by more than one person, each trip is calculated by multiplying the distance by the number of persons. Travel on the InterCity, EuroCity, Rapido, and TR450 trains is possible provided corresponding supplemental fares are paid at the railway stations when reservations are made.

1ST CLASS	2ND CLASS
$289	$181

The Italian State Railways impose an administration fee of $25 on each pass ordered. This fee is already included in the price above. Fee is nonrefundable.

Italy Railcard
Valid for unlimited travel on the entire Italian Rail Network including InterCity, EuroCity and Rapido trains with no surcharge. A supplement is required for ETR Pendolino trains.

Consecutive days	1ST CLASS	2ND CLASS
8 days	$299	$199
15 days	$373	$249
21 days	$433	$289
30 days	$522	$348
Flexi Rail Card		
4 days in 30 days	$239	$159
8 days in 30 days	$334	$223
12 days in 30 days	$429	$286

Children 4–11, half fare; under age 4 travel free.

Norway Rail Flexipass

	ADULT		SENIOR	
	1ST CLASS	2ND CLASS	1ST CLASS	2ND CLASS
3 days in 1 month	$181	$139	$144	$111
4 days in 1 month	$224	$172	$179	$139
5 days in 1 month	$250	$192	$200	$154

Children age 4-16 travel at half the adult fare. Children under age 4 travel free; maximum of 2 children travel free per adult. Senior age 60+. Travel on the Flam Railway Line no longer included. Beginning May 1, 2000, a discount of 30% will be offered on the Flam Line. New "Signatur" Expresstrains run on the Southern Line and Dovreline; Bergen Line added beginning June 2000. Supplement required, includes meals and refreshments.

Le Paris Bus

	ADULT
2 Consecutive Days	$34

Bus makes a continuous loop of the major sights in central Paris. Equipped with English-language commentary. You may get on and off the bus as many times as you wish to see such sights as the Eiffel Tower, Notre Dame, Arc de Triomphe, Louvre Museum, the Opéra, and the Grand Palais.

Paris Plus Pass/Le Paris Visite

	ADULT
3 Consecutive Days	$64

Provides unlimited travel on all zones of the entire Paris Métro (subway), Paris bus routes, RER trains to the airports, Versailles, EuroDisney, and the funicular at the Sacré Coeur. Children under age 5 travel free.

Portuguese Railpass

	1ST CLASS
4 days in 15 days	$105

Children 4–11, half adult fare; under age 4 travel free. Not valid on the Luis de Cameos train.

Prague Excursion

Valid for rail transportation from any Czech border crossing to Prague and returning within seven days.

	1ST CLASS	2ND CLASS
Adult	$55	$35
Youth	$45	$30
Children	$28	$18

Youth 12–25. Children 4–11.

Romanian Railpass

	1ST CLASS
3 days in 15 days	$60

Children 4–11, half adult fare; under age 4 travel free.

ScanRail Pass

Valid for unlimited rail travel in Denmark, Finland, Norway and Sweden.

	ADULT		SENIOR	
	1ST CLASS	2ND CLASS	1ST CLASS	2ND CLASS
5 days in 2 months	$270	$241	$200	$178
10 days in 2 months	$420	$374	$310	$276
21 days	$486	$432	$360	$321

	YOUTH		CHILD	
	1ST CLASS	2ND CLASS	1ST CLASS	2ND CLASS
5 days in 2 months	$203	$135	$150	$100
10 days in 2 months	$315	$210	$233	$155
21 days	$365	$243	$270	$180

Senior 60+. Youth 12–25. Children 4–11.

Spain Flexipass

	1ST CLASS	2ND CLASS
3 days in 2 months	$200	$155
Additional days	$35	$30

Maximum of 10 days. The AVE and Talgo 200 require an additional supplement. Children 4–11, half adult fare.

Sweden Railpass

	ADULT		ADD'L CHILDREN	
	1ST CLASS	2ND CLASS	1ST CLASS	2ND CLASS
3 days within 1 month	$211	$156	$148	$111
4 days within 1 month	$239	$177	$168	$124
5 days within 1 month	$268	$198	$188	$129

Special: Two children (under 16) travel free together with one adult.

Swiss Card (Ideal for Skiers)

Valid for one round-trip rail journey within 1 month.

	1ST CLASS	2ND CLASS
1 month - 1 round trip	$166	$128

Children under 16 free with parent; children 6–15, half adult fare in 2nd class and 40 percent of adult fare in 1st class.

Swiss Museum Pass

Gain entrance to over 180 museums in Switzerland. Valid for one month of unlimited visits.

	ADULT	ADULT + CHILDREN*
Museum Pass	$25	$30

*Valid for one adult and up to five children.

Swiss Pass

	1 ADULT		2 ADULTS*	
	1ST CLASS	2ND CLASS	1ST CLASS	2ND CLASS
4 days	$264	$188	$211	$150
8 days	$316	$238	$253	$190
15 days	$368	$288	$294	$230
21 days	$403	$320	$322	$256
1 month	$508	$400	$406	$320
Flexipass				
3 days in 15	$264	$176	$221	$141
Additional days	$30	$24	$24	$19

Includes unlimited travel on private railways, lake steamers, and city bus lines. Children 6–15, half adult fare; under age 6 travel free.
*Price per person based on 2 people traveling together, includes 40 percent companion discount. Children under 16 free with a parent.

The Vienna Card

	ADULT
3 Consecutive Days	$20

A network ticket valid for 72 hours in zone 100 (except the night buses) and provides transportation on the underground and S-Bahn railways, includes tram and bus travel. Also offers discounts at museums, concert halls, and coffeehouses, the city's famous Ferris wheel, and sightseeing excursions.

Railpass Protection

Entitles traveler to a 100% reimbursement on the unused portion of the railpass if lost or stolen while traveling in Britain or Europe.

$12 per pass

See "Railpass/Rail & Drive Protection" on last page of Appendix.

DRIVE PASSES

BritRail Pass + Car

		3 RAIL & 3 CAR DAYS WITHIN 1 MONTH		6 RAIL & 7 CAR DAYS WITHIN 1 MONTH	
Group	Class	Adult	Senior	Adult	Senior
Manual Transmission					
Economy	1st	$442	$404	$811	$755
Cat B	2nd	$358	—	$688	—
Compact	1st	$469	$432	$876	$821
Cat C	2nd	$386	—	$753	—
Intermediate	1st	$513	$476	$979	$923
Cat D	2nd	$430	—	$855	—
Automatic Transmission					
Compact	1st	$557	$520	$1081	$1025
Cat E	2nd	$473	—	$958	—
Intermediate	1st	$593	$556	$1165	$1109
Cat F	2nd	$509	—	$1041	—
Premium	1st	$681	$644	$1370	$1314
Cat G	2nd	$597	—	$1246	—
Additional Person Rail Supplement					
	1st	$250	$213	$363	$309
	2nd	$166	—	$241	—

Children 5–15, half the adult rail supplement; under age 5 travel free. Includes unlimited mileage and free drop-off. Minimum rental age is 25.

Eurail/Drive Pass

Any 6 days (4 rail, 2 car) within 2 months for travel in any of the seventeen Eurail countries. Add up to 5 additional rail days and unlimited number of car days.

Car Category	2 ADULTS* 1ST CLASS	1 ADULT 1ST CLASS	ADD'L CAR DAY
Economy	$330	$390	$59
Compact	$350	$430	$78
Intermediate	$360	$450	$88
Compact Auto.**	$375	$480	$105
Add'l. Rail Day	$57	$57	

Third and fourth person sharing car $270 per person. *Prices per person based on 2 people traveling together. **Cars with automatic shift are available at selected rental locations. Children 4–11 are $135 for the basic package. Extra rail days are $29 each.

Europass Drive
Any 5 days (3 rail, 2 car) within 2 months for travel in France, Germany, Italy, Spain, and Switzerland. No zones may be added Add up to 7 additional rail days and an unlimited number of car days.

Car Category	2 ADULTS* 1ST CLASS	1 ADULT 1ST CLASS	ADD'L CAR DAY
Economy	$279	$337	$58
Compact	$299	$377	$77
Intermediate	$309	$397	$87
Compact Auto.**	$324	$427	$104
Add'l. Rail Day	$44	$44	

*Prices per person based on 2 people traveling together. Third and fourth person $221 each.
**Cars with automatic shift available at selected rental locations. Children 4–11 are $111 for the basic package. Extra rail days are $22 each.

France Rail 'N' Drive
Any 5 days (3 rail, 2 car) within 1 month for travel in France. Add up to 6 additional rail days and car days. 3rd and 4th persons may purchase rail passes only.

Car Category	1ST CLASS		2ND CLASS		ADD'L. CAR DAY
	2 ADULTS*	1 ADULT	2 ADULTS*	1 ADULT	
Economy	$204	$289	$187	$255	$50
Compact	$232	$345	$214	$309	$75
Intermediate	$249	$379	$232	$345	$95
Compact Auto.	$247	$369	$232	$345	$89
Add'l. Rail Day	$30	$30	$30	$30	

*Price per person.

German Rail/Drive
Any 4 days (2 rail, 2 car) within 2 months for travel in Germany. Add up to 3 additional rail days.

Car Category	1ST CLASS		2ND CLASS		ADD'L. CAR DAY
	2 ADULTS*	1 ADULT	2 ADULTS*	1 ADULT	
Economy	$170	$227	$145	$202	$59
Compact	$190	$267	$165	$242	$78
Intermediate	$200	$287	$175	$262	$88
Compact Auto.**	$215	$317	$190	$292	$104
Add'l. rail day	$40	$40	$30	$30	

*Price per person. Extra person $113 1st Class; $88 2nd Class.
**Cars with automatic transmission are available at selected locations.

Iberic Rail/Drive
Valid for 3 days of unlimited rail travel within 2 months and 3 days of car rental for travel in Spain and Portugal. Up to 2 additional rail days and an unlimited number of car days may be added.

Car Category	2 ADULTS* 1ST CLASS	1 ADULT 1ST CLASS	ADD'L CAR DAY
Economy	$292	$379	$58
Compact	$317	$429	$77
Intermediate	$332	$459	$87
Compact Auto.**	$357	$509	$102
Add'l. Rail Day	$43	$43	

*Price per person. Third and fourth persons or children sharing car need only to purchase railpasses. **Automatics not available in Portugal.

Italian Rail/Drive

Valid for 2 days of unlimited rail travel within 2 months and 2 days of car rental for travel in Italy. Up to 2 extra rail days and an unlimited number of car days may be added.

Car Category	2 ADULTS* 1ST CLASS	1 ADULT 1ST CLASS	ADD'L CAR DAY
Economy	$190	$242	$58
Compact	$210	$282	$78
Intermediate	$220	$302	$88
Compact Auto.**	$240	$342	$104
Add'l. Rail Day	$62	$62	

Third and fourth persons sharing car $138 per person. Need only to purchase railpasses for children.*Price per person. **Automatic transmission available at selected locations.

Spanish Rail/Drive

Valid for 5 days (3 rail, 2 car) within 2 months of travel in Spain. Up to 2 additional rail days and unlimited car days available.

Car Category	2 ADULTS* 1ST CLASS	1 ADULT 1ST CLASS	ADD'L CAR DAY
Economy	$237	$295	$58
Compact	$257	$335	$77
Intermediate	$267	$355	$87
CompactAuto.**	$282	$385	$102

Third and fourth person sharing car $179 each. Need only to purchase railpasses for children.

*Price per person. **Automatic transmission available at selected locations.

Scanrail/Drive

Valid for 5 days of unlimited rail travel and 2 days of car rental to be used within 15 days in the Scandinavian countries of Denmark, Finland, Norway, and Sweden. Unlimited number of car days may be added.

Car Category	1ST CLASS 2 ADULTS*	1 ADULT	2ND CLASS 2 ADULTS*	1 ADULT	ADD'L. CAR DAY
Economy	$304	$359	$242	$297	$60
Compact	$324	$399	$262	$337	$78
Intermediate	$334	$419	$272	$357	$88

Third and fourth person need only purchase railpasses. Car rental not available in Finland. Automatics not available in Norway. *Price per person.

Railpass/Rail & Drive Protection

This program entitles you to a 100 percent reimbursement on the unused portion of a railpass or a combination Railpass/Rail & Drive program if lost or stolen while traveling in Britain or Europe.

$12 per railpass or for the driver
$12 for each additional person

BRITRAIL PASSES

A BritRail consecutive-day or flexipass allows unlimited travel on the entire British rail network spanning England, Scotland, and Wales. At time of publication, the 2000 rates were not available. Folllowing are the prices based on the previous year's products. Please call (800) 772-7151 or visit www.railpass.com for current information or to request a free Info Pack.

BritRail Classic Pass
Valid for consecutive days of rail travel throughout Britain (England, Wales, and Scotland).

	ADULT		SENIOR	YOUTH
	1ST CLASS	2ND CLASS	1ST CLASS	2ND CLASS
8 days	$400	$265	$340	$215
15 days	$600	$400	$510	$280
22 days	$760	$505	$645	$355
1 month	$900	$600	$765	$420

Senior 60+. Youth 16-25. Children 5-15, half adult fare. Children under age 5 travel free.

BritRail Flexipass
Valid for unlimited rail travel for the days chosen within a 60-day period.

	ADULT		SENIOR	YOUTH
	1ST CLASS	2ND CLASS	1ST CLASS	2ND CLASS
4 days in 2 months	$350	$235	$300	$185
8 days in 2 months	$510	$340	$435	$240
15 days in 2 months	$770	$515	$655	$360

Senior 60+. Youth 16-25. Children 5-15, half adult fare. Children under age 5 travel free.

BritRail Pass + Ireland
Valid for travel in England, Scotland, Wales, Northern Ireland and the Republic of Ireland.

	1ST CLASS	2ND CLASS
5 days within 1 month	$528	$396
10 days within 1 month	$752	$566

Children 5-15, half adult fare; under age 5 travel free.
Round-trip Stena Sealink service is included between Holyhead and Dun Laoghaire, Fishguard and Rosslare or Stranraer and Belfast. Reservations are essential for Irish Sea services. Refunds not offered on dated or partially used passes; sea coupons are not refundable if unused. Also includes transportation from both Gatwick and Heathrow Airports to London.

BritRail Family Pass

Receive one free child pass (age 5–15) of the same type when purchasing one adult or senior BritRail Classic Pass, BritRail Flexipass, BritRail + Ireland, BritRail + Car or a BritRail Party Pass (up to 2 children may travel free per BritRail Party Pass; not to exceed total of 5 persons, including child, on the Party Pass). Children under age 5 travel free.

BritRail SouthEast Pass

A Flexipass for a large section of southern England.

	ADULT		CHILD	
	1ST CLASS	STANDARD CLASS	1ST CLASS	STANDARD CLASS
3 days within 8 days	$105	$74	$32	$21
4 days within 8 days	$142	$105	$32	$21
7 days within 15 days	$189	$142	$32	$21

Children 5-15. Children under age 5 travel free.

Freedom of Scotland Travelpass

	STANDARD CLASS
4 days within 8 days	$137
8 days within 15 days	$184
12 days within 20 days	$206

Includes transportation on most Caledonian MacBrayne and Strathclyde ferries to the islands of Scotland. Discounts on some P&O ferry routes and on selected bus companies in Scotland, plus covers Glasgow Underground. Children 5–15, half adult fare. Children under age 5 travel free.

Gatwick Express

FIRST	STANDARD
$28	$18

Travel by train from Gatwick Airport to London Victoria Station. Children 5-15, half adult fare.

British Heritage Pass

Offers entrance to over 500 well-known public and privately owned castles, homes, gardens and other historic properties throughout Britain. Includes colorful guidebook and map.

	ADULT
7 days	$54
15 days	$75
1 month	$102

No discounts for children. The pass is nonrefundable/nonreturnable.

Guide Friday Sightseeing

Booklet of four sightseeing bus vouchers $43

Choice of 24 popular locations: Bath, Birmingham, Brighton, Cambridge, Cardiff, Chester, Cork, Dover, Dublin, Edinburgh, Galway, Glasgow, Hastings, Inverness, Lincoln, Llandudno and Conway, Norwich, Oxford, Plymouth, Stonehenge, Stratford-upon-Avon, Windsor, and York. Flexibility to use for 1 person for 4 different tour days, or 4 people for 1 tour day; each valid for a full day.

London Day Tour

	ADULT	CHILD
	$80	$72

Includes: an experienced guide, a luxury air-conditioned touring coach, pub lunch, cruise of the river Thames with afternoon tea, and all entrance fees. Operates daily. Children 5–15.

London Visitor Travel Card

Valid for unlimited consecutive day travel in the London Underground and on the red double-decker buses. Also includes Heathrow Airport transfer, plus discounts to sites and attractions.

ALL ZONES	ADULT	CHILD
3 days	$31	$14
4 days	$41	$16
7 days	$61	$26

CENTRAL ZONE	ADULT	CHILD
3 days	$21	$9
4 days	$26	$11
7 days	$32	$13

Children 5-15. Children under age 4 travel free.

British Tours

Choose from a wide variety of interesting tours throughout the British countryside; day trips to Paris or Brussels; or Paris overnighters via the Eurostar. Call (888)–TOUR–404 for a free brochure from EuropeanVacation Tours & Groups or visit www.europeanvacation.com for more detailed information and to book a tour.

Station Maps

The following station maps include German terms explained below.

Hamburg Hauptbahnhof (Hbf) Station Terminology

German	English
Abschittskennzeichnung	Sign that indicates the train will serve only a portion of the platform
Ausgang	Exit
Ausgang Steindamm	Exit Steindamm
Autsicht	Supervision
Einkaufszentrum	Shopping center
Gleise	Track
Kirchenallee	Church Avenue
Nordsteg	North
Steintordamm-Brucke	Bridge
Sudsteg	South

Berlin Zoobahnhof (Zoologischer Garten) Terminology

German	English
Gleis	Track
Wahrend der Umbauaarbeiten des Bahnhofs Kann Es Zu Ortlichen Abweichungen Kommen Wir Bitten Um Ihr Verstandnis	During station construction local charges are possible. We ask for your understanding.

Berlin Ostbahnhof (Hbf) Station Terminology

German	English
Am Hauptbahnhof	To train station
Erich-Steinfurth-Strasse	Street name
Gleis	Track
Wahrend der Umbauaarbeiten des Bahnhofs Kann Es Zu Ortlichen Abweichungen Kommen Wir Bitten Um Ihr Verstandnis	During station construction local charges are possible. We ask for your understanding.

Munich Hauptbahnhof (München Hbf) Terminology

German	English
Bahnhofsplatz	Train station place (Street)
Gleis	Track

Luxembourg Terminology

German	English
Gleis	Track
Voie	Track

Berlin Hbf

N

Erich-Steinfurth-Str.

Gleis

11
10
9
8
7
6
3
2
1

enu nihO Kr eşr a Pr ed eßat S

Am Hauptbahnhof

Während der Umbauarbeiten des Bahnhofs kann es
zu örtlichen Abweichungen kommen.
Wir bitten um Ihr Verständnis.

Berlin Zoologischer Garten

Während der Umbauarbeiten des Bahnhofs kann es
zu örtlichen Abweichungen kommen.
Wir bitten um Ihr Verständnis.

Hamburg Hbf

ICE - Gleise 13 und 14
EC/IC - Gleise 5, 7, 8, 11 bis 14
Abschittskennzeichnung

München Hbf

Luxembourg

EC - voies / Gleise 3, 5,
IC - voies / Gleise 2,
IR - voie / Gleis